D1566516

JOHN

Marianne Meye Thompson

John

A Commentary

WJK
Westminster
John Knox Press
Louisville • Kentucky

First edition
Published by Westminster John Knox Press
Louisville, Kentucky

15 16 17 18 19 20 21 22 23 24—10 9 8 7 6 5 4 3 2 1

Book design by Jennifer K. Cox

Library of Congress Cataloging-in-Publication Data

Thompson, Marianne Meye.
John : a commentary / Marianne Meye Thompson.—First edition.
pages cm.—(The New Testament Library)
Includes bibliographical references and index.
ISBN 978-0-664-22111-9 (alk. paper)
1. Bible. John—Commentaries. I. Title.
BS2615.53.T56 2015
226.5'077—dc23

2015002763

♾ The paper used in this publication meets the minimum requirements of the American National Standard for Information Sciences—Permanence of Paper for Printed Library Materials, ANSI Z39.48-1992.

To my students,
who have responded faithfully
to Jesus' call to follow him:
friends in shared work and witness

CONTENTS

LIST OF TABLES

PREFACE

No one comes to the end of such a project as this commentary without the assistance, friendship, and support of a myriad of persons. For more than seventeen years I have taught, written, spoken, preached, and discoursed on the Gospel of John as I worked on this book. Admittedly, I have done other things as well—and they are part of the reason that this manuscript leaves our home, at long last, as the last of our children, and almost old enough to vote.

Now that my labors have come to an end of sorts it is my pleasure to acknowledge the help of so many along the way. I am sure that there are more who should be thanked, but I want to single out a few in particular. I want first to thank those who answered so many questions along the way, including my wonderful colleagues at Fuller. I'm grateful to have learned so much from Jim Butler, who responded patiently and fully to numerous queries about matters of Old Testament interpretation. Thanks are also due to Chris Hays for help with Hebrew translation and transliteration; to Love Sechrest for reading portions of the manuscript; and to Tommy Givens, whose detailed feedback on several questions changed my mind more than once.

Special thanks go also to my longtime friend Ed Cook, who responded graciously to my inquiries about matters related to the Dead Sea Scrolls, the Targums, and Aramaic in general. Maria Doerfler helped with nuances of German translation. Markus Bockmuehl generously discussed a range of issues relevant to Galilee, Simon Peter, rabbinic sources, and the Gospel of John itself. I owe some key aspects of the way I have come to understand the Gospel to Markus, as well as "The Identity of Jesus" discussion group that met over a period of years at the Center for Theological Inquiry at Princeton. (An essay I wrote during the course of those meetings, titled "Word of God, Messiah of Israel, Savior of the World: Learning the Identity of Jesus from the Gospel of John," appeared in *Seeking the Identity of Jesus: A Pilgrimage,* and portions of that essay appear in the introduction to this commentary.)[1]

1. *Seeking the Identity of Jesus: A Pilgrimage,* ed. Richard B. Hays and Beverly R. Gaventa (Grand Rapids: Eerdmans, 2008). Reprinted by permission of the publisher; all rights reserved.

I have had instructors too numerous to name in the study of the Gospel: they have taught me in the classroom, colloquia, conferences, written books, and articles. My debt to them will be obvious, even if not always explicitly acknowledged. However, among my cherished teachers I wish to name and thank especially my doctoral supervisor, D. Moody Smith, a model of wisdom and erudition, for first introducing me to in-depth academic study of this Gospel.

I also owe a great deal to the students who have studied the Gospel of John with me over the years, and for their questions, insights, and commitment to the witness that the Gospel bears. In many ways, this commentary has been written with my students in both the background and the foreground: it has been shaped and often revised in formal and informal discussions with them, and many of my editorial decisions have been made with them first and foremost in view. Ever grateful for the trust that they have put in those of us who teach them, I have dedicated this commentary to them, in the hope they will receive this work with my prayers and blessing for their calling. In our common work and witness, it is my privilege to call them "friends."

The editorial team for the New Testament Library and Westminster John Knox have done yeoman's service in working with the manuscript over the years that I have worked on it. I am especially grateful to my friend and editor, Clift Black, for his competent, patient, and gentle nudging about so many matters, as well as for allowing me to speak with my own voice. Special thanks go also to Dan Braden, who oversaw this project with a steady hand: always peace!

Finally, I want to express my gratitude to my daughters, Allison and Annelise, now grown. They heard a lot from me about the Gospel and the commentary over the years, and they have celebrated with me as various milestones were passed. I especially want to say thank you to my husband, John, for his support. His input, encouragement, commiseration, cheerleading, tech support, editorial suggestions, prayer, and friendship have been invaluable in getting me to the goal. I look forward to the next seventeen years together—this time without a commentary to finish!

It has been a privilege to work deeply in the Gospel over these years and to contribute a commentary to the New Testament Library. Now, at last, the writing is finished: but my reflections on this Gospel surely are not at an end, nor doubtless will they ever be.

Marianne Meye Thompson
Easter 2015

ABBREVIATIONS

Modern Sources and Common Usage

AB	Anchor Bible
ABD	*Anchor Bible Dictionary*. Edited by David Noel Freedman. 6 vols. New York: Doubleday, 1992
ad loc.	*ad locum*, to/at this place
AnBib	Analecta biblica
ANF	*Ante-Nicene Fathers*
ANRW	*Aufstief und Niedergang der römischen Welt*
ANTC	Abingdon New Testament Commentaries
AT	author's translation
ATANT	Abhandlungen zur Theologie des Alten und Neuen Testaments
AThR	*Anglican Theological Review*
AYBRL	Anchor Yale Bible Reference Library
BBR	*Bulletin for Biblical Research*
B.C.E.	before the Common Era
BDAG	Bauer, W., F. W. Danker, W. G. Arndt, and F. W. Gingrich. *Greek-English Lexicon of the New Testament and Other Early Christian Literature*. 3d ed. Chicago: University of Chicago Press, 2000
BECNT	Baker Exegetical Commentary on the New Testament
BGBE	Beiträge zur Geschichte der biblischen Exegese
Bib	*Biblica*
BIS	Biblical Interpretation Series
BJS	Brown Judaic Studies
BNTC	Black's New Testament Commentary
BSRel	Biblioteca di scienze religiose
BTB	*Biblical Theology Bulletin*
BZNW	Beihefte zur Zeitschrift für die neutestamentliche Wissenschaft
c.	century

ca.	circa, approximately
Catena Aurea	*Catena Aurea: Commentary on the Four Gospels Collected out of the Works of the Fathers by St. Thomas Aquinas*. Vol. 4, Parts 1–2. Albany: Preserving Christian Publications, 2000
CBQ	*Catholic Biblical Quarterly*
CBQMS	Catholic Biblical Quarterly Monograph Series
C.E.	Common Era
CEB	Common English Bible
cf.	*confer,* compare
ch(s).	chapter(s)
ConBNT	Coniectanea biblica: New Testament Series
CRINT	Compendia rerum iudaicarum ad Novum Testamentum
d.	died
diss.	dissertation
DNTD	Das Neue Testament Deutsch
D.Phil.	Doctor of Philosophy
DSS	Dead Sea Scrolls
ECIL	Early Christianity and Its Literature
ed(s).	edited (by), editor(s), edition
e.g.	*exempla gratia*, for example
ep.	epistle(s)
EQ	*Evangelical Quarterly*
esp.	especially
ESV	English Standard Version
ET	English translation/version
et al.	*et alii(ae)*, and others
ETL	*Ephemerides theologicae lovanienses*
ExAud	*Ex Auditu*
ExpTim	*Expository Times*
FC	Fathers of the Church. Washington, DC, 1947–
frg(s).	fragment(s)
HBS	Herders biblische Studien
HNT	Handbuch zum Neuen Testament
HTR	*Harvard Theological Review*
HUCA	*Hebrew Union College Annual*
ICC	International Critical Commentary
i.e.	*id est*, that is
Int	*Interpretation: A Journal of Bible and Theology*
IVPNT	IVP New Testament Commentaries (InterVarsity)
JBL	*Journal of Biblical Literature*
JECS	*Journal of Early Christian Studies*

JHS	*Journal of Hellenic Studies*
JJS	*Journal of Jewish Studies*
JQR	*Jewish Quarterly Review*
JSJ	*Journal for the Study of Judaism*
JSNT	*Journal for the Study of the New Testament*
JSNTSup	Journal for the Study of the New Testament: Supplement Series
JSOT	*Journal for the Study of the Old Testament*
JSPSup	Journal for the Study of the Pseudepigrapha: Supplement Series
JTS	*Journal of Theological Studies*
KJV	King James Version
LCL	Loeb Classical Library
lit.	literally
loc. cit.	*loco citato*, in the place cited
LSJM	Liddell, H. G., R. Scott, H. S. Jones, R. McKenzie, et al. *A Greek-English Lexicon.* 9th ed. with rev. supplement. Oxford: Oxford University Press, 1996
LXX	Septuagint
mg.	marginal note/reading
MS(S)	manuscript(s)
MT	Masoretic Text
n(n).	note(s)
NA[28]	*Novum Testamentum Graece*, Nestle-Aland, 28th ed.
NABRE	New American Bible (Revised Edition), 2010
NCB	New Century Bible Commentary
NEB	New English Bible
NETS	*A New English Translation of the Septuagint.* Emended ed. Oxford: Oxford University Press, 2014. http://ccat.sas.upenn.edu/nets/edition/
NIB	*New Interpreter's Bible*. Nashville: Abingdon
NICNT	New International Commentary on the New Testament
NIV	New International Version (2011 update)
NIV84	New International Version (1984)
NKJV	New King James Version
NLT	New Living Translation
NovT	*Novum Testamentum*
NovTSup	Supplements to Novum Testamentum
NRSV	New Revised Standard Version
NT	New Testament
NTD	Das Neue Testament Deutsch
NTS	*New Testament Studies*

OCD	*The Oxford Classical Dictionary*. Edited by S. Hornblower and A. Spawforth. 3d ed. Oxford: Oxford University Press, 1996
ODCC	*The Oxford Dictionary of the Christian Church*. Edited by F. L. Cross and E. A. Livingstone. Oxford: Oxford University Press, 1997
OT	Old Testament
p(p).	page(s)
par.	parallel text(s)
passim	here and there
PEQ	*Palestine Exploration Quarterly*
Peterson	Eugene H. Peterson, *The Message* (NT), 1993
PL	Patrologia latina. Edited by J.-P. Migne. Vols. 1–217, in 1844–55. Indexes, vols. 218–221, in 1962–65. Paris. http://patristica.net/latina/#t001
R.	Rabbi (plus name)
RB	*Revue biblique*
repr.	reprint(ed)
RSV	Revised Standard Version
SBibLit	Studies in Biblical Literature
SBLDS	Society of Biblical Literature Dissertation Series
SBLSymS	Society of Biblical Literature Symposium Series
sec.	section
SNTSMS	Society for New Testament Studies Monograph Series
SP	Sacra pagina
Str-B	Strack, Hermann L., and Paul Billerbeck. *Kommentar zum Neuen Testament aus Talmud und Midrasch*. Vol. 2. Munich: C. H. Beck, 1924
s.v.	*sub verbo*, under the word
TDNT	*Theological Dictionary of the New Testament*. Edited by G. Kittel and G. Friedrich. Translated by G. W. Bromiley. 10 vols. Grand Rapids: Eerdmans, 1964–1976
Tg.	Targum
THKNT	Theologischer Handkommentar zum Neuen Testament
TNIV	Today's International Version
trans.	translated (by), translator
TynBul	*Tyndale Bulletin*
UNT	Untersuchungen zum Neuen Testament
v(v).	verse(s)
vol(s).	volume(s)
WBC	Word Biblical Commentary
WUNT	Wissenschaftliche Untersuchungen zum neuen Testament

WW	*Word and World*
×	(number of) times a form appears
ZNW	*Zeitschrift für die neutestamentliche Wissenschaft und die Kunde der älteren Kirche*

Ancient Sources

Abbreviations of the titles of ancient biblical, Jewish, Greek, and Latin sources conform to *The SBL Handbook of Style for Biblical Studies and Related Disciplines,* 2d ed. (Atlanta, GA: SBL Press, 2014). Below are sources for which the *SBL Handbook* does not provide abbreviations.

Aelius Aristides, *Or.*	*Orations*
Apollodorus, Pseudo-, *Lib.*	*The Library*
Artemidorus, *Oneir.*	*The Interpretation of Dreams*
Curtius Rugus, *Hist. Alex.*	*The History of Alexander the Great*
Cyn. Ep.	*Cynic Epistles*
Dio Cassius, *Hist.*	*Roman History*
Diodorus Siculus, *Hist.*	*Library of History*
Diogenes Laertius, *Lives*	*Lives and Opinions of Famous Philosophers*
Ephrem the Syrian, *Comm.*	*Commentary on Tatian's Diatesseron*
Heraclitus, *Ep.*	*Epistles*, in *Cynic Epistles* (by various authors)
Hist. Aug.	*Historia Augusta*
Livy, *Hist.*	*History of Rome*
Lucian, *Hist.*	*How to Write History*
Martial, *Epigr.*	*Epigrams*
Petronius, *Satyr.*	*Satyricon*
Polybius, *Hist.*	*The Histories*
Thucydides, *War*	*The History of the Peloponnesian War*
Valerius Maximus	*Memorable Deeds and Sayings*

BIBLIOGRAPHY

In the footnotes, all works are cited by author, along with the year if other works from that author are cited.

Commentaries

Augustine. 1988–1995. *Tractates on the Gospel of John*. FC. Translated by John W. Rettig. 5 vols. Washington, DC: Catholic University Press, 1988. Vols. 78–79, 88, 90, 92.

Barrett, Charles K. 1978. *The Gospel according to St. John: An Introduction with Commentary and Notes on the Greek Text*. 2d, rev. ed. Philadelphia: Westminster.

Beasley-Murray, George R. 1999. *John*. 2d ed. WBC. Nashville: Nelson.

Becker, Jürgen. 1979. *Das Evangelium nach Johannes*. Vol. 1. Gütersloh: Gerd Mohn; Würzburg: Echter-Verlag.

———. 1981. *Das Evangelium nach Johannes*. Vol. 2. Gütersloh: Gerd Mohn; Würzburg: Echter-Verlag.

Brant, Jo-Ann. 2011. *John*. Paideia Commentaries on the New Testament. Grand Rapids: Baker Academic.

Brodie, Thomas L. 1993. *The Gospel according to John: A Literary and Theological Commentary*. New York: Oxford University Press.

Brown, Raymond E. 1966. *The Gospel according to John*. Vol. 1, *1–12*. AB 29. Garden City, NY: Doubleday.

———. 1970. *The Gospel according to John*. Vol. 2, *13–21*. AB 29A. Garden City, NY: Doubleday.

Bruner, Frederick Dale. 2012. *The Gospel of John: A Commentary*. Grand Rapids: Eerdmans.

Bultmann, Rudolf. 1971. *The Gospel of John*. Translated by George R. Beasley-Murray. Philadelphia: Westminster.

Calvin, John. 1959–1961. *The Gospel according to St. John*. 2 vols. Grand Rapids: Eerdmans.

Carson, Donald A. 1991. *The Gospel according to John*. Grand Rapids: Eerdmans; Leicester: Inter-Varsity.

Cyril of Alexandria. 1874. *Commentary on the Gospel according to S. John.* Vol. 1, *S. John 1–8.* Translated by Philip Edward Pusey. Library of Fathers of the Holy Catholic Church 43. London: Walter Smith.

———. 1885. *Commentary on the Gospel according to S. John.* Vol. 2, *S. John 9–21.* Translated by Thomas Randall. Library of Fathers of the Holy Catholic Church 48. London: Walter Smith.

Ephrem the Syrian. 1993. *Saint Ephrem's Commentary on Tatian's Diatessaron: An English Translation of Chester Beatty Syriac MS709.* Translated and edited by Carmel McCarthy. Journal of Semitic Studies Supplement 2. Oxford: Oxford University Press for the University of Manchester.

Grayston, Kenneth. 1990. *The Gospel of John.* Narrative Commentaries. Philadelphia: Trinity Press International.

Haenchen, Ernst. 1984. *John: A Commentary on the Gospel of John.* Vol. 1, *Chapters 1–6.* Vol. 2, *Chapters 7–21.* Philadelphia: Fortress.

Hoskyns, Edwyn C. 1956. *The Fourth Gospel.* Edited by Francis N. Davey. London: Faber & Faber.

Keener, Craig S. 2003. *The Gospel of John: A Commentary.* 2 vols. Peabody, MA: Hendrickson.

Köstenberger, Andreas. 2004. *John.* BECNT. Grand Rapids: Baker Academic.

Lincoln, Andrew T. 2005. *The Gospel according to Saint John.* BNT 4. Peabody, MA: Hendrickson.

Lindars, Barnabas. 1972. *The Gospel of John.* NCB. Grand Rapids: Eerdmans.

Malina, Bruce J., and Richard Rohrbaugh. 1998. *Social-Science Commentary on the Gospel of John.* Minneapolis: Fortress.

McHugh, John. 2009. *A Critical and Exegetical Commentary on John 1–4.* ICC. Edinburgh: T&T Clark.

Michaels, J. Ramsay. 2010. *The Gospel of John.* NICNT. Grand Rapids: Eerdmans.

Moloney, Francis J. 1993. *Belief in the Word: Reading John 1–4.* Minneapolis: Fortress.

———. 1996. *Signs and Shadows: Reading John 5–12.* Minneapolis: Fortress.

———. 1998a. *Glory, Not Dishonor: Reading John 13–21.* Minneapolis: Fortress.

———. 1998b. *The Gospel of John.* SP 4. Collegeville, MN: Liturgical Press.

Neyrey, Jerome H. 2007. *The Gospel of John.* New Cambridge Bible Commentary. Cambridge: Cambridge University Press.

O'Day, Gail R. 1996. "The Gospel of John." *NIB* 9:491–865.

Origen. 1993. *Commentary on the Gospel according to John.* Vol. 2, *Books 13–32.* Translated by Ronald E. Heine. FC 89. Washington, DC: Catholic University of America Press.

Ridderbos, Herman N. 1997. *The Gospel of John: A Theological Commentary.* Translated by John Vriend. Grand Rapids: Eerdmans.

Schlatter, Adolf. 1960. *Der Evangelist Johannes*. Stuttgart: Calwer Verlag.

Schnackenburg, Rudolf. 1982. *The Gospel according to St. John*. 3 vols. New York: Crossroad.

Schnelle, Udo. 1998. *Das Evangelium nach Johannes*. THKNT. Leipzig: Evangelische Verlagsanstalt.

Smith, D. Moody. 1999. *John*. ANTC. Nashville: Abingdon.

Talbert, Charles H. 1992. *Reading John: A Literary and Theological Commentary on the Fourth Gospel and the Johannine Epistles*. New York: Crossroad.

Thyen, Hartwig. 2005. *Das Johannesevangelium*. HNT 6. Tübingen: Mohr Siebeck.

Westcott, Brooke F. 1882. *The Gospel according to St. John: The Authorized Version, with Introduction and Notes*. London: John Murray. 2 vols., 1908.

Whitacre, Rodney A. 1999. *John*. IVPNT. Downers Grove, IL: InterVarsity.

Wilckens, Ulrich. 1998. *Das Evangelium nach Johannes*. NTD 4. Göttingen: Vandenhoeck & Ruprecht.

Monographs and Articles

Ackerman, James. 1966. "The Rabbinic Interpretation of Psalm 82 and the Gospel of John." *HTR* 59:186–91.

Alexander, Philip S. 1992. "'The Parting of the Ways' from the Perspective of Rabbinic Judaism." Pages 1–25 in *Jews and Christians: The Parting of the Ways A.D. 70 to 135. The Second Durham-Tübingen Research Symposium on Earliest Christianity and Judaism (Durham, September 1989)*. Edited by J. D. G. Dunn. WUNT 66. Tübingen: Mohr Siebeck.

Allison, Dale C., Jr. 2010. *Constructing Jesus: Memory, Imagination, and History*. Grand Rapids: Baker Academic.

Anderson, Paul N. 1996. *The Christology of the Fourth Gospel: Its Unity and Disunity in the Light of John 6*. Valley Forge: Trinity Press International.

———. 2011. *The Riddles of the Fourth Gospel: An Introduction to John*. Minneapolis: Fortress.

Anderson, Paul N., Felix Just, S.J., and Tom Thatcher, eds. 2007. *John, Jesus, and History*. Vol. 1, *Critical Appraisals of Critical Views*. SBLSymS 44. Atlanta: Society of Biblical Literature.

———, eds. 2009. *John, Jesus, and History*. Vol. 2, *Aspects of Historicity in the Fourth Gospel*. ECIL 2. SBLSymS 44. Atlanta: Society of Biblical Literature.

Anderson, Robert T. 1992. "Samaritans." *ABD* 5:940–47.

Arav, Rami, and Richard Freund. 1995. *Bethsaida: A City by the Northern Shore of the Sea of Galilee*. Bethsaida Excavations Project 1. Kirksville, MO: Thomas Jefferson University Press.

Ashton, John. 2007. *Understanding the Fourth Gospel*. 2d ed. Oxford: Clarendon.

Attridge, Harry. 2002. "Genre Bending in the Fourth Gospel." *JBL* 121:3–21.

———. 2008. "From Discord Rises Meaning: Resurrection Motifs in the Fourth Gospel." Pages 1–19 in *The Resurrection of Jesus in the Gospel of John*. Edited by Craig R. Koester and Reimund Bieringer. WUNT 222. Tübingen: Mohr Siebeck.

———. 2010. "An 'Emotional' Jesus and Stoic Tradition." Pages 122–36 in *Essays on John and Hebrews*. WUNT 264. Tübingen: Mohr Siebeck.

Ball, David Mark. 1996. *"I Am" in John's Gospel: Literary Function, Background, and Theological Implications*. JSNTSup 124. Sheffield: Sheffield Academic Press.

Barton, Stephen C. 1994. *Discipleship and Family Ties in Mark and Matthew*. SNTSMS 80. Cambridge: Cambridge University Press, 1994.

Bauckham, Richard. 1996. "Nicodemus and the Gurion Family." *JTS* 47:1–37.

———. 1997. "Qumran and the Fourth Gospel: Is There a Connection?" Pages 267–79 in *The Scrolls and the Scriptures: Qumran Fifty Years After*. Edited by S. E. Porter and C. A. Evans. JSPSup 26. Sheffield: Sheffield Academic Press.

———. 1998a. "For Whom Were the Gospels Written?" Pages 9–48 in *The Gospels for All Christians: Rethinking the Gospel Audiences*. Edited by Richard Bauckham. Grand Rapids: Eerdmans.

———, ed. 1998b. *The Gospels for All Christians: Rethinking the Gospel Audiences*. Grand Rapids: Eerdmans.

———. 2006. *Jesus and the Eyewitnesses: The Gospels as Eyewitness Testimony*. Grand Rapids: Eerdmans.

———. 2007a. "Did Jesus Wash His Disciples Feet?" Repr. (from 1999) as pages 191–206 in *The Testimony of the Beloved Disciple*. Grand Rapids: Baker Academic.

———. 2007b. "The Holiness of Jesus and His Disciples in the Gospel of John." Pages 253–70 in *The Testimony of the Beloved Disciple*. Grand Rapids: Baker Academic.

———. 2007c. *The Testimony of the Beloved Disciple: Narrative, History, and Theology in the Gospel of John*. Grand Rapids: Baker Academic.

———. 2008. *Jesus and the God of Israel*. Grand Rapids: Eerdmans.

Beirne, Margaret. 2003. *Women and Men in the Fourth Gospel: A Discipleship of Equals*. JSNTSup 242. Sheffield: Sheffield Academic Press.

Bennema, Cornelis. 2002a. "The Giving of the Spirit in John's Gospel—A New Proposal?" *EQ* 74:195–213.

———. 2002b. *The Power of Saving Wisdom: An Investigation of Spirit and Wisdom in Relation to the Soteriology of the Fourth Gospel*. WUNT 2/148. Tübingen: Mohr Siebeck.

———. 2005. "The Sword of the Messiah and the Concept of Liberation in the Fourth Gospel." *Bib* 86:35–58.

———. 2009. *Encountering Jesus: Character Studies in the Gospel of John.* Carlisle: Paternoster.

Berger, Klaus. 1997. *Im Anfang war Johannes*. Stuttgart: Quell Verlag.

Bernier, Jonathan. 2013. *Aposynagōgos and the Historical Jesus in John: Rethinking the Historicity of the Johannine Expulsion Passages*. BIS 122. Boston: Brill.

Beutler, Johannes. 1984. *Habt keine Angst: Die erste johanneische Abschiedsrede (John 14)*. Stuttgart: Katholisches Bibelwerk.

———. 1996. "The Use of 'Scripture' in the Gospel of John." Pages 147–62 in *Exploring the Gospel of John: In Honor of D. Moody Smith*. Edited by R. Alan Culpepper and C. Clifton Black. Louisville: Westminster John Knox.

———. 2001. "Synoptic Jesus Tradition in the Johannine Farewell Discourses." Pages 165–73 in *Jesus in Johannine Tradition*. Edited by Robert T. Fortna and Tom Thatcher. Louisville: Westminster John Knox.

Bieringer, Reimund. 2008. "Resurrection and Ascension in the Gospel of John." Pages 209–35 in *The Resurrection of Jesus in the Gospel of John*. Edited by Craig Koester and Reimund Bieringer. WUNT 222. Tübingen: Mohr Siebeck.

Bieringer, Reimund, Didier Pollefeyt, and Frederique Vandecasteele-Vanneuville, eds. 2001. *Anti-Judaism and the Fourth Gospel*. Louisville: Westminster John Knox.

Black, C. Clifton. 1998. "1, 2, 3 John." *NIB* 12:365–469.

Blomberg, Craig L. 2001. *The Historical Reliability of John's Gospel: Issues and Commentary*. Downers Grove, IL: InterVarsity.

Bockmuehl, Markus. 1994. *This Jesus: Martyr, Lord, Messiah.* Edinburgh: T&T Clark.

———. 1997. "'The Form of God' (Phil. 2:6): Variations on a Theme of Jewish Mysticism." *JTS* 48:1–23.

———. 2000. *Jewish Law in Gentile Churches: Halakhah and the Beginning of Christian Public Ethics*. Grand Rapids: Baker Academic.

———. 2004. "Simon Peter's Names in Jewish Source." *JJS* 55:58–80.

———. 2005. "'Keeping It Holy': Old Testament Commandment and New Testament Faith." Pages 95–124 in *I Am the Lord Your God: Christian Reflections on the Ten Commandments*. Edited by Carl E. Braaten and Christopher R. Seitz. Grand Rapids: Eerdmans.

———. 2010. *The Remembered Peter.* WUNT 262. Tübingen: Mohr Siebeck, 2010.

———. 2012a. "The Baptism of Jesus as Super-Sacrament of Salvation." *Theology* 115:83–91.

———. 2012b. *Simon Peter in Scripture and Memory: The New Testament Apostle in the Early Church.* Grand Rapids: Baker Academic.

Bokser, Baruch M. 1992. "Unleavened Bread and Passover, Feasts of." *ABD* 6:755–56.

Bond, Helen K. 1998. *Pontius Pilate in History and Interpretation.* SNTSMS 100. Cambridge: Cambridge University Press.

Borgen, Peder. 1965. *Bread from Heaven: An Exegetical Study in the Concept of Manna in the Gospel of John and the Writings of Philo.* NovTSup 10. Leiden: Brill.

———. 1968. "God's Agent in the Fourth Gospel." Pages 137–48 in *Religions in Antiquity.* Edited by Jacob Neusner. Leiden: Brill. Reprinted as pages 67–78 in *The Interpretation of John.* Edited by John Ashton. Edinburgh: T&T Clark, 1986.

———. 1969. "Observations on the Targumic Character of the Prologue of John." *NTS* 16:288–95.

———. 1972. "Logos Was the True Light: Contributions to the Interpretation of the Prologue of John." *NovT* 14:115–30.

———. 1996. "The Gospel of John and Hellenism: Some Observations." Pages 95–123 in *Exploring the Gospel of John: In Honor of D. Moody Smith.* Edited by R. Alan Culpepper and C. Clifton Black. Louisville: Westminster John Knox.

———. 2007. "The Scriptures and the Words and Works of Jesus." Pages 39–58 in *What We Have Heard from the Beginning: The Past, Present, and Future of Johannine Studies.* Edited by Tom Thatcher. Waco: Baylor University Press.

Boring, M. Eugene. 1978. "The Influence of Christian Prophecy in the Johannine Portrayal of the Paraclete and Jesus." *NTS* 25:113–23.

Bornkamm, Günther. 1997. "Towards the Interpretation of John's Gospel: A Discussion of *The Testament of Jesus*, by Ernst Käsemann." Pages 97–119 in *The Interpretation of John.* Edited by John Ashton. 2d ed. Edinburgh: T&T Clark. Repr. of *Evangelische Theologie* 28 (1968): 8–25.

Boyarin, Daniel. 2001. "The Gospel of the *Memra*: Jewish Binitarianism and the Prologue to John." *HTR* 94:243–84.

Brown, Raymond E. 1979. *The Community of the Beloved Disciple.* New York: Paulist Press.

———. 1994. *The Death of the Messiah: From Gethsemane to the Grave; A Commentary on the Passion Narratives in the Four Gospels.* 2 vols. New York: Doubleday.

———. 2003. *An Introduction to the Gospel of John.* Edited by Francis J. Moloney. New York: Doubleday.

Brown, Tricia Gates. 2003. *Spirit in the Writings of John: Johannine Pneumatology in Social-Scientific Perspective.* New York: T&T Clark.

Brunson, Andrew. 2003. *Psalm 118 in the Gospel of John.* WUNT 2/158. Tübingen: Mohr Siebeck.

Bryan, Christopher. 2005. *Render to Caesar: Jesus, the Early Church, and the Roman Superpower*. Oxford: Oxford University Press.

Bryan, Steven M. 2005. "The Eschatological Temple in John 14." *BBR* 15:187–98.

Bultmann, Rudolf. 1951. *Theology of the New Testament*. Vol. 1. New York: Scribners.

———. 1955. *Theology of the New Testament*. Vol. 2. New York: Scribners.

Burge, Gary M. 1987. *The Anointed Community: The Holy Spirit in the Johannine Tradition*. Grand Rapids: Eerdmans.

Burkett, Delbert. 1991. *The Son of the Man in the Gospel of John*. JSNTSup 56. Sheffield: JSOT Press.

Burridge, Richard A. 2004. *What Are the Gospels? A Comparison with Graeco-Roman Biography*. 2d ed. Grand Rapids: Eerdmans.

Bynum, William Randolph. 2012. *The Fourth Gospel and the Scripture: Illuminating the Form and Meaning of Scriptural Citation in John 19:37.* NovTSup 144. Leiden: Brill.

Byron, John. 2003. *Slavery Metaphors in Early Judaism and Pauline Christianity: A Traditio-Historical and Exegetical Examination*. WUNT 2/162. Tübingen: Mohr Siebeck.

Byrskog, Samuel. 2002. *Story as History—History as Story: The Gospel Tradition in the Context of Ancient Oral History*. Leiden: Brill.

Carson, Donald A. 1982. "Understanding the Misunderstandings in the Fourth Gospel." *TynBul* 33:59–91.

Carter, Warren. 2006. *John: Storyteller, Interpreter, Evangelist*. Peabody, MA: Hendrickson.

———. 2008. *John and Empire: Initial Explorations*. New York: T&T Clark.

Cassidy, Richard. 1992. *John's Gospel in New Perspective.* Maryknoll, NY: Orbis Books.

Chapman, David. 2010. *Ancient Jewish and Christian Perceptions of Crucifixion*. Grand Rapids: Baker Academic.

Charlesworth, James H. 1995. *The Beloved Disciple: Whose Witness Validates the Gospel of John*? Valley Forge, PA: Trinity Press International.

Childs, Brevard. 1984. *The New Testament as Canon: An Introduction*. Philadelphia: Fortress.

Cohen, Shaye J. D. 1984. "The Significance of Yavneh: Pharisees, Rabbis, and the End of Jewish Sectarianism." *HUCA* 55:27–53.

———. 2001. *The Beginnings of Jewishness: Boundaries, Varieties, Uncertainties.* Berkeley: University of California Press.

Collins, John J., and Daniel C. Harlow. 2010. *The Eerdmans Dictionary of Early Judaism*. Grand Rapids: Eerdmans.

Collins, Matthew S. 1995. "The Question of *Doxa*: A Socioliterary Reading of the Wedding at Cana." *BTB* 25:100–109.

Coloe, Mary L. 2001. *God Dwells with Us: Temple Symbolism in the Fourth Gospel*. Collegeville, MN: Liturgical Press.

———. 2007. *Dwelling in the Household of God: Johannine Ecclesiology and Spirituality*. Collegeville, MN: Liturgical Press.

Conway, Colleen. 1999. *Men and Women in the Fourth Gospel: Gender and Johannine Characterization*. SBLDS 167. Atlanta: Society of Biblical Literature.

Corell, Alf. 1958. *Consummatum est: Eschatology and Church in the Gospel of St John*. London: SPCK.

Crossan, John Dominic, and Jonathan L. Reed. 2001. *Excavating Jesus: Beneath the Stones, behind the Texts: The Key Discoveries for Understanding Jesus in His World*. San Francisco: HarperSanFrancisco.

Cullmann, Oscar. 1967. *Salvation in History*. New York: Harper & Row.

Culpepper, R. Alan. 1983. *Anatomy of the Fourth Gospel: A Study in Literary Design*. Philadelphia: Fortress.

———. 2008. "Realized Eschatology in the Experience of the Johannine Community." Pages 253–76 in *The Resurrection of Jesus in the Gospel of John*. Edited by Craig Koester and Reimund Bieringer. WUNT 222. Tübingen: Mohr Siebeck.

Dahl, Nils A. 1962. "The Johannine Church and History." Pages 124–42 in *Current Issues in New Testament Interpretation: Essays in Honor of Otto A. Piper*. Edited by William Klassen and Graydon F. Snyder. New York: Harper & Row. Repr., pages 147–67 in *The Interpretation of John*. Edited by John Ashton. 2d ed. Edinburgh: T&T Clark, 1997.

Dahl, Nils A., and Alan F. Segal. 1978. "Philo and the Rabbis on the Names of God." *JSJ* 9:1–28.

Daly-Denton, Margaret. 2000. *David in the Fourth Gospel: The Johannine Reception of the Psalms*. Leiden: Brill.

Dark, Kenneth R. 2008. "The Roman-Period and Byzantine Landscape between Sepphoris and Nazareth." *PEQ* 140:87–102.

Daube, David. 1956. *The New Testament and Rabbinic Judaism*. London: University of London, Athlone Press.

De Boer, Martinus C. 2001. "The Depiction of 'the Jews' in John's Gospel: Matters of Behavior and Identity." Pages 241–57 in *Anti-Judaism and the Fourth Gospel*. Edited by Reimund Bieringer, Didier Pollefeyt, and Frederique Vandecasteele-Vanneuville. Louisville: Westminster John Knox.

———. 2013. "Andrew: The First Link in the Chain." Pages 137–50 in *Character Studies in the Fourth Gospel*. Edited by Steven A. Hunt, D. Francois Tolmie, and Ruben Zimmerman. WUNT 314. Tübingen: Mohr Siebeck.

Deines, Roland. 1993. *Jüdische Steingefässe und Pharisäische Frommigkeit: Ein archäologisch-historischer Beitrag zum Verständnis von John 2,6 und der jüdischen Reinheitshalacha zur Zeit Jesu*. WUNT 2/52. Tübingen: Mohr Siebeck, 1993.

Dennis, John A. 2006. *Jesus' Death and the Gathering of True Israel: The Johannine Appropriation of Restoration Theology in the Light of John 11.47–52.* WUNT 2/217. Tübingen: Mohr Siebeck, 2006.

DeSilva, David. 2000. *Honor, Patronage, Kinship and Purity: Unlocking New Testament Culture*. Downers Grove, IL: InterVarsity.

Dettwiler, Andreas. 1995. *Die Gegenwart des Erhöhten: Eine exegetische Studie zu den johanneischen Abschiedsreden (Joh 13,31–16,33) unter besonderer Berücksichtigung ihres Relecture-Charakters*. Göttingen: Vandenhoeck & Ruprecht.

Dodd, Charles H. 1953. *The Interpretation of the Fourth Gospel*. Cambridge: Cambridge University Press.

———. 1963. *Historical Tradition in the Fourth Gospel*. Cambridge: Cambridge University Press.

Dodds, Eric R. 1965. *Pagan and Christian in an Age of Anxiety: Some Aspects of Religious Experience from Marcus Aurelius to Constantine*. Cambridge: Cambridge University Press.

Dunbabin, Katherine M. D. 2003. *The Roman Banquet: Images of Conviviality*. Cambridge: Cambridge University Press.

Dunn, James D. G. 1970. *Baptism in the Holy Spirit: A Re-Examination of the New Testament Teaching on the Gift of the Spirit in Relation to Pentecostalism Today*. Philadelphia: Westminster.

———. 1983. "Let John Be John: A Gospel for Its Time." Pages 309–39 in *Das Evangelium und die Evangelien: Vorträge vom Tübinger Symposium 1982*. Edited by Peter Stuhlmacher. Tübingen: J. C. B. Mohr.

———. 2001. "The Embarrassment of History: Reflections on the Problem of 'Anti-Judaism' in the Fourth Gospel." Pages 41–60 in *Anti-Judaism and the Fourth Gospel*. Edited by Reimund Bieringer, Didier Pollefeyt, and Frederique Vandecasteele-Vanneuville. Louisville: Westminster John Knox.

———. 2006. *The Partings of the Ways: Between Christianity and Judaism and Their Significance for the Character of Christianity*. 2d ed. London: SCM.

Edwards, Mark J. 1995. "Justin's Logos and the Word of God." *JECS* 3:61–80.

Eisler, Robert. 1938. *The Enigma of the Fourth Gospel*. London: Methuen.

Ellens, J. Harold. 2010. *The Son of Man in the Gospel of John*. New Testament Monographs 28. Sheffield: Sheffield Phoenix.

Emerton, John A. 1958. "The Hundred and Fifty-Three Fishes in John XXI.11." *JTS* 9:86–89.

———. 1960. "Some New Testament Notes." *JTS* 2:329–32.

———. 1966. "Melchizedek and the Gods: Fresh Evidence for the Jewish Background of John X.34–36." *JTS* 17:399–401.

Epp, J. Eldon. 1974. "Wisdom, Torah, Word: The Johannine Prologue and the Purpose of the Fourth Gospel." Pages 128–46 in *Current Issues in Biblical and Patristic Interpretation: Studies in Honor of Merrill C. Tenney Presented by His Former Students*. Edited by Gerald F. Hawthorne. Grand Rapids: Eerdmans.

Evans, C. Stephen. 2008. "The Historical Reliability of John's Gospel: From What Perspective Should It Be Assessed?" Pages 91–119 in *The Gospel of John and Christian Theology*. Edited by Richard Bauckham and Carl Mosser. Grand Rapids: Eerdmans.

Evans, Craig A. 1993. *Word and Glory: On the Exegetical and Theological Background of John's Prologue*. JSNTSup 89. Sheffield: JSOT Press.

———. 2001. "Jesus' Action in the Temple and Evidence of Corruption in the First-Century Temple." Pages 319–44 in *Jesus and His Contemporaries: Comparative Studies*. Boston: Brill.

Fee, Gordon D. 1977–78. "Once More—John 7:37–39." *ExpTim* 89:116–18.

Fehribach, Adeline. 1998. *The Women in the Life of the Bridegroom: A Feminist Historical-Literary Analysis of the Female Characters in the Fourth Gospel*. Collegeville, MN: Liturgical Press.

Feldmeier, Reinhard, and Hermann Spieckermann. 2011. *God of the Living: A Biblical Theology*. Translated by Mark E. Biddle. Waco: Baylor University Press.

Fitzgerald, John T. 1997. *Greco-Roman Perspectives on Friendship*. Atlanta: Scholars Press.

Fitzmyer, Joseph A. 1979. "The Languages of Palestine in the First Century A.D." Pages 29–56 in *A Wandering Aramean: Collected Aramaic Essays*. Missoula: Scholars Press.

Fortna, Robert. 1974. "Theological Use of Locale in the Fourth Gospel." *AThR*, Supplementary Series 3:58–94.

Fortna, Robert, and Tom Thatcher, eds. 2001. *Jesus in Johannine Tradition*. Louisville: Westminster John Knox.

Freeman, Kathleen. 1983. *Ancilla to the Pre-Socratic Philosophers: A Complete Translation of the Fragments in Diels, "Fragmente der Vorsokratiker."* Repr., Cambridge, MA: Harvard University Press.

Frey, Jörg. 1997. *Die johanneische Eschatologie*. Vol. 1, *Ihre Probleme im Spiegel der Forschung seit Reimarus*. WUNT 96. Tübingen: Mohr Siebeck.

———. 2000. *Die johanneische Eschatologie*. Vol. 3, *Die eschatologische Verkündigung in den johanneischen Texten*. WUNT 117. Tübingen: Mohr Siebeck.

———. 2004. "Licht aus den Höhlen? Der 'johanneische Dualismus' und die Texte von Qumran." Pages 117–203 in *Kontexte des Johannesevangeliums: Das vierte Evangelium in religions- und traditionsgeschichtlicher Perspektive*. WUNT 175. Tübingen: Mohr Siebeck.

Freyne, Sean. 2004. *Jesus, a Jewish Galilean: A New Reading of the Jesus-Story*. Edinburgh: T&T Clark.

Friesen, Steven. 1993. *Twice Neokoros: Ephesus, Asia, and the Cult of the Flavian Imperial Family*. Leiden: Brill.

Gardner-Smith, Percival. 1938. *Saint John and the Synoptic Gospels*. Cambridge: Cambridge University Press.

Garnsey, Peter D. A. 1999. *Food and Society in Classical Antiquity*. Cambridge: Cambridge University Press.

Gaventa, Beverly Roberts. 1996. "The Archive of Excess: John 21 and the Problem of Narrative Closure." Pages 240–52 in *Exploring the Gospel of John: In Honor of D. Moody Smith*. Edited by R. Alan Culpepper and C. Clifton Black. Louisville: Westminster John Knox.

Giblin, Charles H. 1979. "Suggestion, Negative Response, and Positive Action in St John's Gospel (John 2:1–11; 4:46–54; 7:2–14; 11:1–44)." *NTS* 26:197–211.

Goodman, Martin. 1987. *The Ruling Class of Judaea: The Origins of the Jewish Revolt against Rome, A.D. 66–70*. Cambridge: Cambridge University Press.

Grant, Robert M. 1949. "One Hundred Fifty-Three Large Fish (John 21:11)." *HTR* 42:273–75.

Griffith, Terry. 2008. "The Jews Who Had Believed in Him." Pages 183–92 in *The Gospel of John and Christian Theology*. Edited by Richard Bauckham and Carl Mosser. Grand Rapids: Eerdmans.

Gundry, Robert M. 1967. "'In My Father's House Are Many *Monai*' (John 14:2)." *ZNW* 58:68–72.

Hachlili, Rachel. 1992. "Burials, Ancient Jewish." *ABD* 1:789–94.

Hakola, Raimo. 1999. "A Character Resurrected: Lazarus in the Fourth Gospel and Afterwards." Pages 223–63 in *Characterization in the Gospels: Reconceiving Narrative Criticism*. Edited by David M. Rhoads and Kari Syreeni. JSNTSup 184. Sheffield: Sheffield Academic Press.

———. 2005. *Identity Matters: John, the Jews, and Jewishness*. NovTSup 118. Boston: Brill.

Hanson, Anthony. 1966–1967. "John's Citation of Psalm LXXXII Reconsidered." *NTS* 13:363–67.

Harries, Jill. 2007. *Law and Crime in the Roman World*. Cambridge: Cambridge University Press.

Harstine, Stan. 2002. *Moses as a Character in the Fourth Gospel: A Study of Ancient Reading Techniques*. JSNTSup 229. Sheffield: Sheffield Academic Press.

Harvey, Anthony E. 1976. *Jesus on Trial: A Study in the Fourth Gospel*. London: SPCK.

Haskins, Susan. 1994. *Mary Magdalen: Myth and Metaphor*. New York: Harcourt, Brace.

Hengel, Martin. 1977. *Crucifixion in the Ancient World and the Folly of the Message of the Cross*. Philadelphia: Fortress.

———. 1981. *The Atonement: The Origins of the Doctrine in the New Testament*. Philadelphia: Fortress.

———. 1987. "The Interpretation of the Wine Miracle at Cana: John 2:1–11." Pages 83–112 in *The Glory of Christ in the New Testament: Studies in Christology; In Memory of George Bradford Caird*. Edited by Lincoln D. Hurst and Nicholas Thomas Wright. Oxford: Clarendon.

———. 1989. *The Johannine Question*. Philadelphia: Trinity Press International.

———. 1994. "The Old Testament in the Fourth Gospel." Pages 380–95 in *The Gospel and the Scriptures of Israel*. Edited by Craig A. Evans and W. Richard Stegner. JSNTSup 104. Sheffield: Sheffield Academic Press.

———. 1995a. "The Dionysiac Messiah." Pages 293–331 in *Studies in Early Christology*. Edinburgh: T&T Clark.

———. 1995b. "Jesus as Messianic Teacher of Wisdom and the Beginnings of Christology." Pages 73–117 in *Studies in Early Christology*. Edinburgh: T&T Clark.

———. 1995c. "Jesus, the Messiah of Israel." Pages 1–72 in *Studies in Early Christology*. Edinburgh: T&T Clark.

———. 1995d. "'Sit at My Right Hand!' The Enthronement of Christ at the Right Hand of God and Psalm 110:1." Pages 119–225 in *Studies in Early Christology*. Edinburgh: T&T Clark.

Hera, Marianus Pale. 2013. *Christology and Discipleship in John 17*. WUNT 2/342. Tübingen: Mohr Siebeck.

Hill, Charles E. 2004. *The Johannine Corpus in the Early Church*. Oxford: Oxford University Press.

Hofius, Otfried. 1967. "Die Sammlung der Leiden zur Herde Israels (Joh 10:16; 11:51f.)." *ZNW* 58:289–91.

Hooker, Morna D. 1974. "The Johannine Prologue and the Messianic Secret." *NTS* 21:40–58.

Horbury, William. 2013. "Herod's Temple and 'Herod's Days.'" Pages 83–103 in *Messianism among Jews and Christians: Biblical and Historical Studies*. London: T&T Clark.

Horsley, Richard A., and Neil Asher Silberman. 1997. *The Message and the Kingdom: How Jesus and Paul Ignited a Revolution and Transformed the Ancient World*. New York: Grossett/Putnam.

Hunt, Steven A. 2009. "Nicodemus, Lazarus, and the Fear of 'the Jews.'" Pages 199–212 in *Repetitions and Variations in the Fourth Gospel*. Edited by Gilbert van Belle, Michael Labahn, and Petrus Maritz. Leuven: Peeters.

Hunt, Steven A., D. Francois Tolmie, and Ruben Zimmerman, eds. 2013. *Character Studies in the Fourth Gospel*. WUNT 314. Tübingen: Mohr Siebeck.

Hurtado, Larry. 1988. *One God, One Lord : Early Christian Devotion and Ancient Jewish Monotheism*. Philadelphia: Fortress.

———. 2003. *Lord Jesus Christ: Devotion to Jesus in Earliest Christianity*. Grand Rapids: Eerdmans.

———. 2005a. "First-Century Jewish Monotheism." Pages 111–33 in *How on Earth Did Jesus Become a God?* Grand Rapids: Eerdmans.

———. 2005b. *How on Earth Did Jesus Become a God? Historical Questions about Earliest Devotion to Jesus*. Grand Rapids: Eerdmans.

Hurtado, Larry, and Paul L. Owen, eds. 2011. *"Who Is This Son of Man?": The Latest Scholarship on a Puzzling Expression of the Historical Jesus*. London: T&T Clark.

Hylen, Susan E. 2005. *Allusion and Meaning in John 6*. BZNW 137. Berlin: De Gruyter.

———. 2009. *Imperfect Believers*. Louisville: Westminster John Knox.

Ilan, Tal. 2002. *Lexicon of Jewish Names in Late Antiquity*. Part 1, *Palestine 330 BCE–200 CE*. Texte und Studien zum Antiken Judentum 91; Tübingen: J. C. B. Mohr.

Jensen, Robin M. 2000. *Understanding Early Christian Art*. New York: Routledge.

———. 2012. *Baptismal Imagery in Early Christianity: Ritual, Visual, and Theological Dimensions*. Grand Rapids: Baker Academic.

Jeremias, Joachim. 1969. *Jerusalem in the Time of Jesus*. Philadelphia: Fortress.

Johnson, Luke Timothy. 1989. "The New Testament's Anti-Jewish Slander and Conventions of Ancient Rhetoric." *JBL* 108:419–41.

Johnston, George. 1970. *The Spirit-Paraclete in the Gospel of John*. SNTSM 12. Cambridge: Cambridge University Press.

Jones, Brian W. 1993. *The Emperor Domitian*. London: Routledge.

Jones, Larry Paul. 1997. *The Symbol of Water in the Gospel of John*. Sheffield: Sheffield Academic Press.

Josephus. *See* Mason.

Juel, Donald H. 1988. *Messianic Exegesis: Christological Interpretation of the Old Testament in Early Christianity*. Philadelphia: Fortress.

Kanagaraj, Jey J. 1998. *"Mysticism" in the Gospel of John: An Inquiry into Its Background*. JSNTSup 158. Sheffield: Sheffield Academic Press.

Katz, Stephen. 1984. "Issues in the Separation of Judaism and Christianity after 70 C.E.: A Reconsideration." *JBL* 103:43–76.

———. 2006. "The Rabbinic Response to Christianity." Pages 259–98 in *The Cambridge History of Judaism.* Vol. 4, *The Late Roman-Rabbinic Period.* Edited by Steven T. Katz. Cambridge: Cambridge University Press.

Keck, Leander E. 1986. "Toward the Renewal of New Testament Christology." *NTS* 32:362–77.

———. 1996. "Derivation as Destiny: 'Of-ness' in Johannine Christology, Anthropology, and Soteriology." Pages 274–88 in *Exploring the Gospel of John: In Honor of D. Moody Smith.* Edited by R. Alan Culpepper and C. Clifton Black. Louisville: Westminster John Knox.

Keith, Chris. 2009. *The Pericope Adulterae, the Gospel of John, and the Literacy of Jesus*. Boston: Brill.

Kelly, John N. D. 1972. *Early Christian Creeds.* 3d ed. London: Longman.

Kerr, Alan R. 2002. *The Temple of Jesus' Body: The Temple Theme in the Gospel of John*. JSNTSup 220. Sheffield: Sheffield Academic Press.

Kierspel, Lars. 2006. *The Jews and the World in the Fourth Gospel: Parallelism, Function, and Context*. WUNT 220. Tübingen: Mohr Siebeck.

Kimelman, Reuven. 1981. "*Birkat Ha-Minim* and the Lack of Evidence for an Anti-Christian Jewish Prayer in Late Antiquity." Pages 226–44 in *Jewish and Christian Self-Definition.* Vol. 2, *Aspects of Judaism in the Greco-Roman Period.* Edited by E. P. Sanders, Albert I. Baumgarten, and Alan Mendelson. Philadelphia: Fortress Press.

Klawans, Jonathan. 2000. *Ritual and Moral Impurity in Ancient Jewish Literature.* Oxford: Oxford University Press.

Koester, Craig R. 1989. *The Dwelling of God: The Tabernacle in Old Testament, Intertestamental Jewish Literature, and the New Testament*. CBQMS 22. Washington, DC: Catholic Biblical Association.

———. 1990. "'The Savior of the World' (John 4:42)." *JBL* 109:665–80.

———. 2003. *Symbolism in the Fourth Gospel: Meaning, Mystery, Community*. 2d ed. Minneapolis: Fortress.

———. 2008a. "Jesus' Resurrection, the Signs, and the Dynamics of Faith in the Gospel of John." Pages 47–74 in *The Resurrection of Jesus in the Gospel of John*. Edited by Craig R. Koester and Reimund Bieringer. WUNT 222. Tübingen: Mohr Siebeck.

———. 2008b. *The Word of Life: A Theology of John's Gospel*. Grand Rapids: Eerdmans.

Koester, Craig R., and Reimund Bieringer, eds. 2008. *The Resurrection of Jesus in the Gospel of John*. WUNT 222. Tübingen: Mohr Siebeck.

Köstenberger, Andreas J. 1998. "Jesus as Rabbi in the Fourth Gospel." *BBR* 8:97–128.

———. 2009. *A Theology of John's Gospel and Letters: Biblical Theology of the New Testament*. Grand Rapids: Zondervan.

Kugler, Robert A. 2010. "Patriarchs, Testaments of the Twelve." Pages 2031–33 in *The Eerdmans Dictionary of Early Judaism*. Edited by John J. Collins and Daniel C. Harlow. Grand Rapids: Eerdmans.

Kurz, William S. 1985. "Luke 22:14–38 and Greco-Roman and Biblical Farewell Addresses." *JBL* 104:251–68.

Kysar, Robert. 2005. "The Whence and Whither of the Johannine Community." Pages 65–81 in *Life in Abundance: Studies of John's Gospel in Tribute to Raymond E. Brown, S.S.* Edited by John R. Donahue. Collegeville, MN: Liturgical Press.

———. 2007. *The Maverick Gospel*. 3d ed. Louisville: Westminster John Knox.

Labahn, Michael. 2002. "'Heiland der Welt': Der gesandte Gottessohn und der römische Kaiser—ein Thema johanneischer Christologie?" Pages 147–73 in *Zwischen den Reichen: Neues Testament und römische Herrschaft*. Edited by Michael Labahn and Jürgen Zangenberg. Tübingen: A. Franke.

———. 2013. "Simon Peter: An Ambiguous Character and His Narrative Career." Pages 151–67 in *Character Studies in the Fourth Gospel*. Edited by Steven A. Hunt, D. Francois Tolmie, and Ruben Zimmerman. WUNT 314. Tübingen: Mohr Siebeck.

Langer, Ruth. 2011. *Cursing the Christians? A History of the Birkat HaMinim*. New York: Oxford University Press.

Larsen, Kasper Bro. 2008. *Recognizing the Stranger: Recognition Scenes in the Gospel of John*. BIS 93. Leiden: Brill.

Levine, Lee I. 2010. "Synagogues." Pages 1260–71 in *The Eerdmans Dictionary of Early Judaism*. Edited by John J. Collins and Daniel C. Harlow. Grand Rapids: Eerdmans.

Levison, John R. 1997. *The Spirit in First-Century Judaism*. Leiden: Brill.

———. 2009. *Filled with the Spirit*. Grand Rapids: Eerdmans.

Lieu, Judith. 1999. "Temple and Synagogue in John." *NTS* 45:51–69.

Lincoln, Andrew T. 1998. "'I am the Resurrection and the Life': The Resurrection Message of the Fourth Gospel." Pages 122–44 in *Life in the Face of Death: The Resurrection Message of the New Testament*. Edited by Richard N. Longenecker. MacMaster New Testament Studies. Grand Rapids: Eerdmans.

———. 2000. *Truth on Trial: The Lawsuit Motif in the Fourth Gospel*. Peabody, MA: Hendrickson.

———. 2008. "The Lazarus Story: A Literary Perspective." Pages 211–32 in *The Gospel of John and Christian Theology*. Edited by Richard Bauckham and Carl Mosser. Grand Rapids: Eerdmans.

Lowe, Malcolm. 1976. "Who Were the IOYΔAIOI?" *NovT* 18:101–30.

Lozado, Francisco, Jr., and Tom Thatcher. 2006. *New Currents through John: A Global Perspective*. Atlanta: SBL.

Lukaszewski, Albert L. 2011. "Issues concerning the Aramaic behind ὁ υἱὸς τοῦ ἀνθρώπου: A Critical Review of Scholarship." Pages 1–27 in *"Who Is This Son of Man?": The Latest Scholarship on a Puzzling Expression of the Historical Jesus*. Edited by Larry Hurtado and Paul L. Owen. London: T&T Clark.

Maccini, Robert Gordon. 1996. *Her Testimony Is True: Women as Witnesses according to John*. JSNTSup 125. Sheffield: Sheffield Academic Press.

MacMullen, Ramsay, and Eugene Lane, eds. 1992. *Paganism and Christianity, 100–425 C.E.: A Sourcebook*. Minneapolis: Augsburg Fortress.

Magness, Jodi. 2011. *Stone and Dung, Oil and Spit: Jewish Daily Life in the Time of Jesus*. Grand Rapids: Eerdmans.

Manning, Gary T. 2004. *Echoes of a Prophet: The Use of Ezekiel in the Gospel of John and in Literature of the Second Temple Period*. JSNTSup 270. London: T&T Clark.

Marcus, Joel. 2003. "Son of Man as Son of Adam." *RB* 110:38–61, 370–386.

———. 2009. "*Birkat Ha-Minim* Revisited." *NTS* 55:523–51.

———. 2013. "Passover and Last Supper Revisited." *NTS* 59:303–24.

Marmorstein, Arthur. 1931–32. "Philo and the Names of God." *JQR* 22:295–306.

Martin, Raymond A. 1974. *Syntactical Evidence of Semitic Sources in Greek Documents*. Cambridge, MA: Society of Biblical Literature.

Martyn, J. Louis. 2003. *History and Theology in the Fourth Gospel*. 3d ed. Louisville: Westminster John Knox.

Mason, Steve. 2001. *Flavius Josephus: Translation and Commentary*. Vol. 9, *Life of Josephus*. Leiden: Brill.

———. 2007. "Jews, Judaeans, Judaizing, Judaism: Problems of Categorization in Ancient History." *JSJ* 38:457–512.

———. 2008. *Flavius Josephus: Translation and Commentary*. Vol. 1b, *The Judean War 2*. Leiden: Brill.

McCaffrey, James M. 1988. *The House with Many Rooms: The Temple Theme of Jn. 14, 2–3*. AnBib 114. Rome: Biblical Institute Press.

McCane, Byron R. 2003. *Roll Back the Stone: Death and Burial in the World of Jesus*. Harrisburg: Trinity Press International.

McClaren, James S. 1991. *Power and Politics in Palestine: The Jews and the Governing of Their Land*. JSNTSup 63. Sheffield: Sheffield Academic Press.

McDonough, Sean. 2010. *Christ as Creator: Origins of a New Testament Doctrine*. New York: Oxford University Press.

Meeks, Wayne A. 1967. *The Prophet-King: Moses Traditions and the Johannine Christology*. NovTSup 14. Leiden: Brill.

———. 1997. "The Man from Heaven in Johannine Sectarianism." Pages 169–205 in *The Interpretation of John*. Edited by John Ashton. Edinburgh: T&T Clark.

Menken, Maarten J. J. 1996. *Old Testament Quotations in the Fourth Gospel: Studies in Textual Form*. Kampen: Kok Pharos.

———. 1997. "John 6:51c–58: Eucharist or Christology?" Pages 183–204 in *Critical Readings of John 6*. Edited by R. Alan Culpepper. Leiden: Brill.

Meshorer, Yaʿakov. 1967. *Jewish Coins of the Second Temple Period*. Tel Aviv: Am Hassefer.

Metzger, Bruce M. 1994. *A Textual Commentary on the Greek New Testament*. 2d ed. Stuttgart: Deutsche Bibelgesellschaft / United Bible Societies.

Meyer, Paul. 1996. "'The Father': The Presentation of God in the Fourth Gospel." Pages 255–73 in *Exploring the Gospel of John: In Honor of D. Moody Smith*. Edited by R. Alan Culpepper and C. Clifton Black. Louisville: Westminster John Knox.

Meyers, Eric M., and Mark A. Chancey. 2012. *Alexander to Constantine: Archaeology of the Land of the Bible*. Vol. 3. AYBRL. New Haven: Yale University Press.

Minear, Paul S. 1977. "The Audience of the Fourth Gospel." *Int* 31:339–54.

Moberly, R. Walter L. 2001. "The Christ of the Old and New Testaments." Pages 184–99 in *The Cambridge Companion to Jesus*. Edited by Markus Bockmuehl. Cambridge: Cambridge University Press.

———. 2003. "How Can We Know the Truth? A Study of John 7:14–18." Pages 239–57 in *The Art of Reading Scripture*. Edited by Ellen F. Davis and Richard B. Hays. Grand Rapids: Eerdmans, 2003.

———. 2008. "Johannine Christology and Jewish-Christian Dialogue." Pages 45–58 in *Scripture's Doctrine and Theology's Bible*. Edited by Markus Bockmuehl and Alan J. Torrance. Grand Rapids: Baker Academic.

Moloney, Francis J. 1978. *The Johannine Son of Man*. BSRel 14. 2d ed. Rome: Libreria Ateneo Salesiano.

———. 2003. "Can Everyone Be Wrong? A Reading of Joh 11.1–12.8." *NTS* 49:505–27.

Morris, Leon. 1989. *Jesus Is the Christ: Studies in the Theology of John*. Grand Rapids: Eerdmans.

Motyer, Stephen. 1997. *Your Father the Devil? A New Approach to John and "the Jews."* Exeter: Paternoster.

Moule, Charles F. D. 1962. "The Individualism of the Fourth Gospel." *NovT* 5:171–90.

———. 1977. *The Origin of Christology*. Cambridge: Cambridge University Press.

Newbigin, Lesslie. 1982. *The Light Has Come: An Exposition of the Fourth Gospel*. Grand Rapids: Eerdmans, 1982.

Neyrey, Jerome. 1979. "Jacob Traditions and the Interpretation of John 4:10–26." *CBQ* 41:419–37.

———. 1989. "I Said, 'You Are Gods': Psalm 82:6 and John 10." *JBL* 108:647–63.

———. 2007. "Role and Status in the Fourth Gospel: Cutting through Confusion." Pages 36–56 in *The Impartial God: Essays in Biblical Studies in Honor of Jouette M. Bassler*. Edited by Calvin J. Roetzel and Robert L. Foster. Sheffield: Sheffield Academic Press.

Ng, Wai-yee. 2001. *Water Symbolism in John: An Eschatological Interpretation*. SBibLit 15. New York: Peter Lang.

Nissen, Johannes. 1997. "The New Testament Love Command in Relationship to Hellenistic Judaism." Pages 123–50 in *The New Testament and Hellenistic Judaism*. Edited by Peder Borgen and Søren Giversen. Peabody, MA: Hendrickson.

Nock, Arthur Darby. 1972a. "Deification and Julian." Pages 833–46 in *Essays on Religion and the Ancient World*. Edited by Zeph Steward. Cambridge, MA: Harvard University Press.

———. 1972b. "SŌTĒR and EUERGETĒS." Pages 720–35 in *Essays on Religion and the Ancient World*. Edited by Zeph Steward. Cambridge, MA: Harvard University Press.

Olsson, Birger. 1974. *Structure and Meaning in the Fourth Gospel: A Text-Linguistic Analysis of John 2:1–11 and 4:1–42*. ConBNT 6. Lund: Gleerup.

Painter, John. 1991. "Tradition, History and Interpretation in John 10." Pages 53–74 in *The Shepherd Discourse of John 10 and Its Context: Studies by Members of the Johannine Writings Seminar*. Edited by Johannes Beutler and Robert T. Fortna. Cambridge: Cambridge University Press.

———. 2008. "'The Light Shines in the Darkness . . .': Creation, Incarnation, and Resurrection in John." Pages 21–46 in *The Resurrection of Jesus in the Gospel of John*. Edited by Craig R. Koester and Reimund Bieringer. Tübingen: Mohr Siebeck.

Pancaro, Severino. 1975. *The Law in the Fourth Gospel: The Torah and the Gospel; Moses and Jesus, Judaism and Christianity according to John*. NovTSup 42. Leiden: Brill.

Parsenios, George L. 2005. *Departure and Consolation: The Johannine Farewell Discourses in Light of Greco-Roman Literature*. Boston: Brill.

———. 2010. *Rhetoric and Drama in the Johannine Lawsuit Motif*. WUNT 258. Tübingen: Mohr Siebeck.

Peppard, Michael. 2011. *The Son of God in the Roman World: Divine Sonship in Its Social and Political Context*. Oxford: Oxford University Press.

Phillips, Peter M. 2006. *The Prologue of the Fourth Gospel: A Sequential Reading*. London: Continuum.

Pitre, Brant. 2005. *Jesus, the Tribulation, and the End of the Exile: Restoration Eschatology and the Origin of the Atonement*. Tübingen: Mohr Siebeck.

Poirier, John C. 2008. "Hanukkah in the Narrative Chronology of the Fourth Gospel." *NTS* 54:465–78.

Pollard, Thomas E. 1970. *Johannine Christology and the Early Church.* Cambridge: Cambridge University Press.

Price, Simon R. F. 1984a. "Gods and Emperors: The Greek Language of the Roman Imperial Cult." *JHS* 104:79–95.

———. 1984b. *Rituals and Power: The Roman Imperial Cult in Asia Minor.* Cambridge: Cambridge University Press.

Rainbow, Paul Andrew. 1987. "Monotheism and Christology in 1 Cor. 8:4–6." D.Phil. diss., University of Oxford.

Reed, Jonathan L. 2000. *Archaeology and the Galilean Jesus: A Re-examination of the Evidence*. Harrisburg, PA: Trinity Press International.

Reinhartz, Adele. 1998. "The Johannine Community and Its Jewish Neighbors: A Reappraisal." Pages 111–38 in *What Is John?* Vol. 2, *Literary and Social Readings of the Fourth Gospel.* Edited by Fernando F. Segovia. Atlanta: Scholars Press.

———. 2004. "The Grammar of Hate in the Gospel of John: Reading John in the Twenty-First Century." Pages 416–27 in *Israel und seine Heilstraditionen im Johannesevangelium: Festgabe für Johannes Beutler SJ zum 70. Geburtstag*. Edited by Michael Labahn, Klaus Scholtissek, and Angelika Strotmann. Paderborn: Ferdinand Schöningh.

Resseguie, James. 2013. "The Beloved Disciple: The Ideal Point of View." Pages 537–49 in *Character Studies in the Fourth Gospel*. Edited by Steven A. Hunt, D. Francois Tolmie, and Ruben Zimmerman. WUNT 314. Tübingen: Mohr Siebeck.

Reynolds, Benjamin E. 2008. *The Apocalyptic Son of Man in the Gospel of John*. WUNT 2/249. Tübingen: Mohr Siebeck.

Riesner, Rainer. 1987. "Bethany beyond the Jordan (John 1:28): Topography, Theology, and History in the Fourth Gospel." *TynBul* 38:29–63.

Robinson, John A. T. 1955. "The Parable of the Shepherd." *ZNW* 46:233–40.

———. 1985. *The Priority of John.* Edited by J. F. Coakley. London: SCM.

Ronning, John. 2010. *The Jewish Targums and John's Logos Theology*. Grand Rapids: Baker Academic.

Rösel, Martin. 2007. "The Reading and Translation of the Divine Name in the Masoretic Tradition and the Greek Pentateuch." *JSOT* 31:411–28.

Rousseau, John J., and Rami Arav. 1995. *Jesus and His World: An Archaeological and Cultural Dictionary.* Minneapolis: Augsburg Fortress.

Rubenstein, Jeffrey L. 1995. *The History of Sukkot in the Second Temple and Rabbinic Periods*. BJS 302. Atlanta: Scholars Press.

Runia, David T. 1993. *Philo in Early Christian Literature: A Survey*. CRINT: Sec. 3, Jewish Traditions in Early Christian Literature 3. Minneapolis: Fortress.

Safrai, Shmuel. 1976. "The Temple." Pages 865–907 in vol. 2 of *The Jewish People in the First Century*. Edited by Shmuel Safrai and Menahem Stern. CRINT. Philadelphia: Fortress.

Salier, Bill. 2006. "Jesus, the Emperor, and the Gospel according to John." Pages 284–301 in *Challenging Perspectives on the Gospel of John*. Edited by John Lierman. WUNT 2/219. Tübingen: Mohr Siebeck.

Sanders, E. P. 1985. *Jesus and Judaism*. Philadelphia: Fortress.

———. 1992. *Judaism: Practice and Belief*. Philadelphia: Trinity Press.

Schneiders, Sandra M. 2005. "The Resurrection (of the Body) in the Fourth Gospel: A Key to Johannine Spirituality." Pages 168–98 in *Life in Abundance: Studies of John's Gospel in Tribute to Raymond E. Brown, S.S.* Edited by John R. Donahue. Collegeville, MN: Liturgical Press.

———. 2008. "Touching the Risen Jesus." Pages 153–76 in *The Resurrection of Jesus in the Gospel of John*. Edited by Craig R. Koester and Reimund Bieringer. WUNT 222. Tübingen: Mohr Siebeck.

Schnelle, Udo. 1999. "Die Juden im Johannesevangelium." Pages 217–30 in *Gedenkt an das Wort: Festschrift für Werner Vogler zum 65. Geburtstag*. Edited by Christoph Kähler, Martina Böhm, and Christfried Böttrich. Leipzig: Evangelische Verlagsanstalt.

———. 2001. "Recent Views of John's Gospel." *WW* 21:352–59.

Schroeder, Henry J. 1978. *Canons and Decrees of the Council of Trent*. Rockford: Tan Books.

Schuchard, Bruce G. 1992. *Scripture within Scripture: The Interrelationship of Form and Function in the Explicit Old Testament Citations in the Gospel of John.* SBLDS 133. Atlanta: Scholars Press.

Schwartz, Daniel R. 1992. "Pontius Pilate." *ABD* 5:395–401.

Schwartz, Seth. 1991. "Israel and the Nations Roundabout: 1 Maccabees and the Hasmonean Expansion." *JJS* 42:16–38.

Scott, Martin. 1992. *Sophia and the Johannine Jesus*. JSNTSup 71. Sheffield: JSOT Press.

Segal, Alan F. 1977. *Two Powers in Heaven: Early Rabbinic Reports about Christianity and Gnosticism.* Leiden: Brill.

———. 1980. "Heavenly Ascent in Hellenistic Judaism, Early Christianity and Their Environment." *ANRW*. Part 2, *Principat*, 23.2:1352–89.

Segovia, Fernando. 1982. *Love Relationships in the Johannine Tradition.* SBLDS 58. Atlanta: Scholars Press.

———. 1991. *The Farewell of the Word: The Johannine Call to Abide*. Minneapolis: Fortress.

Sheppard, Beth. 2006. "Another Look: Johannine 'Subordinationist Christology' and the Roman Family." Pages 101–19 in *New Currents through John: A Global Perspective*. Edited by Francisco Lozada Jr. and Tom Thatcher. Resources for Biblical Study. Atlanta: Society of Biblical Literature.

Skarsaune, Oskar. 2002. *In the Shadow of the Temple: Jewish Influences on Early Christianity*. Downers Grove, IL: InterVarsity.

Smalley, Stephen. 1996. "Pneumatology in the Johannine Gospel and Apocalypse." Pages 289–300 in *Exploring the Gospel of John: In Honor of D. Moody Smith.* Edited by R. Alan Culpepper and C. Clifton Black. Louisville: Westminster John Knox.

Smallwood, E. Mary. 1981. *The Jews under Roman Rule from Pompey to Diocletian: A Study in Political Relations.* 2d ed. Boston: Brill.

Smith, Dennis E. 2003. *From Symposium to Eucharist: The Banquet in the Early Christian World.* Minneapolis: Augsburg Fortress.

Smith, D. Moody. 1990. "Judaism and the Gospel of John." Pages 76–96 in *Jews and Christians: Exploring the Past, Present, and Future.* Edited by James H. Charlesworth. New York: Crossroad.

———. 2001. *John among the Gospels.* 2d ed. Columbia: University of South Carolina Press.

———. 2003. "The Contribution of J. Louis Martyn to the Understanding of the Gospel of John. Pages 1–23 in *History and Theology in the Fourth Gospel*, by J. Louis Martyn. 3d ed. Louisville: Westminster John Knox.

———. 2008. *The Fourth Gospel in Four Dimensions: Judaism and Jesus, the Gospels and Scripture*. Columbia: University of South Carolina Press.

Stark, Rodney. 1997. *The Rise of Christianity: How the Obscure, Marginal Jesus Movement Became the Dominant Religious Force in the Western World in a Few Centuries*. San Francisco: HarperSanFrancisco.

Stemberger, Günther. 1977. "Die sogenannte 'Synode von Jabne' und das frühe Christentum." *Kairos* 19:14–21.

Stern, Sacha. 2001. *Calendar and Community: A History of the Jewish Calendar, Second Century* BCE*–Tenth Century* CE. Oxford: Oxford University Press.

Stevenson, J., ed. 2013. *A New Eusebius: Documents Illustrating the History of the Church to AD 337*. Revised by W. H. C. Frend. Grand Rapids: Baker Academic.

Stibbe, Mark W. G. 1992. *John as Storyteller: Narrative Criticism and the Fourth Gospel.* SNTSMS 73. Cambridge: Cambridge University Press.

———. 1994. *John's Gospel.* New York: Routledge.

Thatcher, Tom. 2009. *Greater than Caesar: Christology and Empire in the Fourth Gospel*. Minneapolis: Fortress.

———, ed. 2007. *What We Have Heard from the Beginning: The Past, Present, and Future of Johannine Studies*. Waco: Baylor University Press.

Theissen, Gerd. 1983. *The Miracle Stories of the Early Christian Tradition.* Edinburgh: T&T Clark.

Theobald, Michael. 2002. *Herrenworte im Johannesevangelium.* HBS 34. Freiburg: Herder & Herder.

Thomas, John Christopher. 1991. *Footwashing in John 13 and the Johannine Community*. JSNTSup 61. Sheffield: JSOT Press.

Thompson, Henry O. 1992. "Ephraem (Place)." *ABD* 2:556.

Thompson, Marianne Meye. 1989. "Eternal Life in the Gospel of John." *ExAud* 5:35–55.

———. 2000. *The Promise of the Father: Jesus and God in the New Testament*. Louisville: Westminster John Knox.

———. 2001. *The God of the Gospel of John*. Grand Rapids: Eerdmans.

———. 2004. "The Breath of Life: John 20:22–23 Once More." Pages 69–78 in *The Holy Spirit and Christian Origins: Essays in Honor of James D. G. Dunn*. Edited by Graham N. Stanton, Bruce W. Longenecker, and Stephen C. Barton. Grand Rapids: Eerdmans.

———. 2005. "When the Ending Is Not the End." Pages 65–75 in *The Ending of Mark and the Ends of God: Essays in Memory of Donald Harrisville Juel*. Edited by Beverly Gaventa and Patrick Miller. Louisville: Westminster John Knox.

———. 2006. "Every Picture Tells a Story: Imagery for God in the Gospel of John." Pages 259–77 in *Imagery in the Gospel of John*. Edited by Ruben Zimmerman and Jörg Frey. Tübingen: Mohr Siebeck.

———. 2007. "Jesus: 'The One Who Sees God.'" Pages 215–26 in *Israel's God and Rebecca's Children: Christology and Community in Early Judaism and Christianity; Essays in Honor of Larry W. Hurtado and Alan F. Segal*. Edited by David B. Capes, April D. DeConick, Helen K. Bond, and Troy A. Miller. Waco: Baylor University Press.

———. 2008a. "Learning the Identity of Jesus from the Gospel of John." Pages 166–79 in *Seeking the Identity of Jesus: A Pilgrimage*. Edited by Richard B. Hays and Beverly R. Gaventa. Grand Rapids: Eerdmans.

———. 2008b. "'They Bear Witness to Me': The Psalms in the Passion Narrative of the Gospel of John." Pages 267–83 in *The Word Leaps the Gap: Essays on Scripture and Theology Sparked in Honor of Richard B. Hays*. Edited by J. Ross Wagner, C. Kavin Rowe, and A. Katherine Grieb. Grand Rapids: Eerdmans.

———. 2011. "*Jesus and the Victory of God* Meets the Gospel of John." Pages 21–38 in *Jesus, Paul, and the People of God*. Edited by Nicholas Perrin and Richard B. Hays. Downers Grove, IL: IVP Academic.

———. 2013. "Lazarus: 'Behold a Man Raised Up by Christ!'" Pages 460–72 in *Character Studies in the Fourth Gospel: Narrative Approaches to Seventy Figures in John*. Edited by Steven A. Hunt, Francois Tolmie, and Ruben Zimmerman. Tübingen: Mohr Siebeck.

Torrance, Alan J. 2008. "The Lazarus Narrative, Theological History, and Historical Probability." Pages 245–62 in *The Gospel of John and Christian*

Theology. Edited by Richard Bauckham and Carl Mosser. Grand Rapids: Eerdmans.

Twelftree, Graham H. 2001. "Exorcisms in the Fourth Gospel." Pages 135–43 in *Jesus in Johannine Tradition*. Edited by Robert Fortna and Tom Thatcher. Louisville: Westminster John Knox.

Ulfgard, Håkan. 1998. *The Story of Sukkoth*. BGBE 34. Tübingen: Mohr Siebeck.

Urbach, Ephraim. 1987. *The Sages: Their Concepts and Beliefs*. Cambridge: Harvard University Press.

VanderKam, James C. 1990. "John 10 and the Feast of Dedication." Pages 203–14 in *Of Scribes and Scrolls: Studies on the Hebrew Bible, Intertestamental Judaism, and Christian Origins*. Edited by Harold W. Attridge, John J. Collins, and Thomas H. Tobin. Lanham, MD: University Press of America.

———. 2004. *From Joshua to Caiaphas: High Priests after the Exile*. Minneapolis: Augsburg Fortress.

van der Watt, Jan G. 2000. *Family of the King: Dynamics of Metaphor in the Gospel according to John*. Leiden: Brill.

van der Watt, Jan G., and Ruben Zimmerman, eds. 2012. *Rethinking the Ethics of John: "Implicit Ethics" in the Johannine Writings*. Kontexte und Normen neutestamentlicher Ethik / Contexts and Norms of New Testament Ethics 3. Tübingen: Mohr Siebeck.

von Wahlde, Urban C. 2000. "'The Jews' in the Gospel of John: Fifteen Years of Research (1983–1998)." *ETL* 76:30–55.

———. 2006. "Archaeology and John's Gospel." Pages 523–86 in *Jesus and Archaeology*. Edited by James H. Charlesworth. Grand Rapids: Eerdmans.

Wallace, Daniel B. 1996. *Greek Grammar beyond the Basics: An Exegetical Syntax of the New Testament*. Grand Rapids: Zondervan.

Williams, Catrin H. 2000. *I Am He: The Interpretation of 'Anî Hû' in Jewish and Early Christian Literature*. WUNT 2/113. Tübingen: Mohr Siebeck.

Williams, Peter J. 2011. "Not the Prologue of John." *JSNT* 33:375–86.

Windisch, Hans. 1926. *Johannes und die Synoptiker: Wollte der vierte Evangelist die älteren Evangelien ergänzen oder ersetzen?* UNT 12. Leipzig: Hinrichs.

Wright, Nicholas Thomas. 2003. *The Resurrection of the Son of God*. Minneapolis: Fortress.

Wyschogrod, Michael. 1996. "A Jewish Perspective on Incarnation." *Modern Theology* 12:195–209.

Zimmerman, Ruben. 2004. *Christologie der Bilder im Johannesevangelium: Die Christopoetik des vierten Evangeliums unter besonderer Berücksichtigung von Joh 10*. WUNT 171. Tübingen: Mohr Siebeck.

———. 2008. "The Narrative Hermeneutics of Joh 11: Learning with Lazarus How to Understand Death, Life, and Resurrection." Pages 75–101 in *The*

Resurrection of Jesus in the Gospel of John. Edited by Craig R. Koester and Reimund Bieringer. WUNT 222. Tübingen: Mohr Siebeck.

———. 2012. *Rethinking the Ethics of John: "Implicit Ethics" in the Johannine Writings*. Kontexte und Normen neutestamentlicher Ethik / Contexts and Norms of New Testament Ethics. Vol. 3. Edited by Jan G. van der Watt and Ruben Zimmerman. Tübingen: Mohr Siebeck.

Zumstein, Jean. 2004a. "Die Schriftrezeption in der Brotrede." Pages 123–39 in *Israel und seine Heilstraditionen im Johannesevangelium: Festgabe für Johannes Beutler SJ zum 70. Geburtstag*. Paderborn: Schöningh.

———. 2004b. *Kreative Erinnerung: Relecture und Auslegung im Johannesevangelium*. 2d ed. ATANT 84. Zurich: Theologischer Verlag.

———. 2008. "Jesus' Resurrection in the Farewell Discourses." Pages 103–26 in *The Resurrection of Jesus in the Gospel of John*. Edited by Craig R. Koester and Reimund Bieringer. WUNT 222. Tübingen: Mohr Siebeck.

INTRODUCTION

Readers of the Gospels often move seamlessly from Matthew to Mark to Luke to John, weaving the various narratives together without pause. And why not? Not only do the Gospels tell the story of the same central figure, Jesus of Nazareth; as selective narratives of his public ministry,[1] these Gospels also share a very general framework. After Jesus' public ministry begins with the baptizing ministry of John the Baptist, Jesus calls disciples to follow him; heals the sick, lame, and blind, and raises the dead; teaches the multitudes and confronts other Jewish teachers, particularly the Pharisees, about the interpretation of Scripture and God's will; is put to death on a Roman cross; and subsequently appears to his disciples alive after his death. Within this basic framework a number of similar or identical incidents find their place in all the Gospels: early controversies regarding keeping the Sabbath; the feeding of five thousand, followed by Jesus' walking across the sea of Galilee; a confession of Jesus by Simon Peter on behalf of the Twelve; a public entry into Jerusalem; a demonstration in the temple area aimed at those who sell animals and change money;[2] a closing discourse to Jesus' disciples about what will happen after his death; a last meal eaten with them prior to his betrayal by one of his own disciples and denial by another; Jesus' arrest, trial, and crucifixion by the Romans; and resurrection appearances, first to women who followed him and then to his other disciples. Jesus' ministry repeatedly raises the question of just who he might be: others acclaim him as prophet, Messiah, Holy One, and Son of God; he most typically speaks of himself as "Son of Man."

Yet almost from the earliest days of the church, John's distinctive presentation of Jesus has provoked discussion about its place among the other Gospels. Perhaps the best known of these early assessments was that of Clement of Alexandria (ca. 155–220), who famously opined that after the other evangelists had written down the "bodily things" (*ta sōmatika*),[3] John, "encouraged by his pupils

1. Among the canonical Gospels, Matthew and Luke append "birth narratives," but only Luke includes any account from Jesus' childhood (Luke 2:41–51).

2. This incident appears at the beginning of John (2:13–17) and toward the end of the Synoptics (Matt 21:12–13; Mark 11:15–17; Luke 19:45–46).

3. Or "outward facts"; the phrase is difficult to render into English.

and irresistibly moved by the Spirit, . . . wrote a spiritual Gospel" (*pneumatikon euangelion*).[4] Whatever John was, it had to be distinguished from Matthew, Mark, and Luke not merely by its author, content, or structure, but by its very nature: it is a different kind of Gospel. Modern interpreters continue to puzzle over John, using words such as "maverick," "enigma," or "riddle" to describe John's distinctive account of Jesus' ministry.[5] To be sure, not all of John's readers find it equally enigmatic: but one cannot help but see the differences from the other canonical Gospels and wonder about the origins and character of John. Just how does one account for the Gospel of John? What, exactly, is this Gospel? An eyewitness account of Jesus' life and ministry? A source for otherwise unattested traditions about Jesus? A theological interpretation of Jesus' significance cast as a narrative of his life? A dramatically different view of Jesus than presented in the Synoptic Gospels? Some combination of one or more of these options?

In the following remarks, I do not offer a full-scale critical introduction to the Gospel—such discussions can be found elsewhere[6]—but discussion of some important questions pertaining to John's distinctive presentation of Jesus. These reflections serve to alert the reader to what to expect in this commentary and the perspective adopted in it.

John and the Other Gospels

In its narrative form, John differs, as do the Synoptic Gospels, from the so-called apocryphal gospels, which focus on portions of Jesus' life, such as his childhood (*Infancy Gospel of Thomas*) or his passion (*Gospel of Peter*), or consist almost entirely of sayings of Jesus (*Gospel of Thomas*). Whether taken singly or together, the four canonical accounts have more in common with each other than they do with the noncanonical gospels in both substance and approach.[7] Yet even though Matthew, Mark, and Luke have episodes and material peculiar to them, the extensive overlaps in framework, content, and wording in their presentations of Jesus demand an account of their relationship to each other; it is impossible to think that they were written completely independently of each other. The same cannot be said for John in relationship to its canonical counterparts. Indeed, if the Synoptic accounts converge in spite of some differences, John tends to diverge from them in spite of some similarities.

In the Synoptic Gospels, Jesus' ministry is centered in Galilee, and—with the exception of Luke's accounts of Jesus' presentation in the temple in Jerusalem

4. Reported by Eusebius, *Hist. eccl.* 6.14.7.

5. So Eisler 1938; Kysar 2007. More than once Winston Churchill's description of Russia as "a riddle, wrapped in a mystery, inside an enigma" has been applied to John.

6. See R. Brown 2003; Keener 1:3–330.

7. For discussion of John's relationship to the other Gospels, including the apocryphal accounts, see D. Moody Smith 2001; 2008, various essays.

and visit to it at the age of twelve (2:22–39, 41–50)—Jesus goes to Jerusalem only at the end of his life, when he drives out the money changers from the temple, is arrested, and subsequently crucified. But in John, Jesus' ministry takes place mostly in Judea and Jerusalem, and even in the temple, and Jesus' dramatic action in it occurs early in the narrative. John thus presents a primarily Judean ministry, with Jesus frequently in Jerusalem and the temple, while the Synoptics locate Jesus' public work primarily in Galilee, with his presence in Jerusalem coming only at the end of his life.[8]

Most of the episodes that constitute John's narrative are unique to this Gospel alone: the changing of the water to wine (2:1–11); the encounters with Nicodemus (3:1–13) and the Samaritan woman at the well (4:1–42); the healing of the paralytic at the pool of Bethzatha (5:1–18) and of the blind man sent to wash in the pool of Siloam (ch. 9); the raising of Lazarus from the dead (ch. 11); the washing of the disciples' feet (13:1–11); and Jesus' lengthy encounter and dialogue with Pilate (18:28–19:22).[9] Finally, the resurrection appearance alone to Mary Magadalene at the tomb in the garden, Jesus' "breathing" of the Spirit on the gathered disciples, a subsequent encounter with Thomas, and the appearance by the lake of Galilee and the abundant catch of fish—all are only in John.[10] Key elements of the Synoptic tradition do not appear in John: there are no accounts of casting out demons, healing of leprosy, or encounters with tax collectors or Sadducees; neither are there accounts of Jesus' birth, temptations, or transfiguration; and the institution of the Lord's Supper at Jesus' final meal is missing.

In the Synoptics, Jesus speaks regularly in parables, proclaims the kingdom of God, and teaches across a broad spectrum of topics: almsgiving, anger, marriage, divorce, paying taxes, retaliation, anxiety, and wealth. John's Jesus teaches not in parables but in lengthy discourses, featuring a number of sayings beginning "I am" and followed by an explanatory predicate ("I am the bread of life"),[11] as well as characteristic Johannine vocabulary, including the contrasts of above and below, light and darkness, and such words as "witness," "truth," "world," and "abide." In a nutshell, then, what is most typical of Jesus' teaching in the Synoptic Gospels—the kingdom of God, a variety of topics covering the life of discipleship, teaching in parables and pithy sayings—is lacking in John,

8. Both John and the Synoptics also include episodes located neither in Judea nor in Galilee. Bethsaida and Caesarea Philippi, for example, lie in the region of Gaulinitis, which is part of the tetrarchy of Philip, and not in Galilee, the area assigned to Herod Antipas after the death of their father, Herod the Great.

9. In the Synoptics, Jesus heals a paralytic (Mark 2:1–11 par.), opens the eyes of the blind (8:22–25; 10:46–52 par.), and restores life to the dead (Mark 5:35–42 par.; Luke 7:11–16).

10. There are points of contact with the Synoptic, and especially Lukan, accounts (Luke 24:12//John 20:3–10; Luke 24:36–40//John 20:19–21, 24–27; Luke 24:41–43//John 21:9–13).

11. That is, the Greek *egō eimi* ("I am") with a predicate ("bread of life," "light of the world," "resurrection and the life," etc.). See Matt 14:27; 24:5; 27:43; Mark 6:50; 13:6; 14:62; Luke 21:8; 22:70; 24:39.

whereas what is most characteristic of John (longer discourses and disputes; "I am" sayings; a limited but distinctive vocabulary) tends to be missing from the Synoptics.[12]

How does one account for John's numerous differences from the Synoptics, amid its obvious similarities with them? In a book tellingly subtitled *Wollte der vierte Evangelist die älteren Evangelien ergänzen oder ersetzen?* [Did the Fourth Evangelist Want to Supplement or Replace the Older Gospels?],[13] Hans Windisch proposed that there were four possible explanations of the relationship of John and the other Gospels: John wished to (1) supplement, (2) interpret, or (3) replace the other Gospels. Windisch introduced but dismissed a fourth possibility—that John wrote independently of the other Gospels. His question was not new: already in the early church the question of John's relationship to the other Gospels had been pondered, typically leading to the conclusion that John had written to supplement or interpret the others. Perhaps defending the uniqueness of John, the Muratorian Canon (late 2d c.) states that "though various ideas are taught in the several books of the Gospels, yet it makes no difference to the faith of believers, since by one sovereign Spirit all things are declared in all of them."[14] This statement acknowledges the differences among all the Gospels, essentially adopting the position that all the Gospels implicitly supplement each other, as does Eusebius's suggestion that John recounted the events that happened before the Baptist was imprisoned.[15] Somewhat differently, Clement of Alexandria's designation of John as a "spiritual Gospel" in distinction to the other Gospels proposes a solution to the question of John's relationship to the other Gospels that approximates Windisch's category of "interpretation."[16]

Prior to the twentieth century, many interpreters would have expressed views perhaps most similar to Clement's: that John was written to offer a "spiritual" interpretation in contrast to the "bodily" accounts found in the other Gospels, although the language would more probably have contrasted "theological" or "doctrinal" with "historical." Clement's typology assumed that John was familiar with some or all of the other Gospels[17] and that he wrote to offer his own

12. However, Jesus' identity as king and the character of his kingdom emerge in the Passion Narrative, especially in Jesus' conversation with Pilate (John 18:36–37; cf. 19:14–15).

13. Windisch 1926; his own answer was "ersetzen": John wrote to *replace* the other Gospels.

14. Stevenson 2013, 145 (§124), placing the Muratorian Canon in Rome ca. 190. See also Irenaeus, *Haer.* 3.11.8, who explains the necessity of four Gospels by analogy to the four compass points.

15. Eusebius, *Hist. eccl.* 3.24.7–8.

16. Origen, *Comm. Jo.* 10.2, argued that the discrepancies between the chronologies of John and the other Gospels demanded that they be interpreted "spiritually" or "mystically."

17. Most typically, the Gospel of Mark (D. Moody Smith 2001, 46; see the overview in R. Brown 2003, 94–104). Those who argue that John knew or used one or more of the Synoptic Gospels include Barrett; Bauckham 1998b; Hengel 1989; Hoskyns; Thyen; and Lincoln 2005, 32 (who professed changing his mind in the course of writing his commentary).

distinctive interpretation of Jesus' ministry and person. But in the twentieth century, especially with the work of Percival Gardner-Smith and C. H. Dodd, the theory that John wrote independently of the other Gospels gained favor.[18] Gardner-Smith argued that the similarities between John and the other Gospels could be explained on the grounds of oral tradition and that, in any case, the differences between John and the other Gospels were more difficult to account for if one assumed that John knew and used the other Gospels than if one assumed that he did not, since the differences far outweigh the similarities.[19] Dodd investigated the traditions common to John and the Synoptics, arguing through close analysis that there was little evidence to justify the conclusion that John drew his material from Matthew, Mark, or Luke. If John were written without dependence upon, or perhaps without knowledge of, the other Gospels, then it could be construed neither as a supplement to them nor as a "spiritual interpretation" of them.[20] The view that John's Gospel was probably written independently of the others has gained currency in part because it has proved possible to explain John's narrative without primary recourse to the Synoptics. Although comparison with the Synoptics may illumine certain aspects or emphases of the Johannine narratives, such comparison cannot compel the conclusion that John was dependent on the Synoptic Gospels for his material.[21] Often comparison simply highlights the differences among them. But even if John did not depend on the Synoptics for his material, it is difficult, if not impossible, to rule out the possibility that John knew of the other Gospels but for some reason did not draw more fully on the traditions recorded in them.

While Gardner-Smith and Dodd often appealed to the possibility that John had drawn on oral traditions instead of one or more of the Synoptics, more recent studies of oral traditions have called attention to the complex relationships between oral and written sources. "Oral tradition" could have developed out of the written sources—a feature called "secondary orality"—and in turn could have shaped other written traditions or sources or existed alongside

18. See Gardner-Smith 1938; Dodd 1963.

19. The arguments for a literary relationship among the Synoptic Gospels have typically appealed to the argument that verbatim agreements, in similar material presented in the same order, suggest dependence (or interdependence). But just where John narrates the same incident as the other Gospels (e.g., the feeding of the five thousand), the verbatim agreements between John and the Synoptics are slight; and given the relative lack of overlapping material, the arguments from order remain at a fairly general level.

20. Commentators who advocate Johannine independence (without necessarily dismissing the possibility that John was aware of or had read the other Gospels) include R. Brown 1966; Carson 1991; Keener; Moloney 1998b; O'Day; Ridderbos; D. Moody Smith 1999; and Schnackenburg.

21. John's independence from the other Gospels has sometimes been used as an argument for the historical character of John's unique traditions, on the grounds that if John did not know the other Gospels, it could not be construed as a theological recasting of them. In that event one could entertain the possibility that John bears independent historical witness to Jesus' ministry.

them. Indeed, a number of interpreters have proposed quite elaborate theories to account for the composition of John, positing either John's dependence on or independence from the other Gospels.[22] One recent commentator describes the majority position regarding John's relationship to the Synoptics as advocating John's independence of them, without ruling out John's familiarity with unwritten traditions behind the written Gospels.[23] In other words, no matter how much one appeals to oral or written traditions behind our extant Gospels to explain the relationship of John and the Synoptics, there is some kind of relationship that does not seem aptly described as "independence," especially if "independence" is taken to mean that John wrote in isolation from or ignorance of other early accounts of Jesus.

Perhaps opinion remains divided because of the difficulty of accounting for John's distinctive presentation of Jesus by appealing entirely either to a theory of dependence or independence. Much of John clearly does not come simply from the Synoptic Gospels: many of John's accounts have no parallels there, nor is it easy to explain how at points John could be construed either as supplementing or interpreting one or more of those Gospels. Jesus' words—the substance of his discourses, the vocabulary and imagery used—can often be shown to elaborate upon themes introduced in the other Gospels; yet in John, Jesus' discourses run down new paths hinted at, though not fully charted, in the other Gospels. In Mark, for example, Jesus refers to God as his Father only four times (Mark 8:38; 11:25; 13:32; 14:36); this number increases in both Matthew and Luke. In John, God is designated as "the Father" or "my Father" about 130 times. It would be unfair to say that the relationship of Jesus to God as a son to a father is peripheral or unimportant in Mark (or Matthew or Luke)—but John's Gospel has made it central.

Similarly, Mark and the other Synoptics record Jesus' healing of a paralytic, which comes to a climax with Jesus' pronouncement about the authority of the Son of Man (Mark 2:10); later, when asked about the source of his authority, Jesus essentially refuses to answer the question (11:28–33). When asked why he acts in seeming violation of Sabbath law, Jesus cites his authority as the Son of Man who is "lord even of the sabbath" (2:28), but he does not elaborate further. In John, too, Jesus heals a paralytic on the Sabbath, addressing the paralytic with the same command that one finds in the Synoptics; yet the setting differs.[24] Again, the healing raises the question of Jesus' authority; in John it

22. M.-E. Boismard and Franz Neirinck proffer complicated theories that sketch John's relationship to the Synoptics (see discussion in D. Moody Smith 2001, 141–58); Paul N. Anderson presents a different, complex model of John's multistage composition in relationship to the other Gospel traditions (2011, 125–55).

23. Michaels 29.

24. Note the matching commands: "Rise, take up your mat and walk/go home!" (John 5:8// Mark 2:11 AT).

is followed by Jesus' lengthy discourse explaining its scope and source: God, his Father, has granted him authority to work on the Sabbath, to judge, and to give life. Here Jesus' discourse unfolds in a sophisticated argument that reflects views, found in Philo and later in rabbinic material, that God himself works on the Sabbath without violating his own injunction to rest on the Sabbath. John thus presses an argument from Jewish exegetical literature into making a point about Jesus' all-encompassing authority, which he exercises as a gift from and in dependence on the Father.

How to account for the absence in John of material from the Synoptics poses a different kind of challenge. For example, John lacks the designation of Jesus as "son of David." To be sure, Jesus is the Messiah, but in this Gospel he is such by virtue of being "Son of God." It is easy enough to see *that* this is so: it becomes more speculative to suggest *why* this is so. John may represent a "universalizing" of the traditions of Jesus' Davidic descent: Jesus now exercises his messianic office, not only as "King of Israel" (1:49; 12:13) or "King of the Jews" (18:33, 39; 19:3, 19, 21), but as the King of Israel who has authority over all flesh. Consider also the absence of exorcism from John. In the Synoptic accounts such exorcisms provide evidence of Jesus' overcoming of Satan's power (Mark 3:22–27; Luke 10:17–18); disciples who try to change Jesus' course to the cross speak with the voice of Satan, the tempter (Mark 8:31–33); Satan tempts Jesus, and then his followers, to fall away (Matt 4:1–10; Luke 4:1–13; 22:31). In John, there are no demon exorcisms, and no Satanic temptation faces Jesus. Instead, the devil's power becomes manifested in Judas, the disciple who turns from following Jesus (6:60–71; 13:2, 27), and in those Jews who had once believed in Jesus but did not remain faithful to him (8:30–31). The conflict between the power of God and of Satan (or the devil) is framed in John as the conflict between belief (the faithful disciples) and unbelief (Judas, unfaithful disciples, the world). Jesus overcomes the world (16:33); light overcomes darkness (1:5). Jesus still confronts the powers of darkness, but these powers are construed differently in John than in the Synoptics.

Also absent from John are matters affecting ritual purity: disputes over handwashing (Mark 7:1–12; Matt 15:1–20), the healing of leprosy and of unclean spirits, touching corpses or being touched by the ritually unclean. And yet Jesus himself conducts a baptismal ministry and cleanses his own disciples by word and deed (John 3:22–26; 13:1–12; 15:3). The purification that is needed is not accomplished through ritual washing, either Jewish or Greek or Roman;[25] it is accomplished by Jesus, through his word and his death. Purification is thus less tied to any specific cultural practices; moreover, it is christologically centered. Perhaps in the interest of presenting Jesus to those beyond the confines of Jesus' own time and place, John has also played down the debates over Jewish ritual

25. Ritual washing was part of religious practices in these cultures as well.

practice; but if discussion of these practices was a feature of Jesus' ministry, it is not a feature of his ministry in John.

Even if one were to account for all the possible ways of construing the relationship of this or that bit of material to the Synoptic accounts, one would scarcely account for the totality of the Gospel of John. John, like each of the other Gospels, is greater than the sum of its parts: the narrative is not merely stitched-together bits of tradition; it is a carefully crafted account of a select number of words and deeds from Jesus' life that presents a particular understanding of Jesus, who he was, and what his ministry accomplished. While all the Gospels offer interpreted accounts of Jesus' ministry, the Synoptics have, on the whole, approached their task somewhat differently. John has more thoroughly interpreted and elaborated upon traditional material, especially in Jesus' discourses and dialogue, evincing more freedom in both the arrangement and interpretation of his material to present Jesus as the embodied Word, the Son of God, through whom God's glory is manifested and God is revealed, and through whom God gives life to the world. Still, John's Gospel is not a theological treatise or epistle: it is a Gospel, a narrative of Jesus' life, akin to ancient historical biography. John's interpretive freedom in selecting and ordering events, expanding or contracting material, especially discourses, in order to give an account of what Jesus did and said and how one should understand their significance—all this is exactly what one would expect of an ancient biography.[26] In sum: however one resolves the question of its sources, John bears the distinctive stamp of a creative mind that interpreted received traditions in light of a particular hermeneutical stance and theological convictions about Jesus and the significance of his ministry.[27]

Reading from John's Perspective

Perhaps ultimately at stake in the questions about John's relationship to the other Gospels is John's relationship to the Jesus of history. Typically the Synoptic Gospels have been taken to present "the historical Jesus," or at least to contain materials that enable one to reconstruct that figure, whereas John's Gospel has rarely been employed for that purpose.[28]

26. Burridge 2004. See also the careful discussion, with numerous examples, in Keener 1:11–34. On John's historiographical character, see Bauckham 2007c, 93–112.

27. Similarly Schnelle 1998, 17, 22, 25–26.

28. Here the quest of the historical Jesus is understood to be the effort to reconstruct Jesus "as he really was": what he really did and said and what was done to him, by whom, and why, with the implicit assumption that this reconstructed narrative will differ from the account in any single Gospel or from a "harmonized" account of all the Gospels. For recent discussions of the historicity of the Fourth Gospel, with varying methodological approaches and conclusions, see the two-volume set edited by Anderson, Just, and Thatcher (2007–9); and the work edited by Fortna and Thatcher (2001).

Undoubtedly John would have been puzzled by modern questions of whether he presents "the Jesus of history." In John it matters greatly that Jesus was a figure of the past and that his life displayed very specific contours. But this does not mean that for John the identity of Jesus can be ascertained through historical reconstructions of the "undisputed facts" about Jesus, as though the "real" or "historical" Jesus were other than the Jesus of the Gospel. Even if one could verify every detail in John as "authentic," one would not have therefore grasped the identity of Jesus in the Fourth Gospel, the "what" that makes Jesus who he is. The inadequacy of historical reconstruction is already evident in the opening words of the Gospel, where Jesus the Messiah (1:17) is introduced as the Word through whom the world was made, who became flesh, and who is now ever with the Father. These three statements articulate, respectively, the cosmic identity of the Word as the agent of life; the Word enfleshed among his own, the people of Israel, who as Israel's Messiah is also the savior of the world (4:42); and the one who, subsequent to his death, now lives forever with the Father. These statements encapsulate who Jesus was and is, Jesus as he *really* was and is. This is confessional language, not subject to historical reconstruction or substantiation.

Here we may recall Clement's characterization of John as a "spiritual Gospel," a designation that indicates something about the *kind* of truth John conveys and the *way* that truth is known: a "spiritual" Gospel gives the inner meaning of an event or reality and therefore requires apposite interpretation.[29] In John, the dilemma of understanding Jesus is framed both theologically and chronologically: during his lifetime, Jesus' identity was not grasped, or not grasped completely, because he could not be understood fully through the experiential faculties of sight and hearing. It was only after and in the light of his death and resurrection, the events and realities triggered by them, and the Spirit's instruction, that the disciples would be able to fully articulate what Jesus had intended and accomplished, and who he was and is. Of all the Gospels, John most explicitly articulates the necessity of the postresurrection perspective for understanding Jesus, interpreting Jesus' life retrospectively (see 2:22; 12:16). In John, Jesus is known "from back to front": that is, beginning with the resurrection and reading the significance of his mission and identity from that vantage point.[30] To put it differently, the Fourth Gospel presents an account of Jesus that, all the way through, rolls the results of what happened into the causes

29. Robinson 1985, 344, interprets Clement's description to mean that John gives "the truth of the history really entered into."

30. In an essay translated into English as "Towards the Interpretation of John's Gospel," Bornkamm spoke of John's Gospel as written "von rückwärts aus [from the back]." See Schnelle, 2001, 356: "The retrospective post-Easter viewpoint is for John both a theological scheme and a narrative perspective; it allows the Fourth Evangelist to translate theological insights into narrated history."

of those events and the substance of things that Jesus said and did, along with the witness of human beings and Scripture, into Jesus' self-declared identity. In the Synoptic Gospels, Jesus' identity is slowly unfolded throughout the narrative, to be known cumulatively and vindicated in the resurrection, so that the whole becomes the sum of its parts and more than the sum of those parts; in John, the whole of Jesus' identity already appears in nearly each and every part of the narrative. In John, Jesus is known from the end.

"End" includes not only Jesus' crucifixion and resurrection, but also the events subsequent to them. What happens after Jesus' death and resurrection, and as a result of Jesus' life and ministry—for example, his disciples' conduct of a worldwide mission, his followers' contention with others about how to understand Jesus' identity in relationship to God, Israel, and the world—becomes the lens through which the entire narrative is recounted. Indeed, the results of Jesus' death and resurrection become lodged in Jesus' words and within the narrative itself. Thus, for example, not only did Jesus' death and resurrection lead to his followers' worldwide mission; in John that mission was always already in view in Jesus' own ministry and was, in fact, its goal. John answers certain questions more explicitly than the other Gospels do: "Who then is this? What was he up to? And why did he die?" The answers to these questions are seen from the end of the story, looking back, and they become part of the Gospel's witness and even of Jesus' own words.

While John might thus seem to erase the boundaries between the earthly and postresurrection ministry of Jesus, the Gospel just as clearly distinguishes them: the Word enters into this world (1:14); there is a turning point with the coming of Jesus' "hour," his departure from the world and his disciples, and a "return" to the Father (13:1–4). But even these decisive turning points in the narrative—incarnation, resurrection, return to the Father—do not signal a change in the essential identity of God's Word, who was, is, and will be life for the world. The resurrection is not the aftermath of Jesus' life; rather, what happened through the resurrection and after the resurrection is part of who Jesus is and what his life was all about. To a large extent, this conviction makes the Gospel of John what it is and makes Jesus who he is in the Gospel of John. The one who laid down his life is also the one who took it up again (10:18), the one who *is* resurrection and life (11:25). The claims made for and by Jesus in this Gospel depend for their truth and their substance on Jesus' resurrection to life.[31]

Accordingly John declares that the significance of some events he has narrated could not be understood until later, until after Jesus was raised from the dead (e.g., 2:22; 13:7). After the resurrection, the Spirit of truth was given

31. In M. M. Thompson 2011, I have compared the assumptions underlying John's Gospel in its presentation of Jesus with those of the modern "quest for the historical Jesus."

(14:17; 15:26), and the Spirit instructs the disciples into "all the truth." The Spirit's role is closely correlated with Scripture and sight. On the one hand, Jesus' identity and mission are disclosed through the witness of the Scriptures. These Scriptures provide specific imagery applicable to Jesus (shepherd, king, judge, bread, light). Moreover, these Scriptures speak of the coming of the promised one, of the Messiah (1:45; 5:37, 46); they contain the narratives of Israel's past, such as the wandering in the wilderness; and the promises of the ingathering of God's people and God's presence with his people that come to their fullness in what Jesus offers (Exod 25:8; 29:45; Lev 26:11; 1 Kgs 6:13; Ezek 37:26–28; Zech 2:11). The Gospel also claims that certain scriptural texts actually refer to this Jesus (12:41 alluding to Isa 6:1–6; Ps 69, cited in John 2:19; 15:25; and 19:28–29). In short, the Scriptures of Israel do more than provide the categories and framework for understanding Jesus' identity as the messianic agent of God's decisive act of salvation for his people and for the world. They *bear witness* to Jesus (5:39). To understand the Scriptures' witness *to* Jesus requires that one read them *through* the lens of Jesus' life, death, and resurrection: looking backward, reading retrospectively from back to front.

Thus the Scriptures are not equally understood by all, nor was their significance for understanding Jesus' deeds grasped at the time of Jesus' actions or works. The Spirit, whom Jesus sent from the Father to his followers after his departure, will teach them "all things" and guide them into "all truth" (14:26; 16:13). These "truths" have to do with Jesus' identity: a fuller understanding of his words, signs, and death; and the significance of these for all the world.[32] While John states that he has written his Gospel so that people might believe that Jesus is the Messiah, one cannot arrive at that confession simply by reading it off the surface of Jesus' life and deeds, for his messianic vocation is undertaken, not in terms of the exercise of power against his enemies, but rather as service (13:1–11) and self-giving (10:1–18; 12:23–26) and through his death on the cross. In order to recognize this one as God's Messiah, and to see, enter, and understand the kingdom that is genuinely God's kingdom (3:3, 5; 18:36), the work of the Spirit of God is required: recognition of Jesus as the Messiah is not the product of human logic or reason, but of the revelation, teaching, or witness of God (John 5:36–37; 6:27, 44–45; cf. Matt 11:25–27; 16:17; Luke 10:21–22).[33] The Spirit teaches the disciples, by means of Scripture and in light of the results of Jesus' own mission, how to understand more fully who he is and what he has accomplished. But without the illumination of the Scriptures and the instruction of the Spirit, the events of Jesus' life remain opaque.

32. Robinson (1985, 362) suggests that in writing his Gospel, John is in effect saying, "This is what Jesus was really like; we did not realize it then, but now we know it."

33. See Moberly 2001.

The need for illumination is further documented by the various connotations of "seeing" in the Gospel. On the one hand, "seeing" refers to the simple act of physical sight; on the other, it refers to perception, or "insight." Certain statements—such as "We saw his glory" (1:14), "I have seen and borne witness that he is the Son of God" (1:34), or "We have come to know that [he is] the Savior of the world" (4:42)—show that insight into Jesus' identity cannot be gained entirely by what the eyes can see, but that neither can such insight dispense with what the eyes see.[34] A statement such as "We saw his glory" refers to both levels: some saw in Jesus and his deeds the manifestation of the glory of God. There was something concrete to be seen, but there is something that one cannot see simply by looking. Insight cannot be divorced from sight, although insight does not naturally or inevitably arise from sight (e.g., 9:39). Indeed, at times insight, which might also be termed the perception of a matter through the illumination of God's Spirit, is radically counterintuitive. This is nowhere more evident than in Jesus' death on the cross. Caiaphas urges Jesus' death as a way to placate Roman anxieties and preserve his people (11:48–52); Pilate placates his own worries about losing Caesar's favor by putting a would-be king to death (19:12). Each makes a calculated political decision, in his historical context, that leads to Jesus' crucifixion. But what Caiaphas or Pilate—whether we imagine the "historical" or "Johannine" figures—think about Jesus' death differs considerably from John's assessment of it as the ultimate act of Jesus' self-giving love for the world's salvation. For John, this understanding articulates the *historical* significance of Jesus' death on the cross: this was what Jesus' death meant and means. Modern commentators often distinguish "historical" and "theological," even driving a wedge between them; yet for John, historical and theological significance converge, are mutually interpretive, and are impossible to disentangle. The kind of historical account that bears witness to Jesus does not simply recount his past, but it cannot do without it.

The Gospel of John itself clearly acknowledges that there are other ways to tell the story of Jesus; indeed, the Gospel is shot through with the divisions that arise over differing assessments of him (1:10–13; 6:66; 7:26–42; 9:34). It is clear that those who differed so sharply over Jesus often witnessed the same deeds and heard the same words. But it was within the context of the early gathering of Jesus' immediate disciples and those they taught, a community that was inspired by the Spirit and read the Scriptures as a witness to the risen Lord, that the fullness of Jesus' identity and the significance of his words and deeds came to be articulated.

34. Byrskog's assertion (149) that eyewitnesses were "as much interpreters as observers" squares with the Johannine distinction between the two ways of seeing. Byrskog's point has been amplified by Bauckham 2006 (for discussion of John, see esp. 384–411); see also Keener's discussion (11–34) of the historiographical and interpretative character of ancient biography.

In writing his Gospel, John aims in part to show that "what Jesus *is* to the faith of the true Christian believer, he was in the flesh."[35] Jesus *was* the bread of life, the light of the world, the (embodied) Word and glory of God; and he *is* still the life and light of the world, the Word and glory of God now ever with the Father. The Gospel presupposes the identity of the earthly and exalted Jesus in such a way that neither first- nor twenty-first-century believers may regard their discipleship to be superior—or inferior—to that of others. John recognizes the differences among Jesus' disciples—some were his immediate followers, others came to believe in other times and places—but John neither denigrates nor exalts either kind of discipleship. One of the assumptions of this Gospel, and part of its purpose, is to assure believers who never saw or heard Jesus that their discipleship at second hand is no second-class discipleship. Jesus has one flock, drawn from different times and places, and those sheep have one shepherd. Those who believe in Jesus through the disciples' word, rather than through Jesus' own word, are all one (10:16; 17:20–21).

The Gospel of John does not present the Jesus who was understood by all, but rather the Jesus to whom his disciples and, above all, the "disciple whom he loved" bore witness. We have Jesus as that disciple remembered him, Jesus as all his disciples remembered him, and Jesus as they bore witness to him. The paucity of data in the Jewish and Roman sources of Jesus' day makes it very clear that unless the memories of Jesus' disciples had been preserved, we would know as little about Jesus as we do about "the Egyptian" or Theudas, those revolutionary figures mentioned in Acts (5:36; 21:38)—and that at least some would not have reckoned that much of a loss. Ancient Roman and Jewish sources are not primarily interested in Jesus as a political dissident or social critic, but in a movement that he generated and that lived on until their day. And that is the Jesus in whom John is interested: the living, life-giving Jesus who called and calls people to follow, trust, and love him. This means that to know Jesus, one cannot bypass the memory and witness of those who followed Jesus. Indeed, the Gospel of John might well note that Thomas's error lay not in his empiricist refusal to believe what he could not see, but in his historicist refusal to trust the apostolic witness to the resurrection.

John's Witness to Jesus

In John's Gospel, not only does the resurrection make faith in Jesus possible; it also provides substance to that faith, directed toward the living God who gives life to all the world through his Word, and toward the Word enfleshed as Jesus of Nazareth. Not without reason has the Gospel of John been called "the Gospel of life." "Eternal life" is one of its distinctive themes, not only in terms of the

35. Hoskyns 35.

number of occurrences, but also in terms of its capacity to summarize who Jesus is and what he effects for humankind.

"In the Beginning Was the Word"

John identifies Jesus, the Gospel's central figure, as "the Word" through which the world was made and life was given. This is to enunciate the Word's claim on all humankind, on all creation. Throughout the Gospel there are hints and reminders that, in the words of Jesus, it is the Word, who was with God and was God, who speaks: as the embodiment on earth of Jacob's ladder (1:51), he opens the heavenly realms of glory; he has come "from above" and will return to his previous state of glory; he offers the divine gift of life in the face of death, which pervades the cosmos; as the unique Son, he alone makes God known (1:18). This cosmic aspect of his identity comes to expression in the universal claim of Jesus, the King of Israel, on all the peoples of the world. In every encounter in the Gospel, those who hear, see, follow, or challenge Jesus are in fact coming face-to-face with the agent of their creation: the one through whom the world was made is also its Savior (4:42).

"The Word Was Made Flesh"

It is this Word, made flesh, who heals, teaches, debates, hungers, thirsts, bleeds, and dies, in a specific time and specific places: in the villages in and surrounding Galilee, Samaria, and Judea under the Roman Empire of the first century. Jesus shared the beliefs of his fellow Jews, including the acknowledgment of one living God, the heritage received from the patriarchs, the validity of Torah and the role of Moses in giving it, the sanctity of the temple, the resurrection from the dead, and the promised ingathering of God's scattered children under the Messiah, symbolized in anticipatory fashion by the selection of twelve disciples. John alludes to the halakic regulations that allow for circumcision on the Sabbath (7:22; *m. Šabb.* 18:3–19:4); he is aware of the custom of using stone jars for the waters of purification (2:6; *m. Kelim* 10:1); he knows the Palestinian manna traditions of the Jewish haggadah (6:35–51) and the significance of the last day of the Feast of Tabernacles and the water poured in front of the altar (7:37; *m. Sukkah* 4:1, 8, 9). The designations used for Jesus reflect the categories that come from the Scriptures and the world of first-century Judaism: he is called prophet, Messiah, and King of Israel and of the Jews. His speech is replete with metaphors from Scripture: the vine, shepherd, bread, and light; he interprets scriptural texts (e.g., John 6:32, 45; 10:34–35); he alludes to narratives of Israel's past, such as the sojourn in the wilderness. His public deeds and teaching take place near Passover, on the Sabbath, at Tabernacles and Hanukkah. He disputes with the Pharisees, runs afoul of the chief priests, encounters the Roman governor Pontius Pilate, and dies by crucifixion at the hands of Roman imperial power. Jesus' mission is directed to "his own" (1:11), and he dies in order to save "the nation" and to "gather into one the children of God who had been scattered" (11:48–52). As the Messiah, the one promised in its Scriptures, Jesus both bestows and embodies the fullness of what Israel's various institutions, feasts, and central figures commemorate, promise, or signify: Jesus embodies the fullness of God's grace (1:14,16); joy (3:29; 15:11; 16:24; 17:13); provision (6:13) and life (10:10).

"He Is Ever at the Father's Side"

The Gospel is peppered with promises that the death and resurrection of Jesus will accomplish the hoped-for ingathering of Jesus' own people, yet beyond that will serve to gather all people (3:15; 10:16; 12:32, 47; see also 7:35). As the living one, Jesus sends the Holy Spirit, the Spirit of life, from the Father (14:26; 15:26). Jesus breathes the life-giving Spirit of God into humankind as God breathed the Spirit into Adam, and as God will breathe life into the desiccated bones of the people of Israel (20:23; Gen 2:7; Ezek 37:9). Jesus' risen mode of existence and the sending of the Spirit to bear witness to him make it possible for him to be present and known beyond the boundaries of Judea and Galilee. Jesus, the Messiah of Israel, is also the "Savior of the world" (4:42).

At the end of the Gospel there is also a brief allusion to Jesus' expected return (John 21:22–23), along with a few descriptions of the future that emphasize the twin themes of eternal life and presence—the presence of the Father, and the Son, with the people of God. The Gospel of John thus comprises in itself the whole biblical story from creation (1:1–3) to the second coming of Christ (21:22–23), implicitly identifying Jesus of Nazareth as the one who was, is, and is to come: what can be predicated of the eternal God can also be predicated of him (cf. Rev 1:4).

In John's witness to Jesus, these aspects of Jesus' identity are coordinated in such a way that each determines and shapes the other. It is as the Word made flesh that Jesus is the Messiah: Israel's deliverance is an act of Israel's God, and "Messiah" is defined and redefined in terms of the embodied presence of God's own Word, who speaks words of life to his people. As the agent of creation, the King of Israel delivers his people from the ultimate forces that threaten their very existence—namely, the powers of death—by subjecting himself to the powers of the Roman authorities, who execute him as they had other would-be rebels. Again, it is as the Messiah of Israel that Jesus is the Savior of the world; and it is as the Savior of the world that he is the Messiah of Israel; thus, gathering his flock entails bringing in sheep of other folds (10:16; 11:52). As King of Israel, the Word incarnate accomplishes deliverance from death to life not only for his own, but also for the world, which was "made through him" (1:3).

There is a reason that John 3:16 may be the most repeated and memorized verse of Scripture: its pithy formulations—God so loved the world, that he gave, that they may have life—encapsulate John's declarations about the relationship of God to the world. God's love for the world manifests itself in life for the world: this, in turn, brings glory to God (11:4, 40). John, however, does not present these claims in the form of a letter, dialogue, or treatise, but rather as the narrative of the Word who was with God and was God, who became flesh, and is now ever with the Father. In this Word—who was, is, and will be—there is life; that life reveals God's love for the world; and God's life-giving love glorifies the Father and Son together. Jesus' disciples participate in these realities: they are the recipients of God's love and life; by embodying those gifts in their communal life together, they extend both to the world. In this way they bear witness to Jesus and bring glory to God.

Structure and Structural Features of the Fourth Gospel

A brief and typical overview of the Gospel of John usually divides it into two main parts, with an introductory prologue and a very brief closing epilogue:[36]

1:1–18	An introduction to the Gospel
1:19–12:52	The Book of Signs: Jesus' Public Ministry[37]
13:1–21:22	The Book of the Passion: Jesus' Last Words, Death, and Resurrection
21:23–25	Epilogue[38]

Each constituent "book" includes a summary statement (12:37–50; 20:30–31) that focuses on belief and unbelief. In each book the works of Jesus reveal who he is and what he brings. The book of signs focuses on those works of God done through Jesus, works that embody the fullness of God's gifts: provisions of bread and wine; the gifts of light and life. Many of the discrete episodes in chapters 2–12 include a sign, followed by a dispute or discourse that enunciates Jesus' claims and unfolds his identity as the Messiah and Son of God, whose mission is to deliver his people from death to life. In this first part of the Gospel, the glory of God is revealed through the works and words of Jesus as the work of the living Father that brings life to the world.

36. This is Dodd's well-known outline of the Gospel (1953). R. Brown (1966, 1970) prefers "book of glory" to the "book of the passion," since the hour of Jesus' death is the hour of his glorification (John 12:23, 28; 13:31–32; 17:1, 4). But one cannot limit Jesus' glorification to the second part of the Gospel: Jesus' death and resurrection complete the manifestation of his glory throughout his entire life (2:11; 11:4, 40; 12:28; 17:4).

37. The signs are often numbered at seven; for further discussion, see Excursus 3: "Signs."

38. Others regard all of ch. 21 as an epilogue.

In the second part of the Gospel, the "book of the passion," the glory of God is revealed through the death of Jesus on the cross, an act that shows God's love for the world by demonstrating the lengths to which Jesus will go to bring his life-giving work to fruition. Together, then, Jesus' works and deeds, death and resurrection, manifest God's love, bring life, and manifest God's glory. All these reveal the presence of God and in turn bring glory (*doxa*) to God.

John frequently sets each of the main episodes of the Gospel at the occasion of one of the major Jewish feasts (Passover: 2:13, 23; 6:4; 11:55; 12:1; 13:1; Tabernacles: 7:2; Hanukkah: 10:22). The correlation of certain incidents in Jesus' life with his signs and with the Jewish feasts at which they occur articulates the significance of Jesus' deeds. At Passover, for example, the feast commemorating the deliverance from Egypt that in turn initiates the wilderness wanderings, Jesus feeds the multitudes with fish and bread. His provision recalls the manna, the "bread from heaven," which the Israelites ate during their sojourn in the wilderness; the manna serves as a figure of Jesus as the bread of life. Taken together, the setting (Passover), the deed (Jesus' feeding), and the scriptural context (deliverance from Egypt, God's provision in the wilderness) coalesce to present Jesus as God's bread of life for his people and the world. At Tabernacles, which features ceremonies of water and light, Jesus opens the eyes of a blind man and presents himself as the "light of the world." At Hanukkah, the feast that commemorates the Maccabean recapture and rededication of the temple defiled by the Seleucids, Jesus himself is at the temple, and people wonder whether he is the Messiah, Israel's anointed deliverer; perhaps he will repeat the deeds of the Maccabees.

References to the Jewish feasts provide a chronological framework for the Gospel and give the impression that the duration of the ministry of Jesus was two or three years. These same references point up the Gospel's episodic character: since Passover is in the spring and Tabernacles is in the fall, a year must have elapsed between the events narrated in John 6 and John 11:55. John has deliberately chosen a few episodes, developed them at greater length and with more details than similar scenes in the Synoptics, and placed them in a chronological framework that calls upon texts and festivals within Scripture in order to interpret Jesus' deeds in continuity with God's calling and deliverance of his people. Within the general chronological framework, repeated brief references to the delay of Jesus' hour also convey the sense of movement until the final arrival of the hour in which Jesus completes his work and returns to the glory that he had with the Father before the world was made (2:4; 7:30; 8:20; 12:23; 13:1; 17:1, 5).

Authorship, Date, and Setting

The Gospel stakes its credibility on an eyewitness who had a personal memory of Jesus, namely, "the disciple whom Jesus loved" (19:35; 21:24–25). This disciple is also identified as the author of the Gospel, or at least one connected integrally to its writing (see comments below, at 21:24–25). In my view, this disciple is not one of the Twelve; hence, he is not John, the son of Zebedee. The single oblique reference to "the sons of Zebedee" as among those who were fishing with Peter when Jesus appeared to them by the lakeside (21:2) may allow that "the disciple whom Jesus loved," and who identified Jesus as the Lord to Peter on that occasion, was one of these "sons." But it is equally possible that this disciple should be identified with one of the "two others of his disciples," since elsewhere, when he is paired with Peter, this disciple is also described as "the other disciple" (cf. 20:2–3; 13:23). The Gospel's insistence that "we know" that this disciple's "testimony is true" (21:24) strongly suggests that this disciple's identity was known at some point. The suggestion that he is John the Elder, who is identified in Eusebius (*Hist. eccl.* 3.39.3) as one of two figures named "John" who resided in Ephesus, could account for the early attribution of the Gospel to "John" and for its connections to Ephesus, while also explaining why the Gospel does not identify its author as the son of Zebedee.[39]

In the Gospel itself, "the disciple whom Jesus loved" is explicitly connected with the events of Jesus' passion and thus with incidents set in Jerusalem. He first appears in the narrative at Jesus' Last Supper with his disciples (13:23). He follows Jesus into the high priest's courtyard (18:15).[40] He stands at the foot of the cross as Jesus dies (19:26–35) and is present at the discovery of the empty tomb (20:1–10). Only at the final resurrection appearance of Jesus to some disciples in Galilee (ch. 21) does he appear outside of Jerusalem. There are telling clues that this follower is a Jerusalem disciple, including the disciple's role in scenes set in Jerusalem; the Gospel's familiarity with the topography of Jerusalem and Judea, including such minor locales as Ephraim (11:54), as well as with various locations in or near the temple (its treasury, 8:20; the pool of Siloam, 9:7; Solomon's Portico, 10:23); and explicit details of temple ceremonies, including rituals of water and light associated with Tabernacles (7:37–39; 8:5). Moreover, if more speculatively, his profile suggests someone of priestly lineage.[41] John also pays particular attention to the political situation in Jerusalem, the decisions and actions of the leading priests there (11:48–52), and the fears of the Roman governor, Pontius Pilate—thus simultaneously providing credible Jewish and Roman political motivations for Jesus' execution.

39. For discussions of the arguments regarding authorship, including the external evidence, see Barrett; R. Brown 1966; Keener; Michaels; Schnackenburg; for the view that the disciple whom Jesus loved is also the author of the Gospel and John the Elder (of Ephesus), see Hengel 1989; Bauckham 2006, 416, with bibliography; and more fully, idem 2007, 33–91.

40. This observation depends on whether "another disciple" refers to "the disciple whom Jesus loved" (18:15).

41. In John, notice also Jesus' connection with those of elite status: the description of the wedding at Cana (2:1–11) places it on a well-to-do estate; Jesus meets a royal official in Cana; he is buried by a man of some status, Joseph of Arimathea.

Because the Gospel demonstrates familiarity with Jewish customs, institutions, and interpretive traditions, its background is most typically characterized today as Jewish. Such a characterization represents a change from the viewpoint, dominant in the earlier part of the twentieth century, that John's Gospel should be characterized as a Greek Gospel, that is, arising from a Greek (Gentile) rather than Jewish milieu.[42] But here the discovery of the Dead Sea Scrolls (beginning in the late 1940s) proved pivotal since they provided plausible parallels to much of the language and conceptuality of John that had been commonly assigned in the earlier part of the twentieth century to John's contact with or influence from Greek religion or philosophy. At times John seems to breathe the air of the scrolls. Some of these documents, especially the *Rule of the Community* (1QS), manifest a kind of dualism akin to that in John, with its contrast between light and darkness, truth and error, spirit and flesh (cf. 1QS III, 13–IV, 26). The Dead Sea Scrolls bear witness to a community that spoke of themselves as the "sons of light" and of all those who disdained its ways as the "sons of Beliar" or "sons of darkness." Here too, as in John, God's Spirit is designated as the spirit of truth. Yet in spite of such similarities, not all scholars jumped on the Qumran bandwagon. In the introduction to the second edition of his commentary (1978), a scholar of no less stature than Barrett confessed himself out of step with some of the recent trends in Johannine scholarship when he wrote, "I do not think that Qumran holds the key to John."[43] He may have been prescient, since more recently scholars have called attention to the thinness of the parallels between John and the scrolls.[44] Even so, the discovery of the Dead Sea Scrolls, coupled with increased attention to early Judaism in the last fifty years or so, has certainly changed the discussion, causing interpreters to reevaluate the provenance of John's Gospel and to situate its origins firmly in first-century Palestine.

John presents Jesus as the Messiah, bearing the fullness of God's gifts and God's life, by clarifying the relationship of Jesus to the patriarchs of Israel (4:12; 6:32; 8:53–58), to its festivals and institutions (2:1–11, 19–22; 6:32–41; 7:37–39), and to Moses and the law (1:17; 5:39–40, 45–47; 7:19–23). The consistency and intensity of this line of argument may suggest that the Gospel serves to exhort, encourage, and persuade those readers for whom the symbols and realities of Scripture and Judaism exerted a powerful pull. But one may just as well learn something about the author's own convictions regarding the significance of Jesus, or about the traditions that came to that author. In other words, the conceptual world and rhetorical argument in the Gospel do not necessarily provide a portrait of an "intended audience." The ways in which

42. Dodd's masterly *Interpretation of the Fourth Gospel*, published in 1953, discusses "Hellenistic" and "Rabbinic" Judaism, but he was unable to take into account the DSS.

43. Barrett viii; he adds, "I do not believe that it is a Palestinian work, aimed at Diaspora Judaism."

44. See the articles by Bauckham 1997; Frey 2004.

John employs both Scripture and Jewish interpretive traditions cannot settle the identity of John's "actual" or "real" readers, or perhaps even of its final author. Clearly, however, Scripture, temple ceremonies, and the events they commemorate have shaped John's presentation of Jesus.

Still, while many features of the Gospel are greatly illumined by setting them against the background of Scripture, or of Jewish exegetical traditions, John's basic symbols are universal, fundamental to human life, and part of the landscape of the ancient Mediterranean world: life, water, light, food; vines; sheep; friendship. As will be noted at various points in the commentary, the imagery of the Gospel communicates by appeal to the realities of ordinary life: Jesus is bread and light; he calls his disciples friends; he offers them life. Such realities are part of daily human experience. Against the background of Scripture, however, some of these epithets for Jesus, such as bread and life, align him with the gifts of God, and some, such as shepherd and light, even with God himself.

Additionally, at some points Jesus' teaching and actions are further illumined by setting them against the Greco-Roman world; at times Jesus' teaching has been recast into an idiom to communicate to readers outside the confines of Jesus' own world. For example, some of John's language, such as being "born again," is found in Greco-Roman, but not Jewish, literature (see comments on 3:3); friendship is one of the frequent topoi of non-Jewish moral and philosophical discourse (see on 15:13); and John's Passion Narrative evinces a particular concern to position Jesus with respect to Roman authorities and, possibly, to the claims of Roman imperial cult (see on 20:28).[45]

In light of such characteristics, the Gospel's origins are often sought outside of Palestine, without denying its obvious connections to its Jewish roots, traditions, and imagery.[46] A location in Asia Minor and, more specifically, at Ephesus has commended itself to many for several reasons: (1) Church tradition locates the Gospel in Ephesus (Irenaeus, *Haer.* 3.1.1 = Eusebius, *Hist. eccl.* 5.8.5; Irenaeus, *Haer.* 2.22.5 = Eusebius, *Hist. eccl.* 3.23.3. (2) 1 and 2 John, which are theologically and historically related to the Gospel, combat false teaching apparently denying that "Jesus Christ has come in the flesh" (1 John 4:2; 2 John 1:7). In his letters to various churches in Asia Minor, Ignatius similarly emphasizes the reality of Jesus' flesh against those who apparently deny it (e.g., Ign., *Eph.* 7.2; Ign., *Smyrn.* 3.1–3; 7.1; 12.2). (3) Some early Christian theological developments in Asia Minor seem to draw from the Gospel (e.g., the Logos theology of Justin Martyr; Montanism).[47] (4) The

45. See also Cassidy; Carter 2008.

46. See esp. the arguments of Keener 1:142–49, who demonstrates well the complexity of the arguments about locating John or his readers geographically.

47. After his conversion to Christianity, Justin taught first at Ephesus and then at Rome, developing his Christology of the preexistent Word; he almost certainly cites John (cf. John 3:3, 5 in *1 Apol.* 61.4–5; see also *1 Apol.* 66; *Dial.* 114, 128). Montanism originated with Montanus

Gospel accords particular prominence to John the Baptist, contrasting his baptismal practice with Jesus' ministry more sharply than the other Gospels do. It is striking, therefore, that it is in Ephesus that Paul encounters disciples of John (Acts 19). (5) Domitian, the Roman emperor from 81–96 C.E., was accused by his contemporaries of demanding that certain honors be paid to him (Suetonius, *Dom.* 13; Pliny the Younger, *Pan.* 49.1); and the imperial cult flourished especially in the provinces, including the province of Asia. The book of Revelation, written to the seven churches of Asia, including Ephesus, warns of the designs of the imperial realm on the allegiance of its subjects (13:1–18). John's designation of Jesus as "Lord and God" may counter the claims of Domitian or the imperial cult (see comments at 20:28). (6) Philo comments that there were great numbers of Jews living in every city in Asia Minor and Syria (*Legat.* 245). Later, Josephus speaks of the Jews who dwell in Ephesus (*Ag. Ap.* 2.39) and comments that many Jews emigrated from Palestine in the wake of the first Jewish-Roman War (Josephus, *Ant.* 20.256); numbers of them settled in Asia Minor. Some of the polemical language of John resonates with that of other New Testament documents located in Asia Minor (for sharp criticism of the Jewish synagogue, see Rev 2:9; 3:9). Together these observations plausibly suggest that John's Gospel was ultimately written or published or known quite early in Ephesus.

In the past, John has been dated to the second century, based on assumptions about its dependence on the Synoptics, theological development, and lack of clear evidence of the use of John by early Christian authors. But in 1920 in Egypt, the discovery of a papyrus fragment, $\mathfrak{P}^{52}$ (Rylands Papyrus 457), containing John 18:33–36 and dating to the early second century (between 117 and 138), has provided evidence that John must have been published and circulating by the end of the first century or the very early part of the second. When coupled with the reevaluation of John's dependence on or use of the Synoptics and with the reassessment of schemas that posit a linear development toward a late and "high" Christology,[48] these manuscripts have mitigated the force of arguments for a second-century date of John.

John has typically been dated late in the first century (ca. 90–100), in the reign of the emperor Domitian (see discussion at 20:28).[49] Such a dating has been suggested by the obvious hostility between those Jews in John who believe in Jesus and those who do not, since it has often been alleged that such intense hostility between "messianic" and "nonmessianic" Jews arose only after the

in Phrygia in the latter half of the second century; he believed that the preliminary outpouring of the Paraclete was manifested in the male and female prophets of the Montanist community; see "Montanism," *ODCC* 1107–8.

48. Among many studies, Bauckham 2008; and Hurtado 2003.

49. But Robinson (1985) argues that John was written before the first Jewish-Roman War (66–70 C.E.).

destruction of Jerusalem and the temple. But while the destruction of the temple was a catastrophic event, it is unlikely that it caused an immediate rift between these two groups of Jews. Well before the destruction of the temple, there are other indications in the New Testament and early Christian literature of strained relationships between those who hailed Jesus as Messiah and those who did not.[50] Again, John's "high Christology" has sometimes been offered as an argument for a later dating of John, but contemporary studies in New Testament Christology have demonstrated that "high" Christology need not be dated late and, in fact, emerged quite early (see, e.g., Phil 2:5–11). Still, a date toward the latter part of the first century makes good sense of all the data.

How This Commentary Proceeds

The Gospel of John is a narrative of selected events in Jesus' life and ministry. On the surface such an assertion states an obvious truth about what a Gospel actually is. Indeed, for years readers and interpreters have read John as an account of aspects of Jesus' life, his crucifixion, and his resurrection, and the impact all of these had on his disciples. But with this assertion about the character of John, I intend to signal what this commentary intends to do as well: to trace and explore John's understanding of the ministry and significance of Jesus of Nazareth as presented in this Gospel. To accomplish this, the commentary focuses on the narrative and on the broad cultural milieu out of which it arose.

For those familiar with studies of the Gospel in recent years, I should clarify that I do not take the Gospel to be a cryptic account of a church at the end of the first century, or of the "Johannine community," although the Gospel was undoubtedly shaped by and reflects the experiences and convictions of some who had come to believe in Jesus as Messiah, Son of God. John both explicitly and implicitly delineates the objections to such faith, with the disconsolate acknowledgment that some had abandoned that faith altogether. The Gospel is not a story of Jesus that is either unaware of or unformed by the development of faith communities, and one can at times discern the impact of such developments; but one cannot read the history of those faith communities straight out of the Gospel. What we have in John is a narrative account of who a first-century Christian author understood Jesus to be.

Therefore this commentary focuses on the Gospel's account of Jesus of Nazareth: what he said, what he did, how his life ended, and what happened after his death. One could undertake such a study of the Gospel by considering it to be a self-contained narrative, without attending to the social, cultural, and historical context(s) that produced it. But that would be to misread it, much as if we proceeded to read and interpret the Greek text without knowing Greek.

50. See comments on 9:22 below.

Historical criticism of one sort or another remains crucial because the Gospel recounts the itinerant ministry of Jesus in Galilee, Samaria, and primarily Judea; traces his encounters with Pharisees, high priests, and Roman governors; shows him disputing about proper interpretation of the law and keeping Sabbath; recounts an engagement with a Samaritan woman about the proper place for temple worship; alludes to various rituals of purification, mourning, and celebration of Jewish festivals. We could add to this list, but my point is simply that John's Gospel is the product of a social-cultural world, or worlds, whose language, commitments, and contours must be investigated in order to read John's narrative well. Where various aspects of the Gospel are illumined by appeal to Palestinian Jewish sources, Hellenistic Judaism (e.g., Philo), or Greek religion or philosophy, these sources are brought to bear on its interpretation, without passing judgment on whether such backgrounds necessarily characterize author or reader.

Hence this commentary endeavors to unpack John's witness to Jesus of Nazareth, and to do so by paying attention to the Gospel's narrative, structure, central themes, and the theological and rhetorical arguments that it makes. In short, I aim to articulate John's narratively presented understanding of Jesus—who he was, what he did, and what that means.[51] As already suggested, since the Gospel is the product of its sociocultural world, the commentary will likewise bring to bear on the discussion certain aspects of that world especially pertinent to understanding the text itself, or to suggest possible ways in which first-century readers might have understood the Gospel. At times Synoptic comparisons are introduced in order to illumine John; but this is not a commentary on John in light of the other Gospels. And while I have tried to take into account the historical and cultural contexts of both Jesus and the Gospel, I have not endeavored to reconstruct or pass judgment on the historicity of events, words, or accounts in John. John's Gospel is assuredly a selective, interpreted account of some of the things that Jesus said and did; it presents Jesus and his works and words to be the life-giving deeds of the one God of Israel for all the world. The goal of this commentary is to illumine the witness of that narrative.

This is not a commentary about scholarship on the Fourth Gospel, but I have tried to take into account recent discussion of important issues touching on interpretation of John, such as archaeological discoveries, the shape of Jewish-Christian relationships toward the end of the first century, and the newly refocused attention on Greek and Roman culture and sources for interpreting the Gospel. Still, the literature on the Gospel is enormous and ever growing; I have not sought to catalog or respond to all the options of interpretation for any given verse or issue. I have simply offered my own understanding of the

51. Some central themes and pressing questions in John are briefly treated in nine short excursuses.

text, an understanding that has grown out of interaction with the Gospel itself, informed by consultation of primary and secondary sources.

A Note on the Translation

The New Testament Library prescribes that authors provide their own translations of the biblical text being discussed—a daunting assignment given the plethora of fine translations available today. In my translation I have tried to stick rather closely to the Greek text while at the same time rendering it into idiomatic English. John's is fairly simple Greek, with syntax suggesting that Greek was not his native or primary tongue. The Gospel's Greek lacks the subordinated clauses and participial constructions characteristic of the polished literary style of Luke–Acts or Hebrews. Instead, in its paratactic style various statements are strung together with *kai* ("and");[52] sometimes the statements are simply not connected at all (1:17). I have tried to reproduce John's style. At all times I have tried to convey what I believe the text is saying. For example, John sometimes uses *hina* ("that, in order that"), which typically introduces a purpose clause, when *hoti* ("that") would serve better or seems to be what is needed in the sentence. At other times it is not clear that John has used Greek tenses with the precision that grammarians today accord them. In such instances I have tried to reproduce what I thought was meant, rather than what is written. In that vein, I have also rendered the text into inclusive English, preferring plural pronouns when necessary, when it seems to me that this is what the text intends.

52. John uses *kai* at least twice as often as *de*; Martin (1974) suggests that the pattern is indicative of a Semitic "original," either a document or speaker (or in this case, writer).

COMMENTARY ON THE GOSPEL OF JOHN

John 1:1–18 The Introduction to the Gospel and to Jesus

The opening verses of the Gospel of John constitute one of the most theologically influential passages of Scripture, providing grist for the mill of developing christological reflection. Drawing on the opening words of Genesis, John introduces Jesus, the Messiah and only Son of the Father (1:17–18), as the incarnation of the Word that was with God before all things and through which all things, including life itself, came into being.

Three assertions characterize this Word: the Word was with God, became flesh, and is now ever with God. With these assertions, John further identifies the Word in relationship to God, the world, and humankind.[1] From the beginning, this Word is intrinsic to the identity of God. As the agent of the creation of the world and of all things, this Word relates to the world as the Creator relates to all that is created. Incarnate as a human being of flesh and blood, the Word became part of that created order, subject to the conditions of human frailty. As Jesus of Nazareth, the Messiah, this Word became part of the people of Israel, whose story, as narrated in the Scriptures and now brought to its climactic moment, is the story of all the world. Having suffered death, this same Jesus nevertheless lives with God. If the Word was the agent of God's creation of all life, then the incarnate Word, Jesus of Nazareth, both brought and continues to bring life and light to the world.

It has sometimes been argued that the opening verses of John incorporate an early Christian hymn describing and honoring Jesus as exalted Lord.[2] Early Christians clearly did use hymns in worship (Eph 5:19; Col 3:16; cf. Rev 5:9–10, 12–13). An oft-quoted passage from a letter of Pliny the Younger, governor of

1. Keck (1986) speaks of the three coordinates of Christology: theological, cosmic, and anthropological.

2. Other NT examples of such hymns may include Col 1:15–20; Phil 2:5–11; 1 Tim 3:16.

Bithynia in Asia Minor, to the emperor Trajan (ca. 112 C.E.) speaks of Christians singing hymns "to Christ as to a god" (*Ep.* 10.96–97). But even if these opening verses of John echo phrases from such a hymn, in their present form they constitute a "prose introduction" to the Gospel narrative and its central figure, Jesus; the prologue is not a comprehensive or self-contained summary of the Gospel.[3] For that reason, important aspects of the Gospel, including the postresurrection mission of the Spirit in the church and the world, are not included here.

Yet the prologue introduces, albeit briefly, many of the major themes and much of the imagery of the Gospel, including the coming of the light into darkness, the rejection of the light, the importance of witnesses, the call to believe, the relationship of Moses and the Torah to Jesus, and Jesus' identity as the Messiah and unique Son of the Father in whom there is life. Readers of the Gospel have the key to understanding what characters in the narrative itself repeatedly misunderstand: who Jesus is, and how his identity as the embodied Word of God undergirds both what he claims and what he offers. The Gospel narrative of Jesus' signs, words, and encounters is the narrative of the manifestation of God's glory, life, and love, and of their effects, reception, and rejection. There is no disembodied way to behold the glory of the Word, to receive God's life, or to experience God's love. The opening verses of John show how it is that the Word who was with God and was the agent of creation could also be the subject of a Gospel: this Word became flesh.

1:1 In the beginning was the Word, and the Word was with God, and the
Word was God. **2** This Word[a] was in the beginning with God. **3** All things
came into being through him, and without him not one thing came into
being that has come into being.[b] **4** In him was life: and this life was the
light of all human beings. **5** The light shines in the darkness, but the dark-
ness has not overcome it.

6 There was a man, sent from God, whose name was John. **7** He came
as a witness, to bear witness to the light, so that all might come to believe
through him. **8** He was not the light: rather, he came to bear witness to
the light.

9 The true light[c] that sheds light on every person was coming into the
world.[d] **10** Even though he was in the world, and even though the world
was made through him, the world did not recognize him. **11** He came to his
own home, but his own people did not welcome him. **12** But to all who did
receive him, who believed in his name, he gave the authority to become

3. Cf. Barrett 26–27. P. Williams (2011) shows that early MSS, liturgical systems, and commentators thought of 1:1–5; 1:1–14; or 1:1–17, as the introduction to John. It was not until the late eighteenth century that John 1:1–18 was taken to be a discrete unit and the "prologue" of the Gospel. Michaels (45) speaks of the first five verses of the Gospel as its "Preamble."

God's children. 13 They are not begotten of blood,[e] nor of human desire,
nor of the will of a man; they are begotten of God.[f]

14 And the Word became flesh and lived among us, so that we saw his
glory, glory as of the Father's only Son,[g] full of grace and truth. 15 John
bears witness concerning him and has declared: "This is the one of whom
I said, 'The one who comes after me takes precedence over me, because
he was before[h] me.'" 16 Out of his fullness we have all received abundant
grace;[i] 17 for the law was given through Moses, but grace and truth have
come through Jesus Christ. 18 No one has ever seen God: the only Son,[j]
who is ever at the Father's side,[k] has made him known.

a. The Greek simply has *houtos* ("this" or "this one").

b. Ancient commentators almost uniformly put a full stop (or period) after "not one thing came into being," then began a new sentence with "That which has come into being in him was life" (so also NRSV). But beginning the new sentence with *en* is typical of John's style (1:10; 5:3, 7; 7:37; 9:30, 34; 16:30) and makes good sense in the context of Johannine theology: The Word was the bearer of life for all.

c. The subject of the verb *ēn* could be the Logos (Borgen, 1972), but is here taken to be "the true light" (so RSV, TNIV, NRSV, etc.).

d. The participle *erchomenon* is translated with *ēn* from the opening of the sentence as a periphrastic to modify "the true light" rather than "every person"; hence, "the true light was coming into the world," not "the true light enlightened every person coming into the world"; this translation leads more naturally into the following statement "[The light] was in the world. . . ."

e. *Ex haimatōn* ("of bloods"); Michaels suggests "bloodlines."

f. *Begotten* (as in 3:3, 5) translates the passive of *gennan*, which can mean either "to be born" or "to be begotten"; the Hebrew *yālad* has the same two meanings.

g. "Father's only Son" supplies "Son" in *monogenous para patros,* lit., "the only one from the Father."

h. *Prōtos* ("before") is, lit., "first"; *prōteron* ("former, earlier") may have been intended (Barrett 177).

i. "Abundant grace" renders *charin anti charitos*; there is one grace after another, grace continually taking the place of grace.

j. *Theos* (God) rather than *huios* (Son) is found in $\mathfrak{P}^{66, 75}$א * and other important ancient witnesses, but the reading *huios* follows more naturally on the statement of the relationship of the only Son to the Father in v. 14 (cf. 3:16).

k. *Kolpon*, lit., "bosom, breast, chest"; figuratively, a place of honor (cf. 13:23; Luke 16:23).

[1:1–3] John's narrative opens, like the narrative of Genesis, with a brief account of the creation of the world "in the beginning" (*en archē*, Gen 1:1 LXX).[4] In Genesis, God spoke the heavens and the earth into being; in John, all

4. Borgen (1969; 1972) views John 1:1–18 as a homily on the beginning of Genesis; he is followed by Boyarin.

things come into being by means of the Word (*ho logos*).[5] Few terms in John have been more thoroughly investigated and discussed as providing the key to John's religious and historical contexts, with special consideration of the possibility that *logos* reflects the Greek, particularly Stoic, view of it as the rational principle of the universe. Yet, strikingly, as a designation for Jesus, *logos* appears only in the opening verses of John (1:1, 14), where it is found in assertions about the role of that *logos* in creation, akin to biblical descriptions of God's creation of the world through his word (Ps 33:6) or his wisdom (Prov 8:27–31).

Three things are predicated of this Word: (1) The Word "was in the beginning."[6] Since the Word already existed before the creation of the world, that Word is not part of the created order (1:1–2). (2) Because "the Word" is said to be *with* God, it is clear that the Word can in some way be distinguished from "God." (3) And yet "the Word *was* God" (again using the imperfect tense of *eimi*). The proper designation of the Creator, God (*ho theos*), is also appropriate for the Word (*ho logos*), through whom the world was made (1:1), and signals the distinctive divine functions and identity of the *Logos*. John's identification of the Word as both with God and as God constitutes the heart of the Christology that is unfolded throughout the Gospel.

In John, the twin assertions that "all things" have come into being through the Word (v. 2) and "without him not one thing came into being that has come into being" (v. 3) underscore the Word's agency in God's creation of all things.[7] Particularly important here are the assertions using the preposition *dia* ("through, by means of"): "all things came into being *through* [the Word]" (1:3), a pattern of speech used consistently in the New Testament for the role of the Word (or Christ, or the Son) in creation (1 Cor 8:6; cf. Col 1:16; Heb 1:2). This pattern reinforces the biblical insistence that one God created all that is, and that the Word (or the Son; or the Lord) was the means through which God created all things.[8] God's sole creation of all things in turn articulates the singularity and uniqueness of the one God. In Isa 40–55, for example, God's uniqueness is demonstrated by his creation of the world: "For thus says the LORD, who created the heavens (he is God!), who formed the earth and made it

5. See Excursus 1: "Word and Wisdom in John."

6. The imperfect tense *ēn* ("was") of the verb *einai* ("to be") indicates ongoing action in the past.

7. The God "who lives forever created *all things*" (*ta panta*; Sir 18:1 LXX), is the "creator of *all things*" (2 Macc 1:24–25), the "cause of *all things*" (Philo, *Somn.* 1.67), "the beginning and middle and end of *all things*," and the one who "breathes life into *all creatures*" (Josephus, *Ag. Ap.* 2.190; *Ant.* 1.225; 12.22). For similar sentiments in philosophical texts, see Diogenes Laertius, *Lives* 7.147; Aelius Aristides, *Or.* 43.7.

8. Later, using an image that underscores the unity of the work of the Father and Son (and the Spirit), Irenaeus asserts that the Father created the world with "his own hands," namely, the Word and the Spirit (*Haer.* 3.11.1; 4.7.4; 4.20.1; 5.1.3; 5.6.1; 5.28.4).

(he established it; he did not create it a chaos, he formed it to be inhabited!): I am the LORD, and there is no other" (45:18). God is not only the creator; God is the *sole* creator of the world (Isa 44:24) and of all that is (40:28; 45:7; 48:12–13; cf. 42:5; 44:24; 45:11–12). The assertion that the Word is the sole instrument of God's creation of *all* things aligns the Word uniquely with God's creative work and sovereignty over all things as recounted in Scripture. Greco-Roman Jewish monotheistic rhetoric also emphasizes God's unique creation of and ultimate sovereignty over *all* things; the Gospel of John employs such biblical and Jewish rhetoric to underscore the status and identity of the Son (cf. 3:31, 35; 5:20, 22–23, 26–28; 13:3; 16:15; 17:2).[9]

The statement "and the word was God" (*kai theos ēn ho logos*) poses one of the more challenging problems of translation in John. The absence of the definite article before *theos* (God) has given rise to the translations "the Word was a god" or "the Word was divine."[10] But neither of these affirmations captures John's point. John predicates of the Word what the Old Testament predicates of YHWH: the LORD is God. To call the Word "God" is not to collapse the distinction between "the Word" and "God," as the subsequent distinction between "Father" and "Son" makes clear; it is, rather, to use the highest degree of qualitative predication regarding the subject, the Word: the Word has the quality, the reality, even the identity of God.[11]

[4–5] The Word is the light that continues to shine in the darkness. In Scripture, light is an image for God and for entities that come from or belong to God; light thus serves as a soteriological and ethical image, referring to (1) that which brings salvation; (2) blessedness, salvation, or the heavenly or divine realms; (3) life, when contrasted with the darkness of death; and (4) the path of right conduct. Darkness is the realm of terror, gloom, and death (Job 15:22–23, 30; 17:12–13; Pss 88:12; 91:6; 107:10, 14; 139:11–12), or of lack of knowledge of God or the way to God (Job 5:14; Pss 18:28; 82:5; Eccl 2:13–14; Isa 9:2; 42:7, 16). Because light dispels darkness, or illumines a path in the darkness, it is linked with joy, life, and understanding, and ultimately with God (Pss 4:6; 27:1; 36:9; 56:13; 89:15; 119:105; Bar 4:2; Wis 7:26; *2 Bar.* 17.4; 18.2; 59.2).

Even as God spoke in creating the world and so brought life out of nothing and light out of darkness (Gen 1:3–5), so God's Word enters the world to bring life into being and light into the darkness. Darkness opposes the light's purpose to illumine all people, to bring light into the world and so to bring life

9. Bauckham 2008, 8; Hurtado 2005a, 119–21; M. M. Thompson 2001, 54–55, 74–76.

10. In which case, we might expect either *theou ēn ho logos*, "the Word was of God," or *theios ēn ho logos*, "the Word was divine."

11. Wallace (45–46, 266–69) calls *theos* a qualitative predication that identifies the Word as having the quality of God while yet distinct from God the Father; but Bauckham (2007, 240–42) asserts instead that the statement is one of identity: the Word does not have the quality of divinity or of God; rather, the Word *is* God.

out of death (cf. 3:16–17; 11:25–26). But "the darkness has not overcome" the light. The Greek *katalambanō*, here translated "overcome," may mean (1) to understand, to comprehend; or (2) to overtake, to seize (cf. 12:35); or (3) to attain. Since several other words in the prologue stress human comprehension, including "believe" (*pisteusōsin*, vv. 7, 12), "accept" (*paralambanō*, v. 11), and "receive" (*lambanō,* v. 12), one could understand John to be saying that the darkness did not receive or understand the light. But neither has the darkness "overcome" (i.e., "extinguished") the light; the darkness has not swallowed up the light (cf. 3:19). John thus speaks of the light that *shines* (*phainei*, present tense) in the darkness. The one who *was* the life of the world surely *is* and *will be* its life: the light continues to shine to bring life to all.

[6–8] The first witness to Jesus is "John," who testified to Jesus precisely in order to lead people to believe (vv. 7–8, 15). John—who is never called "the Baptist" or "the baptizer"[12] in this Gospel, but rather simply "John"—has one primary function: to bear witness to Jesus so that "all" might believe in him and have life (1:7–8, 31, 34; 3:26, 32–33; 5:33–36; 10:41). Of the forty-seven occurrences of words cognate with *martyrein* in the Gospel, fourteen refer to John; and his testimony is reported every time he is mentioned (1:6–8, 15, 19, 32–34; 3:26; 5:33–36; 10:40–41). In this Gospel, John does not exhort repentance or call for reform (cf. Matt 3:2, 7–10; Mark 1:4–5; Luke 3:3, 7–9; Josephus, *Ant.* 18.5.2). Rather, his mission is to serve as a witness to Jesus so that others may believe.

The contrast between John and Jesus that runs throughout the Gospel underscores John's function as witness: "[John] was not the light: rather, *he came to bear witness to the light*" (v. 8). In this pattern ("not this . . . but rather that"), which can be found elsewhere in John (3:17; 11:4), the emphasis falls on the end of the statement ("not to condemn the world, *but to save the world*," 3:17). Like Jesus (3:17; 4:34; 5:23, 24, 30, 36; 6:38, 39; etc.), John was "sent from God" (1:6; 3:28), but John was sent in order to bear witness to Jesus, and here he bears witness to the preexistence and preeminence of the Word (1:15, 30). As a "kindled and shining lamp" (5:35), John bore witness to the true light (10:40–41). Augustine shows the relationship of John to Jesus when he writes, "John is truthful, Christ is truth" (*Tract. Ev. Jo.* 5.2).

[9–11] This true (*alēthinon*)[13] light stands in contrast to the Baptist—as well as to any other figure, person, or entity, such as Torah or Wisdom, that might have been spoken of as giving light. It is the true light in that it alone gives life. The cosmological assertion that "all things came into being through

12. Mark uses both "the one who baptizes" or "the Baptizer" (*ho baptizōn*, 1:4; 6:14, 24) and "the Baptist" (*ho baptistēs*, 6:25; 8:28); Matthew and Luke use "the Baptist" exclusively; Josephus refers to "John who was called the Baptist" (*baptistēs*, in *Ant.* 18.116). I use "the Baptist" to distinguish "John" from the Gospel itself.

13. "Real, genuine, or authentic" (BDAG; cf. 1:9; 4:23; 6:32; 15:1).

him" (1:3) thus has an equally all-encompassing soteriological correlate: the light that "sheds light on every person" (*phōtizei panta anthrōpon*) was coming into the world (cf. 3:19; 12:46). Shining in the darkness and shedding light on all, this light makes it possible for all to see, while simultaneously exposing or convicting those who do not come to the light (3:19–21; 9:39–41; 12:46–50).

This Word that was *in the beginning*, through which *all things came into being*, was subsequently also *in the world* (1:10). But although everyone was made through the Word, not everyone believed in him; the statement reflects an estrangement between creator and creature found elsewhere in Scripture (cf. Rom 1:19–25; Isa 44:6–20; 45:18–20). The point is then focused more sharply: this *true light* came to "his own home" (*ta idia*), Israel, but was not received by his own people (1:11). Even as in the Wisdom literature, where wisdom was said to reside with Israel in the form of the Torah, so the Word was embodied and came particularly to Israel (Sir 24; Bar 3:36–4:1). But neither the world nor the Word's "own" believed in him, thus repeating a pattern found in Scripture: God's creation and God's people often fail to heed or respond to God's revelation and will.

[12–13] Still, others did believe, and those who believed came both from the world and from "his own." "To believe in his name" means "to believe in him."[14] All who believed were given the authority (*exousia*)[15] to become God's children (1:12–13). In several places in the Old Testament, the "children of Israel" are called "the children of God."[16] In Jewish literature of the Second Temple period, *Jubilees* expresses the hope that when God creates a new Spirit for the Israelites, they will all be called "children of the living God" (*Jub.* 1.23–25). In the *Psalms of Solomon*, the Messiah brings together a holy people who are all "children of God" (*huioi theou*, 17.27). According to John, God has sent his Son, and God will send his Spirit to accomplish this work of creating and calling together the children of God. The children of God are those "begotten of God" (1:13), by the agency of the Spirit (3:3, 5), because they have "believed in his name."[17] Ultimately it is the death and resurrection of Jesus that will precipitate and enable the ingathering not only of Jesus' own people, but also of all people, the "children of God who had been scattered" (11:52; cf. 3:15; 10:16; 12:32, 47; see also 7:35).

Those who become God's children by God's action and through faith in Jesus are contrasted with those who are begotten "of blood" (*ex haimatōn*) and

14. As a typically Johannine formulation, *pisteuein eis to onoma* (1:12; 2:23; 3:18) is interchangeable with *pisteuein eis* with a pronominal accusative (3:16, 18; 6:29, 40; 7:38, 39; 9:36; 11:25, 48; 12:37). See Excursus 8: "Vocabulary of Faith and Discipleship."

15. *Exousia* can mean "choice, right" or "capability, might, power" or "authority."

16. Children of Israel (MT): Exod 10:20; Deut 4:44, 45; 33:1; Judg 10:8; 1 Kgs 6:13; 2 Kgs 17:34; 2 Chr 7:3; Neh 13:2. For children of God, see Deut 14:1; Hos 1:10 = 2:1 LXX, *huioi theou zōntos*, "children of the living God."

17. See Keck 1996.

of "human [or 'fleshly'] desire" (*ek thelēmatos sarkos*).[18] Here there are echoes of the biblical phrase "flesh and blood" that designates human nature, especially in contrast to God (Matt 16:17; 1 Cor 15:50; Gal 1:16; Eph 6:12; Heb 2:14). It is not physical birth or descent that qualifies one to be a "child of God"; rather, the children of God (*tekna theou*) are those who are now begotten of God, as manifested by their belief in the name of the Son of God (*huios tou theou*, 3:18). Those born of the flesh may become those born of God (*ek theou*), by means of God's generative power. This is the first hint that John reshapes the identity of the "children of God," neither linking that identity to ethnic heritage nor denying it to any on that basis.

[14–18] Those born of flesh may become those born of God through the Word of God, the *Logos*, that has become flesh (*sarx*). In Scripture, *flesh* may denote the frailty and mortality of humankind, often in contrast to divine power and eternity (Isa 40:6–7; Gen 6:17; 7:21; 2 Chr 32:7–8; Job 34:15; Pss 56:4; 73:26; Jer 17:5). By becoming flesh, the Word of God enters this sphere of mortality and frailty and makes it possible for those born of the flesh to become those born of God (1:12–13). John's formulation certainly finds its resonance in Irenaeus, who famously wrote that "the Word of God, our Lord Jesus Christ [did] through his transcendent love, become what we are, that he might bring us to be what he is himself."[19]

In different ways, Greek philosophy and early Christian heresies balked at the central Johannine affirmation, "The Word became flesh." In his *Confessions*, Augustine wrote that although he had found numerous similarities to the doctrine of the *Logos* (Word) in Greek philosophy, "I did not read in them that 'the Word was made flesh and came to dwell among us'" (7.9). But John—and Augustine with him—maintains that the Logos, the very Word of God, who was God, became part of the material realm. Indeed, "he was counted as one of our number, and he paid his dues to Caesar" (*Conf.* 5.3). The Word took on the flesh not merely of humankind, but the particular human flesh of a Jewish subject of the Roman Empire in the first century. Similarly, Irenaeus commented that no heretic held the view that the Word was made flesh (*Haer.* 3.11.3). Some thought the Word *seemed* to become flesh but did not really do so. The affirmation that God's Word truly became flesh distinguishes Johannine Christology in its ancient contexts.[20]

18. Cf. Luke 3:8; Gal 3:7; Rom 4:1; 1 Pet 1:3–5.

19. Irenaeus, *Haer.* 5, Preface. Epictetus (*Diatr.* 2.8.1–2) asks, "What is the essence [*ousia*] of God? Is it flesh [*sarx*]? Certainly not! [*mē genoito*]."

20. The early Christian heresy known as docetism (from the Greek *dokein*, "to seem") thought of Jesus' "flesh" as something of a disguise. A number of early Christian texts suggest that docetism was a threat in the early church in Asia Minor (cf. 1 John 1:1; 4:2; 2 John 7; Ign., *Smyrn.* 2; 3.1–3; 4.2; 5.2; cf. Ign., *Eph.* 7.2; Ign., *Trall.* 10; Irenaeus, *Haer.* 1.10.1–8). For discussion of "incarnational Christology" as marking the divergence of the Christian narrative from its Jewish roots historically and theologically, see Boyarin 261, 265; Wyschogrod.

Because the Word became flesh, it was possible to see "his glory." Here the testimony of the eyewitnesses, those who were witnesses to the life of the enfleshed Word, comes to expression. The first reference to "seeing" in the Gospel is appropriately coupled with the first reference to the Word as the Son (1:14) and the Messiah, Jesus (1:17). As the Gospel now begins to narrate the life of the enfleshed Word, Son and Messiah are the designations that dominate the narrative, while *Logos* disappears.[21] The affirmations "The Word became flesh" and "We saw his glory" introduce the humanity of the Word (flesh) and the historically situated character of his life: Jesus is a common first-century Jewish name; Messiah, a hoped-for deliverer of God's people, Israel.[22]

As a human being, the Word lived with human beings. "Lived" translates *eskēnōsen*, from *skēnoō*, "to live, settle, or take up residence."[23] In the LXX, the tabernacle of God is called a *skēnē*.[24] John may intend an allusion to the rich Scriptural picture of God's dwelling or "tabernacling" with Israel in visible glory, but here with the potentially offensive particularization of God's glory in the enfleshment of the Word.[25] The characteristically Johannine word *doxa* can be translated either "glory" or "honor." John exploits these twin meanings in keeping with Scripture, where "glory" (*doxa*) refers both to the visible presence of God among the people and to the honor that is due to God (see Exod 16:7, 10; 24:16–17; Lev 9:6; Num 14:10; Deut 5:24). Drawing on the scriptural descriptions of luminous manifestations of the glory of God, here the glory of the Son (John 2:11; 11:40; 12:41; 17:24) can be *seen*. "Seeing" does not refer merely to "observation." Not all who physically saw the man Jesus of Nazareth also saw his glory. Sight must be distinguished from insight; while all may "see with the eyes," not all "understand with their heart" (John 12:40, quoting Isa 6:10).

Throughout the prologue, the descriptions of the Word have made clear the Word's divine character, as does John's characterization of the incarnate Word as "the Father's only Son" (*monogenous para patros*, 1:14; cf. 3:16, 18). In a few sentences, John will speak of Jesus as "the only Son who is ever at the Father's side" (1:18; *monogenēs huios ho ōn eis ton kolpon tou patros*). *Monogenēs* means "one and only; only one of its kind or class; unique."[26]

21. For the continuing significance of *logos* in the Gospel, see Phillips.

22. For the translation of Messiah as "Christ" see comments on 1:41; 12:3.

23. The Hebrew verb *šākan* is used of God's dwelling with Israel (Exod 25:8; 29:46; Zech 2:11 [2:14 MT]) and of the dwelling of the bright cloud of God's presence upon the tabernacle (Exod 24:16; 40:35); in such cases the LXX, which often tends toward circumlocutions in describing God, avoids verbs for dwelling or living, so God's glory is said to have "come down" (*katebē*, Exod 24:16) or to have "overshadowed" the tabernacle (40:35).

24. Among many references, see Exod 26:26; 27:9, 21; 29:4; 30:36; Lev 1:1; 4:7; Num 1:1; 2:17; 3:25; see also Josephus, *Ant*. 20.228, *Ag. Ap*. 2.12.

25. See Wyschogrod.

26. The LXX translates *yāḥîd* ("only") both as *monogenēs* (LXX: Pss 21:21; 24:16; 34:17 [MT: 22:21; 25:16; 35:17]) and *agapētos* ("beloved," Gen 22:2, 12, 16; Amos 8:10; Zech 12:10).

When used to describe a relationship to a father, *monogenēs* refers to the only offspring of that father. As the unique Son (*monogenēs huios*), Jesus is thus contrasted to the many children of God (*tekna theou*; vv. 12–13). Furthermore, the affirmation that Jesus is the *only Son* (*monogenēs*, in 1:14, 18; 3:16, 18; cf. also 1 John 4:9) corresponds to this Gospel's characterization of God as the *only God* (or "the one who alone is God," *monos theos*, 5:44). Even as "the only God" reflects typical monotheistic rhetoric, so *only Son* emphasizes the singular status of Jesus.[27]

The mention of the enfleshment of the Word prompts a further reference to the witness of John (the Baptist), who speaks about Jesus in terms of early Christian belief, and especially of his preeminence and preexistence (v. 15).[28] In Christian tradition and confession, John was known as the forerunner of Jesus: here he witnesses to the one who came before him. The present and perfect tense Greek verbs describing John's activity (v. 15) can be translated, "John *bears* [or, "is bearing"] witness and *has declared*." The accent falls on the *ongoing* witness of John to Jesus, begun before Jesus appeared on the scene, continued throughout his ministry (cf. 3:23–30), and still heard in the pages of the Gospel.

Testimony to the benefits received through Jesus Christ continues: grace is mentioned three times in this short paragraph.[29] "Grace and truth" (*charitos kai alētheias*, vv. 14, 17) recall the biblical pair *ḥesed we'ĕmet*, "steadfast love and faithfulness."[30] The LXX translators rendered this phrase in various ways, including *mercy and truth* (*eleos kai alētheia*, Ps 24:10); *mercy and righteousness* (*eleos kai dikaiosynēn*, Gen 24:49); *compassion and truth* (*eleēmosynēn kai alētheian*, Gen 47:29). While John's use of "grace and truth" may reflect this Old Testament pair, the preference for *charis* ("grace") over the septuagintal *eleos* ("mercy") may demonstrate (1) the increasing prevalence of the word *grace* in Christian parlance;[31] and/or (2) John's distinctive translation, based on direct use of the Hebrew text.[32] In particular, John's contention that Jesus is "*full* of grace and truth" may well allude to the characterization of God as "*abundant* [lit., 'great'] in steadfast love and faithfulness" (Exod 34:6 AT).[33]

27. For OT monotheistic rhetoric that emphasizes the "one" or "only" God, see Deut 6:4; 2 Kgs 19:19; Isa 2:17; Mal 2:10, 15; for similar rhetoric in the NT, see 1 Cor 8:6; Eph 4:6; 1 Tim 1:17; Jude 25.

28. For an argument that *prōtos mou ēn* ("he was before me," 1:15) need not refer to preexistence, and thus could reflect the testimony of the "historical" Baptist, see Dodd 1963, 274. To the contrary, see Bauckham 2006, 388: "What John the Baptist says, in the Gospel, is doubtless not a mere report of what even the Beloved Disciple heard him say at the time."

29. In v. 14, "full of grace and truth"; v. 16, "abundant grace"; v. 17, "grace and truth."

30. Josh 2:14; 2 Sam 2:6; 15:20; LXX: Pss 24:10; 35:6; 39:12; 84:11; 88:15, 25; 107:5 (ET: 25:10; 36:5; 40:11; 85:10; 89:14, 24; 108:4).

31. The word "mercy" (*eleos*) does not appear in John; cf. 2 John 3.

32. John's citation of OT texts reflects both Hebrew and Greek text types; for discussion see Menken 1996.

33. In the MT; the LXX lacks an equivalent for "abundant" or "great"; hence, if John is alluding to Exod 34:6, he is likely drawing directly on the Hebrew.

God's plenitude is now manifested in and through Jesus, who is "full of grace" (v. 14); hence, "from his fullness" one may receive "abundant grace," which here translates the Greek *charin anti charitos* (v. 16). The preposition *anti* can be rendered "instead of, in place of"; hence the phrase could be translated "grace in place of grace."[34] This could then mean that the grace found in Jesus followed or replaced the grace found in the law: one grace followed another. But John's emphasis seems rather to fall upon the abundance, the *full* measure, of God's grace that is to be found through Christ (cf. Eph 1:23; Col 1:19; 2:9). It is in the Word made flesh that there is "grace in place of grace," "one grace after another," or "grace abounding."

There is then a contrast between the Torah that came through Moses and the grace and truth that come through Jesus. In contrasting the Torah with Jesus, the Gospel does not deny grace and truth to the law; otherwise it could not serve as a witness to Jesus (1:45; 5:37–39). But the fullness of the divine blessings have come through Jesus: he brings an abundance of wine, water, bread, pasture, Spirit, light, and life. God grants such blessings through the Torah, but God pours them out fully in Jesus. Thus throughout the Gospel, Moses or the law bears witness to Jesus (1:45; 5:45–46).

Yet another way of explicating the significance of the incarnation is found in the closing statement of the prologue: the Son has made the Father known (1:18). Coupled with the assertion that "no one has ever seen God," these two statements point to Jesus as the unique "eyewitness" of God the Father,[35] who alone has "seen" and hence knows God (3:13; 5:38–39; 6:45–46). The Gospel may well be alluding to a commonly received interpretation of Israel as meaning "the one who sees God,"[36] as well as to various Old Testament accounts of seeing God. In Gen 32:30 (32:31 LXX), Jacob saw God "face to face," and so he named the place of their encounter Peniel ("face of God"). Moses, too, is said to have spoken with God "face to face" (Exod 33:11; Deut 34:10; cf. Num 14:14; Deut 5:4). The seventy elders of Israel "saw the God of Israel" (Exod 24:9–11). And Isa 6, Ezek 1, and Dan 7 describe visionary experiences of God, which were echoed in apocalyptic and mystical Jewish texts. How, then, can John say that "no one has ever seen God"?

The bald assertions of such face-to-face encounters were quite often qualified, either within the biblical tradition itself or by translations and interpreters, albeit not in a uniform or consistent manner. For example, while Exod 24:9–10 states that Moses and the elders of Israel saw God, later in that same narrative Moses is denied a vision of God's face on the grounds that no one can see God *and live* (33:20–23). Again, according to Deuteronomy, the people of Israel

34. See also Philo, *Post.* 145: "[God gives blessings] ever new in place of earlier ones [*aiei neas anti palaioterōn*]."

35. See further M. M. Thompson 2007.

36. E.g., Philo, *Deus* 144.

never saw the form of God (4:12–15; 5:4), even though Moses is described as conversing regularly with God "face to face." Philo qualified his own assertion that Israel means "the one who sees God" with the note that one sees God as "through a mirror," that is, not directly.[37] Philo also explains that Moses and Abraham saw the powers of God, but not "the one who is" (*Mut.* 7–17; *Mos.* 2.99–100). The Targums similarly reinterpret most passages that speak of direct apprehension of God or God's face.[38] In other words, there are numerous interpretive moves that seek to explain apparently direct visions of God as mediated or indirect encounters with God.

According to John, the Son alone has an unmediated and direct vision of God, because the Son has been with the Father from the beginning. Only the one who is "from God" (1:1, 18; 8:58), who has been in the presence of God (1:1), and is now "ever at the Father's side," in the position of honor with God, has seen God (6:46) and can in turn make God known: and this happens through Jesus' life, death, and resurrection.[39] Jesus' unique vision of God distinguishes him not only from his contemporaries (cf. 3:13), but also from his disciples, who see the Father in the Son, rather than seeing the Father directly as the Son does (14:8–9).

There is no doubt that in the prologue to the Gospel, John stakes his claim: the central figure of the Gospel, Jesus of Nazareth, is none other than the incarnate Word of God, who was with God, and who was God. Curiously, none of Jesus' claims for himself in the Gospel, and none of the debates over his identity, are formulated in precisely the terms set forth in the prologue. Not until after the resurrection does any confession clearly echo the opening words of the Gospel, "My Lord and my God!" (20:28). Even that reserve is instructive. Although the one of whom the Gospel writes was an agent of the creation of the world and now lives forever with God, the Gospel is the narrative of his dwelling "among us." What follows in the pages of the Gospel is the narrative of the life-giving work of the Word that became flesh. The Gospel is not a series of theological propositions, although certain convictions regarding Jesus' heavenly origins and divine identity are assumed by and voiced in its narrative.

37. *Fug.* 208–13; *Praem.* 44; *Conf.* 72; *Migr.* 201; *Somn.* 1.114; *Her.* 279; *Leg.* 3.15, 186; *Abr.* 54–57.

38. The *Targums Onqelos, Pseudo-Jonathan*, and *Neofiti I* state that Jacob saw an angel or angels; *Onqelos* on Exod 34:10 reads that the elders of Israel saw "the Glory of the God of Israel"; on Num 14:14 it reads, "You are the Lord, whose Shekinah rests among this people, who with their own eyes have seen the Shekinah of your Glory, O Lord"; *Targum Isaiah* at 6:1 reads, "I saw the glory of the LORD resting upon the throne."

39. In Sir 43:31 seeing and describing the Lord are linked; Thyen (106–7) argues that John 1:18 answers the twofold question in Sirach: "Who has seen [the Lord; *heoraken auton*] and who can describe [*ekdiēgēsetai*] him?" The "one whom Jesus loved" reclined "in the bosom of Jesus" or "at Jesus' side" at the Last Supper (13:23, *en tō kolpō tou Iēsou, hon agapa ho Iēsous*), a statement that implicitly authorizes his testimony to Jesus.

But the Gospel is the account of Jesus of Nazareth, his works and his words, and their life-giving power. The story of what he said and did, and how his contemporaries responded to him, is the story that unfolds in the pages that follow.

Excursus 1: Word and Wisdom in John

John's designation of the preincarnate Son as "the Word" (*ho logos*) raises twin questions: the term's conceptual background and John's theological and rhetorical purposes for using it.[40] Some interpreters have proposed that John adopted the Greek philosophical term *logos*, which could refer to the principle of rationality or coherence thought to be immanent in the world, or to the mind or eternal reason regarded as God.[41] Early Christian commentators understood John to adapt this philosophic idea of the *logos* in order to make plain the Word's relationship to God and the created world.[42]

But the explanation of John's use of *logos* has also been sought in scriptural precedents or Hellenistic Jewish speculative theology. The exegetical work of Philo of Alexandria, for example, demonstrates a complex use of *logos* to refer to the means by which the Most High God was visible or known to humankind (*Somn.* 1.229–30; *QE* 2.68).[43] Striking parallels between Philo and John demonstrate that both draw their terminology and conceptuality from Scripture. Even so, however, there are alternative possible origins of John's use of *logos*: (1) the Word of the Lord, which can be further subdivided into the word by which God creates, the prophetic word, and the word of the Scriptures; (2) Wisdom, a preexistent agent of God's creation, a means of instruction and life, and a particular gift to Israel; (3) the translation of various terms that designate God's activity or being in the Aramaic Targums with *Memra* (word).[44] While it is possible and perhaps even likely that no single figure accounts for John's use of *logos*, the most promising options are "the word of the LORD" and the figure of Wisdom, since they best explain the ways in which John develops the portrait of Jesus throughout the Gospel.

According to Gen 1:1, when God speaks, the world is created. That action can be personified: thus, Ps 33:6, "By *the word of the Lord* the heavens were made" (see also Gen 1:3, 6, 9, 11, 14; Wis 9:1; Sir 42:15). Scripture also presents the Word as the subject of active verbs: "The word of the LORD *came to* Abram in a vision" (Gen 15:1, 4). When God speaks to a prophet or king, this speaking may be personified in the phrase "the *word of the LORD* came to . . ." (among many OT references, see 1 Sam 15:1; 2 Sam 7:4; 24:11; 1 Kgs 6:11; 17:8; 18:1; 19:9; Isa 38:4; Jer 1:2, 4, 11, 13; Ezek 1:3; Hos 1:1; Joel 1:1) or even the somewhat redundant "the word that the LORD has spoken" (Isa 37:22;

40. Phillips surveys nearly every possible Hellenistic parallel to John's use of *logos*. He concludes that John echoes a variety of traditions and that he "resemanticizes" the multivalent term *logos* as God, life, and light, and ultimately, Jesus.

41. Heraclitus, frg. 1, states, "All things come to pass according to this word" (*ginomenōn gar pantōn kata ton logon tonde*; in Freeman).

42. Justin, *1 Apol.* 5; Augustine, *Conf.* 7.9.

43. See esp. Dodd 1953, 263–85; Levison 2009, 398.

44. For arguments that the targumic term *Memra* does indeed lie behind *logos*, see Ronning 2010; McHugh (7–9) argues that *logos* "stands for the Memra considered the Holy, Ineffable, Name of God."

cf. Ps 105:19). "The Word of the LORD" comes from God and is the means of God's creation and revelation. It is never separable from the identity of God; yet at the same time it can be spoken of as an active subject. The Word is both *with* God and *is* God.

Much the same can be predicated of the figure of Wisdom, whose contours have also been detected in John's use of "the Word."[45] God's wisdom (*sophia*) and word were often identified or conflated in Jewish exegesis and speculation.[46] Sirach asserts that God's wisdom is God's law (24:23; cf. 15:1); in Bar 4:1 Wisdom is referred to as "the book of the commandments of God, and the law that endures forever"; in Wis 9:1–2 God is said to create all things by his word and his wisdom; Philo of Alexandria assumes the equation of wisdom and the *logos* (e.g., *Leg.* 1.65). Wisdom originates with God (Prov 8:27, 30; Wis 9:4, 9; 18:15; Sir 24:4, 8) and exists before creation (Prov 8:22; Wis 9:9; Sir 1:4; 24:9; cf. John 1:1). More to the point, Wisdom is the agent of God's creation of the world and hence also its life (Prov 3:19; 8:30, 35; Sir 24:8; Wis 7:22; 8:5; 9:1–2; Bar 4:1); it comes to earth and is found particularly although not exclusively in Israel (Sir 24:6–8, 12, 23; Wis 8:1; *1 En.* 42.1; Bar 3:37 [3:38 LXX]). It gives light, or direction, to those who seek its paths (Sir 24:7; Wis 7:30; *1 En.* 42.2).

John is not alone among New Testament authors in depicting Jesus as the wisdom of God. Paul refers to Christ as "the wisdom of God" (1 Cor 1:24, 30); other passages (Col 1:15–20; Heb 1:1–3) may allude to the figure of wisdom to portray Christ as existing with God prior to creation or as an agent of creation or revelation. Yet John never uses the term *sophia* ("wisdom"); he affirms, "The Word became flesh," not "Wisdom became flesh." John's preference for *logos* may arise from several factors.[47] First, John has a particular interest in the relationship of Jesus and the law, "the word of God" (1:17, 45; 5:39, 45–46). As Torah became increasingly important in the self-definition of the Jewish people after the fall of the temple in 70 C.E., it also became increasingly important to specify the relationship of Jesus to the Scriptures of Israel and hence to the God who gave them. *Logos* serves this purpose better than *sophia*. Second, *logos* bridges concepts, prevalent in different Greek philosophical circles, of reason immanent in the universe. Not only does the Word provide coherence for all the world; the mission of the incarnate Word intended for the salvation of all the world also arises from its intrinsic character as universal and immanent reason.[48] Third, in John the emphasis on Jesus as the one who speaks "words of life" (6:63, 68), which are the words of God (8:28; 12:49–50; 14:10; 17:8), and who bears witness to the truth (18:37) explicates Jesus' identity as the *logos*, or Word, of God.[49] Whereas the word *sophia* ("wisdom") never appears in John, outside the prologue *logos* or *logoi* occurs 36 times; *rhēma* ("utterance;

45. Personified wisdom appears in Proverbs, Sirach, Wisdom, Baruch, *1 Enoch*, *4 Ezra*, and Philo. For their impact on the development of Christology, see the particularly rich treatment by Hengel 1995b; 1995d. For more discussion, see Borgen 1996; Epp; Craig Evans 1993; Scott.

46. See the discussion in M. M. Thompson 2001, 130–36.

47. Elsewhere in the NT, the use of *logos* for Jesus is limited to the Johannine literature (1 John 1:1; Rev 19:13).

48. In his effort to explain Judaism with reference to Greek philosophy, Philo demonstrates the utility of the term *logos* to describe the presence and powers of God (see *QE* 2.68; *Fug.* 95–98, 100–101).

49. Phillips 2006.

word") occurs 12 times; *lalia* ("speech, word") occurs twice. Through the Word, God created the world and continues to speak to it.

Both wisdom and word are peculiarly apt figures in the development of Johannine Christology since neither wisdom nor word was considered a being or entity separable from God, such as an angel or prophet, who may choose to do God's will or not. Both wisdom and word refer to something that belongs to and comes from God, something inward or peculiar to God that is externally expressed.[50] These are categories of agency that allow for the closest possible unity of the means of God's revelation and the God who reveals.[51] To speak of Jesus as God's wisdom or God's word is to say that he is God's self-expression, God's thought or mind, God's interior word spoken aloud, or in John's description, "made flesh."[52] While Jesus is also called prophet and Messiah in John, this Gospel deepens the unity between Jesus and God by appealing to categories that portray Jesus not only as the representative of God, but also as the representation of God: the one whose origins lie uniquely in the very being of God. Wisdom and word, coordinated with John's presentation of Jesus as the Son, advance such a Christology.

Early Christian writers subsequently spoke of Jesus especially as the Word, drawing heavily on imagery from Old Testament and apocryphal wisdom texts to round out that picture (among them, Ign., *Magn.* 8.2; Justin, *Dial.* 61.1; 62.1; Tertullian, *Prax.* 7; Theophilus, *Autol.* 2.22; Origen, *Princ.* 1.2.9; Eusebius, *Hist. eccl.* 1.2.2; Augustine, *Tract. Ev. Jo.* 1.16). In a manner without New Testament precedent, patristic theologians often correlated the *logos* with Jesus and the wisdom of God with the Spirit.[53]

50. This is perhaps most explicit in the refined wisdom speculation of Wis 7, where wisdom is said to be "a breath of the power of God, a pure emanation of the glory of the Almighty, . . . a reflection of eternal light, a spotless mirror of the working of God, and an image of his goodness" (7:25–26).

51. Dodd (1953, 275) speaks of wisdom as "the hypostatized thought of God projected into creation, and remaining as an immanent power within the world and in man"; for further discussion of wisdom and word as divine agents, see esp. Hurtado 1988 and the works cited in note 46 above.

52. Dunn 1983, 322–23; and see the comments on 1:14.

53. For contemporary analysis of the Spirit and wisdom, see esp. Bennema 2002b; Levison 2009, 399–404.

John 1:19–4:54
Witnesses to Jesus

The first four chapters of John constitute a thematic and narrative unit that further introduces Jesus, appropriate designations for him, and the gifts that he brings; depict differing but complementary witnesses to him; and show that his work brings to fruition God's promise to create, through the Spirit, a holy people who offer true worship. In style, tone, and content, these chapters differ from the characteristic accounts of Jesus' signs and the ensuing long discourses that make up the christological heart of the Gospel (chs. 5–12).

In these early chapters there are brief accounts of Jesus' signs, unaccompanied by the long discourses in synagogue or temple, such as are found later (e.g., in chs. 5–6). Jesus remains somewhat hidden from public scrutiny (cf. 7:1–10). These early encounters are characterized by questioning, misunderstanding, and tentative positive response to Jesus. However halting, there is a persistent movement toward Jesus and toward grasping just who he is. But in later chapters, as Jesus' claims become more explicit and exalted, responses are characterized by unbelief, hostility, rejection, or desertion. Chapters 1–4 thus lay out some key aspects of Jesus' ministry and work, while also showing early positive response to him. Within that context, we may briefly identify the major themes that are woven throughout these chapters.

First, Jesus is presented as the one who baptizes with the Spirit (1:33; 3:32–34; 4:14); Messiah (1:41, 49; 4:25–26); Rabbi (1:49; 3:2); the one written about in the Law and Prophets (1:45); King of Israel (1:49); the Lamb of God (1:29, 36); the Son of God (1:34, 49; 3:16–18); and the Son of Man (1:51; 3:13). All of these designations are found in the first chapter. Confession of Jesus as the Messiah, the Son of God, does not come only later in the ministry, but already at its outset (contrast Matt 16:13–16; Mark 8:27–31). Nor does Jesus forbid anyone to tell others who he is. Even so, the disciples will grow in understanding Jesus as they follow him, and much of the rest of the Gospel, especially chapters 5–12, lays out Jesus' identity.

Second, the important Johannine theme of witness is introduced. John the Baptist is portrayed entirely in his role as witness to Jesus, rather than as a prophetic preacher of repentance (1:19, 23, 31, 34). Scripture (1:45), Jesus' signs (2:1–11; 4:43–54), the Spirit (1:32–33), and God (1:33; 3:32–34) all bear witness to Jesus. Those who become Jesus' disciples report what they have seen, heard, and understood. They speak from their "sight" and "insight." By testifying to Jesus as the one who speaks and is the truth from God, they participate in the trial of Jesus that occupies the entire Gospel. They will continue that role even after Jesus' death and departure from them (cf. 16:8–11).[1]

Third, these opening chapters narrate several of Jesus' signs (2:1–11; 4:43–54; perhaps 2:13–22) and allude to more (2:1, 23; 3:2; 4:48). Revealing Jesus as the one who manifests the abundant goodness and presence of the life-giving God (2:11, 21; 4:50–53), these signs call for faith in him. However, the response to them is mixed. Some people believe (2:11, 23; 3:2; 4:53), but many simply fail to grasp the import of what they have seen, or question Jesus' authority or power (2:18–20).

Fourth, these chapters introduce the Spirit's role to cleanse and create a new people of God. John the Baptist highlights Jesus as the one who baptizes, or purifies, with the Spirit; in turn, the Spirit revivifies God's people, giving them new birth and life (3:3–8). The biblical promise of the restoration of God's people, also attested in the literature of late Second Temple Judaism, is brought to its initial fulfillment in the creation, through the Spirit, of "the children of God" (1:12–13; 3:3–8). In John, the fulfillment of this promise entails the gathering together of all the children of God, whether they belong to Jesus' "own" (i.e., to Israel [1:11; 3:10]), to the Samaritans (4:5, 42), to the Greeks (7:35; 12:20), or to all the world (1:29; 4:42).

Fifth, the theme of purification partially explicates the Spirit's role, especially in these opening chapters of John. John "baptizes" or cleanses with water; Jesus will baptize or cleanse with the Spirit. Jesus, the Lamb of God, takes away the (defiling) sin of the world. Jesus uses the water for the Jewish rites of purification to provide wine for a wedding feast (2:6). He purifies the temple, polluted by practices arising from human greed. His disciples engage in a dispute with other Jews about the need for purification (3:25). Jesus risks ritual impurity by asking for a drink from a Samaritan's waterpot. In short, these early chapters show Jesus as bringing God's purifying Spirit to his people and their temple, to the Samaritans, and to all the world. Jesus extends the purifying power of God so that people may enter into the realm of God's holiness (17:11).

Sixth, central to the vision of a purified, revivified people of God is worship that is offered "in Spirit and in truth," located in a new, living, sanctified temple. Jesus' cleansing of the temple in Jerusalem (2:13–21) demonstrates his zeal for the holiness of God's house. As the Word of God who "tabernacled" in flesh (1:14), the risen Jesus will be a holy, living temple (2:20–22). True worship of God will be offered neither on Mount Gerizim nor in Jerusalem, for worship of God, who is Spirit, will be offered "in Spirit and in truth" in that living temple (4:21–24).

1. For a reading of the entire Gospel as the trial of Jesus, see particularly Lincoln 2000.

These narratives also recount what happens when Jesus, the incarnate Word of God who brings life and Spirit, encounters a variety of individuals. None of them remains unchanged. Some of those whom Jesus encounters, such as Peter, Nathanael, and Andrew, become his followers and believe in him (2:11; 4:42, 53); others, wanting to know more, struggle with Jesus' claims and challenges (3:1–15); some question Jesus' authority (2:18); still others seem to believe, but with an untrustworthy commitment (2:23–25). But the purposes of God, to seek "true worshipers, who will worship him in Spirit and in truth," will be accomplished. These chapters begin to narrate just how that comes about, then and now.

1:19–34 The Witness of John to Jesus

The familiar picture of John as a fiery preacher of repentance and judgment, dressed in prophetic garb, eating an exotic diet of locusts and wild honey, comes from descriptions found in the Synoptic Gospels (Matt 3:4, 7–12; Mark 1:6; Luke 3:3, 7–17). In the Fourth Gospel, John is portrayed solely as a witness to Jesus. He does not call for repentance, give moral instruction, or warn of judgment. By narrowly defining John's role as witness, the Gospel accomplishes several things: (1) The Gospel identifies John entirely in terms of his role vis-à-vis Jesus, showing that John's ongoing importance derives from his relationship to Jesus; the same is true of various Jewish figures (e.g., Moses) and institutions (e.g., the temple, the law). (2) The Gospel underscores the ongoing significance of John. Not only did he bear witness to Jesus in his own day, but he continues to bear witness through the pages of the Gospel. (3) The Gospel presents John in a role with which other believers, who will also be called on to bear witness to Jesus, can identify.

In bearing witness to Jesus, John joins a large crowd that includes, among others, the Samaritan woman (4:39), Moses (5:46–47), the Scriptures (5:39), Jesus' own works (5:36; 10:25, 32, 37–38), the disciples (15:27), the Paraclete (14:26; 15:26; 16:7–8), and God the Father (5:32, 37–38; 6:57; and 8:14, 17–18). Because John came before Jesus, he stands with witnesses from the Old Testament, such as Abraham, Moses, and Isaiah.[2] The Gospel makes it clear that Jesus' coming "after" John is due entirely to the order of their historical appearance: in truth, Jesus ranks before John, because he existed before John (1:15). Although John "goes before" Jesus, Jesus *was* before John. Throughout the Gospel, John's testimony points to the preeminence of Jesus, who is first in every respect. As the Baptist later states, "He must increase, but I must decrease" (3:30).

2. So Hengel 1989, 129.

1:19 And this is the testimony of John, when the Jews sent priests and
Levites from Jerusalem to ask him, "Who are you?" **20** He confessed—he
did not deny—but rather confessed, "I am not the Messiah." **21** Then they
asked him, "What then? Are you Elijah?" And he said, "I am not." "Are
you the prophet?" And he answered, "No." **22** So then they said to him,
"Who are you? We need to give an answer to those who sent us. What
do you say about yourself?" **23** He said, "'I am the voice of one crying in
the wilderness: 'Make straight the way of the Lord,' even as Isaiah the
prophet said."

24 Now they had been sent from the Pharisees. **25** They asked him, "Why,
then, are you baptizing, if you are neither the Messiah nor Elijah nor the
prophet?" **26** And John answered them, "I baptize with water. Standing in
your midst is one whom you do not know, **27** the one who comes after me.
I am not worthy to loose the thong of his sandals." **28** These things took
place at Bethany beyond the Jordan, where John was baptizing.

29 The next day John saw Jesus coming to him, and he said, "Behold,
the Lamb of God, who takes away the sin of the world! **30** This is the
one of whom I said, 'A man is coming after me, who takes precedence
over me, for he was before I was.' **31** I did not know him; rather, I came
baptizing with water so that he might be revealed to Israel."

32 Again John bore witness, saying, "I have seen the Spirit coming
down as a dove from heaven, and remain upon him. **33** I did not know
him; rather, the one who sent me to baptize with water said to me, 'The
one upon whom you see the Spirit descend and remain, this is the one
who baptizes with the Holy Spirit.' **34** And so I have seen and have borne
witness that this one is the Son of God."[a]

a. The original hand of Codex Sinaiticus and a number of witnesses from the Western tradition read *ho eklektos*, "the Elect One" (favored by Barrett 178; R. Brown 1966, 57; cf. Luke 23:35). If original, the reading may have been changed to the more widely attested "Son of God" (*ho huios tou theou*), a designation that is typical of John and is also found in the accounts of Jesus' baptism in the Synoptics (Mark 1:11; Matt 3:17; Luke 3:22). For "the Elect One" see *1 En.* 49.2–4; Isa 28:16 in 1 Pet 2:6; *Barn.* 6.2; cf. *1 Clem.* 64.1.

[1:19–23] The Gospel begins the public ministry of Jesus with the baptizing ministry of John (cf. Matt 3:17; Mark 1:9; Luke 3:21; Acts 1:22; 10:37). In the Synoptic Gospels, John prepares the way by calling for repentance and announcing the coming of the mighty one who baptizes with the Holy Spirit and fire (that is, with purification and judgment); in the Gospel of John, the Baptizer announces the coming of one whose preeminent status derives from his preexistence.

John identifies himself as a "voice" speaking about another (1:23). But first, and in answer to the queries of the priests and Levites[3] sent by "the Jews,"[4] John denies that he himself is the Messiah (v. 20), Elijah (v. 21), or the prophet (v. 21). Each time he uses a form of the statement "I am not" (*ouk eimi*), anticipating while negatively mirroring Jesus' revelatory "I am" (*egō eimi*) statements. While John's statements about himself are worded negatively, he is nevertheless said to "confess" rather than "deny" what or who he is not. In other words, his statements of his secondary status in relationship to Jesus constitute appropriate acknowledgment, or confession, of his identity and role. John stands in contrast to those who are unwilling to confess their belief in Jesus (9:22; 12:42), and perhaps also to Peter, who three times denies that he is a disciple of Jesus (13:38; 18:17, 25, 27). Both declare what they are not: but Peter denies that he is a disciple of Jesus the Messiah; John denies that he himself is a messianic figure (cf. Luke 3:15).[5]

But John's denial that he is Elijah perplexes in light of the Synoptic tradition, where he is identified explicitly or implicitly as "Elijah" (Matt 11:13–14; 17:10–13; Mark 9:11–13).[6] According to Malachi, Elijah comes—that is, returns—as the messenger who prepares the way before the Lord (3:1; 4:5–6). Elijah's "return" was possible because he did not experience death, but was caught up by God.[7] Sirach anticipates Elijah's coming to "restore the tribes of Jacob," a possible reference to the return of the dispersed tribes to the land (Sir 48:4–12, esp. v. 10; see comments on John 11:52). In the Fourth Gospel, John denies that he is "Elijah," expected to usher in the day of the Lord and restore the tribes of Jacob, because it is Jesus who will "gather into one the children of God who had been scattered" (11:52).

Similarly, John denies that he is the prophet who would fulfill God's promise to "raise up a prophet like [Moses] from among their own people"

3."Priests and Levites" are frequently paired as temple functionaries in the OT (see 1 Chr 13:2; 2 Chr 8:15; 23:4; Ezra 3:12; 7:7; Neh 13:30). While the priests primarily presided over the various sacrifices and offerings, the Levites served as musicians (*m. Tamid* 7:3; 7:4 lists the psalms they are to sing on each day of the week) and watchmen in the temple (*m. Mid.* 1).

4. For further discussion of the term "the Jews," see Excursus 7: "'The Jews' in the Gospel of John."

5. According to Acts, in Ephesus Paul encountered Apollos (18:24–25) and others (19:1–7) who knew of Jesus, but had heard only of the baptism of John, indicating that knowledge of John's mission had spread from Palestinian soil to Asia Minor. Early tradition locates the origins of this Gospel in Ephesus (cf. Irenaeus, *Haer.* 3.1.1; 3.3.4; Eusebius, *Hist. eccl.* 3.1, 3–4).

6. In Luke, the Baptist comes "in the spirit and power of Elijah" (1:17); Jesus himself is compared directly to Elijah (4:25–26).

7. Cf. 2 Kgs 2:11; *4 Ezra* 6.25–26; Mark 6:15; 8:28; according to Justin (*Dial.* 8.4), Elijah returns before the return of Christ; cf. *Dial.* 8.3; 110.1; *m. Soṭah* 9:15 ("the resurrection of the dead shall come through Elijah"); *m. Šeqal.* 2:5; further discussion in Allison 2010, 267–68.

(Deut 18:18).[8] The expectation of a coming prophet can be found in various places, especially in the Dead Sea Scrolls.[9] The Fourth Gospel distinguishes the expectation of the Messiah and of the prophet (7:40–43), and here John denies that he is that prophet who will come as a second Moses, the final interpreter of the law. Neither is John described as "a prophet" in the Fourth Gospel (cf. Matt 11:9; 14:5; 21:26; Mark 11:32; Luke 1:76; 7:26; 20:6); the term is reserved for Jesus.

The three roles—Messiah, Elijah, prophet—are all "final" figures expected to lead and teach Israel, and to gather the tribes of Israel together. John fulfills none of these roles but is "the voice of one crying in the wilderness, 'Make straight the way of the Lord.'" This modified quotation of Isa 40:3 ("A voice cries out: "In the wilderness prepare the way of the LORD, make straight in the desert a highway for our God") differs from that in the Synoptics in two ways: (1) it eliminates the imperative "prepare" and takes "the way of the LORD" as the object of the imperative "make straight";[10] (2) it is put on the lips of the Baptist himself. "The Lord" is surely Jesus himself. John, having just denied that he is the Messiah, Elijah, or the prophet, now cites Scripture to explain who or what he is: he is a voice crying out (cf. 1:15). This self-designation underscores John's role as witness. His importance is captured in what he says about Jesus, so that others might recognize Jesus and follow him. As Origen put it in his commentary, John is "the voice pointing out the Word"; John is voice, but Jesus is speech (*Comm. Jo.* 2.26).

[24–34] The site of John's baptism, "Bethany beyond the Jordan" (1:28), is distinguished from Bethany near Jerusalem, the village of Martha, Mary, and Lazarus (John 11:1, 18; 12:1; Matt 21:17; 26:6; Mark 11:1, 11–12; 14:3; Luke 19:29; 24:50). Later, when Jesus has escaped from those who tried to arrest him, he retreats to this site (John 10:40–41). Origen argued that this Bethany was Bethabara,[11] a known village also named in some ancient manuscripts; this would situate John's baptism about eight miles from Qumran. But others

8. Origen (*Comm. Jo.* 2.8) argues from this passage and the definite article that John was a prophet, but not "the prophet."

9. See 1QS IX, 11; 4QTest 5–13 (4Q175) quotes Deut 18:18–19, linking it with a messianic reading of Num 24:15–17. For a coming prophet, see 1 Macc 4:46; 14:41–47; for help to come from the prophets Isaiah or Jeremiah, see *4 Ezra* 2.18; 2 Macc 15:13–15; for the preference for a prophet over a king as leader, see *L.A.B.* 57.4. Theudas, "a prophet," promised to divide the Jordan and lead the people across it, thus calling Moses to mind and perhaps invoking the promise of Deut 18:15–18 (Josephus, *Ant.* 20.97; Acts 5:36).

10. Isa 40:3 is quoted in Matt 3:3; Mark 1:3; Luke 3:4 as "The voice of one crying out in the wilderness: 'Prepare the way of the Lord, make his paths straight'"; it is used with reference to the community at Qumran in 1QS VIII, 14. John does not include any reference to the "messenger" who "will prepare your way" as do the other Gospels (Mal 3:1; cf. Mark 1:2; Matt 11:10; Luke 7:27).

11. Origen, *Comm. Jo.* 6.24.

have identified this Bethany as Batanea, part of Philip's tetrarchy,[12] and the site of Jesus' retreat later in the Gospel (see comments on 10:40–41). Later John is found baptizing at "Aenon near Salim" (3:23); that is, not at this Bethany. Hence, like Jesus, John seems to have had an itinerant ministry. But if he were neither the Messiah, nor Elijah, nor the prophet, then what was the meaning of his baptizing ministry in the wilderness? John's interlocutors are now identified as those sent by the Pharisees. The central role played by the Pharisees in John and their frequent association with or even identification as the temple authorities likely points to the Gospel's setting after the fall of the temple and the destruction of Jerusalem in 70 C.E. Those who emerged as leaders of the Jewish people at that time are widely regarded as at least descendants of the Pharisees, even if not identical with them.

In its historical setting, John's baptism was likely understood as effecting or symbolizing purification. The discovery of numerous *miqvaʾot* (or *miqwaʾot*, ritual baths) throughout Judea and Galilee, along with discussions of washing and purification in texts such as the Dead Sea Scrolls and the Gospels, point to an increased emphasis on ritual purity in late Second Temple Judaism. Prior to their appropriation in early Christian literature, the Greek words *baptisis* (baptism) and *baptizein* (baptize) could simply mean "wash" or "purify."[13] Someone who called for repentance, and linked that with washing or bathing, would certainly have been understood to be offering some sort of purification; so the Synoptic Gospels associate John's baptism with repentance, confession, and forgiveness of sin (Matt 3:6, 11; Mark 1:4–5; Luke 3:3).

In the Fourth Gospel, John's baptism with water does not deal with sin but bears witness to the one who does: the Lamb of God, who "takes away the sin of the world." To "take away sin" means to remove sin, to purify from sin. John's baptism with water and his words do not cleanse or purify, but they do point to the one who baptizes, or purifies, through the Spirit, his word (15:3), and his death (13:1–11; 19:34). Jesus calls, gathers, and cleanses not only his own (1:11) or Israel (1:31; 11:52), but also the world (1:29), all the scattered children of God (1:12–13; 11:52). John's own ministry is to reveal Jesus to Israel, whose ministry is in turn directed to the world and to the removal of all sin.

While "Lamb of God" (*amnos tou theou*) is a designation for Jesus familiar to Christians in art, literature, and liturgy, and lambs are common in Scripture and Jewish symbolism, no single biblical precedent explains this designation of Jesus (1:29, 36). In Scripture, the scapegoat carries or takes Israel's sin into the wilderness (Lev 16:8–10); but here a lamb "takes away" or removes "the sin of

12. Riesner 1987; Carson 1991, 146–47.

13. See Mark 7:4; Luke 11:38. In the LXX, *baptizein* may refer to washing that removes ritual impurity (cf. 2 Kgs 5:14; Jdt 12:7; Sir 34:25 [34:30 ET]). Josephus, *Ant.* 18.116–17, summarizes John's message as a call to ethical conduct and baptism (*baptismos* and *baptisis*), following upon repentance and a previous cleansing of the soul and a commitment to virtue.

the world." While the Passover lamb[14] is frequently suggested as the template for the "Lamb of God," the Passover lambs, of which there were many, were not killed to atone for sin or to purge uncleanness.[15] Their blood does, however, protect the faithful from death (cf. John 10:11, 15). Twice daily a lamb (LXX *amnos*) was offered "at the entrance of the tent of meeting" (NRSV); this burnt offering was called the *tāmîd* (Exod 29:42–46; Num 28:3–10). Lambs are also offered for atonement, as guilt offerings, and for purification (Lev 9:3–13; Lev 14:2–13; Num passim). Hence the description of Jesus as the "Lamb of God" who "takes away" sin may allude more generally to the various sacrifices of lambs that atone or cleanse. Finally, the servant of Isa 53 is compared to a lamb that "bears the sins of many" (*probaton*, Isa 53:7, 11 LXX), even as Jesus takes away "the sin of the world."

Given the plethora of images that seem to shed light on the work of Jesus as portrayed in John, perhaps no single figure lies behind the description of Jesus as the "Lamb of God." In the multifaceted imagery of the book of Revelation, Jesus is the Lamb (*arnion*) who was slain but now lives, gathers all the peoples of the earth together, leads them to the water of life as a shepherd, conquers his foes, and is the light-giving lamp in the city of God (Rev 5:6–10, 12; 6:1; 7:17; 14:1; 17:14; 21:22–23; cf. the conquering lamb in *T. Jos*. 19.8). In both John and Revelation, the portrait of the Lamb draws on an array of Old Testament images but is, in the end, shaped by the conviction of what Jesus himself was understood to be and to do; here Jesus' work is presented as removing the sin of the world.

John explains that he baptizes to make Jesus known to Israel (1:31). Curiously, the Gospel does not describe or even mention the baptism of Jesus. It does, however, speak of the Spirit's descending and *remaining* upon Jesus (1:32–33). The word *remain* (from *menein*, "to abide, stay") contrasts the permanence of the Spirit's resting on Jesus with the sporadic inspiration of prophets and teachers; it may further reflect the view that the Messiah was the bearer of the Spirit.[16] This one *has* the Spirit, and he has it uniquely and permanently; hence, he subsequently confers it on others as one breathes out one's own breath (3:34; 7:37–39; 20:22).

Unlike the Synoptic accounts, no heavenly voice testifies that Jesus is the "beloved Son." Rather, John the Baptizer asserts that God had told him that he would recognize the coming one by the descent of the Spirit upon him. Human

14. LXX *probaton*, e.g., Exod 12:3–8; goats could be offered as well.

15. The sacrifice of lambs (and goats) "for sins" during the Feast of Unleavened Bread (so Josephus, *Ant*. 3.248–49) does not refer to the lambs slaughtered for the Passover meal.

16. Isa 11:2; *T. Jud*. 24:2–6, perhaps under Christian influence; explicitly in *Targum Isaiah*. According to Philo, the Spirit of God remained with Moses longer than with other human beings because of his "proper reverence, obedience, abstention from evildoing, and contemplation of the one true God" (*Gig*. 47–48, 52, 54).

witness expresses the divine testimony. The Spirit bears witness to the identity of Jesus; John the Baptist makes it known. So Jesus' disciples are to do as well.

The emphasis on the Spirit explains another distinctive feature of the Fourth Gospel's account of John the Baptist. The Synoptic Gospels contrast John's baptism with water and Jesus' baptism with the Spirit: while John baptizes with water but not with the Spirit, Jesus baptizes with the Spirit but not with water.[17] However, in the Gospel of John, Jesus baptizes with both water and the Spirit (3:22; cf. 4:2). John's baptism with water serves to bear witness to Jesus, who would baptize with the Holy Spirit. But since water itself symbolizes the coming Holy Spirit (7:37–39), which Jesus will give, he himself also baptizes with water, anticipating that time when he will confer the Spirit. In other words, John baptizes with water *only*, anticipating the one who will baptize with the Spirit, but Jesus baptizes with *both* water and the Spirit. Baptism with water, whether accomplished by Jesus or John, anticipates the baptizing or purifying work of the Spirit that Jesus alone accomplishes.

1:35–51 The Calling of the First Disciples and Their Witness to Jesus

The witness of John is now shown to bear its firstfruits as he directs two of his own disciples to follow Jesus. Jesus' first disciples follow him for two primary reasons: (1) because Jesus calls them; and (2) because others bear witness to him. Simon Peter will come to Jesus because Andrew declares that they have found the Messiah (1:41), and this pattern of testimony, which leads others to follow or believe, recurs in the Gospel (e.g., 4:39–42). Indeed, the entire Gospel functions as a witness for its readers, so that they may be brought to encounter Jesus through it (20:30–31). It is, of course, also the experience of those bearing witness that their testimony may be rejected (9:24–34; cf. 15:18–21).

> **1:35** The next day John again was standing with two of his disciples, **36**
> and seeing Jesus walking, he said, "Behold the Lamb of God!" **37** His two
> disciples heard him say it, so they followed Jesus. **38** When Jesus turned
> around and saw them following him, he said, "What are you looking
> for?" They said to him, "Rabbi (which, when translated, means teacher),
> where are you staying?"[a] **39** He said to them, "Come and see." So they
> went and saw where he was staying, and they stayed with him that day.
> It was about four o'clock.[b]
>
> **40** And Andrew, the brother of Simon Peter, was one of the two who
> had heard what John said and followed Jesus. **41** Andrew first found his
> brother, Simon, and said to him, "We have found the Messiah" (which is

17. E.g., Mark 1:8, "I have baptized you with water; *but* [*de*] he will baptize you with the Holy Spirit."

translated Christ). **42** He brought him to Jesus. When Jesus looked at him,
he said, "You are Simon, the son of John. You will be called Cephas"
(which means Peter).

43 The next day Jesus wanted to go to Galilee. He found Philip and said to
him, "Follow me." **44** Philip was from Bethsaida, from the village of Andrew
and Peter. **45** Philip found Nathanael and said to him, "We have found the
one whom Moses wrote about in the law, and the prophets wrote about too,
Jesus, Joseph's son from Nazareth." **46** And Nathanael said to him, "Can
anything good come from Nazareth?" Philip answered, "Come and see."

47 Jesus saw Nathanael coming to him and said this about him,
"Behold, truly an Israelite in whom there is no deceit." **48** Nathanael said
to him, "How do you know me?" Jesus answered, "Before Philip called
you, I saw you under the fig tree." **49** Nathanael said, "Rabbi, you are the
Son of God, you are the King of Israel!" **50** Jesus answered, "Have you
believed because I said to you that I saw you under the fig tree? You will
see greater things than these." **51** And then he said, "Amen, amen, I tell
you, you will see the heaven opened and the angels of God going up and
coming down on this Son of Man."[c]

a. "Stay," from *menō*, often translated as "abide."

b. "About four o'clock" translates "the tenth hour," reckoning from 6:00 a.m.

c. Or, "this human being." See Excursus 2: "Son of God, Son, and Son of Man in John."

[1:35–42] The Gospel now introduces John's disciples.[18] Upon hearing John's testimony that Jesus is the Lamb of God, two of them immediately *followed* Jesus, a point stressed three times (1:37, 38, 40). Since the Baptist's mission has been distilled into revealing "the coming one" (1:15, 27, 30) to Israel (v. 31), his role as a witness to identify Jesus has been carried out when his disciples follow Jesus. Here, then, is the first instance of someone serving as a witness to bring others to Jesus, a role so important within the Gospel, anticipating the testimony borne to later generations in order to bring them to believe (1:45; 4:39; 9:25, 30–33; 20:17–18, 29; 21:24).

Jesus asks those following him a simple question: "What are you looking for?" While the question makes sense in the context of the narrative, it also serves to challenge these fledgling disciples, and the reader through them, to deeper insight. For while they initially call Jesus "Rabbi" and want to know where he is staying, if they continue to follow Jesus, they will see the revelation of God in him (1:51), his glory (2:11). The question "What are you looking for?" urges them to move from sight to insight. It has its parallel in the double meaning of the word "follow"

18. See also John 3:25; 4:1; Matt 9:14; 11:2; Mark 2:18; Luke 5:33; 7:18; 11:1; Acts 19:1–7.

(*akoloutheō*). "Following" refers quite literally to the act of following another person, and the Gospel graphically pictures the disciples as walking behind Jesus as they follow him to the place where he is staying for the night (1:38–39; cf. 21:20). But to follow Jesus is to be his disciple (10:27; 12:26; 21:19, 22).[19]

Even as one can see Jesus and not understand who he is, so one can follow him for a period of time yet not become or remain his disciple (6:60–66). When Jesus invites these disciples to "come and see," he is inviting them not only to follow him and to see what he will do, but also to discern in his acts just who he is, and thus to believe and follow on the path of discipleship. John reports that the disciples "stayed with Jesus" because it was late in the day (four o'clock). The word here translated "stay" (*menō*) particularly characterizes disciples who persevere in faith, in contrast to those who desert Jesus or turn away from him (cf. 8:31; 15:4–7, 9–10, 16). The disciples' following of Jesus, their desire to see who or what he is, and their "staying" with him—all foreshadow the kind of discipleship to which Jesus calls them (21:19, 22).

One of John's disciples who followed Jesus is Andrew (1:40, 44; 6:8; 12:22); he testifies that Jesus is "the Messiah" to his brother, Simon, who also becomes a follower of Jesus. Messiah (*messias*), the Gospel explains, is to be translated into Greek as *Christos*, the term in use among the Greek-speaking Christians reading the Gospel (see also 4:25).[20] And while John translates the term, he does not explain it, either here or elsewhere. He does, however, link it twice with Son of God.[21] The connection between "Son of God" and "Messiah" has its roots in God's identification of the king of Israel as "my son" or as "a son to me" (Ps 2:7; 2 Sam 7:14; 1 Chr 17:13; 22:10; 28:6).[22] In John, "Son of God" is once linked with "King of Israel" (1:49). But Jesus is never called "son of David," as he is in the other Gospels.[23] John defines Jesus' messiahship not by his status as the son of David, but by his identity as the Son of God, even as he defines the children of God as those who are born, not of human descent, but of God.

While the double name "Simon Peter" is frequently found in John, it is rare in the rest of the New Testament (Matt 16:16; Luke 5:8; "Simeon Peter" in 2 Pet 1:1).[24] Almost equally as rare is the designation of Simon by the Aramaic

19. See Excursus 8: "The Johannine Vocabulary of Faith and Discipleship."

20. John is the only NT book to use the transliterated *messias*; for further discussion of the origin of the term *christos*, see comments on 12:3 below.

21. John 11:27; 20:31; cf. Mark 1:1; Matt 16:16; 26:63; 2 Cor 1:19; Gal 2:20; also Rom 1:4.

22. Among the DSS, 4QFlor (4Q174) links quotations from 2 Sam 7:10–14 and Ps 2:1–2, texts that speak of the king of Israel as a "son" to God, and identifies the figure in these texts as the "branch of David," a term drawn from the prophets for the coming king of Israel (e.g., Isa 11:1; Jer 23:5; Zech 3:8; 6:12), and eventually a messianic designation.

23. Matt 1:1, 20; 9:27; 12:23; 21:9; Mark 12:35; Luke 18:38, 39.

24. Peter figures in only two scenes in John 1–12 (1:40–42; 6:68–69); he plays a larger role in the second part of the Gospel (chs. 13–21), where he is often paired with the "beloved disciple" (13:18–25; 20:1–10; 21:1–8, 20–24; perhaps 18:15–16).

epithet Cephas (*Kēfā'*), found elsewhere in the New Testament only in Paul (1 Cor 3:22; 9:5; Gal 2:9, 11).[25] Unlike Matthew, John does not offer any explanation of the origin or meaning of Simon's nickname, although he does offer its Greek translation, *Petros* (from the Greek for "stone" or "rock"). Jesus' designation of Simon as "rock" may point to his role as spokesperson for the disciples (6:68–69) and shepherd of Jesus' flock (21:15–19, 22), a role Jesus assigns to Simon after the resurrection (10:3–4, 16; 21:15–19, 22).

[43–51] Accompanied by these disciples, Jesus now heads for Galilee.[26] This is the first explicit association of Jesus with Galilee in John. Since Andrew and Simon Peter come from the town of Bethsaida, it is not surprising that Philip, whom Jesus now calls to be his disciple, also hails from Bethsaida (cf. 12:21), a fishing village on or near the shores of the Sea of Galilee, elsewhere associated with the ministry of Jesus (Matt 11:21; Mark 6:45; 8:22; Luke 9:10, 10:13–15). According to Josephus, Philip the tetrarch, son of Herod the Great, raised the status of Bethsaida from village (*kōmē*, Mark 8:23, 26) to city (*polis*, Luke 9:10; John 1:44), enlarged its population, strengthened its fortifications, and renamed it Julias.[27] It was a Greek-speaking or bilingual area, with a population of both Jew and Gentile.[28] Andrew (*Andreas*) and Philip (*Philippos*) are both Greek names, and Simon is a Greek form of the Hebrew name *Simeon*.[29] These disciples could have been expected to speak Greek. Not surprisingly, later it is to Philip that "some Greeks" appeal to see Jesus (12:21). Just as Andrew found Simon in order to tell him about Jesus, so Philip found Nathanael to report that they had found the one "whom Moses wrote about in the law, and the prophets wrote about too, Jesus, Joseph's son from Nazareth."[30] Those who believe find those who do not, bear witness to Jesus, and so bring others to follow him.[31]

The "law and the prophets" indicate the totality of Scripture (for the phrase, see 2 Macc 15:9; 4 Macc 18:10–18; Matt 5:17; 7:12; 11:13; Rom 3:21). Elsewhere John links Jesus to specific Old Testament passages, especially from

25. For full discussion of Peter's name, see Bockmuehl (2010, 135–57; more briefly, 2012b, 21–23), who suggests Simon was known by the nickname *Petros* (Peter) from his youth; Jesus gave him its Aramaic equivalent, *Kēphas* (Cephas), which is not attested as a name in first-century Hebrew or Aramaic.

26. Bethsaida is technically in Batanea, governed by Philip, and not in Galilee, governed by Herod Antipas.

27. Josephus, *Ant.* 18.28.

28. Whether ancient Bethsaida has been found remains disputed; see Meyers and Chancey 2012, 122–23; Bockmuehl 2010, 158–87.

29. The name Andreas (Andrew) appears in Josephus (*Ant.* 12.18, 24, 50, 53, 86); Philip is the name of Philip of Macedon and Philip, tetrarch of Batanea.

30. In this Gospel, Jesus is said to be "from Nazareth" (*apo/ek Nazaret*, 1:45–46) and is therefore called "Jesus *ho Nazōraios*" (18:5, 7; 19:19)

31. On Andrew's role as witness, see de Boer; Bennema 2009, 47–52.

Isaiah and the Psalms,[32] and there is ample evidence in the New Testament of the early Christian view that Jesus' messianic mission had been written about in the Scriptures (e.g. Matt 1:22–23; Mark 1:1–3; Luke 4:16–30; Acts 2:25–36; 13:34–35; 15:15; Rom 15:3; Heb 10:7). But Nathanael, who hailed from Cana, a small village in Galilee (21:2), scoffs at the suggestion that Nazareth[33] could produce the one promised by the Scriptures. His incredulity foreshadows that displayed later by other Galileans, who wonder how Jesus could be the one who has come down from heaven, since his parents are known to them (6:42). It will soon become evident that to describe Jesus as "Joseph's son from Nazareth" (1:45; cf. 6:42) is to misunderstand him. He is, as Nathanael rightly confesses, the Son of God (cf. Luke 1:35; 2:48–49). As Son of God, Jesus comes "from above," but he is not a heavenly or angelic being whose earthly existence is simply a disguise for his true identity. His true identity is expressed, for John, in the prologue's decisive formulation: the Word was made flesh. He lived in Nazareth, a village with apparently little to commend it. It is this Word-became-flesh, Jesus from Nazareth, who is the Messiah.

Jesus is acclaimed as "King of Israel" by Nathanael, "truly an Israelite in whom there is no deceit." The description contrasts Nathanael with Jacob, who was renamed "Israel" (Gen 32:28–30) and was noted for his cunning and deceit in dealings with his father, Isaac, and his brother, Esau. While Jacob, the conniving father of the twelve tribes of Israel, wrestled with an angel and named the place of his wrestling Peniel, "the face of God," Nathanael, a true Israelite, has seen the Son of God, the King of Israel.[34] Later Pilate asks Jesus whether he is the "King of the Jews" (18:33) and subsequently has him crucified on that charge, inadvertently acknowledging Jesus on those terms (19:19–22). By contrast, here one who is "truly an Israelite" openly and rightly acknowledges Jesus as "the King of Israel" (cf. 12:13). Although in John "the Jews" frequently refers to those who oppose Jesus, "Israel" carries a positive sense, while also indicating Jesus' origins in and mission to "his own people" (1:11, 31, 49; 3:10).

32. John 2:17; 6:31; 10:34; 12:13, 15, 38, 40; 19:24, 28, 37. For discussion of the application of passages from the Psalms to Jesus, see Brunson; Daly-Denton 172–76; M. M. Thompson 2008b.

33. Nazareth was a small Jewish town, given mainly to agriculture; there is little evidence of the adoption of Roman culture, although a good road connected it to the larger and more Romanized towns on the shore of the Sea of Galilee (although not to nearby Sepphoris). Dark suggests that the strongly Jewish and overtly religious identity of Nazareth and communities around it reflect "passive resistance against the Roman state and/or associated cultural change" (98).

34. It is possible that there is an allusion to the tradition that Israel meant "the one who sees God" (see Philo, *Fug.* 208). Nathanael, who is truly an Israelite, sees the Son of God in the place of revelation (1:51) as Jacob (Israel) saw the face of God (Gen 28:12–17; cf. 32:30; 33:10).

Jesus "saw" Nathanael sitting under a fig tree. While in the Old Testament the promise of everyone seated under a fruitful fig tree is a picture of prosperity and peace (Joel 2:22; Zech 3:10), it may not be particularly significant that Nathanael was sitting under a fig tree in a land where figs are common: the point is that Jesus saw him. Jesus promises those who follow him that they will see something greater than a demonstration of his prophetic gift; they will see "the heaven opened, and the angels of God going up and down on this Son of Man" (1:51). The promise is introduced by a doubled "amen" (25 times in John). Although in the other Gospels Jesus also introduces a point with "amen," it is always doubled in John and is followed in every instance by "I tell you" (*legō hymin* or *legō soi*). In the Old Testament "amen" typically comes at the end of a prayer, oath (Neh 5:13), blessing (1 Kgs 1:36; 1 Chr 16:36; Neh 8:6; Ps 41:13), or curse (e.g., Num 5:22; Deut 27:15–16) and means "surely" or "Let it be so!"[35] The unusual appearance of *Amēn* to introduce statements is frequently taken as a marker of a historical peculiarity of Jesus' own speech,[36] a conclusion perhaps bolstered by the fact that throughout the NewTestament *amēn* has been transliterated rather than translated (as with *genoito* or *alēthōs* in the LXX).[37]

The promise of an opened heaven graphically depicts God disclosing heavenly secrets, allowing for the descent of heavenly beings or even the coming of God. In the book of Revelation, an open door into heaven allows John to see the heavenly throne room (Rev 4:1); later, when heaven is opened, the rider whose name is "Faithful and True" and "The Word of God" emerges in judgment (Rev 19:11–16). The "opening" of the heaven allows for entrance into, or visions of, the heavenly realms, as well as the descent or emergence of heavenly figures. Isaiah petitions God to "tear open the heavens and come down" (64:1), and in the Synoptic tradition the heavens are "torn apart" or "opened" at the baptism of Jesus as the Spirit of God comes down upon him. That scene is missing from the Gospel of John, perhaps because the "opened heaven" cannot be limited to a single event or point in time, but rather summarizes the entire ministry of Jesus: his life, death, and resurrection are the revelation of the identity, glory, and presence of God.

The cryptic reference to the angels as "ascending and descending upon this Son of Man" alludes to Jacob's dream of a ladder stretching from heaven to earth, on which the angels ascend and descend (Gen 28:12).[38] In that account,

35. For a doubled *amēn* in prayers and responses, see Neh 8:6; Pss 41:13; 72:19; 1QS I, 20; II, 10, 18.

36. Lindars (48) contends that the doubled *Amēn* underscores the point.

37. While "amen" is sometimes compared to the OT's "thus says the LORD," in the LXX this phrase is translated either *tade legei* (e.g., Exod 4:22; 5:1), *houtōs legei* (e.g., 1 Chr 21:10–11; 2 Chr 34:24; Isa 8:11; 28:16; 30:12; 37:33), or *houtōs eipen* (e.g., 1 Chr 17:4; 2 Chr 12:5; Isa 18:4; 21:6).

38. See the Excursus 2: "Son of God, Son, and Son of Man in John."

the heavens are indeed "opened." Jacob's dream accompanies God's promise to be with Jacob (Israel); Jacob awakens to marvel that God has been "in this place" and names it Beth-el, the house of God (cf. John 2:13–22). But curiously, although Jesus promises heavenly revelation, the disciples will see no heavens torn asunder and no angels: rather, they will become witnesses to Jesus' daily life and work. And here, in his deeds and life, they will see the "heaven opened"; as the "Son of Man" he is the "ladder" who links heaven and earth.[39] Throughout the Old Testament, "son of man" is an idiom for a human being (as in RSV: e.g., Num 23:19; Ps 8:4; Isa 51:12; Ezekiel passim; Dan 7:13–14, 27). In John, "Son of Man" is the Word made flesh, and this Word has come from God to dwell among human beings, to bring the truth, grace, life, and light of God in all their fullness (1:14, 16). Jesus' promise to Nathanael to see "greater things" will be fulfilled initially when Jesus manifests his glory in his first sign (2:11). If the disciples expected to look up in order to see the opened heavens, John invites them instead to look at what is right in front of them: to look at the Word made flesh, the man Jesus of Nazareth, and there to see the revelation of the glory of God.

Excursus 2: Son of God, Son, and Son of Man in John

One of John's distinctive features is the prominence of the designation "Father" for God and "the Son" or "Son of God" for Jesus. By contrast, while in the Synoptics various figures hail Jesus as Son of God, or inquire whether he is the Son of God,[40] he does not speak of himself as "the Son of God." He refers to himself as "the Son" a few times: in the saying about the mutual knowledge of Father and Son, the so-called "bolt from the Johannine blue" (Matt 11:27; Luke 10:22); in his confession of the Son's ignorance of the hour of final judgment (Mark 13:32; Matt 24:36); and in the Great Commission (Matt 28:18–20). He alone speaks of himself as "the Son of Man."

In John, "Son of God" occurs 8 times; "the Son," 15 times; "Son of man," 13 times. Others hail Jesus as "Son of God" (1:34, 49; 11:27; 20:31) but not as "the Son" or "Son of Man." Jesus refers to himself as "the Son" (3:16–17, 35–36; 5:19–23, 26; 6:40; 8:36; 14:13; 17:1, "your Son"), Son of God (5:25; 10:36; 11:4), and Son of Man (1:51; 5:27; 6:27, 53, 62; 8:28; 9:35; 12:23; 13:31); as in the Synoptics, "Son of Man" is found almost exclusively on his lips.[41] John has developed the traditions that refer to Jesus as Son, Son of God, and Son of Man and developed them so that "the Son" becomes the essential, programmatic term for identifying him in relationship to God. "The Son" is

39. Moloney (1978) suggests that Jesus' use of "Son of Man" (1:51) corrects Nathanael's acclamation of Jesus as "Son of God" and "King of Israel" (1:49; cf. Mark 8:29 and 31; 14:61 and 62); R. Brown (2003, 257) sees a "deepening improvement of the titles" allotted to Jesus throughout John 1.

40. For fuller discussion of the distinctive portrayals of God as Father and Jesus as Son and Son of God in all the Gospels, see M. M. Thompson 2000, 87–115, 133–54.

41. The exception is John 12:34, in the query to Jesus about the identity of the Son of Man.

itself a shortened form of "Son of God" and captures Jesus' unique relationship to God; but it may also obliquely allude to Jesus' identity as "Son of Man."

Son and Son of God. In the Old Testament, the king of Israel is characterized as a son to God (2 Sam 7:12–14; 1 Chr 17:13; 28:6; Ps 2:6–9). Israel is known as God's child or son (Exod 4:22–23; Hos 11:1; Jer 31:9); the righteous individual can also be called a child of the Lord (*pais kyriou*) or son of God (*huios theou*; Wis 2:13, 17–18; cf. Philo, *Conf.* 145, commenting on Deut 14:1). In none of these instances does "Son of God" imply deity or even divine origins; to be a "son" or child of God entails a particular relationship: one is elected to a specific vocation (a king, a chosen people), and that vocation requires faithful obedience.

In keeping with the Old Testament's designation of the king of Israel as a son to God, John links "Son" and "Messiah" or "King" (1:49; 11:27; 20:31) as the New Testament does elsewhere (Matt 16:16; 26:63; Mark 1:1; 14:61; Luke 4:41; Rom 1:3–4). As the Son (*huios*) of God, the King of Israel, and Messiah, Jesus is thus distinguished from those who are the children (*tekna* and *paidia*) begotten of God. However, Jesus' identity as the "Son of God" and "Son" cannot be fully summarized in his messianic vocation. Rather, these terms manifest Jesus' origins in and distinctive relationship to God as Father, a relationship that is further characterized by their mutual indwelling (17:11, 20–21, 23) and glorification, or honor (12:23; 13:31; 14:13; 17:1); love (3:35; 5:20); and life-giving mission (3:16–17; 5:21, 25–26; 6:40).[42] "Son of God" and "Son" are used to specify the distinctly *filial* relationship of Jesus to God and play a role in John's presentation of the unity of Father and Son by establishing the dependence of the Son on the Father. How John understands the singularity of Jesus' identity as "Son of God" can be seen in the virtual equation of the charges that "he made himself equal to God" and "he made himself the Son of God" (see comments on 5:18; 10:33; 19:7).[43] Son of God, the absolute "the Son," the singular use of *huios* for Jesus in relation to God, and the attribution *monogenēs* ("unique, one of a kind," 1:14, 18; 3:16) bespeak Jesus' unique divine identity. Although there are other "children of God," there is no other such "Son of God." Jesus is, therefore, simply "the Son."

Son of Man. "The Son" may also allude to Jesus' identity as "Son of Man." Although investigation of this contested phrase has focused on its use by Jesus and its meaning in the Synoptic tradition, its function in the Gospel of John has been equally disputed.[44] The issues can only be summarized briefly here. The Hebrew (*ben ādām*) and Aramaic (*bar ʾĕnāš*) are idioms for "human being" in those languages;[45] the phrase is not idiomatic

42. Greco-Roman emperors who were divinized by act of the Roman senate could be called *divi filius*, "son of the divinized" (see comments on 19:7; 20:28). Human beings born to a god (e.g., Hercules, Perseus) could be called the offspring or sons of God; they were not born immortal, but in mythic accounts they could be made immortal.

43. In the Synoptics, Jesus' blasphemy is linked to his identification as "the Son of Man," who will be "seated at the right hand of Power" (Matt 26:64; Mark 14:62); in John the identification of Jesus as "Son of God" elicits the charge of blasphemy (10:36; 19:7).

44. For a recent survey of the issues involved in interpreting the expression, see the essays in Hurtado and Owen, for which Hurtado provides an apt overview ("Summary," 159–77).

45. For examples in Hebrew, see Num 23:19; Ps 8:4; Isa 51:12; Ezekiel, passim; Dan 8:17; for Aramaic, Dan 7:13.

Greek and does not appear outside the LXX, the New Testament, or texts influenced by them. When the LXX translates either the Hebrew or the Aramaic, it does so rather woodenly, most frequently using *huios anthrōpou.* If the LXX had offered an idiomatic translation, one might have expected *anthrōpos* ("human being") or perhaps *thnētos* ("mortal"; cf. Prov 3:13; Isa 51:12).

In the New Testament the designation "the Son of Man" (*ho huios tou anthrōpou*) occurs primarily in the Gospels (Matthew, 30×; Mark, 14×; Luke, 25×; John, 13×);[46] there and elsewhere, the New Testament typically includes the definite article(s): *ho huios* [*tou*] *anthrōpou*[47] ("the Son of Man" or "the Son of the Man"), perhaps best translated something like "this man." People wonder whether Jesus might be the Messiah or a prophet, but nobody inquires whether he might be the Son of Man, nor does anyone acclaim him as such (cf. Mark 8:28; John 7:40–41). This suggests that in Jesus' day "the Son of Man" did not refer without further qualification to a specific or expected figure.[48]

The question remains why Jesus, and Jesus alone, would have used this phrase to refer to himself and his ministry if it meant simply "human being." Moreover, if Jesus used an Aramaic (or possibly Hebrew) idiom, why was it carried over literally in the Greek to the point of woodenness? Perhaps the best eplanation of the data in the Gospels is that Jesus spoke of himself as "Son of Man,"[49] forging a distinctive self-reference, shaped by biblical terminology and imagery, which gained its meaning from the contexts in which he used it.[50] Its content is best determined from the contexts of the utterances in the Gospels.[51]

But the question remains whether the Gospels draw on specific biblical imagery for conceptualizing their use of "Son of Man." Some interpreters have suggested that the Gospels' "Son of Man" should be explained against the background of either Ezekiel,[52] where God repeatedly addresses the prophet as "son of man," or later rabbinic speculation about Adam;[53] yet perhaps the most common explanation of "Son of Man" has been that it draws on the memorable image in Dan 7:13, where God's kingdom is given to "one like a son of man":[54] a human-shaped kingdom supplants the beastly, destructive kingdoms that have preceded it. This figure, which is "like a son of man," represents

46. For references outside the Gospels, see Acts 7:56; Rev 1:13; 14:14; cf. Heb 2:6 RSV.

47. For the expression without the definite article, see John 5:27; Heb 2:6; Rev 1:13; 14:14.

48. As Hurtado (Hurtado and Owen, "Summary," 166–67) notes, "The expression's primary linguistic function is to *refer, not to characterize*"; "'son of man' designates but does not define Jesus."

49. Some have argued that Jesus spoke Greek, which is indeed a possibility for Jews in first-century Galilee and Judea. But if Jesus did speak of himself *ho huios tou anthropou*, that nonidiomatic usage still requires explanation.

50. See esp. Moule (1977, 11–14), who argues that, while Jesus' usage refers to Dan 7, "son of man" is, nevertheless, not a title but "a symbol of vocation."

51. See Bauckham 2007c, 237: "son of man" carries allusions to Dan 7:13 only in contexts that "make other forms of allusion to" the Danielic passage; so also Hurtado, in Hurtado and Owen, "Summary," 159–77.

52. See the queries raised by Lukaszewski 2011.

53. See esp. Marcus 2003.

54. Dan 7:13, Aramaic, *kĕbar ʾĕnāš*; LXX, *ōs huios anthrōpou.*

"the people of the saints of the Most High": the people of Israel (7:22, 25, 27). The grotesque and destructive beasts of Daniel's vision (7:4–7) could have been supplanted by a lamb or sheep, since Israel is often portrayed as God's flock. But here God grants his people the authority to rule all the other kingdoms that had formerly oppressed them; thus Israel receives the mandate given to humankind to have dominion over the "beasts of the field" (Ps 2:6–7).[55]

In keeping with this variety of possible Old Testament backgrounds, current scholarship suggests four main interpretations of Son of Man in John:

1. "Son of Man" refers to Jesus' humanity. This interpretation has been vigorously defended by Moloney, who argues that the expression for Jesus is "entirely dependent upon the incarnation."[56]
2. "Son of Man" is a designation, drawn from Jewish apocalyptic literature, that implies the heavenly nature of the Son of Man.[57]
3. "Son of Man" refers to the original "divine man," similar to Philo's "the man according to [God's] image" or the "primal" man (Philo, *Conf.* 146; *Leg.* 1.43).[58]
4. "Son of God" or "Son" essentially subsumes "Son of Man."[59]

Of these views, the first is especially well supported by the linguistic data in John. As mentioned, *ben ādām* and *bar ʾěnāš* mean "human being"; *huios anthrōpou* translates these phrases in the LXX. In conjunction with this point, one should note references to Jesus' flesh (1:14; 6:51–58), and the frequent references—sometimes disparaging, sometimes innocent, often ironic—to Jesus as this "man" (*anthrōpos*, 4:29; 5:12; 9:11, 16, 24, 29, 33; 10:33; 11:47; 18:17, 29). John does not argue that Jesus is a human being: it is everywhere assumed that he is. That, in fact, is the point of offense for Jesus' bold claims to have come from heaven or God, or to have been given those divine prerogatives that render him "equal to God" (5:18; 10:33; 19:7).

55. This figure who is "like a son of man" and who is described as "coming with the clouds of heaven" (Dan 7:13 RSV) has been described as apocalyptic, heavenly, and messianic; it is thought that this figure is alluded to in *1 En.* 37–71 and *4 Ezra* 13. In *1 Enoch* a figure described by God as "my/the righteous one" or "my/the elect one" is also called "son of man." It is important to notice that the English translation actually renders three different Ethiopic phrases by "son of man," which inadvertently suggests that "son of man" was a fixed characterization of a known figure; see Darrell D. Hannah, "The Elect Son of Man," in Hurtado and Owen 130–58. In *4 Ezra* 13 there is a deliverer figure described as a "man" with the imagery of Dan 7; the Most High calls him "my Son" (13.32, 37, 52), but he is not called "the Son of man" (or even "a son of man"). In Ezekiel the Tragedian 68–69, God is described in ways that are thought to develop the imagery of Dan 7, but "son of man" does not appear.

56. Moloney 1978, 213.

57. Reynolds; Ellens thinks that John's divine Son of Man stands in marked contrast to the figure in Jewish sources, where "Son of man" is not properly "divine." Drawing on Jewish speculation about Adam, Marcus (2003, 383) remarks that Adam is a figure of great glory, even godlikeness: "In 'the Son of the Man' the godlike one is human; the title, in its implied union of these two aspects, is intrinsically incarnational" (384).

58. Dodd 1953, 43–44; Borgen 1968, 146; Meeks 1967, 70.

59. Burkett.

Put differently, the one who is *anthrōpos* (human) and *ho huios tou anthrōpou* is such by virtue of the "enfleshment" (incarnation) of the Word: Jesus is "Son of Man" because he is the Word made flesh (*sarx*). It is no accident that the Fourth Gospel speaks of the flesh of the Son *of Man* (6:51–56), since "son of man" regularly denotes human beings in Scripture. Precisely this human being will be lifted up (crucified but exalted, 3:14; 8:28; 12:34) and glorified (12:23; 13:31; cf. Acts 2:33–36; 5:30–31; Phil 2:5–11). Thus, even though the Johannine Jesus speaks of the descent of the Son of Man (3:13), "Son of Man" as such does not denote a preexistent being or figure. The Word was in the beginning: "Son of Man" (human being) denotes the Word made flesh. Through this incarnate Word, "the Son of Man," the heavens are opened (1:51), judgment is passed (5:27), and life is given (6:51–58). *This* human being, *this* "Son of Man," is the "ladder" upon which God's angels ascend and descend, the place where God's glory is revealed, because he is God's own Word, incarnate. "Son of Man" "identifies Jesus as the person in whom God is revealed."[60]

In spite of the fact that in biblical usage "son of man" connotes humankind, it is too neat, even misleading, to say that "Son of Man" refers to Jesus in his humanity, while "Son of God" denotes his divinity. "Son of God" can refer either to human figures (as in Judaism) or to divinized or divine beings (as in Greco-Roman literature). More important: all three designations—Son, Son of Man, and Son of God—refer to the same person, Jesus of Nazareth, who is the Word-made-flesh. From his identity as the Word who was with God and who was God, who became flesh, and who in his vocation as the Messiah gives his flesh for the life of the world—from that identity these diverse filial terms derive their meaning.

2:1–11 Jesus' First Sign: The Messianic Provision of Abundance

Having promised Nathanael that he would "see greater things" (1:51), Jesus performs a sign at a wedding in Cana, with the result that the disciples saw his glory (2:11; 11:40). The account of the wedding feast at Cana also serves as a transition to the next portion of the Gospel. John (the Baptist) and Jesus' first disciples have borne witness to Jesus: he is the Lamb of God, the one who baptizes with the Spirit, the Messiah, Son of God, and King of Israel. Now Jesus becomes the central actor in the narrative, and the accounts of his works and words explicate his identity, and what it will mean to do the work and will of the one who sent him. In particular, the sign done at Cana bears witness to Jesus as the one who brings the rich fullness of the messianic age.

Jesus' glory is revealed not in his sheer power to transform water into wine, but in the generous provision of superior wine for the wedding feast. His deed calls to mind the Old Testament promises of the feasting and drinking that

60. Koester 2008b, 97.

will characterize the (messianic) age to come. The one proclaimed by Jesus' disciples to be the Messiah, from whose "fullness we have all received" (1:16), is the host of the feast who provides abundantly for the guests at this wedding. But unlike the revelation of God's glory in a burning bush or a theophany in the temple, the glory that is revealed here remains decidedly hidden, unobtrusive, embodied in a human being, and unseen by most of those at the wedding. To see the "heavens opened" (1:51), to see the manifestation of Jesus' glory (2:11), will mean neither to see angels nor visions; rather, it will be to see the revelation of heavenly glory in and through the act of Jesus' providing plentiful choice wine for the celebration of a wedding. He is the host who provides abundantly.[61]

> **2:1** On the third day, there was a wedding in Cana of Galilee, and the
> mother of Jesus was there. **2** Both Jesus and his disciples had been invited
> to the wedding. **3** When the wine ran out, the mother of Jesus said to him,
> "They have no wine." **4** And Jesus said to her, "Woman, what does that
> have to do with me?[a] My hour has not yet come." **5** His mother said to
> the servants, "Do whatever he tells you."
>
> **6** There were six stone jars, for the Jewish rites of purification, standing
> there. Each held twenty or thirty gallons.[b] **7** Jesus said to them, "Fill the
> water jars." And they filled them up to the brim. **8** Then he said to them,
> "Draw some out now and take it to the manager of the banquet." They
> took it. **9** And when the manager of the banquet[c] had tasted the water that
> had become wine, but did not know where it had come from—although
> the servants who had drawn the water knew—he called the bridegroom
> **10** and said to him, "Every one serves the good wine first, and when they
> have become intoxicated,[d] then the inferior wine; but you have kept the
> good wine until now."
>
> **11** This was the first of the signs that Jesus did in Cana of Galilee. He
> manifested his glory, and his disciples believed in him.

a. Lit., "What to you and to me?"

b. In the Greek, "each holding two or three *metrētas*." A *metrētēs* is a liquid measure of about 39 liters, slightly more than 10 gallons (BDAG s.v.); hence, each jar held ca. "twenty or thirty gallons" (NRSV/RSV).

c. *Architriklinos* is the slave or servant responsible for managing a banquet; often translated "steward" (BDAG s.v.).

d. *Methyskomai* means "to get drunk, to become intoxicated"; cf. Luke 12:45; Rev 17:2.

61. As with the feeding of the five thousand, the sign at Cana is more aptly titled a "gift" or "supply" miracle than a "nature miracle" (Theissen 103–6).

[2:1–2] "On the third day," that is, three days after the events just narrated,[62] Jesus appears at a wedding in Cana of Galilee.[63] Jesus' first sign, his abundant provision of choice wine, takes place at a wedding feast, to which Jesus, his mother,[64] and his disciples have been invited. The subsequent comment that Jesus went to Capernaum with his mother, siblings, and disciples indicates that members of Jesus' family may also have been at the wedding (2:12). There are many unanswered questions in the account: no indication is given of whose wedding it is, why Jesus and other family members were invited, why Jesus' mother would be particularly concerned about the lack of wine, why she expected Jesus to do something, or indeed, what she might have expected him to do. Since Jesus and members of his family have been invited, this may be the wedding of a relative, and on that basis some commentators have suggested that Jesus could have been expected to help supply provisions for the wedding. But the relationship of Jesus to the bride, the groom, or the host of the wedding does not feature in the telling of the story. References to a feast, to several servants, including one who oversees the feast, and to six large stone jars in the house—all indicate the relatively high social and economic status of the host. He could be expected to provide for his guests.

But from beginning to end, the story focuses on the wine that Jesus—not the host—provides and on the origins, the quantity, and particularly the quality of this wine. Wine for the feast has run out (v. 3); but six stone jars, together capable of holding about 120–180 gallons, contain water that will eventually be used to provide wine for the feast. Although plenty of wine has been served up to this point, the wine that Jesus provides proves to be superior. In short, there is a lack of wine, and no one to supply what is lacking; but Jesus can and does provide choice wine in abundance.

[3–5] Commentators have long struggled with the sharpness of Jesus' reply to his mother and have sought to soften it: addressing her as "Woman,"[65] Jesus

62. While "on the third day" recalls the NT's witness that Jesus was raised "on the third day" (Matt 16:21; 17:23; 20:19; par. in Luke; Acts 10:40; 1 Cor 15:4), the phrase does not appear elsewhere in John; here it likely means "on the third day after the previous events" or perhaps "after a short while." The phrase "on the third day" occurs frequently in the OT (e.g., Gen 22:4; 31:22; 34:25; 40:20; 42:18; Exod 19:11, 16; Lev 7:18; 19:7; Num 7:24; 19:12, 19; 29:20; 31:19; etc.).

63. Cana is probably to be identified with contemporary Khirbet Qana, nine miles north of Nazareth; a village flourished there in the first to sixth centuries, due to its favorable location on the Roman road that ran from Ptolemais (Acco, ʿAkko) to Taricheae (Magdala). At least sixty cisterns for storing water have been excavated. See Deines; von Wahlde 2006.

64. In John, the "mother of Jesus" is never called Mary.

65. Note the NIV84's "Dear woman," revised in TNIV simply as "Mother." Although "woman" (NIV, NRSV) seems dismissive, even contemptuous, it appears as a form of address elsewhere in the Gospel (John 4:21; 19:26; 20:13, 15) and in the NT (Matt 15:28; Luke 13:12; 22:57; 1 Cor 7:16, typically translated "wife"), although in these other instances the woman is not known to the speaker; cf. Josephus, *Ant.* 17.74.

essentially tells her to leave him alone,[66] since his hour has not come. But Jesus' reply follows a pattern, typical of John, demonstrating that Jesus acts not at the instigation of others, but at his own initiative; implicitly, he acts in keeping with the Father's will (5:19). When Jesus' mother informs him that the hosts of the wedding have run out of wine, he initially deflects her request, even as he later deflects the petition of the royal official (4:47–48),[67] rebuffs his brothers when they urge him to go up to Judea (7:3–8), and deliberately stays away from Bethany upon hearing of Lazarus's illness (11:5–6). In each account, Jesus does act eventually, but having distanced himself from the original request, he shows that he is not acting under pressure of others' agenda for him (cf. 6:14–15; 7:6–10). In this light, Jesus' statement, "My hour has not yet come," may simply mean that he will act only when he has judged that his time to do so has come.[68]

Jesus thus distances himself from his natural family—here from his mother and later from his brothers—even as he does in the other Gospels (cf. Matt 12:48–50; Mark 3:33–35; Luke 2:49; 8:19–21). Later the dying Jesus entrusts the care of his mother to the "beloved disciple," rather than to his natural brothers, further redefining the contours of his kin (John 19:26–27). After his resurrection, he refers to his disciples as his "brothers" and to God as "my Father and your Father" (20:17–18), showing that the Son (*huios*) has now brought "his own" (*hoi idioi*) into the larger family of the children of God (*tekna tou theou*), a family whose identity is not drawn along natural lines of descent and blood relationships (1:10–13; 3:3–5; 11:52).

[6–10] The Gospel hardly narrates the sign itself. It describes no action of Jesus, such as praying to God, or touching or speaking to the jars or the water. Jesus gives only a simple command to the servants to fill the water jars. Whether the jars were already partially full or entirely empty, how long the filling took, and from where the servants drew the water—such details are not recounted here. Almost in passing, the evangelist refers to "the water that had become wine" (*to hydōr oinon gegenēmenon*, v. 9). The miraculous character of the event remains unexplained, even unobserved and hidden, while the words of the banquet manager, who will be the first to taste the wine, interpret the significance of what has occurred: someone has provided choice wine!

66. "What does that have to do with me?" or "This is no concern of mine" translates a Greek phrase that reads, lit., "What to you and to me?" For the phrase, see LXX: Judg 11:12; 1 Kgs 17:18; 2 Kgs 3:13; 2 Chr 35:21; 1 Esd 1:24 (1:26 ET); and Mark 1:24.

67. See the chart with comments on 4:46–50, showing structural similarities between the two Cana narratives.

68. Elsewhere, Jesus' hour refers to the hour of his death (7:30; 8:20; 12:23, 27; 13:1; 17:1), and glorification (12:23, 27–28; 17:1). Possibly there is a foreshadowing here of the fact that the manifestation of Jesus' glory in his signs (2:11) will eventually also bring about his death: a destiny that Jesus chooses willingly and that cannot be forced on him.

According to the text, "six stone jars" are standing there. Archaeological excavations of Judea and Galilee have discovered bowls, basins, jars, jugs, and other vessels made of limestone and chalk, providing evidence of an industry of manufacturing stone vessels that flourished from the time of Herod the Great (37–4 B.C.E.) to beyond the destruction of the temple (70 C.E.).[69] Here the number and size of these large vessels points to the high status of the household.[70] Stone was preferred for household vessels because, unlike clay or pottery, stone vessels did not so easily contract uncleanness and therefore did not have to be destroyed due to such contamination.[71] John notes that the "six stone jars" are for "Jewish rites of purification": that is, the water can be used for washing for purification because it has been appropriately collected, probably from rainfall, and kept from contamination. The "rites of purification" in question are not those of full immersion, since water for these was collected in cisterns (*ʾōṣārôt*) and/or immersion pools (*miqvaʾot*) specially constructed for such washing; more likely, these rites involve washing various cups and containers and perhaps also the hands before meals (*m. Yad.* 3:1–2; *m. Zabim* 5:12).

The evangelist's comment that there were "six stone jars" to be used for "the Jewish rites of purification" has prompted numerous commentators to interpret Jesus' act to mean that the "wine" of the Gospel has replaced the "water" of the law. The miracle at Cana has even been taken to represent the replacement of the entire system of Jewish purification and sacrifice, and sometimes even the "supersession of Judaism."[72] But the contrast between the "good wine" (*ton kalon oinon*) and the "lesser" (*ton elassō*) wine offered earlier,[73] and especially the emphasis on the abundance of the "good wine," draws on the biblical portrayal of the coming age of salvation as surpassing all previous eras in both the quality and quantity of God's blessings: the "new things" have replaced the "former things" (Isa 42:9; 43:9; 65:17; Rev 21:4). The blessings of this age follow and surpass the bounty of earlier blessings. The move is not lateral, from the old reality of "Judaism" to a parallel and new reality in Jesus, outside of Judaism; rather, the move is forward, from Scriptural hope and expectation to the extravagant provision expected in the coming age.

69. A brief, accessible discussion in English can be found in Reed 44–51, 56–57. For a full treatment, see Deines.

70. Stone jars found in excavations of the temple in Jerusalem hold up to seventeen gallons (Meyers and Chancey 136–37, 175–76); against Haenchen (1:173), who thinks the size of the jars is fictionalized.

71. For biblical texts, see esp. Lev 6:28; 11:32–35; in the Mishnah, see *m. Kelim* 10:1; *m. Parah* 3:2; but contrast CD XII, 15–17, which does not exempt stone vessels from transmitting impurity.

72. For various accounts of John's "replacement theology," see R. Brown 1966, 104; Barrett 191; Dunn 2006, 93–35; Koester 1989, 108; Talbert 92–93; for a discussion of some of the problems with this reading of John, see M. M. Thompson 2001, 190, 217–20; cf. Brant 62–63.

73. See 3:30, where John says that he must decrease or become less (*eme de elattousthai*).

Similarly, the coming of the Messiah in Jewish literature implies a transformation or perfection associated with the arrival of the messianic age that surpasses the previous age. A new (Jewish) temple might replace the current temple in Jerusalem, surpassing the old one in splendor and glory; Jerusalem and its people would be purified (Tob 13:11–17; 14:4–7; Bar 2:27–35; 5:5–9; Sir 36:1–19; *Jub.* 23.27–31; *Pss. Sol.* 17.21–30). In other words, biblical (and Jewish) eschatology has a built-in expectation of "replacement" since the coming messianic age surpasses the former in righteousness, justice, purity, and holiness. But this "replacement" of the old age with the age of abundant blessing in the Messiah is akin to the turning of a page to a new chapter in the narrative, rather than discarding the old story and introducing an entirely new one. Put differently, Jesus does not replace "Judaism": as Messiah, he fulfills the hopes for God's promised blessed age. The choice wine has been saved until the end and is now offered in abundance. This is the next chapter in the story of scriptural hopes and promises.

Specifically, the provision of choice wine at the end of the feast calls to mind those scenes in the prophetic literature of the Old Testament that depict the time of salvation as a time of feasting in abundance and joy, when the mountains shall "drip with sweet wine" (Amos 9:13–14; Isa 25:6–9), and when God shall gather Israel together and provide abundantly for them (Jer 31:10–14).[74] Although there is little evidence that the royal Messiah was expected to be a miracle worker himself, certain apocalyptic texts describe the days of the Messiah as a time when vineyards will become surrealistically fruitful: "on one vine will be a thousand branches, one branch will produce a thousand clusters, and one cluster will produce a thousand grapes, and one grape will produce a cor[75] of wine" (*2 Bar.* 29.5; cf. *1 En.* 10.19).[76] And the wine cup, grape leaf, and grape are frequently found on coins minted during both the first (66–73 C.E.) and second (132–35) Jewish revolts.[77]

It was also expected that "the treasury of manna will come down from on high" in those years (*2 Bar.* 29.7–8). The sign in John 2, with the plentiful provision of wine, should be read in tandem with the feeding of the five thousand in John 6. In each case Jesus provides a surplus, an abundance that sustains life. The visions of plenty in the messianic age are realized in the Messiah, who brings abundant bread and wine as tokens and conduits of God's abundant grace (1:14, 16) and abundant life (10:10). Not only has the good wine been saved till the end, but it also far surpasses expectations. The "lesser" has given way to the

74. In Isaiah, the coming time of Israel's renewed fellowship with God is also pictured as a marriage (54:4–8; 62:4–5); notice also the parables featuring weddings in the Synoptic tradition (Matt 22:1–14; Luke 12:35–38; 14:8–11).

75. About 350–400 liters, or 100 gallons (cf. 1 Kgs 5:2, 25 LXX [4:22; 5:11 ET]; Ezek 45:14).

76. Also found in Irenaeus, *Haer.* 5.33.3.

77. Meshorer 154–69, plates 19–28.

"greater" even as the Scriptures have anticipated. There is therefore both continuity and discontinuity in the Gospel's portrayal of Jesus' relationship to "his own" (1:11), to the law, and to the institutions and practices of worship enjoined in the Scriptures. In the present, as in the past, God provides generously for the sustenance of his people and of the world, to bring joy and gladness.

In the pagan world, wine was connected with the festivals of the god Dionysus. One writer recounts that at a festival of Dionysus three empty pots were sealed in a room and then discovered to be full of wine the next morning.[78] Several authors refer to springs or rivers that inexplicably flowed with wine, and these are sometimes linked with Dionysus (e.g., with his birthplace or a festival).[79] John's account may appear to have some elements in common with such traditions that show Dionysius providing a plentiful supply of wine.[80] Those readers acquainted with such traditions could have read the account of Jesus' sign as surpassing the acts of the pagan deities as well. As often in John, a particular narrative that takes up biblical imagery and subsequent interpretive traditions nevertheless can be understood by those unfamiliar with that milieu and, indeed, by those steeped in other religious contexts. But awareness of the scriptural context not only enriches the texture of the narrative; it also orients the reader to a particular narrative and to the God portrayed in it.

[11] The account closes with the statement "This was the first of the signs that Jesus did in Cana of Galilee.[81] He manifested his glory, and his disciples believed in him." This is the first use of the term "signs" (*sēmeia*) in the Gospel, and it is not surprising to find it linked with "believe" or "trust" (*pisteuō*). John distinctively refers to Jesus' deeds as *signs*, pointers to and manifestations of Jesus' identity as the Messiah and Son of God.[82] While the disciples now believe in him (cf. 20:31), not all those who see signs do so. In fact, later the Evangelist will lament that signs do not lead those who see them to believe (John 12:37–41), citing passages from Isaiah to drive the point home (53:1; 6:10).[83] The disciples' initial responses to Jesus, which entail both acknowledgment of his messianic identity (1:45, 49) and "following" him (1:40, 43–44), now become "trust" or "belief." Having seen Jesus' glory, they "believed" or "trusted" in him.[84]

78. Pausanius, *Descr.* 6.26.1–2; also recorded in Athenaeus, *Deipn.* 1.34.

79. Euripides, *Bacch.* 707; Diodorus Siculus, *Hist.* 3.66.2; Pliny the Elder, *Nat.* 2.231; Philostratus, *Vit. Apoll.* 6.10; Lucian of Samosata, *Ver. hist.* 1.7.

80. See here Hengel 1987; 1995a.

81. Since the only other numbered sign takes place when Jesus is in Cana (4:46, 54), the sense may be that this is the first of two signs that Jesus did in Cana.

82. See Excursus 3: "The Signs in the Gospel of John."

83. *Pisteuō* may mean "believe" with reference to a promise or words spoken, but more typically means "trust" or "rely on" with reference to a person (BDAG).

84. See Excursus 8: "The Johannine Vocabulary of Faith and Discipleship."

The narrative does not indicate what the disciples saw that constituted Jesus' "glory." This is the first reference to Jesus' glory (*doxa*) since the prologue, where "glory" was ascribed to the Word made flesh, the Father's only Son, "full of grace and truth" (1:14), from whose "fullness we have all received" (1:16). Here Jesus has provided fully, and so revealed his glory as the one who provides abundantly for his people. Both in the prologue and here, Jesus' glory can be seen. And yet few of those at the wedding know what has transpired: the steward of the wedding attributes the provision of wine to the bridegroom. The servants apparently know what has happened, but they are not reported to have seen Jesus' glory or to have believed in him. Jesus' glory, his identity as God's agent through whom the fullness of grace and truth are given (1:14, 16), is not manifested to all, but to those with eyes to discern who he is and what he has done. While some discern the truth about Jesus, such discerning faith is never mechanically explained: there is no formula that orders "signs" and "faith" in a predictable or wooden way. If the changing of the water to wine at Cana is the "first" sign that demonstrates the opening of the heavens as Jesus promised (1:51), that revelation remains mysteriously opaque to most.

Excursus 3: The Signs in the Gospel of John

In the Synoptic Gospels, Jesus' acts of healing, feeding, and raising the dead are called *dynameis* ("mighty deeds," Matt 11:20–21, 23; 13:58; Mark 6:2, 5, 14), *thaumasia* ("marvels," Matt 21:15), and *paradoxa* ("remarkable things," Luke 5:26); John refers regularly to Jesus' deeds as *sēmeia*, "signs."[85] Jesus himself speaks of his deeds as the Father's works (*erga*), a point enunciated most sharply in his claim that he works when and as his Father works, to exercise God's authority to give life and to judge, even on the Sabbath (John 5:19–36; 10:25, 38; 14:10–12; 17:4).

"Signs" (MT *ʾōtôt*, LXX *sēmeia*), often linked with "wonders," occurs frequently in the Old Testament to refer to the plagues and other acts accompanying God's deliverance of Israel from Egypt (Exod 4:9, 17, 28, 30; 7:3; 10:1; et al.). But many other things are also called "signs": the rainbow (Gen 9:12–13, 17); circumcision (17:11); the lamb's blood on the doorposts (Exod 12:7, 13); the Sabbath (31:13, 17); the words of God, to be bound on one's hand, forehead, and doorposts (Deut 6:8); the birth of a child (Isa 7:11–14);

85. There is no single Greek equivalent to the English "miracle," nor would NT authors have accepted the rationalist definition that miracles are deeds "contrary to the laws of nature." The Synoptics use "signs" (*sēmeia*) to refer to events that would offer divine ratification—such as a heavenly voice—of Jesus' actions (e.g., Matt 12:38–39; 16:1–4) or the coming of the "end of the age" (e.g., Matt 24:3; Luke 21:11, with *phobētra*, "horrors"; 21:25). False prophets do "signs and wonders" (*terata*, Matt 24:24); Herod hopes to see Jesus perform a "sign" (Luke 23:8). "Signs" can also be used generally to mean "token" or "indicator" (Luke 2:12, 34; 11:30). Elsewhere the NT speaks positively of "signs and wonders" done by the apostles (Acts 4:30; 5:12; 14:3; 15:12; Rom 15:19; 2 Cor 12:12; Heb 2:4) and in keeping with the pair in the OT (Exod 7:3; Deut 4:34; 6:22; 7:19; Ps 135:9; etc.). In Revelation (13:13–14; 19:20), the beast does "great signs" in order to deceive.

the fertility of crops in the land (37:30; 55:13); and heavenly portents (Jer 10:2). Such things are "signs" because they are indicators of God's work in the world. Whether extraordinary (portents in the heaven) or ordinary (the slaying of a lamb; the circumcision of a baby), these things are "signs" because they are not ends in themselves: signs function primarily to point to God's work. "Work" refers more broadly to all that God does. For example, in the LXX creation is God's "work" (*ergon*, *erga*, Gen 2:2–3), as is the exodus (Exod 34:10; Ps 77:12; MT *mĕlāʾkâ* or *maʿăśeh*). While all of Jesus' words and deeds are his "works," or God's work through him, it is less clear what falls under the rubric of "signs" in John. Certain deeds, such as changing water to wine, the healing of the royal official's son, and the feeding of the five thousand are explicitly called signs (2:11; 4:54; 6:14). At other times summarizing comments refer to Jesus' many signs (2:23–25; 11:47; 12:37; 20:30–31), but such summaries do not specify whether some or all of Jesus' deeds, such as the temple cleansing (2:23–25) or resurrection appearances (20:30–31), should be understood as signs.[86] Given the range of meanings of "sign" in the Old Testament and the absence of a clear and univocal use of the term "sign" in John, it is best to cast the net widely: Jesus' signs include his various kinds of miracles (2:11; 4:54; 6:14); actions such as the temple cleansing that point to another event, truth, or reality (2:23–25); and the resurrection appearances, since they are not ends in themselves but testify that Jesus lives (20:27–29). In every case these are signs because they are witnesses to the work of God. As such, they call for faith (10:37–38; 12:37; 20:31).

There are some significant differences between John and the Synoptics in John's use of the tradition of Jesus' miracles. The Synoptics record many deeds of healing and exorcism, typically in short, self-contained narratives; Jesus himself offers little by way of their explanation or interpretation or, if he does, such comments tend to be terse and pithy (e.g., Matt 9:6; 12:12; Luke 13:15–16). Jesus' mighty deeds are reckoned by Jesus or the narrator as manifestations of the inbreaking kingdom or the Spirit (Mark 3:22–30; Matt 12:28; Luke 11:20), Jesus' authority (Mark 1:27; 2:10; 3:15; 6:7; 11:28–33), or the fulfillment of Scripture (Matt 8:17; 11:4–6; 12:15–17; Luke 7:18–23). In the Synoptics, faith is often the premise for healing (Matt 9:2, 22, 29; 15:28; Mark 10:52; Luke 7:50; 8:48; 17:19; 18:42), not the response to Jesus' deeds. Instead, the Synoptics record a variety of responses to Jesus' deeds: awe, fear, amazement, astonishment, wonder, and unbelief.

While John alludes to many signs (2:23–25; 12:37–40; 20:30–31), the Gospel presents a relatively small number of them.[87] Jesus' proclamation and his deeds are not linked with the kingdom, or the power of the Spirit, or the fulfillment of Scripture. Instead, the signs point to Jesus' authority and to his unity with the Father (5:19–30; 10:37–38; 14:10–11). Jesus' signs are often interpreted in lengthy discourses, elaborating these aspects of his identity. Scripture provides imagery—such as Moses' feeding of the Israelites with manna—for interpreting the signs, but otherwise foretells only

86. For various views of the interpretation of 20:30–31, and whether signs include the resurrection appearances, see comments there.

87. John records no exorcisms, healing of lepers, or curing of the deaf, deeds all found in the Synoptics. The lack of exorcisms may perhaps be explained by John's emphasis on Jesus' overthrow of the "ruler of this world" (12:31; 14:30; 16:11), or by his depiction of the primary conflict not between opposed kingdoms or spirits, but between "belief" and "unbelief." See also Twelftree.

the lack of positive response to them (12:37–40). Indeed, there are really one of two responses to the signs: belief or unbelief. One either accepts the testimony of the signs that reveal Jesus to be the one through whom God's life-giving work is accomplished, or one does not (cf. 2:11; 10:37–38; 14:10–11; 12:37; 20:30–31). Faith is not the premise for, but rather the desired response to, Jesus' signs.

Yet the relationship between signs and faith is subtle and complex. Sometimes signs lead to faith (2:11; 3:2; 6:2; 20:30–31), and sometimes they do not (12:37). Sometimes faith is the predisposition necessary to understand what Jesus does (11:4, 40); at other times, Jesus' deeds lead, not to faith, but to misunderstanding (6:14–15, 26) or hostility (9:40; 11:47). Perhaps most vexing, at times John seems to speak positively of believing in Jesus because of his signs (2:11; 20:30–31), but at other times seems to question the genuineness of such faith (2:23–25; 4:48; 6:14–15, 26). Some interpreters have therefore contended that John denigrates faith based on signs when understood as a response to miraculous deeds as displays of power, deeming such faith inferior or provisional (2:23–25; 3:1–2; 4:48–53; 20:29). Response to Jesus based on his miracles could be a first step toward a deeper and more mature discipleship, but it is portrayed in John as fickle, inadequate, or provisional faith at best.[88] Such an interpretation often arises from an emphasis on the "symbolic" aspect of John's presentation of signs, drawn especially from the interpretations of that work offered in the lengthy discourses interpreting the signs.[89] Such discourses are understood to articulate the deeper or genuine meaning of the signs. For example, if Jesus feeds five thousand (John 6:1–13), that "sign" points to his identity as the bread of life (6:35, 48) and to the fact that he can grant eternal life in the resurrection at the last day (6:40, 44, 54): its significance is not found in his ability to multiply bread, or even to feed the hungry, but in his identity as the bread of life for all the world. Thus, when compared to the Synoptic miracle tradition, in John "the reference to spiritual deliverance is primary, and the symbolic element is stronger."[90]

Nevertheless, the description of Jesus' deeds as "symbolic" and of their meaning as "spiritual" must not be taken to mean that Jesus' "signs" are significant apart from what he does in the material realm. Indeed, in a narrative that begins with the creation of the world through the Word (1:1–3) and of the Word's subsequent incarnation in that world (1:14), the signs are revelations of Jesus' identity precisely in the material realm as material deeds.[91] Accordingly, when Jesus raises Lazarus from the dead, his "material" act does not symbolize his "spiritual" power to grant eternal life; these are alternative expressions of his life-giving power. Because he is the one through whom the world was brought to life, he can raise the dead to life, and he can grant the gift of eternal life at the

88. Schnackenburg 1.358; R. Brown 1966, 127. For the contrast between the fickleness of faith arising from signs and perseverance in discipleship, see Barrett 202; Culpepper 1983, 116; Lindars 145.

89. Bultmann argues that John was critical of faith that depended on signs: revelation occurs primarily through the Word, and authentic faith arises from *hearing* rather than seeing (1971, 113, 119, 206, 208; 1955, 44–45, 56–57, 60). Following in Bultmann's footsteps, Becker argues that Jesus' interpretations of the signs through his word rendered the signs superfluous (Bultmann 1971, 452; Becker 1981, 408). For John's emphasis on seeing, see comments on 12:37–43.

90. R. Brown 1966, 529.

91. Schnackenburg 1:525.

last day. When Jesus' "signs" are understood to be "signs" of the Father's indwelling and working through him to bring life, when their witness to the unity of the Father and Son is grasped, then the signs lead to faith.

Those who do not see the work of God in Jesus have not "seen signs," because they have not understood their witness (John 6:26). Instead, they have seen Jesus' deeds as ends in themselves: amazing deeds, wondrous provisions. But to believe that Jesus has power to work amazing deeds is far short of seeing them *as signs*: to see them as revelatory of his glory (2:11) or of God's glory (11:4, 40); as manifestations of Jesus' identity as bread of life (6:35), light of the world (8:12; 9:5), and resurrection and life (11:25–26); and as testimonies to his unity with the Father (14:10–11). Jesus does not do his works in order to evoke faith; he does them because he does the works of God. As works of God, the signs are witnesses to who Jesus is, and as such they call for faith. Both signs and words may lead to faith in Jesus, but they do so only when understood to be the work and word of God through him (3:2; 5:36; 9:3–4; 10:25, 32, 37–38; 14:10–12).

2:12–25 Jesus and the Temple

Even as the temple, situated on a high point in the city, dominated the landscape of Jerusalem, so too it looms large in the pages of the Old Testament. Its construction is anticipated and described in detail; its sacrificial rituals are both celebrated and criticized; its defilement and subsequent destruction by the Babylonians are lamented; and its rebuilding is pressed for and accomplished, with mixed response.[92] Later the temple's profanation by Antiochus IV Epiphanes and subsequent rededication by the Maccabees (168–165 B.C.E.) figure in a narrative of hope and victory that undergirded Jewish identity and expectations. Given the temple's geographical, religious, and political role not only in Jerusalem, but also in first-century Judaism as a whole, it is no wonder that it figures importantly in both Jewish and early Christian texts, including the New Testament.

In the Gospel of John, Jesus is regularly found in Jerusalem, in the temple precincts.[93] As one of the first acts of his public ministry, Jesus clears the temple of money-changers, animals and those who sell them, so that it may be "the house of my Father" rather than a "house of trade" (2:16). Having demonstrated what that temple ought to be, Jesus then also speaks, albeit cryptically, of its destruction and rebuilding in three days. An editorial comment explains that Jesus was actually speaking of "his body" that would be destroyed but raised to life. In brief compass, John presents the need for the expulsion of all trade from the temple so that it may indeed be "my Father's house," but at the same time he points to a future temple. John's account reflects both the conviction

92. On the significance of the temple, see the excellent study by Skarsaune.

93. For studies of the temple in John, see Coloe 2001; Kerr; for the impact of the temple's fall on Judaism and John, see Motyer; Köstenberger 2009, 60–72.

that the temple is the dwelling of the holy God, or of God's glory and name, and the hope, found in Jewish literature of the time, for a new temple that would replace the temple in Jerusalem. Jesus himself is a temple that, like the Jerusalem temple, will be destroyed; yet he will be raised up—and in three days. In John, the risen Jesus is the new, purified, and indestructible temple that is truly the dwelling of God.

2:12 After this, he went down to Capernaum with his mother, his siblings,[a]
and his disciples; and they remained there a few days.
13 Since the Jewish Passover was near, Jesus went up to Jerusalem.
14 In the temple[b] he found those who were selling oxen and sheep and
doves, and money changers sitting there. **15** Having made a whip of rope,
he drove them all out of the temple, both the sheep and the oxen. Then he
poured out the coins of the money changers[c] and overturned their tables.
16 And he said to those who were selling doves, "Take these things out of
here! Stop making my Father's house a house of trade!"[d] **17** His disciples
remembered that it is written, "Zeal for your house will consume me."
18 So the Jews said to him, "What sign do you show us for doing these
things?" **19** And Jesus answered, "If you destroy this temple, in three days
I will raise it up." **20** The Jews said to him, "This temple has been under
construction forty-six years. You will raise it up in three days?" **21** But he
was talking about the temple of his body. **22** So then when he was raised
from the dead, his disciples remembered that he had said this, and they
believed the Scripture and the word that Jesus had spoken.
23 While he was in Jerusalem for the Passover feast, many believed
in his name because they saw the signs that he did. **24** Jesus himself did
not trust himself to them, **25** because he knew all things; he did not need
anyone to testify to him about humankind. For he knew what was within
human beings.

a. Although *hoi adelphoi* is almost always rendered "brothers," by form it may include brothers and sisters (see Mark 6:3).

b. *Naos* is sometimes distinguished as the "sanctuary," perhaps the holy of holies or place where God or the deity is understood to dwell, from the *hieros* or temple precincts; here temple translates both *hieros* and *naos* since the words seem to function synonymously, as they often do in Greek literature (see BDAG and LSJM).

c. John uses two different terms for "money changers": *kermatistēs* (2:14) and *kollybistēs* (John 2:15; Matt 21:12; Mark 11:15; *kollybos* is a small coin).

d. "House of trade" (*oikon emporiou*) contrasts with "my Father's house"; it could be rendered "marketplace" (so NRSV).

[2:12–17] Following the wedding at Cana, Jesus went down to Capernaum with family members and his disciples prior to his journey to Jerusalem for the Passover.[94] Together Passover and the Festival of Unleavened Bread that follow it are one of the three pilgrimage festivals, during which Jews were commanded to go up to Jerusalem (Exod 23:14–17; 34:23; cf. Lev 23:4–7; Num 28:16–25; Deut 16:1–8; Josephus, *Ant.* 4.203).[95] Passover commemorates the deliverance of the Israelites from slavery in Egypt (Exod 12–13; Lev 23:4–8; Num 9:1–15; 28:16–25). As narrated in Exod 12, on the night in which the Israelites fled from Egypt, they were to smear the blood of a lamb on the doorposts of their houses so that the angel of death would pass them by (12:7, 12–13). The Israelites were to eat the roasted lamb while dressed for travel, in haste (12:11), and with bitter herbs, symbolic of the bitterness of bondage (12:8). Some features of the Passover celebration that appear in the New Testament are first attested in the literature of the Second Temple period.[96]

Passover had not always been a pilgrimage feast; the injunctions of Exod 12 do not mention the temple, and at certain times and places the lamb was evidently prepared and eaten in homes (even as the Passover meal is today). But in other Old Testament passages, it is clear that Passover must be celebrated in Jerusalem (Deut 16:1–8; 2 Kgs 23:21–23; 2 Chr 30; 35:1–19).[97] The requirement that the feast was to be kept in Jerusalem, or even within the temple, was tied to the requirement that those keeping the feast would have undertaken appropriate purification (John 11:55–12:1; 18:28). But in John, the focus is on the temple itself and its need of cleansing.

The other two pilgrimage festivals are the Festival of Weeks (Shavuot, or Pentecost) and Tabernacles, or Booths (Sukkot).[98] The Fourth Gospel regularly presents Jesus in Jerusalem on the occasion of the pilgrimage feasts (2:13, 23; 5:1 [?]; 7:2, 14; 11:55–56; cf. also 10:22; Luke 2:41). In the Synoptic Gospels, it was in conjunction with Passover that Jesus went up to Jerusalem, rode into it on a donkey in fulfillment of the prophecy in Zech 9:9, visited the temple, and

94. For similar "vestigial scenes" (Michaels 897), in which a geographical or temporal notice sets a scene but no action is narrated, see 11:54; 12:9, 20–21.

95. Passover and Unleavened Bread are sometimes conflated (see Mark 14:1; Luke 22:1). For their distinction, see Josephus, *Ant.* 3.248; for the feasts described under the single heading of "Unleavened Bread," see *Ant.* 2.317; 9.271; for the feasts together called Passover, see *Ant.* 18.29. On this point, see Sanders 1992, 132–38; Bokser; and Stern 129, esp. nn. 95–96. See also comments on 19:14 below.

96. In John, these include the need for complete purification (11:55) and alms for the poor (13:29; *m. Pesaḥ.* 10:1); elsewhere, scouring the house to remove the leaven (1 Cor 5:6–8); and drinking wine during the Passover meal (*Jub.* 49.6; Mark 14:23; possibly John 6:51–58).

97. *Jubilees* insists that the Passover lamb must be eaten within the temple precincts (*Jub* 49.16, 18, 20–21).

98. Deut 16:16; 2 Chr 8:13. Women, children, and certain others are not required to go up to the temple for pilgrim festivals (*m. Ḥag.* 1:1; see *m. Sukkah* 2:8 for Tabernacles). On the size of the crowds in Jerusalem at Passover and Roman responses to unrest, see Josephus, *J.W.* 6.422–26; *Ant.* 20.106.

began to drive out the money changers and those who bought and sold the sacrificial animals. In John, Jesus' cleansing of the temple (2:13–16) and his entry into Jerusalem on a donkey (12:14–15) are located at two different Passovers, one at the beginning and one at the end of Jesus' public ministry. At the first Passover, Jesus' action in the temple prefigures Jesus' death and resurrection; at the last Passover in the Gospel, Jesus goes to his death.[99]

In John's account, Jesus makes a whip of rope, and drives out the sheep and oxen from the temple; pours out the coins of the money changers; and orders those selling doves to remove them from the temple (2:15–16).[100] Jesus implicitly accounts for his actions with the command "Stop making my Father's house a house of trade!" The business of buying and selling had transformed "my Father's house" (*ho oikos tou patros mou*) into a "house of trade" (*oikos emporiou*), an "emporium" or marketplace (2:16). This contrast indicates what is at stake: either the temple is a house of human commerce, or it is the house of God, a holy place fit for worship of the holy God (cf. 2 Chr 5:14; 6:7–10, 18; 7:1, 3; Ezek 43:4–5; 44:4; Sir 36:19; 49:12; 1 Macc 15:9; Rev 15:8).

This is the first time in the Gospel that Jesus refers to God as "my Father," an identification that also explains his zeal for the temple. As the Father's only Son (John 1:18), Jesus demonstrates a passion, a zeal, for the sanctity of his Father's house (2:18–20). At the outset of the Gospel, then, Jesus demonstrates what the temple ought to be, and perhaps also prepares it as the place where he will conduct much of his teaching as "the Holy One of God," the Son of the Father whose house this temple is (6:69; cf. 2:13; 5:14; 7:14, 28; 10:23; 11:56; 18:20).

The purification of the temple requires the expulsion of traders from it (cf. Zech 14:21). Since pilgrims would have journeyed some distance to the temple, they would have needed to buy animals for their sacrifices. Money changers exchanged the different coins that people brought into a uniform coinage, namely, the Tyrian silver shekel and half-shekel, whose silver content was reliably high (*m. Bek.* 8:7). Such business would have thrived during the three pilgrimage feasts and especially at Passover, when numerous lambs or other animals would be needed.[101] According to Josephus, the temple authorities exploited the wealth

99. For the view that Jesus cleansed the temple early in his ministry, as in John, see Robinson 1985, 127–31; toward the end, as in the Synoptics, see most commentaries and scholars of the historical Jesus, e.g., Keener 1:518–20; or twice, see Blomberg 87–91; Carson 1991, 177–78.

100. According to Lev 1:3–17, there should be animals "from the herd," "from the flock," and an offering "of birds."

101. According to Josephus (*J.W.* 6.420–27), the priests counted 256,500 lambs—a number widely regarded by scholars as inflated (see also *J.W.* 2.280; *Ant.* 17.313; cf. *m. Pesaḥ.* 5:5–7; Philo, *Spec.* 2.146). Jeremias (77–84) estimates the number of lambs at 18,000; Sanders (1992, 136), at about 30,000, but he doubts that oxen and sheep were sold in the temple precincts. But see Bockmuehl 1994, 198 n. 27; Meyers and Chancey 57–58.

that poured into the temple from pilgrims, from the half-shekel tax, and from other gifts (e.g., *Ant.* 20.181; 20.206–7). But here Jesus is not interested in reforming the business practices of those who manage the wealth.[102] Nor is he concerned to put a stop to sacrifice or an end to the sacrificial system. Rather, he protests the business of buying and selling in the temple precincts because such enterprise is incompatible with the temple's identity as "my Father's house" (cf. Isa 4:4–5; Mal 3:1–3; Ezek 43:4–12; Zech 14:20; *Pss. Sol.* 8.12; 17.30).

Jesus' disciples "remembered"[103] Jesus' action in light of Scripture. But the Scripture is not only remembered: it is also reinterpreted. Whereas the relevant passage in Ps 68:10 LXX (69:9 ET; 69:10 MT) reads, "Zeal for your house *has consumed me*" (*katephagen me*, aorist), John has modified the quotation to read, "Zeal for your house *will consume* me" (*kataphagetai me*, future middle).[104] Jesus is now the speaker of the psalm. His words are typically taken as foreshadowing his death: he will be consumed, devoured, or destroyed.[105] But such interpretations move too quickly to the subsequent comment about the destruction and raising up of the temple, where Jesus' body, and his death and resurrection, are clearly in view (vv. 21–22). Jesus is first portrayed not as the temple, but as the one who is zealous for it.

When Jesus disrupts the business of buying and selling in the temple, he expresses the need for the temple's purification, perhaps also foreshadowing the coming of a new, glorified temple. Jewish literature attests to such a hope (Tob 14:5; *1 En.* 90.28; 91.13; *Jub.* 1.17, 27, 29; 25.21; 11Q19 XXIX, 8–10; 4Q174 frg. 1 I, 1–6). In some of these texts God builds a new sanctuary (*1 Enoch*; *Jubilees*; 11QT); in others, perhaps the people themselves build it (Tob 14:5). In still others, the king, the heir to David's throne, or even the Messiah, builds it (2 Sam 7:10–14, cited in 4Q174; Zech 6:12).[106] Developing this biblical trajectory, the Targums explicitly identify the Messiah as the one who builds the temple (*Tg. Zech.* 6:12–13; *Tg. Isa.* 53:5). But here Jesus, the King of Israel, the Son of God (1:49) first zealously purifies his Father's house.

[18–22] As in the Synoptic Gospels, the authorities challenge Jesus' action in the temple (cf. Mark 11:28; Matt 21:23; Luke 20:2). In John, "the Jews"

102. Origen reads this passage as applying to the church's need of purgation: "When are there not some money-changers sitting who need the strokes of the scourge Jesus made of small cords, and dealers in small coin who require to have their money poured out and their tables overturned? When are there not those who are inclined to merchandise?" (*Comm. Jo.* 10.16). Similarly Augustine, *Tract. Ev. Jo.* 10.6.1–4.

103. The Greek word is *emnēsthēsan*, "remembered"; cf. 2:17, 22; 12:16; cf. 13:7; 14:26.

104. *Katesthiō*, "to eat up, devour, consume, destroy," most frequently renders the Hebrew *'ākal* in the LXX (see Ps 68:10 mg. [69:9 ET]); cf. Josephus, *Ant.* 7.163.

105. E.g., Keener 1:528.

106. Herod the Great set out to rebuild the temple in Jerusalem. Although not of the lineage of David, as was Solomon, the son of David, Herod could nevertheless build a temple like a king of Israel; see Horbury.

demand a sign, likely a heavenly voice or miraculous portent, to legitimate Jesus' disruptive demonstration in the temple's precincts (cf. Mark 8:11–12; Matt 12:40). The sign that will be given to justify Jesus' demonstration in the temple is a sign of its destruction and subsequent rebuilding: "If you destroy this sanctuary, in three days I will raise it up." Jesus' questioners misunderstand the point, thinking that he is referring to the temple in Jerusalem still under construction[107]—not a particularly surprising conclusion, given the fact that they are standing in the precincts of the temple, out of which Jesus has just driven the animals.

It is precisely this misunderstanding that the editorial comment corrects: Jesus is not speaking of a miraculous act he will perform if the temple in Jerusalem is destroyed; that is, he says neither "If this temple [of stones] is destroyed, I will rebuild it" or "If this temple [of stones] is destroyed, I myself will be its replacement." Jesus is speaking of another temple altogether: one that was destroyed about the year 30, not the year 70.[108] He is speaking "of the temple of his body." Thus the saying in John has to do with Jesus' crucifixion ("if you destroy this temple") and resurrection ("in three days I will raise it up").

After Jesus' resurrection, but especially after the destruction of the Jerusalem temple in 70 C.E., Jesus was understood to be a temple, the dwelling place of the glory and name of God (1:14). Although destroyed, this temple was raised up. And if Jesus is a new temple, there will be ramifications for understanding proper worship, as Jesus' ensuing encounter with the Samaritan woman will begin to spell out (4:20–25). The presentation of the risen Jesus as the temple of God would also remind early Gentile converts that it was in this temple, and not in the many temples and shrines of their environment, that one was to worship God (Acts 14:13; 17:22–23; 19:27, 35).[109] Jesus is then both the Messiah, the guardian of the temple where the glory of God and the name of God dwell (2:13–17), and himself the locus of that indwelling glory (cf. 1:14; 2:22).[110]

The assertions that it was later, after Jesus' resurrection, that his disciples remembered what he had said, and that they believed both the Scripture and

107. Josephus (*Ant.* 15.380) dates the start of rebuilding the second temple in the eighteenth year of Herod the Great's reign, in 20–19 B.C.E. "Forty-six" years would put the conversation between Jesus and the Jews in 27–28 C.E., two years before the probable date of Jesus' crucifixion in 30 C.E. Josephus implies that the temple was not finished until shortly before the outbreak of war in 66 C.E. (*Ant.* 20.219; cf. *J.W.* 5.36); hence, this temple "has been under construction."

108. See here Robinson 1985, 70; Berger 37; Painter 2008, 35—against Schneiders (2005), who argues that "body" refers only to the risen body of Jesus.

109. In his correspondence with the emperor Trajan, the governor Pliny the Younger happily reports increased worship in Roman temples, apparently due in part to the apostasy of Christians threatened with death (*Ep.* 10.96; cf. comments on 16:2; 18:25–27).

110. Christians also understood themselves to be a temple, a "holy of holies," in which God dwells; 1 Cor 3:16–17; 6:9–20; Eph 2:20–22; 1 Pet 2:4–5; Ign., *Eph.* 9.1; 15.3; Ign.. *Magn.* 7.2; cf. 1QS VIII, 5–9; IX, 6.

the word that he had spoken (2:22), aptly summarize the Gospel's hermeneutical perspective.[111] For the significance of what Jesus did and its implications for who he was are grasped only in retrospect, looking backward from the vantage point of his resurrection and glorification (see this commentary's introduction and comments on 12:27; 14:26; 16:25). Jesus' actions and words are "remembered"[112] by his *disciples*: this Gospel's particular understanding of Jesus is lodged in the corporate, communal memory and interpretation of those who continued to follow him. Their "remembering" connects Jesus' actions or words with "the Scripture." Here, as elsewhere, to believe in Jesus or his word is to believe that Scripture bears witness to him (5:39); conversely, to believe the Scripture is to understand its witness to Jesus. Comprehension of Jesus' action in the temple does not come simply by observing what Jesus did, but from reading the Scriptures in light of the resurrection and the new understanding of Jesus that comes with it, in the context of a community committed to following him, under the tutelage of the Spirit.[113] One cannot dispense with the events of the past—here, the temple action itself—but the mere events cannot and do not lead to full perception of their significance. As ever in John, insight into Jesus' significance includes and demands "sight"; yet "sight" does not guarantee the insight to grasp the identity of Jesus and his work.

[23–25] There are several puzzling features about John's summarizing statement at this point. Although he writes that "many believed" because of the *signs* that Jesus did, it is not at all clear which signs are in view or who these "believers" are. The transformation of the water to wine did not take place in Jerusalem, but in Cana; and the temple cleansing is not called a "sign." If it is, then it is the first and only sign that Jesus has performed in Jerusalem, and the plural "signs" remains puzzling. The statement, therefore, may simply allude to a broader tradition, not recorded in full, in which Jesus was known as one who did signs.[114]

But "Jesus himself did not entrust himself to them, because he knew all things" and "knew what was within human beings." Unfortunately, the text is silent here about exactly what Jesus knew to be within human beings. In the statement that he did not "entrust himself to them" (*ouk episteuen auton autois*), the verb "entrust" (*pisteuō*) is the same verb used in 2:11 ("The disciples *believed* [or, *trusted*] in him") and 2:23 ("Many *believed* in his name").

111. See Carson (1982) for a careful argument that "misunderstandings" are not literary devices and that their resolution depends on the passage of time and events that transpire during that period.

112. Cf. 12:16; 14:26; 15:20; 16:4, 13.

113. In light of Jesus' promise that the Spirit will call his teaching to mind (14:26) and lead them into all truth (16:13), the Spirit can be understood to be the implicit agent of the disciples' remembering and understanding; see further discussion in the Introduction and Excursus 9: "The Holy Spirit in John."

114. See Excursus 3: "The Signs in the Gospel of John."

The statement may be playing on the word: they trusted in him, but he did not entrust himself to them. The rest of the Gospel implicitly and explicitly warns that some will not persevere in faith. Even as Jesus knows who will betray him (6:64), so he can be expected to know who is not trustworthy. Belief, faith, or "putting one's trust in another" (1:12; 2:11; 8:30–31; 20:31) entails an ongoing commitment of faithful discipleship.[115]

John's Gospel reveals Jesus' relationship to the temple as a "pressure point" for understanding him.[116] Other pressure points include the relationship of Jesus to Moses and the law, the ongoing significance of the patriarchs of Israel (Abraham, Jacob), and the identity of the people of God (see terms such as Israel, the Jews, children of God, and the reference to Samaritans, "other sheep not of this fold," and "the Greeks"). Throughout the Gospel, Jesus' relationship to these entities (Scripture), persons (Moses, Abraham), and institutions (the temple, law, purification, Sabbath) causes disputes between him (and/or his followers) and the Jews (chief priests, Pharisees, crowds, and others). The conflicts and disagreements are clearly and primarily among those who identify themselves with the God, Scriptures, worship, and people of Israel. John's Gospel reconfigures each of these in light of the incarnation, death, and resurrection of Jesus. That Jesus does not "entrust himself" to these who have initially believed in him indicates that they will not come to share or continue to hold the interpretations and commitments to which the Gospel bears witness.

Together Jesus' changing of the water to wine at Cana and his demonstration in the temple bear witness to his identity as the one who inaugurates the messianic age of fullness. Already in the first chapter, he has been named as Messiah by those who first follow him (1:41, 45, 49). Jesus has manifested his glory as the one who embodies the fullness of God's grace and truth. He is the true host at the wedding feast at Cana who gives abundantly of God's creation for the joy of all people. Many have come to believe in him (2:11, 23–25). In none of these narratives does Jesus publicly declare who he is: his disciples, his works, and the Scriptures serve as witnesses to him.

3:1–21 The Spirit, New Life, and the People of God

To this point John has portrayed Jesus as God's embodied Word, who is life for the world; the one promised in Scripture: the Messiah, King of Israel, and Son of God who baptizes with God's Spirit. Through him, the abundant blessings of the coming messianic age are now bestowed on the created world (2:1–11).

115. See Excursus 8: "The Johannine Vocabulary of Faith and Discipleship."

116. Dunn (1983, 318) refers to "points of sensitivity" where "an effort is evidently being made to clarify some confusion or to counter opposing views."

As Messiah and Israel's King, Jesus is guardian of the temple; as Son of God, he is zealous for the purity of his Father's house. Unlike Israel's kings, Jesus will do more than build a new temple; after his death and resurrection, Jesus will *be* a new temple for God's people (2:13–22).

Adopting a different metaphor, John 3 reemphasizes the Spirit's work: all people must be "born" by God's life-giving Spirit in order to be God's children and to enjoy fellowship with God. Speaking to a Pharisee and teacher of Israel, Jesus indicates that the time for renewal has come: all Israel, the Messiah's "own" (1:11), must be reborn by God's Spirit (3:3, 5, 8), thus becoming God's children not by physical birth but by the Spirit and through faith in the Son. Such things are possible because the time has come for the world's judgment, which is simultaneously the hour of God's salvation of the world (3:16–18). The light that has come into darkness (1:5, 9–13) is the life that brings people out of death (3:19–21), effected by God's life-giving Spirit.

To participate in this reality that God brings requires a radically new understanding of Jesus and of his teaching, an understanding occasioned by birth "from above," through the agency of God's Spirit. If the initial hunch that Jesus is "a teacher come from God" proves true, it also proves inadequate. For if "no one is able" (*dynatai*) to do signs apart from God's presence (v. 2), neither "is anyone able" (*dynatai*) to enter God's kingdom apart from new birth (3:3, 5). Nicodemus's initial understanding of Jesus, and what he promises and gives, demands drastic revision, a reorientation of his life and commitments as complete as a new birth.

3:1 There was a Pharisee[a] named Nicodemus, a leader among the Jews. **2**
This man came to Jesus at night and said to him, "Rabbi, we know that
you are a teacher come from God. For no one can do these signs that you
do unless God is with him. **3** Jesus said to him, "Amen, amen, I tell you
no one can see the kingdom of God without being begotten from above."[b]
4 Nicodemus said to him, "How can anyone be born after having grown
old? Can one enter a second time into a mother's womb and be born?"

5 Jesus replied, "Amen, amen, I tell you that no one can enter the
kingdom of God without being begotten of water and the Spirit.[c] **6** For
whatever is begotten of the flesh is flesh, and whatever is begotten of the
Spirit is spirit. **7** Do not be amazed that I told you, 'It is necessary for you
to be begotten from above.' **8** The wind blows where it wants, and you
hear its sound;[d] but you do not know where it is coming from and where
it is going. That's how it is with everyone who is begotten of the Spirit."

9 Nicodemus replied, "How can these things happen?" **10** Jesus replied,
"You are a teacher of Israel, and yet you do not understand these things?[e]
11 Amen, amen, I tell you that we are speaking of what we know, and

we are bearing witness to what we have seen. And you do not receive
our witness. 12 If I have spoken to you of earthly things and you do not
believe, then how will you believe if I tell you of heavenly things?[f] 13 No
one has ascended into heaven except the very one who descended, this
Son of Man.[g] 14 Even as Moses lifted up the serpent in the wilderness, so
also must this Son of Man be lifted up, 15 so that everyone who believes
in him will have everlasting life.

16 For God loved the world in this way: he gave his only[h] Son, so that
whoever believes in him should not perish but have everlasting life. 17 For
God did not send the Son into the world to condemn[i] the world, but rather
to save the world through him. 18 No one who believes is condemned;
but those who do not believe have already been condemned, because
they have not believed in the name of the only Son of God. 19 This is
the judgment:[i] that the light has come into the world, but people loved
darkness rather than light, for their deeds were evil. 20 Those who do evil
hate the light and do not come to the light so that their works may not be
exposed. 21 But all who do what is true come to the light, so that it may
become manifest that their works have been worked by God."

a. Compare the Greek *anthrōpos ek tōn Pharisaiōn* ("a man of the Pharisees") with *gynē ek tēs Samareias* ("a woman of Samaria," 4:7).

b. "Begotten from above" translates *gennaō ek anōthēn*. "Begotten of God" points to the generative work of God in creating children, through the Spirit; so also R. Brown 1966, 130; Beasley-Murray 45; Michaels 180 n. 29; differently, Moloney 1993, 109 n. 58.

c. Reading *ex hydatos kai pneumatos* with the preposition *ek/ex* governing both "water and Spirit"; hence, "begotten [or born] of water and Spirit," not "begotten of water *and* begotten of Spirit."

d. "Sound" or "voice."

e. Jesus' reply to Nicodemus (v. 10) can either be a question (as in the present translation) or an exclamation, with the pronoun "you" in the emphatic position: "*You* are a teacher of Israel, and yet you do not understand these things!"

f. Although many translations include vv. 13–15 in the words of Jesus, putting the closing quotation mark after v. 15, it is also possible that one should close the quotation at 3:12; others take the entire discourse to the end of v. 21 (as here).

g. "And no one has ascended into the heaven except the very one who descended, the Son of Man" is attested by $\mathfrak{P}^{66, 75}$ ℵ B. Some MSS add "who is in heaven" (*ho ōn en tō ouranō*), an explanatory insertion that underscores the point that at the present time Jesus is indeed "in heaven" (cf. 1:18, "ever at the Father's side").

h. For *monogenēs*, see comments on 1:14.

i. The various words for judgment and condemnation in 3:17–19 translate the Greek cognates *krinein* and *krisis*; the translation "condemn" in vv. 17–18 indicates that a negative verdict is in view.

[3:1–2] A "leader of the Jews,"[117] a Pharisee, Nicodemus,[118] comes to Jesus "at night" (cf. 9:4; 11:10; 13:30). In view of the obviously symbolic function of "night" in the Gospel, and the scriptural association of darkness with ignorance or lack of understanding,[119] this visit at night may illustrate what will be spelled out later in the chapter: "the light has come into the world" (3:19) to bring people out of darkness; and those who do "what is true come to the light" (3:21). Nicodemus's nighttime visit to Jesus may be an indication of his initial turning toward Jesus, the true Light (1:9). Nicodemus will reappear twice in the Gospel, once to defend Jesus (7:50–51), and again to offer him a royal burial (19:39–42), indicators of a growing understanding of Jesus. As so often happens in the Gospel, initial assessments of Jesus or responses to his work rest on partial or inadequate understanding and must be both corrected and deepened. Such steps, however halting, toward deeper understanding are part of the path of discipleship in the Gospel.[120]

There is no reason to doubt Nicodemus's sincerity and openness to Jesus. His initial assessment is true: Jesus *is* a teacher (*didaskalos*, 1:38; cf. 6:45; 7:16–17; 18:19) who has come from, or been sent by, God (8:40, 42; 9:33; 13:3; 16:30). But the reader knows what Nicodemus does not: that Jesus comes from God not as a teacher, or even a prophet or angel, but as the Word of God, embodied in the flesh. His understanding, while accurate so far as it goes, is partial; as such, it can be a starting point for a fuller confession of Jesus.

[3–5] Jesus responds to Nicodemus's affirmation with the first of three sayings in this section introduced by "Amen, amen, I say to you" (3:3, 5, 11). Jesus now speaks, for the first time, of the kingdom of God,[121] twice linking it with the metaphor of new birth. Jesus' words are somewhat puzzling since his assertion about what is required to see the kingdom of God presupposes a question—"How does one see the kingdom of God?"—that Nicodemus has not

117. "Leader of the Jews" translates *archōn* ("ruler, leader"; see John 7:26, 48; cf. Luke 23:13, 35; 24:20; Acts 3:17). John refers to two authoritative groups, the "chief priests" and "the Pharisees" (mentioned together in 7:32, 45; 11:47, 57; 18:3). In 12:42 "rulers" are contrasted with the Pharisees. Many render *archōn* as "member of the Sanhedrin," but Sanhedrin (*synedrion*, "council") is a term John uses only once (11:47; cf. comments there), where it seems to refer to an ad hoc gathering of the "chief priests" as advisers in a potentially explosive situation (Josephus, *Ant.* 20.202).

118. The name Nicodemus occurs in Jewish sources: Josephus, *Ant.* 14.2.3; *b. Taʿan.* 19b; *Gen. Rab.* 42; *b. Giṭ.* 56a; see Bauckham 1996.

119. E.g., Deut 28:29; Job 23:17; Pss 18:28; 82:5; 112:4; Prov 4:19; Eccl 2:13–14; Isa 29:18. Note also the revelation of heavenly secrets at night: God revealed to Abraham "the end of times, secretly at night" (*4 Ezra* 3.14; cf. 6.12; 10.58–59; 13.1; although the reference is especially to dreams; discussed in Motyer 46).

120. See Excursus 8: "The Johannine Vocabulary of Faith and Discipleship."

121. "Kingdom of God" does not recur in John, although "my kingdom" or "kingship" is found (18:36).

asked. But Jesus' initially enigmatic reply (3:3) echoes, while rephrasing, his visitor's opening declaration:

No one	is able	to do signs	unless God is with him.
No one	is able	to enter the kingdom of God	unless they are born from above.

Nicodemus believes that the signs give evidence of God's presence with Jesus. But if Nicodemus wants to participate in the fullness of all that God brings through Jesus, to enter into the life of God's kingdom, he must receive the new life given through Jesus by means of God's revivifying Spirit. To truly understand the significance of Jesus' signs—that he brings and embodies God's life—requires a reorientation as drastic as a new birth marking a new life: Nicodemus needs to be "begotten from above," or "born again."

"From above" and "again" represent different ways of rendering the Greek *anōthen* (3:3, 7).[122] Since no English word contains both the spatial ("from above") and temporal ("anew") connotations of *anōthen,* translations typically must opt for one sense or the other, raising the question of what Jesus says and how Nicodemus understands—or misunderstands.[123] His question to Jesus about how an old man can be "born again" (v. 4) could be a crass misunderstanding: Nicodemus takes *anōthen* to mean "again," and thus misunderstands Jesus' reference to being "begotten from above," taking it as a second, physical birth ("born again"). While Jesus speaks of this birth spatially but metaphorically ("from above"), that is, from God, Nicodemus thinks temporally and physically ("again"), that is, from his mother.

But the conversation can be construed differently so that issues are not primarily or merely lexical. From the beginning, Jesus speaks of an act of God that brings a new kind of life into being: Nicodemus needs to be born "from above," which will entail being born "anew."[124] Nicodemus lacks the categories or insight to grasp Jesus' words, but he is not entirely off base in imagining that being born anew requires something drastic and difficult, something deemed impossible from the human point of view.[125] Jesus is referring to a new life, one that commences with being "begotten from above," a life that entails a new

122. The Greek *anōthen* can also be rendered "from the beginning" (Luke 1:3). While Jesus speaks directly to Nicodemus ("I say to *you,*" *legō soi,* where *soi* is a second-person sg. pronoun), "unless *any one* is begotten from above . . ." (*ean mē tis gennēthē anōthen,* 3:3) generalizes Jesus' words, as does the pl. pronoun "you" (*hymas,* 3:7).

123. This wordplay depends on multiple meanings of the Greek *anōthen*; there is no equivalent in Hebrew or Aramaic.

124. So also O'Day 549; Moloney 1993, 110; but Michaels (181 n. 32) disputes the common assumption that the word has a "double meaning" and that a speaker would intend both meanings, "again" and "from above," at the same time.

125. Cf. Matt 19:26; Mark 10:27. Malina and Rohrbaugh (82) describe a second birth as "a life-changing event of staggering proportions."

family, identity, and set of commitments. The prologue has already introduced the idea of being "begotten of God" for those who have faith in the name of the Word made flesh, the true light (1:11–13). To be "begotten of God" is now explicated in terms of being "begotten from above," and both figures envision the generative work of God in creating "children of God." The "children of God" do not qualify as such by means of their physical birth, but only by means of their new birth from God.[126] Something as radically new as birth is required, and understanding what is said "requires not a lexicon but insight."[127]

Jesus further explains that to be begotten "from above" is to be begotten "of water and the Spirit" (v. 5). Some commentators assume that two births—one of water, one of the Spirit—are required. Being "born" or "begotten" of water is frequently taken as a reference to baptism.[128] Whether "baptism" then refers to John's baptism or to Christian baptism (or perhaps both, depending on the reader), the point is that such baptism must be joined with or supplemented by the work of the Spirit. But Jesus speaks here of being "born" or "begotten," not baptized. Thus others take "water" to refer to seminal fluid or the natural process of human birth.[129] The point would then be that physical conception or birth ("born of water") does not provide entry into the kingdom of God; one must also be "born of Spirit." The emphasis falls on the Spirit: one who has been born first of water must then be born of Spirit. But why John would have to insist on a first, physical birth remains somewhat opaque, especially since such natural birth, which is linked not to water but to blood and flesh in John (1:12–13), is inadequate to provide entry into the kingdom or qualify one as a child of God.

If in the phrase "of water and the Spirit" the preposition *ek* governs both water (*hydatos*) and Spirit (*pneumatos*), then a single rebirth is in view. In other words "water and Spirit" points to a single birth, not to two births. Tellingly, in the phrase "begotten from above" (3:3), the adverbial "from above" is replaced first by "of water and Spirit" (3:5), and then simply by "of the Spirit" (3:8); these are three ways of asserting the same truth: to be "born" or "begotten" of God implies the Spirit's generative power in creating children of God (1:12–13).

Such a reading draws on the imagery of Ezekiel, where purification with water serves as an image of purification with the Spirit, which re-creates God's people; thus God promises his people: "I will sprinkle clean water upon you. . . . I will put my spirit within you" (36:25–27). When Israel is gathered together, cleansed, and given a new Spirit (36:23–26), then they "will be my people, and I will be your God" (36:27–28; 37:14). God will pour out the Spirit as water

126. Cf. Matt 3:9; Luke 3:8.

127. Keck 1996, 274.

128. So Beasley-Murray 48; R. Brown 1966, 141–44; Bruner 185; Moloney 1993, *Word* 111–13; frequently among patristic authors (Justin, *1 Apol.* 61, 65; Augustine, *Tract. Ev. Jo.* 11, 12); cf. Barrett 209; Hoskyns 213–14; and see Acts 19:1–6.

129. O'Day 550; and see Keener 1:547, esp. n. 138 for further references.

brings life to a dry and thirsty land, so that people may say "I am the LORD's" (Isa 44:3–6; cf. Joel 2:28). Similarly, in the book of *Jubilees*, God promises a coming restoration of his people, through the Spirit, so that Israel may again be God's children: "I shall create for them a holy spirit, and I shall purify them. And I shall be a father to them, and they will be my children" (*Jub.* 1.23–24). An oft-quoted passage from the Dead Sea Scrolls likens the cleansing of water to cleansing by the spirit of truth at the time of judgment:

> At the time of the appointed judgment, God will refine, with his truth, all human deeds, . . . cleansing him with the holy spirit from every irreverent deed. He will sprinkle over him the spirit of truth like cleansing water [in order to cleanse him] from all the abhorrences of deceit and from the defilement of the unclean spirit. (1QS IV, 20–22)

At the time of judgment, now effected through Jesus, who has been given all judgment by God (3:16–19; 5:22, 24, 26–27), God purifies and cleanses people through "the spirit of truth," through "the holy spirit"—two descriptions used of the Spirit also in the Gospel of John (14:17; 15:26; 16:13). With the coming of the one who has the Spirit upon him (1:32), who baptizes with the Spirit, the time for God's Spirit to purify and renew his people has come.

And indeed, throughout the discussion with Nicodemus about the kingdom of God, the work of the Spirit, and the new birth, the formation of a people is in view. To be "born again" or "begotten from above" does not entail having a particular kind of experience, especially not an experience that is interior or private. Even as one is born into a family, tribe, or people, so being "born again" entails identifying with a new people, complete with its own characteristic practices and commitments. Some of these new practices have already been hinted at: this people can expect a new temple, with different rites of purification required to enter it.

Yet the imagery of a second birth, whether being "born again" or "begotten from above," is not found in the Old Testament. Nor is it simply the radical extension of Jesus' words that one must become "as a little child" in order to enter the kingdom of God, where the emphasis falls on identifying with the lowly status of the child (Mark 9:33–37; 10:13–16). There is a closer conceptual parallel to Jesus' pronouncement in the Synoptics that his "family" consists of all those who do the will of God (Mark 3:32–35 par.). Even as Jesus comes from above and does the will of his Father (John 4:34; 5:30; 6:27, 38, 39, 40), so those who are born from above and do the will of God, as revealed in Jesus, are his family constituted by the new birth through the Spirit (3:3, 5).[130]

130. Stoics cherished the idea that all human beings are children of gods/God; see Cleanthes's "Hymn to Zeus," line 4: "We are thy offspring" (cf. Acts 17:28–29) and sources cited in comments on 1:12–13.

John's language has the strongest verbal connections to terminology found in non-Palestinian Judaism, early Christianity, and Greek or Roman religious thought. For example, the Jewish author Philo of Alexandria described Moses' mystical experience in his ascent of Sinai as a "second birth better than the first" (*QE* 2.46). In the New Testament, one finds the language of new birth in 1 Peter (*anagennan*, 1:3, 23) and in the Letter to Titus (3:5, *loutron palingenesis*; cf. Matt 19:28); and it is found quite regularly in 1 John (2:29; 3:9; 4:7; 5:1, 4, 18). The Christian apologist Justin Martyr, a Gentile born in Samaria, who studied Stoic and Platonic philosophy at Ephesus and was martyred at Rome, interpreted John 3:5 (or a variant of it) as a new birth, a regeneration, linked with baptism (*anagennēthēnai*, *1 Apol.* 61). At about the same time as Justin, the pagan writer Apuleius described initiation into the cult of the goddess Isis as being "in a sense, born again and restored to a new and healthy life" (*Metam.* 11.23–24).[131] But in John the "new birth," associated with the kingdom of God and the work of the Spirit, still belongs in the context of the biblical promises of salvation and renewal of the people of Israel.

[6–8] The point that one must be "begotten from above" is further illustrated by what appears to be a truism or a proverb: "Whatever is begotten of the flesh is flesh, and whatever is begotten of the Spirit is spirit" (v. 6); that is, like gives birth to like (cf. Matt 7:16–20; 12:34–35; Jas 3:10–12). In this statement (John 3:6), the first use of "Spirit" likely refers to the Holy Spirit. "Spirit" and "flesh" are not here constituent or conflicting parts of the human being, but refer rather to the Spirit of God and the flesh of humankind. In John, to be "of" (*ek*) something denotes one's origins, and hence one's characteristics and identity: a person "of the Spirit" belongs to the realm of the Spirit. But to be "of" (*ek*) also refer to one's destiny: those who are "of the flesh"—that is, who are flesh—have the destiny of all flesh: mortality[132] (cf. 1 Cor 15:42–54; cf. Gal 5:13–24; Rom 8:5–8). To be "of Spirit" means that one's destiny lies with the Spirit, or participates in the Spirit, and the reality that the Spirit brings: life (6:63).[133] Even as God breathed life into a man of clay so that he became "a living being," so God's Spirit breathes life into fleshly human beings so that they may enter into the kingdom of God, the realm of God. As in Paul's statement that "flesh and blood cannot inherit the kingdom of God" (1 Cor 15:50), no line runs directly from "flesh" to the kingdom of God.

131. Educated in Athens, Apuleius may have written the bulk of his work in Alexandria, which Philo also called home. First Peter is addressed to inhabitants of Asia Minor; the setting for the Epistle to Titus is Crete; and the Epistles of John are traditionally associated with Ephesus. For the argument that certain rabbinic texts imply rebirth, see Keener 1:542–44.

132. Mortality and flesh are also linked in ancient Greek philosophy; e.g., see Epictetus, *Diatr.* 1.3.5–7.

133. See Keck (1996) for discussion of Johannine predications using *ek*.

This then leads to one of the more enigmatic statements in the present discourse: "The wind blows where it wants, and you hear its sound; but you do not know where it is coming from and where it is going. That's how it is [*houtōs*] with everyone who is born of the Spirit" (3:8). There is a striking echo of Eccl 11:5: "Just as you do not know how the breath comes to the bones in the mother's womb, so you do not know the work of God, who makes everything" (cf. Gen 7:15; Isa 31:3). While the wind moves mysteriously, its effects can be discerned. The Spirit cannot be controlled by human beings for their own ends or purposes, but the effects of the Spirit's work can be discerned in creating the children of God, those who "believe in his name" (1:12–13). Human beings do not enter or see or participate in the kingdom of God through natural processes of growth, maturation, or their own efforts; but God's action makes it possible for them to do so (cf. Matt 19:26; Mark 10:27; 14:36; Luke 18:27). With respect to the protest against the possibility of a second birth for those who have grown old, Augustine sagely remarks, "He indeed said that a man cannot do this when he is old, as if he could do it even were he an infant" (*Tract. Ev. Jo.* 12.2).

[9–12] When Nicodemus asks, "How can these things happen?" the answer, at least in part, is that they cannot happen without the Spirit. Since the Spirit is given after Jesus' death (7:37–39; 19:34; 20:22), Jesus' words to Nicodemus are essentially a promise that in turn draws on the promises of the Spirit in the Scriptures, such as a "teacher of Israel"[134] should know, and anticipates the coming of the Spirit after Jesus' death. When Nicodemus expresses puzzlement, Jesus responds on behalf of those who "speak of what we know." Many of the pronouns and verbs in this passage are plural: Nicodemus speaks for himself and others ("we know," 3:2); Jesus uses a plural when he asserts, "You must be begotten from above" (3:7), and refers to "we" who bear witness and "you" (plural) who do not receive it. Jesus represents and speaks for himself and his disciples who accompany him regularly (2:12, 17, 22; 3:22) and who will come after him; Nicodemus speaks for those who share both his initial positive impression and subsequent puzzlement over Jesus.

Just what comprises the "earthly things" (*ta epigeia*, 3:12) that Nicodemus struggles to grasp, however, is difficult to discern.[135] The notion that "heavenly things," God's wisdom and purposes, are unfathomable runs throughout apocalyptic literature. Thus the angel Uriel challenges Ezra, "Your understanding has utterly failed regarding this world, and do you think that you can comprehend the way of the Most High?" (2 Esd [*4 Ezra*] 4:1; see also Isa 55:8–9; Wis 9:16). In John, "earthly things" must refer to those things of which Jesus has just spoken,

134. This is the only occurrence of "teacher" (*didaskalos*) in John that does not refer to Jesus; cf. 1:38; 3:2; 8:4; 11:28; 13:13–14; 20:16.

135. These things are "earthly," not (more negatively) "worldly."

while the "heavenly things" apparently include what Jesus will go on to speak of, namely, his origins in heaven and his eventual return there by means of the cross and exaltation (3:12–14). Later in John, Jesus' audience struggles to understand his claims to come from above (6:42), is offended by his assertions that his flesh and blood give life (6:60), and abandons him when he speaks of returning to where he was before (6:62). The realities of Jesus' heavenly origins and destiny comprise the "heavenly things" that challenge human comprehension. Nicodemus's original hunch that Jesus is a teacher come from God is right; but he does not know just *how* right he is! But by this point in the dialogue, Nicodemus has already faded from the scene as Jesus speaks, as it were, directly to the reader, a feature compatible with John's style elsewhere (e.g., 5:19; 6:35).

[13–15] The emphatic denial that "no one has ascended into heaven" challenges any who claim to have gained knowledge of heavenly things. In the wisdom tradition, the possibility of ascent to heaven to attain knowledge of God's ways and plans is denied to all human beings (Prov 30:4; Bar 3:29; Wis 9:14–18; Sir 43:31–32). But because God's word and wisdom have come down, they may be known by human beings: "the word" of God "is very near" (Deut 30:12–14); God's wisdom has lodged with Israel as Torah (Sir 24:23, 25); God's gift of wisdom and spirit grants understanding of heavenly ways (Wis 9:14–17). In John, the one who has "descended" from heaven and thus may truly reveal God's wisdom and word is Jesus, the "Son of Man" (1:14, 51).[136] Emphasizing Jesus' unique identity and revelation, John insists that no one has entered into God's presence except the one who came from it, an assertion linked to the limitation of the vision of God to Jesus himself (6:46). John's sweeping allegation applies equally to notable biblical figures, such as Enoch, Moses, Elijah, and Ezra, as well as to any contemporary claims to have attained heavenly knowledge through mystical visions, heavenly journeys, or secret revelation.[137]

John now exploits another contrast with Moses. According to Num 21:6–9, when God sent serpents among the Israelites because of their grumbling, Moses set a bronze serpent upon a pole (LXX, *sēmeion*, "sign"), and those who looked upon it were delivered from the venomous serpents and lived (LXX, *zēn*). The story provides a rough analogy to Jesus' being "lifted up" on the cross: even

136. In John, "heaven" denotes the place from which Jesus comes, but it is not explicitly named as the destination of the righteous.

137. For Enoch, see *1 En.* 1.1–3. Philo says Moses ascended the "loftiest" mountain and entered the darkness "where God was" (*Mos.* 1.158; 2.70–71); cf. Ezek. Trag. 67–112; *Jub.* 1.26; *4 Ezra* 14.1–9; *L.A.B.* 9.8; *2 Bar.* 4.2–7; 59.5–11. In 2 Kgs 2:11, Elijah ascends into heaven in a chariot (LXX, *analēmphthē . . . eis ton ouranon*). In contrast, see *4 Ezra* 4.8 and theTannaitic commentary *Mekilta* (on Exod 19:20 [*Baḥodesh* 4.55]): "Neither Moses nor Elijah ever went up to heaven, nor did the Glory ever come down to earth." See here esp. Meeks 1967, 156–58; Segal 1980; Kanagaraj 186–213.

as God had instructed Moses to hold up the bronze serpent on a pole in order to deliver Israel from the peril of death in the wilderness, so will this "Son of Man" be lifted up to deliver the world from the threat of death; those who believe in him will live.

The verb *hypsoō*, which can mean both "lift up" and "exalt," occurs five times in John as a distinctive term for the crucifixion: while human beings "lift up" Jesus to death on the cross, God "exalts" him (3:14; 8:28; 12:32, 34) or, as John writes elsewhere, "glorifies" him (from *doxazein*). John's description of the crucifixion thus takes a page from Isaiah's description of the Lord's servant, who is both "exalted" (*hypsōthēsetai*) and "glorified" (*doxasthēsetai*).[138] The "Son of Man"[139] who is "lifted up" (12:34) is the crucified Jesus: this one is also the subject of Isaiah's vision of the "glory of the Lord" (12:41). Jesus' crucifixion was not in fact the ignominious end of his life, but a revelation of divine glory, of God's life-giving purposes: God sent the Son to *save* the world (3:17; see comments on 12:31–34).

The deliverance that is promised is "everlasting life."[140] "Everlasting" or "eternal" (*aiōnios*) is first a predication of the duration of life (see BDAG s.v.). But "eternal" or "everlasting" life is not simply unending: it is qualitatively different from mortal life in the present world, because it participates in the blessings of the coming age, including being with God, who is living and eternal (17:3). Because it is lived in union with God, such life is characterized by fullness or abundance (1:16; 4:14; 6:33–35; 10:10; 15:5).

[16–17] "Life" and "salvation" are virtually synonymous in John because salvation is construed as deliverance from death and participation in the plenitude of God, both in the present life and in the life that follows resurrection. The basic predications found in 3:16 and 3:17 show this synonymity:

God	gave his Son	whoever [believes]	not perish	but have everlasting life
God	sent the Son	(to) the world	not to condemn	but to save

"The world" refers to all people (1:10–11): God's action through the Son is intended as the salvation of, or life for, all the world and is expressed as deliverance from judgment (3:17–19) or condemnation.[141] Here John uses a rhetorical pattern ("not this . . . but rather that"; cf. 1:8; 11:4) that emphasizes the end of the statement: the Son came "not to condemn the world, *but to save the world*."

God's love for the world is demonstrated by giving the Son for its salvation, to deliver it from death to the life intended for it in creation.[142] Indeed, the

138. For the pairing, see LXX: Isa 4:2; 5:16; 10:15; 33:10; and 52:13.

139. The word *hypsoō* is always linked in John with the Son of Man.

140. See Excursus 4: "Life and Eternal Life in John."

141. "Judgment" and "condemnation" translate the same Greek word, *krisis*; cf. 3:19; 5:24.

142. "For God loved the world *in this way*" (*houtōs*, "in this manner, thus, so").

Gospel speaks of God's love for the world (3:16) in the service of underscoring the dominant and fundamental characteristic of God in this Gospel: God is the living God (6:57), the Creator of the world (1:1–3), who has granted the power to give life into the hands of the Son (5:26–27), the agent of creation (1:3–4). God's love for the world comes to its expression in God's giving life to the world: this is how God loves the world; this is what brings glory to God (11:4, 40).

Only here in John is it said that God "gave" (*edōken*) the Son; otherwise, God is said to send or to have sent the Son (as in 3:17, *apesteilen*). Elsewhere in the New Testament, statements about God's "giving" the Son point to Jesus' death, and the traditional language shapes John's formulation here.[143] Jesus' death is the preeminent and climactic manifestation of his love and life-giving work for the world and for his own (10:11, 13–15; 13:1). But John likely broadens the scope of the verb "gave." While God's giving or sending of the Son into the world for its life comes to its climactic fulfillment, its *telos* (12:27; 13:1; 19:30), on the cross, all of Jesus' works, words, death, and resurrection effect life and the world's salvation.

[18–21] Since the Son is the agent of God's life-giving purposes for the world, trusting (having faith or believing) in him leads to life. While judgment is passed on those who do not believe (v. 18), God does not send the life-giving Son into the world to condemn it. The proper work of God is to give the world life, not death. Similarly, the proper work of God's light is to illumine the truth, not to obscure or hide it. God has sent the true light (1:4–5, 9) into the world so that people may see God by means of that light (9:38–40), but some simply do not come to the light (3:19–20) and so remain in the darkness (9:40–41; 12:40). The Gospel uses strong language here, speaking of those who "hate the light" (3:20). "Hate" is not an internal attitude or emotion of hostility so much as an external expression of distancing oneself from something or being indifferent to it: those who "hate the light" are they who "do not come to the light."[144] They simply do not enter into this light or welcome it (1:9–11). Since the light of judgment has come, the judgment that was expected in the future can be declared now, both for those who believe and those who do not: judgment for life or death has "already" (*ēdē*) been decided (3:18).

The picture of people hiding under cover of darkness serves as a parable of those who do not wish to be exposed to the light.[145] The analogy is natural enough: darkness hides; light reveals; and those who have something to hide

143. In some such formulations, God is the subject (Rom 8:32), and in others Jesus himself is the subject (Gal 1:4; 2:20; Eph 5:2, 25; 1 Tim 2:6; Titus 2:14).

144. So Malina and Rohrbaugh 87; see also BDAG 635, *miseō*; and John 7:7; 15:23–25; as well as Matt 5:43; 6:24; Luke 14:26; 16:13 (for hatred as the opposite of attachment or commitment).

145. "Exposed" here translates *elenchthē*. BDAG notes that both in John 3:20 and Eph 5:11, 13, the word *elenchō* occurs in the context of darkness/light and hence suggests "exposure, with implication of censure."

seek the darkness, not the light, while those who have nothing to hide gladly come to the light. The irony is that while people fear coming into the light, afraid that the exposure of their deeds brings judgment and condemnation, it is there that they find salvation and life. God has not sent the Son to condemn but to save the world, for in him there is light in the darkness and life in the midst of death.

Excursus 4: Life and Eternal Life in John

The Gospel of John is notable for its frequent use of the interchangeable terms "life" and "eternal life" (cf. 3:16; 5:3–40, esp. v. 24; 6:47–48; 10:10, 28; 20:31). John uses the simple noun "life" (*zōē*) 19 times; "eternal life" (*zōē aiōnios*) 18 times; the verb "to live" (*zēn*) 17 times; and "to live forever" (*zēn eis tōn aiōna*) or an equivalent expression 5 times.

While both "life" and "eternal life" feature prominently in John, they are not unique to this Gospel: both terms occur in the Synoptics, although, as elsewhere in the New Testament, "life" occurs more regularly than "eternal life."[146] Given the dominance of the term "kingdom of God" in the Synoptics and of "eternal life" in John, the question arises whether John has simply substituted the one for the other and, if so, how to account for that substitution.

Another term used by John is *psychē*, which may be translated "soul" or "life." It is nearly always found in the context of "losing" or "giving up" one's life or dying for another (10:11, 15, 17, 24; 12:25, 27; 13:37, 38; 15:13; so also Mark 8:35; Matt 10:39; 16:25; Luke 9:24; 17:33). *Psychē* and *sarx* ("flesh") thus overlap each other, since both connote mortality: Jesus lays down his *psychē* (cf. 13:37, 38; 15:13); he gives up his *sarx* for the life (*zōē*) of the world (6:51–58). In contrast to *psychē*, *zōē* is the life that Jesus has and gives, which cannot be taken away; *zōē* comes from the *pneuma* ("spirit"), since the Spirit confers life (3:5–6, 15–16; 6:63).[147]

Daniel 12:2 (LXX) contains the Old Testament's single reference to "eternal life": "Many of those who sleep in the dust of the earth shall rise [*anastēsontai*]; some to eternal life [*zōēn aiōnion*], and some to shame and everlasting contempt [*aischynēn aiōnion*]"; cf. Isa 26:19. In Daniel the phrase *zōēn aiōnion* ("eternal life") translates the Hebrew *ḥayyê ʿôlām*. Both the Greek *aiōnios* and the Hebrew *ʿōlām* can mean a long, unspecified period of time, or a period of time without end, thus suggesting the translation of either the Hebrew or Greek phrases as "everlasting life." Since *zōē aiōnios* refers not merely to the unending duration of life, but also to the quality of life appropriate to the coming blessed age of life with God, "eternal" is typically preferred to "everlasting" in translation (e.g., Dan 12:2 LXX; John 3:16).

146. In the Synoptics, "eternal life" occurs in Matt 19:16; 19:29 (and par. in Mark 10:17, 30–31; Luke 18:18, 30; also 10:25). Outside of the Gospels, "eternal life" is found in Acts, Romans, Galatians, 1 Timothy, Titus, 1 John, and Jude; the absolute term "life," used synonymously with "eternal life," appears in Matthew, Mark, Luke, Acts, Romans, 1–2 Corinthians, Philippians, Colossians, 1–2 Timothy, Hebrews, James, 1 Peter, 1 John, and Revelation.

147. In Gen 2:7 LXX, God breathes the "breath of life" (*pnoēn zōēs*) into Adam ("humankind") so that he becomes a *psychē zōēs* ("living being," which translates the Hebrew *nepeš ḥayyâ*).

Resonating with Dan 12:2, other Jewish texts speak of resurrection, life, and eternal life.[148] Additionally, some texts contrast "this age" with "the age to come" and locate the inheritance of life or eternal life in "the age to come."[149] The Synoptic Gospels associate "eternal life" or "life" with the age to come (Mark 10:29–30) or with the kingdom of God (Luke 18:29–30; cf. Mark 9:43, 45, 47). In John, however, "life" and "eternal life" are not explicitly linked with "the age to come" (a phrase that does not appear in John) even though that age would be attended by or follow the resurrection of the dead.[150] As in Daniel, in John only some are raised to life or eternal life; others are raised to judgment (5:28–29). This twofold resurrection likely refers to the general resurrection of all the dead, following which there are two final verdicts: life or judgment.[151] Those who live do so because Jesus lives (14:19); Jesus will raise up those who believe in him "at the last day" (5:28–29; 6:40, 44, 54; 11:24). John's understanding thus coheres with Paul's view of Jesus' resurrection as the "first fruits" ensuring the future resurrection of believers (1 Cor 15:20–23; cf. 2 Cor 5:5, 10).

But John also asserts that those who believe in Jesus *have* (3:36; 6:47: present tense, *echei*) eternal life; they "have passed from death to life" (*metabebēken ek tou thanatou eis tēn zōēn*, 5:24). Those who believe in Jesus now have that life that is appropriate to the coming age and consequent upon resurrection, and they have it as a present possession rather than—or in addition to—an expectation for the future. John's characterization of "life" or "eternal life" as a present reality has been called "realized eschatology," since the promises of the eschaton (the last day, the last things) are now "realized" or available in the present.[152] In addition to the question of how to account for John's preference for "eternal life" over "kingdom of God," John's "realized eschatology" further presses the question to what extent the Gospel has reinterpreted "eternal life" as well as the resurrection that precedes it.

In John, the promise that eternal life is a present possession seems to preclude the Jewish and Synoptic understanding of "eternal life" as "life of the age to come." Yet this is typically the background proposed for understanding John's view of eternal life, even if one concedes that John thoroughly reworked materials he took over. For example, Dodd held that John reinterpreted the Jewish terminology of life for the sake of a Hellenistic readership and in keeping with Platonic, or Platonizing, tendencies; eternal life was "nei-

148. Among Jewish texts that speak of resurrection or eternal life, or both, are 4Q521; *Pss. Sol.* 3.12; 13.11; 14.10; 2 Macc 7:9 (*eis aiōnion anabiōsin zōēs hēmas anastēsei*, "he shall raise us to everlasting renewal of our life"); 7:14 speaks of "resurrection to life" (*anastasis eis zōēn*); 23, of "life"; 36, of "ever-flowing life" given to the righteous martyrs; 12:43–44, of the resurrection.

149. The contrast between the two ages can be found, for example, in *4 Ezra* 7.113; 8.52; *1 En.* 37.4; 58.3; cf. also 91.10; 103.4; and other apocalyptic literature. This motif is common in the NT (Matt 12:32; Mark 10:30; Luke 18:30; Eph 1:21; Heb 6:5) and frequent in later rabbinic literature (e.g., *m. ʾAbot* 2:7; 4:16–17; *Sipra* 5.85d [on Lev 18:5]; *Sipre* §§47–48; *Mek. Exod.* 13.3; *b. Ber.* 28b; *b. Šabb.* 33b).

150. This is implicit in those Synoptic passages that speak of "entering" or "inheriting life," even when the resurrection is not mentioned (e.g., Mark 9:43, 45); cf. 1 Cor 15:52; *2 Bar.* 30.1–5.

151. John says little about this judgment; see comments on 3:36 and 5:25–29.

152. For a recent discussion of "realized eschatology," see Culpepper 2008. The first volume of the massive study of Johannine eschatology by Jörg Frey (1997) is helpfully summarized in Beasley-Murray cxxvii–cxlii.

ther past nor future, but lived in God's eternal To-day."[153] Focusing on the tension created by asserting that the life of the age to come could be enjoyed in the present age, Cullmann proposed that John *emphasized* the tension between the "already" and the "not yet," such as one finds in the Synoptic statements about the presence and future of the kingdom of God.[154] Similarly, Barrett writes of the "clash and paradox of tense" characteristic of early Christian eschatology that comes to quintessential expression in John's statements "the hour is coming and now is" (4:23; 5:25).[155] Such interpretations generally note that, while John distinctively emphasizes the present blessings of life available through faith, it maintains, even if it does not foreground, the hope for future resurrection and life.

Schnackenburg, however, countered that the proposed connection to the Jewish idea of the life of the age to come "can hardly be right."[156] Instead, he explained the contrast in John between the life of this world and "eternal life" in terms of a qualitative distinction between the earthly and heavenly realms, from which issue two vastly different kinds of life.[157] "Eternal life" is "true divine life": "a share in the life of God" or "communion with the Father and the Son" that provides meaning through the new existence lived in faith.[158] Stated otherwise, the Synoptic framework is temporal, but John's is spatial, grounding its understanding of "life" and "eternal life" directly in the character and life of God.[159]

John's preference for "life" and especially "eternal life," as well as their connection to resurrection, do betray his affinities with Jewish conceptions of eternal life. As R. Brown helpfully puts it, John took over the theme of "eternal life" from the tradition of Jesus' words, where it was linked with "kingdom of God," and made it a central theme of his Gospel, capitalizing on the character of "eternal life" as qualitatively distinct from natural life (*psychē*).[160] In choosing to emphasize "life," John's strategy may be rhetorical: he aims to make his Gospel accessible to readers unfamiliar with the hope of the kingdom of God but all too familiar with the reality of death. The Gospel offers them life, not only in the future, but also in its fullness in the present.

Yet John's understanding of "life" or "eternal life" also differs from its counterpart in the Synoptics in that it is further developed with respect to different coordinates: (1) creation; (2) Christology; (3) the relationship of God (Father), Word (Son), and Spirit; and (4) what believers receive from God in Jesus and through the Spirit.

153. Dodd 1953, 150; see Philo, *Deus* 32; *Fug*. 57. Like pagan sources, Philo generally uses the term *athanasia* ("immortality," "incapable of death") rather than "life" or "eternal life."

154. Cullmann 270; see his entire discussion, on 268–91.

155. Barrett 68.

156. Schnackenburg 2:521 n. 5.

157. Schnackenburg 2:353.

158. Schnackenburg (2:361) alleges that the Johannine idea of life was focused entirely on the individual; likewise Moule (1962). In a similar vein, "eternal life" has been called "spiritual" (Morris 194, 196, 198), "purely religious" (Corell 142), "mystical" (Culpepper 2008, 269). Pursuing a different avenue, R. Brown (1966, lxxxv) suggests that John's emphasis on "realized eschatology" arose from his effort to deal with the problem of the delay of Jesus' return (the Parousia).

159. Cullmann (271) comments that in Jesus' life "the whole history of salvation, past and future, is summed up vertically, and yet this life is incorporated into a horizontal line."

160. R. Brown 1966, 508; he further notes, "The greater adaptability of the theme of life to his emphasis on realized eschatology was undoubtedly a factor in his choice."

1. *Creation.* In John, "life" is first mentioned and presented with respect to creation. "All things came into being" through the Word (1:3), in whom there is "life" (*zōē*, 1:4). R. Brown doubts that *zōē* refers to natural (or created) life: John always uses *psychē* for life that can be given up.[161] But given the proximity and near parallelism of the two statements "all things came into being through him" (1:3) and "in him was life" (1:4), it seems difficult to deny that *zōē* refers to the life that was initially given to all creation. *Zōē* thus refers, not only to life inherited after death, but also to that which is intrinsically in God, and in the Word, and is the source of vitality for all created things. All things were created through him, but some will rise to life through him. Created life is a foretaste and anticipation of eternal life; created life truly images and anticipates eternal life because both come from God. It is through the resurrection that one enters, finally and fully, into "eternal life."[162]

2. *Christology.* Schnackenburg rightly notes that John's understanding of eternal life arises from his Christology.[163] As the source of all life, God spoke the world into being through his Word (see Gen 1:3, 6, 9, 11, 14; Ps 33:6). God has given the Son the same power of life: his word and his deeds bring life (John 4:50; 11:43), and his own resurrection ensures the resurrection to life "at the last day." God alone has life eternally, and this is what he has given to the Son (5:26): Jesus is the bread of life through whom the world is sustained (6:1–15); the good shepherd who gives up his life to protect the lives of others (6:51; 10:10, 17–18); God's living vine through whom God's people are nourished in faith and life (15:1–5; cf. 6:35); the way and truth that lead to life with God (14:6); and the resurrection and life, who raises the dead to life (6:40, 44; 11:25–26; 14:19). From creation, through the revelation in word and deed, to his death and resurrection, the Son[164] is the means through which God gives life in and to the world. This christological coordinate of eternal life especially accounts for John's realized eschatology: those who saw and heard Jesus had contact with the one in whom there is life and who himself is life (cf. 1 John 1:1–4).

3. *Relationship of Father, Son, and Spirit.* But it is not enough to assert that John's emphasis on life has been generated by his Christology, since Christology cannot be articulated apart from its theological coordinate: Jesus is who he is in relationship to God. Distinct from the other Gospels, and more like Paul, John probes the connection between Father, Son, and Spirit with respect to their authority to give life. The living Father is the source of life (5:25; 6:57); the Son is himself life (14:6), in that his words and deeds confer life (4:50; 6:63; 11:43); and the Spirit is the power that effects new life (3:3, 5–8; 20:22).

4. *What believers receive.* Finally, those who receive eternal life share in the life that characterizes and comes from God alone (17:3). Because they have knowledge of and fellowship with this living and eternal God in the present, and are born as children of God to new life by the Spirit, they experience the blessings of eternal life in life lived abundantly (10:10). Created life and eternal life intersect at the point of abundant life

161. R. Brown 1966, 506.

162. For further discussion, see comments on 5:25–29 below.

163. Schnackenburg 2:355.

164. Both word and wisdom are also means of God's life-giving work; see Excursus 1: "Word and Wisdom in John."

in the present (10:10). "Abundant life" has multiple connotations. It looks back toward creation; it anticipates the blessings of the new life of the resurrection, especially the blessing of being in the divine presence; and it lies at the intersection of past and future, while in the present it offers communion with the living God. At the heart of John's understanding of eternal life, one finds a robust view of God who is the sole source of all life, who created and sustains all things in life and who will confer that life upon those who trust in him. What remains consistent in one's experience of eternal life, whether enjoyed in the present or the future, is that it is existence that derives its meaning from the love, fullness, and presence of God.

3:22–36 John Continues to Bear Witness

The Gospel returns once more to the witness of John (the Baptist). As discussed earlier, in the Gospel of John, the Baptist is not so much a forerunner, whose task ends when Jesus comes on the scene, but rather a witness to Jesus. John was baptizing with water so that Jesus might be revealed to Israel (1:31) as the one who would baptize with the Spirit. John continues to bear witness to Jesus as the Messiah (3:28), the Son, who has and gives the Spirit (3:34–35), even as he had done earlier (1:33–34). John's witness does not come to an end once Jesus comes on the scene, and indeed it has still not come to an end. Inscribed now in the pages of the Gospel, John's voice continues to be heard as a voice testifying to Jesus as the one who is above all (3:31).

> **3:22** After this Jesus and his disciples went into the land of Judea, and he
> stayed there with them and was baptizing. **23** John was also baptizing at
> Aenon, near Salim, because there was a lot of water there. And people
> were coming and being baptized. **24** For John had not yet been thrown
> into prison.
>
> **25** There was a dispute between one of John's disciples and a Jew about
> purification. **26** And they came to John and said to him, "Rabbi, you know
> the one who was with you across the Jordan, to whom you bore testimony?
> This one is baptizing, and everyone is going to him." **27** John replied,
> "No one can receive anything except what is given by heaven. **28** You
> yourselves are witnesses that I said, 'I am not the Messiah,' but that I had
> been sent before the Messiah. **29** For the one who has the bride is the bride-
> groom; the friend of the bridegroom stands, listens to him, and rejoices
> greatly because he has heard the voice of the bridegroom. Therefore, my
> joy has been made complete. **30** For he must increase, but I must decrease."
>
> **31** The one who comes from above is above all; the one who comes
> from the earth is of the earth and speaks in an earthly way.[a] The one who
> comes from heaven is above all. **32** This one bears witness to what he has
> seen and heard, but no one receives his witness. **33** The one who does
> receive his witness attests[b] to this: that God is true.

34 For the one sent by God speaks the words of God, for God does not give him the Spirit by measure. 35 The Father loves the Son and has put everything into his hands. 36 Everyone who believes in the Son has everlasting life; but those who disobey the Son shall not see life, for God's wrath rests upon them.

a. The switch from the first-person pronoun ("I") and direct address (vv. 28–30) suggests that at v. 31 there is a transition to the voice of the narrator.
b. Lit., "set a seal," hence, "certify."

[3:22–24] Jesus leaves Jerusalem for the surrounding territory of Judea; according to the Fourth Gospel, there he engages in a ministry of baptizing (but see 4:2), simultaneous with that of John. Now John's baptism is situated not at Bethany beyond the Jordan (see 1:28), but at "Aenon near Salim." Salim is identified with one of two locales, one about eight miles south of Scythopolis (Bethshan) and one a few miles east of Shechem; both are within Samaria, through which Jesus will soon pass on his way to Galilee (4:3).

But why, if the purpose of John's baptism has been to identify Jesus as the coming one, and if he has accomplished this purpose, does John continue to baptize at all (3:23)? Why does Jesus, who is to baptize with the Spirit, take up a ministry of baptizing with water, and why is nothing heard about this in the other Gospels or even later in this Gospel? These brief notices are enigmatic, to say the least.[165] Earlier, John's baptizing work was said to have the goal of making Jesus known (1:31); John continues to baptize *precisely to fulfill his role of bearing witness to Jesus*. In this Gospel, John is a "voice crying in the wilderness," not the one who prepares people for another by calling for their repentance: as long as he baptizes, he bears witness to Jesus. Jesus' own adoption of the practice of baptism in no way conflicts with John's practice, or with his promise that Jesus will baptize with the Spirit. As noted earlier, John baptizes *only* with water, anticipating the one who will baptize with Spirit, whereas Jesus baptizes with *both* water *and* Spirit (see comments on 1:29–34; 3:5). But inasmuch as the Spirit is given after Jesus' death and resurrection, Jesus also baptizes with water during the course of his ministry, anticipating the giving of the Spirit, symbolized by water (7:37–39). The water baptism of both John and Jesus portend the Spirit baptism of Jesus.

[25–30] The reference to the twin baptizing ministries of John and Jesus leads to the comment that a dispute arose about "purification" (*peri katharismou*), indicating that the baptizing mission they carried on was understood as

165. Dodd (1963, 279–87) argues at length that the material is found in John's tradition and somewhat more cautiously labels it "an undigested scrap of genuine information" (cf. R. Brown 1966, 155; Blomberg 96). Others find the evidence inconclusive (Schnelle 1998, 84; Lincoln 2005, 163–66; perhaps also Barrett 219–21).

an act of purification.[166] As we have seen (2:1–25), purification and cleansing are important themes of the Gospel of John, although they surface differently than they do in the Synoptic Gospels. For example, there is no discussion of handwashing (Matt 15:1–20; Mark 7:1–23), and many of the Synoptic episodes that depict persons who are unclean, or things that would defile (the woman with the flow of blood; Jesus' touching a corpse; a man living in the tombs; a demon being cast into pigs) are also missing from John. Even as John gathers up all of Jesus' moral instruction into the command to "love one another," so too purification or cleansing is rolled into the presentation of Jesus as the one who takes away sin (1:29) and cleanses his disciples through his actions (13:1–11) and his word (15:3). Thus when a dispute arises about "purification" (3:25), John bears witness to Jesus, the Messiah (3:27–28), who takes precedence over him (3:30; cf. 1:15, 30). John's work is to make Jesus known.

When the report is brought to John that Jesus is making more disciples than he is, John not only reinforces his earlier witness to Jesus, but also declares that both he and Jesus are simply fulfilling the tasks assigned to them by God (3:27).[167] Jesus is the Messiah, John is the one sent before him; Jesus is the bridegroom, John is the friend of the bridegroom; Jesus is the one who must increase in prominence and importance, while John must decrease.[168] Indeed, from this point onward, he does not appear in this Gospel, although his role as witness is mentioned again (5:33–36; 10:40–41).

The image of Jesus as the bridegroom may reflect the portrayal of God as Israel's bridegroom in the Old Testament (Isa 62:5; Jer 3:20; Ezek 16:32; Hos 1:2; 2:2; for Jesus as the bridegroom of the church, cf. Eph 5:23–32; Rev 19:9). John rejoices as guests and friends do at a wedding. At times in the Old Testament, God's judgment on Israel can be portrayed quite concretely as bringing an end to the joy of a bride and bridegroom (Jer 7:34; 16:9; 25:10; 33:11). But Jesus' ministry brings joy and celebration since the bridegroom, the Messiah, has come. Indeed, Jesus' first sign, the provision of wine at the wedding, ensured that the rejoicing will continue.

[31–36] In John 3:31–36 we seem to have the narrator's remarks, who contrasts the ministries of Jesus and John, culminating with testimony to Jesus as

166. See LXX 2 Kgs 5:14; Jdt 12:7; Sir 34:30, where "baptize" refers to washing for purification or cleansing.

167. Compare Jesus' comment to Pilate in 19:11: while John knowingly operates in the knowledge that "no one can receive anything except what is given by heaven," Pilate does not recognize that his authority comes from above.

168. In 2:10 the wine served first is called "inferior" or "lesser" (Greek, *ton elassō*); in 3:30, John says that he must decrease (or become less; *eme de elattousthai*). The former (wine, the Baptist) pales in comparison with, but also points to, the latter (the wine Jesus provides; the cleansing ministry of Jesus).

the Son in whom there is life. Initially there is a description of "the one who comes from above" and so "is above all" or is preeminent over all, including all persons and likely also all things (3:31). The Greek participle *ho erchomenos*, "the coming one" or "the one who comes," elsewhere in the Gospel refers to Jesus (6:14; 11:27; 12:13); here, Jesus is "the one coming *from above*."[169] The one who "comes from the earth" (3:31) is John. This characterization does not denigrate him or his witness—he is "of the *earth*," not "of the *world*"—but it does subordinate him to Jesus. Although others may be "begotten from above," only Jesus "comes from above." John's "earthly" origin does not undercut the fact that he has been "sent from God" (1:6), and his "earthly way" of speaking does not undermine the witness that he bears to Jesus (1:6–8, 15, 19–34). But as the one who has come from above, Jesus alone can testify fully and completely concerning "heavenly matters" (3:12) and bear witness to God, whom he alone has seen (1:18; 3:11). Thus he testifies to what he has seen and heard from God (see Acts 4:20; 1 John 1:3).

As is typical in the Gospel, the twofold response to Jesus is summarized as either rejection or acceptance of Jesus' witness (John 3:32–33). While in the immediate context it is reported that Jesus is making more disciples than John and that "all" are going to him (3:26), yet it is also clear that not all did "come to him" or become his disciples. Those who accept the word of Jesus in fact accept the truthful witness of God, since Jesus was sent by God and speaks the words of God (cf. 5:24). To accept the truth of Jesus' witness is to accept the truth that God speaks through him, and thus to attest to or certify that God is truthful or true (3:33; 7:28; 8:26). Both those who bear testimony and those who receive that witness attest to God's truthfulness. The Samaritans, whom Jesus will encounter next, exemplify acceptance of Jesus' witness.

The justification for the fact that "the one sent by God speaks the words of God" (3:34) is found in the statement "God gives him the Spirit without measure,"[170] taking God (rather than Jesus) as the implied but unstated subject of the verb "he gives." We have then three parallel statements, each predicating a specific capacity or power of God given to Jesus:

> The one whom God has sent speaks the words of God.
> God has given to the Son the Spirit "without measure."
> The Father loves the Son and has placed all things into his hands.

169. See Matt 23:39; Mark 11:9; Luke 13:35, "the one who comes in the name of the Lord" is the son of David. John's preference for describing Jesus as the Son of God yields the expression "the one coming from above" (3:31).

170. Jesus has the Spirit "without measure" (3:34), as already demonstrated when the Spirit came down and *remained* on him (1:32–33), even as Jesus has eternal "life in himself" because God has given it to him (5:25–26).

As the Son, Jesus has the capacity to speak the very words of God; he has the Spirit of God without limit or measure; and he has been given power over "all things." In the prologue of the Gospel, "all things" are said to have been created through the Word; here, God has given Jesus far-reaching sovereignty over "all things" (cf. Matt 28:18). The Father has bestowed all these prerogatives on the Son: the assertion that the Father entrusts *all things* into the Son's hands marks him out as unique among any and all divinely commissioned agents or spokespersons (cf. comments on 1:3; 5:20–22).

The earlier point that those who believe in the Son have eternal life is repeated, but now with the additional note that disobedience brings God's wrath (*orgē*). This is the sole reference to God's wrath in the Gospel. Elsewhere the Gospel speaks of the judgment (*krisis*) that unbelief brings (3:17–21) and that has been handed over by the Father to the Son (5:22–27; cf. 8:16; 9:39). Judgment is typically linked with death and is the opposite of life and salvation; those who hear the word of Jesus and believe in God are delivered from judgment and pass from death to life (5:24); those who do not believe are the recipients of God's judgment, or wrath (3:36). In short, they do not receive the life that God gives through the Son. John does not speak here or elsewhere of hell or post-mortem punishment; those who do not receive life remain in death. Still, the Gospel repeatedly emphasizes the point that God's work is to bring life and light, not death and darkness. From the opening verses of the Gospel, God is presented as the one who gives life to all things through the Word (1:3–4) and brings light to those in darkness (1:5–9). Here the point is reiterated: God's will for the world is life, salvation, and light, not darkness and death (3:16–21).

4:1–42 The Spirit, True Worship, and the People of God

In John 3 Jesus declares to a law-observant Jewish teacher, whose people can claim descent from the patriarch Abraham, that the time has come for their renewal through God's Spirit. In John 4 Jesus declares to a Samaritan woman, whose people have rejected the Jerusalem temple, that the time has come to offer God true worship—apart from any temple, whether on Mount Zion or Mount Gerizim. True worship, effected by the Spirit, will displace both the Samaritan and Jewish places of worship from the center of their respective religious maps. The dialogues with Nicodemus and the Samaritan woman underscore the Spirit's work in renewing a people for God: the Spirit effects new birth (John 3) and true worship (ch. 4). Characteristics identifying God's people—their ancestry, their worship—are transformed through Israel's Spirit-endowed Messiah.

The movement from the early confession of Jesus as the Messiah, King of Israel (1:17, 41), to the confession of Jesus as the Savior of the world (4:42) mirrors the movement within Jesus' dialogue with the woman at the well: Jesus (a Jew) reveals his status as Messiah to the woman (a Samaritan), whose people come to acclaim him as the Savior of the world. Everything in John moves from Israel to the world. All Israel must be reborn through God's Spirit (3:3–5); through the Jews and their Messiah, salvation will come to the Samaritans and to all the world (4:22). The Samaritans will not come to worship in the Jerusalem temple; but the Father who seeks true worshipers will also seek out the Samaritans to offer true worship in Spirit and in truth.

4:1–15 Jesus, Jacob, and Living Water

At a wedding in Cana, Jesus has supplied wine in abundance for family and friends who are celebrating. Now Jesus offers a source of "living water" to a Samaritan woman who comes in the midday heat to draw water from Jacob's well. Earlier Jesus has used the water intended for rites of purification, transforming it into choice wine for the feast. Now Jesus implicitly compares the water that comes from Jacob's well, the ancestor and namesake of the people of Israel, to the water that he can give. Even as the people at the wedding at Cana received fine wine in abundance, so the woman who encounters Jesus can receive "living water" from Jesus. If Jesus offers more than Jacob was able to offer, is he then "greater than our father Jacob"? The implied affirmative answer once again portrays Jesus as the one whose abundant provision meets and surpasses expectations: indeed, he *is* greater than Jacob.

> **4:1** Now when the Lord[a] knew that the Pharisees had heard that Jesus was
> making and baptizing more disciples than John— **2** even though Jesus
> himself did not baptize but rather his disciples did— **3** he left Judea and
> went again to Galilee.
>
> **4** He had to pass through Samaria. **5** Then he came to the city of Samaria
> that is called Sychar, near the field that Jacob had given to Joseph his son.
> **6** And Jacob's well was there.[b] So Jesus, tired from the journey, sat down
> by the well. It was noon.[c]
>
> **7** A Samaritan woman came to draw water. Jesus said to her, "Give
> me a drink." **8** (His disciples had gone away into the city in order to buy
> food.) **9** The Samaritan woman said to him, "How is it that, even though
> you are a Jew, you ask me, a Samaritan woman, for a drink?" (For Jews
> and Samaritans do not use the same vessels.)
>
> **10** Jesus answered her, "If you knew the gift of God and who it is who
> is saying to you, 'Give me a drink,' you would have asked him, and he
> would have given you living water." **11** The woman said to him, "Sir,[d]
> you don't have anything to draw with, and the well is deep. Where do

you get this living water? 12 Are you greater than our father Jacob, who
gave us this well and even drank from it himself, as did his sons and
cattle?"
13 Jesus answered her, "Everyone who drinks from this water will be
thirsty again. 14 But those who drink from the water that I will give to
them will never be thirsty. The water that I will give them will become in
them a spring of water welling up to eternal life." 15 The woman said to
him, "Sir, give me this water, so that I won't get thirsty or have to come
here to draw water."

a. In v. 1 some mss (𝔓[66*] ℵ D) read "Jesus" instead of "the Lord" (𝔓[66c, 75] A B *al*); the MS evidence is fairly evenly divided; the effort to determine which reading is less awkward leads to no firm conclusion.

b. "Well" translates *pēgē*, "spring, fountain" in 4:6 (BDAG s.v.; cf. 4:14; Jas 3:11); *phrear* is the common word for "well," in John 4:11–12.

c. *Noon* translates "the sixth hour" (cf. 19:14; cf. also 1:39; 4:52).

d. The Greek word *kyrios* can be translated "sir" or "Lord."

[4:1–6] Here again the Gospel refers to Jesus' practice of baptizing (see 3:22–24) but adds the correction that Jesus himself did not baptize; only his disciples did so. This comment may attempt to deal with any awkwardness about Jesus' baptizing, or to prevent anyone from claiming some sort of superior status if they had actually been baptized by Jesus (cf. 1 Cor 1:12–17). In his treatise *Baptism* (11), Tertullian refers to some Christians who, on the basis of John 4:2, denied the need for the rite of baptism on the ground that the text explicitly says that Jesus did not baptize, but his disciples did. Tertullian responds that Jesus authorized but did not participate in the act of baptizing; and that is surely the intent of the note in John 4:2. As Augustine observes, "Jesus still baptizes; and as long as we must be baptized, Jesus baptizes" (*Tract. Ev. Jo.* 15).

Jesus' increasing popularity causes him to leave Judea for Galilee (cf. John 6:14–15; Luke 4:42–43). His work had become known to the Pharisees, who in John are connected particularly with Jerusalem (cf. 1:19, 24; 3:1–2). Later, Jesus will go up to Jerusalem in spite of the potential danger (e.g., 7:1–3; 11:48–53), but meanwhile he avoids conflict until the "hour" has come.

Jesus' journey to Galilee takes him through Samaria.[171] Other routes from Judea to Galilee ran along the sea (via Caesarea) or from Jerusalem down to Jericho, across the Jordan, and northward through the Jordan Valley (see here Mark 10:1, 32–34; Luke 19:1, 28). Josephus (*Life* 269) comments that pas-

171. Samaria refers both to the capital city of the northern kingdom and later to the broader region; cf. Robert Anderson.

sage through Samaria was "necessary" (*edei*, as in John) for a quick journey (of three days) from Galilee to Jerusalem, and elsewhere states that the route was customary for those going up to keep the festivals in Jerusalem (*Ant.* 20.118; cf. *J.W.* 2.232; cf. reference to rabbinic journeys in *Gen. Rab.* 32.10; 81.3). But at this point, Jesus is not on his way to Jerusalem; his route will provide the occasion to demonstrate that his mission will not be limited to the Jews but is intended for all the world. The Samaritan woman's responsiveness, however tentative, foreshadows the responsiveness of those outside of Judea to Jesus.

Weary and thirsty, Jesus sits down by a well.[172] The narratives of the Old Testament recount Jacob's giving land to his son, Joseph (Gen 48:22; Josh 24:32), but make no reference to "Jacob's well." Jacob first encountered Rachel at another well, also in the middle of the day (Gen 29:1–11).[173] The Samaritans viewed themselves as descendants of Ephraim and Manasseh, the sons of Joseph, the beloved son of Jacob (cf. Josh 16:4–17:12; Jer 31:16–20; Zech 9:13; 10:6–12; Josephus, *Ant.* 11:344–46). Thus the references to Jacob and his well, and to the land he gave to Joseph, remind the reader that this conversation takes place in territory once inhabited by the patriarchs—and that Samaritans and Jews share a common ancestry.

[7–9] In a world where water does not flow from taps, women's work often revolves around procuring water for drinking, cooking, washing, and watering, the work of sustaining life. This woman has come alone and in the heat of the day to draw water (cf. Gen 29:6–7). She finds Jesus alone. In her response to Jesus' request for a drink, the woman underscores the barrier between them: he is a Jewish male, she a Samaritan woman (cf. 4:27). Jesus crosses this double barrier, risking reputation and honor and whatever disapproval his actions might occasion, in order to ask something of her.

According to some rabbinic tradition, men—especially sages—should avoid conversation with women (*m. ʾAbot* 1:5; cf. *m. Ketub.* 7:6). There was a history of strained relationships between Samaritans and Jews.[174] Much of the friction can be traced to disputes about the temple and its proper locale. In Ezra, it appears that Samaritans oppose the rebuilding of both the walls of Jerusalem

172. Early Christian authors took the passage as evidence of Jesus' genuine humanity (Irenaeus, *Haer.* 3.22.2; Tertullian, *Prax.* 21.8; 27.11; *Carn. Chr.* 9.7), whereas critics of Christianity, such as Celsus, argued that it disproved Jesus' divinity because gods do not have bodies or physical needs (Origen, *Cels.* 1.70). Augustine finds both a strong Jesus and a weak Jesus: strong, because he is the Word who was in the beginning; weak, because he was made flesh (*Tract. Ev. Jo.* 15.6.2).

173. Isaac (via his father's servant), Jacob, and Moses meet their wives at a well (Gen 24:10–61; 29:1–20; Exod 2:15b–21), leading some interpreters to see this encounter as a type of "betrothal scene"; Neyrey 1979, 425–26.

174. See Sir 50:25–26. Josephus characterizes Samaritans as "apostates of the Jewish nation" (*Ant.* 11.340; cf. 11.346). But elsewhere Samaritans are to be counted among those obliged to say the common Jewish grace together (*m. Ber.* 7:1).

and its temple (Ezra 4:4–5, 24; cf. Neh 4:7–23).[175] Later the Samaritans would build their own temple on Mount Gerizim, which was subsequently destroyed by the Hasmonean ruler John Hyrcanus (in 128 B.C.E.). Even so, Josephus blames the Samaritans for instigating outbreaks of hostility between Jews and Samaritans, some of which ended in violence and murder (cf. *Ant.* 20.118–36; *J.W.* 2.232–44; cf. Tacitus, *Ann.* 12.54). On one occasion, Samaritans defiled the temple grounds in Jerusalem just before Passover by littering them with bones (*Ant.* 18.29). Such incidents reflect the mutual suspicion of Samaritans and Jews of each other, leading to the woman's incredulity that Jesus should ask her for a drink of water, especially since Jews and Samaritans "do not use the same vessels."[176] There is a troubled past between Jew and Samaritan; does Jesus propose simply to ignore it all?

[10–15] In response to the woman's perplexity, Jesus remarks that if she had any idea to whom she was speaking, she would be asking him for a drink, for he can give "living" or "running water," water that is "the gift of God." Later in the Gospel, water is explicitly said to represent the Spirit, which flows like "living water" (7:37–39), and the water likely symbolizes the Spirit here as well. Graphic representations of Jesus' encounter can be found on the walls of several ancient catacombs, sometimes juxtaposed with the raising of Lazarus, perhaps because the account of Jesus' raising of Lazarus depicts Jesus as the "resurrection and the life," while in the story of Jesus' encounter with the Samaritan woman, Jesus promises "living water" that "wells up to eternal life."[177] That is what Jesus offers her; neither her gender, her ethnicity, nor her religious commitments or practices are a barrier to Jesus' gracious gift to her. Neither should they be a barrier to the mission of Jesus' disciples to her and her townspeople, as the narrative will shortly make clear.

Jesus' conversation with the Samaritan woman builds on the contrast between a well and a spring, and on the implicit claim of Jesus to be greater than the patriarch Jacob.[178] For while Jacob had provided a well (*phrear*), fed

175. Josephus, *Ant.* 11.114–15.

176. "Do not use the same vessels" translates *synchrōntai*. Daube (373–82) argues for this now widely accepted interpretation over against "have no dealings with" (RSV); differently, see Lincoln 2005, 168 n. 2. According to the Mishnah, Jews regarded Samaritans as unclean: "R. Eliezer said, 'He that eats the bread of the Samaritans is like to one who eats the flesh of swine'" (*m. Šeb.* 8:10); and Samaritan women were deemed to be in a state of perpetual ritual impurity (*m. Nid.* 4:1), which might explain the Samaritan woman's surprise at Jesus' willingness to ask her for a drink (*m. Kelim* 1:3). Whether these views would have been extant in the time of Jesus is difficult to determine; the narrative itself focuses on the issue of worship, and not explicitly on the issues of purity; cf. Klawans 104–8.

177. See Jensen 2012, 150–52, 159.

178. For "our father Jacob," see 4 Macc 2:19; *Tg. Neof.* 28.10; "our father Abraham" in John 8:53.

by a spring (*pēgē*),[179] to water his cattle and his family, Jesus promises a spring (*pēgē*) of "living water" (*hydōr zōn*) that can quench thirst forever.[180] Not without reason, the Samaritan woman assumes that Jesus is offering something equivalent to what she could give to him: she could draw water, with a bucket, from Jacob's well to give him a drink; he claims to be able to provide some sort of superior water. But he has no bucket: how can he offer her any water at all? The Samaritan woman misunderstands Jesus' word, even as Nicodemus had misunderstood Jesus: Jesus speaks of a new birth, but Nicodemus imagines a second physical birth; Jesus speaks to the woman of "living water," but she imagines a perpetual source of freshwater. Although right in some important respects, she is wrong in others. While the water is provided perpetually, it "lives" not because it is fresh or running, but because it is the means of life. It is "the gift of God."

Jeremiah calls God a "spring of living water" (2:13 LXX, *pēgē hydatos zōēs*; 17:13);[181] and the psalmist compares the longing of a deer for "a spring of waters" (*pēgē hydatōn*) to the heart's longing for God (Ps 42:1 = 41:2 LXX). God provided water for Israel in its wilderness wanderings: Moses made the bitter waters of Marah sweet; later he struck a rock and brought forth water to quench the thirst of the Israelites (Exod 15:23–25; 17:3–6; Num 20:10–11).[182] Because water is essential for life, it is needed not only as part of God's physical provision for his people; it also signifies God's life-giving power and work. Thus Zechariah promises a day when living water (*hydōr zōēn)* shall overflow from a purified Jerusalem (14:8 LXX; cf. Ezek 47:9–12). For John, this life-giving water is to be found in the Father's gift of the Spirit, given to the Son and though him to all peoples of the world.

179. The Hebrew "well of water" (Gen 21:19) becomes a "well of living water" (*phrear hydatos zōntos*) in the LXX, perhaps influenced by the identical phrase at 26:19 ("Isaac's servants dug in the valley and found there a *well of living water*" [AT]). Abraham's servants water his camels from a "well" (*phrear*, 24:11, 20), also called a "spring" (*pēgē*, 24:13, 42, 45; cf. 24:30). Philo contrasts a spring and well (*Post.* 153); the depth of the well of wisdom shows that it is not superficial (*Ebr.* 112).

180. "Living water" (LXX, *hydōr zōn*; John 4:10–11), or running water, is preferred over still or drawn water for the washing that removes the defilement caused by various skin diseases (Lev 14:5–6, 50–52), bodily emissions (15:13), and corpse uncleanness (Num 19:17). In the early Christian document the *Didache*, baptism is to be performed with "living water" (*hydōr zōn*, natural, flowing water) if available; if not, cold water is preferred rather than warm; as a last resort, one may pour water over the head (7:1–3). Tertullian (*Bapt.* 4) tartly remarks, "It makes no difference whether one is washed in a sea or a pool, a stream or a fountain, a lake or a trough."

181. On this passage, Philo declares that "God is something more than life; an ever-flowing spring of living, as he himself says" (*Fug.* 198).

182. In Num 21:18 the place where the water came from the rock is called Mattanah, which means "gift." The text in Numbers does not make this explicit; John's reference to the "gift of God" would be a very subtle allusion.

In some Jewish interpretation, water symbolizes the law[183] or the wisdom that God gives.[184] In keeping with the portrayal of Jesus as both God's embodied word and wisdom, here Jesus gives the living water, the Spirit of life. Other traditions speak of a miraculous flow of abundant water from Jacob's well.[185] If such interpretations were extant when this Gospel was being written, then they would provide a foil for Jesus' implicit claim to be greater than Jacob: Jesus' gift of living water endures to eternal life. The gift of God is the gift of life, and God's Spirit effects life. This is what Jesus, the one greater than "our father Jacob," gives.

4:16–30 Jesus, the Messiah, and True Worship

The conversation now turns from water and thirst to the woman's marital history, Jesus' status as a prophet, and a discussion about "true worship." While the transition seems abrupt, it is Jesus' identity as a prophet that serves both to tie the parts of the narrative together and to provide the basis for his later identification as Messiah. The woman identifies Jesus as a prophet because he knows her past. The Samaritans apparently awaited a prophet-like figure, as Moses was before him. However, the prophet whom they await—one who might restore worship on Mount Gerizim—will turn out to be the Messiah of Israel, and he will initiate worship of another sort altogether.

This passage demonstrates the close connection between worship and the identity of the people of God, traced throughout the pages of the Old Testament as well: Israel, chosen and delivered by God, owes its worship to God alone. Proper worship acknowledges the one true God; in turn, idolatry and other inappropriate forms of worship, including worship in other shrines or places than the temple designated by God, merit God's judgment (see, e.g., Isa 44:9–20). But in the discussion with the Samaritan woman, Jesus makes it evident that the people of God will now be identified by worship tied not to a specific place or building, but rather to the Spirit and to truth. Such worship potentially characterizes all peoples. To put it differently, while salvation comes "from the Jews" (4:22), it is not limited to the Jews.

> **4:16** He said to her, "Go, call your husband, and come here." **17** The woman said to him, "I have no husband." Jesus said to her, "You have rightly

183. CD VI, 2–5; cf. III, 16; XIX, 34, the "well of living waters"; *m. 'Abot* 1:4, 11; 2:8.

184. Prov 18:4; Sir 15:3; 24:25–32; Philo, *Ebr.* 112–13; *Somn.* 2.270–71; *Det.* 117; *1 En.* 48.1; 49.1.

185. Both *Targum Pseudo-Jonathan* and *Targum Neofiti* (but not *Targum Onqelos*) state that when Jacob removed the stone that covered the mouth of the well in Haran, "the well overflowed and came up to its mouth, and was overflowing for twenty years" (*Tg. Neof.* 28.10; cf. *Tg. Ps.-J.* 28.10; cf. *Gen. Rab.* 70.19).

said, 'I have no husband.' 18 For you have had five husbands, and the one
whom you have now is not your husband. You have spoken the truth." 19
The woman said to him, "Sir, I see that you are a prophet. 20 Our fathers
worshiped on this mountain. But you say that Jerusalem is the place[a]
where one must worship." 21 Jesus said to her, "Believe me, woman,[b] the
hour is coming when neither on this mountain nor in Jerusalem will you
worship the Father. 22 You worship what you do not know. We worship
what we know, for salvation is from the Jews. 23 But the hour is com-
ing—and is now here—when genuine worshipers will worship the Father
in Spirit and in truth, for the Father seeks such to worship him. 24 God
is Spirit, and those who worship him must worship him in Spirit and in
truth." 25 The woman said to him, "I know that the Messiah is coming"
(the one called Christ). "When he comes, he will tell us everything."

26 Jesus said to her, "I am he, the one who is speaking to you."

27 And then his disciples came and marveled that he was speaking
with a woman. But no one dared ask him, "What are you looking for?"
or "Why are you speaking with her?" 28 The woman left her water jar and
went into the city and said to the people, 29 "Come and see a man who
told me all that I have done. This can't be the Messiah, can it?"[c] 30 And
they left the city and went to Jesus.[d]

a. "Place" translates the Greek *ho topos*; it refers to the temple (cf. 11:48, "the Romans will take away our holy place").

b. "Woman" translates *gynai*, as in 2:4; 19:26; 20:13, 15.

c. The form of the question expects a negative answer; the woman's question expresses caution or wonder.

d. The imperfect tenses are translated here by the simple past tense ("left, went").

[4:16–20] When Jesus asks the woman to bring her husband to him, he seems to change the subject abruptly (cf. 3:3). Her response ("I have no husband") leads Jesus to reveal the extent of his knowledge about her: not only does he know that she has no husband, but he knows of five past marriages as well.[186] The woman's five marriages would presumably have ended either in the death of a husband or divorce. If previous husbands had died, then the woman would have been left alone and widowed. If previous marriages had ended in divorce, then five times she would have been cast off by her husband.

186. According to Josephus, the Samaritans consisted of five peoples or nations, each of whom "brought their own gods" into Samaria (*Ant.* 9.288–91; cf. 2 Kgs 17:24–41). If the woman's "five husbands" represent five gods or idols, such symbolism might lie behind the transition to the subject of worship (4:19–20) and to Jesus' assertion that the Samaritans worship "what you do not know" (4:22).

On either score, the woman's repeated marriages would not have made her a more desirable candidate for marriage.[187] That she is currently living with a man outside a legally contracted marriage indicates to some commentators her immorality, but to others also her desperation. She needs the protection and support of a husband, but has settled for what she can get. Jesus calls attention to her problematic situation, but he does not condemn her. Subsequently, commentators and preachers have hastened to fill the void!

Even as Nicodemus professed his belief that Jesus was "a teacher come from God," the Samaritan woman rightly judges Jesus to be a prophet, based on his knowledge of her situation. Because she deems him to be a prophet, she questions him about the key issue that divides Samaritans and Jews: the proper place of worship. But even as Jesus' response to Nicodemus shows how much Nicodemus's understanding of Jesus' mission and identity needs revision, so Jesus' response to the Samaritan woman reveals that he will radically reconfigure the entire discussion about the proper place of worship.

While Jews worshiped at the temple on Mount Zion in Jerusalem, Samaritans believed that Mount Gerizim[188] was the mountain where worship of God should properly take place. They continued to observe their rites on Gerizim even after John Hyrcanus destroyed their temple in 128 B.C.E.[189] The Samaritans were awaiting a prophet to instruct them how to handle the various temple furnishings that remained after the destruction. According to Josephus, during the time of Pontius Pilate a certain man promised to lead the Samaritans up to the "most holy of all mountains," Gerizim, and to show them the sacred vessels that Moses had put there. The finding of such vessels could then lead to the rebuilding of the temple (*Ant.* 18.85–87). But Jesus does not hold out hope for a rebuilt temple to the Samaritans, any more than he had earlier to the Judeans; the only temple that will be raised up is the temple of his body (2:21). Jesus counters the woman's reference to the mountain where "our ancestors" (*pateres*, "fathers") worshiped with a declaration about the worship that "the

187. Later rabbinic sources debate whether a woman could remarry two or three times (Str-B 2:437); perhaps this woman was trapped in the custom of levirate marriage (cf. O'Day 567; Tamar in Gen 38; Deut 25:5–10; Luke 20:27–33), with the last male in line refusing to marry her.

188. In Deut 11:29; 27:12, Gerizim is the mountain of blessing; the Samaritan Pentateuch adds a commandment to the end of the Ten Commandments to build an altar and to offer sacrifice on Mount Gerizim (added to Exod 20:17 and Deut 5:21).

189. Josephus (*Ant.* 13.255–56; 18.85–89; *J.W.* 1.63) also notes that Hyrcanus destroyed the city of Samaria and enslaved its inhabitants; cf. 2 Macc 6:2, where (ca. 168 B.C.E.) both the temples in Jerusalem and on Gerizim are defiled at Antiochus's orders. Origen (*Comm. Jo.* 13.80) remarks that the dispute about the proper place of worship continued "even to the present day." The post-Talmudic tractate *Masseketh Kuthim* asserts that the Samaritans will be welcomed back into the people of Israel only when they renounce Mount Gerizim (61b [2:7]).

Father [*ho patēr*]" seeks.[190] Jesus will not adjudicate the long-standing debate over the proper place of worship in favor of either Jew or Samaritan; instead, he characterizes the worship that God desires without regard to either place.

[21–24] And yet the Jerusalem temple has already been identified as "my Father's house" (2:16). Now, identifying himself with the Jews and speaking on their behalf, Jesus asserts, "We worship what we know; for salvation is from the Jews" (4:22).[191] Both assertions assign a primacy to Israel, its temple, worship, Messiah, and God: it is from Israel that salvation comes. But even as the temple in Jerusalem serves as a figure of the temple that is the risen Jesus (2:21), so true worship will soon be localized in *that* temple, located neither on Gerizim nor Zion; the salvation that comes from Israel will flow beyond its borders.

Jesus twice announces that the hour of true worship "is coming" (4:21), but on the second occasion (v. 23) adds the note "and is now here": the hour that is first announced as future is now already present. Since the locus of true worship will no longer be "this mountain" or "Jerusalem," the hour that "is now here" envisions those who worship without a humanly constructed temple, that is, the readers of the Gospel after the fall of the temple. Jesus speaks proleptically of the true worship that will follow his resurrection (2:21) and the giving of the Spirit (7:39; 14:26; 15:26; 16:7–13; 20:22).

The contrast between the "true worship" and worship in a specific temple is neither an argument for the interiorization of worship, as opposed to the practice of various rituals or sacrifice, nor a criticism of the idea of "sacred space" per se.[192] Rather, it finds its proper context in the eschatological assertion that the "hour is coming, and is now here." That hour is, of course, the hour of Jesus' death and return to the Father, after which the Spirit will be given, thus making possible "worship in Spirit," characterized as worship in the truth since the Spirit is the Spirit of truth (7:37–39; 14:17; 15:26; 16:13; cf. 1 John 4:6).[193] Here one finds no sustained criticism of Jewish worship, sacrifice, the priesthood, or even of the temple or conceptions of the temple. Rather, "true worship" belongs to the "hour" that is coming.

190. Cf. John 6:31–32, where Jesus' interlocutors assert, "Our *ancestors* [*pateres*] ate the manna," and Jesus responds, "My *Father* [*patēr*] is giving you the true bread"; and the later contrast between Abraham and God as the Father of the Jews (8:39–42, 44).

191. The neuter relative pronoun ("what," 2× in 4:22) is unusual, given that *ho theos* (God) and *ho patēr* (Father) are masculine nouns. The statement "You worship what you do not know" takes into account both the history of Samaritan worship of multiple gods (2 Kgs 17:24–41) and worship on Gerizim, thus criticizing Samaritan failure to worship the one God of Israel correctly (Hakola 2005, 105). "Salvation is of the Jews" translates *ek tōn Ioudaiōn*; the prepositional phrase with genitive indicates origin or source and is roughly equivalent to *erchesthai ek* (1:44, 46; 7:22, 41, 42; 11:1). See, further, Excursus 7: "'The Jews' in the Gospel of John."

192. *Pace* Ashton 65–66; Borgen 1996, 111–12; Dunn 2006, 93–95.

193. The dative *en pneumati kai alētheia* ("in Spirit and truth") can have locative ("in the realm of the Spirit") or instrumental force ("by means of the Spirit"). These are not mutually exclusive.

That Jesus speaks of alternative worship does not demonstrate that Christian worship of God regards sacred spaces and holy places as outdated or irrelevant. Indeed, earlier in the Gospel, Jesus himself had been identified as a temple (2:21). The reader of the Gospel, then, may make the connection that the alternative "holy place" is Jesus himself, the Holy One of God (6:69).[194] As the locus or "place" of God's presence, Jesus reidentifies the "place" of worship. The holy ground of revelation becomes the sanctified "space" of worship. Here it is that one may "see heaven opened and the angels ascending and descending upon the Son of Man" (1:51): this is "none other than the house of God, and this is the gate of heaven" (Gen 28:12–17). Even as *hoi Ioudaioi* are identified as those who worship at the temple in Jerusalem, and Samaritans as those who worship on Gerizim, so Jesus' followers will be defined by their relationship to yet another temple, the "temple of Jesus' body." This temple will serve as the focal point of worship for Samaritans and Jews, as well as for those Gentiles who have never worshiped either on Gerizim or at the temple on Zion.

In conversation with the Samaritan woman, however, Jesus gives two reasons why one must worship "in Spirit and in truth": (1) "The Father seeks such to worship him" (4:23); and (2) God is Spirit. C. K. Barrett once commented that the statement regarding the Father's seeking true worshipers has "perhaps as much claim as 20:30f. to be regarded as expressing the purpose of the gospel."[195] God seeks those who will offer "true worship," worship that corresponds to the God who "is Spirit" (4:24). In this Gospel, the Spirit of God has been identified as that life-giving power through which God calls a new people into being; through the Spirit, God's people are "begotten from above." Spirit designates God as other than flesh, mortal, and confined in space and time. The life-giving Spirit "blows where it wants" (3:8) and cannot be confined to a single place or to a visible locale, such as the temple on either Gerizim or Zion (cf. 1 Kgs 8:27; Isa 66:1).[196] Once the Spirit that "blows where it wants" has been given, then true worship will not be limited to the temple in Jerusalem, any more than the life-giving breath of God is confined to a single people.

[25–26] The matters disputed between Jews and Samaritans will be explained by the coming Messiah. Only in John do we have the transliteration *Messias* coupled with its translation into Greek, as *Christos* (see 1:41). Inasmuch as the Samaritans accept only the Pentateuch of Moses as authoritative Scripture, and inasmuch as they reject Jerusalem as the holy city, their conception of "the one who is to come" is decisively shaped by the figure of the coming prophet

194. See the fuller discussion in M. M. Thompson 2001, 214–17.

195. Barrett 238.

196. Lincoln 2005, 177.

(Deut 18:15–18), rather than a Davidic king coming to reign in Jerusalem. Corresponding to the hope for a "prophet like Moses" is a Messiah who will instruct the people; hence, the woman's description that he will "tell us everything."

Just at this point, Jesus identifies himself to the woman as that Messiah with the response, "I am he, the one who is speaking to you" (*egō eimi ho lalōn soi*, 4:26).[197] This is Jesus' first use of *egō eimi* ("I am" or "I am he") in John. It is also one of the few places in all the Gospels where Jesus explicitly acknowledges that he is the Messiah. For John, it is significant that he does so in Samaritan territory, for two reasons. First, John affirms certain aspects of the Samaritan expectation of a Messiah. Although greater than Moses, Jesus is both prophet and teacher, as Moses was (1:17; cf. 5:46–47). Second, John underscores the point that salvation originates with the Messiah of Israel: salvation flows from the Jews to the Samaritans (and eventually to the Gentiles; cf. Acts 1:8), from Israel to the nations (John 4:22). The point is dramatically enacted here as the Messiah (of Israel) identifies himself to the Samaritan woman; the scene anticipates what the disciples will later be sent out to do. Jesus bears witness to her that he is the Messiah, a witness that his disciples will eventually carry to all the world.

[27–30] Given the hostilities between the Samaritans and Jews, one hardly expects the comment that it is the woman's *gender* that scandalizes the disciples: Jesus, a rabbi, is speaking with a woman. Somewhat wryly, perhaps, John adds that none of them challenge Jesus on the point! The encounter between Jesus and the Samaritan woman anticipates the witness that women bear, particularly to the resurrection. Even as it is a woman, Mary Magdalene, who first bears witness to the risen Lord, so here the Samaritan woman bears testimony to Jesus as Messiah (cf. 11:25–27). If Jesus' knowledge had impressed Nathanael, a true Israelite, to exclaim that Jesus is the Son of God, King of Israel (1:49), then Jesus' knowledge of the Samaritan woman leads her to acknowledge and bear witness to Jesus as a prophet, the Messiah who has made all things known. Women nearly always have a positive role in John as those who understand, even if haltingly, who Jesus is and bear witness to him.[198]

The Samaritan people come to Jesus because of the woman's testimony to him as Messiah, inviting them to come and see a man with amazing knowledge. There are parallels to the accounts of the calling of the first disciples: having encountered Jesus, the disciples in turn summon others (e.g., 1:41–42, 45; 4:28–29), bearing witness that Jesus is the Messiah (1:41, 45; 4:29), and inviting them to "come and see" Jesus for themselves (1:46; 4:29). The pattern in

197. Cf. Isa 52:6 LXX, *egō eimi autos ho lalōn: pareimi* ("I myself am the one who is speaking; I am here"). C. Williams (257–66) suggests that the language of "knowing all things" resonates with Isaiah's depiction of God's knowing the future.

198. For fuller discussion, see Conway; Maccini.

chapter 4 is the same: the woman encounters Jesus and invites others to see the one who has told her that he is the Messiah. The text's comment that she "left her water jar" may indicate a hasty departure, her hope to return with others, or her excitement; yet on another level it hints that she has accepted Jesus' promise to give her living water that surpasses anything she can draw from Jacob's well.

4:31–42 Jesus and the Samaritan People

Jesus' encounter with the Samaritan woman began with a request for a drink of water, a request that became the grounds for Jesus to offer the woman "living water"—an offer that she does not fully understand. Jesus' own disciples return from the village and offer him food, guessing that he must be hungry (even as he was thirsty earlier). But Jesus counters that he depends for his strength on the one who sent him, just as he, the one sent, offers living water and bread to his followers. Jesus now alerts his disciples to the fact that he is going to send them back to the places where they bought food, in order to offer food of another sort. Even as the Samaritan woman needs to understand Jesus' mission, so the disciples need further instruction on Jesus' mission: as God's Messiah, he calls together a new people; the disciples are part of that people and will, in the future, bear their own witness to the Samaritans. The fields are ripe for harvesting.

4:31 Meanwhile the disciples urged him to eat, saying, "Rabbi, eat."
32 But he said, "I have food that you don't know about."
33 So they said to each other, "Has someone brought him something
to eat?"
34 He said to them, "My food is to do the will of the one who sent me,
and to complete his work.[a] 35 Don't you say, 'There are still four months
before harvest comes?' Look! I tell you, lift up your eyes and see that
the fields are ripe[b] for harvesting already. 36 The one who is reaping gets
his wages, and gathers together fruit that lasts forever, so that the one
who sows and the one who reaps rejoice together. 37 For this saying is
true: one sows and another reaps. 38 I have sent you to reap where you
haven't done any work. Others have done the work, and you have joined
them in it."
39 Many Samaritans from that city believed in him because of the
woman's testimony, "He told me everything I've done."
40 When, therefore, the Samaritans came to him, they asked him to stay
with them. And he stayed there two days. 41 And many more believed
because of his own word. 42 And they said to the woman, "We no longer
believe because of what you have told us, for we ourselves have heard
and have come to know that this man is truly the Savior of the world."

a. "To complete his work" translates *teleiōsō autou to ergon*, using the verb *teleioō* (as in 5:36; 17:4, 23; 19:28); Jesus' final word on the cross in John, *tetelestai* (19:30; "it is finished" or "completed") uses a similar verb *teleō* (also used in 19:28; cf. 13:1).

b. "Ripe" translates *leukai* (white).

[4:31–34] The scene now shifts to an exchange between the disciples and Jesus. Even as the Samaritan woman had misunderstood the nature of the water that Jesus promises her, so now the disciples misunderstand both the "food" of which Jesus speaks and its source: this food comes from God and may be understood as the very presence of the Father with the Son.[199] The Gospel of John elsewhere pairs eating and drinking (e.g., 6:35, 53–56) and uses both as figures of the gifts of wisdom and life that God gives through Jesus. Here, however, Jesus speaks not of the food that he will give to others, but of an altogether different kind of food that sustains him. He is sustained by accomplishing the work, the mission, which God has given him to do. As is typical of John, the dialogue moves on two levels: while the disciples think of food to sustain the physical body, Jesus speaks of food that sustains him in a different way. The dialogue does not denigrate the need for food: Jesus did ask the woman for a drink of water because he was thirsty, and he will feed five thousand who are hungry (ch. 6). But in each case, the gifts of God nourishing the body that perishes can serve as figures of the gifts of God that lead to eternal life, because God is the source of all life. God's work, accomplished by Jesus, leads to eternal life for others.

The one who provides such nourishment is the one "who sent me," the way Jesus regularly characterizes God (4:34; 5:24, 30, 37; 6:38, 39, 44; 7:16, 33; 8:16, 18, 26, 29; 9:4; 12:44, 45, 49; 13:20; 14:24; 15:21; 16:5; cf. 1:33). The phrase aptly conveys the sense that Jesus and God are characterized with respect to the other: the Father is the one who sent Jesus; Jesus is the one who is sent. Simultaneously, the phrase indicates that knowledge of one implies knowledge of the other, as in the statement "Whoever believes in me, believes not in me but in him who sent me" (5:24; 12:44–45; 13:20; cf. 5:23).

[35–38] Reference to the "work" that Jesus must accomplish leads to a discussion of the work in which the disciples participate (see 6:27–29). Jesus describes the work of the disciples as that of reaping (4:36–38); others have sown the seed, whose harvest they reap. In context, the point is that Jesus has sowed the seed among the Samaritans—through his encounter with the woman, who bears witness to her people—and the disciples will reap the harvest of Samaritan faith.

199. In the *Apoc. Ab.* 12.1–2, Abraham says, "We went, the two of us alone together, forty days and nights. And I ate no bread and drank no water, because [my] food was to see the angel who was with me, and his discourse with me was my drink." In John, it is not an angel but the Father himself who is present with Jesus.

Even as the disciples had misunderstood the nature of Jesus' food that sustains him, so too they demonstrate a lack of understanding about the harvest. Jesus quotes a saying, sometimes taken as proverbial, regarding the future harvest: "Don't you say, 'There are still four months before harvest comes'?" Jesus corrects that viewpoint, commenting that harvesttime has arrived: "The fields are [already] ripe for harvest" (cf. "the time is coming and now is," v. 23). In the Synoptic parables, the imagery of harvest pictures judgment, sometimes with an emphasis on sorting or dividing the crop into what is to be kept and what is to be discarded (e.g., Matt 13:24–30), and elsewhere with an emphasis on the abundance of the crop (e.g., Mark 4:8). In John the emphasis falls rather on the imminence of the harvesttime, which is pictured primarily as a time for the ingathering of "fruit" from the mission of God in and through Jesus; so too Jesus "gathers together" the scattered children of God (11:52).

The Samaritan woman had initially wondered if Jesus was the Messiah; her townspeople now acclaim him as the "Savior of the world." *Savior* reflects an Old Testament designation for God that figures especially prominently in the second part of Isaiah (e.g., 43:3, 11; 45:15, 21–22; 49:26; 60:16; 63:8–9; cf. 2 Sam 22:3; Pss 17:7; 106:21; Jer 14:8; Hos 13:4).[200] While these passages particularly emphasize God's deliverance of Israel in times of trouble, there are also promises of the universal scope of God's salvation (e.g., Isa 45:21–22). Jewish sources speak of God as "Savior of all" or "of the world."[201] Pagan deities—such as Zeus, Asclepius, Isis, and Serapis—were called "Savior"; the second-century author Aelius Aristides names Asclepius, the god of healing, as "savior of all" (*sōtēr tōn holōn*) and "savior of all people" (*sōtēr pantōn anthrōpōn*; cf. 1 Tim 4:10).[202] The terms "Savior" and "Savior of the world" also functioned to identify and elevate the emperor in Roman imperial ideology; the terms can be found in Greek and Latin inscriptions and written sources for various emperors, including Julius Caesar, Augustus, Tiberius, Claudius, Nero, Titus, Vespasian, Trajan, and Hadrian.[203] Whether used of deities or emperors, in these descriptions "savior" typically designates a figure of stature

200. "Savior" can also be used of human deliverers (Judg 3:9, 15). In John, "savior" and "salvation" are used only in 4:22 and 4:42. For God as Savior in the NT, see (e.g.) Luke 1:47; 1 Tim 1:1; 2:3; 4:10; Titus 1:3; for Jesus as Savior, see (e.g.) Luke 2:11; Acts 5:31; 13:23; Phil 3:20; Titus 1:4.

201. For God as the "Savior of all" see Wis 16:7. Note also Philo: "savior of all things" (*ho sōtēr pantōn*), in *Fug.* 162; *sōtēr tou pantos*, in *Deus* 156; "Savior of the world" (*sōtēr tou kosmou*), in *Spec.* 2.198; for God as "savior and benefactor" (*sōtēr kai euergetēs*), see *Sobr.* 55; Josephus applies these terms to Vespasian (*J.W.* 3.459; 7.70–71).

202. For gods as "savior," see Aeschylus, *Suppl.* 26 (Zeus), 980 (the Olympian gods); Euripides, *Herc. fur.* 48 (Zeus); Epictetus, *Diatr.* 1.22.6 (Zeus); Aelius Aristides, *Or.* 37.16 (Asclepius); 53.2 (Serapis).

203. For full discussion and further references, see the seminal article by Koester 1990; Cassidy 34–35, 103–4 nn. 20–22; Labahn 2002; Carter 2008, 188–91; Nock 1972b.

and power who consequently delivers people from threats such as physical ailments, war, and death. The threats might vary; but deliverance is needed at the hand of someone who is more powerful than the person who is oppressed and suffering, and more powerful than whatever threatens the person.

By calling Jesus "Savior of the world," by going out to meet him and inviting him to their town, the Samaritans honor Jesus as Jewish towns welcomed and honored emperors, including Vespasian (*J.W.* 3.459; 7.70–71) and Titus (*J.W.* 4.112–14; 7:100–103, 119). But here it is Jesus who merits such acclamation: he is truly (*alēthōs*) the Savior of the world. The Samaritans' welcome further shows that the salvation coming "from the Jews" is intended for all the world. The Samaritans are presumably representative of (the first?) believers from "the world" and therefore appropriately confess Jesus as Savior of the world. They do so initially on the basis of the woman's testimony and then on the basis of Jesus' own words (4:41–42). Even as Jesus gives living water, so his words are "words of eternal life" (6:63). The designation of Jesus as "Savior of the world" expresses the Johannine conviction that Jesus delivers "all people" from the peril of death. The next account of Jesus' raising the official's son demonstrates the power of Jesus' word to heal, to grant life to one on the verge of death—another witness to the identity of Jesus as "Savior of the world."

4:43–54 The Life-Giving Word of Jesus: A Second Sign at Cana

Jesus healing of the official's son at Capernaum is the first of his healing miracles in the Gospel of John. Like the first of Jesus' signs, also set in Cana, it is narrated rather succinctly. No explanatory discourse elucidates the sign or its witness to Jesus. Yet in a relatively short space, this account implicitly emphasizes the efficacy of Jesus' word to bring life to those threatened by death. Jesus' promise, "Your son will live," is fulfilled, and Jesus' deed brings about faith in him as the one who has the power to give life. Later Jesus will stand in front of the tomb of one who has died and command him to live. Again Jesus' word will effect life—but in the case of Lazarus, only after he has died and his loved ones have succumbed to grief. Even then, Jesus remains the hope of those who trust in him; even then, he can speak words of life.

While the current account introduces the life-giving power of Jesus and his word, not all who initially believe in him and his word cling to him: some will desert him when they find his call and his teaching too difficult (6:60–64). But the dogged witness of the disciples is that Jesus has the words of eternal life (6:68). And it is precisely because Jesus can speak life into death that he can ultimately be trusted in the midst of the grieving, and even in the hopelessness and despair, that may accompany the darkness of death.

The story shares similarities with the Synoptic accounts of the healing of the centurion's servant (Matt 8:5–13; Luke 7:1–10). Both the Synoptic and

Johannine accounts involve a healing at a distance, effected through Jesus' word, of someone dear to an important official.[204] In the Synoptic account, the official is a centurion who petitions Jesus to heal his servant or slave (*pais*, Matt 8:5; *doulos*, Luke 7:2), yet he insists that Jesus need not come to his house, because he acknowledges that Jesus has the power simply to speak and what he says will be done. Jesus lauds the man's faith, and the servant is healed. In John, the official begs Jesus to come to his house (4:47) in order to heal his son; but Jesus expresses no admiration of the man's faith (4:48). Still, the man believes Jesus' promise that his son will live, and in the end he believes in Jesus himself. While both Synoptic and Johannine accounts focus, in their own ways, on the power of Jesus' word to heal, the particular emphasis in the Gospel of John falls on the power of Jesus' word to give life. That point will be taken up in the subsequent lengthy discourse in the next chapter, which emphasizes Jesus' divinely given prerogative to give life.

> **4:43** After two days he went from there to Galilee. **44** For Jesus himself
> had testified that a prophet has no honor in his own country. **45** So then
> when he came to Galilee, the Galileans received him, having seen all that
> he had done in Jerusalem at the feast, for they themselves had gone to
> the feast. **46** Then he came again to Cana in Galilee, where he had made
> the water wine.
>
> And at Capernaum there was an official whose son was ill. **47** When
> this official heard that Jesus had come from Judea to Galilee, he went to
> him and asked him to come down and heal his son, for he was about to
> die.
>
> **48** Then Jesus said to him, "Unless you see signs and wonders, you will
> not believe."
>
> **49** The official said to Jesus, "Sir, come before my child dies."
>
> **50** Jesus said to him, "Go. Your son will live." The man believed the
> word that Jesus spoke to him and went. **51** And as he was on his way, his
> servants met him, saying, "Your child lives!" **52** Then he asked them at
> what hour his son had started to get better. They said to him, "His fever
> left him at the seventh hour."
>
> **53** Then his father knew that it was at that hour when Jesus had said,
> "Your son will live." And he and his whole household believed. **54** This
> was the second sign that Jesus did after coming from Judea to Galilee.

[4:43–45] "After two days" Jesus journeys from Samaria to Cana in Galilee, where he receives a welcome from the Galileans who had seen what he did at

204. See the account of R. Hanina b. Dosa's healing of the son of R. Gamaliel at a distance; it has stronger affinities to John's account than to the Synoptic account (see *b. Ber.* 34b).

the feast. "After two days" may simply refer to a short time, yet it picks up the earlier note that Jesus stayed with the Samaritans two days at Sychar (v. 40). The "feast" must refer to the Passover (cf. 2:13, 23), which is the only "feast" mentioned in John to this point. "All that he had done in Jerusalem" includes the temple cleansing (2:13–22) but likely also has in view other deeds, not narrated in John (2:23). Yet John's comments here are puzzling at best, because they suggest that Jesus went to Galilee (4:43; cf. 4:1–3) apparently expecting he would receive no honor, "for Jesus himself testified that a prophet has no honor in his own country" (4:44). This statement seems to explain why Jesus should be rejected in Galilee, if that is indeed "his own country." In that light, the response of the Galileans (4:45) is then quite puzzling: "So then [*oun*] when he came to Galilee, the Galileans *welcomed* him, having seen all that he had done in Jerusalem at the feast, for they too had gone to the feast." Because of the difficulty of reconciling Jesus' expected rejection in "his own country" (v. 44) with the actual welcome he receives (v. 45), many interpreters have concluded that in John, Jesus' "own country" cannot be Galilee, where he *does* receive honor, but Judea, where he does not.[205] But that explanation falters on the facts that (1) John assumes that Jesus is a Nazarene and a Galilean (1:45–46; 2:1; 7:1–9, 41–44, 52; 18:5, 7; 19:19); and (2) Jesus comes to Galilee not from Judea, but from Samaria.

The contrast may well lie not between the receptions that Jesus receives in Judea and Galilee respectively, but between those offered him in Samaria and Galilee. Jesus was well received in Samaria. Initially Jesus was welcomed in Galilee, yet his reception there ends not in acclamation, but in the murmuring of the people and desertion of some of his disciples (6:66). John's comment echoes his earlier statement that Jesus "came to his own home, but his own people did not welcome him" (1:11). The reader who remembers that statement will not expect that the initial welcome of the Galileans will endure, any more than would the initial belief of those who saw his signs in Jerusalem (see 2:23–25).[206]

[46–50] While in Galilee, Jesus encounters the royal official. "Royal official" translates *basilikos*, a word that actually means "royal," and occurs only here in the New Testament (vv. 46, 49). It could therefore refer to a member of the royal (Herodian) family or to an official in Herod's court. It is not clear whether the man is a Jew, but he is not explicitly identified as a Roman or a

205. Some think Galilee is Jesus' "own country" (in 4:44), e.g., R. Brown 1966; Bultmann 1971; Schnackenburg; others say it refers to Judea, e.g., Barrett; Dodd 1963; Hoskyns; Lindars; D. M. Smith 1999.

206. Michaels argues that this statement has in view Jesus' itinerant ministry and essentially means that a prophet cannot stay in any town or village long enough to make it his hometown (cf. Luke 4:43). In *Did.* 11.5, a false prophet may be recognized as such if he stays in one place more than two days.

centurion, and in any case his identity plays no role in this story as it does in the similar accounts of the other Gospels (Matt 8:5–13; Luke 7:1–10). His son (*huios*, vv. 46, 47, 50, 53; *paidion*, v. 49; *pais*, v. 51) is so ill with a fever (vv. 46, 52) that he is near death (vv. 47, 49); hence, the man has come to Jesus asking him to "come down" to heal his son.[207]

There are two curious aspects of this passage: (1) Why does Jesus initially seem to rebuke the official's request but without discernible motivation change his mind and accede to it in the end? Unlike the story of the healing of the centurion's servant in the Synoptic Gospels, there is no reference to the quality of the man's faith. It is not clear that John thinks Jesus is moved by the man's persistence; rather, by now evident as a trait of the Johannine Jesus, Jesus' reply does not seem related to the official's request at all (cf. 2:4; 3:3; 4:16). (2) The word "wonders" appears only here in John (4:48). "Signs and wonders" occurs frequently in the Old Testament accounts of the deliverance from Egypt (e.g., Exod 7:3; Deut 6:22; Jer 32:20–21), as well as in the Synoptics to designate the marvels that false messiahs will promise (Mark 13:22; Matt 24:24); it occurs regularly in Acts as a positive designation of the works of God, of Jesus, and of the apostles (4:30; 5:12; 14:3; 15:12; cf. Rom 15:19; 2 Cor 12:12; Heb 2:4). Jesus' response to the man, "Unless you see signs and wonders you will not believe" (v. 48), has been understood as a criticism or rejection of faith that is based on signs.[208] Why, then, does the account end with the official's believing when the sign is confirmed for him?

The two accounts of signs done at Cana share some features in common: both accounts are quite short, lacking explanatory discourses that clarify the sign's significance. Neither sign occasions hostility or opposition, as does virtually every other sign in John. As noted in the discussion of John 2:1–11, the accounts follow a similar pattern. (See Table 1.)

In brief, Jesus is informed of a situation that requires help or intervention (2:3; 4:47); he appears to rebuff or ignore the request (2:4; 4:48); the request is renewed in some form (2:5; 4:49); and Jesus then responds (2:7–8; 4:50). The sequence of request, rebuff, then (delayed) response demonstrates that it is not the initial request that immediately brings about Jesus' action. As stated above, this sequence narrates John's point, made more explicitly elsewhere, that Jesus acts as the Father tells him and shows him—but only as the Father, and no earthly petitioner, directs him to act. Yet the accounts themselves also make clear that it is the Father's will to intervene for the good of the petitioners. In those instances where Jesus seems initially to refuse to act, but then does act, the result is always for good: generous provision, healing, or the return of

207. Capernaum lies on the shore of the Sea of Galilee, about 640 feet below sea level, while Cana lies in the hills west of the sea; hence, the invitation to "come down."

208. For further discussion, see Excursus 3: "The Signs in the Gospel of John."

Table 1 Two Signs at Cana

The First Sign at Cana	The Second Sign at Cana
1. Jesus' mother reports that the host has run out of wine.	1. The official comes to Jesus with a request that his son be healed.
2. Jesus rebuffs his mother and ignores her request.	2. Jesus rebuffs or ignores the request.
3. Jesus' mother tells the servants to do whatever he tells them.	3. The official renews his petition
4. Jesus commands the servants, "Fill the jars."	4. Jesus commands the official, "Go. Your son will live."
5. The servants obey Jesus' word.	5. The man obeys Jesus' word.
6. The servants "who had drawn the water" know.	6. Corroboration by the servants who know when "his fever left him."
7. The disciples believe.	7. The official and his household believe.

the dead to life. Here John peculiarly dramatizes the dynamics of grace: what is needed by humans is unilaterally initiated by God.

In both accounts of signs done at Cana, Jesus' word brings about the desired result: he commands the servants to draw the water, and they discover it has turned to wine; he tells the official that his son will live, and the father discovers his son has been cured. Each account illustrates the power of Jesus' word and the faith evoked in response to that which Jesus' word accomplishes. Here Jesus speaks a word of promise to the royal official, the promised healing is carried out, and the official and his household come to believe in Jesus (v. 53; see also Acts 10:2; 11:14; 16:15, 31–34; 18:8). There is a parallel here to the story of the Samaritan woman and her people, for even as her faith preceded and led to the faith of all her village, so here the official's faith preceded and led to that of his household. In each case, Jesus' word becomes the occasion for faith in him. Furthermore, the woman and the official each believe because of Jesus' word. Although later the hour of the healing of the official's son will be corroborated, the man believes even before such verification.

[51–54] Jesus' promise, "Your son will live" (*ho huios sou zē*, 4:50, 53), echoes Elijah's words to the mother whose child lived when Elijah pleaded with God (*zē ho huios sou*, 1 Kgs 17:17–24, esp. v. 23 LXX). Elijah is said to "breathe into" (*enephysēsen*) the boy (v. 21).[209] After the child was restored to health upon Elijah's intercession, the woman acknowledged Elijah to be a man of God and "that the word of the LORD in your mouth is truth" (1 Kgs 17:24). Elsewhere John's presentation of Jesus reflects aspects of the ministry of Elijah (1:21, 25; cf. John 6:7–14; 2 Kgs 4:3–6, 42–44). Like Elijah, Jesus provides food for those who have none, and life to those who have none. He speaks, and the boy lives. Jesus' word has the power to give life. While the confession of Jesus as prophet, who speaks the word of God and so effects God's purposes, is true, it is never adequate in John; hence it gives way to recognition of Jesus as Savior of the world (4:19, 42), as Messiah (or king, 4:25, 29; 6:14–15), as Lord and Son of Man (9:17, 35, 38). Still, in drawing the lines between Elijah and Jesus, John demonstrates that the life-giving powers of the Father, given to the Son, are the same life-giving powers that God has exercised throughout Israel's history. The story of God's life-giving work in the world does not begin with Jesus, even if it comes to its dramatic climax here.

This is "the second sign,"[210] or perhaps "the second sign that Jesus did after coming from Judea to Galilee." These are the only two signs that are numbered; both are done while Jesus is at Cana (2:11; 4:46), the home of Nathanael (21:2), who is invited to "come and see" whether "anything good" can come out of Nazareth (1:46) and is then promised that he will see "greater things" (1:51). The signs are two examples of those deeds that comprise "the greater things" that Nathanael will see and that bear witness to Jesus in order to lead people to believe (cf. the comment on 1:51). Just so, the Lord provided two signs to Moses so that the Israelites might believe that the Lord indeed appeared to him: the changing of Moses' staff into a serpent and of Moses' healthy hand into one white as snow (Exod 4:4–9). God gave Moses two signs, with the assurance that if the Israelites did not believe the first sign, they might believe the second. If, however, neither of these suffice, yet more signs will be provided (Exod 4:8–9). Jesus' two signs at Cana do lead people to faith: the disciples believe (John 2:11); the official and all his household come to faith (4:53). Although these two signs do lead some to believe, there will be still more signs, to bear witness to Jesus so that all might believe in him.

The next section of the Gospel of John (chs. 5–12) in many ways constitutes its narrative and christological center. But the groundwork has been laid in the first four chapters of the Gospel. First, Jesus has been identified in various ways, including Word, Son of God, Lamb of God who takes away the sin of the world, Messiah, King of Israel, the one promised in the Scriptures, prophet, the one

209. For the same word describing the breath of life, see Gen 2:7; Ezek 37:9–10; Wis 15:11; John 20:22.

210. See the comments on 2:23–25 and Excursus 3: "The Signs in the Gospel of John."

who baptizes with the Spirit, the bridegroom, Son of Man, and one who does signs that reveal both God's presence with him and his own glory. Just how these various designations appropriately belong to Jesus will be spelled out in the Gospel by means of signs, discourses, and dialogues, and especially in the christologically dense central section of the Gospel (chs. 5–12).

Second, Jesus has begun to gather the children of God (1:12–13; 3:3–8; 11:52). Having come to "his own," he has called disciples to follow him. In his first sign, he also manifests his glory as the one who provides abundantly for his people, with the result that his disciples "believe in him," thus completing the narratives of their calling. The disciples have begun to see "the heavens opened" in Jesus, but they do not yet fully grasp what that means, nor will they do so until after his resurrection and the giving of the Spirit.

Third, the Spirit plays a significant role both in the narrative of these first four chapters and in the characterization of Jesus and his gifts. John the Baptist promises one who will baptize or purify with the Spirit; that Spirit "remains" on Jesus (1:32) who "takes away the sin of the world" (1:29) and so gives life. Subsequently Jesus informs Nicodemus and all Israel with him that the time has come for God's renewing work through the Spirit, so that they may live: all must be "begotten anew" as God's children, by the power of the Spirit from above. Now Jesus promises "living water" that gives eternal life. Descent from flesh and blood, from Jacob and Joseph, do not guarantee entrance into God's life. But God, through his Spirit, wills to bring all into that life-giving realm of light.

And finally, the hallmark of this new people of God is that they offer true worship to him. The dispute between Samaritans and Jews over the proper place to worship God brings this first section of the Gospel to a close. Jesus does not settle the long-running dispute in favor of either the Samaritans or the Jews. Instead, he speaks of the coming time when true worshipers of his Father will not locate their worship on either Mount Gerizim, as did the Samaritans, nor in the temple of Jerusalem, as did the Jews. For the time is coming when the temple of the Jews will be destroyed by the Romans, even as the temple of the Samaritans was destroyed by the Jewish ruler John Hyrcanus. In that hour, true worship will occur in a temple that has been raised up, never to be destroyed again: that temple is the risen Lord. The Messiah's people, including Jews and Samaritans alike, will not need even a purified temple of stone, for the Spirit of God who has created them to be "children of God" also quickens them to worship in that true temple of God.

John 5:1–12:50
The Life-Giving Son of God

The second main section of John (chs. 5–12) presents Jesus as the Son of God, who brings life and light to the world. Through Jesus' work and word, the God who created the world continues to sustain that world in life and to give the light that leads to life, work that brings glory to God. Jesus' words and actions are resolutely oriented toward glorifying God because they are resolutely oriented toward bringing life to God's world.

This section of John is distinguished by several features. First, there are richly textured theological assertions regarding Jesus' identity as the Son who has and offers God's life. Jesus' claim to exercise God's unique prerogative to give life elicits the charges of arrogance and blasphemy (5:18; 10:33). Thus initial enthusiastic response to Jesus (2:23–25; 6:2, 14–15), and even benign misunderstanding of him (3:1–10; 4:7–15), will now give way to open hostility. Jesus claims too much. His climactic sign, the raising of Lazarus, most fully manifests Jesus' identity as the life-giving Son yet leads the Jerusalem authorities to seek his death.

Second, major Jewish feasts play an important role in setting forth Jesus' identity. The Gospel correlates what Jesus has done and said with the significance of the Jewish holy day or feast (Sabbath, Passover, Tabernacles) that provides the setting for those deeds and words. John's exposition of Jesus' signs draws on Scripture and Jewish interpretive traditions to show that Jesus is the one through whom the God of Israel now acts to provide life and light both for his people Israel and for all the world. The story of Israel's God has always been intended to give light and lead to life for all peoples.

Third, the portrait of Jesus is painted not only on the canvas of Israel's festivals, but also on the larger canvas of the creation; indeed, built into the festivals is gratitude for God's creation and sustenance. In these chapters one sees most fully how the Word of God, who was in the beginning with God and through whom the world was created, restores and heals his suffering creation. Jesus gives a man the power to walk (5:8, 9, 11, 12), supplies hungry people with ordinary, daily bread (6:1–15), and uses his own saliva and the dust of the earth to give sight to a blind man. In short, the agent of the world's creation, the very Word of God, uses the stuff of this creation for the benefit of its inhabitants.

Finally, these chapters record the first of Jesus' "I am" sayings with predicates, such as bread of life, resurrection, way, and truth (6:35; 8:12, 58; 9:5; 10:7, 9, 11, 14; 11:25). Again, these sayings reveal Jesus as the one who brings God's life (6:35; 10:7, 11; 11:25) and light (8:12; 9:5) to the world. Through these self-revelatory statements, Jesus sweeps away misunderstandings (6:35), explains his identity (10:7, 9, 11, 14; 8:12; 9:5), and redirects expectations (11:25). Indeed, without Jesus' revelation, he will remain unknown. Without his corrective word, he will be misunderstood. But while Jesus' revelatory words sometimes lead to enlightenment and faith (8:12; 9:5), they may also lead to outright rejection of what he has claimed (8:58–59).

At the end of this section, Jesus' public ministry draws to a close. Jesus will do no more signs such as healing the sick and dying, feeding the multitude, opening the eyes of the blind, and raising the dead. But the work that brings glory to God and life to the world has not ended (12:37–50). That work will now take a different form, as the good shepherd prepares to lay down his life for the sheep. Anticipating his death, Jesus will turn to his own disciples and prepare them for his imminent departure and absence from them (chs. 13–17).

5:1–47 The Life-Giving Prerogatives of the Son: A Sabbath Healing

Jesus' healing of a paralyzed man on the Sabbath serves as the occasion for the demonstration and discussion of Jesus' God-given authority to give life and to judge. In spite of the biblical claims that God rested on the Sabbath (Gen 2:2–3), contemporary Jewish interpreters asserted that God continued his work of sustaining life on the Sabbath. Jesus claims God's prerogative to work rather than rest on the Sabbath, because of the authority granted to him by God. Furthermore, even as Jesus shares God's prerogative to work on the Sabbath day, he also shares other divine powers that belong to God alone: the power to give life and the right to judge all things. On his own, Jesus "can do nothing" (5:19, 30). But he has been authorized by God to judge and to give life, and in doing so he acts in full harmony with the will of the Father, doing only what the Father commissions him to do. God's work is to bring healing and sight, life and light, to the world, which is imperiled by darkness and death. This is precisely the shape and scope of the authority and power that the Father has given to the Son, the work of God that the Son has come to accomplish.

5:1–18 Jesus Heals a Man on the Sabbath

On the Sabbath day Jesus heals a man who cannot walk. Later the healed man is charged with violating Torah's injunctions by carrying his mat on the Sabbath. When the man tells his accusers that it was Jesus who told him to do so, they turn from questioning him to pursuing Jesus, charging him with violating the Sabbath. "The Jews" challenge the man's perceived violation of the Sabbath day, but Jesus bears the brunt of the challenge and must answer for the apparent breach of Sabbath law. Elsewhere in John, those whom Jesus has healed, taught, or called do bear witness to him, recounting and interpreting what he has done (1:32, 41, 45; 3:28–30; 9:15; 11:45–46). But here the man's actions are somewhat ambiguous. By reporting Jesus to the authorities, he has not only borne witness to Jesus' power to heal, but he has also (inadvertently?) become the occasion of escalating hostility toward Jesus. At a later time Jesus says that the disciples will be treated with hostility because of him (15:20–21); here Jesus is treated with hostility because of the claims and actions of others, whether they believe in him and are his disciples, or whether they are only somewhat more distantly attached to him.

5:1 After that there was a festival of the Jews, so Jesus went up to Jeru-
salem. 2 There is a pool by the Sheep Gate in Jerusalem;[a] this is called
"Bethzatha"[b] in Hebrew; it has five porticoes. 3 And there lay a great mul-
titude of invalids—blind, lame, and paralyzed.[c] 5 One man there had been
ill thirty-eight years. 6 When Jesus saw him lying down and knew that he
had been there a long time, he said to him, "Do you want to get well?"

7 The invalid answered, "Lord, I don't have anyone to put me in the
pool when the water is troubled. Even as I am going, someone else gets in
ahead of me. 8 Jesus said to him, "Get up, pick up your mat, and walk!" 9
And at once the man was made well, and he took up his mat and walked.

Now that day was the Sabbath. 10 So the Jews said to the man who had
been healed, "It is the Sabbath. You are not permitted to carry your mat."
11 But he replied to them, "The one who made me well said to me, "Pick
up your mat and walk." 12 They asked him, "Who is the man who said
to you, 'Pick up your mat and walk'?" 13 The man who had been healed
said that he did not know who it was, for Jesus had withdrawn, as there
was a crowd in that place.

14 After this, Jesus found him in the temple and said to him, "Look.
You have been made well. Sin no more, so that nothing worse will hap-
pen to you." 15 The man went and told the Jews that it was Jesus who had
made him well.

16 And this is why the Jews were pursuing Jesus, because he had done
these things on the Sabbath. 17 But Jesus said to them, "My Father is
working even now and I am working."

18 Therefore the Jews sought all the more to kill him, because he not
only broke the Sabbath, but he called God his own father, making himself
equal to God.

a. In the phrase *epi tē probatikē kolymbēthra* , the dative *probatikē* ("sheep") is taken to modify an implied noun, here "gate" (*pylē*): RSV, NIV, NRSV, and ESV, following Neh 3:1; 12:39; hence, "There is by the Sheep [Gate] a pool that is called Bethzatha."

b. There are a number of textual variants for the name *Bēthzatha* (א Eusebius), including *Bēthesda* (A C), perhaps derived from the etymology "House of [Divine] Mercy"); *Bēthsaida* (𝔓$^{66c, 75}$ B), perhaps a scribal assimilation to Bethsaida (1:44); and *Belzetha* (D), a variant spelling of *Bēthzatha*. Josephus (*J.W.* 2.328, 529–30; 5.149–51) speaks of a part or suburb of Jerusalem called *Betheza/Bezetha*, known as "the New City."

c. John 5:4 is missing in a variety of MSS, including 𝔓$^{66, 75}$ א B C* D W^{supp} 33 it$^{d, l, q}$. It is marked by asterisks or obeli, indicating that it is an addition in a number of Greek witnesses. It contains a number of terms otherwise missing from John or the entire NT (*kata kairon, embainō, ekdexomai, katexomai, kinēsis, tarachē, dēpote*, and *nosēma*; Metzger 179). Hence it is recognized as a secondary addition explaining the man's excuse (5:7).

[5:1–2] Throughout John, Jesus is found in Jerusalem at the time of the feasts (2:13; 7:10; 10:23; see comments on 2:13).[1] Since Jesus' presence at Passover and Tabernacles is mentioned elsewhere in John, the unnamed festival could be Pentecost, the third pilgrimage feast. But the discourse that follows develops themes that arise because the occasion is a Sabbath. The pool with five porticoes corresponds to one excavated northeast of the temple grounds, near the Sheep Gate and in the Jerusalem vicinity called Betheza by Josephus. Although now buried beneath later construction, there are actually two large pools, trapezoidal in shape, surrounded by colonnades on each side and divided by a fifth colonnade.[2] Archaeologists suggest that it was a *miqveh*,[3] a pool used for ritual immersion and purification in Jesus' day; later, under the Roman emperor Hadrian (117–138 C.E.), it was dedicated to Asclepius, the god of healing, pointing to its reputation as a place of healing.

[3–5] John's description of the man's helplessness emphasizes the lack of resources at his disposal over against Jesus' initiative and the healing and life-giving power of Jesus' word (4:50, 53; 11:43). The man lies among a great multitude of invalids (v. 3);[4] he has been ill for thirty-eight years (v. 5); and as he tells Jesus, "I have no person [*anthrōpon ouk echō*] to put me in the pool" (v. 7). The comment may be read ironically since Jesus will heal the man by the authority and power of God. Whereas in the Synoptic Gospels people frequently approach Jesus with entreaties for healing and help, John portrays

1. *M. Ḥag.* 1:1 stipulates who must go to Jerusalem for the Feasts of Unleavened Bread, Weeks, and Tabernacles, thus fulfilling Deut 16:16.

2. See further von Wahlde 2006, 560–66.

3. Meyers and Chancey 132. Hundreds of such *miqva'ot* have been found throughout Israel, indicating the widespread concern for purity in late Second Temple Judaism; both the pools of Bethesda and Siloam, which figure in a healing of Jesus, were apparently *miqva'ot*.

4. John describes the man, who is apparently lame (*chōlōn*, 5:3) or paralyzed, as *asthenōn* (cf. 5:3, 5, 7), "weak" or "invalid."

Jesus as either taking the initiative in approaching those in need (5:6; 6:5), disengaging from requests for help (2:4; 4:48), or delaying response to such requests (11:6). Jesus heals in his time and in keeping with the Father's will. And precisely for those reasons, Jesus does indeed heal those in need.

[6–9a] Jesus is aware of the man's situation (v. 6). Jesus' query, "Do you want to be healed?"[5] has often—wrongly—been taken as an indictment of the man's lack of genuine interest in being healed, and hence the cause of his problems. But the man's explanation of his circumstances, and the reference to his inability to get into the pool when the water is troubled, imply an affirmative response: of course he wants to be healed! The fact that for thirty-eight years the man has languished, without assistance, indicts his society, not him. His description of the agitation of the water (v. 7) shows how the healing offered at the pool was understood: whenever the water bubbled or stirred, whoever was able to get into the water would be healed.[6] Perhaps the man imagines that Jesus is offering to help him into the pool.

In any case, Jesus does not wait for the man's answer to his question. Instead, Jesus offers a different avenue for the man's healing: God's agent seeks out precisely those *without* the ability to help themselves, those who are neglected and bypassed by others: those who are dying, cannot see, or cannot walk. Jesus' command, "Get up, pick up your mat, and walk!" has the power to effect what neither human help nor sincere desire nor the unreliable stirring of the waters could do. It is not willpower, desire, or faith that the man lacks: none of these play a role in the man's healing. Whatever the man wants, Jesus wants him to be healed. Jesus' word has power to heal the one who cannot help himself: after thirty-eight years, the man is healed at once (cf. 4:53). Once again divine initiative addresses human need and, without any conditions attached, offers healing: a sign of the fullness of God's grace and truth (1:14, 16).

[9b–13] This is the first reference to Sabbath and the first of two healings on the Sabbath in John (cf. 7:22–23; 9:14, 16). However, it is not Jesus' healing but the man's compliance to Jesus' command to carry his mat that elicits the accusation that the man is doing what is not permitted on the Sabbath (5:10). Both here and in John 9, the authorities initially challenge the one who has been healed, rather than Jesus himself.[7] Jesus' command to carry his mat implicates him in "breaking the Sabbath," and attention now turns to Jesus.

According to biblical injunctions, work is forbidden on the Sabbath.[8] Sabbath keeping is a mark of faithfulness to God's commandments (Isa 56:2, 6;

5. Cf. the somewhat different questions in Matt 20:32; Mark 10:51; Luke 18:41.

6. Although the man does not say that one must get into the water first, the textual variant (v. 4) makes that point. Yet it may well be that the man simply means he cannot get into the water at all.

7. Cf. Matt 9:1–3, 11, 14; Mark 2:16, 18, 23–24; Luke 5:30, 33; 6:1–2.

8. Exod 20:8–11; 31:15–16; 35:2–3; Lev 23:3; 25:2; Deut 5:12–15; Jer 17:21–22, 27.

58:13). A few biblical passages specify what constitutes prohibited "work": fire may not be kindled (Exod 35:3); the land may not be plowed, planted, or harvested (Lev 25:2), nor may animals be put to work (Deut 5:12–15). On the Sabbath one must not gather sticks (Num 15:32), buy or sell (Neh 13:19–22), "bear a burden" or bring it in by the gates of Jerusalem (Jer 17:21–22). This last prohibition covers the man's act of carrying his mat.[9] The healed man is doing "what was not permitted" on the Sabbath; because Jesus has commanded him to carry the mat, Jesus is charged with "breaking the Sabbath."[10] It is Jesus' command, in clear violation of the law, that elicits criticism of him. In the discourse that follows, Jesus argues that by his actions he does not violate the Sabbath since he may work on that day without violating it, even as God does. Jesus, in other words, shares the divine prerogative to work on the Sabbath day.

The belief that God works on the Sabbath can be found in various sources in Second Temple Judaism.[11] Philo, for example, argued that according to the Scriptures (Gen 2:2), God himself did not rest (*epausato*), because God "never ceases making," but God "caused to rest" (*katepausen*) that which he had made (*Leg*. 1.5–6, 16–18).[12] God does not "rest" from his divine creative work, but he does enjoin rest on the Sabbath and participates in it by causing his creation to rest.[13] Without reference to the Sabbath or issues of rest, the *Epistle of Aristeas* (2d c. B.C.E.) asserts that God is continually at work in everything (210), a reflection of the Greek philosophical opinion that God is "ceaselessly active."[14] In short, God works at all times; God may work on the Sabbath day. Jesus claims that prerogative.

[14–15] Jesus then "found" the man in the temple, even as he later finds the blind man who had been healed after he is "driven out" (9:35). In each case, Jesus seeks those whom he has healed in order to press the conversation further, so that they more fully grasp the implications of their healing for understanding Jesus' identity.

9. In the Mishnaic tractate *Šabbat*, 39 classes of work are forbidden on the Sabbath, including taking anything from one domain to another (7:2).

10. Some have interpreted "he broke [or, 'loosed'] the Sabbath" to mean "he abolished the Sabbath"; but in light of the following discourse that vindicates Jesus' authority to work on a day of rest, that connotation is stronger than John intends.

11. See *Jub*. 2.17–33, where Israel alone *keeps* the Sabbath with God "in heaven and on earth."

12. Elsewhere Philo contends that only God truly rests, that rest is not inactivity, but rather "a working with absolute ease, without toil and suffering" (*Cher*. 87).

13. In other and later rabbinic traditions, God carries no burden beyond his own dwelling (understood to be heaven and earth) or to a distance greater than his own stature; therefore his work falls within permissible limits on the Sabbath (*Exod. Rab*. 30.6–9). Similar to the argument in Philo, there is discussion of the kind of work that God did on the Sabbath ("he did not rest from work on the unrighteous and righteous"; *Gen. Rab*. 11.10), as well as denials that God rested at all (*Mekilta* on Exod 20:11 [*Baḥodesh* 7], perhaps to avoid anthropomorphism).

14. On this point, see Dodd 1953, 20.

Jesus exhorts the healed man to "sin no more"[15] so that "nothing worse" will happen (5:14), but he does so only after he has healed the man: neither the man's repentance nor faith in Jesus is a precondition of his being healed. The man has shown some response to Jesus: he responds to Jesus' command to pick up his mat. In John, since sin is nearly defined as unbelief, Jesus may be warning the man regarding the judgment that follows sin, while inviting him to confess faith in Jesus (8:24). But no final account of the man is given.

The Johannine story has a close parallel to the account of Jesus' healing the paralytic in Mark 2, where Jesus both pronounces forgiveness of the man's sin and commands him to walk (cf. Sir 38:9–15; Jas 5:15–16). While some New Testament passages link sin and sickness, not all do; there is no reference to the forgiveness of sins in most Gospel miracle accounts, including the only previous account in John, the healing of the official's son; conversely, in narratives where there is forgiveness of sin (cf. Luke 7:21, 47–48), there often is no reference to healing or sickness. One cannot simply assume that sin produces sickness or that sickness is always the result of sin. While Jesus admonishes the man to stop sinning, warning that "something worse" might happen to the man, the Gospel makes it clear that God's work through Jesus is to heal and to bring light and life into the world.

[16–18] Jesus' various actions on the Sabbath[16] lead "the Jews" to "pursue" or "persecute" him, that is, to seek his death (v. 18).[17] Quite simply, Jesus' teaching has led to violation of the law to honor the Sabbath by refraining from work. Jesus defends himself with the cryptic assertion, "My Father is working even now and I am working," which only exacerbates the problem: he claims not only that God himself has authorized his work, but also that he stands in a distinctive relationship to God, who is his Father. In claiming to imitate God, his Father, he has made himself "equal to God," doing what no human being ought to do (cf. 10:30, 33 and comments there). Jesus' claims are offensive, and consequently the Gospel now sounds the ominous note of the threat against Jesus' life, a threat that will be repeated (7:1, 19–20, 25; 8:22, 37, 40) until it is finally carried out in Jesus' crucifixion.

In biblical and Jewish literature we find a catalog of the empires and rulers who forgot their proper place and claimed divine prerogatives for themselves by making presumptuous claims of one sort or another, including Pharaoh and Egypt (Exod 5:2; Ezek 29–32); Tyre (Ezek 28); Assyria (Isa 10:7–17); Nebuchadnezzar and Babylon (Isa 14:13–14; 47:6–8; Jdt 3:8; 6:2); Antiochus IV

15. *Mēketi hamartane*, 5:14; 8:11; this present imperative can be translated "stop sinning."

16. "He had done" (5:16) translates an imperfect tense (*epoiei*). If the imperfect indicates the kinds of things (*tauta*) Jesus did, one could translate, "he was doing these kinds of things."

17. *Diōkō* (5:16) can mean "pursue, chase," with either positive or negative connotations, or more strongly, "harass, persecute"; "pursuit with intent to harm" is the connotation of the word in this context (cf. 15:20).

Epiphanes (Dan 11:36–39; 1 Macc 1:10); Pompey (*Pss. Sol.* 2.28–32); Caligula (Philo, *Legat.* 22, 74–80, 93–97, and esp. 118, 162; Josephus, *Ant.* 19.4); Nero (*Sib. Or.* 5.33–35, 137–54, 214–21); and Herod Agrippa (Josephus, *Ant.* 19.345, 347; Acts 12:22). The later *Midrash Rabbah* offers a comment on Exod 7:1, "I have made you like God to Pharaoh," excoriating five biblical kings and empires who endeavored to usurp for themselves the prerogatives or status properly belonging to God (the prince of Tyre, Nebuchadnezzar, Pharaoh, Joash [2 Chr 24:17]). These individuals are rebuked for accepting or demanding veneration of some sort, for claiming divine prerogatives or power, including that of creation and sovereignty, or for presumptuous arrogance and failure to acknowledge the supremacy and power of God and the limits of human life.

Similarly, according to 2 Maccabees the dying Antiochus IV learns, through divine punishment, that it is "right to be subject to God, and no mortal should think that he is equal to God" (*mē thnēton onta isothea phronein*, 9:8–12). Philo describes the desire to be "equal with gods" (*isos einai theoi*) as a kind of atheism, as being "without God" (*atheos*), since such a desire or claim fails to recognize one's proper position with respect to God (*Leg.* 1.49). Caligula's desire for divine honors represents "the most grievous impiety" (*Legat.* 118).[18] To claim to be "equal to God," to act as though one had God's prerogatives, or to fail to take one's proper place as a human being before God, is to set oneself up as a rival to the one God, as a second deity alongside the one true God (cf. 2 Thess 2:4; Rev 13:1–6).[19] Autonomy and self-divinization are two sides of the same coin

There is a similar criticism of human presumption in non-Jewish sources. The famous maxim, "Know thyself," attributed to the oracle of Delphi and often put on the lips of Socrates by Plato, was taken as an admonition not to overstep one's bounds.[20] Apollodorus writes of the arrogance of Salmoneus, who in his impiety (*asebeia*) wanted "to make himself equal to Zeus" by substituting the sacrifices to Zeus with sacrifices to himself; he was struck by lightning.[21] Dio

18. For Philo, nothing is equal to God (*oude ison autou*, in *Sacr.* 92); "God himself is equal to and like himself" (*isos gar autos heautō kai homoios ho theos*, in *Aet.* 43); "nothing is equal or better than God" (*oute de ison oute kreissōn esti theou*; in *Leg.* 2.3); nothing is more hostile than the one "who in his arrogance attributed to himself what belongs to God" (*Cher.* 77).

19. Later rabbis chastised those who in any way claimed that there were "two powers in heaven," whether two gods (as the gnostics believed) or the Messiah (thus, Christians) enthroned at God's right hand. On the "two powers" of God: see esp. Segal 1977; Urbach 448–61.

20. Hence "Know thyself!" and "Be temperate" (the other well-known proverb of Delphi) were equivalent (Plato, *Charm.* 164D). Plato's *Republic* includes a story about a shepherd who found a gold ring that made him invisible (2.359e). Using the ring, he seduced the king's wife and killed the king to possess his kingdom. He thus conducted himself as the equal of a god (*isotheos*; 2.360c), determining his own conduct without any external constraints.

21. Pseudo-Apollodorus, *Lib.* 1.9.7. Attributed to Apollodorus of Alexandria (2d c. B.C.E.), *The Library* is now thought to be a second-century-C.E. compilation.

Cassius criticized Gaius (Caligula) for ordering temples and sacrifices in his honor, impersonating the gods, and calling himself "Jupiter."[22] Human beings who wanted divine honors were deemed arrogant and worthy of punishment, even as they were in the Jewish world. If non-Jewish readers read these charges against Jesus, they would likely understand them to include impiety toward God, or the gods, coupled with the arrogance of claiming a status not rightfully his. In short, those of Jewish and Gentile backgrounds would hear the charge that Jesus made himself "equal to God" in quite similar ways: a human being has acted inappropriately and arrogantly.

The charge against Jesus is not simply that he referred to God as his Father; the New Testament tradition makes it clear that human beings can know God as Father (e.g., Matt 6:9; Luke 11:2; Rom 8:15; Gal 4:6; 1 John 3:1–10). Rather, in Jesus' assertion that God is his "own Father" (*patera idion*, 5:18),[23] he claims a distinctive relationship with God precisely by his right to exercise divine prerogatives and power. But as the following long discourse (5:19–47) makes clear, Jesus does not "make himself equal to God" by seizing a status or exercising powers not rightfully his (cf. Phil 2:6–7). Rather, he exercises his authority because God has granted it to him as the Son (5:25–26), and he exercises it in healing a man in need. This is the shape of divine authority demonstrated in Jesus.

5:19–30 The Authority of the Son

The rest of chapter 5 contains this Gospel's most theologically packed account of Jesus' identity with respect to God. The discourse counters the charge that Jesus "makes himself equal to God" (5:18), or that Jesus has set himself up as a rival to the one true God by claiming God's prerogatives as his own. In response, Jesus contends that the Son does not act independently of the Father, but always and only does the work that God has given him to do (5:19). The Son is dependent on the Father. Furthermore, Jesus reaffirms the point that he carries out the divine work of giving life and judging because the Father has granted him the power and authority to do this work (5:21–22, 26–27). Jesus does not *rival* God's power; rather, he *exercises* God's power. Overall, the thrust of the argument for Jesus' dependence on God and authorization by God is an argument for the unity of the Father and Son: not only do Father and Son work in harmony, but the Father also works through the Son and by means of the Son, both to judge and to give life. As Jesus will later say, "The Father and I are one" (10:30).

22. Dio Cassius, *Hist.* 59.26.5; 28.5–6.

23. *Idion* is likely emphatic in 5:18; but see John 1:41: Andrew found "his own [*idion*] brother, Simon," where *idion* is superfluous.

5:19 Jesus answered, "Amen, amen, I tell you that the Son cannot do any-
thing on his own, but only what he sees the Father doing. For whatever
the Father does, the Son also does.[a] **20** For the Father loves the Son and has
shown him all that he does. Indeed, he will show him greater works than
these, that you all may marvel. **21** For even as the Father raises the dead
and makes them live, so also the Son makes alive whomever he wills.

22 For the Father judges no one, but rather has given all judgment to
the Son, **23** so that all may honor the Son even as they honor the Father.
Whoever does not honor the Son does not honor the Father who sent him.
24 Amen, amen, I say to you that the one who hears my word and believes
in the one who sent me has eternal life, and will not come into judgment,
but rather has passed from death to life. **25** Amen, amen, I say to you that
the hour is coming and now is when the dead will hear the voice of the
Son of God, and those who hear it will live. **26** For even as the Father has
life in himself, so also he has granted the Son to have life in himself. **27**
And he has given him authority to judge, because he is the Son of Man.

28 Do not marvel at this, for the hour is coming in which all those who
are in the tombs shall hear his voice **29** and shall come forth—those who
have done good to the resurrection of life, and those who have done evil
unto the resurrection of judgment. **30** I am not able to do anything on my
own; I judge as I hear, and my judgment is just, because I do not seek my
own will but rather the will of the one who sent me.

a. "Also" translates *homoiōs*, "also, likewise, in the same way." The Son not only does the kind of work the Father does; he also does the very work of the Father.

[5:19–21] Jesus opens his discourse with the emphatic statement, introduced by the doubled "amen" (cf. 1:51), that "the Son cannot do anything on his own"[24] (cf. 5:30). Jesus does not work independently of God; indeed, he cannot work without God's authority. Thus Jesus' argument for his dependence on the Father is implicitly an argument for his unity with the Father: the Son never works apart from the Father. Jesus further describes his relationship to God in a picture of a son imitating his father, perhaps as an apprentice who learns his father's trade or craft.[25] The son learns well because the father, in his love, shows or teaches the son all that he himself does. Jesus learns from the Father, sees what he is doing, and puts the Father's own work into practice. Words such as submission, obedience, or subordination do not aptly capture the point of the assertion that Jesus does "nothing on his own," which emphasizes rather Jesus' authority from God and unity in love with God.[26]

24. *Aph' heautou*, 5:19; cf. 5:30; 7:18; 10:18; 11:51; 15:4; 16:13.
25. Many commentators adopt this image, which comes from Dodd 1963, 386 n. 2.
26. Newbigin 66.

Typically, the Gospel underscores the far-ranging scope of Jesus' work: the Son does *all* (*panta*) that the Father does; the Son's subsequent works will be "greater" than those he has just done. Even as *all things* are created through the Word (1:3; cf. comments there), so the Father has given *all things* to the Son (*panta*, 5:20, 22; cf. 3:35; 6:39; 12:32; 13:3; 16:15): these claims lay the groundwork for Jesus' universal mission to all people (1:12; 6:40; 12:32).

The "greater works" are the Father's own work of raising the dead and giving them life (*egeirei tous nekrous kai zōopoiei*, v. 21).[27] Lazarus (12:1, 9, 17) and Jesus (2:22; 20:9; 21:4) are raised from the dead (*ek nekrōn*).[28] They come out of their graves. In these cases the verb is always "raise" (*egeirō*) or "rise up" (*anistēmi*, 20:9). Jesus speaks also of raising people *ek tou thanatou* ("from death"; cf. 5:24). To raise the dead means to bring dead bodies to life; to "give life" means to grant knowledge of God so that one may participate, forever, in God's own life (17:3). Not all the dead who are raised finally receive eternal life (5:29). Eternal life properly belongs to the time following the resurrection, but it is experienced in the present as fellowship with the life-giving God (17:3). Jesus has the twin powers to give eternal life (5:24–25) and to call the dead out of the tombs (v. 28); the latter power will be demonstrated in Jesus' raising of Lazarus, which in turn foreshadows and guarantees Jesus' power to grant eternal life.

In the Scriptures the power to give life uniquely characterizes God. The epithet "living God"[29] contrasts the living Lord who creates with those "dead idols" made by human hands.[30] The living God is the creator and source of life (Deut 32:39; 2 Kgs 5:7; Ps 36:9; Jer 2:13; 17:13; Ezek 37:1–4) and of all that is.[31] This living and life-giving God is the God of resurrection; the God who creates life is also the God who raises the dead to life.[32] In unity with the Father, Jesus exercises the unique divine power to give life.

27. The verb translated "gives life" (*zōopoiein*, 5:21) occurs 6 times in the LXX (Judg 21:14 [MS B]; 2 Kgs 5:7; Neh 9:6; Ps 70:20 [71:20 ET]; Eccl 7:12; Job 36:6) and 11 times in the NT, typically with reference to the future resurrection (John 5:21 [2×]; Rom 4:17; 8:11; 1 Cor 15:22, 36, 45; 1 Pet 3:18), but also with reference to the life-giving work of the Spirit (John 6:63; 2 Cor 3:6; Gal 3:21).

28. Lit., "from the dead ones"; the expression is common in the NT; see Acts 3:15; 4:10; 13:30; Rom 4:24; 6:4, 13. *Nekros* does not necessarily indicate physical death or a corpse; it can refer to a condition of dormancy or inactivity (Rom 7:8; 8:10).

29. Deut 5:26; Jer 10:10; cf. Ps 18:46; Dan 6:20, 26; 4:34; 12:7; Isa 48:12; Pss 41:13; 106:48. See now Feldmeier and Spieckerman.

30. See 1 Sam 17:26, 36; 2 Kgs 19:4, 16; Jer 10:8–10; 23:36; Deut 5:26; Josh 3:10; Pss 42:2; 84:2; Isa 40:18–20; 41:21–24; 44:9–20, 24; 45:16–22; 46:5–7.

31. Isa 40:28; 42:5; 44:24; 45:11–12; 48:12–13; cf. 42:5; 44:24; 45:11–12. For a fuller discussion of God as the one who creates and gives life, including the literature of Second Temple Judaism, see M. M. Thompson 2001, 74–76; cf. Bauckham 2008; Hurtado 2005a, 119–21.

32. See the connection in 2 Macc 7:23: "The Creator of the world, who shaped the beginning of humankind and devised the origin of all things, will in his mercy give life and breath back to you again" (cf. 2 Macc 14:46; Rom 4:17). For further discussion of "the two powers" of God, see comments on 20:28 below.

[22–24] Next Jesus introduces a second divine prerogative that he has been given by the Father: the power to judge[33] or to render a verdict that leads to life or death. Elsewhere Scripture also speaks of God's power to take life (2 Kgs 5:7; cf. Deut 32:39; 1 Sam 2:6), but John emphasizes the life-giving power of God in the face of death. While Jesus has been given the power of judgment, his mission is to save, not to condemn. God does delegate the power of judgment to others in the Scriptures (among many passages, see Gen 49:16; Exod 18:13, 22, 26). But in John the one who judges also has the power to determine who lives; the power of judgment is the power of life. And somewhat astonishingly, the Father has given the Son all authority to judge; the Father "judges no one" (5:22). Jesus' possession of *all* authority distinguishes him from other biblical or Jewish agents, such as kings, to exercise God-given authority in governing and judging.

Because Jesus carries out God's work of giving life and judging, it is appropriate in turn to honor (*timaō*) him even as one honors God. In John's view, failing to honor Jesus is failing to honor God.[34] The Old Testament commands to honor God (*timaō*) and to give him glory (*doxa*, Pss 29:1 [28:1 LXX] and 96:7 [95:7], *doxan kai timēn*) now also include Jesus.[35] Therefore, hearing the word of Jesus is linked to believing the Father who sent him (John 5:24; cf. 4:34 and comments there). For even as the Son does what he has learned to do from the Father, giving life to the dead, so he also speaks what he has heard from the Father, words that give life. Those who hear the word of Jesus "pass from death to life" (5:24) because he is the embodiment of the life-giving Word of God (1:1–3) and speaks the words of eternal life (6:68).

While the Father and Son have different roles—the Father teaches and shows the Son what he is to do—they merit the same honor, further testimony to their unity.[36] Cities or provinces of the Roman Empire often sought permission to offer "divine honors" to a living emperor, and from Augustus onward it was customary for the emperor to refuse such honors.[37] Here, strikingly, Jesus himself calls for such honors: not as an arrogant assertion of his "equality with God" but because of his unity with the Father who has entrusted his work to the Son. The Son gives life in unity with the Father who loves him. For this, the Son is honored as the Father is.

To receive eternal life signals that one has passed from death to life (cf. 1 John 3:14). John's view reflects the expectation of a judgment in conjunction with a general resurrection, when the dead are raised either to life or to

33. *Krinein*, "to judge, to condemn."

34. Hurtado (2003, 52, 363, 373) argues that *timaō* refers to the worship or honor given to a deity; see J. Schneider, *TDNT* 8:169–80.

35. For the conjunction of "glory and honor" owed to Jesus, see also 2 Pet 1:17; Heb 2:7, 9; 3:3.

36. See Neyrey 2007.

37. See Price 1984b, 72–74.

condemnation.[38] In the Gospel of John, the verdict that will be rendered at the final judgment will have already been determined: since the Father's judgment for life is rendered through the Son, those who abide in him have that life now.[39]

[25–30] Jesus explicates the shape of his life-giving work in two ways that, at first glance, might seem to be synonymous: he calls the dead to life (5:25) and brings the dead out of graves (5:28–29). Although these ideas are related, two different facets of Jesus' life-giving work are in view: his authority to bring people into fellowship with God, who is the source of all life; and his authority to call the dead out of their graves at the final resurrection and, at that time, declare the judgment that leads to life or to death. Jesus first states that "the hour is coming and now is, when the dead [*nekroi*] will hear the voice of the Son of God, and those who hear will live [*zēsousin*]." The Son of God, who has life, speaks the words that are spirit and life (6:63); therefore, those who hear him, who trust in him, have passed from death to life (v. 24) and have entered into fellowship with the very source of life, God himself, and so they "live" (v. 25). But Jesus will shortly speak of an hour that "is coming" but is not here. This is the hour of resurrection, when all who are "in the tombs" (*hoi en tois mnēmeiois*) will come out to the "resurrection of life" or the "resurrection of judgment" (*eis anastasin zōēs . . . eis anastasin kriseōs*, 5:28). Graphically, the two sets of assertions compare as follows:

Table 2 Resurrection and Life

5:25 The hour is coming and is now here	the dead [*nekroi*]	shall hear [*akousousin*] the voice of the Son of God	will live [*zēsousin*]
5:28–29 The hour is coming	all [*pantes*] those in the tombs [*hoi en tois mnēmeiois*]	shall hear [*akousousin*] his voice	will come out to the resurrection of life [*ekporeusontai . . . eis anastasin zōsin*] or of judgment

38. For the resurrection, see Dan 12:1–3; 2 Macc 7, esp. vv. 9–10, 14, 23, 29, 35–36; *Pss. Sol.* 2.31–35; 3.11–12; 13.6–12; 14.3–10; 15.10–13; *1 En.* 22–27 (esp. 22, 25); 102–5; *2 Bar.* 15.8; 21.25; 44.11–12; 49–51; 54.16; *4 Ezra* 5.41; 7.26–44 (with explicit mention of the Messiah in vv. 28–29, perhaps a Christian interpolation); Josephus, *J.W.* 2.156–63; *Ant.* 18.14 (portraying the Pharisaic view of judgment and resurrection).

39. The same contrast is found in John 3:16–19, where "eternal life" is the opposite of being judged, or condemned (Greek, *krinō/krisis*, 5:26–27, 29).

These subtle differences are not incidental. While in the present hour one may hear the voice of Jesus and so have eternal life or fellowship with God, the hour has not yet come for the *resurrection* (*anastasis*) of *all* (*pantes*) those who are in the tombs (5:28–29).[40] The reference to those in the graves "coming out" (5:29) is to the raising of all people in the future. Those who have heard the life-giving word (v. 24) and voice (v. 25) of the Son of God ("have done good") will live; they will experience the "resurrection of life" (v. 29). But those who have refused to hear that life-giving voice ("have done evil") emerge from the grave to judgment. That judgment is not further described. There is no description in John of punishment for the dead; the typical New Testament words for hell or hades do not appear. God's "wrath," or "judgment" (3:36; 5:29), leads to death.

"Resurrection" and "life" are thus not simply equivalent terms,[41] as is demonstrated by the fact that the resurrection can lead to life *or* judgment. Those who believe in Jesus have eternal life in the present; they have already received the verdict that leads to life (5:24), and through fellowship with God they participate in the blessings of eternal life with God (17:3). The fullness of that participation, however, comes with resurrection (5:28–29), which seals the verdict passed in the present. Those who believe in Jesus have life, as both present blessing and future promise, but they have not yet experienced resurrection.[42]

Jesus' authority to give life and to judge are further explained as God's "granting" these powers to him. In the statement "Even as the Father has life in himself, so he has granted the Son to have life in himself" (5:26), we find the epitome of John's Christology. God, the living Father, has no prior and external cause; now the Son is similarly said to "have life in himself." The Son has life as God does, but he has it because God has granted (or, "given," *edōken*) it to him. The first formulation ("life in himself") points to independence; the second formulation ("for the Father has granted him") points to dependence. The Father gives his own kind of life to the Son; the Son in turn gives life to the world.

John is often said to present Jesus as God's agent, along the lines of the rabbinic figure of the *shaliakh* (from "to send"). In later rabbinic texts, a *šālîaḥ*, "one who is sent," represents "the one who sent him" in a legally binding relationship, authorized to carry out a specific commission on behalf of the

40. The same juxtaposition between "life" and "resurrection" can be found in John 6:54: the one who (already) has eternal life will be raised at the last day; cf. 11:25–26. For recent discussion of the resurrection in John, see the collection of essays in Koester and Bieringer, with extensive bibliographies. See also Excursus 4: "Life and Eternal Life in John."

41. As some have argued: e.g., Bultmann 1971, 403; Schnackenburg 2:331.

42. So also Moloney 1996, 17; Talbert 126.

sender, so that "a *šālîaḥ* is as the one who sent him" (*m. Ber.* 5:5; *b. B. Meṣiʿa* 96a; *b. Ḥag.* 10b, 93b; *b. Menaḥ.* 93b; *b. Naz.*12b; *b. Qidd.* 42b, 43a). As God's *šālîaḥ*, Jesus has life in himself and can give it to others.[43] In many ways, Jesus does appear as God's *šālîaḥ*, God's sent one: he is sent by God and does the works of the Father, so that to hear him is to believe the Father, and to see him is to see the Father. The one who is sent is as the one who sent him. But John pushes toward a Christology that locates the distinctive work of Jesus not merely in the Father's authorization and commission given to him, but also in the Father's giving to him that life which he has as the eternally existent Word of God.[44] Such predications will compel later theological formulations in ontological terms. Here we have descriptions of what the Father and the Son *do*; yet *precisely as such*, these are also predications of who and what the Father and the Son *are*: life for the world.

God has given Jesus the power to judge "because he is the Son of Man."[45] "Son of Man" alludes to the one who is "like a son of man" (a human being) in Daniel, and to whom God *gives* dominion, glory, and kingship (Dan 7:13–14, 27). In Daniel, this human figure supplants all the beastly kingdoms that fail to offer proper homage to God and that persecute God's people. After the demise of the beastly kingdoms, the human-shaped kingdom receives everlasting dominion, glory, and kingship. In John, Jesus is the "Son of Man" who has come down from heaven (3:13) and will in turn be "lifted up," or crucified on the cross (3:14; 12:23, 34; 13:31), so that he may give life (6:27, 53). This "Son of Man" is the King of Israel (1:49), the one who may properly exercise God's rule. He exercises that rule because it has been given to him by God (5:22, 27), who indeed distributes all power to govern or rule (19:11). And although Jesus has the power to judge, to acquit or condemn, he always exercises that power as the Son who does the work of the living God, the life-giving Father. The one who has life in himself acts to bring life to the world. This is his commission, his mission, and his identity.

Jesus then (1) repeats the opening statement, that "the Son can do nothing on his own" (vv. 19, 30), and (2) asserts that the Son *hears* what "the one who sent [him]" has told him. Jesus' just judgment depends on hearing the same verdict that the Father renders and declaring that verdict. Jesus' judgment mirrors and enacts God's judgment. Jesus does not elevate himself to a status equal to or independent of God; rather, he hears and does the will of God, even as he does what the Father shows him (5:19). Jesus is both dependent on and one with God.

43. See also comments on 6:53: "You have no life in you." Those who believe may also have life within (6:54), but they cannot bestow it to others.

44. For further discussion, see M. M. Thompson 2001, 126–30.

45. For further discussion, see Excursus 2: "Son of God, Son, and Son of Man in John."

5:31–47 Witnesses to Jesus

Jesus' discourse now turns to the theme of witness, which figures prominently throughout the Gospel of John.[46] Jesus marshals an impressive array of witnesses who will speak on his behalf, including John the Baptist, Jesus' own works, the Father, the Scriptures, and Moses. Nowhere is the specific content of their witness restated or elaborated; for example, how and what the Scriptures say about Jesus (5:39) is not explained, nor is it explained just how God bears witness to Jesus (5:37). But Jesus calls to his defense those very witnesses—Moses, the Scriptures—who might have been enlisted as his accusers, based on his Sabbath healing and his assertion of his God-given prerogatives and unity with God. It was, after all, Moses and the Scriptures that spoke of God's resting on the Sabbath; yet Jesus calls them to his defense. Similarly, his work of healing the man on the Sabbath and commanding him to pick up his mat was held up as accusing evidence against his claim to be doing God's work, and it is precisely this work, God's work, that Jesus calls to his defense.

> **5:31** If I bear witness concerning myself, my witness is not true. **32** There
> is another who bears witness[a] about me, and I know that the witness that
> he bears[a] is true. **33** You sent to John; and he has borne witness[a] to the
> truth. **34** But the witness that I receive is not from human beings; rather,
> I speak these things in order that you may be saved. **35** That one was a
> kindled and shining lamp, and you rejoiced for a while in his light. **36**
> But I have a witness greater than John's. The works that the Father has
> given me to complete—these works bear witness that the Father has
> sent me. **37** And the Father who sent me has borne witness about me. But
> you have never heard his voice, and you have never seen his form. **38**
> You do not have his word remaining in you, because you do not believe
> the one whom he has sent. **39** You search the Scriptures, because you
> think that through them you have eternal life. But they themselves bear
> witness concerning me! **40** And you do not want to come to me in order
> that you might have life.
>
> **41** I do not welcome[b] glory[c] from human beings. **42** But I know you, that
> you do not love God.[d] **43** I have come in the name of my Father, and you do
> not receive me. But if another were to come in his own name, you would
> receive him. **44** How can you believe when you welcome glory from each
> other, but do not seek the glory that comes from the only God? **45** Do not
> think that I will accuse you to the Father; it is Moses who accuses you, on
> whom you have set your hope. **46** For if you believed Moses, you would
> believe me, for he wrote about me. **47** But if you do not believe what he
> wrote, how will you believe my words?

46. See esp. Harvey; Lincoln 2000.

a. The Baptist bears witness (*martyrōn*, present tense) and has borne witness (*memartyrēken*, perfect tense, connoting past action with continuing results in the present).

b. Or "receive" (cf. 1:11, "his own did not receive/welcome him").

c. *Doxa* may also be translated as "honor" or "praise."

d. "Do not love God" translates *tēn agapēn tou theou ouk exete en heautois* ("You do not have the love of God in you"). This could also be rendered, "You do not have God's love in you."

[5:31–35] Although Jesus judges justly because he listens to and seeks the will of the one who sent him (5:30), he concedes that his own witness about himself cannot establish its validity. According to the Scriptures a single witness cannot provide sufficient testimony for conviction of a crime (Num 35:30; Deut 17:6; 19:15), especially in capital cases. Later Jewish sources broaden this proviso, so that the witness of a single person cannot constitute valid testimony at all, particularly if the witness concerns oneself.[47] On that principle, no single witness can ensure a favorable verdict. Therefore Jesus calls on other witnesses, including John the Baptist (vv. 33–35), Jesus' works (v. 36), and the Scriptures (v. 39). Through their testimony to Jesus, one may hear and accept God's own testimony (v. 37).[48]

Jesus turns first to invoke the witness of the Baptist (vv. 33–35). From the beginning of the Gospel, John "has borne witness" (*memartyrēken*) and "bears witness" (*martyrei*, 1:15; cf. 5:32) to Jesus as the Son of God, the Lamb of God, the one on whom the Spirit has descended, the one sent by God (5:36–37; cf. 3:26–27). Ironically, while people "were willing" (*ēthelēsate*, 5:35) to rejoice in John's light, they are not willing (*ou thelete*, 5:40) to come to Jesus, even though John was a lamp that was lit and went on shining precisely so that people would see the "true Light" (cf. 1:7–8). Because John's human testimony (5:34) might seem inadequate to confirm that Jesus speaks on behalf of God, Jesus turns to a witness "greater than John's" (v. 36). Even so, John's human testimony about Jesus was intended to lead people to have and see the true light of life and "be saved" (v. 34).

[36–40] In summoning witnesses, Jesus next calls on his own works, on God, and on the Scriptures to bear witness to him. Jesus' works, including the healing narrated in 5:1–9 and the work of giving life and judging, constitute the witness "greater" than John's because these are "the works that the Father has given me." As works that embody the divine prerogatives of giving life and of final judgment, they are part of the Father's witness to Jesus, testimony that the Father has indeed given this Son these distinctive divine prerogatives (v. 36).

47. Josephus, *Ant.* 4.219; *Life* 256; *m. Roš Haš.* 1:7; 2:6; 3:1; *m. Ketub.* 2:9.

48. For God as a witness, see Gen 31:50; 1 Sam 12:5–6; Jer 42:5; Mic 1:2; and in the NT, Rom 1:9; 2 Cor 1:23; Phil 1:8.

While Jesus next refers to the witness of the "Father who sent me" (v. 37), the text does not specify exactly how the Father bears such witness. But Jesus does emphatically deny that his accusers have ever heard the Father's testimony.

Three statements—you have never heard his voice, you have never seen his form, you do not have his word dwelling in you (vv. 37–38)—evoke, apparently by denying, the traditions of God's speaking the law to Israel at Sinai. According to Deuteronomy, God spoke to Israel so that they "heard the sound of words but saw no form [LXX, *homoiōma*]; there was only a voice" (4:12, 15, 33, 36). But in John, Jesus denies that "the Jews" have heard God, seen God, or have his word within them, because they do not believe in the one whom God has sent (5:38). John does not thereby discount the entirety of the "historic revelation to Israel,"[49] but he links the manifestation of God with the mission of Jesus, so that to see the Son is to see the Father; to hear the Son is to hear the Father. Jesus' sweeping assertions do not deny that there has ever been knowledge of God in Israel, but they inextricably link knowledge of God with Jesus since his advent. In seeing Jesus' signs and hearing his word, one sees and hears the Father because Jesus both embodies and speaks God's word.[50]

Exactly what it means to "see God" (v. 37) is not spelled out. There are numerous biblical descriptions of various visual encounters with God: Jacob saw God face-to-face; Moses saw a burning bush and God, passing by in his glory; Isaiah had a vision in the temple; Ezekiel saw a heavenly chariot; Daniel spoke of seeing the Ancient of Days.[51] While God can be seen in certain forms, such visions of God are radically different from seeing a fellow creature: they are difficult to describe and often disorienting. Here God is spoken of as having "form"[52] but not as having flesh or body. The "form" of God makes it possible to "see" God, although how and what one sees are not further explained.[53] But any and all such visual apprehensions of God are denied to Jesus' opponents here. In Jesus, the embodied Word of God, one may see the Father, mediated and indirectly (14:9). There are no other visions of God available. Similarly, those who have not attended to the words of Jesus cannot claim now to be hearing a word from God, either in "the Scriptures" or from Moses, that does not finally point to Jesus (5:39, 47). These sweeping claims for the singularity of

49. As D. Moody Smith rightly notes (1999, 141).

50. On "seeing" and "hearing" in John, see also 1:18; 6:46; 8:38; 12:37–43; 14:9; and comments there.

51. See also Matt 5:8, "They will see God"; 1 John 3:2; Rev 4–5.

52. According to Gen 32:30, Jacob calls the place where he has seen God face-to-face "Peniel"; according to 32:31 LXX, Jacob calls it "the form of God [*eidos theou*], for I have seen [*eidon*] God face-to-face." Cf. Bockmuehl 1997.

53. Regarding Deut 32:39 LXX ("Behold! Behold! It is I!" [*idete idete hoti egō eimi*]), Philo denies that the living God can be seen with one's eyes, but should rather be perceived "by the eyes of our mind, through his mighty works done in the world" (*Post.* 167–68).

the knowledge of God made available through and in Jesus are grounded in his identity as the incarnation of God's own Word (1:1–3, 14).

Because Jesus has both heard and seen the Father, because Jesus thereby has full knowledge of the Father, he can speak the truth. Jesus' accusers have not believed the witness of Jesus' works (v. 36), nor have they received God's witness (v. 37), because they have failed to heed the revelation and word that Jesus has brought (5:38–40, 43).[54] They have neither the knowledge of God gained by direct apprehension (as Jesus does) nor indirect apprehension (through listening to Jesus, the Scriptures, or other witnesses to him).

They "search the Scriptures" (5:39).[55] Thus they are portrayed, like Ezra the scribe, as one who has "set his heart to study [*lidrôš*] the law [*torah*]" (Ezra 7:10; cf. Isa 34:16). Scripture, properly understood, bears witness to Jesus (John 5:38–39);[56] but unless one is taught by God (6:45), reads Scripture in light of the resurrection of Jesus (2:17, 22), and is guided by the teaching of the Spirit of truth (14:26; 16:13, 14), one hears the Scripture not as a witness to the identity of Jesus as the life-giving Word of God, but as an accusing witness, a judge.[57] These are strong and potentially offensive claims, underscoring the point that emerges repeatedly from John: there is no neutral perspective on Jesus. Obviously not all persons who read the Scriptures, then or now, read them as pointing ultimately to Jesus. But the claim that Scripture bears witness to Israel's Messiah, Jesus of Nazareth, is foundational to the Gospel of John, the entirety of the New Testament witness, and the early Christian apologetic tradition.[58]

[41–47] Having invoked the witness of the Baptist, Jesus now calls upon Moses, who bears witness to Jesus. Jesus does not, however, seek human adulation or praise. The glory or honor (*doxa*) which he would welcome consists of the proper acknowledgment of his mission as the one who comes in the name of the Father, the one to whom prophets and Scriptures bear witness. The evidence for Jesus' stinging assessment that his questioners do not love God is that they fail to welcome the one whom God has sent (5:23). Since honoring Jesus and honoring God are two facets of one response, those who do not welcome and honor Jesus violate the basic command to love God (Deut 6:4).

54. For the superiority of seeing to hearing as the basis for witness in the ancient world, see Byrskog 2002, 146–76, on "The Eyewitness as Interpreter."

55. *Eraunate* can be imperative or, as the context demonstrates, indicative: they search *because* they think they have eternal life in or through them. Philo invites his readers to "examine" or "investigate" (*ereunēsōmen*) some aspect of Scripture (*Det.* 141; *Cher.* 14); cf. the Hebrew *dāraš*, "to seek, ask," which in the DSS refers to the interpretation of Scripture (1QS V, 11; VI, 6; VIII, 15; 4Q174 (4QFlor) I, 11, 14; CD VI, 7; XX, 6).

56. John 1:45; 2:22; 7:38, 42; 10:35; 13:18; 17:12; 19:24, 28, 36–37; 20:9.

57. Lincoln 2000, 54–56.

58. See, e.g., Justin, *Dial.* 58.11; cf. also 78.10; 92.1; 100.2; 119.1.

But some obviously believe that to honor Jesus as one honors God is to participate in Jesus' own blasphemous act of making himself equal to God. For their defense, they may well have called on Moses, Israel's great prophet and leader, the friend of God, who bore witness to *the only God* (v. 44).[59] But John portrays Moses as the accuser and not the defender of those who do not honor Jesus, for Moses actually wrote about Jesus (v. 46). Moses appears in the law-court as a witness for Jesus and against those who do not believe in him. While Moses was traditionally known to intercede for Israel, and thus protect it from God's judgment, here John turns Jewish tradition on its head.[60] Still, Jewish authors also knew that Moses could be called as a witness *against* the people of Israel (*L.A.B.* 19.4–5), that they sometimes did not believe him (*4 Ezra* 7.106) and often paid no attention to the prophets sent to them.[61] If they had believed Moses and the prophets, they would have believed Jesus. Throughout the Gospel, Moses, the Law, and all the Scriptures bear witness to Jesus, so that to hear Moses' words (John 5:47) and to be Moses' disciple is in fact to hear Jesus' words and become his disciple (9:28). As elsewhere, "Moses and the prophets" (1:45) point forward to Jesus. Unless they are grasped in that way, those texts will not be rightly interpreted, and to press John's point, God cannot be fully known. The word of God that came to Israel has its climactic turning point in the narrative of the Word embodied (1:14–18).

The healing of the man at the pool and the subsequent discourse lay out the heart of Johannine Christology pointedly and succinctly, underscoring who Jesus is and how he is known. First, in relationship to "the only God," Jesus is the one who has and exercises the prerogatives of God, specifically the unique divine prerogatives of giving life and passing final judgment on all things, which God has granted to him. Second, Jesus is known through the witness that others—John the Baptist, Moses, the Scriptures, and ultimately God—bear to him. One must search the testimony of Scripture, hear the words of Moses, and receive the witness of God in order to grasp the identity of Jesus. For John, receiving Jesus does not repudiate Israel's God, its Scriptures, or its people; rather, receiving Jesus properly honors God, hears the Scripture aright, and orients the people to their Messiah. That this is so cannot simply be read off the surface of Jesus' ministry or assertions or the texts of Scriptures. This is the

59. For various descriptions emphasizing the singularity or uniqueness of God (*monos*), see Deut 6:4; 2 Kgs 19:15, 19 (*kyrios ho theos monos*); 2 Macc 1:24–25; 7:37; Pss 71:18 (72:18 ET); 85:10 (86:10); Isa 37:16, 20; Dan 3:45 LXX (Pr Azar 22).

60. For Moses as Israel's intermediary or defender, see *Jub.* 1.19; Philo, *Mos.* 2.166; *4 Ezra* 7.106; *L.A.B.* 12.8–9; *T. Mos.* 11.17. Satan is traditionally Israel's accuser (e.g., Zech 3:1; Rev 12:10).

61. For Israel's rejection of its prophets, see 1 Kgs 18:13; 19:10, 14; 2 Kgs 17:13, 23; 21:10; 24:2; 2 Chr 24:9; Jer 7:25–26; 25:4; 26:5–11; 29:19; 35:15; 44–45; Neh 9:6–38 (esp. v. 26); *Jub.* 1.12; in the NT, Matt 23:37–39; Luke 11:47; 13:34.

witness from faith for faith; but for John, it is the witness of faith to the historical significance of Jesus' mission and person.

6:1–71 Jesus, the Bread of Life: Signs at Passover

The feeding of the five thousand and Jesus' discourse on the bread of life draw on the biblical account of God's provision of manna for the people of Israel, thereby presenting Jesus as the true "bread from heaven" who gives life to the world. Even as God provided manna for Israel in the wilderness, so God now provides the "bread from heaven" that grants eternal life. While Jesus' discourse looks back to God's provision of heavenly manna for his people, it may also allude to a promise found in Jewish literature anticipating the return of manna from on high in the age to come. The narrative of God's provision for Israel in the past and the anticipation of God's blessings in the future are both reconfigured in Jesus and his life-giving work for all the world. This work climaxes in Jesus' death and resurrection; it is remembered by his followers as they eat the Lord's Supper. Jesus' action is presented in John not merely as a deed in the past, but also as an act that was further explicated by, although not limited to, eating and drinking (the Lord's Supper) together, where those who eat and drink remember that they are still fed by Jesus. Even as God fed the Israelites in the wilderness, so God continues to sustain his people.

The narrative of Jesus' "walking on the water," or crossing the sea, lies between the account of the feeding of the multitudes and the discourse on the bread of life. In this account, Jesus comes to the disciples struggling in crossing the lake, and when they do not first recognize him, speaks the reassuring words identifying himself to them: "It is I" (*egō eimi*). This simple self-identification anticipates the first of Jesus' characteristic "I am" sayings in the Gospel ("I am the bread of life," 6:35).[62] Echoing patterns of divine speech in the Old Testament, this group of sayings underscores the identity of Jesus as the one who lives and remains with his people, and through whom the one sovereign God's life-giving work is accomplished.

But just as the Israelites murmured and grumbled, even after God had delivered them, so in his long discourse Jesus' claims to give God's life to the world provoke increased murmuring and grumbling about him (6:41, 60). Their grumbling increases the more that Jesus focuses on his identity as the means of receiving God's life, and on the necessity of his death in his life-giving work (6:41, 52), leading even many of Jesus' own followers to abandon him (v. 66). The chapter sounds a final ominous note when, for the first time, it mentions

62. John 6:35; 8:12; 9:5; 10:7, 11; 11:25; 14:6; 15:1. See Excursus 5: "The 'I Am' Sayings of John."

"the Twelve" (v. 67), but also indicates that one from among this chosen group will betray Jesus (v. 70).

While Jesus' work aims to bring life to the whole world, the more that Jesus speaks of his heavenly origins, presents himself as the means and source of eternal life, and asserts the need to "eat and drink" his body and blood, the more offensive people find him. Jesus' claims may sound familiar to Christian readers accustomed both to thinking of Jesus as God's Son "come down" from heaven and to hearing the "words of institution" at the Lord's Supper, but John portrays them as divisive when uttered by Jesus to his contemporaries. Thus what transpires in this chapter again echoes the prologue's assertion that the one who was life and light for all the world was received by some and rejected by others. Never abandoning God's commitment to Israel, the Gospel constantly portrays the scope of God's work on a cosmic canvas. The one promised in the Scriptures (1:45), the King of Israel (1:49), is the "Lamb of God, who takes away the sin of the world" (1:29).

6:1–15 The Feeding of the Five Thousand

The narrative of the feeding of the five thousand appears in all four Gospels. Although sometimes referred to as a "nature miracle," Jesus' action is more aptly characterized, along with the transformation of the water to wine, as a miracle of "gift" or "supply."[63] In this category, it belongs among the works of the prophets such as Elijah and Elisha, who generously supplied meal, oil, and bread to those in need. No wonder John depicts the people acclaiming Jesus as a prophet (6:14). But the sign is misunderstood: John reports that, in response to what they have seen, the crowd wants to "seize Jesus to make him king." Since Jesus' act has demonstrated his ability to provide for his people, it is not surprising that they are eager for him to take up the role of king, continue to provide for them, and perhaps do even more than that. And while, in the Gospel of John, Jesus is a king, his authority comes not from human beings, but from God. Hence, the shape of his kingship is not determined by any human agenda, but by God's life-giving purposes for the world. Precisely for that reason he feeds those who hunger.

> **6:1** Then[a] Jesus went to the other side of the Sea of Galilee, or Tiberias.[b]
> **2** A large crowd followed him, because they saw the signs that he did on
> those who were sick. **3** And Jesus went up on the mountain, and there he
> sat down with his disciples. **4** Passover, a festival of the Jews, was near. **5**
> When Jesus saw the large crowd coming to him, he said to Philip, "Where
> shall we buy bread in order that they may eat?" **6** He said this to test Philip;
> for he already knew what he was going to do.

63. Theissen 103–6.

7 Philip answered, “Two hundred denarii of bread would not be enough
for each of them to have just a little.”
8 Then one of the disciples, Andrew the brother of Simon Peter, said
to him, **9** “There is a boy here who has five barley loaves and two fish.
But what are these for so many?”
10 Jesus said, “Make the people sit down.” There was a lot of grass in
that place. The men who sat down numbered five thousand.
11 Jesus took the bread and, having given thanks, distributed it to those
sitting down; likewise also the fish, as much as they wanted. **12** And when
they were filled, Jesus said to his disciples, “Gather up the pieces that are
left over, so that nothing may be lost.” **13** They gathered them up and filled
twelve baskets with pieces from the five barley loaves, left by those who
had eaten.
14 So when the people saw the sign[c] that he had done, they said, “This
is truly the prophet who is coming into the world!” **15** Jesus, knowing that
they were going to come and seize him in order that they might make him
king, withdrew again to the mountain alone.

a. *Meta tauta*, “after these things”; cf. John 3:22; 5:1, 14; 6:1; 7:1; 19:38; 21:1; the singular *meta touto* occurs in 2:12; 11:7, 11; 19:28. The phrase “after these things” does not indicate how long or short the lapse of time between the events.

b. Lit., “the Sea of Galilee of Tiberias” (*tēs thalassēs tēs Galilaias tēs Tiberiados*). To avoid the awkward reading with two genitives referring to the same sea, some MSS omit “of Tiberias” (cf. “sea of Tiberias” in 21:1); others read “of Galilee and Tiberias”; still others, “of Galilee in the regions of Tiberias.” The troublesome double genitive (as in 𝔓[66c, 75] A B) is likely original.

c. Although most MSS have a singular (“the sign that he had done”), some (including 𝔓[75] and B) read “the signs that he had done,” probably in assimilation to the plural in 6:2 (see also 2:23).

[6:1–6] The scene is set on “the other side” of the Sea of Galilee, or Tiberias.[64] Even as the Gospel jumps over large periods of time in order to correlate Jesus’ work with significant festivals of the Jewish calendar, so now it has moved from Jerusalem (ch. 5) to the eastern shore of the Sea of Galilee (6:1).[65] That it was “near Passover” presumably indicates a passage of time since the previous Passover (2:13, 23). John calls Passover a “festival of the Jews.”[66]

64. John is unique in the NT in referring to the sea (or lake) of Galilee as “Tiberias” (6:1, 23; 21:1), but Josephus calls it *hē pros Tiberiada limnē* (*J.W.* 3.57) and *hē Tiberieōn limnē* (*J.W.* 4.456). For names of the sea in ancient Jewish, Greek, and Christian sources, see Freyne, “Galilee, Sea of,” *ABD* 2:899–900.

65. On John’s use of the feasts to provide the chronological framework for this Gospel, see the discussion of John’s structure in the introduction to this commentary.

66. On Passover, see also the notes and comments at 2:13; 19:14.

While Passover commemorates God's deliverance of the Israelites from Egypt, it is actually God's provision of manna during the wilderness wanderings, after the departure from Egypt, that provides the literary and theological context for Jesus' interpretive discourse in this chapter.

A crowd follows Jesus "because they saw the signs that he did" (6:2). Whether this statement refers to Jesus' signs in Galilee (2:1–11; 4:46–54) or in Jerusalem (5:1–9), it indicates that Jesus' reputation as a miracle worker is bringing "a large crowd" to him (cf. 2:23, 25; 4:45; see also 4:46–47; 5:15). John's account underscores both Jesus' initiative in feeding the crowd and his abundant provision for them: he goes up on the mountain;[67] sits down; sees the multitudes; and in order to "test" (*peirazō*) Philip, asks how he and his disciples are to feed them. Although often in the New Testament *peirazō* (or its related noun) carries the negative connotation of "tempt, trap, entice, or lead astray" (e.g., Matt 4:1, 3; 6:13; 1 Cor 7:5), here it means to "examine, try, prove" (e.g., 2 Cor 13:5; Jas 1:2–4). Jesus "tests" Philip to see whether he understands what Jesus is able and willing to do, so that Philip may see and understand Jesus rightly.

[7–9] The disciples' responses underscore their meager resources, five barley loaves and two fish, and the great need: two hundred days' wages, the value of two hundred denarii, would scarcely buy enough food for all the people. While the disciples see the need, they think their resources are too slight to help; they do not understand that Jesus can provide abundantly beyond what they imagine. This brief narrative echoes and trumps the story in 2 Kgs (4:42–44) where, in spite of his servant's doubts, Elisha feeds a hundred people with twenty loaves of barley,[68] with bread left over. Jesus feeds thousands, and there is an abundance left over.

[10–13] Again Jesus takes the initiative, ordering the people to sit down and distributing bread and the fish to them. Jesus is the host at this meal, even as he became the (unseen) host of the wedding feast at Cana by providing wine for it. After distributing the bread, Jesus commands that the pieces be gathered up "so that nothing may be lost," and his disciples do as they are bidden.[69]

Several points are notable in this brief narrative. First, Jesus prays ("having given thanks," 6:11) before distributing the bread and fish, perhaps in keeping with the Jewish prayer of thanksgiving: "Blessed art thou, O Lord our God, king of the universe, who brings forth bread from the earth" (*m. Ber.* 6:1).

67. Which "mountain" is not specified; cf. John 6:15; Mark 6:46; Matt 15:29.

68. *Artous krithinous* (2 Kgs 4:42 LXX). A staple of the ancient Mediterranean diet, barley was less expensive than wheat (cf. 2 Kgs 7:16) and sometimes associated with the poor by Roman and Jewish authors alike; see Pliny the Elder, *Nat.* 18.74; Josephus, *J.W.* 5.427; on the use of barley and wheat, see Garnsey.

69. For the distinctive Johannine note that Jesus does not lose any of those God has given to him, see 6:39; 17:12; 18:9.

Second, John's description reflects the words spoken over the bread and cup at the Lord's Supper as recorded elsewhere: "And he took bread, and when he had given thanks he broke it and gave it to them" (Luke 22:17–19; Matt 26:26–27; Mark 14:22–23; 1 Cor 11:24). Although Jesus here distributes bread and fish (cf. 21:9), he will go on to speak of eating and drinking (v. 35) his flesh and blood (vv. 51–58) and eventually will mention the one who will betray him (cf. 1 Cor 11:23, "on the night when he was betrayed"). Jesus' provision of bread foreshadows his giving of his flesh in death (6:51).

Third, the five loaves and two fishes (v. 9) spectacularly contrast with the leftover twelve baskets of bread (v. 13) recalling the abundant provision of wine in John 2:1–12: from six stone jars of water, Jesus provides far more wine than the wedding guests require. The "twelve baskets" call to mind the twelve tribes of Israel, now reconfigured in the twelve disciples, representative of Jesus' followers (cf. 6:67). All the scattered children of God will be gathered together (11:5; 17:21–22); none of them will be lost (6:39; 10:28–29; 17:12): there will be "one flock, one shepherd" (see comments on 10:12–16; 11:52; 17:21–22).

In its prayer of thanksgiving over the Eucharist, the early Christian catechetical document the *Didache* (late first or early second c.) also interprets it in terms of the feeding miracle and, further, as the gathering of the church into one: "Even as what was broken was scattered over the hills, and was gathered together and became one, so let your church be gathered together from the ends of the earth into your kingdom" (9.4; 10.5).[70] In John, the feeding miracle also serves as a figure of the Lord's Supper and of the gathering of God's people. Jesus gave his body and blood to gather his people together; hence, even as the bread is scattered, so must it be gathered; even as there are many pieces, there is also one loaf (cf. 1 Cor 10:14–17; 11:27–34).

Finally, Jesus' feeding of the five thousand foreshadows his provision of bread and fish to his disciples by the Sea of Tiberias after his resurrection (21:1–13). As Jesus fed the multitude in the wilderness, so the risen Lord feeds his disciples (10:9–10; 21:12–13). Once again, the Gospel of John draws a parallel between the experiences of those who are with Jesus during his earthly ministry and those who will follow him after his resurrection (e.g., cf. 1:43 and 21:19, 22). The same Lord provides for his own.

[14–15] Having seen the sign, the people hail Jesus as the coming prophet (6:14), most likely referring to the expectation of a prophet like Moses (Deut 18:15–18; cf. John 1:21–25; 4:19; 6:32; 7:40). The transition from prophet (6:14) to king (v. 15) can perhaps be explained by the designation of Moses as both prophet and king in Jewish tradition, though it may also link hopes for two

70. The *Didache* (9–10) and the *birkat ha-mazôn* ("blessing for the nourishment") of the Passover meal draw on different parts of Sir 36:10–23; see discussion in Skarsaune 406–13.

messianic figures in Jesus.[71] Jesus is both prophet, one who speaks God's truth, and king, the "anointed" one (see 1:41, 49; 4:19, 29, 44; 7:40–41).[72]

Also relevant here are Josephus's accounts of men such as Theudas (*Ant.* 20.97–98) and "the Egyptian" (*Ant.* 20.168–70). Both claimed to be prophets; Josephus judges both as deceivers. He similarly criticizes a number of figures that, in one way or another, sought royal power or honors, because they improperly seized kingship or exercised "tyrannical power."[73] While all these movements either dissipated on their own or were put down by the Romans, each seemed to have exercised some hold over the popular imagination. John's statements that the crowds take Jesus for a prophet and want to "make him king" portray altogether predictable responses in this first-century context. Jesus is implicitly contrasted with those who deceive others and with their self-aggrandizing aspirations.

Jesus withdraws from the crowd because his authority and kingly office come not "from himself" or from the eager and restive crowd, but from God (18:33–36; 19:11). The crowd's desire to make Jesus king "is not faith, but unbelief. They have not understood who Jesus is."[74] Jesus did not make himself equal to God (5:1–18); he will not make himself king. At the triumphal entry, Jesus will receive the acclamations of the crowd who hail him as "King of Israel" (12:13, 15), but the road through Jerusalem leads to the cross, and only in that way to a throne and scepter—a path that the crowd clamoring to crown Jesus could scarcely have imagined.

6:16–21 A Revelation of Jesus' Identity

The surprisingly terse account of Jesus' walking on the lake follows the note that Jesus has withdrawn "to the mountain alone" (6:15). The disciples are without their leader, and for a time Jesus is the "great Absent One" in the story.[75] When Jesus comes to them, his presence first elicits fear because they

71. On Moses as prophet, see Hos 12:13; Wis 11:1; *L.A.B.* 35.6, "first of all the prophets"; *T. Mos.* 11.16, "divine prophet for the whole earth"; Philo, *Mos.* 1.175; 2.187, 292; Josephus, *Ant.* 4.329. For Moses as ruler or king, see *L.A.B.* 9.16; 20.5; Philo (*Mos.* 1.334; 2:2–7) refers to Moses' royal, prophetic, and priestly offices; see also *Mos.* 2.187, 292; *Praem.* 53; Josephus, *Ant.* 4.327; Meeks 1967; Hylen 2005.

72. Since kings were anointed, the promised future king who would deliver Israel became known as "the anointed one," that is, "the Messiah," where Messiah translates the Hebrew and Aramaic words for anointed; see comments on 1:41 and 12:3.

73. Regarding those who claimed power for themselves, see Josephus on Judas (of Sepphoris, Galilee; *Ant.* 17.271–72; *J.W.* 2.56); Simon of Perea (*Ant.* 17.273–76; *J.W.* 2.57); and Athronges, the shepherd of Judea (*Ant.* 17.278). For those who exercised "tyranny," see *J.W.* 4.389–93 on John of Gischala; and on Simon bar Giora of Gerasa, *J.W.* 2.652; 4.508; 5.11; 7.32.

74. Newbigin 76.

75. Ridderbos 216.

do not recognize him until he identifies himself and speaks words of comfort. Jesus' presence is not always discerned: he must disclose himself in order to be recognized. And even though the storm is apparently not stilled, the disciples arrive safely to their destination.

> **6:16** When evening came, his disciples went down to the sea, **17** got into
> a boat, and started across the sea to Capernaum. And when it was dark[a]
> and Jesus had not yet come to them, **18** the sea grew rough because a
> great wind was blowing. **19** When they had been rowing about three or
> four miles, they saw Jesus walking on the sea and drawing near the boat,
> and they were afraid. **20** And he said to them, "It is I. Do not be afraid."
> **21** Then they wanted to take him into the boat, but at once the boat was at
> the land to which they were going.

a. Perhaps reflecting both John 1:5 and 12:35, some MSS (א D) read *katelaben de autous hē skotia* ("darkness had overtaken them"), accenting the perilous character of the disciples' situation without Jesus.

[16–19] The account begins with the note that, at evening, the disciples started across the sea toward Capernaum, that it grew dark, and that "Jesus had not yet come to them": he had not rejoined them after withdrawing from the crowd (6:14–15). Yet the comment indicates that although Jesus was absent for a time, he will not remain so. John then sketches the plight of the disciples as they struggle, in Jesus' absence, to row across the sea under difficult conditions (vv. 16–19).[76] The darkness, the stormy sea, and the distance that the disciples have rowed emphasize the obstacles in the way of Jesus' being present with the disciples. When Jesus does come to them, the disciples are terrified (v. 19): they do not know who is walking across the sea to meet them. Indeed, why should they? Why should they expect Jesus or anyone else to meet them in the midst of the lake?

[20–21] Jesus identifies himself to the disciples with the simple words "It is I" and encourages them, "Do not be afraid." "It is I" or "I am" translates the Greek *egō eimi*, which can be a simple way of identifying oneself to another; hence, the blind man acknowledges that he is the person "who used to sit and beg" with *egō eimi* (9:9; cf. 4:26; 18:5, 8).[77] Jesus thus reassures the disciples

76. The disciples are "about 25 or 30 stadia" out to sea; one stadium = ⅛ of a Roman (or English) mile = about 600 Greek, 625 Roman, or 607 English feet = 192 meters (see BDAG; LSJM). Today the lake is 8 by 13 miles (Rousseau and Arav 246); these measurements differ significantly from Josephus's report that the lake is 40 by 140 stadia (4.5 by 15.6 miles; *J.W.* 3.506). Rousseau and Arav also (246) describe winds that can roil the lake, raising waves of 6–7 feet.

77. Asahel responds to Abner's question, "Is it you, Asahel?" with *egō eimi* (2 Sam 2:20 LXX; MT, *ʾānōkî*). See Excursus 5: "The 'I Am' Sayings of John."

that they have not seen a ghost or apparition, but Jesus himself: since he is no longer absent from them, but now with them, they need not be afraid.

But in Scripture, God frequently encourages his people with the words "Do not be afraid," often grounding them in the promise of his presence (Gen 15:1; 26:24; Isa 41:10; Jer 1:8). God's people are not to fear because God is and will be with them. Surely the one who has just walked across the waves of the stormy sea can now be understood to be speaking as God has spoken, promising his anxious disciples his protective presence. But curiously, the disciples do not respond with wonder or worship: they are simply willing to take him into the boat. For now, they recognize Jesus, and they welcome his presence in their midst. Fuller recognition of who he is, Lord and God, will come after the resurrection (20:28).

John enigmatically reports that the boat reaches the shore immediately. Here it is not clear whether Jesus gets into the boat (cf. Matt 14:32; Mark 6:51). A number of patristic commentators believed that Jesus does not since the boat is immediately at its destination: a point thought to heighten the miraculous character of this event in John's narrative.[78] Others thought that, in keeping with his divine nature, Jesus continues on the sea to the shore.[79] Still others assume that Jesus gets into the boat, demonstrating that Jesus' presence with the disciples ensures their safe arrival at their destination.[80] Following this last suggestion, one hears echoes of Ps 107:28–30: "Then they cried to the LORD in their trouble, and he brought them out from their distress; he made the storm be still, and the waves of the sea were hushed. Then they were glad because they had quiet, and he brought them to their desired haven." Like the psalmist, John describes the distress and trouble of God's people on the sea, and then their arrival at a safe haven.[81] Like Isaiah, John pictures Jesus as the Lord who is with his disciples when they "pass through the waters" (Isa 43:2), who "makes a way in the sea, a path in the mighty waters" (43:16; Ps 77:19; cf. Job 9:8).

Curiously, given the potential of the Old Testament allusions for depicting Jesus in terms of God's own actions, John remains remarkably silent on the meaning of Jesus' walking across the sea. John does not call Jesus' crossing the sea "a sign," although like the signs it demonstrates God's deliverance of those in need. But clearly, walking across the sea manifests Jesus' identity as the one who is with his disciples in the most perilous of situations: he will not

78. Theodore of Mopsuestia, *Commentary on John* 3.6.21; on John 6:21, cf. Bultmann 1971; Moloney 1996.

79. John Chrysostom, *Hom. Jo.* 43.1. If Jesus is presumed not to have gotten into the boat, the point may be that he traversed the entire sea *on* the water, whereas the Israelites, led by Moses, crossed the Red Sea on land that had been *beneath* the water, on dry ground (though this would not aptly characterize the disciples' sea crossing).

80. Ridderbos 218; Schnackenburg 2:27.

81. There is no explicit mention that the wind ceases, as in Matt 14:32; Mark 6:51.

abandon his disciples; he will come to them (14:18) and bring them safely to their destination (14:2–3).

6:22–34 Bread from Heaven

After eating their "fill of the loaves" (6:26), the people now want more: more bread, more miracles, more of what Jesus can offer. They follow him across the sea, looking for more of what he has given them earlier, bread that fed them for a day. When they find Jesus, he redirects their quest to a different kind of bread, bread that will feed them for eternal life. Even as the Samaritan woman asked for the living water that Jesus can give, not understanding that he was speaking to her of the gift of the Spirit, so now the people ask for Jesus "always" to give them the "bread of God" that "comes down from heaven" and "gives life to the world" (vv. 33–34). They are right to ask for it; but they do not yet understand what Jesus wants to give them. That remains to be explained further.

> **[6:22]** On the next day, the crowd that had remained on the other side of the
> sea saw that there was no other boat there,[a] and that Jesus had not entered
> the boat together with his disciples, but that only his disciples had gone
> away. **23** Other boats from Tiberias came near the place where they had
> eaten the bread after the Lord had given thanks. **24** So when the crowd
> saw that Jesus was not there, nor his disciples, they themselves got into
> the boats and went to Capernaum, looking for Jesus. **25** And when they
> found him on the other side of the sea, they said to him, "Rabbi, when
> did you come here?"
>
> **26** Jesus answered them, "Amen, amen, I say to you, you seek me, not
> because you saw signs, but because you ate your fill of the loaves. **27** Do
> not work for the food that perishes, but rather for the abiding food that
> gives eternal life, which[b] this Son of Man will give to you. For the Father,
> God,[c] has set his seal on him." **28** They said to him, "What should we do
> in order to work the works of God?" **29** Jesus answered them, "This is the
> work of God: believe in that one whom he sent."
>
> **30** They said to him, "So what sign will you do, that we might see and
> believe in you? What work will you do? **31** Our ancestors ate manna in
> the wilderness; as it is written, 'He gave them bread from heaven to eat.'"
> **32** Jesus said to them, "Amen, amen, I say to you, it was not Moses who
> gave you bread from heaven, but my Father is giving you the true bread
> from heaven. **33** For the bread of God is that which comes down[d] from
> heaven and gives life to the world." **34** They said to him, "Lord, give us
> this bread always."

a. Lit., "no other boat there except one" (*allo ouk ēn ekei ei mē hen*), perhaps the one the disciples have used.

b. Grammatically, *hēn* ("which") can refer to *tēn brōsin tēn menousan* ("abiding food") or to *zōēn aiōnion* ("eternal life"); here it clearly refers to "abiding food," i.e., the bread of heaven that is the subject of the discourse.

c. "The Father, God," translates *ho patēr . . . ho theos*, an explicit collocation unique to John and to the NT, although see John 20:17 ("my Father and your Father, my God and your God"); 2 Cor 1:3; 11:31; Eph 1:3 (all, "the God and Father of our/the Lord").

d. The phrase *ho katabainōn ek tou ouranou*, "coming down from heaven," uses a masculine participle that (grammatically) can refer either to bread ("the bread that is coming down from heaven") or (implicitly) to Jesus or the Logos ("the bread of God is *the one* who is coming down from heaven"). Both the present tense "coming down" (*ho katabainōn*, vv. 33, 50) and the aorist (*ho katabas*, vv. 41, 51, 58) are used in this discourse without apparent difference.

[6:22–25] On the following day the crowd that had been fed by Jesus discovered that he had disappeared (v. 22). Using "some boats from Tiberias," the people cross the sea to Capernaum, apparently expecting to find Jesus there, understandably eager to see and hear more from him. John surely does not mean that all five thousand men, not to mention women and children, found boats and crossed the sea. Rather, many who were fed by Jesus continued to seek him. Yet their first question to Jesus once they find him seems decidedly banal: "Rabbi, when did you come here?" The answer is to be found in the crossing of the sea—an event that they did not witness. But the question allows Jesus to redirect their seeking.

In this passage, John refers to Jesus as "the Lord" (v. 23), which becomes a frequent designation for him, especially later in John (chs. 11, 13–14, 20), as it is in the New Testament generally. John uses "Lord" for God only when it occurs in biblical quotations (12:13; probably 12:38), but in some quotations "Lord" clearly refers to Jesus (1:23). "Lord" can simply mean "sir" and be a form of respectful address, and it may be that a number of times Jesus is addressed in that way in John (4:11, 15, 19, 49; 5:7; 6:34). But even these places are open-ended, and the reader may intuit what the figure in the Gospel does not: Jesus is indeed "the Lord" (for such open-ended passages see 4:15, 49; 9:36; 20:15). In John, "Lord" typically denotes the one who commands the allegiance of his disciples by virtue of his authority in relationship to God and particularly by virtue of the resurrection (e.g., 9:38; 11:27; 13:13–14; 20:18, 20, 25, 28).

[26–29] Throughout the Gospel, many persons seek Jesus, often for the wrong reasons or unaware of what they are looking for or why (cf. 1:38–51; 7:34–36; 8:21; 13:33; 18:4, 7; 20:15). In such cases, Jesus guides them into a new understanding of the goal of their quest. Here the people are seeking Jesus because they ate their "fill of the loaves." They are hungry, and he has satisfied their hunger. But if they had sought him because they had "seen signs," they would be seeking him because they understood Jesus' feeding of the multitudes as a witness to him as the one who gives not only bread, but also "the abiding food that gives eternal life."

The contrast between two kinds of food is a contrast between food that is eaten to sustain life in this world and food that provides life for the world to come. Jesus does not feed people with bread merely as an object lesson to show that he can give them food for eternal life. Rather, Jesus can give food that sustains human life in this world and that provides eternal life because he is the agent of God's creation of all life (1:1–4; 11:25; 14:6).[82] Furthermore, Jesus can and will give[83] his disciples "the abiding food that gives eternal life" because the Father, the very one whom Jesus and his fellow Jews know as God, has set his seal on him. A seal can serve as a means of identification, or of certification or attestation (BDAG, *sphragizō*). Here the sense is similar to statements that God has given Jesus authority to perform certain functions or tasks (5:26–27) and that God bears witness to him (5:36–37).[84] The living and life-giving God authorizes the Son to give life.

Jesus has told the people to work for, or devote their energies to, the food that brings eternal life. They inquire what constitutes the "works of God," meaning the deeds that God desires and commands.[85] Jesus compresses the plural "works" (*erga*, 6:28) into a singular "work" (*ergon*, v. 29): God desires faith in the one whom he has sent (cf. 4:23). As elsewhere in the New Testament, what people are to seek above all else is more than food, drink, or clothing, even though they clearly need these things that God provides (Matt 6:19–34; Luke 12:33–34; 16:13; 12:22–32; cf. Rom 14:17).

[30–34] The people ask for a sign so that they may believe: their "work" (of faith) would then be a response to Jesus' "work," his sign (v. 30). Their request for a sign that would lead them to believe, ironic as it is given what Jesus has just done and said (6:26), nevertheless expresses John's view that Jesus' signs, properly understood, call for faith in him. The idea is scarcely unique to John; elsewhere in Scripture, signs are given to lead to faith (Gen 9:12–17; Exod 4:8–9, 17; Isa 7:11, 14).[86] But while Jesus' words and deeds are to lead to faith, they are not unambiguous or unequivocal: people who hear and see Jesus sometimes believe, but often do not.

82. Schnackenburg (1:515–28) rightly insists on the "solidly material aspect" of the signs of Jesus. See Excursus 3: "The Signs in the Gospel of John."

83. In 6:27, the future tense *dōsei* ("will give") anticipates Jesus' death.

84. In 6:27, the aorist *esphragisen* ("has set his seal") need not be taken to refer to a specific event or point in time, such as the incarnation (Moloney 1996, 45), the descent of the Spirit at baptism (Barrett 287), or God's attestation of Jesus through the signs (Keener 1.678); it may simply refer to God's authorization of Jesus.

85. Cf. 4Q266 II, 14–15, "I will open your eyes so that you may see and understand the works of God, and choose what pleases him and reject what he hates."

86. Somewhat differently, in Mark 8:11–13 seeking "for a sign" carries a negative valence because such a search for corroboration impedes faith; cf. Luke 23:8.

The crowds who have followed Jesus understand what he can do, but they do not understand what it means, so they ask for a sign so that they may believe, quoting Scripture ("as it is written") to justify their request: "He gave them bread from heaven to eat" (6:31). The exact source of the Scriptural quotation is uncertain (so also in 7:37); there are affinities to Exod 16:4, 15; Ps 78:24; and Neh 9:15, and John may have combined elements of texts for his own purposes.[87] While in these texts God is the one who gave the manna, Jesus' reply suggests that the people took Moses to be the subject of the statement, "He gave them bread from heaven," for Jesus corrects their reading: "It was not Moses who gave you bread from heaven, but my Father is giving you the true bread from heaven." The crowds apparently appeal to the bread that Moses gave "our ancestors" ("our fathers," *hoi pateres hēmōn*) to eat; Jesus speaks of the bread that "my Father" (*ho patēr mou*) is giving. As elsewhere in John, Jesus is presented as Scripture's authoritative exegete (6:45; 7:38; 8:17; 10:34–35; 13:18; 15:25); here he corrects the way the people are reading the text: "Do not read 'Moses' but read 'my Father'; do not read the 'bread from heaven' as manna, but 'the true bread from heaven'; and do not read 'gave' but read "gives.'"[88] Jesus reminds the people that it was not Moses who gave their ancestors the bread from heaven: it was God; and that same God, Jesus' Father, is now giving them the true (*alēthinon*) bread from heaven. The manna, given in the wilderness to sustain God's people, is a type of the *true* bread now given by God.[89]

An explanatory gloss further characterizes the bread: it is the bread *of God*, and it is "coming down from heaven and giving life to the world," a reference not just to the feeding of the five thousand but even more to the incarnation of the Word in flesh (cf. 6:51–58, emphasizing the flesh of this human being, this "Son of Man"). Although the people do not understand the full significance of Jesus' promise to give "life to the world," any more than the woman at the well

87. See Exod 16:4, "I am going to rain bread from heaven for you"; 16:15, "It is the bread that the LORD has given you to eat"; Ps 78:24, "He rained down on them manna to eat, and gave them the grain of heaven"; Neh 9:15: "For their hunger you gave them bread from heaven." The context of the quotation in Ps 78 is esp. interesting: manna is given in spite of the people's lack of faith and trust in God (cf. 78:22–29).

88. Borgen (1965, 61–67) shows that John uses the *'al-tiqrê* . . . ("Do not read *X*, but rather read *Y*") method of interpreting a text; Barrett 302. In 6:32, the Greek perfect *dedōken* renders the Hebrew *nātan* ("he gave"); the Greek present *didōsin* ("he is giving") matches the Hebrew present participle *nōtēn*. These Hebrew forms have the same consonants but differing vowel points (added in the early Middle Ages), so one can legitimately read *ntn* either way.

89. Borgen (1965) stresses the contrast between Jesus and the manna that Moses gave; Hylen stresses their continuity (as here). Provocatively, Martyn (123) concludes that in the end John does not seek to establish Jesus' identity via typological or midrashic arguments; he is not trying to correct exegetical missteps in order to show how the Scriptures bear witness to Jesus. Rather, "faith has only one essential presupposition: the presence of Jesus and his self-authenticating word." But for John, Scripture does point to Jesus when read retrospectively, through the instruction of the Spirit; see the introduction to this commentary.

understood Jesus' promise of "living water," they ask Jesus to provide this gift: "Lord, give us this bread always." They are right to ask. But they do not yet see that the bread is not something that Jesus gives but rather is Jesus *himself*, and that because he is God's life-giving agent and Word, Jesus not only can offer them the bread that gives life eternally, but is himself also that bread.

6:35–59 "I Am the Bread of Life"

Beginning with his declaration, "I am the bread of life," Jesus' discourse expounds the quotation from Scripture, "He gave them bread from heaven to eat," in three parts, as follows:

6:35–40	"He gave them bread": Identification of Jesus as the true bread of life
6:41–51	"From heaven": Explication of the (potentially scandalous) description "come down from heaven"
6:52–59	"To eat": Explication of "eating" this heavenly bread

In the first two parts of the discourse (6:35–40, 41–51), eating and drinking are metaphors for ingesting and imbibing God's word or instruction; hence, interwoven through these two parts one also finds the call to understand, to hear and learn from God, and to have faith in the one who instructs (6:36, 45–47). To eat is to learn, to understand, to know, to ingest God's word. One feasts on God's wisdom, on God's instruction. In the third section of the discourse (vv. 52–59), there is a shift from eating bread and drinking water or wine[90] to eating the flesh and drinking the blood of the Son of Man, this human being who is speaking such enigmatic words. The language of eating and drinking flesh and blood evokes the Lord's Supper. Even as the Lord's Supper recalls the death of Jesus—the giving of his very self, his flesh and blood, for the life of the world—so one now "ingests" and "imbibes" life by taking into oneself the life-giving benefits of Jesus' death. The discourse produces a divided response: some disciples defect, but Simon Peter, speaking for the Twelve, confesses that Jesus, the Holy One of God, has the words of eternal life.

> **6:35** Jesus said to them, "I am the bread of life. The one who comes to
> me will never hunger, and the one who believes in me will never thirst.[a]
> **36** But I tell you that you have seen me and do not believe. **37** Everyone
> whom[b] the Father gives me will come to me, and the one who comes to

90. In Prov 9:5, Wisdom issues an invitation to "eat of my bread and drink of the wine I have mixed"; in Sir 15:3, Wisdom supplies the "bread of learning" and the "water of wisdom."

me I will never drive away, 38 because I have come down from heaven
not to do my own will, but rather the will of the one who sent me. 39 This
is the will of the one who sent me: namely, that[c] I should lose nothing
of all that[d] he has given to me. And I will raise it[d] up on the last day. 40
For this is the will of my Father, that all who see the Son and believe
in him will have eternal life. And I will raise them[d] up at the last day."

41 The Jews grumbled about him because he had said, "I am the bread
that has come down from heaven," 42 and they said, "Isn't this Jesus, the
son of Joseph, whose father and mother we know? How then can he say,
'I have come down from heaven'?" 43 Jesus replied, "Do not grumble
among yourselves. 44 No one is able to come to me unless the Father
who sent me draws them, and I will raise them up at the last day. 45 It is
written in the prophets: 'And they shall all be taught by God.' Everyone
who hears and learns from the Father comes to me. 46 Not that anyone
has seen the Father except the one who is from God; this one has seen
the Father."

47 "Amen, amen I say to you, whoever believes in me has eternal life.
48 I am the bread of life. 49 Your ancestors ate manna in the wilderness,
and they died. 50 This is the bread that has come down from heaven,
which someone might eat of and not die. 51 I am the living bread that
has come down from heaven. If anyone eats this bread, they shall live
forever, and the bread that I will give for the life of the world is my
flesh."

52 The Jews disputed with each other, saying, "How is this one able
to give us his flesh to eat?" 53 Then Jesus said, "Amen, amen, I say to
you, if you do not eat the flesh of this Son of Man and drink his blood,
you have no life in you. 54 Whoever eats my flesh and drinks my blood
has eternal life, and I will raise them up at the last day. 55 For my flesh
is true food and my blood is true drink. 56 Whoever eats my flesh and
drinks my blood abides in me, and I abide in them. 57 Even as the living
Father sent me, and I live because of the Father, so the one who eats me
will live because of me. 58 This is the bread that has come down from
heaven, not as your ancestors ate and died. The one who eats this bread
will live forever."

59 He said these things as he was teaching in the synagogue in
Capernaum.

a. With *ou mē*, one expects a subjunctive (such as *peinasē*, "will never hunger") rather than a future indicative (such as *dipsēsei*, "will never thirst"); but the indicative is found in such instances in Matt 26:35; Mark 13:31; John 4:14.

b. The neuter singular *pan ho* ("all that"), translated here to reflect its assumed referent to "all people" or "everyone."

c. Not infrequently in John, *hina* introduces an explanatory clause or indirect discourse (e.g., 2:25; 4:34, 47; 5:7; 6:29).

d. Nothing "of all that" (*pan ho*) and "it" (*auto*, 6:39) render neuter-singular forms; "them" (*auton*) translates a masculine-singular form. The neuter forms show that the author views those whom Jesus receives and raises up as a whole.

[6:35–36] Jesus has just instructed the crowd that God, his Father, can give them the "true bread from heaven" that "gives life to the world." When they then petition Jesus for this bread, he redirects their seeking by identifying himself, in the first full "I am" statement of the Gospel, as "the bread of life."[91] The discourse that follows draws on the identification of bread, and particularly manna, the "bread from heaven," as a symbol for the nourishment provided by God's wisdom, teaching, or word (Deut 8:3; Prov 9:5; Isa 55:10–11; Sir 17:11; 24:19–22; 45:5).[92] Wisdom invites people to a feast of bread and wine, of instruction and learning, that leads to the path of life; according to the book of Sirach, that wisdom is embodied most fully in the Torah (Prov 9:5; Sir 24:19–21). Drawing on such traditions, the Jewish exegete Philo interprets the manna as the divine gift of wisdom.[93] In addition to serving as a figure of Torah and wisdom, manna was associated with the age to come. According to *2 Baruch* 29.6–30.1, the messianic age will be marked by the return of manna from on high and the resurrection of the dead.[94]

In John one hears echoes of the interpretation of bread and manna as figures of wisdom and the law, and of manna as the gift of end-time blessing. As the bread of life, Jesus embodies the instruction offered by wisdom and law; he is the bread that gives life both now and in the resurrection at the last day.[95] Those who accept his implicit invitation to come to him and to believe in him[96] will have their hunger and thirst to know God and to have the life that God gives fully satisfied (cf. Pss 42:2; 63:1; 143:6; Isa 55:1).

91. Here see Excursus 5: "The 'I Am' Sayings of John."

92. According to Deut 8:3 LXX, manna was given to show "your ancestors" (*hoi pateres*) that "one does not live by bread alone, but by every word that comes out of the mouth of God." Water can also stand for the law, wisdom, or God's instruction (cf. Ps 1:3; Prov 13:14; 18:4; Sir 15:3; 24:21, 23–27; 1QH VII [formerly XV], 4, 16; CD VI, 2–5; III, 12–17a; XIX, 32–35; *2 Bar.* 77.13–16; *m. ʾAbot* 6:1).

93. In commenting on Exod 16:4, Philo (*Mut.* 259–60), replaces manna with wisdom (*sophia*), yielding the following comment: "And indeed it says, 'Behold I rain upon you bread from heaven.' Of what food can he rightly say that it is rained from heaven, save of heavenly wisdom which is sent from above?" See also *Her.* 191; *Leg.* 3.162–64.

94. Later rabbinic traditions, which cannot be dated much earlier than the third century, expect the righteous to eat manna in the age to come; see *Mekilta* on Exod 16:25 and some texts from the *Midrash Rabbah* (*Num. Rab.* 11.2; *Ruth Rab.* 5.6; *Eccl. Rab.* 1.9; *Exod. Rab.* 2.6; *Deut. Rab.* 9.9).

95. See Dodd 1953, 336–37; Epp 136–37; Childs 137. Carson (1991, 289) argues that Isa 55:1–2, 10–11, adequately explains John's intertextual allusion; cf. R. Brown 1966, 521.

96. John 6:31, 35, 50, 52, 53, 54, 55, 56; cf. 7:37–38.

[37–40] Jesus then elaborates the relationship of his own work to that of the Father, who sent him (v. 38), whose purpose it is to give life (vv. 39–40). John again unites the work of Father and Son: those who respond to the Son in faith have been "given" to the Son by the Father; the Son will not cast out any given to him by the Father (v. 37).[97] Jesus' words account for the appalling actions of those disciples who turn away from him as well as Judas's betrayal: they have not been "given" to Jesus by the Father (6:66, 70–71). These statements make God ultimately responsible for drawing people to Jesus. But they also reiterate the point that the Father's will (vv. 39–40) is that none should be lost, but that all should be given eternal life, so that they may be raised at the last day (vv. 39–40). God wills resurrection and life, not death.[98] Because Jesus does the will of his Father, he gladly receives all those whom God has given to him. He gladly gives them the bread of life.

[41–47] "The Jews" deem Jesus' claim that he is the "bread that came down from heaven" to be both ludicrous and offensive. Surely Jesus' earthly origins (6:42, 52) undercut his claims to heavenly origins: he cannot be "from above." Thus the people grumbled (*egongyzon*, vv. 40, 43, 61; 7:32) even as did the Israelites in the wilderness—an action that indicates not so much dissatisfaction as disobedience or unbelief (Exod 15:24; 16:2, 7, 8, 9, 12; 17:3; Num 11:1; 14:2, 27; 17:5, 10 [20, 25 LXX]). "The Jews" fail to acknowledge Jesus' true identity: the one who is sent *by* God is the one who comes *from* God, who comes "down *from heaven*" (1:14).[99]

Even as Jesus has "come down from heaven," from the Father, so those who come to Jesus are drawn by the Father (6:44) or taught by God (v. 45). The verb "draw" (from *helkō*) can mean "to pull or drag by force" (e.g., John 21:6, 11; Acts 21:30) or "to attract" (BDAG s.v.). In John the emphasis on God's love for the world argues strongly for the latter meaning. According to Jer 31:3 (38:3 LXX), because God loves Israel with an eternal love, God has drawn them (*heilkysa*) with compassion; later Jeremiah promises that God himself will write the law on the hearts of his people so that they no longer need teachers (31:33–34; cf. 24:7; 32:38). In Ezekiel, the people of God are given a new heart and a new spirit, with the result that they heed all God's instruction (36:23–28; John 3:3–8). In other words, the prophets envision a future time when God restores his people, renews their heart and spirit, and becomes their teacher, drawing them to himself, so that they live in accordance with God's will and purposes (Jer 24:7; 31:33; 32:38; Ezek 11:20; 14:11; 36:28; 37:23, 27; Zech

97. "I will never cast out" or "drive away," *mē ekbalō exō*, 6:37; contrast 9:34, where the Pharisees "cast out" or "drove out" the blind man (*exebalon auton exō*).

98. For the distinction between life and resurrection, see comments on 5:25–28.

99. There may be an implicit allusion to the tradition of Jesus' virginal conception (so Barrett 184), but it is not further elaborated; cf. 8:41: "*We* were not born of fornication."

8:8; cf. 2 Cor 6:16; Heb 8:10; Rev 21:7). That prophetic vision comes to fruition in God's drawing people to Jesus.

Those whom God draws "shall all be taught by God" (John 6:45; Isa 54:13 LXX).[100] John has widened the scope of the text in Isaiah from Israel ("all your children") to "all" (*pantes*), a movement typical of the Gospel. But how is one taught by God? Earlier Jesus has pictured himself as an "apprentice" to the Father and as only doing "what he sees the Father doing" (John 5:19; cf. 8:28). Here, however, the Gospel rules out the possibility of a direct vision of God on the part of the would-be believer: one may *hear* from God, but no one but Jesus *has seen* God. Implicitly this assertion denies any such claims for Moses, or for any other figure who might have been thought to have attained a vision of God (see on 1:18; 3:13; 5:37), thus also denying to them a status as revealer or teacher superior or even equal to that of Jesus (cf. 3:2). In fact, the point is already made in Exod 33, which says that although Moses once *spoke* with God "face to face, as one speaks to a friend" (33:11), he was not allowed to *see* the face of God (33:23) since "no one may see me and live" (33:20).[101] Jesus, however, has seen God, learned from God, and can therefore make God known (John 1:18). It is through Jesus' teaching and deeds, then, that one is taught by God, that one hears God (7:16–17). Thus the two scriptural texts, "He gave them bread from heaven to eat" (6:31) and "They shall all be taught by God" (6:45), interpret one another: the bread is God's word, instruction, or wisdom, both brought by and embodied in Jesus.

[48–51] Jesus reiterates his identity as "the bread of life," the bread that can give life (v. 48) because he has been sent by "the living Father" (6:57; cf. "living God" in Deut 5:26; Jer 10:10). He has come "down from heaven" so that people may have life with God. The manna had also been "bread from heaven," but it was temporal, had to be gathered daily, and sustained life only in this world; thus, after "your ancestors" (*hoi pateres hymōn*) ate it, they still died (John 6:49, 58). But those who eat of this bread from heaven will never die: they can be assured that they have life with God that cannot be taken away by death (5:25; 11:26).

The discourse takes a new turn when it introduces the term *sarx* (flesh, 6:51), which occurs repeatedly in the next section (vv. 51–58), and explains that the life-giving "bread" is Jesus' own flesh, his very self, ultimately given in death. "Flesh" (*sarx*) especially indicates humankind in its mortality (1:13; 3:6; 8:15;

100. John 6:45 reads, *esontai pantes didaktoi theou*; Isa 54:12–13 LXX reads, *thēsō . . . pantas tous huious sou didaktous theou*, "I will cause all your sons/children to be taught by God," emphasizing God's role more directly; cf. *theodidaktoi*, "taught by God" (1 Thess 4:9); *didaktois pneumatos*, "taught by the Spirit" (1 Cor 2:13). In the DSS, CD XX, 4 speaks of "the disciples of God."

101. For the same contrast between "hearing" and "seeing" in John, with a preference for seeing and emphasis on Jesus' unique vision of God, see 8:38; comments on 1:18; 5:37; 12:37–43; M. M. Thompson 2007.

17:2) and so is appropriately used of Jesus' flesh as given in death. Moreover, the verb *[para]didonai* ("to hand over, give, give up") with the preposition *hyper* ("for, on behalf of") is regularly used in the New Testament with reference to Jesus' death, as in the memorable formulation, "[God] gave him up for us all" (Rom 8:32).[102] Flesh alone, death alone, does not lead to life. But Jesus' "flesh" (*sarx*) gives life for the world because he is the incarnate (John 1:14) Word of God, in which there is life (1:4). It is through his "coming down" from God, becoming flesh, and through his words, his deeds, and his death, that Jesus makes God known, because each of these points to the life-giving work of God: in his signs, Jesus feeds those who hunger; through his words, he imparts wisdom; in his dying, he gives life.

[52–58] As Jesus' assertions shift from themes of eating and drinking, understood as believing in and coming to Jesus, to the more graphic and specific imagery of "eating the flesh" and "drinking the blood" of Jesus, the responses shift from grumbling to dispute.[103] While the reference to "flesh" evokes the assertion that the Word became flesh (1:14), the addition of blood (*haima*, 6:53–56) shows that the death of Jesus is also in view, and that "eating the flesh" and "drinking the blood" constitute an allusion to the Lord's Supper (cf. 19:34).[104] While the Pauline and Synoptic accounts of the Lord's Supper speak of the *body* and blood, not the *flesh* and blood of Jesus, other early Christian authors did speak of the Eucharist in terms of "the blood" and "the flesh of our Savior Jesus Christ" (Ign., *Smyrn.* 6.1–2).[105]

But the pairing of "flesh and blood" is also found throughout biblical literature. "Flesh and blood" may refer to (1) the flesh and blood of a sacrificial animal, often coupled with the warning that one is not to eat the two together because "the life of the flesh is in the blood" (Lev 17:11; Deut 12:23); (2) human beings, particularly in their physicality or mortality;[106] or (3) the slaughter of human life, sometimes further described in cannibalistic terms of feasting, eating, or drinking the flesh and blood of those conquered.[107] Against the backdrop

102. *Hyper hēmōn pantōn paredōken auton*; see also Luke 22:19; Gal 1:4; 2:20; Eph 5:2, 25; 1 Tim 2:6; Titus 2:14.

103. In this portion of the discourse, John uses *trōgō* (6:54–58) rather than (the aorist) *phagō* for eating. Used of animals (BDAG, "chew, nibble, munch"), *trōgein* may place graphic emphasis on the act of eating. But John never uses the present tense *esthiein*, so *trōgein* may be his substitute for it (Barrett 299). Cf. Ps 41:9, with *esthiōn* (40:10 LXX), but cited at John 13:18 with *trōgōn*.

104. For blood as a figure for Jesus' death on the cross, see also 1 John 1:7; 5:6; Rev 5:9; Matt 27:24–25; Acts 20:28; Rom 3:25; Eph 1:7; Heb 13:12; Ign., *Smyrn.* 1.1; *1 Clem.* 7.4.

105. Ign., *Rom.* 7.3, the incorruptible bread and drink of God are the flesh and blood of Jesus Christ; Ign., *Phld.* 4.1; Justin (*1 Apol.* 66) also describes the Eucharist as the flesh and blood of the Lord.

106. Matt 16:17; 1 Cor 15:50; Gal 1:16; Eph 6:12; Heb 2:14; Sir 14:18; 17:31.

107. Deut 32:42; Isa 49:26; Jer 19:9; Ezek 5:10; 32:5; 33:25; 39:17–18; 44:7; Mic 3:3; 4 Macc 6:6. See also Eph 2:13–14 for descriptions of Jesus' death in terms of his blood (2:13) and flesh (2:14); Col 1:20–22 ("blood of his cross," v. 20; "in his body of his flesh," v. 22).

of any of these uses of the phrase "flesh and blood," "eating flesh" and "drinking blood" would be abhorrent: the act either violates commandments of the Torah or denotes cannibalism, sometimes in horrifically violent imagery.

In John 6, "flesh and blood" refer quite literally to Jesus portrayed as a sacrificial victim. But continuing the imagery of the earlier part of the discourse, "eating" and "drinking" refer to taking these into oneself through faith.[108] Earlier, "eating" and "drinking" have referred to taking into oneself the word of Jesus; here, they refer to taking into oneself the benefits of Jesus' death, commemorated in the practice of eating the Lord's Supper. John does not include an account of the "institution" of the Lord's Supper at his last meal with his disciples. Instead, the meal that first anticipated and then commemorated the death of Jesus has been set in the narrative of Jesus' life, showing that Jesus' entire life, his whole self, his "flesh and blood," were given to be life for the world. To put it differently, the eucharistic language in John 6:52–58 shows that the significance of the bread and cup of the Lord's Supper arises not only from Jesus' death, but also from his whole life as the Word that became incarnate and subsequently died on a cross, in order to give life to the world (cf. Luke 22:19; 1 Cor 11:24).

In partaking of the Lord's Supper, a bond is forged between believers and the risen Lord. When Jesus insists, "If you do not eat the flesh of the Son of Man and drink his blood, you have no life in you" (John 6:53), he is not speaking of the need to partake of the Lord's Supper in order to have life, but of the necessity of communing with the one who is that life.[109] Jesus' flesh, both his life and death, is "true food" and his blood "true drink" in that it accomplishes the ends of food and drink: it gives life (6:54–55). Those who do not eat do not have life within them (*en heautois*, 6:53). This phrasing echoes earlier statements where Jesus claims that "as the Father has life in himself, so also he has granted the Son to have life in himself" (*en heautō*, 5:26). Here is a parallel between Jesus and believers: the living Father[110] has life in himself, which he

108. The psalmist exhorts one to "taste and see that the LORD is good" (Ps 34:8) and declares that he "thirsts for God" (Pss 42:2; 63:1; 143:6). God's word or Torah provides nourishment (Deut 8:3; Isa 55:1–3); the failure to hear it can be described as a famine (Amos 8:11).

109. Ignatius famously asserts that the "one bread" is "the medicine of immortality [*pharmakon athanasias*], the antidote we take in order not to die but to live forever" (Ign., *Eph.* 20.2); in the *Didache*, the Eucharist is "spiritual food and drink [*pneumatikēn trophēn kai poton*], and eternal life" (10.3). On the connections between Passover and Eucharist in early Christian liturgy, see the excellent discussion in Skarsaune 399–422.

110. For the "living God," see 1 Sam 17:26, 36; 2 Kgs 19:4, 16; Jer 10:8–10; 23:36; Deut 5:26; Josh 3:10; Pss 42:2; 84:2; Isa 40:18–20, 28; 41:21–24; 44:9–20, 24; 45:16–22; 46:5–7; for the living God as the creator and source of life, see Ps 36:9; Jer 2:13; Ezek 37:1–16. Diogenes Laertius comments that the Stoics call the deity "*dia* ['on account of' or 'because of'] because all things are due to him; Zeus [Zēna] insofar as he is the cause of life [*zēn*, the verb 'to live'] or pervades all life" (*Lives* 7.147); so also Josephus, *Ant.* 12.22. For further discussion of the significance of this description of God, see M. M. Thompson 2001, 73–77.

grants to the Son, who may in turn give life to believers (4:14; 7:37). Those who eat the bread of life have taken life into themselves, but they do not become the source of life for others.

Various images of bread are layered over each other to bring out the significance of Jesus as the "true bread of life": bread to feed the five thousand, manna given the Israelites in the wilderness, the figurative bread of Torah, God's word and wisdom, the bread of the Eucharist, and Jesus himself.[111] Together, these various images of bread, of feeding and provision, show that what God gave to Israel, he now gives through Jesus; that what Jesus gave the hungry, he still gives as the living one; that what Jesus gave during his earthly life, he gave also in death; and that what he was in the creation of the world, he is now and will be on the last day. No matter which aspect of God's work in the world, or of Jesus' ministry and person, is taken into account, or whether creation or eschatology is in view, the same truth shines through: "in him was life, and this life was the light for all people" (1:4).

[59] It may come as a bit of a surprise to discover that Jesus has been speaking in a synagogue! This is actually the first and only place in this Gospel where Jesus is shown *in* a synagogue, even though he later claims that he has "always taught in synagogues and in the temple" (18:20; cf. 9:22; 12:42; 16:2). In the first century the synagogue was both the center of communal activity and the primary place in which the law was read, as the religious role of the synagogue gained in importance after the fall of the temple in 70 C.E.[112] The synagogue is the appropriate setting for the single longest interpretation of the Scriptures found in John and, indeed, in all the Gospels (cf. Luke 4:16–27; Acts 13:14–15; 15:21).

Excursus 5: The "I Am" Sayings of John

Characteristic of Jesus' speech in the Gospel of John are a number of revelatory sayings that begin with or include the Greek phrase *egō eimi* ("I am," "I am he," "it is I").[113] In these various sayings, Jesus speaks in formulations and imagery aligning himself with God's self-revelations as creator and sovereign in Isaiah. In John, Jesus' *egō eimi* statements point to his "unique role as the revelatory and salvific presence of God."[114]

111. In 1 Cor 10:3–4, perhaps 20–30 years earlier than John, Paul interprets the Lord's Supper in light of the biblical traditions of God's provision of manna and a well in the wilderness. While eating the Passover lamb was central to the remembrance of Passover, throughout John 6 the emphasis falls on eating bread: the five thousand ate bread; the Israelites ate manna, bread from heaven, in the wilderness; and Jesus' followers eat the bread that reminds them of his flesh, the bread that "has come down from heaven."

112. Both Philo (*Legat.* 156; cf. *Hypoth.* 7.12) and Josephus (*Ag. Ap.* 2.175) speak of regular gathering for religious instruction. See Levine 1260–61; comments on 9:22 below.

113. Particularly to be commended for further study are Ball and Catrin Williams.

114. Catrin Williams 255 n. 2.

The Old Testament context is of the utmost importance for interpreting these sayings since, on its own, *egō eimi* can simply be an ordinary way in which a speaker identifies oneself. The phrase can be used this way in John, but this is not its most distinctive usage.

The various sayings in John can be distinguished and categorized as follows:

1. There are seven "I am" (*egō eimi*) sayings with a predicate,[115] in which Jesus reveals who he is, and what he brings or offers to the world:

> I am the bread of life. (6:35)
> I am the light of the world. (8:12; 9:5)
> I am the door for the sheep. (10:7, 9)
> I am the good shepherd. (10:11, 14)
> I am the resurrection and the life. (11:25)
> I am the way, the truth, and the life. (14:6)
> I am the vine. (15:1)

These are statements in which Jesus identifies himself with a particular entity or figure and, more specifically, with entities that give life or can be identified as life itself (11:25; 14:6).

2. There are sayings without a predicate in which *egō eimi* is the speaker's way of acknowledging himself in response to an explicit or implicit query such as, "Who is it?" or "Who is there?" or "Is that you?" Thus, when the blind man's neighbors doubt that he is the man who was healed, he insists: "It is I!" (*egō eimi*, "I am the one" or "I am he!"; 9:9; cf. 2 Sam 2:20).

Several times in the Gospel, Jesus uses *egō eimi* simply to acknowledge his presence:

> I am he [*egō eimi*], the one speaking to you. (4:26)
> It is I [*egō eimi*]; do not be afraid. (6:20)
> I am [*egō eimi*] the one who bears witness. (8:18)[116]
> I am he [*egō eimi*]. (18:6)
> I told you that I am he [*eipon hymin hoti egō eimi*]. (18:8)[117]

In such statements, "I am" is an ordinary means of self-identification in Greek. Without the other categories of such "I am" statements, they would probably not call attention to themselves.

3. In four other statements, Jesus uses *egō eimi* without any predicate. In three of these statements, a verb for know or believe is followed by *hoti* ("that") and *egō eimi* ("I am"):

> For if you do not believe [*pisteusēte*] that I am [*egō eimi*], you will die in your sins. (8:24)

115. Cf. Matt 24:5, "Many shall come in my name, saying, 'I am the Messiah'" (*egō eimi ho Christos*); cf. Mark 13:6; Luke 21:8.

116. This statement is quite similar to those in the first category (*I am* with predicate).

117. Jesus' responses to these queries may belong in the third category or at least overlap with it.

> When you have lifted up the Son of Man, then you will know [*gnōsesthe*] that it is I [*egō eimi*]. (8:28)[118]
>
> Before Abraham was, I am [*egō eimi*]. (8:58)
>
> So that . . . you will believe [*pisteusēte*] that I am [*egō eimi*]. (13:19)

It is this third group of sayings, in which *egō eimi* is used as the object of what one believes, that raise questions about the meaning of all Jesus' "I am" sayings in John. The starting point for their interpretation, and perhaps for all the "I am" sayings, is the Old Testament, and particularly God's self-identification in a number of places, including Exod 3:14; Deut 32:39; and Isaiah (esp. 43:10, 11; 45:3).[119]

First, the "I am" sayings of John are often taken to reflect God's identification of himself in the memorable formulation "I am who I am" (*ʾehyeh ʾăšer ʾehyeh*) or "I will be who I will be" (Exod 3:14 and mg.). The LXX renders the Hebrew of Exod 3:14 as *egō eimi ho ōn*, "I am the one who is," thus characterizing God or God's identity in terms of ongoing existence (cf. John 5:26). In spite of the fact that Moses asks God what his name is, the Hebrew verb form *ʾehyeh* does not recur as a name for God; neither is the Greek *egō eimi* found as God's name elsewhere in the LXX.[120]

Alluding to the LXX, the first-century Jewish exegete Philo repeatedly refers to God either as *ho ōn* ("the one who is") or, more frequently, as *to on*, "that which is." On Exod 3:14, Philo even comments, "[God] has no proper name, . . . for it is not the nature of him that is to be spoken of, but simply to be" (*Somn.* 1.230–33; *Mut.* 11–15; *Deus* 62; *Det.* 160; *Decal.* 58). In other words, the LXX, and Philo's use of it, show that the revelation of God in Exod 3:14 was understood to emphasize God's sheer existence, the fact that God simply is. There are instances in John where Jesus' "I am" sayings particularly emphasize that he has, and can give, that sort of divine life; that he "is" as God is (e.g., John 8:58).

Second, there are numerous places in Scripture where God identifies himself to Israel and its patriarchs with statements such as "I am the LORD" (Gen 15:7); "I am the God of your father Abraham" (Gen 26:24) or "I am God, the God of your father" (Gen 46:3); or "I am the LORD your God" (Exod 6:7; 16:12; 20:2; and frequently in Leviticus). The Septuagint translates the various underlying Hebrew expressions[121] either with *egō eimi* or *egō* ("I") and the appropriate predicate; English translations use "I am." It is a characteristic of divine speech in the Old Testament for God to describe and present himself by means of such declarations. But without the predicates, the Greek *egō eimi* (and its underlying Hebrew) would be neither particularly revelatory nor characteristic

118. Perhaps this might be interpreted, "You will know that I am the Son of Man," "You will know that I am he," or "that I am."

119. For *egō eimi* in the Synoptic Gospels, see Matt 26:22, 25 (KJV, "Lord, is it I?"). For *egō eimi* used by Jesus to acknowledge himself, see Mark 14:62; Luke 24:39; used by others, Mark 13:6; Luke 21:8; 22:70; 24:39. *Egō eimi* is also spoken by Jesus in conjunction with the sea crossing (Matt 14:27; Mark 6:50).

120. Aquila and Theodotion rendered the Hebrew of Exod 3:14 with the future tense *esomai (hos) esomai* ("I will be who I will be").

121. E.g., *ʾănî YHWH*, Gen 15:7; *ʾănî-ʾĒl Šadday*, Gen 17:1; *ʾānōkî ʾĔlōhê ʾAbrāhām*, Gen 26:24.

of divine speech. As with the first category of sayings, it is the predicates themselves that are significant.

Third, other passages in the Old Testament are particularly suggestive for John's use of the absolute *egō eimi* (8:24, 28, 58; and perhaps 4:26; 6:20; 18:5, 8), where the underlying MT expression is *'ănî hû'*, often best translated not merely as "I am" but as "I am he." In particular, there are several important passages in Isaiah, as well as the only MT occurrence of *'ănî hû'* outside Isa 40–55: "See now that I, even I, am he; there is no god besides me. I kill and I make alive; I wound and I heal; and no one can deliver from my hand" (Deut 32:39). The statement calls for recognition of God in light of his self-declaration as "I am he" (*'ănî hû'*, *egō eimi*), while simultaneously acknowledging God to be the one who has the power over life and death. God's declaration in Deut 32:39 casts light on Jesus' "I am" sayings since, in John, God's power over life is given to the Son. The "I am" sayings with predicates (the first category above) underscore the same point.

A number of sayings in Isa 40–55 reflect the rhetorical pattern where God speaks in the first person, emphatically asserting his uniqueness, such as these:

> I, the LORD, am first, and will be the last. (41:4)
> I, I am the LORD, and besides me there is no savior. (43:11)
> I am God, and also henceforth I am He. (43:13)
> I am the LORD. (43:15; see also 46:4; 48:12; 52:6)[122]

In such statements one finds different Hebrew expressions for these first-person assertions, including *'ănî*, *'ănî hû'*, or *'ānōkî, 'ānōkî 'ānōkî*. These forms are translated in the LXX either with *egō* or with *egō eimi*. Again, the predicates are needed to complete the thought.

But particularly striking are the parallels between Isa 43:10 LXX and the absolute Johannine sayings that use the verbs "believe" or "know" (John 8:24, 28; 13:19):

> *hina gnōte kai pisteusēte kai synēte hoti egō eimi*, that you may know and believe and understand that I am. (Isa 43:10 LXX)
> *ean gar mē pisteusēte hoti egō eimi*, if you do not believe that I am. (John 8:24)
> *tote gnōsesthe hoti egō eimi*, then you will know that I am. (8:28)
> *hina pisteusēte hotan genētai hoti egō eimi*, that you will believe when it happens that I am. (13:19)

According to Isaiah, people are to know, believe, and understand that God is (LXX, *hoti egō eimi*; MT, *kî 'ănî hû'*). In John, people are called to believe or know that Jesus is (*hoti egō eimi*). Like the Father before him, the Son now reveals himself as the one who is.[123]

Not only is the pattern of Jesus' speech in John redolent of Old Testament patterns of divine speech in grammatical form; Jesus' assertions also duplicate the object of what one is to believe or know ("that I am he," *hoti egō eimi*). In Isaiah, God's declaration

122. Cf. other places in the LXX where God says *egō eimi*: Isa 43:25; 45:8, 18–19; 46:9; 48:17; 51:12; Babylon's false claims (47:8, 10) are couched in the same form.

123. See Schnelle 1998, 125.

"that I am he" is followed by the emphatic denial "Before me no god was formed, nor shall there be any after me" (43:10). These assertions are typical of monotheistic rhetoric, not only in Isaiah, but also in Jewish apologetic literature, in which God is depicted as declaring emphatically that he alone is God.[124] In John, Jesus' various declarations, using *egō eimi* ("I am"), underscore his unique status with respect to his role in conferring the Father's gift of life: there is no other bread of life, no other light for the world, no other vine. The definite article (*the* bread of life, *the* light of the world) identifies Jesus with these realities exclusively. What he offers is himself: he offers the bread of life because he himself is life (John 1:4).

Both the form and content of Jesus' *egō eimi* statements, with and without a predicate, reflect the form and content of divine speech in Isaiah: Jesus' statements are like the monotheistic rhetoric of Isaiah that declares God to be the only God because God alone is the living God, creator of all. The Johannine "I am" statements, particularly those with predicates (life, bread, resurrection, vine), reinforce Jesus' identity as the one who mediates the life of the living Father (6:57). Together these patterns of speech illumine the "absolute" *egō eimi* sayings. They show that Jesus speaks as God does, making similar claims for his unique identity, an identity located above all in the power to give life. But apart from context, neither the Hebrew *'ănî hû'* nor the Greek *egō eimi* carries those connotations: they simply mean "I am" or "It is I." While Jesus speaks the way God speaks, it is what he asserts about himself that links him to God (cf. the assertions of those kings who boast in their powers in Ezek 27:3; 28:2, 9; and see the extended comments on "equal to God" at John 5:18). Even as God declares his uniqueness, so also Jesus presents himself as God does: as the one in whom there is life for all and hence as the object of faith.

6:60–71 The Response to Jesus' Discourse

The response to Jesus' words is mixed, as indeed it is throughout the Gospel. Now some of Jesus' own disciples find his teaching unbearable and stop following him. Even more ominous is the note that one of Jesus' own disciples not only is going to abandon him but also to betray him (6:71). To be sure, the opening verses of the Gospel have foretold a mixed response to Jesus' mission (1:10–13). In the present context we have a painful and poignant turn of events: some who once were Jesus' disciples turn away from him. But the Twelve, confessing that Jesus has the "words of eternal life," remain faithful—except Judas. "The Twelve" represent the kind of response that the Gospel elsewhere cultivates: initial belief must lead to perseverance and faithfulness, to "abiding" in Jesus.[125]

6:60 When many of his disciples heard this, they said, "This is a hard word! Who is able to hear it?" **61** Jesus, knowing that his disciples were

124. Hurtado 2005a; Catrin Williams.

125. See, further, Excursus 8: "The Johannine Vocabulary of Faith and Discipleship."

grumbling to one another about this, said to them, "Does this give you
offense? **62** What then if you see this Son of Man ascending to where he
was at first? **63** The Spirit is the one who gives life; the flesh profits noth-
ing. These words that I have spoken to you are spirit and life. **64** But there
are some of you who do not believe." For from the beginning Jesus knew
who would not believe, and who it was who would hand him over.[a] **65** And
so he said, "This is why I have said to you that no one is able to come to
me unless it has been given to them by the Father."

66 After this many of his disciples withdrew and no longer went about
with him. **67** Then Jesus said to the Twelve, "Do you also wish to leave?"
68 And Simon Peter said to him, "Lord, to whom shall we go? You have
the words of eternal life. **69** And we have believed and come to know
that you are the Holy One of God."[b] **70** Jesus answered them, "Have I
not chosen you twelve? And one of you is a devil." **71** He said this about
Judas, the son of Simon Iscariot.[c] For he—one of the Twelve—was going
to hand Jesus over.[a]

a. The word translated "handed over" comes from *paradidōmi*, "hand over, turn over, give up" a person; "surrender" a person into the custody of another; or "hand over" with implied treachery (see BDAG; LSJM). Elsewhere in the NT it refers to the handing on of tradition (1 Cor 11:23; 15:3) or to God's giving the Son up to death; it occurs in the Gospels most frequently with reference to Judas's act of delivering or "betraying" Jesus to death (cf. John 6:64, 71; 12:4; 13:2, 11, 21; 18:2, 5; 19:11; 21:20). To demonstrate the parallelism of the actions of Judas with the Jewish (18:30, 35–36; 19:11) and Roman (19:16) authorities in the Passion Narrative in "delivering" or "handing over" Jesus to be crucified, the translation "hand over" is used here (so also 6:71); see comments on 13:2; 19:11, 16; similarly, see R. Brown 1994, 1:211; Keener 2:1127.

b. Here *ho hagios tou theou* is attested by 𝔓^{75} ℵ B D; numerous variants harmonize Peter's confession here with the Synoptics (Matt 16:16; Mark 8:29; Luke 9:20).

c. The textual evidence of 𝔓$^{66, 75}$ B C L W Ψ 33 *al* favors the genitive case *Iskariōtou*, agreeing with *Simōnos* ("Judas, son of Simon Iscariot"), rather than the accusative *iskariōtēn* agreeing with *Ioudan* ("Judas Iscariot, son of Simon").

[60–66] Heretofore Jesus' audience has been described either as the crowd (6:2, 5, 22, 24), people (6:10, 14), or the Jews (6:41, 52); now his own disciples come into view (6:60). Some of Jesus' followers respond to him with incredulity and unbelief. When Jesus' own followers are offended (*skandalizō*) at his words, he speaks of a yet greater offense: the "ascent" of this human being to the Father (1:51; 3:11–13). If people struggle to understand how Jesus can be the bread of God that has come down (*katabainō*) from heaven, how will they possibly understand that he will return (ascend, *anabainō*) to the Father? Jesus' return presupposes the events of his death (13:1) and his resurrection (20:17), after which he "ascends" to his Father.

Given the emphasis on Jesus' flesh as necessary for the life of the world (6:52–58), the statement that "the flesh profits nothing; the Spirit gives life" (v. 63) is jarring. A similar contrast between flesh and Spirit occurs in John 3, where Jesus tells Nicodemus, "Whatever is begotten of the flesh is flesh, and what is begotten of the Spirit is spirit" (3:6). Flesh is mortal; it can neither receive nor give eternal life. Only the Spirit can give life, and the one reborn of the Spirit enters the kingdom and lives (3:5–6; 6:63). "The flesh profits nothing" refers not to Jesus' flesh, but to the human person apart from the life-giving work of the Spirit.[126] Those who do not have the Spirit "do not believe" (v. 64); they have not been "given" to the Son by the Father (vv. 39, 65); they have not been "taught by God" (v. 45). Like Nicodemus, they seek Jesus because of his deeds (3:2; 6:26) but find Jesus' claims to have come from God and to be returning to him offensive and mysterious. Jesus' explanation—that he must be lifted up and so give life to the world (3:14–16) or that, having died for the world, he will return to the Father (6:51–62)—lies beyond their comprehension, at least apart from God's teaching (6:44–45) and the giving of the Spirit. Without the Spirit that gives life, people cannot know the one who is life.

[67–71] As a result of Jesus' discourse and claims, there is a division among his followers as many desert him (cf. 7:40–44). Among those who remain with Jesus are the Twelve, here referred to for the first time in the Gospel (cf. 20:24), although no list of their names or account of their selection is ever provided (cf. Matt 10:2–4; Mark 3:14–19; Luke 6:13–19, where they are also called apostles; and Rev 21:14). John frequently refers to the "disciples" of Jesus, mentioning a number of followers not attested in the Synoptics by name, including Nathanael (1:45–49), Nicodemus (3:1–13; 7:50; 19:39), Lazarus (John 11:1–44), as well as the unnamed Samaritan woman and the "disciple whom Jesus loved" (13:23; 19:26, 35; 20:10). Jesus' disciples are larger than the circle of "the Twelve" (cf. also 10:16; 17:20).

Still, Jesus states that he has chosen (*exelexamēn*) the Twelve (6:70), echoing Scriptural language for God's "choosing" of Israel (Deut 4.37; 7:7; 10:15; 14:2; Pss 33:12; 135:4; Isa 49:7; Ezek 20:5), Abraham (Gen 18:19; Neh 9:7), and David (2 Sam 6:21; 1 Chr 28:4). As is evident from biblical precedent, to be chosen means to be called and designated by God for a particular vocation (see comments on 15:16–19). As is also evident from God's choosing Israel, such "choice" does not guarantee faithful obedience. Judas may be among those chosen by Jesus; but he is not among those who persevere in following after him.

Those who remain with Jesus do so because they believe that Jesus' words are the words of life, even as he has said (6:63), and confess him as "the Holy One of God." The designation *ho hagios tou theou* is not a known messianic title, but it is attributed to Jesus by demons in the Synoptic accounts (Mark 1:24;

126. Schnelle 1998, 139.

Luke 4:34). The Holy One of God will "cast down" the ruler of this world, even as he drives out demons in the other Gospels (John 12:31; 14:30; 16:11; cf. Rev 21:8, 27; 22:3, 15–19). Sent by God, the Holy Father (John 17:11), he gives the Holy Spirit (1:33; 14:26; 20:22). Given the fact that John elsewhere attributes to Jesus a number of the roles or designations of God (e.g., Lord, Savior, Creator, King, God; cf. esp. Isa 43:10–16), the identification of Jesus as the Holy One of God connects him with the Holy One of Israel, a designation for God especially common in Isaiah, without simply collapsing their identities into each other: John consistently distinguishes the Father and the Son, even when or perhaps especially when speaking of their unity (10:30; 17:11, 21).

Here it is not Peter whom Jesus labels a devil (or Satan; cf. Mark 8:33), but Judas, the son of Simon Iscariot. Although the phenomenon of abandoning an initial interest or faith in Jesus was surely to be found in Jesus' own day,[127] there is in the Gospel of John a particular horror of disciples who fall away from or desert Jesus, hand him over to the authorities, or otherwise fail to persevere in their allegiance to him. Indeed, the most negative rhetoric in the Gospel will be directed against "Jews who had believed in him" (8:31). Having abandoned their initial faith, they are said to belong to the devil (8:44; cf. 1 John 3:10, "children of the devil"), even as Judas himself is here called "a devil" (6:70). Jesus' discourse produces a division among his followers, leading some to turn away; his faithful followers are represented by the Twelve.

John's portrait of Jesus in chapter 6 fuses traditional material about Jesus' ministry; allusions to the Scriptures and interpretive traditions about manna, word, and wisdom; the practice of celebrating the Lord's Supper; and John's own deep convictions about Jesus—all to present him as the "true bread of God" that gives life to the world. The events of the chapter are set at Passover. Like the first Passover, there is also a miraculous crossing of the sea, followed by a period of time during which God provides manna in the wilderness, a provision that prefigures what God now gives through Jesus. The traditions that read manna as a figure for both Torah and instruction or wisdom, expecting its return as an eschatological gift and sign, are woven throughout the discourse, in order to present Jesus as the one in whom God's life-giving word, law, and wisdom are given here and now, and through whom life will be given "at the last day." The meal that remembers the death of Jesus became a distinctive practice of the church; John provides graphic imagery of eating and drinking the "flesh" and "blood" of Jesus, another way of ingesting the bread that comes from God, of taking the very life of God into oneself. Jesus' acts of provision in his own day were remembered by the church in its day; and its memory of what he had done and the experience of his ongoing presence became the hermeneutical lens

127. See the parable of the sower in the Synoptic Gospels for a mixed response to the word of God (Matt 13:3–8; Mark 4:3–8; Luke 8:5–8).

through which God's gifts to Israel were interpreted and understood as prefiguring God's abundant gifts both to his people and to all the world.

7:1–10:21 Jesus, the Light of the World: Words and Deeds at Tabernacles

Chapters 7:1–10:21 comprise a connected series of narratives and discourses set during the Feast of Tabernacles (7:2; cf. 10:22).[128] Given the fact that in its celebration both the exodus from Egypt and the return from exile in Babylon were remembered at this feast, it could arouse hopes for subsequent deliverance. Not surprisingly, the questions raised throughout these chapters are whether Jesus might be the Messiah, or the prophet (7:26–27, 31, 41–42; 9:22; cf. 10:24), and how that vocation is to be exercised. Jesus presents himself as one from God, whose teaching is certified by God (7:16–17). As the one who comes from God, he speaks and acts as the light, opening the eyes of the blind and directing people to the pathway that leads to life: not only for his people, Israel, but also for all the world (8:12; 9:5). He is the light of life because he is the Son, who existed before Abraham ever came into being (8:58) and who commits himself as the Messiah, the shepherd of the sheep, to protecting them from death (10:1–18). Ultimately he will exercise his messianic vocation and accomplish the purposes of his mission in giving himself up for his flock. A multitude of titles and epithets are predicated of him: Prophet, Messiah, light, life, teacher, Lord, Son of Man, and shepherd. Collectively, these designations show what it means to confess Jesus as Messiah in the Gospel (9:22–23), as the one who speaks and acts on behalf of the Father who sent him.

Given Jesus' bold declarations, the people are divided in their assessments of him (7:43; 10:19). Some honor Jesus as a prophet (7:40, 52; 9:17); others, as the Messiah (7:26–27, 31, 41–42; 9:22). Some charge him with deceiving the people; others regard him as a sinner who breaks the law (7:12, 19, 21–24; 9:16, 24–25, 29). He is even accused of being possessed by a demon (7:20; 8:48, 49, 52; 10:20–21). Although many believed (7:31; 8:30; 9:38), others did not (7:41, 43–44), including Jesus' brothers (7:5), the Pharisees (7:32), and the chief priests (7:45). No matter what Jesus does or says, his actions and words lead to differences among the people over fundamental questions about just who he is (10:19–21).

These chapters illustrate the warning of Jesus: "Do not judge by appearance, but judge with right judgment" (7:24). These judgments have to do with whether Jesus comes from God and so speaks truthfully about who he is and what he can offer. Much is at stake. Jesus challenges "the Jews" regarding their claims to be descendants of Abraham (8:39), a cherished status and privilege, and by

128. Poirier argues that from 8:12 onward, the setting is Hanukkah.

implication undercuts their very identity as those who name God as their father (8:41). As Jesus' own rhetoric throughout these chapters becomes increasingly pointed and polemical, the response becomes increasingly resistant and hostile (8:33–59). And when Jesus heals on the Sabbath, the right judgments that must be passed have to do with what it means to keep or to violate the law, what constitutes sin or lawbreaking, and whether Jesus or his opponents best understand and interpret Moses. In short, the debates have to do with the relationship of Jesus and his followers to Moses and the law (9:25–29), the meaning of Jesus' signs (9:16), his identity as prophet (9:17) and Messiah (9:22), and whether he indeed comes from God (9:33) and is to be confessed as Lord (9:38).

7:1–13 Jesus and His Brothers: Invitation to the Feast

Tabernacles, perhaps the greatest of the temple feasts in late Second Temple Judaism, was the perfect occasion for Jesus to reveal himself and press his claims publicly—or so his brothers urge him. Yet their urging is not evidence of their belief in Jesus, any more than was the desire of the crowds to make Jesus king (6:15) or the grumbling of his own disciples (6:60–61). The episodes of the Gospel regularly illustrate the contention of the prologue that "he came to his own home, but his own people did not welcome him" (1:11). Even so, the motifs and themes associated with Tabernacles become the backdrop against which Jesus' claims and identity are portrayed in John 7, showing who he is for Israel and for all the world, and thereby inviting trust in him.

> **7:1** And after these things, Jesus went about in Galilee, for he did not
> want to go about in Judea, for the Jews were seeking to kill him. **2** Now
> it was Tabernacles, the feast of the Jews. **3** His brothers said to him: "Go
> up from here to Judea, so that your disciples may see the works that you
> do. **4** For no one who wants to be known openly acts in secret. If you do
> these things, then show yourself to the world." **5** For his brothers did not
> believe in him.
>
> **6** Jesus said to them, "My time is not yet here. Your time is always
> here. **7** The world cannot hate you, but it hates me, because I bear witness
> that its works are evil. **8** You go up to the feast; I am not[a] going up to this
> feast, for my time has not yet fully come." **9** Having said these things, he
> remained in Galilee.
>
> **10** When his brothers went up to the feast, then he himself went up,
> but in secret, not openly. **11** The Jews were seeking him at the feast, say-
> ing, "Where is he?" **12** And there was great grumbling about him among
> the people. On the one hand, some were saying, "He is a good man," but
> others were saying, "No, he deceives the people." **13** But no one spoke
> openly about him for fear of the Jews.

a. The adverb *oupō*, "not yet," rather than *ouk*, "not," found in some early papyri such as 𝔓[66, 75], alleviates the tension between Jesus' refusal to go to the feast (v. 8) and his ensuing appearance there (v. 10) and is probably to be judged as secondary.

[7:1–2] "After these things" Jesus "went about" in Galilee, avoiding Judea because "the Jews were seeking to kill him." The chronological indicators and descriptions of Jesus' activities are somewhat vague, but the threat against Jesus' life, introduced earlier (5:18), is now repeated. And yet at least six months have passed in the implied chronology of the Gospel. These events here are set "near Tabernacles" (7:2), in the fall, while the feeding of the five thousand is set near Passover (6:4), in the spring. The distinct episodes of the Gospel are nevertheless connected by John's narrative of the mixed, but increasingly negative, reception that Jesus receives, leading ultimately to his death in Jerusalem. From here on in the Gospel, the intent to put Jesus to death will intensify (7:1, 19–20, 25; 8:22, 37, 40).

Jesus' brothers apparently expect that he will accompany them to Jerusalem for the Feast of Tabernacles.[129] In the Old Testament, Tabernacles, one of the three pilgrimage festivals,[130] is a harvest festival (Lev 23:34–44; Exod 23:16; 34:22; Deut 16:13–15; 31:10–13; Zech 14:18–19). Because the festival came to commemorate the wilderness wanderings after the exodus from Egypt, when the Israelites had no fixed dwellings, it was called the Festival of Booths, Sukkot (Greek, *heortē skēnōn*; Hebrew, *ḥag hasukkōt*). Elsewhere it is referred to as "the festival of the LORD" (Lev 23:39; Hos 9:5) or, more simply, "the festival" (*ḥag*, 1 Kgs 8:2; Ezek 45:25). There are different regulations for observing it in the Pentateuch. According to Leviticus the people are to live in "booths" or "huts" as a reminder of God's provision during the years of wilderness wandering (Lev 23:42–43; Neh 8:14–17). On the first day of the feast, people are to take fruit and branches of various trees, including palms and willows, and "rejoice before the LORD" (Lev 23:40). Numbers prescribes extensive sacrifices

129. John 7:2 calls it *hē heortē hē skēnopēgia*, as does LXX in Deut 16:16; 31:10; 1 Esd 5:50; 1 Macc 10:21; 2 Macc 1:9, 18; Zech 14:16, 18; also Josephus, *Ant.* 4.209; 8.100, 123, 225; 11.77, 154; 13.46, 241, 372; 15.50; *J.W.* 2.515. It is also called *hē heortē tōn skēnōn*, "the Feast of the Tabernacles" or "tents," in LXX at Lev 23:34; Deut 16:13; Ezra 3:4. For recent studies of Tabernacles, see Rubenstein; Ulfgard. In a rare description of a Jewish feast in a pagan source, Plutarch describes Tabernacles (*skēnē*) as "the greatest, most sacred holiday of the Jews," notes its Dionysiac character, and refers to the practice of living in huts, carrying branches in procession, and using "little trumpets to invoke their god" (*Quaest. conv.* 4.6.2 [*Mor.* 671D–E]; cf. *m. Sukkah* for descriptions).

130. On the crowds who gathered for Tabernacles, see Philo, *Spec.* 1.69; Josephus, *J.W.* 2.515; *Ant.* 17.254. Tabernacles is celebrated on days 15–21 of the seventh month, Tishri (September–October), preceded by Rosh Hashanah (on day 1) and Yom Kippur (day 10).

for Tabernacles (29:12–38); Deuteronomy dictates that the law is to be read (31:10–13; Josephus, *Ant.* 8.100).

Ezra connects the resumption of sacrifice in the temple after the return from Babylon with the Feast of Sukkot, because the dedication of Solomon's temple occurred then (Ezra 3:4; 1 Kgs 8; 2 Chr 5–7; 2 Macc 1:18; cf. *m. Sukkah* 3:12). In Nehemiah, Tabernacles is linked to rediscovering, reading, and obeying the law, including the proper celebration of Tabernacles itself, after the return from exile. Nehemiah reports that "from the first day to the last day" of the festival, Ezra read from the law, "from the book of the teaching of God" (*bĕsēper tôrat hāʾĕlōhîm*; Neh 8:13–18; Ezra 3:4). According to Zechariah, Tabernacles will be celebrated after God's judgment and the restoration of Jerusalem. Its celebration will entail (1) the purification of the city of Jerusalem, so that all vessels are clean and commerce is banished from the temple (14:16–21; cf. John 2:13–21), and (2) the universal pilgrimage of the nations to Jerusalem to worship the God of Israel, where they too will keep the feast.

Tabernacles is characterized by joy and celebration. In the book of *Jubilees* the feast is also called the feast of rejoicing (16.20; cf. 16.27, 29; 2 Macc 10:6). According to *Jubilees* 16, Abraham celebrated the first Feast of Tabernacles by building booths, sacrificing, praying, and marching around the altar he had built, waving branches of palms, willow, and fruit.[131] Josephus calls Tabernacles an "exceedingly great and holy feast" (*Ant.* 8.100), observing that the eight-day feast included various sacrifices, a procession with branches or *lulavs*, and the citron (presumably in keeping with Lev 23:40; *Ant.* 3.244–47). He refers to the festival as "Lights" (*Ant.* 12.325). The later Mishnaic regulations of *Sukkah* cover the building of booths, sacrificing, and gathering of branches (including the citron), the singing of psalms, rejoicing at the place of water drawing, a ceremony with pouring water, flute playing, and the lighting of golden candlesticks.[132] Additionally, dancing, singing, and the playing of instruments were part of the celebration and rituals of Tabernacles.

Of the practices associated with Tabernacles in various sources, three in particular resonate with John's presentation of Jesus' actions in the temple at this feast: the reading of the law or "teaching of God" (7:16–24), the drawing and especially pouring of the water (7:37–39), and the lighting of the golden candlesticks (perhaps also Josephus's reference to the feast as "lights";

131. Jacob also keeps the feast (*Jub.* 32). Philo indicates in passing that in the Diaspora booths were built at the time of the festival (*Flacc.* 116). See also 11QT XI–XIII; XXVII, 10–XXIX, 6; XL, 10–17; and XLIV, 6–16, according to which booths are built *within* the confines of the temple (11QT XLII, 10–17; following Neh 8:16, where the booths are built "in the courts of the house of God.")

132. On the lighting of the candlesticks, see comments on 8:12.

8:12; 9:5). Neither the ritual of pouring nor of lighting candlesticks occurs in biblical descriptions of the feast; however, these seem to be reflected in Jesus' promise to give living water (7:37–39) and his claim to be the light of the world (8:12; 9:5). While the Gospel reflects knowledge of ceremonies in the temple, drawn not from Scripture but from traditions of celebrations of Tabernacles, both light (Pss 43:3; 119:105, 130; Prov 6:23; Isa 2:5) and water (Sir 24:21) are images for divine instruction or wisdom, which, according to Deuteronomy and Nehemiah, is to be read at Tabernacles. Jesus' claims to offer living water and to be light for the world figuratively express his further claim that his teaching is of God. The various themes, drawn from biblical descriptions and regular celebration of Tabernacles, provide the backdrop to depict Jesus as the teacher of God's truth, as light and salvation for all people.

[2–9] Jesus has been in Jerusalem for Passover (2:13) and on the occasion of another feast (5:1). Urging him to go to Jerusalem, Jesus' brothers assert that he ought not to work in secret (*en kryptō*) but rather to act openly or in public (*en parrēsia*), that he should "show himself" to the world (7:4, *phanerōson*; cf. *phanerōs*, 7:10).[133] Among Greek philosophers, *parrēsia* referred to freedom, boldness, or frankness in speech, perhaps in potentially intimidating circumstances (see BDAG s.v.). John contrasts speaking "openly" (or with *parrēsia*) and speaking figuratively (10:24; 11:14; see comments on 16:25, 29), characterizes Jesus as speaking publicly and openly (7:26; 18:20), and indicates that at times Jesus was not able to work publicly (11:54) or that people were unable to speak publicly about him (7:4, 13) or were fearful of doing so. When Jesus does not work or speak with *parrēsia*, publicly or openly, he is waiting for "his hour" to arrive or refusing to seek his own honor.

While Jesus' brothers urge him to be "known openly" (NIV, "to become a public figure"; NRSV, "to be widely known"), Jesus does not seek to enhance his own reputation (7:18). Nor will he "show" himself to the world at his brothers' urging, any more than he would acquiesce to his mother's request (2:4). That his time has not yet come (7:6, 8; 2:4) indicates that he will act only as his Father commands (7:18). When Jesus' hour does come, it will not bring public acclamation and glory—at least not as the world measures glory. The world does not welcome him; instead, the world "hates" Jesus because he reveals the character of its deeds (7:7).[134] Following his resurrection, he will indeed become openly

133. Matthew and Mark name Jesus' brothers as James, Joseph (Joses), Simon, and Judas (Jude), and refer to "his sisters" (Matt 13:55; Mark 3:21; 6:3). According to early Christian tradition, Jesus' brothers and their descendants later became leaders in the early church (Acts 12:17; 15:13; 21:18; 1 Cor 15:7; Gal 1:19; 2:9–12; Jas 1:1; Jude 1; cf. Eusebius, *Hist. eccl.* 3.11, 20).

134. "Hate" (*misein*) and its cognates (scarce in LXX, with fewer than two dozen occurrences) lack the affective connotations that the English terms "hate" and "hatred" carry: hence, "hold in disfavor" or "have relatively little regard for" (BDAG). The term functions nearly as the opposite of *doxein* ("to give glory; honor"; see, e.g., 7:18; comments on 3:20 above).

(or widely) known. While ultimately blessings will flow from Jerusalem to all the world (7:38),[135] the world is at this moment not hospitable to God's agent. Jesus puts it quite starkly: "The world hates me" (7:7; 15:18–19).

[10–13] After telling his brothers that he is not going to the feast (v. 8), Jesus *does* go after his brothers have departed (v. 10). Here one finds the same contrast between what is done in public (openly) and in secret (hidden) that his brothers had used earlier, although the values placed on each are reversed: Jesus will go, but not openly (*phanerōs*), as they had urged him; he will go only in secret (*en kryptō*), which they disdain. While they see public revelation as an opportunity for fame or glory, it is exactly these aspirations that Jesus eschews, seeking instead only his Father's glory.

The argument over Jesus' identity continues with the question whether he is "good" or whether he deceives the people with false teaching. But these assessments are not offered "openly . . . for fear of the Jews" (v. 13), here meaning the authorities who seek Jesus' life (7:1; cf. 19:38; 20:19). Indeed, potential deliverers are generally distrusted. Josephus labels several as "deceivers."[136] The Gospels warn against false Messiahs and false prophets, who lead many people astray (Matt 24:4–5, 11, 24; Mark 13:21–22). Other early Christian literature reports that Jesus was characterized as "a deceiver" (cf. Matt 27:62–66; Justin, *Dial.* 69). Many promised deliverance; few made good on the promise.

In reporting the allegations made against Jesus, John clearly recognizes that there are other ways to tell the very story he recounts; indeed, John's account regularly and deliberately refers to the divisions that arise because of differing assessments of Jesus (1:10–13; 6:66; 7:26–42; 9:34). There is no neutral presentation of Jesus; no report of who he might be, if severed from his interpreters' faith or lack thereof. Without some sort of commitment to, even belief in or about, this figure from Nazareth, he would have been remembered much as Josephus, the Jewish historian, remembers him: a dot on the timeline of the history of perpetually tense relationships between the Romans and the Jews.

7:14–36 The Middle of the Feast: Jesus' Teaching from God

At the midpoint of the celebration of the eight days of Tabernacles, Jesus enters the temple to teach. As noted earlier (see on 7:1), the reading of God's law, God's "teaching," was a feature of some biblical descriptions of Tabernacles. In John a dispute arises, not over the content of Jesus' teaching, but over its source and then also over Jesus' identity. The origin of the law is not in dispute; rather,

135. For Jerusalem as "the center of the nations/earth," cf. Ezek 5:5; 38:12; *Jub.* 8.19; *1 En.* 26.1; Rev 20:8–9; cf. Philo, *Legat.* 281.

136. *Goēs,* "swindler, cheat"; Josephus, *Ant.* 20.167; *J.W.* 2.264; 6.288; see also comments on John 6:15 and 10:8.

the origin of Jesus' teaching is questioned. Even as the people have earlier disputed Jesus' heavenly descent because they claim to know his genealogical origins (6:42), here they dispute the identification of Jesus as Messiah because they know his geographical origins. In both cases, the people are mistaken: Jesus' identity can only be fully known and grasped when he is understood as the one who comes uniquely from God.

> **7:14** When it was the middle of the feast, Jesus went up to the temple and
> was teaching. **15** And the Jews marveled, saying, "How does he have such
> learning when he has never studied?" **16** Jesus responded, "My teaching is
> not mine, but the teaching of the one who sent me. **17** If anyone desires to
> do his will, they will know whether this teaching is from God or whether
> I am speaking on my own. **18** The one who speaks on his own seeks his
> own glory. The one who seeks the glory of the one who sent him—this is
> the one who is truthful and in whom there is no unrighteousness.
>
> **19** "Didn't Moses give you the law? And yet none of you keeps the
> law! Why do you seek to kill me?" **20** The crowd answered, "You are pos-
> sessed! Who is seeking to kill you?" **21** Jesus responded, "I did one work,
> and you all marveled. **22** Moses gave you circumcision—not that it was
> from Moses, but from the fathers—and you circumcise on the Sabbath.
> **23** If you will circumcise a man on the Sabbath so that the law of Moses
> is not violated, then why are you angry that I made a man well on the
> Sabbath? **24** Do not judge by appearance, but judge with just judgment."
>
> **25** Some of those in Jerusalem said, "Is this the one they are seeking
> to kill? **26** See, he speaks openly, and no one says anything to him. Can it
> be that the authorities truly know that he is the Messiah? **27** But we know
> where he comes from. When the Messiah comes, no one will know where
> he comes from."
>
> **28** When Jesus was in the temple teaching, he said, "So you know
> me, and you know where I come from? But I do not come on my own;
> rather, the one who is true sent me, and you don't know him. **29** I know
> him because I come from him and he sent me." **30** Then they were seek-
> ing to seize him, but no one laid a hand on him, because his hour had
> not yet come.
>
> **31** Many of the crowd believed in him and said, "When the Messiah
> comes, will he do more signs than this man has done?" **32** The Pharisees
> heard the crowds muttering these things about him, and the chief priests[a]
> and the Pharisees sent servants to seize him. **33** Jesus said to them, "I am
> with you for yet a little while, and then I am going to the one who sent
> me. **34** You will seek me, and you will not find me, and where I am going
> you will not be able to come." **35** The Jews said to him, "Where is he going
> that we will be unable to find him? He is not going to go to the Diaspora

of the Greeks in order to teach the Greeks, is he? 36 What does he mean when he said, 'You will seek me and you will not find me, and where I am you will not be able to come'?"

a. English translations distinguish *ho archiereus* (sg.) and *hoi archiereis* (pl.) in John (and the other Gospels) as "high priest" and "chief priests," respectively; the distinction in translation is retained here, but a recognition of the similarity in the Greek may help to explain the fact that both Annas and Caiaphas are called "high priest" (*ho archiereus*, 18:13, 15–16, 19, 22, 24, 26; cf. comments at 18:13).

[7:14–18] At the middle of the feast, Jesus entered the temple in order to teach (v. 14). Amazed by his teaching, the authorities wonder among themselves how Jesus acquired his knowledge, since "he has never studied" (*mē memathēkōs*). Since in the context, Jesus speaks of Moses and the law (7:19, 22–23), the "learning" (*grammata*) that they deny to Jesus is likely formal study of the law, rather than basic education. Jesus defends his teaching, as he defends his action and teaching elsewhere, as coming "from God" and not "from myself" (*ap' ematou* or *aph' heautou*; cf. 5:19, 30; 8:28; 10:18; 12:49; 14:10).[137] In the previous discourse Jesus had spoken of the need to be "taught by God" (6:45); here he declares that, in order to discern the source and truth of his teaching and whether it comes from God, one must "desire to do God's will": that is, have a willing disposition toward the truth.[138] By implication, the one who speaks (or teaches) from God, rather than "on his own," does so because he seeks not his own glory but the glory of the one who sent him. So while Jesus calls attention to himself and his teaching here and elsewhere in John, he also places himself alongside those who desire to do God's will, those who seek God's glory and not their own. Ultimately Jesus' commitment to God's will and God's glory will be manifested in acceptance of the destiny of the cross: a stance of self-emptying, not self-aggrandizement (10:18; 12:26–28).[139] To desire to do God's will thus also entails acknowledging Jesus' path of service (13:1–11), in giving his life for the world, as the way of God's prophet and Messiah.

[19–24] The discussion then turns to Moses and the law, with Jesus charging that those who truly believe Moses would not seek to kill him, which they are doing because of his "one work" (v. 21) of healing a man on the Sabbath (v. 23; 5:1–19). Moses and the law, rightly understood, bear witness to and not against Jesus, even when his actions seem to put him at odds with both (5:45–47). The countercharge that Jesus has a demon reflects similar accusations in the

137. According to Philo (*Spec.* 1.65), a true prophet says nothing of his own (*ouden oude*), but is truly possessed and inspired, serving as an "interpreter of God."

138. Augustine here cites Isa 7:9 LXX, "If you do not believe, you will not understand."

139. With good reason, Grayston (34) draws a parallel to Jesus' prayer "Not my will, but yours be done" (Luke 22:42); on this whole passage, see Moberly 2003.

Synoptic tradition that Jesus was possessed by an unclean spirit and so cast out demons by the power of Beelzebub rather than the power of God's Spirit (Mark 3:22, 30; Matt 12:24; Luke 11:15). John's Gospel includes no accounts of demon possession or exorcism, and the charge that Jesus himself has a demon is applied to his claims to speak the truth from God (cf. 8:48). If Jesus "has a demon," then he is a deceiver of the people; but if he is sent by God, then he is "good," true, and there is no unrighteousness in him (7:12; 18).

In appealing to Moses for justification of his Sabbath healing, Jesus actually alludes to the halakic regulations that allow for circumcision on the Sabbath (7:22; *m. Šabb.* 18:3–19:5). While the obligations to circumcise and to keep the Sabbath are both found in the law of Moses, here circumcision is understood as the greater of these obligations and is carried out in order not to violate the law that requires it (John 7:23). Sometimes in order to keep the law, it becomes necessary to set aside or "override" an injunction of it. Thus, if one can remove the foreskin of a single body part on the Sabbath, and so "override the Sabbath," surely one may make an entire man well on the Sabbath. There were differences of opinion among Jewish interpreters of the law as to which actions could legitimately "override" the Sabbath. For example, the rabbis allowed that saving the life of someone in danger also overrides the Sabbath, even when one is uncertain whether that life is endangered (e.g., *m. Yoma* 8:6; *Mekilta* on Exod 22:1–2; cf. Luke 14:3–5). By contrast, the earlier *Damascus Document* (among the DSS) stringently forbids offering aid to animals or persons on the Sabbath (CD XI, 12–16; cf. Luke 13:15). To "judge with right judgment" means to discern that the healing of the man at the pool is in keeping with the principle that such an act is allowed on the Sabbath, even though a life is not in immediate danger.

[25–30] The people of Jerusalem are divided, wondering what the authorities actually think about Jesus (cf. Matt 21:46; Mark 12:37; Luke 23:47–51). Skepticism arises because of Jesus' origins. For the people, the question whether Jesus is the Messiah turns on the question of his "earthly" origins; for Jesus, the question is whether he has been sent from God (cf. 6:41–51).

"The Jews" object that Jesus cannot be the Messiah since "when the Messiah comes, no one will know where he is from" (7:27). Since they claim to know where Jesus comes from (7:41–42, 52), he cannot be the Messiah. In response to their assertion, Jesus asserts that they do not know where he comes from if they do not understand that he comes from God (7:28–29); the same point is made in the designation of Jesus, the Messiah, as the Son of God, rather than the son of David. Certain Jewish texts speak of the revelation of the anointed or chosen one at a time known only to God (*2 Bar.* 29.3; 39.7; 72.2; *4 Ezra* 7.28; 13.26, 32, 52; *1 En.* 48.6; 62.7). In some of these texts, the Messiah exists with God prior to his appearance: that is, the Messiah is with God, awaiting God's revelation of him, but until that time he is unknown, or hidden. The ministry of the Baptist served "to reveal him to Israel," so that he can now be known (John 1:31; cf. 1:26).[140] And in John, he is to be known as the one who comes from God.

[31–36] In spite of the objections, many believe in Jesus because of his signs. While, for John, this is the appropriate response to signs (12:37; 20:31), there is little evidence in the Scriptures or in Jewish literature that the Messiah would be known as a miracle worker. Miracles are more typically associated with prophetic figures, such as Elijah and Elisha (cf. comments on 4:48–54; 6:14); the expectation of the coming prophet like Moses may have colored messianic expectation. Yet there is also first-century evidence for the expectation that the time of the Messiah would be marked by healing, deliverance, and abundance (Matt 11:4–5; Luke 7:22–23; 4Q521; cf. comments on 2:1–11).[141] Although there may be no explicit evidence for the expectation of a miracle-working Messiah, Jesus' deeds surely raise the question of just who he might be, and "the Messiah" is one of the possibilities.[142] In any case, John takes Jesus' deeds as witnesses to his messianic identity because they manifest God's life and because, as Messiah, Jesus gives himself to protect his people from death.

The "chief priests and Pharisees" send servants (*hypēretas*). "Chief priests" and "Pharisees" is an odd combination, since priests refers to those who, by heredity, serve in the temple, whereas Pharisees refers to a "party" who are not associated with the temple unless they are also priests. John's regular use of "the Pharisees" to indicate authorities in Jerusalem may well reflect the Gospel's post-70-C.E. setting when the temple has been destroyed and its priests have faded in importance.

The servants find Jesus readily enough in the temple. Jesus foreshadows his death when he warns that in a short while he will return to the one who sent him, and they will be able neither to follow nor to find him. He is speaking of his return to God; again they are thinking in strictly geographical terms, even as they have with respect to his origins. They assume that he intends to go to the Diaspora, where he would presumably be beyond the jurisdiction of the temple authorities. Ironically, following Jesus' death, his disciples will carry the message of his life, death, and resurrection to the Diaspora, and in that way Jesus will "go to the Greeks" (see 12:20, 32). But Jesus' point here is that while looking for his identity in terms of his parentage, or his origins, they miss the fact that he can only be known in relation to the God who sent him.

140. See Matt 16:17: "Flesh and blood has not revealed this to you, but my Father in heaven." In Justin's *Dialogue with Trypho*, the revelation of the Messiah depends on Elijah's anointing and manifestation of him to all (8.4; cf. 110.1).

141. In the *Mekilta* on Exod 15:11, Moses promises the people that God will do more signs and wonders for their offspring than he did for their fathers.

142. R. Brown 1966, 313.

7:37–52 The Last Day of the Feast: Living Water

The Festival of Tabernacles comes to its climactic moment, the "great day of the feast," with Jesus' promise to give living water and his revelation of himself as the light of the world. Both images—water and light—play a role in the celebration of Tabernacles. Earlier, John has drawn on key institutions (temple), holy days (Sabbath), and persons (Moses, Jacob) to explicate who Jesus is and what he brings. Here the pattern continues. The ceremony of drawing water from the pool of Siloam and then pouring it over the altar (see below) provides the backdrop for Jesus' claim to give living water; the lighting of golden candlesticks in the precincts of the temple becomes the backdrop for Jesus' claim to be light of the world. John has drawn from some elements of Tabernacles that particularly fit the themes of these chapters in order to show that what was hoped for and commemorated in the celebration of the Feast is now being realized and given through the person of Jesus.

7:37 On the last great day of the feast, Jesus stood and cried out, "Let
anyone who is thirsty come to me and drink. **38** The one who believes in
me, even as the Scripture says, 'Out of his belly will flow rivers of living
water.'" **39** He said this about the Spirit, which those who believed in him
were to receive; for the Spirit had not yet been given,[a] because Jesus was
not yet glorified.

40 When they heard these words, some of the people said, "This is
truly the prophet!" **41** But others said, "This is the Messiah." And others
said, "But the Messiah doesn't come from Galilee, does he? **42** Doesn't
the Scripture say that he is from the seed of David and that he comes from
the village of Bethlehem, where David was?" **43** So there was a division
among the crowd about him. **44** Some of them wanted to seize him, but
no one laid a hand on him.

45 The servants went to the chief priests and Pharisees, who said, "Why
didn't you bring him?" **46** The servants answered, "No one ever spoke
like this man!" **47** And the Pharisees answered, "Are you also deceived?
48 Has any one of the authorities or the Pharisees believed in him? **49** This
crowd, which doesn't know the law, is cursed."

50 Nicodemus, who had gone to Jesus earlier, and who was one of
them, said to them, **51** "Our law does not judge people without first giv-
ing them a hearing to find out what they are doing, does it?" **52** And they
responded, "Are you also from Galilee? Search, and you will see that no
prophet[b] arises from Galilee."

a. The Greek reads "the Spirit was not yet [*oupō gar ēn pneuma*]." Several textual variants sought to alleviate the embarrassing implication that the Holy Spirit did not exist at this time, including these: (1) "The (Holy) Spirit was not yet given [*dedomenon*]" (B and many others); and (2) "The Holy Spirit was not yet upon them" (D*). The more difficult reading in the text best explains the origin of the others, but it is understood rightly by the variants in B and elsewhere.

b. Here 𝔓[66] reads *ho prophētēs* ("Search and see that the prophet is not to arise from Galilee"); but this reading is not widely attested and may be due to scribal assimilation of 7:52 (*prophētēs*) to the reading *ho prophētēs* at 7:40.

[7:37–39] The action now moves from the middle of the feast to the last day of the celebration of Tabernacles.[143] According to the Mishnah, on each of the seven days of Tabernacles the priests filled a golden vessel with water from the pool of Siloam (cf. 9:7) and then poured it over the altar (*m. Sukkah* 4:9–10).[144] Although John makes no explicit mention of this water libation, the water ceremony of Tabernacles provides a backdrop for the introduction of Jesus' invitation to all who are thirsty to come to him and drink so that they will never thirst (4:13–14; 6:35).

A quotation from Scripture explains Jesus' invitation (7:38). Depending on how one punctuates the sentence, the quotation could be attributed to Jesus (as in the present translation) or to the narrator. But the citation does not correspond to any known Scriptural text (so also John 6:31). There are Old Testament passages that speak of water flowing out of a sanctified Jerusalem and/or the temple within it (Zech 13:1; 14:8; Ezek 47:1–12; Joel 3:17–18) as well as from the rock in the wilderness given to quench the thirst of the Israelites (Exod 17:6; Num 20:8–11; Pss 78:16, 20; 105:41; Isa 48:21; Neh 9:15, 20). But no biblical text has the phrase "rivers of living water" or pictures the water flowing from within a person.[145] From whose "belly" do the "rivers of living water" flow?[146]

Some translations and interpreters render Jesus' invitation thus: "Let the one who is thirsty come to me, and let him drink, whoever believes in me. As the Scripture has said, 'Out of his belly shall flow rivers of living water.'"[147]

143. According to some sources, the festival lasted seven days (Deut 16:13, 15; Lev 23:34; Ezek 45:25); but it was followed by a "holy convocation," a day of rest, on the eighth day (Lev 23:36, 39) so that it is also called a festival of eight days (2 Macc 10:6; Josephus, *Ant.* 3.245, 247; *m. Sukkah* 4.8). In the Mishnah, some rites of Tabernacles are celebrated for seven days, and some for eight; since the water libation is performed seven days, John apparenty identifies the seventh day as the "last day" of the feast.

144. The water libation is not mentioned outside rabbinic sources.

145. In several passages in Isaiah, God gives water to the thirsty (43:20; 44:3, in which God gives water and spirit; 55:1).

146. On *koilia* in 7:38, Levison (2009, 372–78) compares the cave of Gihon, the source of the waters in the pool of Siloam, and the "cavity" of the human body from which the living water flows.

147. E.g., NRSV, CEB, NEB; Beasley-Murray 115–16; R. Brown 1966, 319; Keener 1:728–29; Lincoln 2005, 254–57; D. Moody Smith 1999, 174.

While in this translation it remains ambiguous whether Jesus' words end with "believes in me" or include the Scriptural citation, that citation provides the explanation why people may drink and be satisfied: living water flows from Jesus (cf. 19:34; 20:22). But in the translation offered here—"Let anyone who is thirsty come to me and drink. The one who believes in me, even as the Scripture says, 'Out of his belly will flow rivers of living water'"—the one who is thirsty, who drinks, and who believes is the one from whom flow the "rivers of living water."[148] On this reading, the passage has a clear parallel to Jesus' promise in John 4:14: "Those who drink from the water that I will give to them will never be thirsty. The water that I will give them will become in them a spring of water welling up to eternal life" (see also Isa 58:11). Both passages in John 4 and 7 assume that Jesus gives the "living water," which becomes a "never-failing, self-replenishing stream" within the believer.[149]

Water serves as a figure of the Spirit, which those who believed in Jesus were going (*emellon*) to receive at a future time; they could not receive the Spirit because (1) the Spirit "had not yet been given" (lit., "was not yet"), and (2) Jesus had not yet been glorified. These statements point forward to the time of the giving of the Spirit, the Paraclete (14:26), after the death of Jesus and his glorification.[150] Since the Old Testament speaks of the Spirit of God active in the world, John's statement that "the Spirit was not yet" must refer to the particular giving of the Spirit as the Paraclete to bear witness to Jesus, call him to remembrance, and to teach the disciples after his departure (14:26; 15:26; 16:13–15). For those reading the Gospel, the passages about the Spirit are statements of their present reality: after Jesus' death and resurrection, the Spirit has been given, and all that the Gospel has promised would happen through the Spirit is now coming to fruition.

[40–44] Once again, Jesus' teaching and claims lead to a "division" (7:43). There are different assessments of him (prophet, Messiah), opposing responses of belief and unbelief, and efforts to arrest and to defend him. Oddly, here the crowd raises an objection to Jesus' messianic status—he comes from Galilee rather than Bethlehem—that seems flatly to contradict their earlier contention that "when the Messiah comes, no one will know where he is from" (7:27). But these objections share one thing: in neither case do the people know that Jesus comes ultimately from God. Therefore, any attempt to deny who he might be by means of appeal to geography or his

148. In 7:38, the disputed sentence reads: "The one who believes [*ho pisteuōn*] in me [*eis eme*], . . . out of *his belly* [*ek tēs koilias autou*] will flow rivers of living water." This reading takes the pronoun *autou* in the phrase *ek tēs koilias autou* as referring to the subject of the sentence, "the one who believes," not to the object of belief (Jesus); see KJV, RSV, TNIV, ESV; Barrett 327; Carson 1991, 322–25; Fee; Michaels 463–65; Talbert 148.

149. Michaels 465.

150. See Excursus 9: "The Holy Spirit in John."

origins "from below" fails to grasp his identity, which in John is known with respect to Jesus' ultimate origins.

If Jesus is from Bethlehem[151] in Judea, the village of David, that would allow him to be the Messiah who is to come from the house of Judah (Rev 5:5; Heb 7:14; Gen 49:9–10; *T. Jud.* 21.2; 24.5; the Targums on Gen 49:9–10). But that, for John, would not explain the kind of Messiah that Jesus is; he is the Messiah and "King of Israel" as the Son of God (1:49; 11:27; 19:7–9, 14–15; 20:31). Those who followed in the line of David were reckoned by God as "sons" and knew God as "father" (2 Sam 7:12–14). In John, Jesus is not like a son of God; he is the (only) Son of God (3:18) who comes from above and who knows God as his "own Father." John's citations of and allusions to various passages of the Old Testament regularly show how Jesus can be understood by analogy with various biblical figures or entities, even if he surpasses what is promised in or through them.

Since it is clear that those who dispute that Jesus is the Messiah do not judge with right judgment (7:24), they have not assessed the matter of Jesus' origins rightly either. Earlier they had claimed to know where he comes from (7:27) but in fact do not know that he actually comes "from above," from God (3:31; 7:28). Here they claim to know that Jesus is from Galilee and so cannot be the Messiah. But they err in that judgment as well, and so there is a "division in the crowd."

[44–52] Such division also runs through the ranks of the "chief priests and Pharisees" (cf. comments on 1:24; 7:32; 11:47). These authorities send servants to arrest Jesus, who return without him, all the while marveling at his teaching. At least one Pharisee, Nicodemus, defends Jesus, desiring to hear and learn what he does (v. 51). Nicodemus had first come as an eager but uncomprehending inquirer (v. 50; 3:1–21); now he appears as Jesus' advocate, contending that the law demands for Jesus to be heard (v. 51). According to Deuteronomy, judges appointed by God are to "judge justly" (*krinate dikaiōs*, Deut 1:16 LXX; cf. 19:16–18), even as Jesus has exhorted the people to judge with "right" or "just" judgment (*tēn dikaian krisin krinete*, 7:24). But it is precisely on the basis of the law that the Pharisees spurn Nicodemus's suggestion, claiming that those who believe in Jesus are not the authorities who know the law, but the crowd that does not (vv. 48–49). In their ignorance of the law, these crowds are led astray or deceived (7:12, 47) by a man who himself has never studied the law (7:15). As careful observers of the law, the Pharisees know it well, assuming that it will speak for them and against

151. The likely reference here is Mic 5:2, speaking of the one who will come from Bethlehem to "rule in Israel"; the Targum on Micah specifically names the Messiah; cf. Matt 2:1–6. Although the tradition of Jesus' birth in Bethlehem is not found elsewhere in John, it may be alluded to here; it is unlikely that John would introduce an objection from the Scriptures if he did not think it could be answered, since the Scriptures bear witness to Jesus.

those who defend Jesus. But in the Gospel of John, the law properly interpreted and understood bears witness to Jesus (1:45; 5:37–39). When read as a witness *against* Jesus, the law is not properly interpreted (10:34; 15:25; 18:31; 19:7).

Yet the Pharisees further dismiss their fellow Pharisee, Nicodemus, by asking whether he too is from Galilee and challenge him that "no prophet" comes from Galilee. Strictly speaking, the statement is untrue; Jonah the prophet was from Gath-Hepher, a village in Galilee (2 Kgs 14:25); Nahum came from Elkosh, in the northern part of the land (Nah 1:1). Perhaps, then, the statement has in view the origins of the "prophet like Moses," since Moses was never associated with Galilee. But more likely the Pharisees' comment is a broadside against Jesus and his followers, since both are accused of breaking the law (5:10; 9:16, 24, 28). And because Jesus was known as the one from Nazareth (*apo ho Nazaret*, 1:45) and "the Nazarene" (*ho Nazōraion*, 18:5, 7; *ho Nazōraios*, 19:19), and the Galileans are presented initially as those who welcomed him (4:45), the Pharisees' comment derides Galilee and both Jesus and those who follow him. It is typical of John's irony that when characters in the narrative speak of Jesus in ways that either question or mock his identity, they are in fact unknowingly speaking the truth. Earlier Nathanael wondered whether anything good can come from Nazareth (1:46); he is invited to "come and see." That invitation continues to be extended throughout the pages of the Gospel.

Excursus 6: 7:53–8:11 Jesus and the Woman Caught in Adultery

The pericope known as "the woman caught in adultery" (John 7:53–8:11)[152] is missing from significant early manuscripts of the Gospel, including $\mathfrak{P}^{66, 75}$ ℵ B, early Syriac versions in the East (syr$^{c, s}$), and from several Old Latin manuscripts in the West (it$^{a, l*, q}$). The predominant witnesses for the passage's inclusion come from the Western manuscript tradition: it is found in some Old Latin texts; Ambrose and Augustine knew it; Jerome included it in the Vulgate; and it appears in the fifth-century Codex Bezae (D). Its varied placement—after John 7:36; 7:44; or 21:25; or even after Luke 21:38 (in f^{13})—suggests that it had no fixed place in transmission. Where the passage does appear in ancient manuscripts, it is often marked with asterisks or other notations, indicating that the copyists who included the account knew of its problematic textual status. Although the passage does appear in a number of manuscripts—and thus became part of the Vulgate, the Byzantine text, the critical Textus Receptus and translations based on it, such as the KJV—it is not a part of the Gospel of John as first circulated but was introduced into it at some later point.

Stylistically the passage is unlike the rest of the Gospel. For example, only here does John refer to "scribes" (8:3), and only here is Jesus addressed as "teacher" (*didaskale*, 8:4; elsewhere *didaskale* is given as the translation of "rabbi": 1:38; 20:16). The passage is somewhat intrusive, interrupting the flow of Jesus' discourses in the temple at the

152. Keith offers a recent comprehensive survey of this passage.

Feast of Tabernacles, and it does little to inform the discourses of Jesus at this point or the complaints against him. It is strangely disconnected from both what immediately precedes (the skepticism over Jesus' status, in 7:40–52) and what follows (Jesus' declaration of himself as the light of the world, in 8:12).

Probably this self-contained pericope was inserted here because (1) it pictures Jesus as teaching in the temple, the setting of the discourses delivered at Tabernacles (chs. 7–8); (2) it serves as an instance of "judging with right judgment," demonstrating Jesus' refusal to enforce a law with which he does not explicitly disagree (cf. 7:22–24); (3) it may illustrate Nicodemus's point that the law does not judge without first giving someone a hearing (7:51); and/or (4) it anticipates Jesus' assertion "I judge no one" (8:15). Although it is sometimes alleged that the passage was excised because it was considered too lenient regarding adultery, there is little evidence for that view.[153] Indeed, Jesus tells the woman what he tells the man at the pool of Bethzatha/Bethesda: go and "sin no more" (*mēketi hamartane*, 5:14; 8:11). Jesus does not sanction the stoning of the woman, but neither does he condone or excuse her actions.

Just here the story has the ring of authentic Jesus tradition, reminiscent of many stories in Luke where Jesus welcomes a known sinner without condemnation.[154] Perhaps most similar are the story of the woman weeping at Jesus' feet (Luke 7:36–50), accounts of Jesus' table fellowship with sinners (5:30; 7:34; 15:1–2), parables that feature a generous portrayal of sinners (15:11–32; 18:9–14), and narratives where Jesus calls, welcomes, and forgives sinners (5:20–23, 30–32; 7:48). Even if not an original part of John's Gospel, the story of Jesus and the adulterous woman may well be an actual reminiscence of Jesus' actions. Its witness coheres theologically and historically with the canonical portrait of Jesus, as well as with certain Johannine emphases and themes. Most important, it has been read as Scripture by large portions of the church for years. That fact invites some brief comments on it here.

[7:53] And they all went to their own homes. **8:1** And Jesus went up to the Mount
of Olives. **2** Early in the morning he again went to the temple, and all the people came
to him; and he sat down and taught them. **3** Then the scribes and Pharisees brought a
woman who had been caught in adultery, and they put her in their midst. **4** And they
said to Jesus, "Teacher, this woman was caught in the act of committing adultery! **5** In
the law, Moses commanded us to stone such women. So what do you say?" **6** They said
this to trap him, because they wanted to bring a charge against him.

Jesus bent down and wrote on the ground with his finger. **7** And as they continued to
ask him, he stood up and said to them, "Let the one among you without sin cast the first
stone." **8** And again he bent down and wrote on the ground.

9 And when they heard what he had said, one by one they began to leave, beginning
with the oldest, so that only the woman was left there. **10** And Jesus stood up and said
to her, "Woman, where are they? Does no one condemn you?"

11 And she said, "No one, sir." And Jesus said to her, "Neither do I condemn you.
Go, and sin no more."

153. See Keith 210–13.

154. As noted above, the passage does appear after Luke 21:38 in a group of ancient MSS (*f*[13]).

[7:53–8:5] Jesus retires to the Mount of Olives (mentioned only here in John) and returns from there to teach at the temple. These notes fit Luke's description of Jesus as lodging on the Mount of Olives at night and returning to the temple in the mornings (21:37–38, perhaps accounting for the story's placement after 21:38). As Jesus was teaching, the "scribes and Pharisees" brought an adulteress to him. While the combination of "scribes and Pharisees" occurs often in the Synoptic tradition (Matt 5:20; 12:38; 23:13, 15, 23, 25, 27, 29; Luke 5:21, 30; 6:7; 15:2), "scribes" do not otherwise appear in John. An adulteress was likely a married woman, as the law of Moses, to which her accusers refer, covers illicit sexual relationships primarily between men and married, not unmarried, women (Lev 20:10–12; Num 5:11–31; Deut 22:21; Ezek 16:38–40).

The law also forbids men to commit adultery (Exod 20:14; Lev 20:10; Deut 5:18; 22:22), but the scribes and Pharisees bring only one of the guilty parties, letting the man off the hook and reminding Jesus that the law of Moses condemns "such women." Their report—"This woman was caught in the act of committing adultery!"—may reflect the presumption that, since there are witnesses, they can move directly to the proper sentence (Num 5:13). The law does not explicitly command stoning for adultery, although it does stipulate that those who commit adultery shall die (e.g., Lev 20:10; Deut 22:22; but cf. Ezek 16:40). In any case this is not a formal trial but a test of how Jesus will respond to a case about which Moses is quite explicit, apparently reflecting suspicions about Jesus' adherence to the law. The authorities' declaration highlights the possible conflict with Moses: "In the law, *Moses* commanded us to stone such women. So what do *you* say?" (John 8:5; cf. 9:28–29).

[6–11] Jesus explicitly challenges neither their report nor their understanding of the appropriate punishment. Instead, he responds with an action that has always puzzled interpreters: he "bent down and wrote on the ground with his finger" (8:6, 8). The text nowhere indicates what Jesus wrote, and that silence has fueled rampant speculation.[155] Many have sought the answer in contextual clues from the Gospel itself, even though the passage is unlikely to have been in John originally.[156]

The description of Jesus' writing "with his finger" calls to mind the description of the tablets of the law written by "the finger of God" (LXX: *tō daktylō tou theou*, Exod 31:18; Deut 9:10). Notice that the two references to Jesus' writing on the ground (John 8:6, 8) bookend an apparent allusion to the death penalty that the law requires.[157] One may further observe the use of the verbs *katagraphō* (8:6) and *graphō* (8:8). While *graphō* is common in the New Testament, this is the only place where it describes

155. Keith (12–21) catalogs 38 possible explanations for Jesus' actions. Several MSS explain that Jesus wrote on the ground "the sins of every one of them" (*henos hekastou autōn tas hamartias*), likely derived from 8:7–9 (Metzger 190).

156. E.g., given the reference to living water in John 7:38, some suggest an allusion to Jer 17:13: "Those who turn away from thee shall be written in the earth, for they have forsaken the LORD, the fountain of living water" (RSV).

157. The statement "Let the one among you without sin cast the first stone" (8:7) may combine the injunctions of Deut 13:9–10 and 22:21. For the history of this interpretation, traceable to Ambrose, see Keith 176, 181–82.

an action of Jesus, and *katagraphō* does not occur elsewhere in the New Testament. Here both verbs are used—and both appear in the LXX to describe the writing of the Decalogue (Exod 32:15).[158] If Jesus was writing something from the law, or if his writing was understood to parallel God's writing of the law on stone tablets, then his action follows quite naturally from the reference to Moses and the law (v. 5). Perhaps Jesus was tracing out the words of the law, or writing down his own interpretation of it, or even writing the very words he speaks: "Let the one among you without sin cast the first stone" (v. 7). In any case, Jesus does not endorse the woman's punishment.

As R. Brown points out (1966, 338), Jesus recognizes that the woman's accusers are using her as a pawn to trap him. While Jesus accepts the report of the woman's adultery and apparently also the law's dictate that an adulteress should be put to death, he stipulates that only those without sin may cast stones. Jesus does not contradict the law, but since it is not Jesus' purpose to condemn (12:47), he does not read the law in a way that brings condemnation to sinners.

But neither does Jesus acquit the woman of the charges brought against her.[159] He does offer her a path for the future that honors God's will: "Go, and sin no more." Thus Jesus exercises "right judgment" (7:24). In doing so, the Gospel resists, here as elsewhere, the stark contrast between Moses and Jesus, between what the law says and what Jesus teaches. Instead, John presents Jesus as accepting the law's dictates while turning the tables on the women's accusers, implicitly asking whether Moses might not end up as *their* accuser (thus 5:45: "Do not think that I will accuse you to the Father; it is Moses who accuses you").

8:12–20 Jesus, the Light of the World

After the Feast of Tabernacles, Jesus continues his dialogues with the people, the Pharisees, and others with his declaration "I am the light of the world." Jesus promises that his disciples will have "the light of life," the light that shows the pathway to God, the source of life (8:12; cf. 1:4), the light that itself is life. Jesus' claims again press the question of the source and truth of his teaching (8:13) and of his relationship to the one he names as his Father (v. 19). In preceding discourses and narratives, Jesus' identity as Messiah and prophet has created division among the people; now his insistence that there is no life and no knowledge of God apart from him provokes an intensified negative reaction. The Gospel implicitly acknowledges the offensiveness of Jesus' claims when it reports, "No one arrested him, because his hour had not yet come" (v. 20). As is typical of John, the more exclusive or exalted Jesus' claims, the more

158. As Keith (27–52) points out, the use of these verbs rules out suggestions that Jesus was simply "doodling" or drawing pictures on the ground.

159. He does not explicitly forgive her sin; indeed, nowhere in John does Jesus explicitly forgive sinners (see comments on 20:23; cf. Mark 2:5, 9, par.; Luke 7:48).

hostile the response (5:18; 6:60–66; 10:31–33). Before long, Jesus' claims will become even more offensive and the response to him more antagonistic, leading to further attempts on his life (8:58–59).

8:12 And again Jesus spoke to them, saying, "I am the light of the world. The one who follows me will not walk in darkness, but will have the light of life."

13 The Pharisees said to him, "You are bearing witness to yourself. Your witness is not true."

14 But Jesus answered them, "Even if I bear witness concerning myself, my witness is true because I know where I come from and where I am
going. But you do not know where I come from or where I am going. **15**
You judge according to human standards, but I do not judge anyone.

16 "Even if I do judge, my judgment would be true, because I am not
alone; rather, the Father who sent me is with me.[a] **17** And in your law, it is
written that the witness of two persons is true. **18** I am the one who bears
witness about myself, and the Father who sent me bears witness about me."

19 They said to him, "Where is your father?"

Jesus answered, "You do not know me or my Father. If you knew me,
you would know my Father also." **20** He said these things in the treasury
in the temple, where he was teaching. And no one arrested him, because his hour had not yet come.

a. Lit., "I am not alone; rather, I and the Father who sent me"; thus perhaps, "I do not bear witness alone, but I and the Father who sent me bear witness together."

[8:12] In his second "I am" saying, Jesus presents himself as the "light of the world" (8:12; 9:5). Light itself is many faceted: as an object that shines, like the sun or a lamp, it can be seen; it is also the medium that dispels darkness or illuminates one's path in it. It is the arena in which one sees. In the Old Testament, light is an image for God as salvation,[160] as well as for various divine gifts and attributes, such as God's guidance, salvation, truth, Word, or Torah.[161] Light and darkness serve as figures of life and death, as they do also in the Greek classical tradition.[162] In John the light dispels the darkness (1:5, 9; 3:19–21; 12:35–36, 46) and is thus an image for salvation and truth, and even the object of faith (12:36, 46). It provides illumination so

160. E.g., Ps 27:1; Mic 7:8.

161. As in Pss 36:9; 44:3; 119:105, 130; Prov 6:23; Isa 9:2; 58:8–10; 60:1; Mic 7:9.

162. Job 33:30; Ps 56:13. At death "darkness enfolded [one's] eyes" (Homer, *Il.* 4.461; 5.47; 13.672; cf. Euripides, *Alc.* 266; Aeschylus, *Eum.* 72). For linking light and life, see Homer, *Il.* 18.61; *Od.* 4.540 (with the classical *phaos* or *phōs*; LSJM); Euripides, *Alc.* 272.

that people may find their way (11:9–10) or is simply the sphere in which one lives (9:4; 12:35). Thus the unusual phrase "light of life" has both soteriological and ethical dimensions: light confers life and illumines the path of right conduct.[163]

This life-giving light was earlier identified with God's Word made flesh (1:4, 5, 7, 8, 9; 3:19); as the incarnate Word, the one who comes from and is going to God, Jesus imparts salvation and illumines the way that leads to life. Jesus assures those who follow him that they will indeed find their way to life.[164] While "following" (*akolouthein*) Jesus often entails his physical presence (21:20), following can refer more generally to discipleship (1:43); hence it does not require Jesus' physical presence but also describes discipleship in the postresurrection period (21:22).[165] The light "shines" (*phainei*, present tense) in the darkness (1:5); one may continue to have "the light of life" (8:12). As the light, Jesus gives light on the path to life, and he himself is that life: to live in the light that he brings is to live in his life, to live in him (15:2–7). The multifaceted character of the image of light lends itself to various ways of understanding the relationship of the disciple to Jesus, including seeing, following, being illumined or guided by, and living in Jesus.

As the "light of the world," Jesus enacts the role of the Isaianic Servant, who was to be a "light for the peoples" (Isa 42:6; 49:6).[166] The immediate setting for Jesus' declaration that he is the light of the world may be a ritual of Tabernacles, first attested in the Mishnah: the ceremonial lighting of golden candlesticks in the Court of the Women in the temple, at the close of the first day of the festival.[167] The golden candlesticks had four golden bowls, reached by ladders; young men of priestly lineage poured the oil into these bowls; the wicks were made from priestly garments. Thus these candlesticks were in every way holy.[168] When the candlesticks were lighted, "there was not a courtyard in Jerusalem that did not reflect the light" (*m. Sukkah* 5:2–3). Now the light emanating from the temple, for all the world, is Jesus himself. In John, Jesus' identity as the "light of the world" also alludes to Torah, read at Tabernacles:

163. For "light of life," see Ps 56:13; Job 33:30; 1QS III, 7.

164. In 8:12b the Greek is emphatic: *ou mē peripatēsē en tē skotia* ("shall surely not walk in darkness!").

165. See, further, Excursus 8: "The Johannine Vocabulary of Faith and Discipleship."

166. In LXX of Isa 42:6 and 49:6, *phōs ethnōn*; as also in Acts 13:47.

167. There are no references to this ceremony in Jewish sources earlier than John, nor any direct reference to the ceremony in John. It occurred on the first day of the festival, whereas the events of John 8–9 are set after "the last great day of the feast" (7:37). Cf. Poirier, who connects John 8 with Hanukkah (10:22).

168. Elsewhere Jesus uses water for Jewish rites of purification (2:6); cleanses the temple, which then symbolizes his risen body; and heals two persons at a *miqveh* (Bethesda/Bethzatha, ch. 5; Siloam, ch. 9). The things that are holy point to the Holy One of God.

God's teaching, God's revelatory word, finds its fullest embodiment in Jesus, who is the Word that is the light of life for all the world.[169]

[13–19] The Pharisees challenge Jesus that his testimony cannot be true (*alēthēs*) on the grounds that the law requires the evidence of two (or even three) witnesses (v. 17).[170] Jesus offers two responses. First, his testimony is true because "I know where I come from and where I am going" (v. 14); second, he does have a second witness, "the Father who sent me" (v. 16). Yet it is not immediately apparent how Jesus' awareness of his origin and destiny qualifies him to be a witness at all, whether a sole or second witness, or validates the truth of his testimony. The answer lies not so much in Jesus' knowing his origin as in that origin itself. Jesus comes from God, knows God, and is going to God (7:28–29, 33). Because he has come from God, and God is the ultimate source of truth, Jesus may then truthfully testify to himself. But Jesus' various interlocutors do not know his origins or destiny; they do not know that he is from God and going to God. They judge *kat' opsin*, by what they see ("by appearance," 7:24), rather than from the insight of faith or from the perspective of God, the one who sent Jesus and so testifies to him (8:18). They judge *kata tēn sarka*, by human ("fleshly") standards (8:15), rather than by the Spirit, who would enable understanding of Jesus' origins and thus his identity (3:3; 6:63). For them, Jesus is an unknown and therefore an unreliable witness.[171] If Jesus comes from and is going to God, and if they neither see nor grant this, then they do not know who he is (8:19). They have not been born of the Spirit (3:3, 5) or taught by God (6:45). They cannot judge with right judgment (7:24), and they do not see by means of the light of life. In John's terms, they walk in darkness.

[20] John notes that Jesus spoke these things while teaching in the temple; specifically, in the "treasury" in which money from dues and contributions to the temple were kept (cf. Mark 12:41–44; Luke 21:1–4). Josephus refers to "chambers" for storage, where the wealthy stored their possessions during the siege of Jerusalem in 70 C.E.[172] The exact location of these chambers is somewhat uncertain; they may be within the Court of the Israelites, that part of the temple complex into which male, but not female, Israelites could enter, or in the less restricted and more public Court of the Women. In either case, Jesus is once again teaching within the temple court. Even as the light of the golden

169. In Wis 18:4, those without the "light of the law" (*phōs nomou*) are imprisoned in darkness. In Matt 5:14, disciples whose deeds reflect Jesus' interpretation of Torah righteousness are "the light of the world"; in John, the law points to Jesus, who is the light of the world (cf. Theobald 269–70).

170. Deut 17:6; 19:15; Num 35:30; Matt 18:16; 26:60; 2 Cor 13:1; 1 Tim 5:19; Heb 10:28; Rev 11:3; *m. Roš Haš.* 3:1; *m. Ketub.* 2:9.

171. Cf. *m. Roš Haš.* 2:1: a witness unknown to a judge cannot offer testimony.

172. See *J.W.* 6.282; Josephus's most detailed description of the temple is found in *J.W.* 5; *m. Šeqal.* 2:1 and 6:5 refer to "shofar-chests" for storing money.

candlesticks shone "for all Jerusalem" from within the temple, so Jesus claims to be the "light of the world" while in the temple. Even as a river will flow from the temple for the healing of the nations, so the light streams from the temple for all the world to receive life (John 7:37–39; Ezek 47:12; Rev 22:2). It is from God's holy place, now embodied in God's Holy One (John 2:21–22; 4:21–24), that life and light are given for all the world.

8:21–30 Sin, Death, and Departure

In a brief exchange laden with irony, Jesus cryptically informs the people that he is going away: he speaks of his crucifixion and subsequent return to the Father. But Jesus is misunderstood. The people wonder whether Jesus means that he is going to the Diaspora—a speculation not unfounded, for after Jesus' death, resurrection, and return to the Father, the message about him will be taken to the Diaspora. But what they must come to understand is not only how Jesus will depart but, even more, what the departure means. If they understand that Jesus will not simply die, but that he is going to God, they will also understand that he has come from God. They will then understand his teaching as coming from God, because they will understand that he comes from God.

8:21 And he said to them again, "I am going away, and you will look for
me, and you will die in your sins. Where I am going, you will not be able
to come."

22 The Jews said, "Is he going to kill himself? Why is he saying,
'Where I am going, you will not be able to come'?"

23 And he said to them, "You are from below, I am from above. You
are of this world, I am not of this world. **24** Therefore I said to you that
you will die in your sins. For if you do not believe that I am,[a] you will
die in your sins."

25 They said to him, "Just who are you?" Jesus said to them, "Why do
I even speak to you!"[b] **26** I have many things to say and judge with respect
to you, and the one who sent me is true, and I speak the things that I have
heard from him to the world." **27** They did not know that he was speaking
to them about the Father.

28 Jesus said to them, "When you have lifted up this Son of Man,[c] then
you will know that I am, and that I do nothing on my own, but that I speak
these things even as the Father taught me. **29** And the one who sent me is
with me, and he has not left me alone; for I always do what is pleasing to
him." **30** And when he said these things, many believed in him.

a. *Hoti egō eimi* could be rendered "that I am he" or "that it is I."

b. The clause *Tēn arxēn ho ti kai lalō hymin* can be taken in various ways:

1. As a question, taking *ho ti* as *hoti*, translated as "why?" (cf. Mark 9:28), and *tēn arxēn* adverbially: "Why do I speak to you at all?" (NRSV).
2. As a statement, supplying *egō eimi*, reading *ho ti* as "what," and translating *tēn arxēn* adverbially as "from" or "at the beginning"—yielding one of the following translations: "[I am] from the beginning what I am telling you," or "[I am] what I have told you from the beginning." Barrett accepts the first reading; but one might then have expected John to use *ex arxēs* (6:64; 16:4) or *ap' arxēs* (8:44; 15:27).

c. Or, "lifted up *this* man"; see Excursus 2: "Son of God, Son, and Son of Man in John."

[8:21–24] While the discussion of Jesus' origins and destiny continues, a new note is introduced with reference to "death" and "sin." The link between sin and death (vv. 21, 24) is biblical (Gen 2:17; 3:3; Rom 6:23). Ironically, "the Jews" think that Jesus' assertion of his "going away" may indicate that he is planning to kill himself.[173] His pathway will lead to his death, but at the hand of others, while their unbelief will lead them only into the realm of death. The "sin" that leads to death is specifically the sin of not trusting or believing in Jesus (8:24); unbelief demonstrates that one is "of this world," having not received the new birth of the Spirit, or birth from above. The contrast between "this world" and the world "above" is a variation on the contrast found elsewhere in the New Testament between "this age" (*aiōn houtos*) and "the age to come" (*aiōn ho mellōn* or *ho erxomenos*).[174] But the contrast in John is expressed in spatial rather than temporal terms: the one who brings life, the pathway out of sin and death, has in the present come from God.[175]

Jesus calls people to believe "that I am he" or "that I am" (*pisteusēte hoti egō eimi*, v. 24; cf. Isa 43:10).[176] Here one might have expected an "I am" saying with a predicate, specifying what one is to believe about Jesus (e.g., "I am the light of the world). But there is a striking parallel between certain statements in Isaiah and Jesus' words here. In Isaiah, people are to know or to believe that God is (*hoti egō eimi*), a statement that encompasses all that God is: the LORD, Savior, God, the Holy One, Creator, King, the one who makes a path in the sea (Isa 43:10–16). Each of these descriptions also characterizes Jesus in the Gospel of John. Even as God calls on Israel to bear witness to his unique identity as God—the one who is, who creates and saves all that is—so Jesus declares he is the one who is; by implication, he creates and saves all that is. As the point

173. Josephus notes that those who take their own lives are "received by the darkest place in Hades," punished by "God their father" (*J.W.* 3.375–80).

174. See Matt 12:32; Mark 10:30; Luke 18:30; 20:34–35; 1 Cor 1:20.

175. In Isa 55:8–11 God is pictured as being in the heavens, high above the earth; God's word comes forth, accomplishes his purposes, and returns to him there.

176. For a fuller discussion of the "I am" sayings, including the absolute sayings in 8:24, 28, and 58, and their reflection of passages in Isaiah, see Excursus 5: "The 'I Am' Sayings of John."

of his declarations become clearer, the responses will become more sharply negative; at present, no reaction to Jesus' assertions is reported.

[25–27] Jesus' use of *egō eimi*, redolent as it is of divine speech and coupled with the assertion that one must believe in him in order to live, leads naturally to the inquiry, "Just who are you?"[177] Jesus' response—"Why do I speak to you at all!"—suggests that the answer has already been given in the various discourses (chs. 5–7) where Jesus has asserted his identity as the Son who exercises God's prerogatives, who has come down from heaven, and who speaks the words and does the will of God. Both Jesus' identity and the substance of his teaching are grounded in "the one who sent me" (v. 26), a description of God particularly common in chapters 5–8 (17 of 31 Johannine occurrences). Jesus reiterates earlier assertions that his teaching is from the God who sent him (7:16), that he does not speak on his own authority (7:18), that those who hear him do not know his true origins or identity (7:28; 8:14, 23), that he alone truly knows God (7:28–29; 8:19), and that he has the power to give life (7:37–38; 8:12). But, as elsewhere in John, the fact that they do not yet know who he is (8:25) means that they cannot know the one who sent him, "the Father" (v. 27), for knowledge of the one implies knowledge of the other (v. 27; cf. 5:24; 12:44–45; 13:20; 15:21).

[28–30] Jesus then asserts that, after lifting up of the Son of Man, they will know (1) "that I am" (*hoti egō eimi*), (2) that he does not act on his own, and (3) that he teaches as the Father has taught him. "Lifting up" refers to Jesus' crucifixion ("when *you* have lifted up"), which anticipates his resurrection and return to the Father. The resurrection will testify that Jesus has "life in himself" (5:26), that he can appropriately speak of himself as living and thus can declare, in the present tense, "I am" (*egō eimi*; 8:28; cf. 1:18). Just as God lives, so Jesus also lives (6:57). Still, the one who makes these claims asserts that he does nothing on his own authority or power; he speaks only as the Father has instructed him. In every way he is dependent on God; in every way God is with him, never abandoning him (v. 29; cf. 17:21–23). It is precisely this mutual relationship of Father and Son, expounded in John in terms of the Father's own work and words being fully entrusted to and carried out by the Son (5:19–22, 26–27; 17:6–8, 10), which allows Jesus to use the language that God uses in Isaiah. These bold claims now lead "many" to believe in him, even as he has invited them to do.

8:31–47 Children of Abraham, Children of God

The various disputes about Jesus raise questions about the status of his disciples. If Jesus' teaching is truly of God, then one ought to listen to him, as one would listen to any prophet of God (see Deut 18:18–20). But Jesus' words

177. In 8:25, "Just who are you?" renders *Sy tis ei?* with *sy* ("you") in the emphatic position.

and actions appear to challenge the law (John 5:10–11) and Moses' status as a teacher and prophet (5:45–47; 6:14–15, 32; 7:22–23), all of which put him at odds with the authorities' wisdom (7:48). To heed and to follow one who himself does not heed Moses' teaching would threaten one's identification with those to whom the law was given: the descendants of Abraham, Isaac, and Jacob. Already Jesus has been presented as greater than Jacob, the father of the twelve tribes (4:12); now he will be portrayed as greater even than Abraham, the ancestor of all Israel (8:53). That entails a reconfiguration of the identity and privileges of those who claim Abraham as their ancestor. What remains to be explored in this dialogue, however, is in just what way Jesus is "greater than Abraham" and what that means for those who have long and rightfully claimed to be Abraham's children.

8:31 Then Jesus said to the Jews who had believed in him, "If you remain
in my word, you are truly my disciples, **32** and you will know the truth,
and the truth will make you free."

33 They said to him, "We are the offspring of Abraham. We have never
been enslaved to anyone! How can you say, 'You will be free'?"

34 Jesus answered them, "Amen, amen, I tell you that everyone who
does sin is a slave of sin. **35** The slave does not remain in the household
forever; the son remains forever. **36** So if the Son makes you free, you
will truly be free. **37** I know that you are Abraham's offspring. But you
are trying to kill me, because my word finds no room in you. **38** What I
have seen with the Father, I speak; and you do what you have heard from
your father."

39 They answered him, "Abraham is our father."

Jesus said to them, "If you really are children of Abraham, you would
do what Abraham did.[a] **40** But now you are trying to kill me, a man who
has told you the truth that I heard from God. Abraham would not do that.[b]
41 You are doing what your father did."

They said to him, "*We* were not born of fornication.[c] We have one
father—God."

42 Jesus said to them, "If God were your father, you would love me, for
I have come from God and I am here. For I have not come on my own,
but that one sent me. **43** Why do you not understand what I say? Because
you are not able to hear my word. **44** You are of your father, the devil,[d]
and you want to do what your father does. That one was a murderer from
the beginning, and he does not stand in the truth, because there is no truth
in him. Whenever he speaks a lie, he is speaking from what he is, for he
is a liar and the liar's father.[e]

45 "But because I tell you the truth, you do not believe me. **46** Which of
you accuses me of sin? If I speak the truth, why do you not believe me?

47 The one who is from God hears the words of God. This is why you do not hear me, because you are not from God."

a. The best attested reading has "If you really are Abraham's children, you would do what Abraham did" (*ei . . . este* in the protasis, and *epoiete* in the apodosis, as in $\mathfrak{P}^{66, 75}$ ℵ B D; later MSS read, "If you *were* Abraham's children" (*ēte*): a contrary-to-fact condition that may go further toward denying "the Jews" the status of "children of Abraham."

b. The Greek reads *touto Abraam ouk epoiēsen*, "Abraham did not do this."

c. Standing first in this sentence, the pronoun "we" (*hēmeis*) is emphatic and perhaps alludes to the traditions of Jesus' birth (cf. comments on 6:42; and CEB at 8:41, "Our ancestry isn't in question!").

d. In the clause *hymeis ek tou patros tou diabolous este* ("You are of your father, the devil"), "father" and "devil" are taken in apposition to each other (not, "you are of the father of the devil").

e. In the phrase "the liar's father" the singular genitive *autou* is understood to refer to the preceding "liar" (*pseustēs*; CEB) rather than to *pseudos* ("lie[s]"; NRSV).

[8:31–32] Jesus' address to "the Jews who had believed in him" (cf. 7:31) demonstrates that "the Jews" are not portrayed monolithically in the Gospel as "unbelievers." Yet even those who believed in Jesus (7:31) are divided over his identity (7:40–43). In the present context the conversation between Jesus and these professed disciples quickly takes a puzzling turn. After only a brief interchange, Jesus asserts that they are seeking to kill him because his word has found no place in them (8:37). In what sense, then, can they be said to have believed in him? The problem is alleviated somewhat if we take the perfect participle (*hoi pepisteukotes*, v. 31) with the sense of the pluperfect ("those who *had* believed in him"), referring to disciples who had *formerly* believed but have not persevered in their belief.[178] Such erstwhile disciples appear elsewhere (6:66) as aligned with Judas, who "would hand him over" (6:64) and was labeled "a devil" (6:70–71; see comments on 8:44; 13:2). Jesus' partners in dialogue and debate thus are those who had once believed but have abandoned their initial commitments (see also 1 John 2:19–24). By the end of the present discourse, they will be said to have the devil as their father. The strongest negative rhetoric in the Gospel characterizes not those who have never believed, but rather those who had once believed, who once were aligned with Jesus and his disciples, but who now have abandoned such commitment, as did Judas.[179]

This point is strengthened by the contrast between *believing* and *abiding* (v. 31). Those who believe must abide in Jesus' word so that they will truly

178. See Carson 1991, 346–49; D. Moody Smith 1999, 185; Griffith. Falling away is a kind of unbelief; there is no need to imagine a particular (schismatic) group in view (so Hakola 2005, 185–86).

179. Hylen (59–74, 113–30) argues that the boundaries between "groups" in John are thus blurred; no group is monolithic in its response to Jesus.

(*alēthōs*) be his disciples. While the Greek word *menein* ("to abide") can mean simply to stay or reside in a certain location (1:38; 2:12; 4:40; 7:9; 10:40), in John it connotes permanence, endurance, or faithfulness, particularly in following Jesus (1:32, 33; 5:38; 6:27, 56; 14:10; 15:4). In the present passage there is an implied contrast between initial belief and the perseverance that is characterized as "continuing" or "abiding."[180] Those who continue or endure in their faith, who do not abandon Jesus, are genuinely (*alēthōs*) his disciples. Such disciples know the truth and are set free by it. Freedom is freedom from sin and death. Sin is not simply conduct that needs forgiving; freedom from sin implies a new beginning and new life (3:3, 5).[181]

[33–38] The Jews, surprised at Jesus' promise that they would be made free, protest that as Abraham's offspring they have never been enslaved to anyone.[182] Considering the captivity of "Abraham's offspring" in Egypt (and later Babylon), and the fact that the Feast of Tabernacles looks back to the time in the wilderness after God brought the Israelites out of Egypt (Lev 23:39–43), one might judge their protest to be unwittingly ironic or simply false. Jesus offers no overt corrective but instead redirects the conversation. Here he reinterprets the meaning of slavery altogether as slavery to sin (John 8:34; cf. vv. 21, 24, 51). Jesus then explains to these would-be disciples how they can receive freedom from sin and death (vv. 34–35), but the argument is very compressed. First, there is the assertion that a slave does not "abide" forever in "the house," but a son does.[183] The statement is not explicitly christological; rather, it simply asserts that a son, as offspring and heir, enjoys a permanent place in his parental home. In the next statement, however, the son in the household is Jesus himself. Second, Jesus asserts that "the Son," precisely because he is free and so has a permanent place in the household, can make others free. The Son confers his own freedom on those who are receptive to his word and "continue" in it (8:31, 37; 6:68).

Given the contrast between a slave and a son, and the protest that "the Jews" are legitimate descendants of Abraham (8:41), the story of Ishmael and Isaac may inform this conversation. Both are descendants of Abraham, but the child of the slave woman does not inherit; only the true son does (Gen 21:10; cf. Gal

180. So also John Chrysostom, *Hom. Jo.* 54.1; Augustine, *Serm.* 84.1: "To be a disciple, it is not enough to come, but to continue." See comments on 2:23–25 above.

181. Talbert 155. Epictetus, the Stoic philosopher who was born a slave (55–135 C.E.), mused on the character of "slavery" and "freedom." If the free person "lives as he wishes," then no one is truly free, since people are enslaved by their desires (sorrow, fear, envy, and pity) and by their moral and rational errors (*Diatr.* 4).

182. For discussion of various ways that Jewish authors proposed to reconcile their status as "slaves of God" with enslavement to human masters, see Byron 37–143.

183. Epictetus (*Diatr.* 4.12–13) comments that since Caesar is "the common master of all," all should consider themselves as "slaves in a great household."

4). Ishmael, the son of Abraham by a slave woman, was considered illegitimate by at least some Jewish authors.[184] The Jews in John 8 contend that they are genuine offspring, the "seed" of Abraham,[185] neither slaves nor the offspring of slaves; therefore they are descended legitimately from Abraham (v. 41). Jesus grants the point that they are descendants of Abraham (v. 37), but they do not act as he did: they do not welcome a messenger from God as Abraham did (Gen 18). They do not show themselves to be true descendants of Abraham, but Jesus shows himself to be a true Son of the Father, since a genuine son imitates his father's actions (John 8:38–39). These Jews do what they have learned from some other father, since the desire to kill Jesus could hardly be attributed to Abraham (vv. 40–41, 56).

There are two ways of being a child of Abraham: by descent and by imitation. It was a shared idea of ancient writers that children reflected their parents, not merely in appearance, but also in conduct and character; the theme is found in ancient philosophers, moralists, and the teaching of Jesus.[186] In John's Gospel, Jesus does not deny that "the Jews" are the "descendants of Abraham" (*sperma Abraam*, 8:37; cf. v. 56), but he maintains that they are not acting as Abraham's children (*tekna tou Abraam*, v. 39). The contrast is not between physical descent and spiritual identity, but between conduct that belies one's parentage and conduct that demonstrates that parentage. Descendants of Abraham cannot, simply by virtue of their descent, live in their paternal home forever: they must do what Abraham did: rejoice in Jesus' coming and be set free from slavery to sin by the Son, the heir in the household (vv. 34–37, 56). Just as the "works of God" (*erga tou theou*) are reinterpreted as the single "work" of believing in Jesus (6:28–29), so also "what Abraham did" (lit., "the works of Abraham," *erga tou Abraam*, 8:39) is epitomized in Abraham's glad welcome of Jesus (v. 56).

Both Abraham's hospitality[187] and his exemplary piety and righteousness were often commended for imitation.[188] For example, the author of 4 Maccabees exhorts the Israelites (*paides Israēlitai*), the offspring of Abraham's seed

184. Philo, e.g., speaks of Ishmael as illegitimate (*nothos*) because he was the son of an Egyptian woman (Gen 16; *Sobr*. 8; *Migr*. 94; *Mut*. 147; cf. *QG* 3.59). Interpreting Ishmael to mean "hearkening to God" and Israel to mean "the one who sees God," Philo deems the knowledge gained through seeing as superior to the knowledge gained through hearing. That contrast may be implicit in John 8:38 (see Philo, *Fug*. 208; comments on 12:37–43 below).

185. For the Israelites as the "seed [descendants] of Abraham" (*sperma Abraam*), see 2 Chr 20:7; Ps 104:6 LXX (105:6 ET); Isa 41:8; 3 Macc 6:3; 4 Macc 18:1; *Pss. Sol.* 9.9; 18.3–4.

186. As in Matt 5:44–48; 4 Macc 15:4; Sir 22:3–5; Plutarch, *Aem*. 2.1 [*Mor*. 495A–B, 496C]).

187. Gen 18:1–8; cf. Heb 13:2; Philo, *Abr*. 107, 114–16; Josephus, *Ant*. 1.196.

188. See *Jub*. 11.15–12:27; Sir 44:20; 1 Macc 2:52; 4 Macc 16:20; Heb 11:8–12, 17–19; cf. *1 Clem*. 17.1–18.1; 31.2. The "merits of the patriarchs" belong to those who act like the patriarchs (Philo, *Virt*. 206); cf. *L.A.B.* 33.5: "Do not hope in your fathers; for they will not profit you at all unless you be found like them."

(*apogonoi Abramiaiōn spermatōn*), to obey the law and exercise piety (18:1). Abraham was deemed to have kept "the works of the commandments" before they had even been given (*2 Bar.* 57.2). In the Mishnah "the disciples of Abraham our father" are contrasted with the "disciples of Balaam the wicked" by their virtues and dispositions (*m. ʾAbot* 5:19). Jesus thus calls on an apparently shared conviction that those who are Abraham's offspring must live as he did, in order to urge his hearers to follow Abraham's example and joyfully welcome the one whom God has sent.[189]

[39–43] Responding to the allegation that they are not truly Abraham's children, "the Jews" reassert their claim, "Abraham is our father" (v. 39).[190] Again, the Jews' claim that they are descendants of Abraham *by birth* is not denied; it is countered with the claim that they are not children *by imitation*: they do not do as Abraham did.[191] Abraham's true children are children by imitation, not merely by physical descent. It is because they seek to kill Jesus, not because they are descendants of Abraham, that they are said to be "of the devil."[192] In seeking to take Jesus' life, these inconstant disciples demonstrate that they do not truly have Abraham as their father, for Abraham's response to Jesus was quite different. Instead, they follow the pattern of another father (v. 41).[193] Challenging the possible implication that they are illegitimate children ("*We* were not born of fornication," *ek porneias*; cf. translation note) the Jews now declare not only that Abraham is their father, but also that they have only one Father, God himself (v. 41).

Although no Scriptural texts are cited here, such could be provided to bolster the claim that the children of Abraham, the Israelites, are the children of God (Jer 3:4–5, 19; 31:9; Deut 32:4–6; Mal 1:6; 2:10).[194] These texts also emphasize that those who name God as Father ought to act accordingly, by being obedient to God and faithful to one another (Jer 3:19; Mal 2:10). If, indeed, those "who had believed in him" have God as their Father, as they claim, then that ought to be manifested appropriately in response to the Son of the Father. In other

189. Early Christian literature elsewhere speaks of Abrahamic descent (1) as demonstrated in *actions* (Matt 3:8–10; Luke 3:8–9; 19:9); (2) as limited to descent through Isaac, and through Abraham's true heir, Jesus himself (Matt 1:2; 8:11; 22:32; Acts 7:8; Heb 11:18; Ign., *Mag.* 10.3); and (3) as expressed by faith in the Messiah, Jesus (Rom 4:11–18; Gal 3:7–9). These categories also overlap, as they do here (John 8:56; *1 Clem.* 31.2; *Barn.* 13.7).

190. "Our father Abraham" or similar phrases occur frequently in rabbinic texts. See *m. Taʿan.* 2:4–5; *m. Qidd.* 4:14; *m. ʾAbot* 3:12; 5:2–3, 6, 19; also see Isa 51:2; Josephus, *Ant.* 14.255; 4 Macc 16:20; Rom 4:1, 16; Jas 2:21; *1 Clem.* 31.2.

191. Note this chapter's frequent use of *poiein*, "to do" (8:28, 29, 34, 38, 39, 40, 41, 44, 53).

192. Moberly 2008, 57.

193. In the ancient Mediterranean world, honor was ascribed to a person for a number of reasons, including descent or lineage; it was insulting to impugn one's ancestry (see Matt 3:7, "offspring of snakes" [AT]; Mark 6:3, "son of Mary," i.e., without a known father).

194. For fuller discussion, see M. M. Thompson 2000, 35–48.

words, they ought to love Jesus (John 8:42) and accept his word (v. 43). The twin claims to have Abraham and God as "father" are validated by those who live in imitation of Abraham and thus manifest their obedience to God.

[44–47] The argument continues. Those who rightfully claim God as Father truly love Jesus (v. 42), hear and understand his word (v. 43), and believe him (vv. 45–46). Because they honor or receive the Son, they are the true children of God (1:12–13), the true children of Abraham, the true "brothers" of Jesus (contrast 7:5 and 20:17). But those who do not hear or love God's Son belong to another family with a different father; they are "of [their] father, the devil," who is a murderer and a liar: he kills the righteous, and he neither hears nor does that which is true (8:44). In biblical and Jewish literature, the primary role or task of the devil, or Satan ("the adversary"), is to accuse the righteous, to deceive people, or lead them to abandon faith in God.[195] The devil—the source of war, tyranny, demon worship, and murder—works death; thus the devil's purposes are contrary to the life-giving purposes of God.[196]

In John's Gospel, the devil, or Satan, appears in connection (1) with Judas Iscariot (6:70–71; 13:2, 27; 17:12) and (2) disciples who abandon Jesus, in contrast to those who "remain" in Jesus' word (6:60–71). John's exclusive link of the devil with Judas and inconstant disciples fits with the elimination of demon exorcisms from the Gospel: the powers of darkness are characterized not in terms of demonic possession but rather in terms of unbelief and (here) the abandonment of belief.[197] Those who seek Jesus' life, who do not hear or accept his words, belong to the family to which Judas, "a devil," belongs (6:70; 13:2). They belong with those who abandon or betray Jesus, thus imitating their "father," who stands over against the purposes of God.[198]

There are striking conceptual and verbal parallels between this passage and the assertions of 1 John, where a schism in the community has led to the departure of some members, now characterized as "antichrists," who deny the Son and the Father (2:18–23): they are guilty of sin, subject to death, "of the devil," and "murderers" (3:4–15). In the Gospel of John, "the Jews who had once believed" in Jesus are slaves to sin: because they seek to kill Jesus, they are "of the devil." In both this Gospel and 1 John, those who are branded most sharply

195. See Gen 3:13; *Jub.* 1.11; 10.1; 15.31; 1QS, esp. II, 17–24; *T. Job* 3.5–6; *T. Dan* 3.6; *T. Zeb.* 9.7–8; Luke 8:12; 1 Pet 5:8. Acts labels the magician Elymas a "false prophet," and Paul calls him a "son of the devil," the enemy of righteousness, a deceiver (13:8–11).

196. Wis 2:24; *L.A.E.* 9–17; *Jos. Asen.* 12.9–10; *Jub.* 10.5; *T. Sol.* 6.1–4.

197. In 8:48, Jesus is accused of having a demon on account of his claims; 13:27 says that Satan "entered into" Judas—John's sole example of "possession" (yet satanic not demonic).

198. Origen writes that Jesus' words "make it very clear that one is not a child of the devil as a result of creation, . . . and it is also clear that one who was previously a child of the devil can become a child of God" (*Comm. Jo.* 20.106–7). Similarly, Augustine denies the Manichaean interpretation that those "of the devil" were born evil by nature (*Tract. Ev. Jo.* 52.10).

as "of the devil" are those who once believed, who were once disciples, but who did not continue in Jesus' word.

Here Jesus' polemic particularly resonates with God's indictment of his people in Isaiah for their lack of knowledge (John 8:14, 19, 24, 27–28, 55; Isa 43:10, 26; 48:8), their refusal or inability to hear (and later, to see; John 8:43, 47; Isa 6:9–10; 42:18–20, 23) or to grasp the thoughts of God who is above the earth (John 8:23; Isa 55:8–11), and their slavery because of sin (John 8:33–34; Isa 50:1).[199] If, indeed, those who are addressed in this discourse are former disciples, then the note in Isa 65:11 LXX may be additionally pertinent, for it says that those who forsake the Lord set a table for *tō daimoni* ("the demon," or "the devil"). Those who are "of the devil" are those who, like Judas, forsook the Lord (6:70–71). Minimally, the Gospel's rhetoric clarifies what is at stake in turning from Jesus: in the cosmic conflict between the powers of "God" and "the devil," there is no neutral ground on which to stand.[200]

Later Jewish literature includes rhetoric that bears even greater resemblance to the language of John 8 than that of Isaiah. For example, the "sons of Israel" who do not practice circumcision are called "sons of Beliar" (*Jub.* 15.33–34); the descendants of Dan who abandon the Lord and act like Gentiles show that their "prince is Satan" (*T. Dan* 5.6); the Israelites who do not heed the law as do the members of the *Yaḥad* (the community of the DSS) are the "sons of darkness" and followers of Belial (1QM I, 1–16; 4Q266 frg. 3 II, 1–18). While the language of prophetic critique is typically aimed at the people as a whole and is designed to bring them to repentance, the language of these later Jewish texts draws boundaries between various groups within Israel and their practices.[201]

Here Jesus addresses "his own" (1:11), as the prophets of old addressed their people, and in the sharpest terms warns against the consequences of turning from him. Repeatedly in John the intensification of Jesus' claims elicits the strongest negative reaction. This pattern will soon be demonstrated again, as the ensuing discourse gives voice to claims for Jesus' identity in terms resonant with the Gospel's opening affirmation that the Word through whom the world was made was in the beginning with God and was in fact God. Now Jesus will be presented as the one whose word can confer eternal life (8:51), because he was before Abraham ever came into existence. That claim will lead to the attempt to stone Jesus as guilty of blasphemy.

8:48–59 "Before Abraham Was, I Am"

Jesus' long and polemical discourse now reaches its climactic point with the declaration "Before Abraham was, I am." But prior to this assertion, Jesus

199. Lincoln 2005, 272–73.
200. See Carter 2008, 86–92.
201. For insightful discussion of how such polemics function, see Johnson; and Hakola 2005.

makes three points: (1) He knows God and seeks his Father's honor (or glory, *doxa*; 8:49–50, 54–55). (2) His word can give life (8:51) because he himself keeps God's word (8:55). (3) He offers eternal life, the life from God, because—in words reminiscent of the Gospel's opening verses—Jesus himself has been before Abraham ever was (8:58; 1:1–3). Once again, Jesus' claim to have and to give the very kind of life that God has provokes incredulity and ultimately an attempt to stone him (8:58; 5:18; 10:31–33). Thus, although Jesus repeats and reasserts claims he has made earlier, his continued insistence, coupled with an escalation of the rhetoric that divides him from those who do not believe in him, catalyzes open hostility.

8:48 The Jews said to him, "Aren't we right in saying that you are a Samaritan and have a demon?"
49 Jesus answered, "I do not have a demon; rather, I honor my Father,
and you dishonor me. **50** I do not seek my own glory. There is one who
seeks it and who judges. **51** Amen, amen I say to you, if any one keeps
my word, that one will never see death."
52 The Jews said to him, "Now we know that you have a demon!
Abraham died, and so did the prophets, and you say, 'If anyone keeps
my word, that one will never taste death.' **53** You are not greater than our
father Abraham, who died, are you? And the prophets died. Who do you claim to be?"[a]
54 Jesus answered, "If I glorify myself, my glory is nothing. It is the
Father who glorifies me, of whom you say, 'He is our God.'[b] **55** And you
do not know him, but I know him. Even if I say that I do not know him, I
would be a liar, like you. But I know him and I keep his word. **56** Abraham,
your father, rejoiced to see my day; and he saw it and was glad."
57 Then the Jews said to him, "You are not yet fifty years old,[c] and you have seen Abraham?"[d]
58 Jesus said to them, "Amen, amen, I say to you, before Abraham was, I am."
59 Then they picked up stones to throw at him. But Jesus was hidden and went out from the temple.

a. Or, "who do you make yourself?" with the verb *poiein*, as in 5:18; 10:33; 19:7.

b. Some MSS (א B* D) read *hymōn* instead of *hēmōn* (𝔓[65, 75] A B[2]), thus reading (in indirect discourse), "You say he is *your* God" rather than "You say, 'He is *our* God'" (direct discourse). There is no substantial difference in the assertions.

c. Instead of "fifty" (*pentēkonta*), some MSS read "forty" (*tesserakonta*), perhaps to harmonize with Luke's witness that Jesus was "about thirty" when he began his ministry (3:23).

d. Instead of "You have seen [*heōrakas*] Abraham?" some MSS read "Has Abraham seen you [*heōraken se*]?" This would make Abraham the subject of two successive statements: "Abraham saw my day" and "Abraham has seen you." The variant is probably the result of scribal emendation.

[48–55] Jesus is charged with being a Samaritan, those characterized by false worship and lack of knowledge of God (4:22), and with having a demon, of deceiving the people.[202] Whereas in the Synoptic tradition Jesus' exorcisms suggest collusion with Beelzebub (Mark 3:22 par.), here the charge of demon possession is raised because of his claims for himself and his teaching. Jesus denies this accusation of being in collusion with the devil on the basis that he honors his Father and seeks only God's glory, something the devil would never do (John 8:49–50). Jesus' claim that he can give eternal life (v. 51) leads to further unbelief, since all the great figures of the past—Abraham, the prophets—are dead. As the *Testament of Abraham* acidly puts it, after noting Abraham's exemplary righteousness and hospitality, "Even to him came the common and inexorable bitter cup of death and the unforeseen end of life" (1.3). Even Abraham, the father of the people of Israel, and the prophets, who were especially commissioned by God, were mortal. Does Jesus claim that he will somehow escape their fate? Is he greater than the one who is the ancestor of all Israel, greater than the prophets who spoke the word of God?

The prophets who declared the word of God died, but Jesus asserts that those who keep his word "will never see death." His audience correctly understands that he is making a claim about the kind of life he gives; therefore they rightly ask him, "Who do you claim to be?" Jesus replies, much as he has elsewhere in this Gospel, that he claims nothing for himself: he does not seek his own glory and need not do so, since God glorifies, or honors, him (5:41, 44; 7:18). This is the very God whom these Jews claim to worship and serve. Since that God glorifies Jesus, the conclusion is that those who do not honor Jesus are not children of God. Put most forcefully, the claim to belong to God without honoring Jesus is a lie. The heart of this debate is not a general or theoretical claim to know God, but a christological claim: if one dismisses Jesus as the light who reveals God, the source of eternal life, then one has not "judged with right judgment" (7:24). The specificity of the claim here, as elsewhere in John, is undeniably offensive, even blasphemous, to those who do not grant Jesus' unique status and identity in relationship to the one true God. From John's point of view, it is equally offensive to deny that identity.

[56–59] Jesus next implicitly summons Abraham as witness: "Your father Abraham rejoiced to see my day." "The Jews" should show themselves worthy of the privilege of being "children of Abraham" by doing as Abraham did:

202. For further discussion of the Samaritans, and animosity between them and Jews, see comments on 4:6, 7–9, 16–20 above.

rejoicing in Jesus' coming.[203] According to *4 Ezra* 3.14, God revealed to Abraham "the end of the times"; it may be that such a tradition is in view here.[204] However, "the Jews" understand Jesus to mean that he saw Abraham, that he was alive when Abraham was alive; they are thinking merely of chronological time. That is a misunderstanding, typical of the Gospel, as is the fact that Jesus corrects it, not with a direct explanation or rebuttal, but by shifting the ground and showing that their misunderstanding is corrected when they understand who he is (4:14–15, 25–26; 6:34–35). Abraham might have anticipated Jesus' coming with joy; but he was not in fact anticipating someone who would come long after him, but rather someone who existed before he ever did. Jesus' affirmation, "Before Abraham was, I am," contrasts Abraham's existence with Jesus' existence: Abraham "was" or "came into being" (aorist: *genesthai*); but Jesus *is* (present: *eimi*; 8:58).[205] This takes the reader back to the opening verses of the Gospel, to the existence of the Word in the beginning, and the creation of all things through the Word.

Jesus' declaration, "Before Abraham was, I am," echoes divine speech in the Old Testament, where God speaks in various statements beginning with "I am" (Exod 3:14; Isa 43:11, 13, 15, 25; 42:6; 44:24; 45:5–6; 48:12).[206] Earlier in this discourse, Jesus has twice told the crowds that they must believe "that I am" or that they will believe "that I am" or "I am he" when they have lifted him up (John 8:24, 28; where "I am" translates *egō eimi*). Curiously, in those places, when Jesus uses the absolute "I am," he is not charged with blasphemy, nor does anyone seek to stone him. There, the only response is puzzlement. It is not until Jesus promises that whoever believes in him will "never taste death" (vv. 51–52) and claims to have existed *before* Abraham ever was (8:58) that anyone tries to stone him. For with these assertions Jesus has claimed that he can give eternal life because he shares in it, and it is Jesus' participation in the eternal life of God that comes to expression in the assertion "Before Abraham was, I am." As the response of "the Jews" indicates, it is no less blasphemous than to make oneself equal to God (5:18; 10:33).[207] This climactic statement of Jesus reveals what is at stake in believing "that I am" (8:24, 28).

In his encounter with "the Jews," including "the Jews who had believed in him" (8:30–31), Jesus warns that appealing to Abraham as their father avails nothing if they do not act as Abraham did. The true children of Abraham

203. So also John the Baptist rejoiced in the coming of the one greater than he (3:29–30).

204. See also *T. Levi* 18.11–14, where the Lord and the patriarchs Abraham, Isaac, and Jacob rejoice at the coming of the eschatological priest; in *2 Bar.* 4.4 God shows Abraham the tabernacle to be built in the new Jerusalem.

205. See the discussion of verb tenses of *eimi* and *ginomai* at 1;1, 14, 18.

206. See Excursus 5: "The 'I Am' Sayings of John."

207. For stoning as both judicial penalty and mob reaction, see various accounts in Philo, *Flacc.* 66; *Mos.* 1.235; 2.218; *Legat.* 127; and Josephus, *J.W.* 2.225, 445, 492.

welcome the one that he welcomed; Abraham's rejoicing in Jesus' coming becomes a model for them. Abraham's rejoicing is warranted because Jesus is "greater than our father Abraham," since he existed before Abraham ever came into being. Jesus' superiority to Abraham neither negates nor overturns the status of Abraham as the forefather of "the Jews." Abraham is not written out of the story of Jesus, but his place in that story is reconfigured.[208] The same is true for Moses and Jacob, the law and the temple, the feasts and rites celebrated by Jesus' contemporaries: none of these is written out of the story of Jesus, for all of them point ahead to Jesus.

The contentious debate in John 8 is not between two religions, Christianity and Judaism, nor does Jesus condemn Jews or Judaism per se, although there is no doubt that the text has been read this way—and with harmful consequences. One can account for the style of the Gospel's rhetoric by setting it in its historical contexts; it is far more difficult, if not impossible, to soften John's point that receptivity and response to Jesus, the Son of God, determine whether one is a child of God. The point is christological, and all christological claims are ultimately theological in the proper sense: they have to do with the identity of God. In John, Jesus speaks the words of God because he is the incarnation of the revelatory and life-giving Word of God, itself intrinsic to the identity of God. The narrative of Israel and of its chief institutions and figures cannot be told apart from this Word, because there is no way to speak of Israel's identity, its narrative, its temple and law, its prophets and patriarchs, apart from God. These claims regarding Jesus' identity are the impetus for the Gospel itself.

These are also claims that divide "his own," even as the prologue has indicated: the Word came "to his own" but was not welcomed by all; those who did receive him were granted the privilege of becoming "children of God" (1:11–13). Jesus' coming brings division within Israel, a point found not only in John but also in the Synoptic traditions: towns and villages are judged for failure to respond to Jesus (Matt 10:14–22; 11:21 par.); wheat and weeds, good and bad fish, and sheep and goats are sorted (Matt 13:24–30, 47–50; 25:31–46); members of families are set against each other (Matt 10:34–37; Luke 12:51–53), as Jesus is "destined for the falling and rising of many in Israel" (Luke 2:34). In John, Jesus gathers the scattered children of God, the children of Abraham who rejoice in the coming of the day of the Messiah. But the consequence of that ingathering is division: there are different assessments of Jesus' role—neutral, positive, and hostile—and rejection and acceptance of his most exalted claims (John 6:64–66; 7:43; 8:59; 10:19, 33, 39, 41–42). Jesus is the light of the world, but not everyone comes to the light (1:4, 9; 3:19–21).

208. In disagreement with Moloney's statement: "There was a time when he [Abraham] belonged to a narrative. His story is finished; he has come and gone" (Moloney 1996, 113).

Excursus 7: "The Jews" in the Gospel of John

Few puzzles in New Testament scholarship have proved to be as resistant to solution as the meaning, referent, and function of *hoi Ioudaioi* in the Gospel of John, some form of which occurs 71 times, almost always in the plural (68 times). Most English translations render *hoi Ioudaioi* as "the Jews," in keeping with the way in which the phrase is typically rendered when translating other ancient sources, such as books in the LXX and Apocrypha, Philo, and Josephus. But such translations presuppose, rather than articulate, an answer to the question of "the Jews'" identity. To some extent the difficulty of both understanding and translating *hoi Ioudaioi* in John reflects the larger question of the proper understanding and translation of *hoi Ioudaioi* in other ancient sources.

Hoi Ioudaioi may be translated—virtually transliterated—as "the Judeans," construed geographically as referring to the inhabitants of the region of Judea, as opposed to Galilee or Samaria (John 4:3, 47, 54; Acts 1:8), even though "Judea" can also designate a broader geographical area that includes Galilee and Samaria.[209] When Josephus writes that the "Jews" (*Ioudaioi*) were called such "from the day that they came up from Babylon, which is taken from the tribe of Judah, which came first to these places, and there both they and the country gained that appellation,"[210] he reveals the term's originally geographical connotations and, by extension, its application to the people who come from *Ioudaia.*

References to "the Jews" are found in ancient literature written by Jews when speaking of themselves, whether the literature is directed to other Jews or to non-Jews. One finds the term frequently throughout the Maccabean literature and in other texts of the Greek Old Testament, especially Ezra, Nehemiah, and Esther.[211] Similarly, Philo frequently speaks of "the Jews," without clearly identifying himself as one of them. His use of the term assumes that *hoi Ioudaioi* live throughout the ancient world, including Egypt and Rome, and are characterized by a particular ancestry, set of laws, religious practices, and various customs.[212] Josephus regularly refers to the people whose history he narrates as "the Jews," only sometimes explicitly including himself among them,[213] while describing their peculiar commitments (*Ant.* 1.4; 1.200; *Ag. Ap.* 1.1; 2.180). Both Philo and Josephus thus refer to "the Jews," as do non-Jews.[214]

"The Jews," therefore, is the ordinary way in which Jews and, to a lesser extent, non-Jews refer to the people who originate from *Ioudaia* ("Judea"), whether they came to be

209. Thus, Strabo, *Geogr.* 16.2.34–36; cf. Acts 2:9.

210. Josephus, *Ant.* 11.173; in context, "these places" refers to Jerusalem and its environs.

211. E.g., Esth 3:6; 4:13–16.

212. E.g., Moses is "the lawgiver of the Jews"; Gaius harbored an excessive hatred toward "the Jews" (Philo, *Legat.* 133; used throughout this work); "the high priest of the Jews offers up [prayers and sacrifices]" (*Spec.* 1.97; cf. 1.167; 4.179, 224). Philo also speaks of "our nation" (*hemeteros ethnos*, in *Decal.* 1.1; *to genos hēmōn*, in *Spec.* 2.217).

213. Josephus, *Ant.* 15:384; *Ag. Ap.* 1.130: *to genos hēmōn.*

214. But such references are harder to find; cf. Strabo, *Geogr.* 16.2.2; 16.2.34–36; Suetonius refers to the inhabitants of Judea as *Iudaei* (*Judaei*, e.g., *Vesp.* 4; cf. Tacitus, *Ann.* 12.54; *Hist.* 5.1); but he also says that Claudius banished "the Jews" (*Iudaei*) from Rome (*Claud.* 25; see *Dom.* 11).

part of "the Jews" by birth or conversion, whether they continue to dwell in Judea or not, and who have a peculiar heritage, ancestry, customs, and religious practices. Thus while *Ioudaioi* originally meant Judean, and never entirely loses its geographical connotation, it comes also to bear a wider meaning, evident in the English translation "Jew."[215]

The Use of "the Jews" in John

The term *hoi Ioudaioi* is not univocal in John.[216] An overview of the patterns of usage in John reveals the substantial ways in which John's depiction of the Jews fits within the ancient sources just surveyed.

1. The genitival form of "the Jews" (*tōn Ioudaiōn*) characterizes certain rituals (purification, 2:6) and festivals, including Passover (2:13; 6:14), the Sabbath (5:10), and Tabernacles (7:2). While at first glance these descriptions appear redundant, since feasts such as Passover and Tabernacles are not associated with other peoples, the descriptors are in fact analogous to patterns found especially in Josephus.[217]

2. In John, although Jesus includes himself among "the Jews" (4:22), he is called "a Jew" only by a Samaritan woman and a Roman governor (4:9; 18:35). "The Jews" accuse Jesus of being "a Samaritan" (8:48), and "the chief priests of the Jews" ask Pilate not to identify Jesus as "King of the Jews." Thus, while Jesus and non-Jews call Jesus a Jew, "the Jews" themselves do not.

3. Jesus' disciples seem to be distinguished from "the Jews," although it is not always clear who is included among "the Jews" (11:19, 31, 33, 36, 45). John sometimes writes that "some of the Jews" or "many of the Jews" (11:45; 12:11; cf. 12:42) believed in Jesus. At least some of the time, then, John distinguishes those among "the Jews" who believed in Jesus from "the Jews" overall.

4. Whereas the Synoptic Gospels speak of Jesus in conflict with Pharisees, Sadducees, and chief priests, in John the opposition to Jesus comes primarily from "the Jews" (5:16, 18; 8:57–59; 10:31; 11:8).[218] "The Jews" are also adversaries of Jesus' disciples; several times the Gospel states that people—presumably, Jews themselves—are afraid to confess their faith in Jesus openly "for fear of the Jews" (7:1, 13; 9:22; 20:19).

5. While "the Jews" often denotes Jesus' opposition, that term does not appear in the Farewell Discourse (chs. 14–17), where Jesus describes the situation of the disciples after his death and departure. Here opposition always comes from "the world," not "the Jews." It is not only "the Jews" who are hostile to Jesus; "the world" demonstrates its antagonism as well.

215. So Cohen 2001, 3; Mason (2007) disputes the expanded meaning, emphasizing instead its enduring ethnic sense.

216. Especially emphasized by Schnelle 1999. Somewhat differently, Hylen (2009, 117–21) treats "the Jews" as a single, conflicted character.

217. Josephus refers to the feasts that "the Jews" call "the Passover" (*J.W.* 2.10; cf. *Ant.* 17.213; 18.29) and "Pentecost" (*J.W.* 2.42).

218. "The Jews" occurs in Matthew 5 times; in Mark, 6×; in Luke, 5×, predominantly in the phrase "the king of the Jews" in the Passion Narrative (in Matthew, 3 of 5 uses; in Mark, 5 of 6 uses; in Luke, 4 of 5 uses).

Proposals for Understanding John's Use of "the Jews"

In recent years there has been vigorous discussion of how one ought to construe the preceding data in John, and even how one ought to translate *hoi Ioudaioi*.[219] Some interpreters, looking primarily at the patterns of usage within the Gospel, conclude that John uses "the Jews" in a limited way to refer to some, but not all, of those who could be called Jews. For example, some allege that *hoi Ioudaioi* are Jewish authorities and ought to be translated as such.[220] These authorities, not the crowds, are the source of opposition and hostility to Jesus; those who feared "the Jews" (7:1, 13; 9:22; 20:19) feared the authorities and their power. Others take *hoi Ioudaioi* to refer to the inhabitants of the limited geographical territory of Judea, contending that John portrays Jesus' opponents as the inhabitants of Judea, who did not welcome Jesus, while the Galileans and Samaritans did (4:41–42, 54; 7:1, 9).[221]

Other interpreters look outside the narrative to the historical context of John and to various possible historical referents of "the Jews." Some scholars understand *hoi Ioudaioi* to be a rigorist subgroup of Jews, with particular ties to the key institutions (e.g., the synagogue) of Judaism, who were seeking to define what it means to be "Jewish," particularly after the fall of Jerusalem.[222] John's presentation of "the Jews" is also taken to reflect the factionalism of post-70 Judaism, and sometimes more particularly the increasing hostility between Jews who did not accept messianic (and other) claims for Jesus and those who did.[223] There are disagreements whether the disputes between these two factions can still be called "inner-Jewish" or whether they have moved to such a stage that John is not willing to place either Jesus or his followers among "the Jews."[224]

In light of both the internal and external evidence of John, it is best to take *hoi Ioudaioi* as designating the people whose ancestry, worship, laws, and customs identify them as belonging to the people who originated in Judea, even if they no longer dwell there. Thus in John, *hoi Ioudaioi* are characterized as they are in other ancient literature: they worship one God, whom they call upon as their Father (4:21–24; 8:41, 54); their (early) father (*patēr*) is Abraham (8:39), and they are the people of Israel (3:10; 12:13); they adhere to the law given through Moses and are faithful students of the Scriptures (5:39, 45–46; 7:19–23; 9:28–29), observing its various statutes, including those related to circumcision (7:22); they honor the temple in Jerusalem and make pilgrimages there (2:13–14); and they keep the Sabbath (5:10–18; 9:14–15) and feasts commemorating

219. Among more recent studies with surveys of the literature, see Motyer; von Wahlde 2000; Bierenger, Pollefeyt, and Vandecasteele-Vanneuville; Kierspel; Hakola 2005; Schnelle 1999.

220. Von Wahlde (2000) claims that this is the consensus view and that virtually every instance of "the Jews" in John (except in 6:41–52) refers to the authorities; see also Hylen 2009, 185 n. 4. The NLT, NIV, and CEB are among translations that sometimes translate *Ioudaioi* with "Jewish leaders" (e.g., 1:19; 2:18; 5:10, 15, 16, 18) and sometimes with "Jews" (e.g., 4:9, 22); NLT sometimes substitutes "people" for "Jews" (e.g., 6:52; 8:31; 10:19; 11:19); for discussion, see Dunn 2001, 53–55.

221. See the seminal study by Lowe.

222. Ashton 131–59; Motyer.

223. This view has particular resonance with Martyn's reconstruction of the conflicted situation between "church" and "synagogue" that can be detected in John.

224. See, e.g., Dunn 2001.

God's deliverance of and faithfulness to them (2:13, 23; 7:2; 10:22; 11:55; 18:28).[225] These are simply the markers of the people known as *hoi Ioudaioi.*[226]

On these points Jesus differs with *hoi Ioudaioi* in John in two primary ways: (1) he disputes the claims of "the Jews" to be the proper representatives of their ancestors (Abraham, Israel), various characteristic practices (law, worship, Sabbath, Scriptural interpretation), and institutions (temple); because (2) he reinterprets each of these characteristic identity markers—such as descent from Abraham, adherence to Moses' law, proper Sabbath observance—locating their significance in his own mission and the messianic fullness that he brings. To the extent that *hoi Ioudaioi* are marked by claims, commitments, and practices that Jesus challenges or reinterprets, John does not, without qualification, use the term of Jesus' followers. Jesus' disciples come from among the Jews, but they are "the Jews who believed in him."[227]

Jesus the Jew and the Children of God

Those "who believed in his name" are called "the children of God" (1:12). Like *hoi Ioudaioi,* they are described in relationship to Abraham, Jacob, Moses, the law, and the temple. John does not separate Jesus or his followers from their heritage in Israel.[228] Jesus himself is identified by others as a Jew (4:9; 18:35); and he associates himself with the Jews and their worship in the Jerusalem temple (4:22). Jesus defends the temple even if he also foresees its end (4:22–24), attends pilgrimage feasts there while interpreting Jewish ceremonies as witnesses to God's ongoing deliverance and provision through him (2:13–21; 6:31–35; 7:10, 37–39; 8:12; 9:5; 10:25–38); uses the waters intended for purification to furnish wine for a wedding (2:1–11) and to wash the eyes of the blind

225. "The Jews" is sometimes taken to have lost any particular historical or geographical sense and to mean, simply, "representative of unbelief" or "the unbelieving world in general": Bultmann 1971, 86; Moloney 1998b, 40–41. Others take it as a stereotyped expression, covering all subgroups typically distinguished in the other Gospels, such as sinners, tax collectors, Herodians, Sadducees, scribes, and elders: they are now all simply "the Jews" (so Fortna; Culpepper 1983).

226. According to 2 Macc 6:1–11 the practices of the Jews that were forbidden by Gentiles included temple sacrifices, observance of the Sabbath and ancestral festivals, and circumcision, as well as the simple confession that one was a Jew (*haplōs Ioudaion homologein einai*, v. 6). Philo notes that Moses commanded his *ethnos* to welcome proselytes because "they had left behind every privilege, including their blood-relatives, ancestral home, customs, sacred rites, and images of the gods" (*Virt.* 102–3; cf. *Spec.* 4.178). For the association of kinship and worship in the Greek world, compare Herodotus, *Hist.* 8.144.2, who speaks of the kinship of Greeks in "blood and speech, and the shrines of the gods and the sacrifices that we have in common."

227. One can see the differences between John and the shape of the conflict in such early Christian documents as the epistles of Ignatius ("It is outlandish to proclaim Jesus Christ and practice Judaism"; *Magn.* 10.3), *Barnabas* ("Do not become like some people . . . saying that the covenant is both theirs and ours. For it is ours"; 4.6); or *Diognetus* ("Christians are right to abstain from the vulgar silliness, deceit, and meddling ways of the Jews, along with their arrogance"; 4.6).

228. Israel is a positive though limited term: John's baptism makes Jesus known to Israel (1:31); Nathanael, "truly an Israelite" (1:47), hails Jesus as "King of Israel" (1:49), as do "many of the Jews" when Jesus enters Jerusalem (12:12–13). Jesus himself upbraids Nicodemus, a Pharisaic ruler of the Jews (3:1), for not understanding what might be expected of him as a "teacher of Israel" (3:10).

man (9:6–11); and reads the Scriptures as the unbreakable word of God that, in turn, bears witness to the course of his own mission (5:39; 10:35).

But it is precisely at these points—ancestry, temple, festivals, rites of purification, Scripture, and the like—that Jesus' disciples are distinguished from *hoi Ioudaioi* as "the Jews who believed in him." Some of these differences may be cataloged as follows:

1. "The Jews" claim Abraham as their father; Jesus' disciples claim the ancestry of Abraham insofar as they do as Abraham did, joyfully welcoming Jesus, and in that way become children of God by being begotten of God through the Spirit (1:12–13; 3:3–5).

2. The Jews worship in the temple; Jesus is himself the temple in which his followers worship in Spirit and in truth (4:20–24).

3. The Jews journey to Jerusalem to keep the pilgrimage feasts (Passover, Booths) in the temple; they celebrate the feast that commemorates the temple's purification and rededication (Hanukkah); Jesus' followers receive from him the gifts to which these feasts point (God's deliverance and provision for his people) because these are now embodied in what Jesus is and gives (bread of life, light of the world, living water).

4. The Jews observe the laws of purification through washing with water; Jesus baptizes with water, pointing to the purification he will accomplish by means of baptism with the Spirit, his word (15:3), and his death (13:1–11).

5. The Jews, or their teachers, claim to be "disciples of Moses" and to study the Scripture or the law of Moses (9:27–29); Jesus' followers acknowledge Moses and the law, but as witnesses that point to Jesus (1:17–18; 5:39, 45–47). For "the Jews," it is impossible to be both a disciple of Moses and of Jesus; for Jesus' followers, to be a true disciple of Moses entails becoming a disciple of Jesus.

Jesus' followers identify with, or are related to, Abraham, Jacob, Moses, the law, and the temple through Jesus and by means of faith in him. From John's point of view, even if some who believe in Jesus were born Jewish or are proselytes to Judaism, *hoi Ioudaioi* does not fully characterize them: Samaritans do not need to adopt Jewish temple worship to belong to those who worship God rightly;[229] Gentiles belong to the children of God by believing in Jesus' name, do not become proselytes (first or later) to Judaism, and in this sense are not called *Ioudaioi*.[230] *Ioudaios* ("Jew" or "Judean") describes and locates Jesus in a way that it does not characterize his later disciples, since they do not share the identifying markers of worship, law, the patriarchs, and the Jewish festivals with the *Ioudaioi*, but only as these are reinterpreted through and in Jesus—a reinterpretation rejected by *hoi Ioudaioi* themselves.[231]

229. Cf. comments on 4:20.

230. Translators struggle to find an appropriate English word, since no term fully embraces the cultural, ethnic, geographical, and religious aspects of the ancient term *Ioudaioi*. In order to preserve the original geographical sense of the term, and to render it in keeping with other ancient designations of peoples (*ethnoi*), the translation "Judean" ought to be preferred. But since *Ioudaioi* came to apply to people living outside of Judea, and since "the Judeans" is not transparently connected to the people historically known as "the Jews," "the Judeans" ought to be retranslated, as it were, as "the Jews."

231. Keener (1:218–19) argues that John employs "the Jews" ironically as "a response to his opponents' functional claims that the Johannine Christians are no longer Jewish"; similarly, de Boer 2001.

The use of "the Jews" in the Gospel of John suggests a time and situation removed from that of Jesus himself. John's Gospel stresses that which has come to fullness in Jesus and does so by relating him and his followers to his Jewish identity. If Jesus' followers are no longer called *hoi Ioudaioi*, they are nevertheless connected to them because they are connected to Jesus, a Jew (4:9) and King of the Jews (19:21). Jesus is the pivot on which the narrative turns: those among "his own" (1:11), *hoi Ioudaioi*, may be ushered into the hour of fullness through Jesus; those who do not come from among *hoi Ioudaioi* are nevertheless connected to Israel's heritage through Jesus.

9:1–41 Light in Darkness

One of the most memorable narratives in John is that of the Sabbath healing of a man born blind (9:1–41). Jesus' healing instigates a verbal sparring match with the Pharisees, who question the man and his parents in order to discover what was done, who did it, and what it means. Although Jesus appears only at the beginning and end of the narrative and is never directly interrogated by the Pharisees, he is clearly the ultimate subject of the investigation. In apparent breach of the law, Jesus has healed on the Sabbath, calling into question his faithfulness to the law and implicitly to God (1:17, 45; 5:45–46; 6:32; 7:19, 22–23). As the man defends Jesus, he also becomes the target of the Pharisaic indictment of Jesus as a sinner who has abandoned the law of Moses (9:13, 16, 24, 28–29, 31, 34).

As part of the ongoing trial of Jesus and his disciples in the Gospel, questions about the man and about Jesus propel the story: Was the man blind? Who opened his eyes? How did he do it? Where is he now? Since it is a Sabbath, has Jesus violated the law? Is Jesus, then, a sinner or from God? How can a sinner do such signs (see 9:12, 15, 16, 17, 19, 26, 27, 34, 35, 36, 40)? Numerous affirmations about Jesus answer this barrage of questions: He is a prophet (v. 17) from God (v. 33; cf. 1:1, 14); he is Son of Man and Lord (9:35, 38). The entire story graphically illustrates Jesus' exhortation to "judge with right judgment" (7:24): the man's witness provides a concrete example of doing so.

In order to judge rightly, one must see rightly, and the narrative also raises a question: What does it take to see? The dominant motif in the passage is blindness (vv. 1, 2, 3, 13, 17, 18, 19, 20, 24, 25, 32, 39, 40, 41). While on one level the blindness is physical, by the end of the story blindness has acquired a figurative meaning as well. The once-blind man now "sees," whereas some with physical sight are blind (9:41; cf. 8:24). As the man gains his sight, he also gains greater insight into Jesus' identity: sight becomes a figure for the insight that perceives the significance of what Jesus has done and who he is. The narrative thus demonstrates what happens when light comes into darkness (1:4–5, 8, 12). And though the light has come into the world for salvation and not for judgment, not all will see or want to see (3:17–21).

9:1–12 Jesus Heals a Man Born Blind

While walking near (or perhaps in) the temple, Jesus heals a blind man by putting mud, made from dirt and saliva, on his eyes and sending him to wash in the pool of Siloam. The healing evokes an unusual reaction from those who have known him: they doubt that the man who now sees is the same man who was once blind. Although he insists that he has indeed been healed, he is unable to tell them much about the one who healed him. Thus begins the investigation into the healing and the healer.

> **9:1** And as he was passing by, he saw a man blind from birth. **2** And the
> disciples asked him, "Rabbi, who sinned, this man, or his parents, that
> he was born blind?"
>
> **3** Jesus answered, "He was not born blind[a] because he or his parents
> sinned, but that the works of God might be revealed in him. **4** We must[b]
> work the works of the one who sent me as long as it is day. The night is
> coming when no one is able to work. **5** While[c] I am in the world, I am the
> light of the world."
>
> **6** When he had said these things, he spat on the ground and made mud
> with his spittle and put[d] the mud on the man's eyes **7** and said to him, "Go,
> wash in the pool of Siloam" (which is translated as "sent"). So he went
> and washed and came back seeing!
>
> **8** Then his neighbors and those who had seen him[e] before as a beggar
> said, "Isn't this the one who sat and begged?"
>
> **9** Some said that it was, but others said, "No, but he is like him."
>
> The man kept saying, "It is I!"[f]
>
> **10** They said to him, "Then how were your eyes opened?"
>
> **11** He said to them, "The man called Jesus made mud and put it[g] on my
> eyes and told me, 'Go to Siloam and wash.' So, I went, and when I had
> washed, then I could see."
>
> **12** And they said to him, "Where is he?"
>
> He said, "I don't know."

a. Lit., "Neither this one nor his parents sinned, but rather in order to reveal the works of God in him"; this English translation supplies what is implicit in the Greek.

b. Instead of "we must" (*hēmas dei*, $\mathfrak{P}^{66, 75}$ ℵ* B), some MSS read "I must" (*eme dei*, $ℵ^{a}$ A C $f^{1, 13}$), likely a copyist's alteration since Jesus is speaking and is the agent of the man's healing.

c. Greek *hotan*, "whenever."

d. Here B reads *epethēken* ("put"); *epechrisen* ("anointed"), found in $\mathfrak{P}^{66, 75}$ ℵ A, may be an assimilation to *epechrisen* in 9:11.

e. Or, "Those seeing him before as a beggar." The Greek has a present participle, *hoi theōrountes*, perhaps indicating how recently the man has been seen begging.

f. Greek, *egō eimi.*
g. *Epechrisen*, "anointed, smeared"; see note d.

[9:1–5] Jesus' healing of the man born blind[232] does not take place in the temple (8:59), although the public venue of the temple precincts was considered an appropriate locale for begging (Acts 3:2–3, 10; Josephus, *J.W.* 2.10; *Ag. Ap.* 1.305). The narrative opens with the disciples' question to Jesus, "Rabbi, who sinned, this man or his parents, that he was born blind?" (John 9:2). The disciples express a common view that various physical ailments can be the result of sin (see comments on 5:14). But here the question is, Whose sin accounts for the blindness of an infant? The view that one can suffer the consequences of the sins of one's parents or ancestors can be found throughout the literature of the ancient world.[233] Later rabbinic commentary assumed that one's disposition may already have been fixed in the womb[234] or that a fetus could commit idolatry if his mother entered the temple of an idol.[235] Such later views might explain the disciples' question here.

Jesus does not explicitly refute the general connection between sin and sickness, but he shifts the focus from consideration of what the man or his parents have done to the works of God. Jesus' statement that the man was born blind "*that* the works of God might be revealed[236] in him" (v. 3; cf. 11:4) indicates that God's work is not to condemn people to darkness: it is to bring light to them, as the ensuing narrative makes clear. The man was not born blind as a punishment for or as the result of sin; the man's blindness will show that God's purposes are to bring light into the darkness of human existence.

"The works of him who sent me" are the works of God that Jesus does.[237] The plural "works" encompasses the imminent healing of the man born blind,

232. BDAG shows that *ek genetēs* ("from birth") is frequent in Greek literature; Pausanias (2d c. C.E.) mentions that Ophioneus, the Messenian seer "blind from birth" (*typhlos ek genetēs*), had received his sight; cf. *Descr.* 4.10.6; 4.12.10; see Lev 25:47 LXX). *Ek koilias mētros*, "from the mother's womb," is a more common biblical idiom (Judg 16:17; Pss 21:11 [22:10 ET]; 70:6 [71:6]; Job 1:21; 38:8; Isa 49:1; Matt 19:12; Luke 1:15; Acts 3:2; 14:8; Gal 1:15).

233. See Exod 20:5; Deut 5:9; 2 Kgs 5:27; Jer 31:29; Jdt 7:28; Tob 3:3–4; Josephus, *J.W.* 3.375; also Hesiod, *Op.* 281–84; Apollonius of Rhodes, *Argon.* 2.475; Valerius Maximus 1.1.ext.3.

234. See *Gen. Rab.* 63.6–7 on Gen 25:22: that Esau and Jacob "struggled together" in Rebekah's womb signals Esau's antenatal tendency toward idolatry and wickedness.

235. *Song Rab.* 1.41.

236. *Hina* with the subjunctive typically denotes purpose ("in order that"); but it is possible that in both vv. 2 and 3, *hina* introduces a result clause: "Who sinned [with the result] that this man was born blind?" (9:2) and "[with the result] that the works of God might be revealed in him" (9:3) rather than "[in order] that the works of God might be revealed in him." The interpretation of the *hina* in 9:3 was already disputed in the fourth century (John Chrysostom, *Hom. Jo.* 56.1–2).

237. For Jesus' work as God's "work," see 4:34; 17:4; as God's "works," 5:20, 36; 10:25, 32, 37–38; 14:10–12; 15:24.

all other healings, as well as Jesus' "work" of bringing life. Jesus includes his disciples—"*We*[238] must work the works of the one who sent me"—in his mission of bringing light to darkness: as those who follow the light (8:12; 12:35–36), as witnesses to the light of the world, they are part of God's work and will continue God's work in the world. But night is coming (cf. 13:30). Anticipating his death, Jesus warns of an end to this particular phase of his work; the awareness of the approaching end lends urgency to his mission. Yet as long as he is in the world, he will persist in doing God's light- and life-giving work (9:5; 11:9–10; 12:35–36): there is still time for Jesus to work and for people to see and come to the light.

But Jesus' caveat regarding the approaching end of his time inevitably raises questions: If he is the light of the world (only?) as long as he is in it, how can John also speak of the light's perpetual shining in the darkness (1:5)? If Jesus' work as the life-giving light will soon come to a close, how then will people be able to come to the light, to follow him, after he has departed? Here Jesus speaks as one whose work has a temporal limit. The approaching end constrains him to do the work of God (cf. Luke 12:50). But he is also for all time the light of the world: he was the light in creation (1:4–5) and will be the light that continues to shine in the world after his resurrection. John acknowledges the boundaries between Jesus' earthly and risen existence.[239] But at the same time the Gospel assumes the continuity of the work and the identity of the preresurrection and postresurrection Lord. Jesus does not *become* the light of the world upon his resurrection, nor does he cease to be that light; he already *is* the light for the world and will continue to be so.

[6–7] Typical of Johannine narratives, Jesus takes the initiative in approaching the man (5:6; 6:5; contrast Mark 8:22; 10:47–51). Jesus makes mud with his own saliva and dirt, spreads the mud on the man's eyes, and commands him to go and wash in the pool of Siloam. In the ancient world, saliva was thought to have curative properties, although there is perhaps less evidence for the view in Jewish tradition (e.g., *b. B. Bat.* 126b). Several Roman historians report that Vespasian cured a man of blindness by spitting in his eye,[240] and Pliny the Elder enumerates prophylactic and curative properties of human spittle (*Nat.* 28.7). No one would have thought it particularly surprising for Jesus to make use of spittle in healing (see Mark 7:33; 8:23).

238. For the inclusion of the disciples in Jesus' work, both present and future, see 3:11; 4:2, 38; 6:5; 14:12; 20:21.

239. So Ridderbos 334; Schnelle (1998, 154) rightly notes that John presupposes the "identity of the earthly with the exalted" Jesus; differently, Theobald (270–71) contends that Jesus speaks here as the exalted Christ.

240. Tacitus, *Hist.* 4.81; 1.3; Suetonius, *Vesp.* 7.2–3; Dio Cassius, *Hist.* 65.8.

Mud alone, in itself, does not effect the man's cure (v. 11).[241] Jesus sends the man to wash in the pool of Siloam, which according to John means "sent" (*apestalmenos*), an interpretation of the pool's name not otherwise attested.[242] The pool of Siloam, fed by the spring of Gihon, is the pool from which water was drawn for the water libation at the Feast of Tabernacles (*m. Sukkah* 4:9), thus linking the man's washing to Jesus' promise of living water (cf. John 7:37–39). This man will have the light of life (8:12). The pool of Siloam, partially uncovered in recent archaeological investigation, was apparently very large (200 meters long), with steps leading into it on all sides. Its structure and position below the temple suggest that it was a *miqveh*, a pool for ritual immersion and cleansing before entering the temple.[243]

[9–12] After the man washes in the pool, he is able to see. But the man's neighbors disagree whether the healed man is their formerly blind neighbor: Jesus' actions have (again) divided them (cf. 7:40–42). Their inability to recognize the formerly blind man parallels their inability to discern Jesus' identity through the witness of his sign (cf. 4:54; 6:14). While the man persists in his testimony—"The man kept saying, 'It is I!'" (9:9; *egō eimi*)—his neighbors persist in their doubt and uncertainty. Jesus' works provoke disagreements about his origins, his identity, and his relationship to God—and here these disagreements involve the one he has healed.

The man's neighbors then inquire *how* he has been cured, a question that provides the occasion for him to recount yet again what "the man called Jesus" has done (v. 11; cf. vv. 14–15, 26): Jesus made mud, spread it on the man's eyes, sent him to Siloam, and told him to wash; and the man went, he washed, and now he sees. This is "how" the man was healed: he was the recipient of Jesus' action and responsive to Jesus' commands. But when pressed regarding Jesus' whereabouts, the man cannot answer: he does not know where Jesus is. Indeed, from this point in the story, Jesus is strangely absent. Even though his actions have generated the controversy that dominates the narrative, Jesus does not take center stage. Rather, the main conversations occur between the man and his neighbors, between the man and the Pharisees, and between the man's parents and the Pharisees. Jesus returns only after the Pharisees drive

241. According to Ephrem the Syrian, the man is healed by Jesus' command (*Comm.* 16.29); this interpretation is not widely adopted by modern commentators.

242. John may have derived this etymology for Siloam from the Hebrew verb *šālaḥ* ("send"), thus playing on Jesus as the one who is "sent" by the Father and who in turn "sends" the man to wash. In Isa 8:6 there is reference to "the waters of Shiloach" (*mê hašilōaḥ*), which the LXX translates as *to hydōr tou Silōam*; Neh 3:15 refers to the pool of Shelach (*bĕrēkat hašelaḥ*; not in the LXX), but no interpretation of the name is given. Josephus (*J.W.* 5.140) refers to Siloam as a "sweet spring" (*pēgē glykeia*).

243. Meyers and Chancey 132. The pool at the exit of Hezekiah's tunnel, often pictured in books and commentaries, is from the Byzantine era.

the man out (9:34). The man's testimony to Jesus is cast into sharp relief in Jesus' absence. Indeed, bearing witness to Jesus in his absence is what Jesus' disciples must do.

9:13–23 The Pharisees Question the Man

The man's neighbors take him to the Pharisees, who are particularly interested in what Jesus did and the fact that he did it on the Sabbath. They ask for the man's account of his healing and interpretation of its significance. Initially doubting that this healing had actually taken place, they summon the man's parents, who refuse to speak up for fear of what might happen to them. This brief episode shows that bearing witness to Jesus as the Messiah of God divides families and communities.

> 9:13 They took the man who had been blind to the Pharisees. 14 Now the
> day on which Jesus made the mud and opened the man's eyes was the Sabbath.
>
> 15 So, again the Pharisees asked the man, "How did you get your sight?"
>
> He said to them, "He put mud on my eyes, and I washed, and I see!"
>
> 16 Then some of the Pharisees said, "This man is not from God, because he does not keep the Sabbath."
>
> But others said, "How can a man who is a sinner do such signs?" And there was a division among them.
>
> 17 They said again to the blind man, "What do you say about him, since he opened your eyes?"
>
> The man replied, "He is a prophet."
>
> 18 But the Jews did not believe that he had been blind and received
> his sight, so they summoned the parents of the man who had received his
> sight 19 and asked them, "Is this your son? And you say that he was born
> blind? Then how does he now see?"
>
> 20 The parents answered them, "We know that this is our son, and
> that he was born blind. 21 But how he now sees, we do not know; nor do
> we know who opened his eyes. Ask him; he is of age; he will tell you himself."
>
> 22 His parents said this because they were afraid of the Jews. For the Jews had already agreed that if anyone were to confess Jesus to be the Messiah, he would be cast out of the community.[a]
>
> 23 Therefore his parents said, "He is of age; ask him."

a. *Synagōgē* can mean "gathering, assembly" (as frequently in the LXX) or "synagogue building" (John 6:59; 18:20); see comments on 9:22.

[9:13–15] The man's neighbors took him "to the Pharisees," but it is not clear what they were expected to do. As devout laypersons, the Pharisees had a reputation for careful observance of the law (Josephus, *Ant.* 17.41; *J.W.* 2.162; *Life* 191), and behind the ensuing dialogue lies the question whether Jesus' healing has violated the law. The earlier Sabbath healing (ch. 5), followed by Jesus' lengthy discourse regarding his identity as the authoritative and unique life-giving Son, led "the Jews" to attempt to put Jesus to death. Here, however, Jesus has disappeared from the scene, and the blind man is on trial. He repeats his simple testimony to Jesus, bearing witness by recounting what Jesus has done ("He put mud on my eyes"), how he himself had responded to Jesus' command ("I washed"), and what the result was ("I see").

[16–17] Predictably, Jesus' action leads to a division: some of the Pharisees believe that he has not kept the law; therefore, he is a sinner who cannot have been sent by God, since God's law forbids work on the Sabbath.[244] Later the Mishnah will specify thirty-nine classes of forbidden work. Among the forbidden work is kneading: possibly Jesus is accused of "kneading" as he makes mud (*m. Šabb.* 7:2; 24:3). John, however, does not specify the accusation; the charge is simply that Jesus does not observe the Sabbath (9:16): he has not kept God's law.

Others, however, think that Jesus cannot be a sinner because, as Nicodemus, another Pharisee, had put it earlier, "No one can do such signs unless God is with him" (3:2; 9:16). In keeping with that assessment, the healed man calls Jesus a prophet, a confession expressing incipient faith (9:17; cf. 4:19; 6:14; 7:40, 52). In the subsequent dialogue between the man's parents and the Jews, the question will be whether Jesus is the Messiah (9:22–23; cf. 7:40–43); by the end of the chapter, this man Jesus will be confessed as Lord. While "prophet" correctly identifies Jesus as one sent by God to declare God's word, "prophet" will be supplemented by more appropriate designations for Jesus.

The debate about Jesus' status as a sinner is initially framed as a question of whether Jesus has broken the law. On this point, the Pharisees are divided: Jesus appears to be a sinner, a lawbreaker, since he has not observed the Sabbath, but a sinner cannot do such signs. According to many commentators, John concedes the point that Jesus has not observed the Sabbath but draws a different conclusion than some of the Pharisees: Jesus is *not* a sinner (loc. cit.: Bultmann 1971; R. Brown 1966; Barrett; Beasley-Murray). But John's Gospel does not even concede the charge that Jesus violates the Sabbath (so also Keener 1:784).

244. See comments on John 5:10; cf. Exod 20:8–11; 31:15–16; 35:2–3; Lev 23:3; 25:2; Deut 5:12–15; Jer 17:21–22. Patristic writers understood "opening the eyes" of the blind man as an act of creation; so Irenaeus: "What the creating Word had neglected to form in the womb, this he supplied openly"; *Haer.* 5.15.2; John Chrysostom, *Hom. Jo.* 56.2; 57.1; Ephrem the Syrian, *Comm.* 16.28; Athanasius, *Inc.* 18.4. If this interpretation be accepted, Jesus would be exercising his power to create, in keeping with John 1:1–4 and 5:26–27.

Part of what it means to "judge with right judgment" is to discern that, when Jesus works on the Sabbath, his work reveals that his Sabbath works are God's Sabbath works: they are done with God's authority (5:19–20, 26–27) and are the kind of life-giving and sustaining work that God himself does on the Sabbath (cf. 5:17). Jesus does "the works of him who sent me" by bringing light to darkness, even on the day of rest.

This debate indirectly reflects disagreements in first- and second-century Jewish sources regarding the kinds of work, if any, that could "override" the Sabbath or the prohibition against working on the Sabbath (cf. comments on 7:19–24). In John 7:22 it is apparent that circumcision can "override the Sabbath" (*m. Šabb.* 18:3–19.5). The Mishnah allowed certain acts of mercy to "override the Sabbath" for the sake of saving a life (*m. Yoma* 8:6; but cf. *m. Šabb.* 22:6). Not all agreed with such a stance: at least one leader of a synagogue thought that the other six days of the week provided ample opportunity for healing (Luke 13:14), and the DSS stringently prohibit violation of the Sabbath in order to offer aid to animals or persons in need (CD XI, 12, 16).

To be sure, the blind man's life is not in immediate danger. Yet the man's healing demonstrates the urgency of Jesus' work because it points to the fact that those who remain in the darkness of unbelief are in danger of death. Jesus' work is urgent, since life indeed is in danger; Jesus' work must be undertaken "while it is day" (9:4), even if that day is the Sabbath. Yet here the debate does not turn on allowable exceptions to the law, but on Jesus' identity and appropriate response to him. It is typical of John that debates concerning the interpretation of Scripture are ultimately settled by appeal to Jesus' identity and his authority to interpret Scripture (5:39, 45–47; 6:31–35, 45).

This narrative is therefore shaped by the definitions of sin and sinner, and how sin is understood with respect to the law and to belief in Jesus (vv. 2, 16, 24, 31, 34). Initially the man born blind is deemed a sinner or the child of sinners (vv. 2, 34); now Jesus is called a sinner; and at the end of the account, the Pharisees are labeled sinners for their failure to see that Jesus is the one who has done God's work by bringing sight to the blind, light to the world (1:4–9; 3:19; 8:12; 9:5). The basis for "right judgment" has thus shifted from keeping the law to response to Jesus. The law is neither set aside nor dismissed, but "right judgment" (7:24) entails acknowledging that Jesus is God's divinely sent emissary because the kind of work that Jesus does, bringing light into darkness, is God's own work. The law may forbid work on the Sabbath, but it does not and cannot prohibit the life-giving work of God. Thus God's witness to Jesus through his signs calls for the judgment that this healing "overrides" the Sabbath, even if the case cannot finally be adjudicated by appeal to the law.

[18–23] Now "the Jews" turn to question the man's parents, who refuse to comment on their son's healing, claiming that they know nothing about it and that the man, who is of age (that is, at least 13 years old), must speak for himself.[245] Moreover, the Gospel explains that they are afraid to speak, because they are "afraid of the Jews" who "had already agreed that if anyone were to confess Jesus to be the Messiah, he would be cast out of the community" or "put out of the synagogue" (*aposynagōgos genētai*, v. 22). The word *aposynagōgos* appears only in John (cf. 12:42; 16:2): it is not found elsewhere in the New Testament, in the LXX, or in any nonbiblical literature. It may have been coined to describe a situation for which John had no word ready to hand. Such coinage might suggest that, whatever these parents fear, there is no obvious precedent for it in first-century Judaism. In the LXX, *synagōgē* regularly occurs with reference to the gathering or congregation of Israel rather than to a building or institution; in that light, the parents fear being excluded or cut off from the social and communal networks of the "congregation [*synagōgē*] of Israel."[246]

The explanation offered for the parents' silence appears to be an intrusion into the narrative because it envisions a scenario not actually narrated: nobody has asked the man or the parents whether they believe Jesus to be the Messiah; the scene is not obviously set in the synagogue; and the man is eventually driven away (v. 34) for his presumption, not his confession of Jesus as Messiah. Precisely because this editorial explanation describes a situation that does not fit naturally with the narrative to this point, it has occasioned considerable discussion. In recent decades it has even been taken to be the key for unlocking the puzzle of the Gospel's historical provenance. Briefly, the historical reconstruction posited to explain this situation is as follows:

> "The Jews," actually the Pharisees, are understood to refer to an authoritative body that has made a formal agreement[247] that if anyone confesses Jesus to be the Messiah, that person will be expelled from the synagogue (*aposynagōgos genētai*). Since it is deemed unlikely that such expulsions took place already in Jesus' day, the account in John 9 is taken to depict the situation of later Jewish believers in Jesus, particularly after the destruction of the temple in 70 C.E.[248] Some interpreters have suggested, moreover, that John's situation reflects the adoption of an official policy of Jewish authorities, probably those gathered under the leadership of Joḥanan ben-Zakkai at Yavneh (Jamnia) after the fall of the temple, who sought to tighten the boundaries of Judaism by identifying or silencing *minim* (sectarians). This policy is thought to be reflected in the promulgation

245. For more on the meaning and identity of "the Jews," see Excursus 7: "'The Jews' in John."

246. So also Brant 166–68; Hoskyns 356; Hurtado 2005b, 70; Levine 1260. Thyen (466) contends that "synagogue" here refers not simply to a building, or to a religious fellowship, but rather to "the locus of communal life" (*Lebensgemeinschaft*). *Synagōgē* can also designate a place or building (6:59; 18:20; Marcus 2009, 533 n. 42).

247. The Greek *synetetheinto* is often rendered "had already agreed," suggesting the existence of a formal policy.

248. In a 2013 monograph, Jonathan Bernier contends that informal pressure could have kept Jesus' followers from synagogue participation.

of the so-called *birkat ha-minim* ("blessing" [in reality, a curse] of the "*minim*," "sectarians" or "heretics"): the twelfth benediction in a series of eighteen blessings and curses (Shemoneh Esreh, Eighteen Benedictions) regularly pronounced in the synagogue. According to later rabbinic tradition, a rabbi named Samuel the Small composed a "blessing" against the *minim*.[249] The story of its composition, but not the text of the prayer, is found in the Talmud (*b. Ber.* 28b–29a). The story also states that anyone who falters while reading the prayer is suspected of being a *min* and removed from his post as reader or lector.

Here, then, is an official decree designed to identify *minim* ("sectarians") and to remove them from public responsibilities in the synagogue. Interpreters of John draw the connection between that decree, its use to detect heretics, and the expulsion of those professing Jesus as the Messiah from the synagogue. The cost for confession of Jesus was high: those cast out from the synagogue are cut off from the social networks of family and community. It is then further suggested that the Gospel of John assumes the experiences of a group of Christians, often called "the Johannine community," who have suffered the trauma of such expulsion and are now cut off from families, friends, and neighbors who do not share their messianic confession. The story of these Johannine Christians is obliquely told in the narrative of the encounters of the man born blind, his parents, and "the Jews."

While such a historical reconstruction has been highly influential in Johannine studies in the past decades,[250] nearly every aspect of it has been challenged.[251] A number of scholars have doubted that the council of Yavneh had the authority to promulgate and enforce a policy that would expel Jewish messianists from the synagogue; that it sought to "tighten" the boundaries of orthodoxy at all; or that it had extensive influence in the late first century.[252] The date of the formulation of the *birkat ha-minim*, when it first specifically targeted *Notsrim* (*nôṣrîm*, Nazarenes, or Christians) and on what grounds, has also been vigorously discussed.[253] And some have questioned the view that the destruction of the temple provoked the sharp rift between "Jews" and "Christians" often presupposed by this hypothesis.[254]

But having said all that, and setting aside for the moment the explanation at 9:22–23, the entire encounter between the healed man and the Pharisees or "the Jews"—within the text, not behind it—envisions a rift, or division, if only in

249. For further traditions about this benediction, see *t. Ber.* 3.25; *y. Ber.* 2.3, 4b–5a; *b. Meg.* 17b.

250. It is closely associated with the work of Martyn; and R. Brown 1979.

251. The literature is extensive; see esp. Hakola 2005, 41–86; and Langer. For a summary of the response to Martyn's thesis, see D. Moody Smith 2003; for a nuanced discussion more sympathetic to the historical basis of Martyn's reconstruction, see Marcus 2009.

252. Cohen 1984; Hakola 2005.

253. Stemberger 1977, 15–16; Kimelman 233–34; Katz 1984, 65–69; Alexander; Marcus 2009. For a complete history of the *birkat ha-minim*, see Langer 2011.

254. The addition of the *Notsrim* (*nōṣrîm*, Nazarenes) to the twelfth benediction seems to have come at a later time; Katz 1984; Reinhartz 1998.

the form of the dismissal of the man and his witness to Jesus as a prophet who has come from God (3:2; 4:19; 6:14–15; 7:40, 52). John frequently reports the people's division of opinion about Jesus.[255] The controversy here recalls earlier differences about whether Jesus is "a good man" or a deceiver (7:12), assessments apparently arising from Jesus' Sabbath healing (7:19–23), which leads to Jesus' entreaty to "judge with right judgment" (7:24). In the blind man's encounter with the Pharisees, the key disputed issue is, once again, adherence to the law of Moses and the potential implications of the Sabbath healing for assessing it. Which judgment about Jesus, the law, and the Sabbath healing constitutes "right judgment" when there are apparently conflicting data? While Jesus has done God's work in bringing sight to the blind, some think he has violated God's law in doing that on the Sabbath. Exactly how the law is to be observed is not simply a matter of debate between Jesus and his contemporaries, or between early Christians and Jews; it is in fact a matter of considerable discussion in Jewish sources as well.

The dispute between the man and the Pharisees is not simply whether Jesus is the Messiah, a question disputed elsewhere in John but one that need not have led to fracturing the synagogue community.[256] While "Messiah" does refer to the promised deliverer in the line of David, it has also become a shorthand term to summarize Jesus' identity in John. When the Gospel invites its readers to believe that "Jesus is the Messiah, the Son of God" (20:31), it has in view the full range of claims made for Jesus. He is the one of whom Moses and the prophets spoke (1:45) and to whom Moses bears witness (5:45–46). Again, it is not merely the question of Jesus' status as Messiah but also of his allegiance to the law and his relationship to Moses and Abraham, key figures of Jewish identity, that divide his contemporaries, particularly in the narratives of John 5–9.

The man's healing, his witness to Jesus, and the Pharisees' dismissal of that witness and of the man presage Jesus' own warning to his disciples that, after his death, they will be put out of the synagogue, excluded in some way from "the congregation" or "assembly" (*aposynagōgos*, 16:2; cf. also 12:42; 15:18, 20; cf. Matt 10:17; 23:34; Mark 13:9; Luke 12:11; 21:12).[257] While it is difficult to determine exactly what this entailed, the practice of exclusion from the community is not without precedent in the Old Testament (Ezra 10:8) and later Jewish literature (see 1QS VI, 24–VII, 25, where disciplinary exclusion ranges from 10 days to 2 years; permanent exclusion, for uttering the divine name, is

255. The Synoptic Gospels also testify to the division that Jesus' ministry effects among the people of Israel (e.g., Matt 13:38–43, 47–50; Luke 2:34; 12:51–53).

256. According to *y. Taʿan.* 4.5, Rabbi Akiba said that Simon Bar-Kosiba (Bar Kokhbah) was the Messiah—a claim for which he was ridiculed, but not threatened with expulsion from the synagogue (so also *Lam. Rab.* 2.2.4).

257. This could refer to a localized action against Jewish believers in Jesus; D. Moody Smith 1990, 86; Marcus 2009, 551.

also possible).[258] What is in view is not so much "excommunication," being put outside the bounds of a recognized and defined institutional expression of a religion, but exclusion from the community of family and friends in which one has lived, learned, and worshiped.

The idea that one's commitment to God determines, even overrides, all other allegiances can be found in various Jewish authors, such as Philo of Alexandria (20 B.C.E.–50 C.E.):

> But as for these kinships, as we call them, which have come down from our ancestors and are based on blood-relationship, or those derived from marriage or other similar causes, let them all be cast aside if they do not seek earnestly the same goal, namely, the honor of God, which is the indissoluble bond of affection which makes us one.[259]

In Philo, as in early Christian thinking, allegiance to the one God bound the faithful not only to that God, but also to one another. Likewise, the Cynics, a school of ancient Greek philosophy, held that the ideal philosopher was free from all worldly distractions brought about by the duties of family and home, so that he could be free to be "wholly devoted to the service of God" and to the universal family.[260] In other words, certain religious or philosophical commitments entailed the subordination of family ties, yet produced identification with and belonging to a new community.

John's account calls attention to the shape of the family that is both lost and established when the social networks that ordinarily bind parents to children are disrupted and replaced by new ties of kinship (cf. Matt 10:35–37; 19:29; Mark 3:31–35; 10:29–30; Luke 12:52–53; 14:26; 18:28–29). The man healed by Jesus demonstrates exactly the kind of exemplary courage and faith in confessing Jesus that others in the Gospel, including the man's parents, lack (cf. 12:42–43). Since the man's parents are willing to make him an orphan, he will need a family and a place to belong. Jesus' subsequent act of seeking and finding the man (9:35) embody his promise to his followers that he will not leave them as orphans (14:18). In his ministry, Jesus gathers together those who have been cast out or scattered by others and makes of them one flock (see 9:34–35; 10:11; 11:52).

258. While two Jewish disciplinary bans, *niddui* and *ḥērem*, are sometimes thought to offer an explanation for the threat of being made *aposynagōgos*, there is no reference to the more severe ban, *ḥērem*, before the third century; furthermore, *niddui* was a temporary disciplinary ban within the synagogue; so Martyn 51; Katz 2006, 271–76.

259. Philo, *Spec.* 1.316–17. Noting the cost of converting to Judaism, Philo describes a proselyte as one who, having "joined a new commonwealth" has thereby "turned his kinsfolk . . . into irreconcilable enemies" (*Spec.* 4.178; see 1.51–52). For fuller discussion of similar passages in ancient literature and comparison to the Gospels, see Barton; comments on 19:25–27 below.

260. Epictetus, *Diatr.* 3.22.69–72.

9:24–41 The Pharisees Question the Man Again

When the parents refuse to speak, the Pharisees renew their questioning of the man, now concentrating on the question of sin, the apparent violation of the Sabbath, and the implications for understanding Jesus in his relationship to the law of Moses. Unconvinced by the man's witness that Jesus is a prophet from God, the Pharisees end the questioning simply by dismissing him, driving him out from their presence. But Jesus seeks him out, identifying himself as the one who healed him, which leads to the man's confession, "I believe, Lord." Jesus' sign has led the man to faith because he has understood its witness to Jesus as the one who does God's work in the world.

9:24 Then they summoned the man who had been blind a second time
and said to him, "Give glory to God. We know that this man is a sinner."

25 He answered them, "Whether he is a sinner, I do not know. One
thing I know: I was blind, now I see."

26 They said to him, "What did he do to you? How did he open your
eyes?"

27 He answered them, "I already told you, and you did not listen. Why
do you want to hear it again? Do you want to become his disciples too?"

28 But they reviled him and said, "You are a disciple of that one; we are
disciples of Moses. **29** We know that God spoke to Moses, but we don't
know where this man comes from."

30 The man said to them, "This is amazing! You don't know where he
comes from, yet he opened my eyes! **31** We know that God does not listen
to sinners, but if anyone fears God and does his will, then God listens to
him. **32** Not since the beginning of time has it been heard that someone
opened the eyes of anyone born blind. **33** If he were not from God, then
he could do nothing."

34 They answered, "You were born in utter sin, and you want to teach
us?" And they drove him out.

35 Jesus heard that they had driven him out and found him and said,
"Do you believe in this Son of Man?"[a]

36 He answered, "And who is he, Lord, that I might believe in him?"

37 Jesus said to him, "You have seen him, and he is the one speaking
with you."

38 And he said, "I believe, Lord." And he worshiped[b] him.

39 And Jesus said, "For judgment I came into the world, so that those
who do not see may see, and those who see may become blind."[c]

40 Some of the Pharisees who were with him heard these things and
said to him, "We are not blind, are we?"

41 Jesus said to them, "If you were blind, you would have no sin. But
now that you say, 'We see,' your sin remains."

a. Instead of *huion tou anthrōpou* (as in $\mathfrak{P}^{66,75}$ ℵ B D W syr^{s} $\text{cop}^{sa, bo[ms], ach[2], fay}$ *al*), some texts read *huios tou theou*, likely appropriating John's own language (20:31) and Christian confession of Jesus.

b. See BDAG, *proskyneō*. The word can refer to prostrating oneself before another, often in connection with making a petition or request (e.g. Matt 8:2; 9:18; 15:25; 18:26; 20:20). But here *prosekynēsen auto* means "he worshiped him" or "knelt before him in reverence."

c. A number of MSS ($\mathfrak{P}^{75}$ ℵ* W $\text{it}^{b,(1)}$ cop^{ach}; Diatessaron^{v} lacks all of vv. 38–39) are missing the text in vv. 38–39: "And he said, 'Lord, I believe.' And he worshiped him. And Jesus said.'" These are likely accidental omissions.

[9:24–25] The questioning continues. "The Jews" challenge the man to "give glory to God," which can mean to give praise to God—rather than to Jesus, who as a sinner presumably does not honor God.[261] As noted earlier, this discourse is punctuated by queries about who can properly be called a "sinner": the healed man (9:2–3, 34), Jesus (vv. 16, 24, 25, 31), or the Pharisees (v. 41)? The connection between "sin" and "sight" shows that the true sinners are those who fail to perceive God's work of giving light in darkness through the work of Jesus. Even as "the works of God" were redefined as the singular "work" of having faith in Jesus (6:29), so here the work that does not please God, that which is sin, is *not* to heal on the Sabbath, but to reject the one sent by God who has done such a healing. Those who do not believe are not labeled wicked, immoral, or unjust: their sin is unbelief (cf. 8:24).

In any case, the man either refuses to say or does not know whether Jesus ought to be called a sinner. He knows only one thing: he can now see. This fact trumps all arguments that can be mounted against Jesus. Jesus has brought light into his darkness: this is the work of God, and "no one can do such signs unless God is with him" (3:2; 9:16, 33). When understood as the works of God, the signs of Jesus lead to faith. Hence, faith that is occasioned by Jesus' signs requires discernment of the kind of work that God does in the world. Such faith requires that one judge with right judgment (7:24).

[26–28] Again the Pharisees wish to hear the report of *how* the man was healed, which may indicate that it was the mode of healing that was problematic and perceived as a potential violation of the Sabbath and of the law (cf. comments on 9:16–17). When the man ironically asks them whether they want to become Jesus' disciples, too, they counter that one can be either a disciple of Jesus, as this man apparently is, or of Moses (v. 28). One cannot be both. But for John, Moses serves as a witness to Jesus, and so a true disciple of Moses

261. See Pss 28:1 LXX (29:1 ET); 95:7 LXX (96:7); Isa 42:12; Jer 13:16; 4 Macc 1:12; Luke 17:18; Rom 4:20; Rev 4:9; 14:7; 19:7. When Achan sins and hides what he has done, Joshua exhorts him to confess his sin and thus "give glory today to the Lord God of Israel" (*dos doxan sēmeron tō kyriō theō Israēl*; Josh 7:19 LXX).

becomes a disciple of Jesus (5:45–46). Moses stands with and witnesses to Jesus. The question, then, is, "Whose appeal to Moses is justified?"[262] The Pharisees revile (*eloidorēsan*) the man for his confession; the hostility between the "disciples of Moses" and of "that one" (*ekeinou*) is intense.

[29–33] A second charge is then raised against Jesus: since his origins are unknown, there is no clear way to discern whether he is from God. This accusation actually restates Jesus' earlier point: "the Jews" do not know where he is from; they do not know that he is from God (8:14; cf. 7:28). Again the man appeals to Jesus' act of opening his eyes as testimony to Jesus' divinely ordained mission; whatever scruples and objections there might be ought to disappear in the face of the witness of this sign.

In further defense of Jesus, the man maintains that Jesus must be sent by God, since God does not listen to sinners, but only to those who fear God (*theosebēs*) and do God's will.[263] "Sinners" refers to those who deliberately violate God's law; God's refusal to hear their prayers is evidence of judgment upon them.[264] But Jesus' signs are evidence of his God-given mission to bring light to the world, and the man correctly interprets his own healing as evidence of Jesus' coming from God (*para theou*, 9:33; cf. vv. 3, 16). Neither this man, nor the Jews, nor anyone else who saw what happened to him had ever seen such a sign: why do they doubt its divine origin?

The man's insistent testimony leads the Pharisees to chastise him for the sin that supposedly led to his blindness, to sneer at his attempts to instruct them regarding the ways of God, and to drive the man out (*exebalon auton*, 9:34) from the ad hoc trial they have convened.[265] "Born in utter sin" recalls the description of him as *born blind* (*typhlos ek genetēs*, 9:1), as well as the disciples' suspicions that either he or his parents had sinned and thereby brought it about. By echoing the disciples' opening query (9:2), the Pharisees show that they have learned nothing from Jesus' sign or the man's testimony to it. He has spoken for himself, and in response the Pharisees have dismissed him from their presence. This is not precisely an expulsion from the synagogue (9:22), although it foreshadows such later acts.

[35–38] Jesus now finds the formerly blind man and asks him, "Do you believe in the Son of Man?" Not surprisingly, the healed man inquires to whom the expression "Son of Man" refers, since it can simply mean "human being." Earlier in this chapter, Jesus has three times been referred to as a

262. D. Moody Smith 1999, 197; Barrett 362.

263. *Theosebēs* occurs only here in the Greek NT; *theosebeia*, meaning godliness, reverence, or piety, occurs in the NT only in 1 Tim 2:10, but both the adjective and noun are common in Hellenistic texts (see BDAG).

264. Isa 1:15; 1 Sam 2:25; Jer 7:16–18; 11:14; 14:11–12; 15:11; *Pss. Sol.* 5.2, 5, 12; 7.7; 15.1; 16.1–15; *1 En.* 14.7; 97.3, 5; *L.A.B.* 27.7.

265. So also R. Brown 1966, 375.

human being, or man, an identification of Jesus found elsewhere in John.[266] When Jesus asks the healed man, "Do you *believe* in the Son of Man?" he moves the man from confessing things about him (that he is a prophet, from God, the Messiah) to believing in him, to believing in this man who stands before him now.The healed man expresses his belief visibly and audibly: he kneels before Jesus in reverence or worship as he utters his confession, "I believe, Lord." The man thus completes his confession of and identification with Jesus (cf. 11:27, 32; 20:28).

The expression "Son of Man" has appeared earlier in the Gospel, especially in contexts where Jesus refers to his divine origins (1:51; 3:13–15; 6:51–58)—the very issue in dispute between the healed man and the Pharisees. Even as "the Messiah" designates the deliverer descended from David but reconfigured by the actual course of Jesus' mission, so the term "Son of Man" means "human being," but implies that fundamental aspect of Jesus' identity: he is flesh, human, by virtue of his incarnation. The formerly blind man now confesses this man, Jesus, as Lord, a confession particularly common in resurrection encounters with Jesus (20:13, 16, 18, 25, 28; 21:7). The healed man thus becomes a model for all disciples who bear witness to Jesus as Lord in hostile circumstances and at the cost of ostracism from their social communities.

[39–41] Given Jesus' earlier statements that the Father has entrusted all judgment to him (5:22, 27), his declaration here that he has come for judgment (*eis krima*) follows naturally. Jesus judges "with right judgment," and he urges others to do the same (see esp. 3:19–21; 7:24). Here the blind man exemplifies what it means to "judge with right judgment" or "to see"; it is to make the appropriate confession of Jesus as Lord. The Pharisees claim to see the truth about the law, the Sabbath, and Jesus and to understand these things rightly, but since they do not believe that Jesus has done the work of God, that he has come from God and is not a sinner, they are actually blind. Their sin remains. Jesus' words anticipate John's later quotation of Isaiah, which explains the unbelief of Jesus' contemporaries in terms of the judgment of blindness that falls on unbelief (Isa 6:9–10, cited in 12:40).[267] The blind gain their sight, but those who claim to see are judged to be blind.

At the end of this narrative, then, the blind man and the Pharisees have exchanged places. In the beginning of the narrative, the man was blind, and his condition was attributed to either his sins or to sins of his parents. As the light of the world, Jesus opens his eyes. By means of that deed, the man comes to see Jesus as one who has come from God, to do the work of God, and he comes to

266. "The man called Jesus," *ho anthrōpos ho legomenos Iēsous*, 9:11; "this man," *houtos ho anthrōpos*, v. 16; "a man who is a sinner," *anthrōpos hamartōlos*, v. 16. See, further, Excursus 2: "Son of God, Son, and Son of Man in John."

267. John 9:39 reads, "so that those who do not see may see, and those who see may become blind" (*hoi mē blepontes blepōsin kai hoi blepontes typhloi genōntai*).

confess, "I believe, Lord." But from beginning to end, the Pharisees pass a different judgment: they believe the man to be a sinner, they doubt that the healing ever took place, they question the means by which it was done, they discount its significance for understanding who Jesus might be, and finally they brush off the man's insistent confessions and eject him from their presence. Though they have physical sight, it does not lead them to "see signs" (cf. 4:48) or to see the healing as a sign that points to Jesus as the light of the world.

These conclusions have implications for understanding the law and how Jesus and his followers relate to it. The law itself is not the problem, but the law must be read and interpreted as a witness to Jesus. It forbids work on the Sabbath, but it cannot forbid the work of the life-giving God on the Sabbath; and if Jesus does the work of God, then he has not violated the law. The verdict turns on the answer to this question: Has Jesus done the work of God? The man utters a resounding yes; others answer with an equally emphatic no; still others register uncertainty. In John's estimate, those who refuse to accept the implication of the man's testimony, "I was blind, and now I see," are those who do not judge with right judgment: they are blind to the work of God in and through Jesus.

10:1–21 Jesus, the Good Shepherd

The long, dramatic narrative of Jesus' healing of the blind man and the ensuing interrogation lead into a discourse in which Jesus presents himself as (1) the good shepherd who protects his sheep and (2) the door by which the sheep go in and out of the sheepfold, to find security and pasture. While this discourse contains no direct Old Testament citations, it nevertheless draws on the extensive scriptural imagery for both God and the king as Israel's shepherd. The people of Israel are God's flock; in his fold they may safely dwell; in verdant pastures they find nourishment for life. As shepherd of the sheep, Jesus protects his sheep from death; as the door for the sheep, Jesus provides access to the rich pasture that sustains life. Both images, door and shepherd, accent Jesus' authority and will to give life, and to give it fully.

Jesus' discourse implicitly offers a critical assessment of the Pharisees' treatment of the man born blind. By driving him out from their midst, they have left him alone, outside the community (9:34); by seeking to discredit Jesus, they have potentially separated the man from the source of life and light. By contrast, the good shepherd protects his sheep from predators and neglect, feeds them, calls them by name, and thus gathers them together into his flock, and so sustains them in life within that one flock. And even as the good shepherd calls together, guards, and sustains his flock, so Jesus calls together, guards, and sustains his people who no longer have a sure place within the synagogue, but who hear and respond to the voice of this good shepherd.

10:1 "Amen, amen, I tell you that the one who does not enter into the
sheepfold through the door, but rather climbs in from elsewhere—that
one is a thief and an outlaw. 2 The one who enters through the door is
the shepherd of the sheep. 3 The doorkeeper opens to this one, and the
sheep hear his voice. He calls his own sheep by name and leads them
out. 4 When he has brought out all his own sheep, he goes before them,
and the sheep follow him, because they know his voice. 5 They will not
follow a stranger, but rather they will flee from him, for they do not know
the voice of strangers."

6 Jesus used this figure of speech, but they did not understand what he
was talking about. 7 So again Jesus said, "Amen, amen, I tell you that I
am the door for the sheep. 8 All those who have come [before me][a] are
thieves and outlaws, and the sheep did not hear them. 9 I am the door.
Whoever enters through me will be saved, and will come in and go out
and find pasture. 10 The thief comes only to steal and kill and destroy. I
have come in order that they might have life, and have it abundantly.

11 I am the good shepherd. The good shepherd lays down his life[b] for
the sheep. 12 The hired hand, who is not the shepherd, to whom the sheep
do not belong, sees the wolf coming and leaves the sheep and flees. 13
And the wolf seizes and scatters them, for the hired hand does not care
about the sheep.

14 I am the good shepherd, and I know my own and they know me, 15
even as the Father knows me and I know the Father, and I lay down my
life for the sheep.

16 And I have other sheep, which do not belong to this fold. It is neces-
sary for me to lead them out,[c] and they will hear my voice, and they shall
be one flock, [with] one shepherd.[d]

17 For this reason the Father loves me, because I lay down my life, in
order that I may take it up again. 18 No one takes[e] it from me, but I lay it
down on my own. I have this authority to lay it down, and I have authority
to take it up again. This command I have received from my Father."

19 Again there was a division among the Jews because of Jesus' words.
20 Many of them said, "He has a demon and is mad. Why even listen to
him?" 21 But others said, "These are not the words of one who is demon
possessed. Is a demon able to open the eyes of the blind?"

a. "Before me" (*pro emou*) is sometimes missing, or found before or after *ēlthon* ("have come"). It was likely added to explain the otherwise cryptic phrase "all who have come," or deleted to avoid a "blanket condemnation of all Old Testament worthies" (Metzger 195).

b. The MS reading at 𝔓45 ℵ*, "give [*didōsin*] one's life," in place of "lay down [*tithēsin*] one's life," corresponds to the Synoptic formulation (Matt 20:28; Mark 10:45) and suggests how some early scribes (rightly) understood the typically Johannine phrase (10:15, 17; 13:37–38; 15:13; 1 John 3:16).

c. 𝔓[66] reads *synagagein* ("gather together") rather than *agagein* ("lead them out"). The reading is preferred by Martyn (165–66), who interprets Jesus' words to refer to the "gathering together" (11:52) of Jewish Christians expelled from various synagogues.

d. *Genēsontai*, "they shall be one flock," is found in 𝔓[45] ℵ[c] B D; the singular *genēsetai*, "there will be one flock," in 𝔓[66] ℵ* A may be a correction to read more smoothly with "one shepherd."

e. The aorist *ēren* ("took, has taken") is the more difficult reading, but the present *airei* ("takes, is taking") has wider external support.

[10:1–2] Jesus' indictment of the Pharisees for their sin and blindness (9:41) continues (10:1–2). A doubled "amen" introduces a short *paroimia* (v. 6), a "figure of speech" depicting a sheepfold (*aulē*, an enclosed courtyard used for keeping animals) with a door, a shepherd who keeps his sheep there, a doorkeeper who allows him to enter, and "a thief" and "outlaw" who attempts to enter the sheepfold illegitimately. Unlike the "thief" (*kleptēs*) and "outlaw" (*lēstēs*, v. 8), the legitimate shepherd is no stranger to either the doorkeeper or the sheep. A *kleptēs* is simply a thief; John uses it of Judas (12:6). It is more difficult to define *lēstēs*, later used of Barabbas (18:40; see comments there). BDAG offers (1) "robber, highwayman, bandit," with evidence from the New Testament (e.g., Luke 10:30, 36) and Josephus, and (2) "revolutionary, insurrectionist, guerilla" as another possible meaning. In the LXX a *lēstēs* is a lawless or violent person, but certainly not a revolutionary, let alone a freedom fighter (Hos 7:1; Obad 5; Jer 7:11; 18:22; Ezek 22:9). Josephus uses the term derogatorily to characterize robbers, the *sicarii*, who "murdered people in the daytime and in the midst of the city" (*J.W.* 2.254), insurgents (*stasiastai*), deceivers (*goētes*, *J.W.* 2.264), tyrants (*tyrannos*, *J.W.* 2.275), and his own political opponents. In John, "thieves and outlaws" or "marauders" are those whose actions destroy the sheep (vv. 8, 10); they enter the fold surreptitiously and illegitimately (v. 1).

[3–5] The shepherd enters the fold through the door because he is known both to the doorkeeper[268] (*ho thyrōros*, v. 3; cf. 18:16–17) and to the sheep, who recognize his voice when he calls them by name to lead them out of the fold, presumably to pasture that sustains life (cf. Isa 43:1, "I have redeemed you; I have called you by name"). Although the sheep will not follow a "stranger,"

268. Most contemporary interpreters describe the doorkeeper simply as an "undershepherd" or "watchman" in Jesus' parable (Carson 1991, 381; Lincoln 2005, 293); others, reading the figural speech allegorically, suggest that the doorkeeper is the Father (Calvin 1959, 259); Moses or Scripture (John Chrysostom, *Hom. Jo.* 59.2); the Holy Spirit (Bruner 609); the Spirit acting through appointed ministers (Westcott 2:51); the "watchmen" of Israel who should acknowledge Jesus as Messiah (Robinson 1955); or John the Baptist (Painter 1991, 57–58).

including the outlaw who climbed in over the walls, they follow the shepherd who calls his own (*ta idia*, v. 4; cf. 1:11; 16:32) sheep by name (v. 4). The point is not that this shepherd separates his own sheep from others in the fold,[269] but that the sheep and shepherd know each other. This shepherd can be trusted to take care of his own.[270]

[6–10] Up to this point, there is no explicit identification of the figures in Jesus' picture of the shepherd, his sheep, and the sheepfold; not surprisingly, John comments that some of those listening to Jesus' *paroimia* ("figure of speech, parable") did not understand it. Jesus' assertion "I am the door for the sheep" (v. 7) does not immediately clarify matters. Having just sketched a picture of the shepherd's legitimate entry into the sheepfold, Jesus might be expected to drive the point home with an explanation such as he will use later: "I am the good shepherd" (cf. v. 11, 14). The image (*paroimia*) would then provide commentary on the healing of the man born blind and his subsequent encounters with the Pharisees by showing how Jesus, the good shepherd, knows his own sheep and leads them out of the fold. Having never seen Jesus before his healing, the man nevertheless "knew" his voice and confessed faith in Jesus (9:35–38; cf. 20:16; 21:15–19).

Instead of immediately identifying himself as the good shepherd, Jesus first declares, "I am the door for the sheep" (10:7, 9). Although the previous parable indeed has a door, it is the means by which *the shepherd* enters the sheepfold (vv. 1–5). Presumably that shepherd is Jesus, as later in the discourse (vv. 8, 10, 11–18, 27–30). But now Jesus identifies himself as the door by which *the sheep* enter and leave the sheepfold (vv. 7–9). Jesus' explicit identification of himself as the door lessens the oddity of the contrast of this door with human figures ("thieves and outlaws") and explains the implicit description of the sheep "listening" to the door rather than to others (v. 8).

The depiction of Jesus as a door by which one "comes in and goes out" may recall promises found in the Psalms: the righteous enter into salvation through the "gate of the Lord" (*pylē tou kyriou*, 118:20–21 [117:20–21 LXX]). When the sheep enter (presumably, into the fold) through that door, they find salvation or protection from death (John 10:9), but they also have access to pasture that nourishes and sustains life "abundantly" (*perisson*, v. 10).[271] Even as Jesus provided wine (2:1–12) and bread (6:1–14) in abundance, so he generously provides abundant pasture, once again illustrating the Gospel's affirmation "from his fullness we have all received" (1:16). Such abundant life consists of fellowship with God (17:3) and others (17:20–26) that issues in fullness of love

269. Carson 1991, 382; Keener 1:806; Schnackenburg 2:279–80.

270. R. Brown 1966, 392; Michaels 579; Talbert 165; Ridderbos 354.

271. Note the Synoptic parallels, where the "narrow gate" leads to life (Matt 7:14) or salvation (Luke 13:23–24).

(13:34–35; 15:13; 17:26), joy (3:29; 15:11; 16:24; 17:13), and peace (14:27; 16:33). This "abundant life" is what created life ought to be (1:3–4), and it anticipates the blessings of eternal life (3:16–17). Abundant life is found at the intersection of created life and eternal life: each is given by God through the Son (or Word) and experienced as knowledge of and union with God (17:3; see Excursus 4: "Life and Eternal Life in John").

Because Jesus gives life abundantly, he can be contrasted to those "thieves and outlaws" who come to "kill and destroy" (10:8, 10). The characterization of "all who have come before me" as "thieves and outlaws" raises the question of just who these others might be. They can scarcely include the likes of Abraham, Moses, and John the Baptist, since these are presented in the Gospel as trustworthy witnesses to Jesus. But "all" could include any authorities or leaders who do not bear witness to Jesus, or whose mission or work does not lead or point to Jesus. "All who have come before me" could also include messianic pretenders, whose failed missions might be easily summarized in the description that they came only to kill and destroy. In any case, Jesus states that the sheep "did not listen to them" (v. 8).

In light of their treatment of the man born blind, however, the Pharisees who have "cast him out" are surely among those who have come to "steal and kill and destroy." These are harsh words: certainly the Pharisees did not set out to destroy the lives of others. But where life and death are stark opposites, as they are in John, whatever does not lead to life leads to death, and those who lead others away from following Jesus, the light of life, inadvertently lead them to their death. The early Christian catechetical document known as the *Didache* (2d c.) manifests the same worldview in its opening lines, "There are two ways, one of life and one of death; and there is a great difference between the two ways" (1.1; cf. Ps 1:6, "The way of the wicked will perish").

[11–13] For the first time in the discourse, Jesus makes explicit what has only been implicit heretofore: "I am the good shepherd" (John 10:11). As the good shepherd, Jesus enters the fold legitimately, knows, gathers, and leads the sheep out (vv. 1–5, 11–18, 27–30). He also protects the sheep from death (vv. 1–5, 11–18). Here is where the image of Jesus as the good shepherd overlaps with the image of Jesus as the door: apart from access to food, the sheep will die, just as they will perish if left without the shepherd's protection.

Jesus is the "good shepherd" who protects the sheep, as the Old Testament so often pictures God as the shepherd of Israel, leading and protecting his people (Pss 78:52–54; 79:13; 80:1; 95:7; 100:3). Like a shepherd, God feeds his flock, gathers the lambs, and gently carries and leads them (Isa 40:11; Jer 23:3–4; Ezek 34:11–16; Zech 10:3). Those returning from exile are fed so that they neither hunger nor thirst (Isa 49:9–11). If at times God seems not to care for his sheep, failing to protect them and allowing them to be scattered (Ps 74:1; Jer 31:10), God's identity as Israel's shepherd means that he will again deliver them. God is also portrayed as the shepherd of individuals in leading them through all the vicissitudes of life (Gen 48:15; Ps 23).

"Shepherd" also designates human authorities: some faithfully carry out their tasks, and others do not.[272] Joshua is to lead God's people "out and bring them in, so that the congregation of the LORD may not be like sheep without a shepherd" (Num 27:17). David becomes a shepherd of Israel (Ps 78:70–72). Faithful shepherds will feed Israel with "knowledge and understanding" (Jer 3:15). By contrast, those kings or priests who do not care for the people are blind (Zech 11:17; Isa 56:10–11) or wicked shepherds (1 Kgs 22:17; Jer 10:21; 23:1–2; Ezek 34:5–6). Israel's "rulers" (*archontes*) are compared to wolves that seize and kill their prey (Ezek 22:27; cf. Zeph 3:3).

John's picture of Jesus as the good shepherd has particularly strong resonance with the depiction of God as shepherd of the people of Israel in Ezek 34. There God's sheep are said to be scattered, becoming food for wild animals, because they had untrustworthy shepherds (34:5–6, 8). God indicts these worthless shepherds for their failures, announcing that he himself will shepherd his people, gather them from the various lands to which they have been scattered, bring them to their own land, and care for them there (34:11–16). When God has saved and gathered this flock, he will appoint David—that is, a king or, perhaps, the Messiah—as the "one shepherd" to protect them from wild animals, and feed them with abundant food (Ezek 34:24–29; cf. Jer 23:4–5; 29:14; Mic 2:1–12; 5:1–5; *Pss. Sol.* 17.21–45). The sheep belong to God (Ezek 34:31), but David is their shepherd (34:23–24). In John, Jesus' identification of himself as shepherd will lead "the Jews" to ask if he is the Messiah (10:24). In his implicitly positive response, Jesus also testifies to the unity of his work as shepherd with the work of the Father, who holds all things securely in his hand (vv. 28–29).

As the good or even "ideal" shepherd,[273] Jesus is contrasted with a hired hand, and the shepherd's role is now also described in terms of the actual course of Jesus' ministry and specifically with reference to his death and resurrection. This shepherd can be called good because he "lays down his life for

272. The image of a ruler or leader as a shepherd is widespread in the ancient world. Philo likens the emperor to "a shepherd and protector of the flock" (*Legat.* 44); Moses had the skills of a shepherd (*Det.* 25; *Mos.* 1.62; *Ios.* 2–3; and cf. *Somn.* 2.152–54). In Hesiod's *Theog.* (444), Hermes has charge of and rules over the flocks of sheep and herds of goats (Homer, *Hymn 4: To Hermes* 567–71; Pausanius, *Descr.* 9.22.2); Apollo was called "attendant of the sheep" (*opaōna mēlōn*, in Pindar, *Pyth.* 9.5.64). Dio Chrysostom characterizes a king as a "shepherd," who should care for and protect his people (*1 Regn.* 13, 15–16; *4 Regn.* 43–44). Jensen (2000, 37–44) observes the difficulty of distinguishing shepherds in ancient art as Christian or pagan.

273. As Bultmann (1971, 364) notes, John could have called Jesus a "true" or "genuine" (*alēthinos*) shepherd since he is contrasted to all pretenders, but *kalos* ("good") underscores the shepherd's "being for" the sheep; Lincoln (2005, 296–97) aptly characterizes the good shepherd as the one who dies nobly or well (*kalōs*).

the sheep" (*tēn psychēn autou tithēsin hyper tōn probatōn*; cf. 10:15b, 17–18). The phrase "to lay down one's life" means "to give oneself up to death, to die"; later the same idiom is used to speak of Peter's willingness to "lay down his life" for Jesus (13:37–38) and to characterize dying for another as a supreme manifestation of love (15:13). These expressions use the preposition *hyper* ("for, on behalf of"). When used with any verb meaning "to die," *hyper* signals that such a death is "for the benefit of others," without specifying that benefit more precisely. One might die instead of the other, or die to benefit the other in some way. It is the shepherd's death, and not merely the shepherd's willingness to fight off predators, that protects the sheep from death.[274] Not all shepherds die for their sheep—in fact, a dead shepherd would not seem to offer much hope for his sheep's ongoing protection! But *this* shepherd dies for his sheep. The actual course of Jesus' life determines the depiction of this shepherd.

The contrast between the good shepherd as one who "lays down his life for his sheep" and the hired hand who flees at the first sign of danger further underscores the lengths to which the true or good shepherd will go for the sake of his sheep. The hired hand deserts the sheep, leaving them vulnerable to predators. Precisely because the shepherd faithfully guards his sheep, he puts himself in their place, willingly facing death so that they may live. The shepherd does so because the sheep belong to him (10:12, 14) and he cares for them (v. 13): a hired hand has no vested interest in the sheep.

Here is the heart of John's theology of Jesus' death: death threatens the world, but Jesus' death brings life to it.[275] Ordinarily, the prospect of a dead shepherd would not appear to be very promising for the sheep he is charged to protect, any more than a dead king would encourage his subjects that he would yet save them from their enemies. But in this case the death of the shepherd is the very means by which his work of protecting the lives of the sheep is accomplished. Because he is the good shepherd, Jesus gives his life so that the sheep may live; because he gives his life so that the sheep may live, Jesus is the good shepherd. While the role of shepherd is explicitly assigned to Jesus, it is clear from statements later in the chapter that Jesus' shepherding tasks embody God's protecting and saving work as the shepherd of his people (10:18, 28–30). As the "good shepherd," Jesus is neither simply one among other shepherds nor simply the first among equals. He is, rather, the only shepherd, the genuine shepherd, and the depiction of him in these verses attests his "absolute significance, both christological and soteriological."[276]

274. Bultmann (1971, 371 n. 5) suggests that *tithenai tēn psychēn* should be understood to mean "to stake one's life, to risk it, to be prepared to lay it down"; see Peterson's translation: "The Good Shepherd puts the sheep before himself, sacrifices himself if necessary."

275. See also the comments on Jesus' death at 12:20–26.

276. Ridderbos 360.

[14–16] Jesus now repeats his claim, "I am the good shepherd," elaborating it in terms of (1) the mutual knowledge of the sheep and shepherd, as well as the mutual knowledge of the Father and Jesus; (2) his voluntary death for his sheep; and (3) his task of gathering "other sheep" into one flock. Scripture envisions the gathering of all God's people under one shepherd, that is, the unification of Judah and Israel under the messianic shepherd designated by God: a theme continued in Jewish literature (*Pss. Sol.* 8.28–34; 11.2–3; chs. 17–18; see comments on 11:52). John's Gospel draws on that motif in presenting Jesus as the good shepherd who protects the flock and "gathers together the scattered children of God" (11:52). Those "children of God" include all who "believe in his name" (1:12), thus enlarging God's flock to include, at least potentially, "all people" (12:32).

Here Jesus speaks of the necessity (*dei*, v. 16) of including the "other sheep not of this fold." Who are these "other sheep"? If the children of God whom Jesus gathers now include "all people," then surely the Gentiles are in view. As elsewhere in the New Testament, God's saving work is "to the Jew first and also to the Greek" (Rom 1:16; 15:8–9; cf. Matt 15:24; 28:19–20). But the "other sheep" may simply refer to all those who did not enjoy either temporal or physical proximity to Jesus: those who neither saw nor heard him, including Diaspora Jews, Gentiles, and second-generation Jews or Gentiles—any and all who came to believe in Jesus (cf. John 17:20–21; 20:29). These, too, belong to Jesus' one flock, because Jesus' death and resurrection expand the scope of his work as shepherd to gather, protect, and nurture his flock (cf. 7:35; 12:32). Jesus' statement, "I must lead them out" (*kakeina dei agagein*), indicates that finding and gathering these "other sheep" completes his work as shepherd. All those who hear Jesus' voice, wherever and whenever they do, belong to him and to each other: there will be only one flock; they have only one shepherd. Through his death Jesus gathers together all God's children (11:52) and draws all people to himself (12:32).

[17–18] The Father loves Jesus, the shepherd who is willing to give his own life for the sheep. But Jesus' death is not final: he lays down his life "in order to take it again." Typically the New Testament says that God raised Jesus from the dead (Acts 2:24; 10:40; 13:30; Rom 10:9; 1 Cor 15:4). In John, Jesus is an active agent in his own resurrection: he has the authority (*exousia*) both to lay down his life and to take it up again (10:18), because he has been given life "in himself" as the Father has it (10:18; 5:26), and this power remains his, independent of human actors in the drama. Although there are efforts to arrest or kill Jesus throughout the Gospel, none succeed because "his hour had not yet come" (7:30, 44; 8:20, 59; 10:39). Jesus will indeed die for his sheep, in accordance with the Father's command (v. 18), but he will do so only when "his hour" comes.

In a play on words, Jesus further makes it quite clear that he lays down his life willingly: "No one takes it from me [*ap' emou*], but I lay it down on my own [*ap' emautou*]" (v. 18). Throughout the Gospel, Jesus does nothing on his own (*ap' emautou*) but only what the Father tells him to do (5:30; 7:17, 28; 8:28, 42; 12:49; 14:10). Even Jesus' authority to lay down his life is a charge or command (*entolē*) from the Father (v. 18; cf. 6:38; 12:49; 14:31; 15:10). To put it differently, Jesus dies willingly and in accord with God's life-giving purposes. Jesus' death is not the result of human design, even though religious authorities conspire to put him to death (11:48–53) and Roman power puts him on the cross. It is the Father's will that, through Jesus' death, life should come to all who become part of his flock (cf. 12:50). Jesus' death does not threaten the security of his sheep because his death and his resurrection are the Father's will: the living Father gives the Son life in himself, and the Son may then lay down and take up his life so that others live. The good shepherd does not remain dead: he lives.

[19–21] But again the people are divided (as in 7:43; 9:16). What ultimately divides Jesus' hearers is the disputed source of Jesus' authority and power. Some think he speaks like a madman and has a demon, but others appeal to the opening of the blind man's eyes to counter that charge: "A demon cannot open the eyes of the blind" (cf. 10:22). The kind of work that Jesus does, bringing light and life, testifies that he cannot be driven by demons. As Nicodemus earlier put it, "No one can do these signs that you do unless God is with him" (3:2). The man born blind has essentially repeated that same declaration: "If this man were not from God, then he could do nothing" (9:33). Finally, that is the question: Is this man from God? Its answer divides Jesus' hearers.

And so the events set at Tabernacles draw to a close (7:1–10:21). All the festivities of Tabernacles—the reading of the law, the water libations, and the lighting of golden candlesticks—form the backdrop for John's presentation of Jesus as the true teacher of God's word, the provider of living water, and the one who shines the life-giving light for all the world. As the light of the world, Jesus opens the eyes of a man born blind; but his sign provokes a hostile response since it was done on the Sabbath, as was the healing of the lame man (ch. 5), and thus stirs up questions about Jesus' allegiance to the law, which forbids work on the Sabbath. If Jesus' teaching truly comes from God (7:16)—indeed, if Jesus himself truly comes from God—then how does he justify his actions? How should Jesus' relationship to Moses and the law be construed? Can one be a disciple of both? Or must one choose between them? Since God's people, the children of Abraham, are those who follow the law, what happens to their identity if the law is no longer a defining marker of that identity?

In the course of this long series of discourses, God's people, Abraham's children, are now redefined as those who welcome Jesus, as Abraham did (8:56). To act as Abraham did is to judge rightly that Jesus is the one who was before Abraham (8:58), to believe his word and thereby never die. Sin is now redefined in terms of *response to Jesus*: sin is failing to judge with right judgment (7:24); refusing to acknowledge Jesus as the Son, whose word can give freedom and life (8:30–32) and whose works bring God's light to shine in the darkness (9:30–33); and who is God's Messiah for the salvation of his people. Jesus' messianic mission is further defined in terms of his death and resurrection, extending beyond Israel to include "other sheep . . . not of this fold" (10:16 RSV). In short, the discourses and events of Tabernacles (John 7:1–10:21) extend Jesus' claims while sharpening the conflicts between Jesus and his contemporaries. Jesus does not reject Moses and the law, the temple and its festivities, or Abraham and his people, but he does subordinate them all to himself. Their validity is now established by their relationship to Jesus and how they testify or lead to Jesus as the one who embodies God's work to give light and life to the world.

10:22–42 Jesus the Messiah: The Feast of Dedication

The scene now shifts from the Feast of Tabernacles, celebrated in the fall, to the Feast of Dedication, or Hanukkah, celebrated in the winter months, but the location is still the temple. Though set several months later, Jesus' dialogue with "the Jews" returns to the image of Jesus as the shepherd of the sheep without missing a beat. And now the implications of that biblical image are underscored, as Jesus' interlocutors ask him directly whether he is the Messiah. The question of Jesus' messianic identity recalls the reluctance of the blind man's parents to acknowledge that Jesus has healed their son and that Jesus might be the Messiah (9:18–22).

Several interrelated aspects of Jesus' role and identity as the shepherd of the sheep are sharpened here. First, while the earlier portion of the chapter has emphasized the shepherd's role in feeding and protecting his sheep so that they might live, now it becomes clear that this shepherd gives his sheep eternal life (10:28). Second, he does so because he works in perfect unity with God, who is the source of all life, protecting and nourishing the sheep through Jesus' work and mission (10:29–30). Finally, Jesus' identity as the Son of God is made explicit. The king of Israel was sometimes designated as God's son (2 Sam 7:12–14; Ps 2:7). Here Jesus' messianic identity is confirmed in the statement that he is the Son of God (10:36). Additionally, this title is given its peculiar Johannine coloring, with emphasis falling on the unity of Father and Son, particularly in their work of bringing life to the world.

> **10:22** It was the Feast of Dedication in Jerusalem; it was winter, **23** and
> Jesus was walking in the temple in Solomon's porch. **24** Then the Jews
> gathered around him and said to him, "How long will you keep us in
> suspense? If you are the Messiah, tell us openly."
>
> **25** Jesus answered, "I told you, and you do not believe. The works that
> I do in my Father's name, these testify to me. **26** But you do not believe,

because you do not belong to my sheep. 27 My own sheep hear my voice,
and I know them, and they follow me. 28 And I give them eternal life, and
they will never perish, and no one will seize them from my hand. 29 My
Father, who has given them to me, is greater than all,[a] and no one is able
to seize them from my Father's hand. 30 I and the Father are one."

31 Again the Jews picked up stones in order to stone him. 32 Jesus said
to them, "I have shown you many good works from the Father. For which
of these works do you stone me?"

33 The Jews replied, "We do not stone you for any good work, but
rather for blasphemy and because, although you are a human being, you
make yourself God."

34 Jesus replied, "Is it not written in your law,[b] 'I said, you are gods?'
35 If he called them gods to whom the word of God came—and the Scrip-
ture cannot be broken[c]— 36 how can you say, 'You are blaspheming,'
to the one whom the Father sanctified and sent into the world because I
said, 'I am the Son of God'? 37 If I do not do the works of my Father, do
not believe me. 38 But if I do, even if you do not believe me, believe the
works, so that you may know and understand[d] that the Father is in me and
I am in the Father."

39 Again they tried to arrest him, and he slipped through their hands.

40 And once more he went across the Jordan to the place where John
first baptized, and he remained there. 41 And many came to him, and they
said, "John did no sign, but everything that John said concerning this one
is true." 42 And many believed in him there.

a. Some MSS have a neuter relative pronoun ("*what* my Father has given me is greater than all") while others have a masculine relative pronoun ("my Father, *who* has given [them] to me, is greater than all"). The first reading, however difficult, probably best accounts for the origin of the others; but Barrett and other commentators conclude that it makes no sense and prefer the second, adopted here.

b. "Your" is omitted from "in your law" (*en tō nomō hymōn*) in a number of MSS, such as $\mathfrak{P}^{45}$ ℵ* D; it may have been added by assimilation to 8:17.

c. Or "destroyed."

d. "Know" and "understand" render, respectively, the aorist (*gnōte*) and present (*ginōskēte*) subjunctives of the verb *ginōskein*.

[10:22–24] The Feast of Dedication (*enkainia*, "renewal") is Hanukkah. Hanukkah is not a pilgrimage feast, but Jesus is again in the temple in Jerusalem. According to Josephus, when Herod enlarged the Temple Mount, he built a magnificent roofed colonnade or portico (*stoa*; *Ant.* 15.396–401; 20.221). It was associated with Solomon, although the temple he had built had been destroyed much earlier (cf. Josephus, *J.W.* 5.184–85). Early Christians seemed to have gathered in its precincts as well (cf. Acts 3:1; 5:12).

Celebrated in the ninth month, Chislev (December), Hanukkah commemorates the Maccabean victories over the Syrian forces of Antiochus IV Epiphanes at the conclusion of the Jewish revolt in 168–165 B.C.E. According to the account in 1 Maccabees, because the altar and the temple had been profaned by the pagan sacrifice of unclean animals and setting up an idol—"the desolating sacrilege" (cf. Mark 13:14; Dan 9:27)—the Jews tore down the defiled altar and erected a new one, rebuilt and refurbished the interior of the temple, and fashioned new sacred vessels once they recaptured the temple (1 Macc 4:45–61). The dedication of the renovated temple was celebrated in the Feast of "Dedication," or Hanukkah, mentioned only here in the New Testament. The Hebrew word *ḥănukkâ* and cognates of the Greek *enkainia* (*enkainismos*, *enekainisen*, "renewal, restoration") are used in the MT and LXX, respectively, to refer to the dedication of the altar in the tabernacle (Num 7:10–11), and in the first (1 Kgs 8:63; 2 Chr 7:5) and second temples (Ezra 6:16). Although the rededication of the altar and temple in the second century B.C.E. was thus one in a series of such dedications, the Feast of Hanukkah specifically commemorates the victory of the Maccabees. It served as a visible reminder that the temple was holy and was to be kept holy for the worship of the one God of Israel.

Inasmuch as Hanukkah commemorated the triumph of the Jews over the Syrians that led to the temple's reconsecration, it provides an appropriate context for the question whether Jesus is the Messiah who will free Israel from foreign oppression. Jesus' self-identification as the "good shepherd" also evokes the portrayal of the king as a shepherd in the Bible. Hence "the Jews" entreat Jesus to declare "openly" ("boldly, plainly")[277] whether or not he is that Messiah, and not to "keep them in suspense." Presumably their challenge to Jesus is twofold: they wish both that he would speak directly, rather than in figures, and that he would give an answer to the question that others are now frequently raising: Is Jesus the expected Messiah?

[25–28] However, characteristic of Jesus in all the Gospels, he does not answer that question directly or in public. Jesus' first followers had acknowledged him to be the Messiah (John 1:41, 45), and Jesus had affirmed his messianic identity to the Samaritan woman (4:26). But these acknowledgments were not public proclamations on Jesus' part, and in any case the inhabitants of Jerusalem were not privy to these private encounters. Hence Jesus' claim that he has already told them raises the obvious question: When has he told them that he is the Messiah?

It is possible that the reader is to imagine that Jesus has made just such a declaration, although it is not narrated elsewhere in the Gospel. John does present Jesus as referring to words that he has spoken (10:36; 14:2) that are not recorded in the Gospel in the form cited. But, perhaps more likely, Jesus

277. On speaking "openly" or "boldly," see John 7:13–26; 10:24; 11:14, 54; 16:25, 29; 18:20.

clarifies his identification as the good shepherd as a veiled messianic claim. The fact that "the Jews" ask him whether he is the Messiah implies that they have detected just such a hint in the image of the shepherd (see comments on 10:11); now they entreat Jesus to relinquish figurative speech for open announcement.

Jesus' discourse has not met "the Jews'" criterion of speaking plainly. But Jesus' reproach, "I told you, and you do not believe," suggest that their judgment lies not in Jesus' failure to speak plainly, but in "the Jews'" failure to believe (10:25). In fact, Jesus could not provide the evidence they desire, since he is not a king by any conventionally recognizable criteria, Jewish or pagan. His messianic vocation is undertaken, not in terms of the exercise of power against his enemies, but as service (13:1–11) and self-giving (10:1–18; 12:23–26), culminating in his death on the cross. As elsewhere in the New Testament, recognition of this Jesus as the Messiah depends upon God's revelation (John 6:44–45; see also Matt 11:25–27; 16:17; Luke 10:21–22). Jesus' words here are in keeping with his earlier declarations that entry into God's kingdom (John 3:3, 5; 18:36) requires the work of God's Spirit, and that God's witness to Jesus enables confession of Jesus as Messiah (5:36–37; 6:27).

Jesus also singles out the works done "in my Father's name" (10:25; cf. comments on 14:13–14; 17:6, 12) as providing testimony that he is the Messiah. But which of Jesus' works bear such testimony? In the context of the Gospel, the most likely referent is the healing of the man born blind as an exemplar of Jesus' other signs. But in neither biblical nor Jewish thought was the Messiah expected to be a miracle worker, although miraculous occurrences were believed to characterize the eschatological age (Isa 35:5–6; Matt 11:2–6; Luke 7:21–23; 4Q521; cf. comments on 6:1–15; 7:31–36). When Jesus refers to his works, he may well include all the words and deeds that bear witness to him as the one who brings life and light to the world. But these works are not clearly or specifically messianic works that Israel's coming king would do, unless the messianic vocation be construed, as John does, as the provision of light and life in darkness and death. John does not call Jesus the son of David; rather, he emphasizes that Jesus is the Son of the Father. Jesus exercises his messianic vocation as the Son of God and by virtue of the Father's authority. Since that vocation includes the works given to him by the Father, these works bear witness to his identity.

Jesus' works cannot compel faith. Just as Jesus called his first disciples, he continues to do so, and those who belong to his flock hear and follow him. Even as the Gospel implicitly distinguishes between the phenomena of "sight" and "insight," so too it distinguishes between "hearing" and "responding." Not all who see the signs come to the insight of faith; not all who have heard Jesus respond to his voice. Those who respond to him are his sheep. As the shepherd provides food and shelter to his sheep so that they may live rather than die, so Jesus provides eternal life to his own. Jesus' statements to this effect are emphatic: neither his gift nor his protection is temporary. The life that Jesus grants the sheep is eternal; the sheep will never perish; and no one can take the sheep from him, or "seize them from his hand" (John 10:28). As the Gospel elsewhere insists, with an obvious glance at Judas's inexplicable betrayal of Jesus, Jesus does not "lose" any of those given to him by God (17:12; 18:9).

While John's emphasis falls most squarely on Jesus' unique role in protecting the sheep, it also becomes clear that Jesus' power to defend and protect his sheep depends ultimately upon God, "my Father," who holds the sheep. This is true for two closely related reasons. First, the Father has "given" the sheep to Jesus; second, the Father is "greater than all." Elsewhere in this Gospel, the Father has granted Jesus the power to give life and to judge (3:34–35; 5:19–22, 26–27; 12:49–50; cf. 18:11). In the present instance, Jesus' sheep belong to God, the Father, who has in turn entrusted their care to Jesus. Since Jesus' Father is "greater than all" (*pantōn meizon*, 10:29), there are no forces or powers, human or satanic, that can wrest these sheep from the Father's protection.

[30] Few passages have played a more important role in the formulation of christological confessions than the statement "I and the Father are one." Patristic commentators found this verse a bulwark against views that discounted the essential unity of the Father and Son (e.g., Arianism) or that emphasized their unity to the point of denying their distinction (e.g., Monarchianism).[278] In its immediate context, the statement "I and the Father are one" emphasizes the unity of the saving work of Jesus and God.[279] Calvin boldly asserted, "The ancients misused this passage to prove that Christ is *homoousios* [of the same substance] with the Father. Christ is not discussing the unity of substance, but the concord He has with the Father; so that what Christ does will be confirmed by His Father's power" (1:273). Jesus and his Father are one in their work: specifically, in guarding the sheep. What the Father does, the Son does, and the Son does the work of the Father. Herein lies their unity: the Father never works apart from the Son or at odds with the Son; and the Son never works against or apart from the Father's purposes. The point is nearly identical to one Jesus had made earlier when charged with making himself equal to God (John 5:18): the Father has given the Son his own prerogatives to grant life and to judge; therefore the Son does the Father's work, and the Father does his work through the Son. In other words, Jesus and the Father "are one." The charge that Jesus "makes himself equal to God" (5:18) or that he "makes himself God" (10:33) could be restated, "You make yourself one with God" (10:30).

John characterizes the identity of Jesus in the same way that the Old Testament defines the identity of God as God—by emphasizing the kind of work that

278. Father and Son are "one" (*hen*, neuter), that is, "one thing" (*unum*), not "one person" (*unus*, Tertullian, *Prax.* 22); the plural verb "are" also indicates two persons (Origen, *Dial.* 124).

279. Cf. 1 Cor 3:8, "The one who plants and the one who waters are one" (*hen eisin*).

each does. When the Old Testament speaks of God's uniqueness, it underscores especially God's identity as creator and sovereign. The powers to give life and to judge, the powers of the Creator and Sovereign, are the very powers of God. Thus, to speak of the Word as active in creation (John 1:1–3), or of the Son's power to give life (1:1–3; 5:25–27), to exercise judgment (5:26–27), or to save from death (as is the case here) is in fact to characterize Jesus in terms of the distinctive works that characterize the one God (cf. comments on John 1:3). Jesus does not simply do works that are like the Father's works; he does the Father's works (vv. 37–38) because the Father is in him (v. 38). The christological scandal of John is not that Jesus has made himself equal or one with God, but that God has chosen to make himself one with Jesus.

"I and the Father are one" expresses one particular facet of the comprehensive unity of the being, revelation, and work of the Father and Son. As Augustine put it, "What Christ does with the Father, the Father does; and what the Father does with Christ, Christ does. Neither does the Father do anything apart, without the Son; nor the Son apart, without the Father: inseparable love, inseparable unity, inseparable majesty, inseparable power" (*Tract. Ev. Jo.* 5.3). Later in John the unity of the Father and Son is described in categories that do not immediately refer to works or deeds. Jesus prays that the disciples may be "one, as we are one" (17:11, *ōsin hen kathōs hēmeis*; 17:22, *ōsin hen kathōs hēmeis hen*). While such unity includes the unity of will and mission, it is not limited to that: the emphasis falls on the mutual or reciprocal indwelling of Father and Son (10:38; 14:1, 11).

[31–33] The statement that "the Jews" *again* sought to stone Jesus refers to the attempt to stone him earlier, following his dramatic self-disclosure in the statement "Before Abraham was, I am" (8:59). In that discourse Jesus claimed both to have and to give what God alone has and gives: eternal life. Still earlier, "the Jews" had charged Jesus with making himself equal to God because he claimed the prerogatives and authority of God to do God's work on the Sabbath (5:18). Now Jesus has claimed that he gives the sheep eternal life, that they will never perish, and that no one can "seize them from my hand" because no one can "seize them from my Father's hand." In all three of these instances (chs. 5, 8, and 10), the charges of falsely claiming equality with God are based on what Jesus claims to be able to do: specifically, to give eternal life to his followers. Thus, Jesus asks, which of his "good works"—works that bring life and light and are done by God's authority—merit such hostility? "The Jews" deny that any of Jesus' "good works" has stirred their antagonism and claim that it is rather his blasphemy: though a human being, he is making himself God (cf. Ezek 28:2; Hos 11:9).[280]

The charge of blasphemy (*blasphēmia*) occurs only here in the Gospel of John (10:33, 36). Generally speaking, in the LXX as well as in the writings of

280. In each case, the charge has to do with what Jesus "makes" (from *poiein*) himself to be.

Josephus and Philo, *blasphēmia* has a broader meaning than it would later acquire; the Mishnah, for example, limits blasphemy, or at least blasphemy that merits death, to pronouncing the divine name (*m. Sanh.* 7:5). By claiming that he and the Father are one, Jesus is "making himself God." In other words, impugning God's sovereign and unique identity is tantamount to blasphemy (see comments on John 5:18). At Jesus' trial, he is said to be worthy of death, not because he is guilty of blasphemy, but because he has made himself "the Son of God" (19:7)—a charge that reflects Jesus' defense of himself in those terms (at 10:34–36). In view of the setting of this discourse at Hanukkah, the charge that Jesus "makes himself God" may recall the charge that Antiochus IV Epiphanes was guilty of blasphemy for thinking himself to be "equal to god." But according to at least one source, as he was dying in anguish, he confessed that he had learned, "It is right to be subject to God; mortals should not think they are equal to God" (*isothea phronein*; 2 Macc 9:12). Strikingly, Jesus manifests a dependence upon God that other usurpers of divine prerogatives did not (cf. 5:18); his dependence is revealed in part by Jesus' identification of himself as God's Son and in his completion of God's works.

[34–36] Jesus further replies to the accusation that he is making himself God by (1) appealing to a scriptural text in which God addressed someone as "gods" and (2) arguing that this text allows him to present himself as the Son of God, whose works bear witness to the fact that he is one with God. The scriptural text is Ps 82:6, which Jesus quotes as "your law," in other words, as Torah. This designation is emphatic and serves rhetorically to make the point that Jesus' position can be substantiated by texts deemed authoritative by "the Jews." As elsewhere in John, Jesus makes his point by calling on shared commitments and beliefs to show how these demand the conclusions drawn by Jesus rather than by his opponents (5:45–46; 7:19–22; 8:17; cf. 8:53–54).

In Ps 82 God addresses some whom he calls "gods" (v. 6). The exact identity of these "gods" (*ʾĕlōhîm*) was also an issue for early Jewish interpreters of this psalm, who variously took them to be angels, judges, Melchizedek, or Israel at Sinai. This last interpretation is found in the Jewish midrashic tradition and may well be reflected in John's description of those who are called "gods" as "those to whom the word of God came" (10:35).[281] These Israelites were "gods" because at Sinai they received the word of the one who is alone God. The term *ʾĕlōhîm*, "gods," is therefore a secondary or derivative status by virtue of Israel's reception of the word of God.

The psalm continues, even if Jesus' citation of it does not, by further identifying these "gods" as "children of the most high" (82:6, *bĕnê ʿelyôn* = 81:6 LXX, *huioi hypsistou*), who shall nevertheless "die like mortals" (82:7). To explain

281. Cf. *Mekilta* on Exod 20:15–19 (*Baḥodesh* 9.80); *Sipre* 320; *Num. Rab.* 16.24; for discussion, see Emerton 1960; Hanson; Neyrey 1989.

how "gods" can "die like mortals," the midrashic tradition posited that the Israelites were called "gods, children of the most high" when they received the law at Sinai, but they became subject to death and hence mortal because of their sin with the golden calf. John's allusion to Ps 82 draws specifically on the designation of the children of the Most High as "gods" who still die; but Jesus, the Son of God (*huios theou*), can give eternal life to those children of God threatened by death (10:18, 28–30, 32, 37–38). If this reasoning holds, the argument here would be quite similar to Jesus' earlier statements, "Your ancestors ate manna in the wilderness, and they died; this is the bread that has come down from heaven, which someone might eat of and not die" (6:49–50). Though Scripture, which cannot be broken, calls the Israelites "gods," they are subject to death; but now the Son of God does God's work in giving life (3:16; 10:28–30). Would "the Jews" stone him for doing God's life-giving work? Jesus claims this unique prerogative precisely as the Son who can free Abraham's descendants, who themselves ate manna and received the law at Sinai, from sin and death (8:36–37, 52, 58).

This Scripture quotation presents "the Jews" a puzzle regarding Jesus' identity, similar to those found elsewhere in the Gospels (cf. Mark 12:35–37, citing Ps 110:1). The puzzle cannot be solved by exegetical expertise, but only by recognition that Jesus is the Messiah (John 10:24–25) precisely as the Son of God (1:17–18, 49; 11:27; 20:31). Jesus comes from God, from above; he is sent by God; he does the works of God; therefore, he is one with God, and in his unity with God, he is the Son of God. The charge against Jesus, that he has made himself the Son of God (19:7), is essentially equivalent to the charge that he makes himself equal to God. The Gospel answers both charges in the same way: Jesus has not made himself anything; what he possesses, he has been given by God ("sanctified and sent into the world," 10:36). If "the Jews" want an answer to the question whether Jesus is the Messiah (10:24), they will find it in recognizing the Messiah as the life-giving Son of God (20:31).

[37–42] Jesus then further appeals to his works to corroborate his unity with the Father. Because Jesus' works bring light, life, and salvation, they are the works of God and, as such, testify that "the Father is in me and I am in the Father" (10:38). The works of Jesus call for belief, not because they are miraculous, but because they are the Father's works, that is, they offer what God offers: light and life (vv. 25, 32, 37). Jesus' claim to do the works of God is not simply a claim to be a prophet, or even the Messiah, as is clear from the response: "they tried to arrest him" (v. 39).

But since Jesus' hour has not yet come, he escapes from their hands and goes to the place where John has been baptizing earlier ("Bethany beyond the Jordan," 1:28). Once again "many" came to Jesus, recalling the earlier complaint by John the Baptist's disciples that "all are going to him" (3:26).

The Baptist's own insistence that he has come to bear witness to the Messiah is echoed here in the affirmation of his testimony to Jesus: "Everything that John said concerning this one is true," even though the Baptist has done no sign to corroborate the truth of his witness. Just as John has claimed nothing for himself but to bear witness to Jesus, neither does he do any signs that might lead people to believe in him. He points to Jesus. Even the recollection of the Baptist's witness leads many to believe in Jesus, thus fulfilling John's mission: he came that Jesus might be revealed to Israel, so that all would believe in him (1:7–8, 31; 3:28–30).

Jesus' appearance in the temple at Hanukkah, the feast celebrating the rededication of the temple after its capture and desecration by the Seleucid king Antiochus IV, provides the setting for "the Jews" to ask Jesus to make his intentions known: Is he the Messiah, a promised shepherd-king in the line of David, who will defy the current foreign powers as Judas Maccabaeus did of old? Jesus does not answer the question directly. Rather than presenting himself as the son of David, Jesus presents himself as the Son of God, who does the works of God, and who is one with God. Unlike Antiochus IV, however, Jesus does not make himself equal to God; he is what and who he is by virtue of the mutual indwelling of Father and Son. Their unity explains how he does the works that he does and how he can call himself the Son of God without thereby committing blasphemy. While Jesus' words are an implicit acknowledgment of his messianic role, they also show that he carries out that vocation as the good shepherd who gives his life for the sheep, in order that they might live and be gathered together into one flock (10:11, 18, 28–30; 11:48–52). Jesus will demonstrate his life-giving power by raising Lazarus from the dead. Caiaphas will gather advisers, who will respond in an effort to protect their temple and people by sacrificing Jesus to the Romans. But it will be Jesus' death, not the defensive actions of the Jewish authorities, that protects and unifies God's people (11:48–52).

11:1–54 Jesus, the Resurrection and the Life: The Final Sign

The climactic sign of Jesus' ministry, the raising of Lazarus from the dead, bears witness to him as the Son of God, who has the power to give life because he acts with the authorization and prerogatives of God. Jesus' life-giving work has been manifested in his feeding the five thousand and healing the man born blind, and explicated in various discourses in which he presents himself as the bread of life, which comes from God; the life-giving Son, who sets people free from sin and death; the light of the world, which shows people the way from death to life; and the good shepherd, who protects his sheep from danger by giving his own life for them. Together these words and deeds bear witness to Jesus' claim "I and the Father are one" (10:30). The raising of Lazarus testifies that Jesus, who is resurrection and life, exercises God's own power over death, in love, and for the glory of God.

The conflict between life and death shapes the narrative of the raising of Lazarus, as it shapes the entire Gospel. Virtually from the beginning of the narrative, death hovers over this whole narrative. Word comes to Jesus that Lazarus is ill (11:1–3) and later that Lazarus has died (11:10–14). Jesus journeys to Bethany, knowing full well the risk to his life inherent in the journey (11:4, 8). Even the disciples anticipate that their lives may be threatened by Jesus' return to Judea (11:7–8, 16). Because of the notoriety that this sign brings to Jesus, the Jewish authorities, led by Caiaphas, determine to have Jesus put to death in order to save the people (*ethnos*) and the temple (11:48–54). Jesus' action of bringing life to Lazarus will bring death to himself, but what brings death to Jesus will bring life to the world: there is no life apart from death (10:18; 12:24).

The raising of Lazarus, and the council's action in response, provide the narrative corroboration of Jesus' earlier words that the good shepherd willingly lays down his life for the sheep that he loves, in order that they might have life and have it abundantly. The narrative also dramatically depicts Jesus' power to do the works of the "living Father," who sent him so that the world might have life (6:57; 3:16). The account of Jesus' raising of Lazarus thus serves as a fitting climax to the cluster of signs in the Gospel's central part (chs. 5–11), which presents Jesus as the life-giving Son of the Father. God's love for the world is manifested through Jesus' life-giving works that, in turn, bring glory to God.

11:1–16 "The One You Love Is Ill"

A man named Lazarus, loved by Jesus, has fallen gravely ill. His sisters, Martha and Mary of Bethany, send a message to Jesus, presumably to ask for his help. Jesus' enigmatic response and delay in going to aid Lazarus will reveal that Jesus acts for the glory of God, so that people might come to believe in him (11:4, 15). As will become evident when Jesus raises Lazarus, it is Jesus' life-giving work that brings glory to God.

> **11:1** Now a certain man was ill, Lazarus of Bethany, the village of Mary
> and her sister Martha. **2** (It was Mary who anointed the Lord with perfume
> and wiped his feet with her hair; her brother Lazarus was ill.) **3** So the
> sisters sent to him, saying, "See, Lord,[a] the one you love is ill."
>
> **4** But when Jesus heard it, he said, "This illness does not lead to death;
> rather, it is for God's glory, so that the Son of God might be glorified
> through it." **5** Now Jesus loved[b] Martha and her sister and Lazarus. **6** So
> when he heard that he was sick, he stayed in the place where he was for
> two days.
>
> **7** Then after this he said to his disciples, "Let us go to Judea again."

8 The disciples said to him, 'Rabbi, just now the Jews were seeking to
stone you; and you are going there again?"
9 Jesus said, "Are there not twelve hours in the day? Those who walk
in the day will not stumble, but will see the light of this world. 10 But those
who walk in the night, stumble, because they do not have the light in them."
11 He said these things, and then he said, "Lazarus our friend has fallen
asleep. But I am going in order to awaken him."
12 The disciples said to him, "Lord, if he has fallen asleep, he will
recover."[c]
13 Jesus had been speaking about [Lazarus's][d] death, but they thought
he was speaking of lying down to sleep. 14 So Jesus told them plainly,
"Lazarus has died. 15 And I rejoice for your sake that I was not there, so
that you may believe. But let us go to him."
16 Thomas, the one called "Twin," said to his fellow disciples, "Let us
also go, so that we may die with him."

a. Although a few early witnesses (B and syr[s]) do not have the address to Jesus as "Lord" (*kyrie*), and its addition would be easily explained as assimilation to 11:32, the majority of witnesses testify to its inclusion in the text.

b. A few mss (D a e) read the Greek synonym *ephilei* instead of *ēgapa*, perhaps to make the statement conform more closely to the description of Lazarus as the one whom Jesus loves (*hon phileis*, v. 3).

c. Instead of *sōthēsetai*, 𝔓[75] reads *egerthēsetai*, anticipating the later reference to resurrection.

d. Lit., "Jesus had been speaking about his death"; the pronoun *autou* ("his") must refer to Lazarus, not Jesus.

[11:1–6] The narrative begins with the introduction of two sisters, Mary and Martha, and their brother, Lazarus, all friends of Jesus, who reside in the village of Bethany.[282] As disciples and witnesses to Jesus, the two sisters feature prominently in this chapter, as women do elsewhere in John. About two miles east of Jerusalem, the Bethany of Mary, Martha, and Lazarus should be distinguished from "Bethany beyond the Jordan" (1:28), where Jesus apparently is when he hears the news about Lazarus (10:40; see also comments on 11:18). It is in her hometown that Mary will anoint Jesus' feet with costly perfume before his triumphal entry into Jerusalem (12:1). Even though the actual narrative of the anointing comes later in the Gospel, the reference to Mary calls on the reader's familiarity either with her or the anointing itself to identify one by means of the other (11:2; cf. 12:1–8).[283]

282. For Bethany, see Matt 21:17; 26:6; Mark 11:1, 11; 14:3; Luke 19:29; 24:50. For recent discussions about Lazarus, with bibliography, see M. M. Thompson 2013.

283. In Mark and Matthew, an unnamed woman anoints Jesus' head, not his feet. The terse allusion to Mary here (11:2) likely refers to the account as known from John 12.

In John, Jesus has a circle of disciples or admirers located in or near Jerusalem, including the family of Mary, Martha, and Lazarus, as well as Nicodemus, Joseph of Arimathea, and the unnamed beloved disciple. The family of Bethany may be relatively wealthy, given Mary's ability to procure a quantity of expensive perfume, the presence of many mourners from Jerusalem (vv. 18–19), and Lazarus's burial in a tomb rather than in a simple ditch. Although Lazarus is the Greek form of "Eleazar," which in Hebrew means "God has helped," there is little if any indication that John has in view the etymological significance of this name.[284] No matter what Lazarus's social status might be, he figures in the narrative not because he is distinguished by status, but because he is the beloved friend of Jesus, and because he shares the common fate of all humankind: mortality. In a nutshell, this narrative recounts how Jesus' love for one of his own overcomes the power of death.

When Lazarus becomes ill, his sisters send Jesus a simple message: "Lord, the one you love is ill" (v. 3). This intriguing reference to Lazarus not as "our brother" or as "Lazarus," but rather as "the one you love" (*hon phileis*) introduces him entirely in his relationship to Jesus, as the recipient of Jesus' love and friendship. The sisters' description may constitute a subtle rhetorical appeal to Jesus: if Jesus does indeed love Lazarus, then presumably he will respond to their request. Lazarus is the first individual in the Gospel who is said to be loved by Jesus, a description repeated several times (vv. 3, 5, 11, 36). And while it will shortly be stated that Jesus also loves Martha and her sister (v. 5), Lazarus does seem to be singled out, even by his sisters, as "the one whom you love." This description raises a question: Is Lazarus the one who is elsewhere referred to as "the disciple whom Jesus loved" (cf. 13:23; 20:2–8; 21:7, 20)?[285]

That identification is further suggested by the fact that this beloved disciple appears in the narrative (13:23) only after Lazarus's introduction. In the disciple's first appearance in which he is so identified, he is reclining at Jesus' side at the Last Supper (13:23), even as Lazarus is earlier depicted as reclining at table with Jesus (12:2). Additionally, when Lazarus emerges from the tomb, his feet and hands are bound or wrapped, and a *soudarion*[286] ("facecloth, cloth") covers his face (11:44). Later the Gospel describes in some detail how Peter and the beloved disciple both see the linen wrappings and the *soudarion* that Jesus has left behind, but that only the beloved disciple is said to believe when he sees

284. Eleazar was the third most common male name among Palestinian Jews from 330 B.C.E. to 200 C.E.; see Ilan.

285. This disciple is regularly described in the Gospel as the recipient of Jesus' love: "whom you love" (*hon phileis*, 11:3); "whom Jesus loved" (*hon ēgapa ho Iēsous*, 13:23); "that disciple whom Jesus loved" (*ho mathētēs ekeinos hon ēgapa ho Iēsous*, 21:7, 20). For identification of Lazarus as the otherwise unnamed beloved disciple, see Hunt 207–9; Stibbe 1992, 79–80, 168.

286. Only John uses *soudarion* to describe a burial cloth (11:44; 20:7; differently, Luke 19:20, Acts 19:12).

these things (20:5–8). Perhaps the implication is that he believed Jesus had been raised because he had himself been released from burial wrappings such as he now saw lying before him. Finally, it is possible that the rumor that the beloved disciple would not die (21:23) arose from a misunderstanding of Jesus' words (that "everyone who lives and believes in me will never die," 11:25–26) to mean that Lazarus, after dying and being raised to life, will not die again. Perhaps the chief objection to the identification of the beloved disciple with Lazarus is simply that throughout the Gospel this disciple remains anonymous, whereas Lazarus does not. If Lazarus is indeed the "disciple whom Jesus loved," why is he not explicitly identified as such?

Although Mary and Martha implicitly request Jesus' help, Jesus does not go to Bethany, but "stayed in the place where he was for two days." Needless to say, Jesus' response jars with John's comment that "Jesus loved Martha and her sister and Lazarus" (v. 5).[287] Jesus' delay and his reference to God's glory (v. 4) again emphasize that his actions are not coerced: Jesus acts in his own time and in order to bring glory to God (see 2:3–5; 4:47–50; 6:5–6; 7:6–10; and comments there). God's glory will be revealed in an act, motivated by love, that brings life to the dead (see 3:16).[288] And when God is glorified, so is the Son of God: they are one in their life-giving work (10:30).

[7–10] Jesus makes his intentions plain to his disciples: he will return to Judea (v. 7). The disciples protest Jesus' decision on the grounds that his life is in danger there (v. 8; 10:31, 39).[289] Jesus' disciples do not grasp that Jesus' death is not the temporal end of his life and ministry, but rather their ultimate goal. Jesus explains his return to Judea with a cryptic question: "Are there not twelve hours in the day?" (v. 9). Both Jews and Romans divided the day into twelve parts, reckoned by "hours" of daylight. In the daylight, one may see clearly and walk without stumbling; during the night, it is easy to stumble since there is no light to illumine one's path (vv. 9–10). Jesus' remarks indicate that there is still daylight enough for him to carry out his work and that, although he is fully aware that some seek his death, darkness will not prevent him from doing that work (cf. 9:4–5). But in any case "night" is a danger only for those who do not have light to illumine their way. Those who see the "light of the world" (11:9) do not stumble: they have the daylight to illumine their path.

But Jesus is speaking on another level as well. As the light of the world himself (8:12; 9:5), his work will continue in the face of opposition, hostility,

287. "Loved" translates *ēgapa* (from *agapan*), whereas earlier (v. 3) the verb was *philein* (as in 11:36). The alternation of these two Greek words occurs elsewhere in John and is not theologically significant (see comments on 21:15–19).

288. See also Lincoln 2008, 218.

289. In 11:8 "the Jews" are those hostile to Jesus, who seek his life; but elsewhere in this chapter, "the Jews" are those who come to mourn with Mary and Martha; some come to faith in Jesus.

or any threats against it. Those who see by this light will be able to work in the darkness without stumbling or being overcome by it (1:5). In sum, Jesus maintains that, for him, it is still daylight, even if the hours of night are pressing—and that even these hours of darkness, real as they are, are not a genuine threat to the true light. God's work can and will continue in spite of the darkness. His disciples will do well to pay heed to Jesus' exhortation, underwritten by the implicit promise of the ongoing presence of his light.

[11–16] Jesus must go to Judea in order to "awaken" (*exypnisō*) Lazarus, now described as "our friend," that is, a friend of Jesus and his disciples (*ho philos hemōn*, v. 11). In 3 John 15, the Elder sends greetings from and to "the friends," which, like *adelphoi* ("brothers and sisters"), describes those who follow Jesus. In the Johannine literature, calling others "friends" echoes Jesus' address to his own disciples as "friends" (15:13–15). The disciples misunderstand Jesus' statement that Lazarus "has fallen asleep" (*koimasthai*, v. 11). But Jesus' metaphor for death is found in biblical and Jewish writings, as well as early Christian literature; it cannot have been unfamiliar to them.[290] The parallelism is found also in Greek and Roman mythology, where Sleep (*hypnos*, *somnus*) and Death (*thanatos*, *mors*) are said to be brothers.[291]

The disciples miss the point, objecting that if Lazarus is asleep, then he will surely recover. The Greek word *sōthēsetai*, which may be translated as "will recover" or "will be saved," suggests that the disciples think, that since Lazarus is sleeping, he is past the crisis and on the mend. But Jesus clarifies his meaning: Lazarus has died. There can be no expectation of "improvement" or "natural recovery." What is true for Lazarus will also be true for Jesus and for all his followers threatened by death: there is no "natural recovery" from death. The dead will live again, not by their own power, but by the intervention of the one who created and sustains all life.

Jesus' sign will reveal that those who are "asleep," that is, those who have died, will nevertheless be "saved" or raised to life. John does not use his typical words for raising the dead, *anastasis* or *anistanai* (5:29; 6:39, 40, 44, 54; 11:24), because Jesus' "awakening" (*exypnisō*, v. 11) of Lazarus is a resuscitation, rather than the resurrection anticipated "at the last day." But because Lazarus is dead and Jesus gives him life, the raising of Lazarus foreshadows the resurrection of the dead, even if it is not itself that resurrection. The one who

290. See, e.g., the OT phrase "slept with his fathers" throughout 1–2 Kings and 2 Chronicles; *Jub.* 23.1; *T. Mos.* 10.14. For death as "sleep" (sometimes "eternal/everlasting sleep"), see Dan 12:2; Sir 30:17; 2 Macc 12:45; *4 Ezra* 7.31–32; *2 Bar.* 11.4; 21.24; 36.11; *T. Iss.* 7.9; *T. Zeb.* 10.6; Matt 9:24; 27:52; Mark 5:39; Luke 8:52; KJV: Acts 7:60; 13:36; 1 Cor 15:6; 1 Thess 4:13; 5:10 (*katheudōmen*); 2 Pet 3:4; Ign., *Rom.* 4.2; *1 Clem.* 44.2.

291. Hesiod, *Theog.* 756–59; Homer, *Il.* 14.231; Pausanias, *Descr.* 5.18.1; Cicero, *Nat. d.* 3.17; Seneca, *Herc. fur.* 1063; in several of these texts, Night (*Nyx*) is their mother or nurse.

can restore life to Lazarus in the present is the one who gives life to the dead at "the last day" (11:24; and 6:40, 44, 54; 12:48).

Jesus' determination to go to Judea induces Thomas[292] to exhort his fellow disciples to follow Jesus, even if they must also die with him.[293] That is an ironic comment: this journey to Judea will indeed lead to Jesus' death, yet when that moment comes, none of the disciples die with him. The Gospel foresees a time when Jesus' followers will be put to death for their allegiance to him (16:2; 21:19). Although the Gospel describes several attempts of "the Jews" to stone Jesus, he is actually put to death by Roman crucifixion.

11:17–44 The Raising of Lazarus

When Jesus does travel to Bethany, he encounters Martha and Mary, the grieving sisters of Lazarus, who has died in Jesus' absence. Each of the sisters comes separately to Jesus, lamenting that his presence would have prevented Lazarus's death: "If you had been here, my brother would not have died." As the one who is the life of the world, Jesus' presence gives life. To be sure, the narrative indicates that even those who believe in Jesus can expect to die. But death will not have the final word over them, for those who believe will be raised to life by the one who is the resurrection and the life. As the fearful prospect of Jesus' death looms ever more darkly over the narrative, he is still the light that shines in the darkness, the life that overcomes death.

> **11:17** When Jesus arrived, he found that Lazarus had already been in the
> tomb for four days. **18** Now Bethany was near Jerusalem, about two miles
> away, **19** and many of the Jews had come to Martha and Mary in order to
> console them about their brother. **20** When Martha heard that Jesus was
> coming, she went and met him. Mary stayed in the house.
>
> **21** Martha said to Jesus, "Lord, if you had been here, my brother would
> not have died. **22** But even now I know that whatever you ask God, God
> will give you."
>
> **23** Jesus said to her, "Your brother will rise."
>
> **24** Martha said to him, "I know that he will rise in the resurrection at
> the last day."

292. *Didymos* means "twin" but is also a proper name. So also is "Thomas," which derives from the Aramaic (*tĕʾōmaʾ*) or Hebrew (*tāʾôm*) for "twin." Since the Gospel does not specify whose twin Thomas was, some early traditions designated him as Jesus' twin (*Acts of Thomas* 31). This alleged relationship may have provided the basis for the claim in the *Gospel of Thomas* (Preface; 1) that Thomas was the recipient of special revelation from the risen Lord.

293. While the pronoun "him" (*autou*) in the phrase "die with him" (*apothanōmen met' autou*) could refer grammatically to Lazarus, in context Thomas expects that Jesus' return to Judea might result in a successful attempt on Jesus' life (11:16).

25 Jesus said to her, "I am the resurrection and the life. Those who
believe in me, even though they die, will live, 26 and those who live and
believe in me will never die. Do you believe this?"

27 She said to him, "Yes, Lord, I believe that you are the Messiah, the
Son of God, who is to come into the world."

28 When she had said these things, she went away and called Mary,
her sister, saying privately, "The Teacher is here and is calling for you."

29 And when she heard it, she got up quickly and went to him. 30 Now
Jesus had not yet come into the village, but was still at the place where
Martha met him. 31 So when the Jews who were with her in the house,
consoling her, saw Mary get up quickly and go out, they followed her,
thinking that she was going to the tomb to weep there.

32 When Mary came to where Jesus was, and saw him, she fell at his
feet, saying to him, "Lord, if you had been here, my brother would not
have died."

33 When Jesus saw her weeping, and the Jews with her weeping, he
was deeply disturbed[a] in spirit and troubled. 34 He said, "Where have you
laid him?"

They said to him, "Lord, come and see."

35 Jesus wept.

36 So the Jews said, "See how he loved him!" 37 But some of them said,
"Could not the one who was able to open the eyes of the blind have kept
this man from dying?"

38 Jesus, again greatly disturbed, came to the tomb. It was a cave, and
a stone was lying on it. 39 Jesus said, "Take away the stone." Martha, the
sister of the dead man, said to him, "Lord, the smell![b] It has been four days."

40 Jesus said to her, "Did I not say to you that if you believed, you
would see the glory of God?"

41 So they took away the stone. And Jesus lifted up his eyes and said,
"Father, I thank you that you have heard me. 42 I know that you always
hear me, but I said this on account of the crowd standing here, so that they
might believe that you have sent me."

43 When he had said these things, he cried out with a great voice,
"Lazarus! Come out!"

44 The man who had been dead came out, his feet and hands bound
with strips of cloth and his face wrapped in a cloth. And Jesus said to
them, "Unbind him, and let him go."

a. A number of MSS insert *hōs* ("as") before *embrimoumenos*, i.e., "*as if* deeply disturbed," softening the description of Jesus' deep distress.

b. The word *ozō* means simply "smell, emit an odor," whether foul or sweet; in the context, the point is that the stench of decay will be strong.

[11:17–22] Upon his arrival in Bethany, Jesus learns that Lazarus has been in the tomb four days (vv. 17, 39). Since it is Jewish custom to bury the dead on the day of their death, Lazarus had apparently died even before Mary and Martha's message reached Jesus. Martha, after hearing that Jesus has at last come, declares: "Lord, if you had been here, my brother would not have died"—a sentiment reiterated by Mary (11:32) and echoed later by the mourners who ask whether Jesus, who opened the eyes of the blind man, could not also have made Lazarus well (11:37). Martha, Mary, and the mourners all make the same point: Jesus could have prevented Lazarus's death.[294] Undoubtedly: yet Jesus does not promise that he will prevent death, but that he has the power to raise the dead to life. Human lives run their course; but as the one in whom there is life, and who is the life, Jesus can confer life—even on the dead. Jesus is not caught off guard; he has already told his disciples that Lazarus is dead (v. 14); upon his arrival in Bethany, the report has corroborated his assertion. Bethany is about "fifteen stadia" (slightly less than two miles) from Jerusalem (see comment on 6:19), the home of "many of the Jews" who have come to console Mary and Martha at the death of their brother.

Martha apparently believes that Jesus can help even now, because she also believes that God will give him whatever he asks (11:22). If she expects Jesus to ask God to restore Lazarus's life to him, it is difficult to explain her barely concealed reproach of Jesus (v. 21) and her later protest at the tomb that Lazarus's body will be well along in the process of decay (v. 39). Her conviction that God will grant Jesus whatever he asks is correct, but she has not fully grasped just what that means.

[23–26] Jesus promises Martha, "Your brother will rise," a promise that she understands to refer to the resurrection of the dead "at the last day" (v. 24; 6:39, 40, 44, 54; 5:28–29). "Your brother will rise" could also portend Jesus' imminent raising of Lazarus; but Martha misses the possible double meaning of Jesus' words. Jesus' subsequent declaration, "I am the resurrection and the life," is the heart and pivot of the narrative. With that declaration, Jesus reinterprets, but does not undercut, the common expectation of resurrection, by tying it inextricably to himself and to what he can effect both in the future and in the present. The one who can bring dead bodies out of the tombs is the one "in whom there is life" (1:4) and to whom the Father has given "life in himself" (5:26). He is, therefore, also the one who will effect the resurrection "at the last day." All life comes from and through God's Word, whether this be created

294. Koester (2003, 65) comments that the sisters' poignant words would resonate with readers "as they experienced sickness and death in a time when Christ was not visibly present, and as they turned to a seemingly absent Christ for help and received no timely answer." Bruner (659) writes, "Jesus' delays always hurt. Our text is honest."

life (1:1–4), the fullness of life and communion with God in the present (10:10; 17:3), or the coming resurrection to life (5:29).

When Jesus says, "I am the resurrection and the life," he again claims the power and authority to raise the dead and to give them life (5:25–26), both in the present hour and at the last day. In calling Lazarus from the tomb, Jesus will graphically demonstrate that "the hour is coming" when "all who are in the tombs will hear his voice" and "will come out" (5:28). Jesus will call to Lazarus, and Lazarus will come out of the tomb—but not, at present, to the resurrection. Jesus' raising of Lazarus foreshadows the resurrection of the dead, even as elsewhere Jesus' own resurrection guarantees that final resurrection (14:19).

Jesus explains the meaning of his claim to be the resurrection when he says, "Those who believe in me, even though they die, will live" (v. 25). That is to say, those who have faith in Jesus are not kept from dying ("even though they die"), anymore than Lazarus was; even if Lazarus's death was preventable, death ultimately comes to all flesh. But those "who believe in me" will live: they will live by means of the resurrection, which Jesus has the power to effect. And this clarifies the meaning of the second part of Jesus' revelatory statement, "I am the life." For those "who believe in me," the resurrection will be a resurrection *to life*, to eternal life with God (17:3). Jesus has the power to call the dead from the tombs, both now and at the last day; he has the power to grant them eternal life, anticipated and enjoyed now, and fully experienced with the resurrection at the last day (see comments on 5:25–26; 14:19; Excursus 4: "Life and Eternal Life in John").

Here Jesus binds the hope for life to that which he is and does, to himself as the one who has power over all the dead. For John, as for Paul, death is the final enemy (1 Cor 15:26): but it has been and will be overcome by God through the resurrection in Jesus Christ. Jesus' promises are made as he is on his way to death; indeed, the specter of death—for Lazarus, for Jesus, and for his disciples—has hovered over this entire scene (vv. 4, 8, 14, 16). Jesus will share Lazarus's fate, but even as he can in the present confer life on those who believe, after being raised to life, he will raise those who believe in him in the resurrection at the last day (John 6:39–40, 44, 54, 57).

[27] As a response to Jesus' question, Martha's confession that she believes that Jesus is the Messiah, the Son of God, the one coming into the world, establishes the proper work of that Messiah as delivering people from death to life. Although there are a few hints in Jewish traditions that the messianic age will be attended by the resurrection of the dead to life, nothing points to the expectation of a Messiah who will himself raise the dead.[295] Martha's affirmations about Jesus cannot be understood simply in light of contemporary messianic expec-

295. In 4Q521 the resurrection is a feature of the coming "messianic" age; it is not clear that the Messiah accomplishes this.

tation. Here the two beliefs—that Jesus is the Messiah, Son of God, and that he can and will raise the dead—are brought together, so that to confess Jesus as Messiah is to confess him as the one who has the power of life. This is the shape of the messianic mission that Jesus carries out as the Son who has come from God (see 5:25–26; 8:36, 55; 10:15–18, 25, 28, 30). Martha fails to fully grasp the implications of what she has just confessed; but initially inadequate confession, or confession made with partial faith, is often the basis for subsequent deepening insight about Jesus in the Gospel (3:2; 4:19; 6:14; 7:40; 9:17).

[28–30] Martha then summons her sister, Mary. Martha has addressed Jesus as "Lord" (*kyrie*, 11:27),[296] but now she informs her sister that "the Teacher" is calling her.[297] Whatever else Jesus may be, he is certainly honored and known as a teacher, and those who address him as such expect him to speak and act with authority (see 1:38; 3:2; 13:13–14; 20:16; also 8:4). Jesus himself links together the designations "Teacher and Lord" when he washes the disciples' feet, telling his disciples that they rightly acknowledge him as such (13:13–14). At the tomb, Mary Magdalene will respond to Jesus by calling him "Rabbouni!" which, as John points out, is translated "Teacher" (*didaskale*, 20:16; cf. 1:38).[298]

[31–37] Mary responds to Jesus' summons and, kneeling at his feet either in entreaty or reverence, essentially repeats her sister's words, "Lord, if you had been here, my brother would not have died" (11:32; cf. v. 21). Mary was followed by "the Jews," those from Jerusalem who came to console her and her sister (v. 30). There is no reason to question their motives or their sincerity: they have come to grieve the death of Lazarus with his sisters during the seven-day period of mourning (see Sir 22:12; Jdt 16:24), and they follow her because they think she is going to the tomb to grieve there.[299] Here Mary of Bethany is weeping because of the death of her brother; later Mary Magdalene will weep because of the death of her Teacher and Lord (20:11–13). Jesus' response to Mary Magdalene outside his own tomb is instructive for understanding the present account. There he asks, "Why are you weeping?" (20:13). Mary need not weep, since the living Jesus is standing before her: she needs only to recognize him. But when Jesus encounters Lazarus's sister, Mary, at Bethany, he asks no such question: it is obvious that Mary mourns the death of her brother. Jesus does not scold her for grieving the dead. After all, Lazarus is not standing alive in front of her, but is dead and in a tomb. Seeing Mary

296. This address occurs frequently in John's Gospel, both with the common meaning "Sir" and the richer confessional meaning "Lord"; see the comments on 6:23.

297. Note the picture of Mary, sitting at Jesus' feet in the posture of a learner, in Luke 10:39.

298. See Köstenberger 1998.

299. Since impurity could be contracted by contact with a corpse (Num 19:11–16; Lev 11:31–32; 22:4; Ezek 44:25), tombs were located outside residential areas and marked (e.g., whitewashed, as in Matt 23:27) so that unnecessary contact could be avoided.

weeping, "[Jesus] is greatly disturbed in spirit" (*enebrimēsato tō pneumati*) and "troubled" (*etaraxen heauton*, or "troubled in himself," 11:33), and Jesus himself weeps (v. 35).

Jesus' reaction has puzzled many interpreters. After all, from the beginning of this story, it is clear that Jesus acts in keeping with his perception of God's purposes; that he is entirely committed to enacting and bringing glory to God, whatever the path; and that as the sovereign agent of a sovereign God, he has the power of life and death. Jesus knows what will happen to Lazarus and what he will do in response to Lazarus's death. And yet Jesus is twice described as being "greatly disturbed" (vv. 33, 38) and weeping at the tomb of Lazarus. But if Jesus has known all along that Lazarus's illness will "not lead to death" (v. 4), why does he weep at the tomb? And why is he "greatly disturbed"? "Greatly disturbed" renders the Greek *enebrimēsato* (from *embrimaomai*); BDAG states that it indicates anger and displeasure, but allows that *embrimōmenos* (also from *embrimaomai*; v. 38) can mean "deeply moved."[300] Similarly, *etaraxen* (from *tarassō*, here translated as "troubled," v. 33) means "to cause inward turmoil, stir up, disturb, unsettle."[301] Some interpreters maintain that Jesus is angry or agitated over the lack of faith demonstrated by the grieving of Lazarus's family and friends;[302] others say he is angry at death itself.

Another line of interpretation, not necessarily incompatible with the first, emphasizes Jesus' demonstration of compassion for those grieving the loss of their brother and friend.[303] Quite simply, Jesus weeps when he sees that those whom he loves are also weeping; and he weeps because one whom he loves has died.[304] Thus the mourners rightly observe, "See how he loved him!" Here, then, is the penultimate expression of Jesus' love for Lazarus, which has been part of the narrative since Mary and Martha's initial message to Jesus: "the one whom you love is ill." Because Jesus loves Lazarus, he weeps at his tomb; and he weeps with and for those who love Lazarus. That Jesus will soon raise Lazarus to life, and so manifest God's glory, does not mute the genuine sorrow that he experiences and expresses.

300. So also *LSJM,* which indicates that the word can be used of the snorting of horses, or of strong rebuke, as in the Synoptic Gospels with reference to exorcism (Matt 9:30; Mark 1:43).

301. Jesus is also said to be "troubled" in the face of his own death (12:27), and by the treachery that leads to his betrayal (13:21).

302. Bultmann 1971, 405; Schnackenburg 2:336; Beasley-Murray 192–93; emphasized by Moloney (1996, 166–68), who overstates when he speaks of Jesus' "frustrated and angry disappointment . . . and deep, shuddering, internal emotion." For discussion of Jesus' emotions, esp. as related to ancient philosophical ideals, see Attridge 2010.

303. "I know that our nature asks and seeks for its friends and daily companions; it cannot but be grieved [at the loss of one of them]. And this Christ demonstrated as well, for He wept over Lazarus" (John Chrysostom, *Hom. Jo.* 62 on John 11:35).

304. "He is as much affected by our ills as if He had suffered them in Himself" (Calvin 2:11).

Jesus' weeping at the tomb of Lazarus demonstrates that grief over death is not an inappropriate response. As Ridderbos puts it, "As the Son of God he does not come to redeem the world from imaginary grief or to make grief over death imaginary. Therefore he joins the mourning procession for the friend whom he is to raise from the dead, and he weeps."[305] While the story is sometimes read as a demonstration of Jesus' human nature, "humanity" and "divinity" are not separable aspects of Jesus' identity in John: he is always the incarnate Word of God, and it is the Word-made-flesh, the life-giving Son confronted by death, who weeps at the tomb of his friend.

[38–40] The tomb in which Lazarus was buried is described as a "cave," with a stone sealing the entrance. Archaeological excavations in Jericho, Jerusalem, and at Qumran testify to different types of tombs and ways of burying the dead, so it is difficult to say precisely what sort of tomb is in view here.[306] Lazarus may have been buried in a *kokh* (Hebrew pl., *kokhim*; Latin, *loculus*, "a little place"; pl., *loculi*) tomb, a family tomb with multiple horizontal shafts, or perhaps in an individual tomb;[307] the entrance would be blocked or sealed with a rectangular stone. Jesus commands that the stone be taken (not rolled) away, leading Martha to protest that there will certainly be a strong smell, since Lazarus's body has now been decaying for four days.[308] Jews did not embalm the dead but wrapped the bodies with spices (see 19:39–40; contrast Gen 50:2–3, 26); while the spices do not prevent decay, especially in a warm climate, their aroma can mask the odor of decay. But after four days, the strong odor indicates the extent of the corpse's decay. There is no doubt in Martha's mind: Lazarus is dead, and his body already rotting. In spite of her earlier acknowledgment that Jesus is "the resurrection and the life," and that God will grant to Jesus whatever he asks, she scarcely expects that Jesus will bring Lazarus out of the tomb to life. She has not fully understood what she has confessed.

Jesus' response to her protest, "Did I not tell you that if you believed, you would see the glory of God?" (11:40), raises the question of the relationship of Martha's belief to "seeing" God's glory. What kind of faith is in view? Faith in Jesus as Messiah? In his power to raise the dead? And how does Martha's faith enable her to "see the glory of God"? All who are at the tomb see Lazarus come out; but not all will see that deed as pointing to Jesus as the resurrection and life. To understand Jesus' action as the life-giving work of God means that

305. Ridderbos 402.

306. See Hachlili; McCane; Reed 47–49 (with illustration); Meyers and Chancey 40–41, 79–80, 104–5.

307. Crossan and Reed (245) describe such a tomb as a rectangular shaft "sunk between 5 and 7 feet into the ground, with a lengthy burial niche at the bottom where a body could be laid out horizontally."

308. According to *m. Yebam.* 16:3, identification of a corpse should be made within three days of death; otherwise the body might be unidentifiable due to decay.

one has seen the glory of God. In Jesus' deed, Martha will see the enactment of the words spoken to her: Jesus is resurrection and life. If she truly understands this, she will then see, in and through Jesus, the manifestation of God's glory (see 1:14; 2:11; 12:41; 17:24).

[41–44] So "they took away the stone," and Jesus "lifted up his eyes," or "looked upward," the posture of prayer (see Mark 6:41 par.; Luke 18:13). Jesus' prayer is not a petition for God to act but a thanksgiving that he has been heard, which may in turn imply that Jesus has already made just such a petition, unrecorded in the Gospel. Jesus' prayer bears witness to his unity with God, a unity that explains on what grounds he can call Lazarus out of the tomb: Jesus and the Father are one in their purpose of giving life to the world. Therefore Jesus gives thanks (*eucharisteō*; cf. 6:11, 23) that God has heard him and will act so as to bring life to Lazarus. God's response is visible, not audible: the emergence of the dead man from the tomb demonstrates the truth of Jesus' assertion that the Father always hears him and has sent him to do God's work in the world.

Lazarus comes out, still bound in the cloths in which he was buried. "No tomb can be so tightly sealed that the voice of Jesus cannot enter it."[309] Although Lazarus is frequently portrayed wrapped as a mummy, it is not clear that the "strips of cloth" were wound around him in that fashion. Rather, there may have been a single large cloth that covered the body and was bound at the feet; additionally, the jaw and hands were bound to the body. The description of Lazarus's hands and feet bound in "strips of cloth," with his face "wrapped in a cloth," provides a striking contrast to the later description of Peter's discovery of the empty tomb of Jesus, with "linen wrappings lying there" and "the cloth" rolled up in another place (20:5–7). Even as Jesus will leave his death shroud behind, he now commands the people at the tomb to unbind Lazarus, so he can leave his death shroud behind.[310] Jesus effects the removal of the trappings of death because he is the resurrection and the life, who calls the dead forth to life.

In this Gospel, Lazarus is presented entirely in terms of what happens to him and how others respond to him because of his mortality: because he is dying, his sisters solicit Jesus' help, and because he dies, Mary, Martha, Jesus, and "the Jews" from Jerusalem mourn for him; because Jesus raises him from the dead, the curious wish to see him, and therefore the chief priests seek Lazarus's death (12:9–10); and ultimately and most significantly, because Lazarus dies, Jesus risks his own life, journeying to Bethany to bring the dead man back to life. Mortal and frail, Lazarus represents all human beings faced with the threat of death; but as one who has received life, Lazarus represents all who are given life

309. Zimmerman 2008, 101.

310. Regarding Jesus' command "Unbind him, and let him go" (11:44), Barrett writes, "Lazarus came out of the tomb alive under the bandages. It is unlikely that John saw allegorical significance in this statement. The story ends here, abruptly; there is no more to say" (403).

by the One who has and gives life. Jesus' raising Lazarus to life is the climactic sign of Jesus' life-giving power.

The raising of Lazarus discloses how God resolutely counters the pervasive threat of death: God's Word-made-flesh enters fully into and assumes the conditions of humanity, including suffering and mortality; yet in his resurrection Jesus reveals that death's pernicious grip on human life is not ultimate. Death is powerful; but it is not all-powerful. The raising of Lazarus redounds to God's glory because it reveals God's love and life-giving purposes for the world. This account puts the assertions of John 3:16 into narrative form: God's love for the world is expressed through the giving of life. Although the death and resurrection of Jesus will further reveal God's life-giving power, its full disclosure awaits "the last day," with the resurrection to life and the judgment when Jesus' identity as the life-giving Son of God will be vindicated.

In early Christian art and interpretation, the raising of Lazarus was juxtaposed with imagery and episodes related to the new life received in baptism. Like those who were baptized, or a newborn child (see John 3:3–8), Lazarus is frequently depicted as nude. Lazarus has thrown off the winding sheet of death: he therefore begins life anew, as a new child (and hence is also depicted as quite small when compared to other figures in a given work of art). Or, to put it the other way around, the new life given to Lazarus becomes a figure of the new life given to those who are initiated into the fellowship of Christ.[311] The raising of Lazarus is linked to the creation of Adam (Gen 2:7), the raising of Jairus's daughter (Mark 5:35–42 par.) and the widow of Nain's son (Luke 7:11–16), as well as the deliverance of Jonah (Jonah 2:1–10), the three youths from the furnace (Dan 3:19–28), and Daniel (6:19–23).[312] That the raising of Lazarus should have an important place in early Christian art may be due simply to its subject matter and representation of the hope for life after death. But it surely occupies that prominent place in part due to the drama of the narrative in John: here the main characters have names; Lazarus's family and friends—and Jesus himself—mourn for him; and Lazarus's death and restoration to life supply the backdrop for Jesus' declaration that he is the resurrection and the life (11:25). Both in terms of its placement in the Gospel and its revelation of Jesus, this narrative presents the climactic summary of John's witness to Jesus: he is the Messiah, the Son of God, who raises the dead in the resurrection and confers life.

11:45–54 The Council Gathers in Jerusalem

The raising of Lazarus creates yet another division among the people (vv. 45–46). Those who do not believe in Jesus determine that his life must be

311. See Jensen 2012, 150–52, 159.
312. See, e.g., the third-century *Apos. Con.* 5.1.

sacrificed for the sake of preventing Roman action against the temple and city (vv. 47–53). Now Jesus withdraws from his public ministry (v. 54). There will be no more signs and no extended public discourses. The Gospel has come to the final Passover of Jesus' life, and the hour of his death will soon arrive. But even though the authorities meet to discuss what should be done to stem Jesus' rising popularity, in the end they do not determine the course of events or their outcome. If Jesus had been seeking to avoid his death in Jerusalem, he would never have gone to Bethany and to the tomb of Lazarus, his friend. His willingness to return to Judea, where he put his life in danger for a friend, even as the good shepherd would do for his sheep—that willingness is but a precursor to his final journey to Jerusalem, where he will lay down his life for his friends.

11:45 So many of the Jews who had come to Mary, and who had seen what
he did, believed in him. **46** But some of them went to the Pharisees and
told them what Jesus had done.

47 Then the chief priests[a] and the Pharisees gathered the council
together and said, "What are we to do? For this man does many signs. **48**
If we permit him to do so, all will believe in him, and the Romans will
come and take away both our temple[b] and our nation."[c]

49 But one of them, Caiaphas, who was high priest that year, said to
them, "You don't know anything! **50** You don't understand that it is better
for you[d] that one man should die for the people, than that the entire nation
should perish."

51 He did not say this on his own, but rather because he was high priest
that year, he prophesied that Jesus was to die for the nation, **52** and not for
the nation only, but to gather into one the children of God who had been
scattered. **53** From that point on, they purposed together to kill him.

54 Then Jesus no longer went about openly among the Jews, but rather
he withdrew from there into the region near the wilderness, into the city[e]
called Ephraim, and there he remained with his disciples.

a. For "chief priests," see the comments on 7:32; 18:10–14; cf. 7:45; 12:10; 18:3, 35; 19:6, 15, 21.

b. "Our temple": lit., "our place" (*hēmōn . . . ton topon*).

c. "Our nation," or "our people" (*hēmōn . . . to ethnos*).

d. Instead of the second-person plural *hymin* ("for you"), some MSS read *hēmin* ("for us": A W vg sy), and א omits it (probably accidentally). "For you" fits Caiaphas's disparaging remark, "You don't know anything!"

e. John uses *polis* ("city") for town or village.

[11:45–48] While the raising of Lazarus leads "many of the Jews" to believe in Jesus, others report to the Pharisees what Jesus had done. Presumably, those who report Jesus' action believe that he raised Lazarus to life, but even this deed does not lead them to faith. They did not see God's glory in Jesus' deed. The argument is circular: the sign can lead people to faith, but faith can itself lead people to see the sign in such a way that they understand its significance. Coming to faith in Jesus follows neither a simple linear progression nor a fixed process, whether here or elsewhere in the Gospel narrative.[313]

John distinguishes "the Jews" from "the Pharisees,"[314] who together with the "chief priests" meet as a "council." "Chief priests" and "Pharisees" are an odd combination: priests inherited their positions, but Pharisees constituted a "party" within Judaism. The Greek word for council, *synedrion*,[315] is used only here in John but occurs in the Synoptics with reference to local courts (Matt 5:22; 10:17; Mark 13:9); to the gathering of priests, scribes, and others in connection with Jesus' trial (Mark 14:55; 15:1; Matt 26:59; Luke 22:66); and in Acts to the gathering of the high priest, elders, scribes, and others who discuss the appropriate response to early Christians (e.g., Acts 5:21; 6:12; 22:30; 23:1; 24:20). Recently the view that the Sanhedrin was a formal standing body—of seventy-one members, according to the Mishnah (*m. Sanh.* 1:5)—with legislative and judicial authority has been vigorously challenged.[316] Under Roman oversight, the chief governing power in Judea was the high priest. In the present passage, and in keeping with the power and authority of the high priest, Caiaphas determines what ought to be done with Jesus. But Josephus and the Gospels indicate that the high priest could and did gather other priests and laypeople for consultation, trials, and decisions—although there is no evidence that any votes were taken.[317]

John associates both the chief priests and the Pharisees, who would have had no official functions in the temple unless they were also priests, with the temple (7:15, 32, 45; 10:23–24). The authorities are collectively concerned with the possible consequences of Jesus' ministry: if they allow Jesus to continue "performing many signs," they run the risk of attracting attention and incurring Roman destruction of "this place and our nation." "This place" (*ton topon*) designates the temple, although it may include Jerusalem as well.[318] For readers of the Gospel, the statement is tragically ironic. Jesus' public ministry of doing signs has already come to an end, but not because of the council's decision.

313. See, further, Excursuses 3: "The Signs in the Gospel of John"; and 8: "The Johannine Vocabulary of Faith and Discipleship."

314. Elsewhere John seems to identify priests and Levites with the Pharisees (1:19, 24).

315. The Greek word, *synedrion*, was rendered in Hebrew as *sanhedrîn*, from which we derive the English term "Sanhedrin."

316. So Sanders (1992, 472–90); for judicious discussion of the evidence in the NT and Josephus, see R. Brown 1994, 342–43; Keener 2:1073–76.

317. Josephus, *J.W.* 2.331, 336; 5.532, 570–71; *Ant.* 4.218; 11.105; 14.167–80; 20.200–202, 216–17.

318. For "place" with reference to temple, see Jer 7:14, with "place" parallel to "house" (= temple); "holy place," 2 Macc 5:19; "place": John 4:20; Acts 6:14; 21:28.

And while Jesus will soon be crucified, the Romans will nevertheless destroy the temple and "take away our people" several decades after Jesus' death. In spite of Caiaphas's machinations, he and the council are powerless to genuinely determine the course of events.

[49–54] Caiaphas, the high priest at the time, pushes a course of action (mistakenly) designed to ensure the survival of the people (or, nation; *ethnos*): Jesus must be sacrificed in order to protect the people from the Romans who have the will and the power to subdue troublesome subjects. Jesus' death would be "better" for the nation, since it would prevent its destruction. Rome typically did not look favorably on public gatherings, especially at major pilgrimage festivals such as Passover. Any rumors that Jesus was held by some to be the Messiah, a deliverer or king, would only compound Rome's tendency to react—or to overreact with force.[319] In the face of such very real danger, Caiaphas seeks to protect his people—even as Jesus has argued that a good shepherd should.[320] But while Caiaphas is willing to hand Jesus over to death, he is apparently not willing to sacrifice himself. Caiaphas does not know that Jesus' death will be "better" for his people in ways that he has never imagined, since through Jesus' death comes life of a very different sort than Caiaphas seeks to protect.

Caiaphas served as high priest from 18 to 36 C.E. By law the high priest held his position for life, but in the time of the Seleucids and the Romans, the high priest served at the pleasure of Syria or Rome and sometimes was replaced during his lifetime. John's statement that Caiaphas was high priest "that year" has sometimes been taken to reflect John's mistaken understanding that high priests were replaced annually. But more likely "that year" refers to the year of Jesus' death and thus accentuates the solemnity of Caiaphas's statement (cf. 11:51; 18:13).[321] This is not simply any year; neither is Caiaphas's plan of his own devising.[322]

Indeed, in that fateful year, the high priest unwittingly utters a prophecy that correctly illumines the deeper significance of Jesus' death: Caiaphas prophesies that "Jesus was about to die for the nation, and not for the nation only, but to gather into one the children of God who had been scattered" (11:51–52).[323]

319. E.g., see Josephus, *J.W.* 2.10–13, 224–27; *Ant.* 20.112—discussed briefly at 12:12–13.

320. To preserve the peace of the nation and the city for the Romans, certain Jewish leaders entreated Gessius Florus, the Roman procurator of Judea in 64–66, to pardon a few wrongdoers who had insulted him (Josephus, *J.W.* 2.302–4). Instead, Florus had many of the residents of Jerusalem arrested, tortured, and crucified.

321. Cf. statements regarding Jesus' "hour" (e.g., 2:4; 7:30; 8:20; 12:23; 13:1; 17:1) or Jesus' "time" (7:6, 8)

322. According to Josephus (*Ant.* 18.64), Jesus was condemned by Pilate "at the suggestion of the principal men among us," a statement that coheres with John's description here of the role of the chief priests and Pharisees in Jesus' death.

323. Josephus (*J.W.* 1.68–69; *Ant.* 11.327; 13.299) states that John Hyrcanus was given the gift of the priesthood and prophecy.

Even though Caiaphas becomes the agent of Jesus' condemnation, his prophetic speech rightly announces what Jesus' death will accomplish. Much biblical and Jewish literature testifies to the hope that God will again gather together the twelve tribes. John's testimony that Jesus' death will gather the "scattered" children of God recalls especially certain biblical texts that promise a gathering of the scattered sheep of God's flock.[324] Jesus dies *hyper* ("for, on behalf of") the people; as the good shepherd, he gives his life for (*hyper*) the sheep (10:11, 15), so that they will not be scattered and destroyed.

The hope for the gathering of God's people, the twelve tribes of Israel, comes to expression in the New Testament understanding of Jesus' mission (e.g., Matt 8:11; 15:24) and constitutes a particular feature of the Johannine understanding of Jesus' death. Jesus' death and resurrection lead to the proclamation of his resurrection to all the world, and the gathering of all the children of God,[325] both Jew and Gentile, into one people (10:16). John's view of Jesus' death fits well with the view, current in much contemporary historical Jesus research, that Jesus' aim was the eschatological restoration of Israel.[326] But John has focused Jesus' ingathering work particularly on the cross and on its effects, which extend beyond the children of Israel, to all those who are "children of God." The scattered children who will be gathered include Israel ("his own," 1:11), Samaritans (4:39–42), Gentiles (cf. 7:35; 10:16); indeed, all the world (3:16; 12:32). The Gospel's interpretation thus joins the political motives for Jesus' death with its saving effects: while the council intends that Jesus should die *instead of* the people, by their unwitting collusion, he dies *for* them.[327]

The Gospel reports that, because of Caiaphas's plan, Jesus no longer goes about in public but instead withdraws to a town called Ephraim, "in the region near the wilderness." It is uncertain exactly where Ephraim was located, but Jesus retreats there with his disciples because it provides safe haven.[328] It is not that Jesus fears death: his journey to Bethany in Judea has indicated his willingness to venture into territory where his life is in peril (11:7–8).[329] And he will soon return to Jerusalem to face the cross. John's note that Jesus goes to Ephraim, "near the wilderness," where he "remained with his disciples,"

324. For the theme of the gathering of Israel, scattered throughout the nations, see Isa 43:1–8, 15; 44:6; 45:18–25; 52:7; Jer 31–33; Ezek 34; 37:15–18; Mic 2:12–13; Zeph 3:15–20; Obad 21; Tob 13; Sir 36:1–17; 48:10; 2 Macc 1:27; *Pss. Sol.* 8.28–34; 11.2–3; chs. 17–18. See also Dennis.

325. For "children of God," see comments on 1:12 above; cf. 1 John 3:1, 10; 5:2.

326. See esp. the seminal works of Meyer; and Sanders 1985.

327. Cf. Dennis 67.

328. For a discussion of options, see H. Thompson.

329. In *Contra Celsum* (9.1), Origen reports Celsus's charge that, "when we had convicted him, condemned him, and decided that he should be punished, [Jesus] was caught hiding himself and escaping most disgracefully." Origen denies that Jesus ever fled to hide himself, or that he was caught against his will (citing John 18:4–8 to establish the latter point).

seems rather to imply a period of waiting—waiting until his hour comes at last. It does so with Passover.

11:55–12:50 Summary of Jesus' Signs, Anticipating Jesus' Death: The Final Passover

Once again it is near Passover: the third and final Passover of John's Gospel, during which Jesus will be arrested and crucified. No longer does Jesus do signs that embody and confer God's life. Now the actions of friends and foes alike, as well as Jesus' own words, portend and lead inexorably to his death: Mary's anointing prepares Jesus for his burial (12:1–8); Jesus rides into Jerusalem on a donkey, enacting Zechariah's vision of Israel's coming king (12:12–16); and Jesus himself reiterates the necessity of his death to bring life to the world and to complete God's work (12:20–28). Citations from Isaiah explain the unbelief of Jesus' contemporaries as foreseen by the prophet (12:38–41).

This material (11:55–12:50) serves as a transition between Jesus' public ministry and his death, which is not the grim end to his life and mission. Rather, it is an integral part of his life-giving work as the good shepherd, the Messiah, who achieves his victory not by defeating Roman occupying power, but by overcoming the powers of death (12:44–50). In giving himself to death so that life may come to all the world, Jesus manifests God's glory and accomplishes God's purposes (12:28–33, 49–50). Jesus heeds God's charge to lay down his life and take it up again (10:18; 12:49); as the good shepherd, he does so of his own volition, out of love for his friends and for the life of the world.

11:55–12:11 Preparation for Jesus' Burial

Now that the moment of Jesus' death has drawn near, Mary of Bethany, Lazarus's sister, pours a large quantity of expensive perfume on Jesus' feet, anticipating his burial (12:1–8). Hers is an act of costly devotion that stands in sharp contrast to the unbelief of the Jewish council, which intends to have Jesus killed. In spite of their different aims and intentions, the two scenes and the two deeds belong together: the authorities plot to put Jesus to death, while Mary prepares him for his burial.

> **11:55** Now the Passover of the Jews was near. Many went up to Jerusalem
> from the countryside before the Passover in order to purify themselves. **56**
> They were looking for Jesus, and saying to each other, as they stood in the
> temple, "What do you think? He won't come to the feast, will he?" **57** For
> the chief priests and the Pharisees had given orders that whoever knew
> where he was staying should inform them, so that they could seize him.

12:1 So six days before Passover, Jesus went to Bethany, where Laza-
rus was, whom Jesus had raised from the dead. 2 They made supper for
Jesus[a] there. Martha was serving, and Lazarus was one of those reclining
at table with him. 3 Then Mary took a pound of costly perfume of pure[b]
nard, rubbed[c] Jesus' feet, and wiped his feet with her hair. The house was
filled with the fragrance of the perfume.
4 Judas Iscariot, one of his disciples (the one who was about to hand
him over), said, 5 "Why was this perfume not sold for three hundred dena-
rii and given to the poor?" 6 He said this, not because he was concerned
about the poor, but rather because he was a thief, and he had the money
box and would take what was put into it.
7 But Jesus said, "Let her alone, so that she may keep it for the day of
preparation for my burial.[d] 8 The poor you always have with you; but you
do not always have me."
9 When the great crowd of the Jews learned that he was there, they
came not only because of Jesus, but in order to see Lazarus, whom Jesus
had raised from the dead. 10 So the chief priests planned that they would
also put Lazarus to death, 11 because on account of him many of the Jews
were going away[e] and believing in Jesus.

a. Although the Greek has *autō* ("him"), Jesus and not Lazarus is meant, as the rest of the sentence makes clear: "Lazarus was one of those reclining at table with *him*."

b. *Pistikēs*, that which belongs to *pistis* ("faith") and is therefore "faithful, trustworthy," is an unusual characterization for perfume or ointment; it is typically translated "pure" ("genuine, unadulterated"); but Augustine and others assumed that it must (also) be a place name (see also BDAG, *pistikos*).

c. "Rubbed" for *ēleipsen*, also translated "anointed" (NRSV, CEB).

d. The textual variant that replaces *hina . . . tērēsē* ("so that she may keep it") with the perfect tense *tetērēken* (A Γ Δ $\mathfrak{P}^{65}$ f^1 f^{13}; "she has kept it") tries to explain how Mary, having just poured out the perfume, can still be said to keep it.

e. Some translations render *hypēgon* as "deserted" (NRSV, CEB); Barrett (415), suggests, "left their former Jewish allegiance and way of life." But these translations are too strong; *hypagein* ("to go, go away") is frequently used in John (cf. 6:67).

[11:55–57] All the Gospels locate Jesus' crucifixion at the time of Passover. John reports that sojourners go up to Jerusalem before the Passover, one of three pilgrimage feasts,[330] so that they can "purify themselves" (*hagnisōsin*): that is, undergo the appropriate sprinkling (for impurity due to contact with a corpse) and immersion (for other impurity) so that they will be ritually pure for entrance

330. See the comments on 2:13.

to the temple and participation in the sacrifice of the Passover lambs.[331] Later John states that the chief priests will not enter the Praetorium so that they will not be defiled (*mianthōsin*) or become ritually impure (18:28).[332] Only so could one properly keep the Passover.

The Gospel of John speaks of Jewish rites of purification in several places (2:6; 3:25; 11:55; 18:28). These rites prefigure Jesus' cleansing of his followers accomplished by his word, his death, and the Holy Spirit.[333] Following his entry into Jerusalem, Jesus washes his disciples' feet, foreshadowing the cleansing effected by his death. At an earlier Passover, Jesus has purified the temple; at this final Passover, he will complete the cleansing of his disciples. If the pilgrims at Passover need to undergo ritual purification to celebrate the feast, Jesus' disciples will be purified or cleansed by Jesus' death at this final Passover. In preparation for his death, Jesus, the "holy one of God" (*ho hagios tou theou*, 6:69) "sanctifies himself" (*hagiazō emauton*, 17:19) so that his disciples may be sanctified (*hēgiasmenoi*, 17:19) by means of his death. As the Lamb of God who takes away sin, Jesus is without blemish (cf. Lev 1:3, 10; 3:1, 6; etc.) and has no need of cleansing: God's Holy One brings others into the realm of God's holiness.

[12:1–3] Jesus, however, is not to be found in Jerusalem—or at least not yet. Rather, he is once again at the home of Lazarus in Bethany. The curious crowds press to see both Jesus and Lazarus, with the result that Lazarus's life is now also in danger (11:47–48; 12:1, 9, 10–11). Martha serves Jesus and her brother, Lazarus, who is "reclining" (*anakeimenōn*) or "at table" with Jesus.[334] In both Luke (10:38–42) and John, Martha appears as the woman in charge of the household while her sister, Mary, offers Jesus "unconventional expressions of devotion,"[335] which Jesus subsequently defends against her detractors. In John's account, Mary took a pound (*litran*) of the costliest perfume and "rubbed" (*ēleipsen*) Jesus' feet, and then wiped (or dried, *ekmassein*) them with her hair. Mary's posture of attending to Jesus' feet (see 11:32) anticipates Jesus' kneeling at and washing the feet of his own disciples.

331. On the need for purity at Passover, see Num 9:6–12; 2 Chr 30:17–18; Philo, *Mos.* 2.224; *Spec.* 1.261; 2.145–49; Josephus, *Ant.* 6.427. Josephus describes all those who were present at the feast as "pure and holy" (*katharoi kai hagioi*, in *J.W.* 6.425).

332. *Miainō* can refer to the stain or defilement caused both by ritual and moral impurity; see BDAG.

333. Several word groups are used: *hagnizō* ("purify," 11:55); *hagiazō* ("sanctify," 10:36; 17:17, 19); *katharizō, katharismos, katharos* ("cleanse, cleansing, clean," 2:6; 3:25; 13:10, 11; 15:3); *louō* ("bathe," 13:10); *niptō* ("wash," 13:5, 6, 8, 10, 12, 14; cf. 9:7, 11, 15); and perhaps also *baptizō* (since in the LXX *baptizein* refers to washing for the cleansing of ritual impurity; cf. John 1:24–34). See also Bauckham 2007b.

334. Lazarus reclines with Jesus but not necessarily next to him; the "disciple whom Jesus loves" "reclines" next to Jesus (13:23; 21:20); the difference may suggest that Lazarus is not this disciple. For "reclining" at table, see also comments on 13:23.

335. Bauckham 2007c, 179.

While the skin was often anointed or rubbed with oils after bathing, Mary pours perfume on Jesus' feet apparently without first washing them with water.[336] If she or someone else has washed his feet, that act is not mentioned. Mary's pouring of perfume on Jesus' feet, then wiping it off, seems to be a substitute for washing,[337] though perhaps Mary's action should be understood as washing Jesus' feet with perfume. In the *Satyricon*, Petronius (1st c. C.E.) recounts an "unheard-of piece of luxury" when, during a banquet, slaves brought in ointment in silver basins and rubbed it on the feet of those who were reclining at table.[338] Plutarch recounts a magnificent banquet at which the feet of the guests were bathed in spiced wine.[339] Similarly, John portrays Mary as bathing or washing Jesus' feet with costly perfume.

Mary's wiping of Jesus' feet has struck some commentators as odd: Why wipe the perfume off as soon as it is put on? Presumably she is wiping away the excess. Later (John 13) Jesus washes the disciples' feet and dries them with a towel; here Mary pours perfume on Jesus' feet and wipes them with her hair. Mary's anointing of Jesus' feet with costly perfume serves as a counterpoint to Jesus' washing of the disciples' feet: Jesus does not require the cleansing that the disciples need (13:10–11), but he is worthy of this lavish expenditure and act of humble devotion. The narrative stresses not only the perfume's cost and abundance, but also the luxuriousness of Mary's act: the perfume's fragrance filled the whole house, in contrast with the stench of decay about which Martha warned Jesus at Lazarus's tomb (11:39). Although Mary's act prepares Jesus for his burial, his death will not lead to the decay of his body, but to his resurrection. In an oblique way the perfume's fragrance suggests that Jesus would not experience corruption but would be raised to life and to the glory he has had with his Father.

Mary's act of costly devotion prepares Jesus for his burial, but it is not a royal or messianic "anointing."[340] She uses perfume, not oil, as was customary for the "anointing" of Old Testament kings; she rubs the perfume on Jesus' feet, not his head. Furthermore, to describe her act, John uses the verb *aleiphein*. The verb occurs in the New Testament nine times; both Luke and John use it to describe a woman's act of pouring oil or perfume on Jesus' feet (Luke 7:38, 46 [2×]; John 11:2; 12:3).[341] Although *aleiphein* is typically translated

336. For washing or bathing followed by "anointing," see Ruth 3:3; 2 Sam 12:20; Ezek 16:9.

337. In Luke 7:44 Jesus implies that the woman who wept at his feet has effectively washed them. The same passage indicates that, though a standard cultural custom, footwashing was apparently not always practiced: "I entered your house; you gave me no water for my feet." Cf. the comments on the practice of footwashing at 13:1–11.

338. Petronius, *Satyr.* 70.2.

339. Plutarch, *Phoc.* 20.2 (mid 1st c. to early 2d c. C.E.).

340. So also R. Brown 1966, 2:454; Lincoln 2005, 337. Barrett (409) describes it as "a means of expressing the royal dignity of Jesus."

341. Other references in the NT include anointing one's head while fasting (Matt 6:17), anointing the sick (Mark 6:13; Jas 5:14), and anointing Jesus' body at the tomb (Mark 16:1).

"to anoint," another verb may also be translated as "to anoint": *chriein*,[342] from which *Christos* ("the anointed one") is derived.[343] In the LXX these same two verbs, *aleiphein* and *chriein*, are used for various acts of "anointing"—the anointing of one's body after bathing, of sacred objects, or of a priest or king—although *aleiphein* is far less common.[344] When the ceremonial anointing of a king is in view, the verb *chriein* is always used (throughout LXX in 1–2 Samuel; 1–2 Kings; 1–2 Chronicles; Psalms). In these cases, *chriein* typically translates *māšaḥ* ("to anoint"); conversely, *māšaḥ* is almost always translated *chriein*. Consequently, the one who has been anointed is called *māšîaḥ* ("the anointed one") in Hebrew, sometimes translated as (*ho*) *christos* in Greek.[345] In the LXX this term often refers to the currently reigning king of Israel (e.g., 1 Sam 2:10; 24:6 [7 LXX]; 2 Sam 1:14). Although Jesus is unquestionably *ho Christos* (the Messiah) in John, here Mary rubs or smears (*ēleipsen*) Jesus' feet with perfume; she does not anoint (*echrisen*) his head with oil as one would do for a king.

Mary's is an act of devoted service to Jesus, whom she has already addressed as "Lord" and acknowledged as "Teacher" (11:28, 32). When Jesus, rightly called Teacher and Lord (13:14), in turn stoops to wash his disciples' feet, the incongruity is striking: here is the one whose feet were just bathed in the costliest of perfumes! Why, then, should he now take up the task of washing the feet of his own disciples? As we shall see, Jesus' actions arise from both his love of his disciples and his refusal to be bound by cultural norms of honor and status in expressing that love for them.

[4–6] Judas, described both as "one of his disciples" and "the one who was about to hand him over," values the pound (*litran*) of perfume that Mary has poured on Jesus' feet at three hundred denarii.[346] If one denarius is regarded as a day's wage (see Matt 20:2 mg.), then this perfume was worth about a year's wages (allowing Sabbaths and feast days for rest). Mary's is an exorbitant expenditure. She treats Jesus with the honor due to one of high status, even as Nicodemus will prepare Jesus' body for burial by wrapping it in linen along with a hundred pounds (*litras*) of myrrh and aloes (19:39). Mary honors Jesus

342. The verb is found in Luke 4:18; Acts 4:27; 10:38; 2 Cor 1:21; Heb 1:9.

343. Except for its use in 2 Cor 1:21 to describe God's "anointing" Paul and perhaps his fellow apostles, *chriein* always occurs in the NT with reference to God's anointing Jesus.

344. LSJM defines both *aleiphein* and *chriein* as "[to] anoint the skin with oil, as was done after bathing." Each word can also be used to mean "smear" or "cover" (see BDAG; LSJM).

345. In 1 Sam 24:6 ET, e.g., David refuses to harm Saul, "the Lord's anointed" (24:7 MT, *māšîaḥ* YHWH; LXX, *christos kyriou*; cf. *ho kechrismenos*, "the one who has been anointed," Lev 4:3). Apparently in order to avoid the term *christos*, Aquila, a Jewish proselyte who translated the OT into Greek, rendered *māšîaḥ* with *eleimmenos*, a participle cognate with the Greek infinitive *aleiphein*.

346. A *litra*, a Roman pound = 327.45 grams or 12 ounces (BDAG; LSJM); as a liquid measure, about ½ pint (LSJM).

while he is living; Nicodemus honors Jesus through solicitous treatment of his body.

According to John, Judas protests the extravagance because he kept the money box and was a thief (*kleptēs*; see 10:9–10). He is not really interested in giving the money to the poor; he is interested only in having access to the money himself (13:29). Although John calls Judas a thief, he does not mention that Judas betrays Jesus for money (Matt 26:15; Mark 14:11; Luke 22:5). Throughout John, Judas epitomizes those who have fallen away: if they had once believed in Jesus, they do so no longer. Judas thus stands in contrast to Mary: she spends generously what she has to honor Jesus, while Judas greedily grasps what does not belong to him. Mary honors Jesus; Judas betrays him.

[7–8] Jesus rebukes Judas: "Let her alone, so that she may keep it for the day of preparation for my burial." Jesus' defense of Mary is based on her preparation of him for his death and burial. In John's narrative the anointing of Jesus' feet precedes his entry into Jerusalem; his impending death thus becomes the lens that brings his entry and acclamation as king into focus. Jesus is a king whose sovereignty is defined by death and its defeat.

Even so, the statement "that she may keep it [*auto*] for the day of preparation for my burial" is obscure. Presumably "it" refers to the ointment or perfume; however, since Mary has just poured it out on Jesus' feet, how can she also keep it? The problem may be alleviated somewhat if *entaphiasmos* (often translated "burial") is understood as the act of preparing the body for burial, rather than the actual entombment.[347] Because Jesus' death is now imminent, preparation for his burial has already begun. This understanding of *entaphiasmos* in turn implies that the cryptic purpose clause (*hina . . . tērēsē*, "so that she may keep it") does not refer to her keeping this perfume for some future occasion; rather, it explains the purpose of her action here.[348] We could then paraphrase: "Leave her alone. She has kept it for the day of preparation for my burial."[349] Jesus' further statement, "You always have the poor," reflects the sentiment of Deut 15:11: "The poor will never cease out of the land" (RSV)—from which the conclusion may be drawn that one ought to be generous in giving to them (cf. John 13:29). But since Jesus' death is imminent, there is not much more time to render him appropriate honor in this very tangible way.

347. So also R. Brown 1966, 449; and Lincoln 2005, 339 (who cites Gen 50:2–3 LXX). Moloney (1996, 182) cites LSJM (575) for the translation "laying out for burial." BDAG suggests, "the performance of what is customary for burial, preparation for burial or burial itself," citing Mark 14:8; John 12:7. See also Lindars 418–19; Talbert 184.

348. The (admittedly not original) textual variant, "She has kept it," captures the sense of the difficult Greek clause here (so also R. Brown 1966, 449; and Beasley-Murray 205).

349. This reading reflects the explanation given in the Synoptics: that Jesus' body has been anointed *beforehand* (Matt 26:12, *pros to entaphiasai*) or in order to prepare it for burial (Mark 14:8, *eis ton entaphiasmon*).

[9–12] Lazarus has become a curiosity.[350] Not only does a "great crowd of Jews" come to see Jesus; they also want to see the one who has been raised from the dead. The raising of Lazarus has led many to believe in Jesus, thus simultaneously accomplishing the function of the signs in John and exacerbating the very problem that Caiaphas sought to solve by recommending that Jesus be handed over to death. Although the "chief priests" also planned to put Lazarus to death, there is no indication that the plan was carried out. But their intention hints at the fate that Jesus' disciples might expect, since "a servant is not greater than his master" (13:16; 15:20; see 15:18; 16:2; 21:18–19).

Mary's act of devotion is at once unique and exemplary: unique in her preparation of Jesus for burial, exemplary in demonstrating lavish honor of Jesus. Her devotion contrasts sharply with the authorities' unbelief and Judas's treachery, and these varying responses to Jesus again demonstrate the "division" among the people (11:56–57). This division extends to the way in which Jesus' death is perceived: the authorities assume that Jesus' death will discredit him; Judas's eventual betrayal of Jesus will further their designs. Crucifixion was considered by the Romans to be a dishonorable and shameful way to die, and later Roman historians assumed Christianity to be a superstition, discredited in part by the shameful death of its founder.[351] But Mary's lavish gift prepares Jesus for his death: she wishes to honor him, to bring him the glory (*doxa*) due to him (5:23; 11:4; 12:16, 23, 28, 43). In one way or another, all three of these acts—Mary's gift, Judas's betrayal, and the authorities' decision—are oriented toward Jesus' death, even though their understanding of his death varies greatly.

12:12–19 The Coming of the King

After Mary's lavish pouring out of perfume on his feet, Jesus rides into Jerusalem on a donkey while the crowds welcome him with palm branches and royal acclamations. John rather tersely narrates the triumphal entry, remembered on the Christian calendar as Palm Sunday. In fact, in John's narrative the responses of the crowds, Jesus' disciples, and the Pharisees take up more actual space than the account of the entry itself. Furthermore, the entry is framed by responses to Jesus' raising of Lazarus from the dead. Those who were there when Jesus called Lazarus from the tomb bear testimony (vv. 11–12, 17); news of Jesus' great deed lures crowds from Jerusalem (v. 18); the Pharisees react with despair to the enthusiastic response to Jesus and his signs (v. 19).

350. Theophylact imagines that they hoped "Lazarus might bring back a report of the regions below" (*Catena aurea*, ad loc.).

351. Cicero, *Rab. Perd.* 16: "For it is not only the actual occurrence of [the acts constituting crucifixion] but the very mention of them, that is unworthy of a Roman citizen and a free man" (cf. Heb 12:2).

By framing the narrative of the entry itself with these assessments of Jesus' sign in Bethany, John makes it clear that the one who "comes in the name of the Lord" and who is the "King of Israel" comes from God to bring life to his people. Not all perceive this, of course, and there are varying reactions to Jesus, ranging from curiosity (vv. 9, 12, 18) to eager acclamation (vv. 13, 17) to an almost cynical resignation regarding his popularity (v. 19). The significance of what he has done and who he is becomes clear only later, to his disciples, and in light of the Scripture that they come to understand later (v. 16). The acts of Jesus can be reported, but without the lens of Scripture and subsequent reflection on it, they will never be fully understood.

[12:12] On the next day the great crowd that had come to the feast, having heard that Jesus was coming to Jerusalem, **13** took palm branches and went out to meet him, crying out, "Hosanna! Blessed is the one who comes in the name of the Lord, the King of Israel!"

14 Jesus found a young donkey[a] and sat on it, even as it is written, **15** "Do not fear, daughter of Zion. Look, your king is coming, sitting on a donkey's colt!"

16 His disciples did not understand these things at first, but when Jesus had been glorified, then they remembered that these things had been written about him and that they had done these things to him.

17 The crowd who was with him when he called Lazarus out from the tomb and raised him from the dead bore witness. **18** On account of this, the crowd went out to meet him, because they had heard that he had done this sign.

19 Then the Pharisees said to each other, "See, you can do nothing. Look, the world has gone after him!"

a. *Onarion* is the diminutive of donkey; hence, "young donkey."

[12:12–13] Since it is near Passover, a "great crowd" has gathered in Jerusalem. Upon hearing that Jesus is coming, they gather palm branches to welcome him into Jerusalem. Josephus claims that there were about 2,700,200 pilgrims in Jerusalem for Passover (*J.W.* 6.425; cf. 2.280, "not fewer than three million"). While these numbers are assumed to be exaggerations, the numbers of people in Jerusalem did swell during Passover and other pilgrimage feasts. It is not entirely clear whether this is the same "great crowd" that has made its way to Bethany to see Jesus when they heard of the raising of Lazarus (12:9) or who are described as witnesses to it (12:17; 11:19, 31, 45). Because of that deed, Jesus increasingly attracts crowds—many of whom come to believe in him (11:45; 12:11, 17–18). The council's fears about Jesus' ever-increasing notoriety following his raising of Lazarus are proving to be well founded (11:47–48).

Since Passover commemorates the deliverance of the people of Israel from Egypt, it occasioned various protests and uprisings against the ruling powers—a threat intensified by the sheer numbers of pilgrims in the city. For example, Josephus reports that under Archelaus,[352] some Jews protested the execution of their compatriots who, viewing the Roman eagles that had been set up over the entrance to the temple as a pagan defacement of the holy place, had surreptitiously taken them down. A riot ensued, troops were sent in, and several thousand worshipers were killed. As a result, the Romans cancelled the temple sacrifices, including the preparation of the Passover lambs (*J.W.* 2.10–13). Later, under the procuratorship of Cumanus (48–52 C.E.), a Roman soldier infamously "bared his backside" to the Jewish people, leading again to a riot and the subsequent deaths of thousands (*J.W.* 2.224–27; *Ant.* 20.112).[353] Because of the fear of such uprisings, and the possibilities for turmoil and unrest, the Roman procurator and additional troops were typically in residence in Jerusalem during the time of Passover.

A great crowd advanced to meet Jesus with palm branches (*ta baia tōn phoinikōn*) in their hands and the words of the psalmist on their lips. The Greek word *baia* refers to palm branches; the *phoinix* (phoenix) is the date-palm tree.[354] It is John's account that gives us the picture of pilgrims waving palm fronds as Jesus enters the city, in turn giving rise to the day's designation as "Palm Sunday." Palm trees are not common in Jerusalem, although Josephus mentions palm trees (*phoinika*) in abundance at Jericho (*Ant.* 14.54; 15.96). Yet palms appear regularly in ancient accounts of events set in Jerusalem, particularly in association with festive occasions or events at the temple. According to 2 Macc 10:6–7, when the temple was rededicated (165 B.C.E.) after having been retaken in the course of the Maccabean revolt, the Jews came to the temple carrying "fronds of palm" (*phoinikas*); when Judas Maccabaeus's brother Simon captured the citadel and "cleansed it from its pollutions," the Jews entered with "palms" (*baiōn*, 1 Macc 13:51). Palm branches appear frequently on various coins, including those minted by the Hasmoneans, Herod Antipas, and by Bar Kochba in the course of his revolt (132–35 C.E.)—which failed to recapture Jerusalem or rebuild the temple.[355]

Not surprisingly, then, John portrays the crowds carrying palm fronds, hailing Jesus as "King of Israel":[356] the one who might preserve the temple and

352. A son of Herod the Great, Archelaus was ethnarch of Samaria, Judea, and Idumea from his father's death in 4 B.C.E. to his deposition by Rome in 6 C.E.

353. Josephus puts the deaths at 30,000 and 20,000 persons, respectively.

354. Technically, then, the explanatory genitive *tōn phoinikōn* is unnecessary (12:13); but see *T. Naph.* 5.4 and 2 Macc 10:7 for *phoinikas*; 1 Macc 13:51 for *baiōn*.

355. The coins are discussed in Ulfgard 252–56.

356. Palm branches were also linked with Tabernacles (*Jub.* 16.31; Josephus, *Ant.* 3.245; 13.372); Simon bar Kosiba (bar Kokhba) asked for palm branches for Tabernacles from Ein Gedi; and the Mishnah states that Ps 118:25 was recited once a day for 6 days during the Feast of Tabernacles, but 7 times on the 7th day as branches were waved (*m. Sukkah* 4:5). Such details prompt some scholars to place Jesus' entry at Tabernacles: Rubenstein 86–87; Brunson.

the people from foreign threats such as those posed by the Babylonians, the Seleucids, and now the Romans. Little do the crowds who hail Jesus as king know that the authorities have already plotted a different way in which Jesus might save both temple and people. But neither they nor the disciples expect that instead of vanquishing the Romans to accomplish his royal vocation, Jesus will die on a Roman cross.

A quotation from the last of the Hallel Psalms (113–18), "Blessed is the one who comes in the name of the LORD!" (118:26), is found in all four Gospels.[357] In John, as in Mark and Matthew, the citation of the psalm begins with the acclamation "Hosanna!" a transliteration of the petition "Save us" (*hôšîʿâ nāʾ*, 118:25 MT; *sōson dē*, 117:25 LXX). But by the first century, "hosanna" had become an acclamation of praise, rather than a petition for deliverance, as is apparent in its coupled statement, "Blessed [*eulogēmenos*] is the one who comes in the name of the Lord!" (12:13).[358] In the psalm, "the one who comes in the name of the LORD" refers to the pilgrim coming up to Jerusalem, but here Jesus is the one who comes in the name of the Lord. Elsewhere "the one who comes" refers to the coming deliverer, either a king or a prophet (Mal 3:1; Matt 11:3, 14; John 6:14). The crowds in Jerusalem rightly acclaim Jesus as the "King of Israel," echoing Nathanael's acknowledgment of Jesus in those terms early in the Gospel (1:49).[359] In the Old Testament, "King/king of Israel" designates both God as the ultimate sovereign of Israel (Isa 44:6; Zeph 3:15) as well as the earthly king, God's anointed (passim), but in the New Testament it refers only to Jesus (Matt 27:42; Mark 15:32; John 1:49; 12:13). Jesus' identity as king figures prominently throughout John's Passion Narrative (18:33; 19:19–22). What is at stake is not whether Jesus is king, but how he will assume and exercise his sovereignty.

[14–15] Jesus responds to the crowds' acclamations that he is "the King of Israel" by finding a young donkey on which to ride into the city. While Jesus' action is explained by reference to that which "is written," the source of the scriptural quotation is once again puzzling. Although ostensibly a condensed form of Zech 9:9, which urges "daughter Zion" to rejoice because her triumphant king is coming, in John "daughter Zion" is exhorted, "Do not fear," a common scriptural admonition often arising from the assurance of the Lord's presence with his people (cf. Zeph 3:16–17). Throughout John, Jesus' presence

357. According to the Mishnah, the Hallel (Pss 113–18) is closely associated with preparing the Passover Lambs (*m. Pesaḥ.* 5:5–7) and eating the Passover meal (10:6–7).

358. This is one of the rare instances in John where "Lord" refers to God, not Jesus (see comments on 1:23; 6:23).

359. In John there is no mention of David, David's kingdom, or Jesus as the son of David in the account of Jesus' triumphal entry (see Mark 11:10; Matt 21:9, 15; cf. Luke 19:38). As in Nathanael's earlier confession, Jesus is the King of Israel, the Messiah, as the Son of God (see 11:27; 20:31). Brunson (267) also affirms that the crowd expresses "true belief rather than a misguided sense of nationalistic messiahship."

instills courage and hope, especially in the face of hostile forces that might rightly cause fear (6:20; 14:27; cf. also 7:13; 9:22; 12:42; 19:38; 20:19).

The description of Jesus' riding into Jerusalem on a donkey is sometimes understood to correct the misguided hope that Jesus would be a conquering king; as such, he could be expected to ride into Jerusalem on a warhorse, not a humble beast of burden.[360] Indeed, earlier in the Gospel, after the crowd had seen the sign of the multiplication of loaves and fishes and wanted to seize Jesus to make him king, he had withdrawn to be alone (6:14–15). Jesus will not be made king "by force" (6:14 NRSV), and he will not exercise his kingship by force. He comes, as the prophet Zechariah says, "sitting on a donkey's colt," a king who overcomes not by might or power, but by God's spirit (Zech 4:6). As such a king, Jesus welcomes the crowds' accolades.

[16] But the disciples understood all this only later, after Jesus' death and resurrection, when they "remembered" that these things "had been written about him."[361] Their "remembering" is an act of interpretation, rereading this Scripture in light of Jesus and his actions (cf. John 2:17, 22). Here, as elsewhere in the first part of the Gospel (1:1–12:16), John introduces Old Testament quotations with the phrase "as it is written."[362] Jesus' identity as the King of Israel who comes to his people, riding on a donkey and receiving their praise, is written in Scripture. But the fact that his disciples "remember" the Scripture only after Jesus' death and resurrection indicates that now the course of Jesus' life, of the way that events unfolded, will shape *what they remember* and *how they read* the Scriptures. While the texts from the Psalms and the Prophets cited here bear witness to Jesus as the King of Israel, it has become clear in John that he does not seek to become king by force (6:14–15); that as Israel's shepherd Messiah, he exercises his vocation by giving his life in death (10:11–30); and that his "anointing" presages not ascension to a powerful throne but to his death on a cross (12:1–8). Such "remembering" does not merely recall events in the past; it also shapes how those events are remembered and consequently also shapes the corporate life of those who follow the one who is remembered (13:34–35; 15:13).

[17–19] Because a large crowd follows, welcomes, and testifies to Jesus (12:9, 12–13, 17), the Pharisees lament that "the world" might follow him as well (12:19). "The world" derogatorily but ironically characterizes the many

360. Matthew, the only other Gospel to cite Zech 9:9 upon Jesus' entry, retains the description of the king as "humble, and mounted on a donkey" (Matt 21:5). In a culture where most people walked, donkeys or mules are regularly specified as royal mounts (Gen 49:11; Judg 5:10; 2 Sam 13:29; 18:9; 1 Kgs 1:33, 38, 44).

361. See 2:17; 14:26; 15:20; 16:4, and comments at 2:22 above.

362. With the verb *graphein*, 6:31, 45; 8:17; 10:34; 12:14; so also 15:25; cf. *teleioō* with *graphē* in 19:27–28. In connection with Jesus' death, scriptural quotations are introduced primarily with *pleroō* ("fulfill," as in 17:12; 19:24, 36); see comments at 12:38.

who have believed in Jesus. Earlier Caiaphas had upbraided the council for failing to understand the dangers posed by Jesus' actions; now, precisely what the council had feared—that Jesus' actions would continue to draw and incite crowds over which they had no sway—has come to pass. But their fear that "the world had gone after him" will soon come to be realized in a way, and to an extent, that they had not anticipated, as the crowds of Jewish pilgrims in Jerusalem swell to include "the Greeks" who represent the peoples of the world. Rather than bringing an end to Jesus' works and influence, Jesus' death—and resurrection—will signal the beginning of a new, worldwide mission, whose purpose is "to gather into one the children of God who had been scattered" (11:52).

12:20–36 Anticipating Jesus' Death

The hour of Jesus' death and glorification, anticipated almost from the beginning of the Gospel (2:4), has come (12:23). Although others have sought Jesus' life more than once, they have been unable to arrest or kill him precisely because "his hour had not yet come" (7:30; 8:20). That hour would come only in Jesus' proper time, determined in harmony with the will of the Father, from whom Jesus has received the command to both lay down his life and take it up again (10:18). In keeping with the portrayal of Jesus in the Gospel as sovereign over his own destiny, Jesus now sets the course of the final events of his life in motion. The request of "some Greeks" to see Jesus induces him to declare that his death no longer lies in the future; indeed, it is imminent. His hour has come.

> **12:20** Some Greeks were among those who had gone up to worship at
> the feast. **21** They went to Philip, who was from Bethsaida in Galilee,[a]
> and made a request: "Sir, we want to see Jesus." **22** Philip went and told
> Andrew; and Andrew and Philip went and told Jesus.
>
> **23** Then Jesus said, "The hour has come for the Son of Man[b] to be
> glorified. **24** Amen, amen, I say to you, unless a grain of wheat falls into
> the earth and dies, it remains alone. But if it dies, then it bears much fruit.
>
> **25** "Those who love their lives will lose them, and those who hate their
> lives in this world will keep them for eternal life.
>
> **26** "If anyone wants to serve me, let them follow me; where I am, there
> will my servant be. If anyone wishes to serve me, the Father will honor
> them.
>
> **27** "Now I am troubled. And what shall I say? 'Father, save me from
> this hour'? No indeed; for this very reason I have come to this hour. **28**
> Father, glorify your name!"
>
> Then a voice came from heaven, "I have glorified it, and I will glorify
> it again." **29** Then the crowd that was there and heard the voice said that
> it was thunder; but others said that an angel had spoken to him.

30 Jesus answered, "This voice has not come for my sake, but for yours.
31 Now is the judgment of this world; now is the ruler of this world cast
out. 32 And if I am lifted up from the earth, I will draw all people[c] to me."
33 He said this in order to show by what sort of death he would die.

34 Then the crowd said to him, "We have heard from the law that the
Messiah remains forever. How then can you say that it is necessary for
the Son of Man[b] to be lifted up? Who is this Son of Man?"[b]

35 Jesus said to them, "The light is with you only a little while longer.
Walk while you have the light, so that the darkness may not overtake you.
Those who walk in darkness do not know where they are going. 36 While
you have the light, believe in the light, so that you might be children of
the light." After Jesus said these things, he went away and hid from them.

a. Bethsaida (on the northeast side of the Sea of Galilee) was in Batanea, the region governed by Philip the tetrarch; but ancient authors used "Galilee" as a general designation (as in "the Sea of Galilee").

b. Or, "this man."

c. The reading *panta* ("everything, all things") has strong external attestation (including 𝔓[66] א*), but the reading *pantas* ("all people, everyone") has good attestation as well.

[12:20–26] Following the despairing observation of the Pharisees that "the world has gone after him" (v. 19), the introduction of the "Greeks" (v. 20) anticipates the spread of Jesus' following to all the world. Although some understand the "Greeks" as Gentiles, their presence in Jerusalem at Passover suggests that they are Greek-speaking Jews. According to Acts 6:1, the early church contained both "Hebrews" and "Hellenists," Jews distinguished at least by their different native tongues (Aramaic and Greek). Given the character of Bethsaida, the home of Philip and Andrew, as a bilingual town (see comments on 1:44), it is not surprising that they are sought out by those who themselves speak Greek.[363]

They ask simply to "see" or meet Jesus. When Jesus' disciples report this request to him, he seems neither to grant nor deny it, but enigmatically declares that the hour for the glorification of "the Son of Man" (or, "this man")[364] has arrived (cf. 13:1). Earlier, when Jesus declared that he was going away, his interlocutors questioned whether he was going to the Diaspora to teach the Greeks (7:35). The time has now come for that to happen—but only after Jesus' death, when witness may be borne to him in all the world by the power of the Spirit. Following his death, Jesus will indeed draw "all people" to himself (see on 12:32). Since this worldwide mission happens only after Jesus' death, in this Gospel the approach of "some Greeks" indicates

363. See Bockmuehl 2010, 164–65.

364. See Excursus 2: "Son of God, Son, and Son of Man in John."

that the hour of his death and of the consequent extension of his work has now come.

A series of statements interprets the significance and effects of Jesus' death (see also comments at 10:11). First, the "hour" of Jesus' death is the hour of his "glorification" and return to the Father (12:23; 17:5). As noted earlier, crucifixion was considered dishonorable and shameful, but in John's Gospel the cross brings honor or glory—both of which may translate the Greek term *doxa*—to Jesus and to God, because the cross expresses God's love for the world and brings to completion the life-giving work of the Father through the Son.

Second, Jesus' death is necessary (12:24). Even as a grain of wheat must "die" in order to produce fruit, so Jesus must die in order to give life to others. To be sure, a grain of wheat does not actually die; but when it is buried in the earth, an entirely new plant, laden with fruit, may spring up from it.

Third, life comes through death (12:25–26). The good shepherd lays down his life (*psychē*, 10:11) for the life (*zōē*, 10:10, 28) of the sheep. Even as Jesus' death brings life to the world, so those who wish to enter into the eternal life (*zōē*) that Jesus gives do so by losing their own lives (*psychē*), so that God's life becomes their own (12:25; cf. Mark 8:36; Luke 9:25).

Fourth, those who want to serve Jesus must "follow him," and that may require following him on the path to one's own death. The point is graphically illustrated in the encounter of the risen Jesus with Peter. After Jesus cryptically foretells Peter's death at the hands of others, he exhorts Peter, "Follow me" (21:18–22). If Peter wants to serve Jesus, he must follow him, even to his own death.

[27–30] The next section of Jesus' words presents a brief soliloquy, echoing Jesus' prayer in Gethsemane as reported in the Synoptics, but with a decided Johannine twist. Jesus' impending death distresses him ("Now I am troubled," 12:27). In the Synoptic Gospels, Jesus prays for God to remove the cup of suffering and death from him; but in John, Jesus refuses to pray for such deliverance: "And what shall I say? 'Father, save me from this hour'? No indeed; for this very reason I have come to this hour." The obvious differences between Jesus' prayer in Gethsemane, not recorded in John, and his words here manifest John's explicitly retrospective narration of events. The Synoptics recount these events "front to back," so that one reads of the agony of Jesus as he wrestles with his destiny until he ultimately resolves to do God's will, however mysterious or difficult it may be. In John, the events are recounted "back to front," and begin rather than end with Jesus' determination to do God's will. Jesus' distress is recorded in the light of the eventual outcome, namely, that Jesus did God's will in dying to bring life to the world. In his prayer Jesus expresses the result of his life as its very purpose. And the life-giving purpose of Jesus' death cannot be the occasion for grief or agony, even if Jesus will experience both as he carries out God's purposes.

John's style of narrating such events thus coheres with his presentation of the disciples' faith. The disciples comprehend Jesus' mission only retrospectively, because its significance can only be understood when it has been completed in his death, resurrection, and return to the Father. From that vantage point the Gospel recounts Jesus' life and mission; from that vantage point one may grasp who Jesus is, if one is also guided by Scripture and the Spirit. John's narrative is both shaped by and gives witness to the perspective gained from "back to front."[365]

Jesus asks that God will "glorify his name," that is, to glorify God's *own* name or bring honor to himself by means of all that Jesus is about to do (cf. Matt 6:9; Luke 11:2).[366] Clearly the cross is a significant stumbling block in the way of accepting Jesus as God's anointed one. As Paul acknowledges, to speak about a crucified man as God's Messiah sounds exceedingly foolish in the ears of his contemporaries (1 Cor 1:18–25). Paul even counters the charges that Jesus was cursed by God as one who had died on a tree by lodging his "cursed" death in the purposes of God (Gal 3:10, 13, referring to Deut 21:23). John boldly presents the cross as a means of the glorification of God's name, because Jesus' death is the means by which God draws all people to himself. God's glory comes to expression in the cross because God's life-giving purposes are brought to fruition there.

In dramatic response to Jesus' prayer, "a voice came from heaven." God speaks—the only such occasion in John—but, typical of the divided responses to Jesus in the Gospel, some hear an angel while others hear thunder. Elsewhere Scripture does portray God as speaking through an angel or by means of thunder (Exod 19:19; Job 37:2, 5; 40:9; Rev 4:5; 14:2; cf. Sir 43:17); hence the crowds may intuit a divine communication. But their ultimate failure to interpret the voice as God's own, and to discern in Jesus the one through whom God speaks, indicates that, even as the Pharisees are blind to the light of God in Jesus (9:40–41), so here the crowds are deaf to the voice of God (5:37–38). They can neither see nor hear God because they do not see or understand the one who speaks on his behalf and comes in his name. Yet "this voice" has come for their sake. God has spoken so that people may hear the divine confirmation of Jesus the Son. God sends light and speaks his word, not to conceal the mission and identity of Jesus, but precisely to reveal who he is and what his life and death effect.

[31–34] As the means by which both Father and Son are glorified, Jesus' death on the cross signals God's victory over the prince of this world and "will draw" all the peoples of the world to faith in Jesus. Although human powers, both Roman and Jewish, pass judgment on Jesus and condemn him to death, in reality the world's negative judgment upon Jesus becomes a judgment against the world. Because the world has not judged with right judgment (7:24),

365. See "Reading from John's *Perspective*" in the introduction, above.
366. Cf. 13:31; 17:1, 5, where God *glorifies* Jesus.

judgment is passed upon the world. Although the "world" can refer, positively, to those whom God loves (3:16), it also designates those who have rejected the work and mission of Jesus; the world "hates" or rejects Jesus and his disciples (7:7; 15:18–19). Yet this is one and the same world: the world that rejects Jesus is the world that God loves.

Even as "the world" is judged, so is its "ruler."[367] Although there is no explicit identification, the "ruler of this world" is also referred to as "the devil" (8:44; 13:2), a liar and murderer (8:44), and Satan (13:27).[368] Here the world is judged and the ruler of this world is cast out through Jesus' death on the cross (see 16:11; Rev 12:9). With the death of Jesus, it might appear that the forces of evil have conquered, that those who betrayed Jesus have won. But in fact, by means of Jesus' death, the "ruler of this world" is judged, overthrown, cast out. The overthrow and downfall of the powers of evil—be they embodied in Satan, demons, or earthly "principalities and powers"—are part of Jewish and early Christian eschatological expectations (e.g., Col 2:15; Rev 12:9; 20:2). That expectation is echoed here, but also radically revised. In John, the powers of evil are not judged and overthrown by physical force or military might, but by the death of Jesus, itself the manifestation of God's love for the world. The God who loves the world has sent his Son into the world to bring life to it and thus to triumph over the powers of death and darkness. All this happens through and on the cross, where the Son of God is "lifted up" ("exalted") and "glorified" ("honored") as God's life-giving agent. Even as the future judgment is sealed in the present (3:17–18; 5:24), so the future final judgment against evil has been passed in the cross.

By means of his death, Jesus draws "all people" to himself. When coupled with Jesus' previous assertion that only those who are drawn by the Father come to him (6:44), the statement that Jesus draws "all people" links Jesus' sovereign initiative in drawing people to himself to God's own work, as often in the Gospel (cf. 5:26; 10:28–30). "All" (*ta panta*) emphasizes the scope of the divine work: God created all things through the Word (1:3); the true light enlightens all people (1:9); all things are given into Jesus' hands (3:35); and the Father shows the Son all that he is doing (5:20) and has given all judgment to him (5:22).[369] In the work of creation and salvation, the work of the Father and Son is one unified work. The God who creates the world is the God who saves the world.

The point of Jesus' statement that he will draw[370] "all people" to himself is not that he will draw every single person, a point difficult to square with other

367. John refers to the prince/ruler of this world three times (12:31; cf. 14:30; 16:11; *archōn tou kosmou toutou*). In the DSS, Belial stands over against the "prince of lights" (CD V, 18; 1QM XIII, 10; XV, 2–3; XVII, 5–6); in *Jubilees*, Mastema is often called "Prince Mastema" (17.16; 18.9, 12).

368. For the role of the devil in Jewish literature and the NT, see comments on 8:44–47.

369. For further discussion of *panta*, "all things," see comments at 1:3.

370. On the meaning of "draw," see comments on 6:44.

assertions in John (3:18; 5:29; 8:24), but that his work encompasses all the world's peoples (cf. Rev 5:9; 13:7). The extent of that work to "all" people (cf. 10:16) shows the fullness of God's love poured out for the life of the world. The coming of the "Greeks" to see Jesus foreshadows the inclusion of those persons who are not the children of God by virtue of their natural descent but by virtue of their birth from God (1:12–13; 3:3–5; 8:39–40).

Once again Jesus speaks of "being lifted up from the earth" (*hypsōthō ek tēs gēs*, 12:32; cf. 3:14; 8:28). To be "lifted up" refers to the manner of Jesus' death by crucifixion: a cross is physically "lifted" or "raised up" from the earth (see comments on 3:14). To be "lifted up" also signifies the exaltation of Jesus. In the LXX the Greek word *hypsoō* renders a number of Hebrew words that denote "lifting high" in either a physical or figurative sense; in Isaiah, the servant of God is both "lifted up" (*hypsōthēsetai*) and "glorified" (*doxasthēsetai*, 52:13). Thus, when John writes that Jesus speaks of being lifted up "to show by what sort of death he would die," he refers, in the first instance, to the mode of Jesus' death by crucifixion. It is not too far a stretch to imagine that he also intends a secondary reference to Jesus' crucifixion as an elevation to glory.

But the crowd is puzzled at the very mention of Jesus' death. In particular, two challenges or questions are raised having to do with the identity of the Messiah or Son of Man of whom Jesus speaks. First, the crowds assert that "the law" states that the Messiah will "remain forever." Elsewhere in John, "law" can refer to parts of Scripture other than the five books of Moses, as it may here (e.g., 10:34 referring to Ps 82). There are Old Testament passages that speak of the permanent establishment of the Davidic line (e.g., 2 Sam 7:13; 1 Chr 22:10; Pss 89:3–4, 36–37; 110:4; Isa 9:7; Ezek 37:25), and this may be in view here.[371] At least the crowds cannot comprehend a Messiah who would die before completing his messianic task, or whose mission would be accomplished by means of his death on a cross: a Roman instrument of political subjugation and torture.

Second, the crowds seek the identity of "this man" or "Son of Man,"[372] this Messiah who must be "lifted up." Interestingly, here Jesus has spoken of "the Son of Man" but not of the Messiah (12:23); the crowds identify the two figures (v. 34). Whether "Son of Man" in itself designates a heavenly or divine deliverer is greatly contested (cf. *1 En.* 45.3–46.4; 48.2–6; *4 Ezra* 13), but here the phrase clearly refers to Jesus, who will be lifted up on the cross. The answer to the questions "Who is this Son of man?" or "Who is this man who will be glorified and exalted to draw all people to him?" is Jesus (John 12:34), God's agent of judgment (5:27), who lives forever.

371. Echoes of that point are found in *Pss. Sol.* 17.4; *T. Reu.* 6.12; *1 En.* 49.2. In *4 Ezra* 7.28, the Messiah lives 400 years before dying. *Sib. Or.* 3.48–50 speaks of an "immortal king."

372. Greek *ton huion tou anthrōpou* ("the Son of Man"); see Excursus 2: "Son of God, Son, and Son of Man in John."

[35–36] Jesus does not obviously reply to their query, but instead he invites his questioners "to walk in the light" (3:21; 8:12; 11:9–10), because the light will soon be taken away. The point is not that after Jesus' departure there will be neither light nor the possibility of turning toward that light (cf. 12:46), but that the intensity of the light will soon be taken away. With the arrival of Jesus' "hour," the urgency of the call to believe has intensified as well. Jesus' death and the end of his earthly ministry are imminent.

12:37–50 The Summary of Jesus' Public Ministry

John now draws the narrative of Jesus' public ministry to its conclusion. Jesus will turn from signs and public discourse and dialogue to private instruction of his disciples as events unfold that lead to his arrest, trial, and crucifixion. In light of Jesus' coming crucifixion, it may not be surprising that John summarizes Jesus' work by noting the unbelief of his contemporaries: "they did not believe" (v. 37) and "they could not believe" (v. 39). Yet there were some who believed (v. 42; 1:11–13). Jesus came as a light into the world (12:46), to save and not to condemn (v. 47), to speak the words of God (vv. 48–49), and so to bring eternal life (v. 50). Now as always, the light "shines in the darkness" (1:5; 12:46).

12:37 Even though Jesus had done so many signs before them, they did
not believe in him. **38** This was to fulfill the word that the prophet Isaiah
spoke, "Lord, who has believed our report? To whom has the arm of the
Lord been revealed?"

39 Therefore they could not believe, for Isaiah also said, **40** "He has
blinded their eyes and hardened their heart, lest they should see with their
eyes and understand with their heart and turn, and I should heal them." **41**
Isaiah said these things because he saw his glory and spoke about him.

42 Nevertheless, even many of the authorities believed in him, but
because of the Pharisees they did not confess him, so that they would not
be ostracized from the community.[a] **43** For they loved human glory more
than God's glory.

44 And Jesus cried out and said, "Whoever believes in me does not
believe in me but in the one who sent me; **45** and the one who sees me
sees the one who sent me. **46** I have come as a light into the world, so that
no one who believes in me should remain in darkness. **47** I do not judge
anyone who hears my words and does not keep them, for I did not come
to judge the world but rather to save the world. **48** The one who rejects me
and does not receive my words has a judge; the word that I have spoken
will judge that one on the last day. **49** For I have not spoken on my own.
Rather, the Father who sent me has himself commanded what I should say

and speak. 50 And I know that his commandment is eternal life. Whatever I say, therefore, I say even as the Father has told me."

a. Or, "cast out from the synagogue" (Greek, *aposynagōgoi genōntai*; cf. 9:22; 16:2).

[12:37–43] Jesus has done many signs, but as elsewhere in biblical narratives, God's gracious and saving work on behalf of his people does not inevitably produce understanding or faith. Moses laments that although God had done "signs and great wonders" in the land of Egypt, Israel had neither seen nor understood what the Lord had done for his people (Deut 29:2–4). Isaiah speaks of the lack of belief or response to the work and word of God, and John includes two Isaianic quotations here that underscore the negative response to Jesus: "Lord, who has believed our report? To whom has the arm of the Lord been revealed?" (Isa 53:1); "He has blinded their eyes and hardened their heart, lest they should see with their eyes and understand with their heart and turn, and I should heal them" (Isa 6:10).[373] Through Jesus' signs and words, "the arm of the Lord" (God) has been revealed: the Son has made the Father known (see comments on 1:18; 5:37; 6:46; 14:9). Some people have responded with faith (John 1:10–13). But others have not "believed our report," thus fulfilling Isaiah's words that God has "blinded their eyes and hardened their heart." These difficult utterances echo the Johannine note that no one sees or responds to Jesus unless they are taught or drawn by God, unless their eyes are opened to see (see comments on 6:44, 65; 9:38–41; and Excursus 8: "The Johannine Vocabulary of Faith and Discipleship").

Up to this point, citations of Scripture have been introduced with some variation of the formula "as it is written." Now, as the Passion Narrative begins, scriptural citations are regularly introduced with a variation of the phrase "that the Scripture might be fulfilled" (with a form of the verb *plēroō* or *teleioō*).[374] It is particularly important for John, as for other early Christian writers, to stress that Jesus' crucifixion was not an unforeseen or chance happening. Collectively, all these quotations interpret Jesus' death and the unbelief of his contemporaries as reflective of things written in Scripture.

All four Gospels, and also the book of Acts, quote Isa 6:9–10 to explain the lack of response to Jesus or his emissaries. In the Synoptic Gospels this quotation accounts for the failure to understand Jesus' parables; in Acts, it explains the rejection of Paul's preaching.[375] John has recast the prophetic rebuke not as

373. On the function of these dual quotations from Isaiah, see Hengel 1994, 392–93.

374. John 17:12; 19:24, 28, 36–37. There are no explicit quotations from Scripture in chs. 20–21; the only reference to "scripture" is found in 20:9, "For as yet they did not know the Scripture that it was necessary for him to rise from the dead."

375. Matt 13:14–15; Mark 4:12; Luke 8:10; Acts 28:26–27. All these citations maintain the parallelism between hearing and seeing: the people have failed to both hear (understand) and see (perceive) what God has done.

a failure to *hear* and *see*, but entirely as a failure to *see*. Isaiah's word of judgment links or equates hearing and seeing as means of knowing or apprehending the truth:[376] the people will hear, but not understand, see but not perceive; their ears will be heavy and their eyes closed; they will neither see nor hear in order to turn and be healed. John condenses the passage from Isaiah so that it refers only to *seeing*, not to hearing: "He has blinded their eyes and hardened their heart, lest they should see with their eyes and understand with their heart and turn, and I should heal them" (John 12:40, citing Isa 6:10). John then adds the editorial remark, "Isaiah said these things because he saw his glory and spoke about him" (12:41). By eliminating the references to "hearing" in his citation of the passage from Isaiah, and adding the note that Isaiah *saw* Jesus' glory, John highlights the failure of Jesus' contemporaries to see his glory (cf. 1:14; 2:11)—something that Isaiah had not missed. Scripture accounts for the unbelief of Jesus' contemporaries: they "could not" believe, because in writing about those who could not believe, Isaiah had written of them, even as he wrote of Jesus' glory. In Scripture, God's glory refers to a *visual* phenomenon; it appears or is revealed or seen (Exod 33:22; Num 14:22; Isa 66:18–19; Ezek 39:13, 21). John uses the passage from Isaiah to emphasize "seeing" or discerning the glory of Jesus; judgment falls on those who do not perceive it, on those who do not understand him as the one sent (John 2:11; 6:36, 40) to do God's work of bringing light into darkness, life into death.[377]

Greek philosophers and historians also distinguished between the knowledge gained through hearing (secondhand reports) and seeing (firsthand experience). The dictum of the Greek philosopher Heraclitus, "Eyes are surer witnesses than ears," was echoed by ancient Greek historians.[378] But while Dio Chrysostom echoes the sentiment, he also recognizes the greater difficulty of convincing the eyes: "The popular saying that the eyes are more trustworthy than the ears is perhaps true, yet they are much harder to convince and demand much greater clearness; for while the eye agrees exactly with what it sees, it is not impossible to excite and cheat the ear" (*Dei cogn.* [*Or. 12*] 71).

The Jewish exegete Philo also quoted Heraclitus's pronouncement (*Ebr.* 82). He speaks of "the more certain testimony of sight" and declares that "hearing

376. As also in Deut 29:2–4: the people have neither eyes to see nor ears to hear the signs that "the LORD" has done.

377. Thus Hurtado (2003, 380): "Not only is [Jesus] associated with the glory of God, he *is* the glory of God *manifest*."

378. Cited in Diels-Kranz, 22B frg. 101a; ET, "The eyes are more exact witnesses than ears" (in Freeman 131). Heraclitus's observation is cited by Polybius, *Hist.* 12.27.1; cf. 4.2.1–2; see similar sentiments in Herodotus, *Hist.* 1.8; Thucydides, *War* 1.73.2; Lucian of Samosata, *Ver. Hist.* 29; Josephus, *Ag. Ap.* 1.55; *J.W.* 1.1, 3, 22. On the role of the eyewitness as interpreter, see esp. Byrskog 146–76; with specific relationship to the Gospel of John, see M. M. Thompson 2001; and comments on 1:18; 5:37; 6:45–46; 19:35.

stands second in estimation and below sight, and the recipient of teaching is always second to him with whom realities present their forms clear to his vision and not through the medium of instruction" (*Conf.* 57, 148; cf. *Abr.* 57, 61). Philo also draws a contrast between Ishmael and Israel in terms of hearing and seeing, to the detriment of the former:

> "Ishmael" means "hearkening to God." Hearing takes the second place, yielding the first to sight, and sight is the portion of Israel, the son freeborn and firstborn; for "seeing God" is the translation of "Israel." It is possible to hear the false and take it for true, because hearing is deceptive, but sight, by which we discern what really is, is devoid of falseness. (*Fug.* 208)

However valued personal access to an event or person in the form of "seeing" might be, seeing does not guarantee understanding or insight. In John, "sight" becomes the "insight" of faith through God's work and instruction that is granted through reading Scripture, in the community of disciples, following the resurrection of Jesus, and under the tutelage of the Holy Spirit. But as Isaiah lamented, even the Lord's signs "in their presence" (*emprosthen autōn*, John 12:37)[379] did not lead to faith.

And yet "many of the authorities" do believe in Jesus (v. 42). Fearing ostracism from their community, being "put out of the synagogue," they do not confess that faith. Since the Greek *doxa* can be rendered as either "glory" or "honor," here is wordplay not visible in English: John writes that Isaiah saw "his glory" (*ten doxan autou*, v. 41), but that the authorities love "human honor" (*tēn doxan tōn anthrōpōn*) more than "God's honor" (*tēn doxan tou theou*, v. 43). Wanting to preserve their own honor in the eyes of their neighbors, and fearing the dishonor and disgrace that would be theirs as followers of Jesus, these would-be disciples cannot take the step of publicly identifying themselves as those who believe in Jesus. They cannot confess that they see what Isaiah saw. The public ridicule of the man born blind, the threat of being made *aposynagōgos*, and the rift created with his parents—all amply testify that there is a price to be paid for following Jesus, that it is paid in the coin of social ostracism, and that such a price is high indeed.

[44–50] The closing words of Jesus' public ministry summarize his identity and his mission with a series of by-now familiar assertions that present him as the one who represents God, who speaks on behalf of God, and who brings God's light into the world. Not only is he the *representative* sent by the Father (vv. 44, 49); he is also the *representation* of the Father: to see, hear, and believe Jesus is to see, hear, and believe in the Father who sent him

379. See 20:30, "Jesus did many other signs in the presence of his disciples" (*enōpion tōn mathētōn*).

(cf. Excursus 1: "Word and Wisdom in John"). Here, too, Jesus emphasizes that his mission is to save and not to condemn: to bring light (v. 46) and life (v. 50). God's work is ultimately a mission of love for the world (3:16–17), of bringing light in the darkness (9:3–5) and life to counter death (11:4, 40). Eternal life is God's "commandment," what God purposes for the world, and what he has shown and commanded Jesus to say and to do (5:19, 26–30; 6:38–40, 45–47; 7:16; 10:18). Although elsewhere in John the future judgment is brought into the present hour, here that judgment is deferred to "the last day." At that time, Jesus' word will serve as judge (12:48): how one has responded to Jesus' word determines what judgment will be passed, because this word has come from the Father and has been spoken by the embodied Word of God.

The second major section of the Gospel (5:1–12:50), presenting Jesus as the life-giving Son of God, now comes to a close. Repeatedly in this densely packed section of John, Jesus' deeds have borne witness that he is the Son who gives life and gives it abundantly. He enables a man to walk, feeds a multitude of hungry people, accompanies his disciples through stormy seas, opens the eyes of a blind man, and finally, calls Lazarus back from the grave. These signs are God's works since they bring light, wholeness, and life into the world; as such, they bring glory to God, the living Father (6:57).

Jesus' signs are complemented and interpreted by five "I am" sayings ("I am the bread of life," 6:35; "I am the light of the world," 8:12 and 9:5; "I am the door for the sheep," 10:7, 9; "I am the good shepherd," 10:11, 14; and "I am the resurrection and the life," 11:25). These sayings point to Jesus as the one who grants life because he himself has and is the very life of God (1:5; 5:25–26; 11:25). Concentrated in this section are also the so-called absolute "I am" sayings (that is, those with no predicate), which echo God's absolute claims that he is the only God, creator of all that is. Ultimately Jesus' claims to have and to give the eternal life that God alone has and gives, and that he is one with God in the unity of their saving work, are deemed blasphemous, leading to attempts to stone him (8:58; 10:30–31).

Jesus' claims demand a reconfigured perception of God's identity so as to include Jesus. His claims also redefine God's people, heretofore identified as the descendants of Abraham (8:37–58) and those faithful to the law of Moses (5:45–46; 7:19–23; 9:28–29). Because the Father and Son are one, God's people are now defined not only as those who rightfully claim Abraham as their father, but also as those who imitate Abraham in welcoming Jesus; they believe in the Son as they believe in the Father. God's people are those who believe that Moses and the law are ultimately pointers to Jesus and interpreted by Jesus, and they follow him as the one true teacher and prophet of God.

Jesus' signs and words are set against the background of major feasts on the Jewish calendar, including Sabbath, Tabernacles, Hanukkah, and Passover. The rituals and ceremonies that mark these days are now understood to prefigure Jesus in terms of what God gives and accomplishes through him. Hence they are properly understood in their relationship to the messianic mission and identity of Jesus. They, too, play a role in John's redefinition of the contours of the people of God. Each festival commemorates God's gifts to and deliverance of his people, as well as adumbrates the gifts of God in Jesus for his people and for all the world.

The more that Jesus presses his claims, the more the disciples desert him—and the more the authorities seek to silence him. Although Jesus' work and word continually divide the people, ultimately he intends to gather all God's children together (11:52). His mission includes "his own," the people of Israel, the offspring of Abraham, but it is not limited to them; he seeks "the other sheep not of this fold" (10:16), those beyond the boundaries of Israel, so that they too may be numbered among the children of God (1:12–13), because the Word of God has become flesh to give light and life to all the world (6:51; 8:12; 9:5). God's love for the world created through the Word manifests itself in God's life-giving purposes: in those purposes one sees the glory of the Father and of the Son.

John 13:1–17:26
Jesus and His Disciples

Jesus' hour, anticipated throughout the Gospel (2:4; 7:30; 8:20), has come at last (12:23; 13:1). Knowing that his death is imminent, Jesus prepares his disciples for his departure in deed, word, and prayer. For the first time in the Gospel, the disciples are told that they will be unable to find or follow Jesus (13:33, 36): he will be absent from them. This stands in marked contrast to the call of the first disciples, who were invited by Jesus to "come and see" (1:39) and to "follow me" (1:43; cf. 10:27; 12:26). Yet Jesus promises that he will continue to be present with them, albeit in new ways. Preparing his disciples for his absence, Jesus instructs them on how they are to live.

First, however, Jesus eats a last meal with his disciples. During this meal, Jesus disrupts the ordinary course of events by taking up a basin and towel and washing his disciples' feet. In doing so, Jesus exemplifies the disposition of self-giving love that must characterize their life together. But this act makes its lasting impact because it is a figure of Jesus' death (13:34–35; 15:12–13). In it, Jesus leaves the disciples with an image of the service rendered to them, epitomized in his death on the cross, urging them to serve one another out of love and without regard to preservation or enhancement of their own status (13:1–20, 34–35; 15:13; 17:21–22).

Second, Jesus speaks at great length about his departure from this world, his absence from the disciples (13:33, 36; 14:1–5, 28; 16:5, 16–20, 28; 17:11) and their need to remain steadfast, to abide in him (15:1–9), if they are to exercise their vocation of bearing faithful witness in and to the world. In bearing witness they will endure the hostility of "the world," as he has (15:19–24; 16:1–2). Although Jesus will depart, the disciples will not be alone: Jesus himself will be with them (14:18–20, 23, 28), as will his Father (14:23), and the Paraclete, who will continue to guide them in understanding the truth that has been embodied in Jesus (14:16–17, 26; 15:26–27; 16:8–13).

This discourse belongs to a genre called either "farewell speeches" or "testaments," found in biblical, Jewish, and Greco-Roman sources.[1] Such speeches,

1. They share features with other literary genres, such as the literary symposium; for discussion of genre, see Segovia 1991, 5–20; Attridge 2002, 10, 17–18; Parsenios 2005; and comments below.

often uttered on the brink of one's own death, provide a vision of hopes for the future, through a combination of warnings, exhortations, and blessings. These words of farewell are rhetorically crafted not simply to say "good-bye," but also to elicit a certain kind of conduct from one's family or people and to leave the vision of such conduct as a legacy. So Jesus leaves his disciples a legacy that begins with his love for them and issues in their mutual love.

Finally, Jesus prays for his own consecration for what lies before him (17:1–5) and for the consecration of the disciples, so that they might remain unified and steadfast in his absence (17:9–23); the unity for which he prays will be an outgrowth of his unity with the Father. But the disciples are not only to look inward or to each other. Empowered by the Spirit, and in their communion with the Father and the Son, they are to look outward to the world that God loves. They are sent into the world even as Jesus was sent, bearing witness to the light and life of God (17:18).

Thus in deed, word, and prayer, Jesus portrays the kind of community that he wishes the disciples to cultivate after his departure. Numerous exhortations are directed toward inculcating the behaviors and dispositions that the disciples need to fulfill the mission given them by Jesus. They are to remain steadfast in faith in him, imitating his generous love, and guided by the Spirit of truth, in order that they might bear witness to Jesus' life-giving love. But these discourses also make it evident that in order to sustain their commitments, the disciples will need the constant presence of Jesus, his Father, and the Spirit. In fact, without the life that flows from the Father, to and through the Son, enlivened by the Spirit, the disciples will fail to bear fruit: they will die. But Jesus' last words, while admonishing the disciples in face of troubles to come, intend to encourage, console, and assure the disciples that they will not be alone and that they can be confident of Jesus' presence and of their eventual participation in the life of God with him.

13:1–30 Jesus' Final Meal with His Disciples

All four Gospels narrate a final meal of Jesus with his disciples immediately before his arrest. In the Synoptic Gospels, the meal is Passover (Mark 14:12–14; Matt 26:17–18; Luke 22:8) and includes the "words of institution" over the bread and cup that signify Jesus' body and blood. In John, the meal is not described as Passover (see comments on 18:28; 19:14–16, 31, 42),[2] and neither the bread and cup nor the "words of institution" are part of the meal. Earlier in the Gospel, Jesus had promised that his flesh and blood provide true life (6:35–51); but at the point where the other Gospels describe Jesus as giving

2. John thus apparently sets the events of Jesus' last week 24 hours earlier than do the Synoptics; for arguments to the contrary, see Blomberg 186–88, 246–48, 254–56; Ridderbos 454–57.

his disciples the bread and cup, John features Jesus washing his disciples' feet (13:1–11). These are two such different accounts of Jesus' last meal that it is easy to argue that these are simply two different last meals, if it were not that each leads directly to Jesus' arrest, trial, and crucifixion.[3]

There are some particularly striking resonances between John's account and Luke's account of the Last Supper that show how, in their different ways, Luke and John offer theological interpretations of Jesus' death as they recount Jesus' last meal with his own. Luke sets the dispute about greatness, found at an earlier point in Mark's Gospel, at the Last Supper (cf. Mark 10:32–45; Luke 22:24–27). Jesus' instructions to serve one another are epitomized in his own example—"I am among you as one who serves" (Luke 22:27)—recalling his earlier, surprising benediction on those faithful slaves who will be served by their master (Luke 12:37). Jesus' words of instruction and blessing to his disciples in the Gospel of Luke are enacted in John's description of Jesus washing his disciples' feet: the master upsets the commonly accepted social hierarchy, acting as a servant of his disciples. In both the Lukan and Johannine accounts, Jesus' actions and words at his last meal with the disciples presage and interpret his death on the cross in ways congruent with his earthly ministry.

13:1–20 Jesus Washes His Disciples' Feet

Footwashing was practiced in both Jewish and Greco-Roman contexts, and for many of the same reasons:[4] as a means of personal cleanliness, as an act of hospitality, and as part of ritual purification for priests and worshipers in cultic settings. As an act of personal hygiene, hands and feet were washed more frequently than the rest of the body since they also become dirtier more easily.[5] As an act of hospitality, footwashing offered guests the opportunity, such as they would have had in their own homes, to wash their feet after travel. Footwashing could be done by the guest or by a servant or other person for the guest.[6] Finally, footwashing was often part of the preparation of a priest or religious functionary for participation in cultic rituals. For example, according to the Mosaic law, priests are to wash their hands and their feet "so that they

3. Paul also locates the supper in which Jesus set forth the bread and cup as his body and blood on "the night in which he was betrayed" (1 Cor 11:23–25).

4. See Thomas; Bauckham 2007a.

5. Seneca, *Ep.* 86.12 (in LCL, *Seneca the Younger*, 5:317–19).

6. Eurycleia, Odysseus's aged nurse, washes his feet when he arrives in disguise (*Od.* 19.344–48, 353–60, 376, 505); Abraham requests water so that his guests may wash their feet (Gen 18:4; cf. 19:2; 24:32; cf. Tob 7:9; Luke 7:44). Abigail offers to wash the feet of David's servants (1 Sam 25:41). In the Jewish novella *Joseph and Aseneth*, Joseph's feet are washed by servants before a meal (*Jos. Asen.* 7.1), and then later by Aseneth, the Egyptian princess, who declares herself to be Joseph's maidservant (*Jos. Asen.* 20.1–5).

may not die" (i.e., because they had entered the holy place unwashed; Exod 30:19, 21).

Here Jesus performs an act of service typically rendered by a slave: he will soon die a death suffered by slaves, death by crucifixion. But this very death completes the disciples' cleansing by Jesus. Jesus walks this path, and he walks it willingly, because of his love for his disciples. In turn he calls them to imitate his service of love as they follow him. In washing his disciples' feet, Jesus makes it plain that the structures of status and honor that govern society, played out in customs of hospitality where those of inferior status wash the feet of their superiors, are not to hold sway among his followers. Jesus' disciples are to follow him and, in doing so, to learn the patterns of their life together from him (13:14–16; cf. 13:34–35; 15:13).

Earlier in the Gospel, Jesus had spoken of the necessity of "eating his flesh" and "drinking his blood" in order to have life (6:51–58). Now he insists that he must wash the feet of his disciples in order for them to have "a part with him" (13:8). While the footwashing clearly provides a model for the disciples to emulate, its function is not merely exemplary: it also prefigures Jesus' death as an act of service and self-giving love that completes his cleansing of his disciples through his word, deed, life, and death, thus binding them for all time to him. The footwashing shows that Jesus' death completes the purification of the disciples, even as in the Synoptic accounts Jesus' body and blood are given for the forgiveness of sins (Matt 26:28) and to seal his covenant with his disciples (Matt 26:28; Mark 14:24; Luke 22:20).

13:1 Before the Feast of the Passover, when Jesus knew that his hour had
come to leave this world to go to the Father, having loved his own who
were in the world, he loved them to the end. **2** And during supper, when
the devil had already decided that Judas, son of Simon Iscariot,[a] would
hand Jesus over,[b] **3** Jesus—knowing that the Father had put all things into
his hands and that he had come from God and was going to God—**4** stood
up from supper, laid aside his garments, and taking a towel, wrapped it
around himself.

5 Then he put some water into a basin and began to wash the feet of
his disciples and to dry them with the towel tied around him. **6** He came
to Simon Peter, who said to him, "Lord, are *you* going to wash *my* feet?"

7 Jesus replied, "At present you do not understand what I am doing,
but you will understand later."

8 Peter said to him, "You shall never wash my feet!" Jesus replied, "If
I do not wash you, you will have no part in me."

9 Then Simon Peter said to him, "Lord, not my feet only but also my
hands and my head!"

10 Jesus replied, "The one who has bathed does not need to wash, except
for his feet,[c] for he is clean all over. And you are clean—but not all of you."
11 For he knew the one who would hand him over; therefore he said,
"Not all of you are clean."

12 When he had washed their feet and had taken up his garments and
reclined again, he said to them, "Do you know what I have done for you?
13 You call me 'Teacher' and 'Lord,' and you are right, for indeed I am
[both]. 14 If I, then, your Lord and Teacher, have washed your feet, you
also ought to wash one another's feet. 15 For I have given you an example
so that you will do what I have done for you. 16 Amen, amen, I tell you,
the slave is not greater than the master nor is the one who is sent greater
than the one who sent him. 17 If you know these things, blessed are you
if you do them.

18 "I am not speaking about all of you: I know whom I have chosen.
But the Scripture must be fulfilled: 'The one who has eaten my bread has
lifted his heel against me.' 19 I tell you this now, before it happens, so that
when it happens you will believe that I am. 20 Amen, amen, I tell you,
whoever receives one whom I sent receives me, and whoever receives
me receives him who sent me."

a. Reading the nominative *Ioudas*, as in $\mathfrak{P}^{66}$ B א. *Ioudas* is then the subject of the *hina* clause ("that Judas, [son of] Simon of Iscariot, would hand over [Jesus]"). Further, "[son] of Simon Iscariot" rather than "Judas Iscariot" is also found in $\mathfrak{P}^{66}$ א B and is supported by readings elsewhere in John (6:71; 13:26) that take "Iscariot" as the modifier of "Simon," Judas's father, and not of Judas himself.

b. For the translation of *paradidōmi* as "hand over" rather than "betray," see textual notes at 6:64; 18:30; 19:11, 16.

c. Many important MSS, including $\mathfrak{P}^{66}$ B C D, include "except for his feet" (*ei mē tous podas*); that qualification is missing in א. Commentators who favor the longer reading include Thomas 1991, 19–25; Carson 1991, 464–66; Ridderbos 462; Keener 2:909 n. 126; Lincoln 2005, 369–70; and Michaels 729–30.

[13:1–4] It is almost Passover (v. 1). Jesus eats a last meal with his disciples, but it is not the Passover meal, which will be eaten after Jesus has been crucified and buried (18:28; 19:14). Throughout the Gospel, Jesus' hour has been anticipated but deferred (2:4; 7:30; 8:20); now it has come. Earlier the hour of Jesus' death had been called the hour of his glorification (12:23, 27–28); now it is the hour of his return to the Father. Once again, John has narrated the events of Jesus' life "back to front," already taking into account the resurrection of Jesus, and assigning to these events the meaning that they would come to have in early Christian interpretation of them. Jesus' death is not the end of life, but the completion of his mission and return to the Father from whom he has come.

Neither is his life taken from him: he laid it down "on his own" (10:18) because of his love for "his own."

John is the only Gospel that speaks of the death of Jesus in terms of love, be it the love of God for the world (3:16) or the love of Jesus for his own (13:1, 34–35; 15:13; cf. Gal 2:20; 1 John 4:7–21). In context "his own" (*tous idious*) refers to Jesus' disciples but does not deny that the people of Israel are "his own" (cf. 1:11 and comments there) or that God's love reaches to the whole world (3:16). The phrase here translated "to the end," *eis telos*, may have either a temporal sense ("to the end [of his life]") or an adverbial sense ("fully, completely"). In John, since Jesus' final words from the cross are "It is finished" (*tetelestai*, 19:30), *eis telos*[7] may well mean "to the end of his life." Jesus has loved his own and will continue to love his own until his death, but precisely in that death he will reveal his love in the fullest way possible: by giving up his life for his friends (15:13). His disciples are to love as he loved, by giving themselves for each other (13:34–35). In the Greek, 13:1 contains a single long sentence with multiple prepositional phrases and subordinate clauses, all modifying the main verb and its object: "he loved them [his own]" (*ēgapēsen autous*). Everything else modifies and explains that simple declaration: the grammar of John's sentence is the logic of Jesus' passion.

Not only does Jesus know that the hour of his departure (his death) has come, but he is also aware that the events that will bring it about will be set in motion by one of his own disciples. Anticipating Jesus' betrayal, "the devil" intrudes into the narrative (13:2)—not surprisingly, since elsewhere Judas is named "a devil" (6:70), and those who do not remain faithful in following Jesus are said to have the devil as their father (8:30–31, 44; see comments there). "The devil" is later called "Satan" (13:27; cf. Rev 12:9, "that ancient serpent, who is called the Devil and Satan") and is also referred to "as the ruler of this world" (12:31; 14:30; 16:11). As in Revelation (12:9), the "devil" or "Satan" is the great deceiver of the world: the devil's work leads to defection and unbelief.[8]

Yet it is difficult to discern exactly what the devil is understood to do here. The Greek phrase *diabolou ēdē beblēkotos eis tēn kardian*, if rendered quite literally, yields the translation "the devil had already put it into the heart," without specifying whose heart is in view: is it the heart of Judas or the heart of the devil himself? This may be a way of stating that "the devil had already decided" (that is, "put it into his [the devil's] own heart"), and that is the translation adopted

7. *Telos* and *tetelestai* are cognates.

8. See comments on John 8:44–47; 12:31; cf. Matt 4:1–11; Luke 4:1–13; 8:12; Acts 13:10; Eph 6:11; 1 Tim 3:6–7; 2 Tim 2:26; 1 John 3:8–10; 1 Pet 5:8–9; Rev 12:9; *Jub.* 10.1–4; 11.5; *1 En.* 54.6; 4 Macc 18:6–8.

here.[9] This reading takes the *hina* clause ("that Judas would hand over") as indicating the content of what the devil decided, with *Ioudas* as the subject of the verb "hand over"; thus the entire sentence would read, "The devil had already decided that Judas . . . would hand Jesus over."[10] But for John, that does not let Judas off the hook; Judas is not merely a pawn of the devil. As noted, the devil often leads to and incites sin, especially in the form of disobedience or apostasy. But even if the source or cause of sin lies outside the individual, that does not excuse the sin. In fact, sinful deeds demonstrate the need for release from the powers that determine or incite sinful behavior that incurs guilt or punishment (8:34; Rom 3:9; 6:6–10). Hence the ruler of this world must be judged and overthrown (12:31; 14:30; 16:11).

Jesus knows "that the Father had given all things into his hands," a statement that echoes other assertions in the Gospel (cf. 3:35; 5:20; 6:37, 39; 10:29; 12:32; 15:15; 16:15; 17:10); he has the power to lay down his own life and take it up again (10:18). Although numerous other human agents act in the drama that leads to Jesus' crucifixion, he will "lay down his life," as he now lays aside his garments in order to wash the feet of his disciples. He does so in full knowledge of his origins and destination: he has come from God to carry out his mission and, having carried it out, he will return to God. The cross is not an impediment to that mission, but the means by which he carries it out.

[5–11] During supper, Jesus begins to wash his disciples' feet.[11] Peter objects. The address to Jesus as "Lord," and the emphatic placement of the Greek pronouns *sy* (you) and *mou* (my) at the beginning of the question, articulate Peter's objection: "Lord, are *you* going to wash *my* feet?" (*Kyrie, sy mou nipteis tous podas?* 13:6). In the strongest possible terms, Peter then also declares that *the Lord* will "never wash *my* feet!" (v. 8). A person of superior status—be it master, parent, husband, or teacher—does not wash the feet of a subordinate—servant, child, wife, or pupil.[12] Although the degrading or humiliating aspect

9. See LXX: Job 22:22, *analabe . . . en kardiai sou* ("Lay up . . . in your heart"); 1 Sam 29:10, *mē thēs en kardia sou* ("Put no evil in your heart" = "Do not think evil thoughts"). So also Moloney 1998a, 13 n. 39.

10. So, e.g., Barrett 439. But if one adopts one of the textual variants (in 13:2) that declines "Judas" in the genitive case and takes "the heart" (*tēn kardian*) as referring to Judas's heart, then one could translate, "The devil had already put it into *the heart of Judas* to hand Jesus over." Most modern versions adopt this second way of construing the Greek but vary in rendering "put into the heart." Thus the NABRE reads "induced," but other versions (NIV, TNIV, NLT) soften that verb to "prompted"; CEB reads "provoked."

11. Ordinarily footwashing takes place upon arrival in the house, or before the meal (see Luke 7:44; Tob 7:9); that Jesus does this "during supper" points to the deliberately symbolic and provocative character of the action.

12. Still, such an act might in theory be contemplated, at least among friends or peers: "In friendship, those who are superior should lower [*submittere*] themselves, so, in a measure, should they lift up their inferiors" (Cicero, *Amic.* 72).

of this task should not be overemphasized, Jesus' action clearly demonstrates a reversal of role and status,[13] in which he identifies with those of lowly status, those who serve others.[14]

When Peter protests Jesus' action, Jesus informs Peter that later ("after these things," *meta tauta*, v. 7) he will understand what Jesus is doing. Peter seems to understand well enough that Jesus is breaking the boundaries of normal social conventions in washing his disciples' feet, serving when he ought to be served. What, then, remains for Peter to understand, and when will he understand it? Elsewhere in John, the capacity to understand certain incidents follows Jesus' resurrection (2:22; 12:16), or depends on insight into the Scriptures (2:22; 12:16; 20:9), or the giving of the Spirit (14:26; 16:13). "After these things" must refer to the time after Jesus' death and after sufficient time has passed for its significance to register.

What Peter does not understand, what he will comprehend only "after these things," is that even as washing another's feet cleanses them, so Jesus must cleanse his disciples so that they may belong to him (v. 8). The footwashing itself signifies, but does not accomplish, that cleansing. It is Jesus' death on the cross, constantly in view in the Gospel since the raising of Lazarus, that completes their cleansing. Footwashing, a service that a slave can be expected to render to a master, foreshadows and interprets Jesus' death, because even as Jesus performs the service of a slave, on the cross he will die the death of a slave; even as he willingly washes his disciples' feet, so he willingly lays down his life for them. Such insight would not be evident from the spectacle of Roman crucifixion, any more than Jesus' washing of his disciples' feet would suggest anything other than that he was performing this menial task for them. But like one of Jesus' signs, it points beyond itself: footwashing and crucifixion become mutually interpretive.

Jesus' death, interpreted as a selfless act of service and sacrifice, provides a model for the disciples to emulate (John 15:13; 21:17–19). The disciples are to love one another as Jesus has loved them (13:34–35). Such love will include acts of service, such as washing another's feet; and it may be manifested supremely, as Jesus' love was, in death (15:13; 1 John 3:16). Peter cannot now know that someday his path will follow that of his "Teacher and Lord," and that his fate will mirror his master's (John 21:18–19). Jesus' promise to Peter that "later you will understand" refers not only to a time after the Last Supper, but also to "a dimension of the story that [Peter] will only learn to understand over a long period and in a way that is painful."[15] Peter will understand what

13. See Mark 9:35; 10:42–45; Matt 18:1–4; 23:11; Luke 9:48; 22:24–26.

14. One of Pompey's companions, Favonious, washed the statesman's feet when Pompey had no servant to perform the task (Plutarch, *Pomp*. 73.6–7).

15. Ridderbos 459.

Jesus has done in laying down his life for him as he himself serves his fellow disciples and lays down his own life for his master (cf. 1 Pet 2:21). Jesus' words that Peter will understand "later" refer not only to insight gained through time and understanding of the Scripture, but even more to the lived experience of costly discipleship.

In response to Peter's emphatic objection, "You shall never wash my feet!" Jesus insists, "Unless I wash you, you will not belong to me." "Belong to me" translates *ouk echeis meros met' emou* ("you will have no part with me," John 13:8). *Meros* may mean "part, share, portion"; at a number of places in the New Testament, it refers to the "share" or "part" one has either in final judgment or condemnation (Matt 24:51; Luke 12:46; Rev 20:6; 21:8; 22:19).[16] To have a share in Jesus is to belong to him, and belonging to Jesus depends on his cleansing death. Peter's reply—"Lord, not my feet only but also my hands and my head!"—expresses his sincere desire to remain a follower of Jesus. If Jesus wishes to wash his feet, why not his hands and head as well! But Jesus pushes the conversation and action back toward the original act: he desires only to wash Peter's feet. In other words, Jesus is resolutely determined to carry out *this* act that demonstrates his love for his own, portraying it in the form of service that overturns human categories of judging (7:24) and human standards of glory or honor. In his last action among them, he will "present himself to his disciples, as he leaves them, for all time to come in the form of a servant."[17]

In many ways, Jesus' reply to Peter in 13:10 ("The one who has bathed does not need to wash, except for his feet, for he is clean all over. And you are clean—but not all of you") determines the meaning of the footwashing. Yet understanding these words is complicated by important textual variants. In spite of the strong textual evidence for adopting the so-called longer reading that includes the phrase "except for his feet," a number of commentators have argued that it is a later addition that actually misconstrues the meaning of Jesus' footwashing.[18] Citing the Johannine penchant for synonyms, they understand the verbs for washing (*louō* and *niptō*, "bathe" and "wash") as interchangeable. Jesus then effectively says, "The one who has bathed [*ho leloumenos*] has no need to wash [*nipsasthai*] again because he is already clean." Understanding the footwashing to symbolize Jesus' death on the cross, they interpret Jesus' insistence that he must wash Peter's feet so that Peter may "have a share" in him, to mean that Jesus' death on the cross accomplishes Peter's salvation. Nothing further is needed. By this argument, whoever added "except for

16. The LXX speaks of the Lord as "my portion [*meris*]" (Pss 15:5 [16:5 ET]; 118:57 [119:57]). Ignatius prays that his "portion" (*meros*) may be in God (Ign., *Pol.* 6.1). Here, the "portion" of the disciples is "with" Jesus.

17. Ridderbos 460.

18. Hoskyns 438–39; Bultmann 1971, 469; Barrett 441–42; R. Brown 1970, 567–68; Schnackenburg 3:20–22; Lindars 451; Beasley-Murray 229; Moloney 1998a, 15 n. 44.

his feet" failed to see that the two verbs (*louō*, *niptō*) are synonymous and thus failed to understand that the footwashing symbolizes all that Jesus' death accomplishes. Furthermore, the addition of the phrase "except for his feet" is thought to intrude into the context, since it undercuts the declaration that one who has washed "is entirely clean."

But the shorter reading ("whoever has bathed has no need to wash") does not explain what Jesus is actually doing: washing the disciples' feet. He is not "bathing" the disciples. The so-called longer reading, "The one who has bathed [*ho leloumenos*] has no need to wash [*nipsasthai*] *except for his feet*," fits perfectly with the practices of footwashing. One bathes the whole body less frequently than one washes the body's extremities. Whether undertaken for cultic purity, as an act of hygiene, or as a sign of hospitality, footwashing is a necessary if limited washing. Moreover, there is ample evidence that the verbs *louein* ("to bathe") and *niptein* ("to wash") were commonly distinguished, and distinguished exactly as here in John: one *bathed* the body; one *washed* the feet.[19]

But if the disciples need to have their feet washed, then how are they "clean all over"? "Clean all over" does not need to mean that every part of the body is as clean as it can be. Rather, that phrase suggests that the disciples have previously "bathed" and so "are clean all over," but now need to have their feet "washed." Those who have taken a bath before leaving home are "clean all over" and only need to wash their feet upon arriving at their destination. In the context of John's Gospel, the disciples have been "bathed" or made clean by the words of Jesus, words that have led them to believe in him and thereby have life (15:3). One of the disciples, however, has abandoned Jesus and so turned away from those life-giving words (6:66–71). That one is, of course, Judas; hence, "not all of you are clean."

How, then, does the footwashing depict the death of Jesus? Here we again take our cue from John 19:30, "It is finished!" Jesus' words from the cross indicate that his death brings the mission entrusted to him by the Father to its completion. That mission is to make the Father known (1:14; 17:6), to glorify the Father (12:28; 17:4), to manifest the Father's love (3:16; 17:26), and to bring life to the world (3:16; 10:10). All these things are accomplished by means of Jesus' life, from incarnation to final glorification, including his words,

19. See the entries under *louō* and *niptō* in BDAG, which show that *louō* regularly refers to bathing, while *niptō* refers to washing parts of the body, including those contexts in which they are used together; see also LSJM under *louō*, and this comment under *nizō* (the earlier classical form of *niptō*): "[The word is] commonly used of persons washing part of the person, while *louomai* is used of bathing, *plynō* of washing clothes." In Exodus, priests take a complete bath (*louō*, 29:4), followed by the (partial) washing of hands and feet (*niptō*, 30:17–21; reference to the routine observance of this requirement can be found in 40:30–32); so also *T. Lev.* 9.11: "Before you enter the sanctuary, bathe; while you are sacrificing, wash; and again when the sacrifice is concluded, wash"; and *m. Yoma* 3:2–4, 6; 4:5; 7:3.

signs, death, and resurrection. Jesus' death completes his mission (19:30) as the life of the world gives himself over to death, even as the shepherd gives up his life for the sheep (10:11, 15, 17–18), or as a grain of wheat falls into the earth and dies (12:23–25), so that there may be an abundant and fruitful life (10:10). Without that death, without the cross, the work remains unfinished; there will be no life. Jesus must undertake this act of service for his disciples' sake.

[12–15] When Jesus has finished washing the disciples' feet, he takes his place again at the table with them and instructs them that what he has done is to serve as an example (*hypodeigma*, "pattern, model," v. 15) for them. Jesus has willingly laid aside the prerogatives and dignity accorded his status as Teacher and Lord in order to wash his disciples' feet. Similarly, in the community of Jesus' followers, conduct toward the other is to be governed by love rather than the preservation of one's own status or honor. Jesus' disciples are to think not of what is due to them—in Jesus' case, proper regard for him as Teacher and Lord—but instead to serve one another in the mundane practices of life. Washing someone's feet is neither heroic nor remarkable. The love and service to which Jesus calls his disciples will work itself out primarily in the routines of daily living.

But what does Jesus actually intend for his disciples to do? There are at least three options, not necessarily exclusive. First, Jesus' command to do what he has done for them can be taken literally, so that the disciples are to wash each other's feet in the course of their ordinary life together, as an act of extending hospitality and care for the other.[20] Second, the command can be taken literally to institute a churchly practice alongside baptism and the Lord's Supper.[21] Third, the command can be taken to refer to acts of service generally: even as Jesus has washed his disciples' feet in humble service, they are to perform similar acts of kindness for others whenever the need arises. Jesus' words are typically interpreted as a general admonition to "serve each other" in various forms; yet it would be odd indeed for Jesus to have commanded his disciples to "wash one another's feet" unless he had meant that they were to undertake this particular task for others that he had just undertaken for them.[22] Even as Jesus had been willing to disregard social conventions in order to perform a necessary task expected only of those of servile or subordinate status, so also Jesus' disciples are to do for others as he has done for them. And even as Jesus' action represents his death for those whom he loves, so too the disciples' practice of washing each other's feet will serve to remind them continually of what Jesus will give for them on the cross. The simplest task, washing another's feet, and

20. In 1 Tim 5:10 footwashing is a specific instance of the hospitality extended to others.

21. See esp. Thomas 126–85. Although footwashing would become part of the ritualized practices of the church, evidence for it in the early period (it is not mentioned, e.g., in the Apostolic Fathers) is either lacking or ambiguous at best. For the later practice, see *ODCC*, "Pedilavium."

22. Bauckham 2007a, 204.

the costliest gift, dying for another—both reflect Jesus' life-giving mission and work for others. The disciples are to do these things in remembrance of him.

[16–20] A number of sayings underscore the charge that Jesus' disciples should follow his example:

- A doubled-amen saying emphasizes that servants or those who are sent (the disciples) are not superior to their masters or the one who sent them (v. 16).
- A blessing falls on those who emulate Jesus (v. 17).
- A warning indicates that not all the disciples are among the blessed (vv. 18–19).
- A second doubled-amen saying makes the point, found elsewhere in the Gospel, that those who receive or respond to Jesus are in fact responding to the God who sent him; and in turn, those who receive Jesus' emissaries receive Jesus himself (v. 20).

Taken together, this material emphasizes what is at stake in hearing Jesus' word and following his example.

The saying that "the slave is not greater than the master nor is the one who is sent greater than the one who sent him" states the obvious (v. 16). Certainly in the ancient world it was believed that society functioned smoothly when people adhered to the norms that governed the stations or positions that they occupied. As the Stoic philosopher Epictetus once wrote: "Remember that you are an actor in a drama, of such a kind as the author pleases to make it. If short, of a short one; if long, of a long one. If it is his pleasure you should act a poor man, a cripple, a governor, or a private person, see that you act it naturally. For this is your business, to act well the character assigned you; to choose it is another's."[23] One should do what one is given to do. But here Jesus has subverted normal expectations: he has acted as a slave and not as a master. Therefore, if the disciples are to follow his example, they too will conduct themselves as slaves and not as masters. Jesus' words can, of course, be misused to demean or subjugate those who have neither power nor opportunity to do other than to serve. To tell a slave to wash his master's feet requires nothing out of the ordinary of the slave; to tell a master to wash the feet of his slave requires a radical reorientation of values on the part of the master. Jesus' disciples are to follow in his pathway of generous self-giving love, even as he himself has done. In following Jesus, in adopting his way of life, they will be blessed.

Elsewhere in the Gospel, Jesus has regularly made the point that the Father sent him, that the Father tells him what to do and say, and therefore that to respond to him is to respond to the Father (5:37; 6:44; 7:28; 8:16, 18, 26, 29;

23. Epictetus, *Ench.* 17.

12:49; 14:24; cf. 9:4). But now, anticipating the time when he will send out his disciples, Jesus makes the same point about the relationship of the disciples to him: he will send them and tell them what to do and say; therefore a response to them will actually be a response to Jesus, and hence to the Father who sent him. One is again reminded of the Mishnaic dictum that "the one who is sent is like the one who sent him" (*m. Ber.* 5:5), but the reference is now to the disciples of Jesus as those who are sent by him, rather than to Jesus as the one sent by the Father. If the disciples are to bear witness to the world, they must emulate and embody the pattern of Jesus' life (15:13–17) as the one sent by God. Jesus has just raised the stakes for his disciples.

Throughout the Gospel it is also clear that Jesus knows particularly that one of his own disciples will desert and hand him over to the authorities. Here there seem to be two specific reasons given for Judas's action: The one who hands Jesus over (1) has not been chosen by Jesus and (2) acts in accordance with Scripture (13:18). In many ways these two explanations of Judas's betrayal raise as many problems as they solve. Jesus statement "I know whom I have chosen" implies that he has not chosen all of them; his (true, faithful) disciples are those whom he chose (15:16, 19). Earlier the Twelve, none excepted, are characterized as "chosen" (6:70); following that statement Jesus immediately acknowledges, "One of you is a devil" (6:70–71). In other words, Jesus knew even when choosing Judas that he would not remain faithful. Judas will show that he is not to be reckoned among "the chosen."

Jesus' foreknowledge is now coupled with a quotation from Scripture. While in Matthew and Mark, Jesus states that "the Son of Man goes as it is written of him,"[24] John supplies a text to explain Judas's betrayal: "The one who has eaten my bread has lifted his heel against me" (Ps 41:9 [40:10 LXX; 41:10 MT]).[25] Even as David was betrayed and exposed to death by his close associates, so too Jesus is handed over to his death by those who are among his "chosen," his intimate friends (cf. 15:18, 25).[26] And yet Jesus is not caught off guard. He has told his disciples what will happen before it does happen so that they "will believe that I am" (13:19).[27] His identity as the divine life-giving one, expressed in the absolute "I am" statements, might seem to be threatened by certain events, particularly the subversive action of his disciple that leads to his death on the cross; yet even here Jesus will manifest his divine identity for those who have eyes to see (cf. 8:28). Not only does he demonstrate his foreknowledge; he also

24. Matt 26:24; Mark 14:21; Luke 22:22: "going as it has been determined" (*hōrismenon*).

25. The citation in 13:18 does not correspond exactly either to the MT or to the LXX; as in 6:51–58, John uses the verb *trōgein* rather than the *esthiein* in Ps 40:10 LXX (41:9 ET).

26. Schuchard (114–16) shows parallels between the accounts of Ahithophel's betrayal of David in 2 Sam 15–17 and Judas's betrayal of Jesus.

27. Or "that I am he"; see Excursus 5: "The 'I Am' Sayings of John."

alerts the disciples that his death on a cross does not obscure God's glory but reveals that glory.

Again John's Gospel painfully bears witness to the horror of having one's own friends or associates deliver one up to earthly powers. The introduction of Judas lends an ominous overtone to Jesus' next statement ("Amen, Amen, I tell you, whoever receives one whom I sent receives me; and whoever receives me receives him who sent me"). Jesus' disciples can also expect that they will not always be welcomed and that, like Jesus himself, they might find themselves betrayed by their close associates.

13:21–30 Jesus Predicts His Betrayal

Jesus foretells both his imminent betrayal and the means by which his betrayer will be known. This account, somewhat longer than those found in the other Gospels, involves both Simon Peter and the disciple whom Jesus loves. Peter asks the "disciple whom Jesus loved," now for the first time explicitly designated as such, to find out from Jesus how they will be able to identify the disciple responsible for delivering Jesus to the authorities. This beloved disciple is in a position to know something from Jesus that no one else knows and, in turn, to make it known to others, including (or perhaps especially) Simon Peter. And alongside Peter and the beloved disciple, the role of Judas himself looms large in this account. When compared to the other Gospels, more space is given to the description of identifying Judas as the one who will hand him over: what Luke reports in a pithy sentence (22:21), John narrates at some length, dwelling, as it were, on the inconceivable fact that one of the Twelve will hand over his master.

> **13:21** When Jesus had said these things, he was troubled in spirit, and he
> testified and said, "Amen, Amen, I say to you that one of you will hand
> me over." **22** The disciples looked at each other, uncertain of whom he
> was speaking.
>
> **23** One of his disciples, the one whom he loved, was reclining at table
> right next to Jesus. **24** Simon Peter signaled to him to inquire about whom
> Jesus might be speaking. **25** So the one who was reclining upon Jesus'
> breast said to him, "Lord, who is it?"
>
> **26** Jesus answered, "It is that one to whom I give this piece of bread
> that I have dipped." And when he had dipped the piece of bread, he gave
> it to Judas, son of Simon Iscariot.
>
> **27** After the piece of bread, then Satan entered into [Judas].[a] Then Jesus
> said to him, "What you are going to do, do quickly." **28** None of those
> reclining at table knew why he said this to him. **29** Some thought that,
> since Judas carried the money box, Jesus was telling him, "Buy what we

need for the feast" or "Give something to the poor." **30** When he had taken the piece of bread, he went out immediately.

And it was night.

a. Here the Greek *ekeinon* means "that one," i.e., Judas.

[13:21–26] Although Jesus was aware that one of his own would be instrumental in handing him over to his death, and cites Scripture to corroborate the point, he is nevertheless "troubled in spirit" (*etarachthē tō pneumati*). So too Jesus is "troubled" when standing in front of Lazarus's tomb ("greatly disturbed . . . and troubled," 11:33) and when contemplating his own death ("I am troubled" or, more lit., "my soul is troubled," 12:27). The three statements are interesting for what they share in common: in each case where Jesus is deeply troubled, it has nevertheless also been made quite clear that Jesus knows what he will do, what is coming next, or that what is about to unfold will do so in harmony with God's purposes and the Scriptures (cf. 11:4, 11 with 11:35; 12:27a with 12:27b; 13:18–19 with 13:21). Jesus' foreknowledge does not suppress his genuine distress.

John never explicitly explains what Judas does or why he does it (cf. 18:2); although earlier Judas had been branded "a thief," John does not say that Judas sold Jesus for money (cf. Matt 26:15). Yet Judas hands Jesus over to the authorities (19:11), and finally Pilate hands him over to his death (19:16). Jesus' announcement that one of his disciples will hand him over perplexes them: who among them would do such a thing? At Peter's instigation, the "disciple whom Jesus loved," who is "reclining next to Jesus,"[28] asks Jesus of whom he is speaking. This "beloved disciple" is never identified by name; he appears first and almost exclusively in narratives set in Jerusalem and is thus linked primarily with the events of Jesus' Last Supper, crucifixion, and resurrection (13:23; 18:16; 19:26–27, 35; 20:1–8; 21:7, 20–24); and he is often paired or contrasted with Peter.[29] When the beloved disciple and Peter appear together, the beloved disciple is shown to have greater proximity and faithfulness to Jesus and earlier recognition of Jesus as the living Lord: he reclines next to Jesus in a position of honor (13:23); remains faithfully at the foot of the cross and is appointed guardian of Jesus' mother (19:27); understands the significance of the empty tomb (20:8); and identifies Jesus to Peter in a resurrection appearance

28. Reclining at festive meals and banquets, a marker of wealth, was a table custom shared by Greeks, Romans, and Jews. Ordinary meals in Galilean villages were eaten while sitting on the ground, not reclining on couches; texts from the DSS speak of sitting according to one's rank at meals (1QS VI, 3–5; cf. 11QT XXXVII, 8–9). Jesus is described as reclining at meals and "banquets" (*katakeisthai*, Mark 2:15; 14:3; Luke 5:29; 7:37; see Magness 81–82; Dennis Smith, esp. 14–18, 133–72). For illustrations of reclining and banqueting, see the art collected in Dunbabin.

29. See 13:18–25; 20:1–10; 21:1–8, 20–24; perhaps 18:15–16, if he is "the other disciple."

(21:7). While demonstrating many of the traits of a model disciple, he remains unnamed. His absence from preresurrection narratives set in Galilee suggests that he is not one of the Twelve.[30]

The short exchange between Jesus and the beloved disciple does not clarify for them what is about to happen (v. 28). Jesus identifies his betrayer as the one to whom he will give a piece of bread that he has dipped in the dish. Here the connection to the quotation from Ps 41:9 (cited in 13:18) becomes clear: Jesus will give Judas a piece of bread, and Judas will become "the one who ate my bread" but then "lifted his heel" or turned against Jesus. The narrator makes explicit the identification that the "devil," the one who will hand Jesus over, is Judas son of Simon Iscariot (6:71; 12:4; 13:2, 26; 18:2, 5).

[27–30] The short account of what happens next raises the vexing question of what John means by stating that Satan "entered" into Judas. Luke also speaks of Satan's "entering" into Judas (Luke 22:3, *eisēlthen de Satanas*); there is a parallel to demons "entering" and "leaving" a person (or a herd of swine, as in Luke 8:30, 33). John, however, includes no accounts of casting out demons; the description of Satan's "entering into" Judas is the sole example of (satanic) possession (see comments on 8:44, 48). A substantively different parallel to the assertion that "Satan entered" into someone can be found in the descriptions of the Father, Son, or Spirit as "being" or "abiding" *in* the believer who keeps the commandments of Jesus (14:16–17, 23; 15:4; 17:23). Even as this divine indwelling or abiding makes it possible for the believer to remain faithful (15:4), so now Satan "enters into" Judas, demonstrated by Judas's faithlessness.

Still, Jesus maintains control of the situation, telling Judas to go and do quickly what he has intended (13:27). The disciples misunderstand Jesus' words (13:28), thinking that Jesus is commanding Judas either to gather some provisions for the feast or to give some money to the poor.[31] These guesses are, of course, deeply ironic. Judas will not return to the feast, and he has already been branded as a thief who does not care for the poor (12:6). It seems highly unlikely that Jesus would therefore send Judas on an errand to "give something to the poor" (13:29). But at this point in the narrative, the disciples do not understand what is transpiring: even as they will understand the meaning of the footwashing only later, here they remain ignorant about Judas's role in the events about to unfold.

Finally, then, Judas leaves the company of the disciples. The narrator's statement that "it was night" could simply be a comment on the time of day. But since throughout the Gospel "darkness" indicates the absence of the light

30. For a contrary view, see Thyen 597. For arguments that Lazarus is the beloved disciple, see comments on 11:1–6 and also on 21:20–24; cf. the introduction, above, on "Authorship."

31. Giving alms to the poor is among the Mishnaic regulations for observance of Passover (*m. Pesaḥ.* 10:1).

brought by Jesus, it is likely that the statement "It is night" also marks Judas's final turning from Jesus. Even as Nicodemus had earlier come by night to the light, Judas has turned from the light to enter the darkness. Like Cain, who turned against his brother, Abel (John 8:44; 1 John 3:9–16), Judas has deserted both Jesus and his fellow disciples.

13:31–16:33 Jesus' Final Words to His Disciples

Having washed his disciples' feet, commanded them to follow his example, and warned them that one of their company would betray him, Jesus turns to explain the significance of his imminent departure for his disciples. In a long discourse, interrupted periodically by questions from his often-uncomprehending disciples, Jesus instructs them that even though he is "going away" (14:1, 4, 19, 28; 16:5, 7, 16, 28), he will "come again" (14:3). He will not abandon them (14:18), but will reveal himself to them (14:21), and dwell with them (14:18, 23) and in them (14:20; 15:4–5). Indeed, "presence in absence" is the great theme of Jesus' so-called Farewell Discourse.[32] Even though Jesus must depart, he will be with the disciples, although obviously not as he has been with them: the Word who "became flesh and lived among us" (1:14) and has made God known (1:18) now returns to the Father. He will no longer be with them. How, then, does this life-giving Word continue to mediate life and to give light in darkness, to make the Father known, and to provide protection for his imperiled flock? It is the burden of the Farewell Discourse to interpret Jesus' departure to the Father as inaugurating a new period in which Jesus will be present with and among the disciples in new ways.

Jesus also instructs the disciples on the hallmarks of faithful discipleship that must characterize their life in this new era: they must continue to believe (14:1, 10–11, 29; 16:30–31), cling closely to Jesus (15:1–11), and bear witness to him (15:1–8, 16) in the face of the world's hostility (15:18–16:2; 16:8–11, 33). They must love each other as he has loved and will love them (13:1, 34; 14:15; 15:12–13, 17), because their love for each other will be a witness to the world, to "all people," that they are disciples of Jesus, who gave his life for them and for the world (13:35). For their communal life in this period of Jesus' "absence," the disciples will not only have Jesus' own continued presence, but also the abiding presence of the Paraclete, the "Spirit of truth," who will both make Jesus' words and person ever present to them and lead them into the as yet unknown future. In short, Jesus' Farewell Discourse encourages, exhorts, and instructs the disciples with respect to this new era, unsought and unwelcome but inevitable and near, in which they must discern Jesus' presence precisely in his absence.

32. See Ashton 456; Attridge 2002, 17–18; Parsenios 2005, 7.

Jesus' Farewell Discourse, his final words gathered together in 13:31–16:33,[33] shares some features with various "farewell speeches" or "testaments" of biblical and Jewish literature.[34] Such speeches, often uttered on the brink of one's death, provide visions of the speakers' fears and hopes for the future, through a combination of warnings, exhortations, and blessings, thus giving expression to the legacy that a particular testator wishes to leave. A prime biblical example is Jacob's farewell: he gathers his sons, the representatives of the twelve tribes of Israel, warns them of "what will happen" in the days to come, and offers each a blessing (Gen 49:1–28). Similarly, in bidding farewell to the people of Israel on the eve of his own death, Moses recounts Israel's history, exhorts Israel to keep the law, and offers a blessing to each of the tribes in light of their roles within Israel and in the land they will inhabit (Deut 33).[35] Later Jewish literature develops these farewell speeches in testamentary literature, such as the *Testaments of the Twelve Patriarchs*, the *Testament of Moses,* and the *Testament of Job*.

Alongside the biblical and Jewish models, one may adduce Plato's *Phaedo*, the account of the condemned Socrates's final words and death, as the exemplary farewell scene of classical literature.[36] In it Echecrates petitions Phaedo, "I wish you would tell me about [Socrates's] death. What did he say in his last hours?" (57a). Jesus' Farewell Discourse shares a number of features with Greco-Roman farewell addresses modeled on the *Phaedo*, including emphasis on "the speaker's impending death, care of those remaining, regulation of discipleship, thanks to the gods, an account for his life, [and] consolation to an inner circle."[37]

Jesus delivers his discourse at a meal, not on his deathbed. John's account evinces the influence of the literary symposium, in which a meal provides the setting for various dialogues.[38] Friendship is a frequent topic in such dialogues,

33. Some commentators locate the beginning of the discourse proper at 13:31 (Barrett 449; R. Brown 1970, 608–9; Beasley-Murray 244; Lincoln 2005, 386); others, at 13:36 (Michaels 763) or 14:1 (O'Day 735; Moloney 1998a, 29; D. Moody Smith 1999, 262). While various scholars have proffered theories of a complex composition history of the material in John 14–16, Jesus' words constitute a single, long discourse, as they are interpreted here. For various reconstructions of the composition history, see R. Brown 1970, 582–603; Segovia 1991; for the view that certain "base texts" of the discourse are subject to "rereading" (*Relecture*) in order to address changing circumstances and problems, see esp. Dettwiler.

34. For discussion of genre, see Kugler 2010; Segovia 1991, 5–20; Attridge 2002, 10, 17–18; Parsenios 2005.

35. See also the accounts of the final words of Joshua (Josh 23–24); Samuel (1 Sam 12); David (1 Kgs 2:1–10; 1 Chr 28:1–29:20); Tobias (Tob 14:3–11); Mattathias (1 Macc 2:49–70); Moses (*Ant.* 4.309–31); and in the NT, Paul's farewell to the Ephesian elders (Acts 20:17–38).

36. See Kurz for analysis of the similarities and differences between Greco-Roman, biblical, and later Jewish farewell speeches.

37. Kurz 253–54.

38. E.g., the dialogues with Socrates written by Plato and Xenophon, called *Symposia.* The symposium was both a social custom (a drinking party following the evening meal, or *deipnon*) and a literary genre (in which the symposium provides the narrative setting for extended dialogue and discourse); see Parsenios 2005; Dennis Smith 219–77.

since the meal both provides the setting for making friends and is itself an expression of friendship (cf. John 13:34–35; 15:13–15).[39] Of course John's account of Jesus' Farewell Discourse also reflects the Gospel tradition that, just before his arrest, Jesus ate a last meal with his disciples. But in the Synoptic accounts of that last meal, Jesus says relatively little to his disciples about what to expect or how they are to live after his death (yet cf. Luke 22:24–38). Some such instructions have already been given (Matt 24–25; Mark 13; Luke 21). But John's account of Jesus' last meal and last words differs notably in its concentration on the situation of the disciples in Jesus' absence. Jesus' Farewell Discourse also differs from typical farewell speeches by anticipating not only his death but also his resurrection: these are the last words, not of a dying man, but of one who will soon be raised to new life.

What does Jesus say in his last hours? Jesus promises that he will not abandon his own. The crisis facing the disciples is Jesus' death, which he interprets to them as his departure: he is "going away" (13:33; 14:2–3, 28–31; 16:16–17); the disciples will grieve and mourn. But their distress will be taken away when, "in a little while," they see him again (14:19; 16:16; 20:18, 25, 29) because he has been raised to life; then their grief will give way to joy (16:20–24). This is the promise of Easter: the crucified Lord has risen to new life. Jesus' resurrection grounds the many promises in the Farewell Discourse that he will continue to be with the disciples (14:18, 19, 23): because he is living, he may be with them. Yet things are changing, and he will not be with the disciples as he has been, as is made clear by the explanation that while they will "see" him, the world will not (14:19). Even though absent from them, the disciples will see him; Jesus will "come to them" (14:18) and be "in them" (14:20; 15:4; 17:21); they will abide in him (14:20; 15:5–7; 17:21). As the risen one, Jesus will continue to be present with disciples. To be sure, he will be present in new ways, but promises of his presence pervade the forewarnings of his absence.

Jesus further promises his disciples the presence of another, the Paraclete, the Holy Spirit, who will come to be with them, to teach them, and to defend them (14:16–20, 26; 15:26; 16:7–15). The Paraclete does not replace Jesus but serves to bear witness to him and to bring his words to mind—in short, to make Jesus present to his disciples.[40] Even as God's Word became flesh in Jesus, now God's Spirit becomes newly present as the Paraclete. This is the fulfillment of the promise of the coming of God's Spirit, who bears witness to the Son (1:33) and provides ongoing guidance to the community of faith.

Finally, in the Farewell Discourse Jesus also speaks, albeit ever so briefly, of "coming again" (cf. also 21:22). In fact, Jesus' discourse to his disciples opens

39. Plutarch speaks of *to philopoion tēs trapezēs* ("the table that makes friends") and writes that the meal, together with conversation, leads "to friendship" (*philophrosynē*); cf. Plutarch, *Mor.* 612D, 660B.

40. For elaboration of this point, see Excursus 9: "The Holy Spirit in John."

with the promise that he is going away to "prepare a place" for the disciples, but that he will "come again and take you to myself." Here the Gospel gives voice to the New Testament hope of the return of Jesus (14:3, 18, 28).

The disciples may thus hope for Jesus' resurrection (16:17, 20–22), his postresurrection presence with them (14:18, 23, 28), and the ongoing ministry of the Paraclete (14:16, 26; 15:26–27; 16:7–14), as well as for Jesus' return to take them to be with him (14:3). The disciples hope for Jesus to come back so that they may be with him *there*, in the future, but all the while he assures them that he will be with them *here*, in the present. John does not thereby simply erase the boundaries between the present and the future, but he reinterprets time christologically. Even as the hope of eternal life includes the expectation of an abundant life in the present, so also the hope of being with Jesus in his Father's house includes the expectation of Jesus' presence, as well as that of the Father and of the Spirit,[41] with them now. Jesus is going away; yet as the living Lord he will be present with them in new ways. The disciples can live in joy and peace as they await his return. Easter (Jesus' resurrection) and Parousia (Jesus' return) bookend the promises of Jesus' abiding presence with his own.

13:31–38 Jesus' New Commandment

Jesus elaborates upon his departure: First, he reiterates that all that is about to happen will bring glory to God. Second, he introduces the commandment that the disciples are to love one another. And third, Jesus explains to Peter that Peter cannot follow him now. Having responded to Jesus' call to follow him, having declared his desire to belong to Jesus, Peter now finds that Jesus intends to leave them all. Before addressing the crisis created by his imminent departure, Jesus gives the commandment by which his disciples are to order their lives together, because it is the commandment that best reflects Jesus' life among them. His love for them must be embodied in their love for each other.

> 13:31 So when [Judas] had gone out, Jesus said, "Now the Son of man is
> glorified! And God is glorified through him. 32 [And if God is glorified
> through him],[a] then God will glorify himself through him, and he will
> glorify himself at once.
>
> 33 "Little children, I am with you for a little while. You will look for
> me, and even as I said to the Jews, 'Where I am going you cannot come,'
> so I say to you now.
>
> 34 "I give you a new commandment, that you should love each other;
> even as I have loved you, so you are to love each other. 35 This is how
> everyone will know that you are my disciples, if you love each other."

41. The promised presence is thus incipiently, but unmistakably, Trinitarian in character.

36 Simon Peter said to him, "Lord, where are you going?"
Jesus answered, "Where I am going you cannot follow me now, but you will follow later."
37 Peter said to him, "Lord,[b] why can't I follow you now? I will lay down my life for you."
38 Jesus answered, "You will lay down your life for me? Amen, amen, I tell you, the rooster will not crow before you have denied me three times."

a. The reading in brackets is found in ℵ^{c} A C^{2} K Δ Θ Ψ *f*^{13} 28 33, but is missing in a wide range of excellent MSS, including 𝔓^{66} ℵ* A B C* D L W X Π *f*^{1} *al.* Although typical of John's repetitive style, the addition smooths out a rougher reading and thus may be secondary.

b. "Lord" (*kyrie*), absent from ℵ* 33 565 vg syr^{s} and other early MSS, may have been added so that Peter's requests in 13:36 and 13:37 parallel each other.

[13:31–33] Judas's departure from dinner has set into motion the events that will lead to Jesus' trial and crucifixion. John describes crucifixion as "glorification" to counter the perception that it was a shameful or dishonorable means of death. Jesus will not be discredited; he will not bring shame upon his Father as he faces an ignominious death at the hands of Roman occupiers.[42] To the contrary, the Father will honor or glorify Jesus through his death on the cross.

Addressing his disciples as "little children" (*teknia*, v. 33),[43] Jesus tells them that before long he will depart from them. The disciples are called "little children" not because of their youth but because of the spiritual authority of the speaker: as Teacher and Lord (13:13–14), Jesus is both instructor and master.[44] Although Jesus later refers to his disciples as "friends" (15:15) and "brothers" (20:17), he also continues to call them "children" (21:5). Retaining his position of authority, Jesus exercises it to instruct his disciples that they are to treat each other, not as inferiors, but as friends and family, even as he treats them.

Earlier Jesus had told "the Jews" that a time would come when they would not be able to find him, because he was going where they could not follow (7:34, 36; 8:21–22). Now the disciples find that the warnings regarding Jesus' absence pertain also to them. Not only will the Jews be unable to find Jesus; Jesus' own disciples will look for him and be unable to follow after him. But Jesus does not

42. See the comments on 1:14; 2:11; 5:23; 12:16, 20–26, 28, 43.

43. *Teknion,* the diminutive of *teknon*, appears in the Gospel and Epistles of John in direct address to the disciples (John 13:33) or readers (1 John 2:1, 12, 28; 3:7, 18; 4:4; 5:21). John prefers *teknon* ("child"; plural *tekna*, "children") for "offspring" and for "children of God" (e.g., 1:12; 8:39; 11:52; cf. 1 John 3:1, 2, 10; 5:2; 2 John 1, 4, 13; 3 John 4); *paidia* ("children") in 21:5 and 1 John 2:14, 18.

44. In biblical Wisdom literature, pupils were often addressed as "children" (or "sons"): Prov 1:8, 10, 15; 2:1; 3:1, 11, 21; Sir 2:1; 3:12, 17; 4:1; 6:18.

say that they will be unable to know or "see" him, and much of the discourse that follows explains how they *will* be able to know and perceive him once he is gone, thus gaining a new understanding of what it will mean to "follow" him. For now, it is clear that the situation of the disciples is changing, and Jesus therefore instructs his disciples how they are to live after his departure.

[34–35] Anticipating his imminent departure and resulting absence, Jesus gives his disciples "a new commandment."[45] It is "new" because it is the first time that Jesus has commanded his disciples to love one another. Up to this point, Jesus has frequently spoken of believing in him (5:46; 8:45; 10:37–38); now he turns to the conduct that must govern the disciples' lives together when he is no longer present among them to provide explicit guidance. Faith and love belong together in the Gospel, as they do also in the Epistles of John, and can be said to summarize what God commands: "And this is his commandment, that we should believe in the name of his Son Jesus Christ and love one another, just as he commanded us" (1 John 3:23; cf. Gal 5:6; Ign., *Eph.* 14.1, "The beginning of life is faith, and the end is love"). The commandment is also new because from now on the measure of the disciples' love for one another must be Jesus' love for them, manifested ultimately and supremely in his impending death on the cross for them.

In farewell speeches in the ancient world, those facing death often commended the pattern of their lives to their friends or disciples. When Seneca was condemned to death and forbidden to write out a will, he told his friends that he would leave them only "the pattern of his life" (Tacitus, *Ann.* 15.62). Jesus does command his disciples to love one another, but his legacy to them is not just a principle of behavior but the very "pattern of his life" among them (cf. 1 John 2:5–6; 3:14–16; cf. Eph 5:2).[46] To live as Jesus called them to live will require knowing not only his words, but also knowing, following, and abiding in him.

Jesus' new command is that the disciples are to love "one another." According to the Synoptic Gospels, Jesus asserted that the "greatest commandment" of all is to love God (quoting Deut 6:5) and that the commandment next to it in importance is "Love your neighbor as yourself" (quoting Lev 19:18).[47] Indeed, "all the law and the commandments" depend on these two commands (Matt 22:34–40).[48] Early Christian tradition reiterated Jesus' point when it epitomized

45. "Maundy" Thursday, the day on the Christian calendar that marks Jesus' Last Supper with his disciples, takes its name from the Latin word for "command," *mandatum.*

46. Some of the *Testaments of the Twelve Patriarchs* emphasize the importance of family unity and love for one another (*T. Zeb.* 8.4–6; *T. Jos.* 17.2–8).

47. See Matt 19:19; 22:39; Mark 12:28–31; Luke 10:27; Rom 13:9.

48. Philo writes of the two laws that stand at the head of all the others: "the regulating of one's conduct toward God by the rules of piety [*eusebeia*] and holiness [*hosiotēs*], and of one's conduct toward human beings by the rules of philanthropy [*philanthropia*] and justice [*dikaiosynē*]" (*Spec.* 2.63; *Virt.* 51; *Abr.* 208; *Decal.* 50, 106–10, 121; *Her.* 168, 172). Josephus prizes the same two

love as the pinnacle or summary of the law's instructions or of Jesus' teaching, or both, insofar as behavior toward others was concerned (Rom 13:9–10; Gal 5:14; 6:2; Col 3:14; Jas 2:8; see also *Did.* 1.2; *Barn.* 2.8; 19.5; Pol., *Phil.* 3.3). In John, Jesus' instructions are gathered under the single command to love one another, now given flesh and bones in his own exemplary love. After Jesus has departed, the disciples will need to embody his love, from washing each other's feet to giving their lives for others. The Gospel aims to form Jesus' disciples into a community where love for the other is learned by following the example of those who imitate Jesus' love (13:34–35; 15:13).

Some interpreters of John have contended that his ethic has sacrificed a concern for the other who is *outside* the household of faith, refocusing the wide range of Jesus' instruction entirely on the one who is *inside* the household.[49] But John is not alone in foregrounding the paramount importance of love of one's fellow believer. Early Christian paraenesis stressed the importance of doing good to those in the household of faith (Gal 6:10), of loving "the family of believers" (1 Pet 2:17; 1 Thess 4:9), or of loving "one another" (Rom 12:10; 13:8; Gal 5:13; Eph 4:1; 1 Thess 3:12; 1 Pet 1.22; 3:8; 4:8). Sometimes such paraenesis appends the command to love "all" (1 Thess 3:12) or instructs that one should "do good to one another and to all" (1 Thess 5:14; Gal 6:10); or that one should "honor everyone" while also loving "the family of believers" (1 Pet 2:17). Love moves from the household of faith outward, from the community to the world. In commanding the disciples to love one another, Jesus does not envision a love that shrinks from risk, rejection, and suffering, or that is limited only to each other (see comments on 3:16–17; 15:16–20). Love for one another impels love for the world.

If the mutual love of Jesus' followers bears witness to their identity as Jesus' followers, then the nagging question is simply this: Does it work? The second-century Christian author who penned the epistle known as *2 Clement* lamented the failures of Christian love and, hence, witness: "When they see that we not only do not love them that hate us, but not even them that love us, they laugh us to scorn, and the Name is blasphemed" (13.4). Yet there is scattered but persistent evidence from the ancient world that the care of Christians for one another was now and again evident to outsiders. Strikingly, even when it was evident, it did not always evoke a positive response, let alone faith in Jesus.[50]

An oft-quoted comment of Tertullian's (ca. 200 C.E.) indicates that the love of Christians for one another was noticed by those around them: "It is our care

---

virtues, which are exhibited by Jews and Gentiles alike (*J.W.* 2.139; 7.260; *Ant.* 6.265; 9.236; 15.375; 16.42, 172; 18.117; *Ag. Ap.* 2.146).

49. For discussion, see the essays in van der Watt and Zimmerman.

50. But Stark argues that Christianity thrived in part because its values of love and charity were manifested in social service and community solidarity, thus ensuring higher survival rates in the face of catastrophes, such as plague, and attracting converts.

of the helpless, our practice of loving-kindness, that brands us in the eyes of many of our opponents. 'Only look,' they say, 'how they love one another!'" (*Apol.* 39.7). Interestingly, Tertullian does not speak of these critics of Christianity as admiring it, only that they noticed its communal commitments. In fact, he also lamented that whenever there are natural disasters—earthquakes, famine, or pestilence—people blame Christians and wish them sent "straightaway to the lions" (*Apol.* 40).[51] Lucian of Samosata's (ca. 125–180 C.E.) slightly earlier satirical account (*The Passing of Peregrinus*) narrates how Peregrinus easily took advantage of the gullibility and generosity of Christians, who believed that they were "brothers of one another." Even though they took care of those in prison, visiting and providing for them (11–13), Lucian does not admire these Christians. Later the emperor Julian (r. 361–363) worried that Christianity was growing because of Christian practices: "Their benevolence to strangers, their care for the graves of the dead, and the pretended holiness of their lives . . . have done most to increase atheism."[52] He added, "It is disgraceful that, when no Jew ever has to beg and the impious Galileans not only care for their own poor but ours as well, all people should see how our people lack aid from us."[53]

Ancient records are thus punctuated with observation of Christian benevolence and charity. While the mutual love of Jesus' disciples was intended to bear witness to the world that they were *his* disciples, these records also show that even the demonstration of such love did not necessarily lead others to assess the character of Christian life together as demonstrating the self-giving character of Jesus himself; in fact, ancient evaluations of Jesus are typically as negative as are evaluations of early Christians. Outside of Christian circles, Jesus was not admired. But in the Gospel of John, Jesus calls his disciples to persist in the kind of love that he has showed for them and for others, regardless of the response. After all, Jesus healed a paralytic who had never expressed faith and whose report of his healing to the authorities sparked their pursuit of Jesus (5:8–16). Love within the Christian community, and for the world as well, bears witness to the love of God in and for an unresponsive and even hostile world (3:16). The lack of recognition or response cannot serve as a measure of the success of the church's witness; but the failure of the Christian community to offer such a witness blasphemes the Name, as *2 Clement* lamented centuries ago.

[36–38] Simon Peter now renews the question, "Lord, where are you going?" Even as Jesus has told them that they cannot come with him at present, so now

51. In the third century, Origen stated that Christians were not widely admired but rather "hated by all the nations" (*Comm. ser. Matt.* 39).

52. By "atheism," Julian means lack of belief in the Roman gods.

53. Julian, *To Arsacius, High-Priest of Galatia*, in MacMullen and Lane 271–72; Julian includes the Judeans (Jews) as well. On these and other texts, see Dodds 135–38; Stark 73–94, esp. 82–88.

he makes the point specifically to Simon Peter that he cannot (*ou dynasai*) follow Jesus. It is not time for Peter's death, his own "departure" to the Father. Later Peter will indeed "follow Jesus" in giving his life as a martyr (21:18–19).[54] But at present, Peter lacks the ability or strength to confess Jesus in the face of danger: he will be like those who fear to confess Jesus openly "for fear of the Jewish authorities" (9:22; 12:42). Although Peter protests that he will lay down his life for Jesus, he will soon deny that he even knows Jesus, and he will deny that he follows Jesus.

Excursus 8: The Johannine Vocabulary of Faith and Discipleship

Jesus' disciples are described as those who "believed" or "believed in him" or "in his name"; readers of the Gospel are called to the same commitment (20:30–31).[55] How does one come to faith? What is faith? What does believing entail? What does it mean to live as Jesus' disciple?

Most basically, disciples are called to follow (*akolouthein*) Jesus (1:43; 21:22; frequently also in the Synoptics). While the word *akolouthein* can refer to a literal or physical "following after" (1:37; 21:20), it is frequently used for being a disciple: "following" in the sense of listening and attending to someone (8:12; 10:4–5, 27; 12:26). This usage is found in other Greek literature (see BDAG s.v.). Following refers both to the initial turning toward Jesus—a response to his invitation, a disposition toward Jesus put into action—as well as to the continued commitment to "follow after" him. At the beginning of the Gospel, Jesus summons would-be disciples to follow him (1:43); at the end of the Gospel, he again calls Peter to "Follow me!" (21:22). Those who follow Jesus are further invited to "come and see" (1:39, 46): such seeing will lead to faith in, and understanding of, who Jesus is. John uses "seeing" to cover both "sight" and "insight." Those invited to "come and see" are invited to be with him to see all that he says and does ("sight"), as well as to discern, in what is seen, just who Jesus is ("insight").

Following Jesus, accepting his invitation to "come and see," ideally leads to believing in him (2:11). Various formulations use the quintessentially Johannine verb, "believe" (*pisteuein*):

- Without an object, one is simply said to "believe" (1:50; 3:12; 4:42; 6:47, 64; 20:31).[56]
- With a prepositional phrase, one believes "in his name" (*eis to onoma autou*, 1:12).

54. In 13:36 the verbs where Jesus addresses Peter specifically are in the second-person sg.

55. John uses the verb *pisteuein* ("to believe") more than all the other Gospels combined (98 times in John; 34 times in the Synoptics). *Pisteuein* may be translated as either "to believe" or "to have faith." While in English "believe," "believing," "believer," and "belief" are cognates, there are no comparable equivalents for the word group of "faith." John does not use the noun *pistis* ("faith, belief"); the Synoptics use it 24 times.

56. In Mark 9:42 a textual variant adds *eis eme* to the absolute *tōn pisteuontōn*; in Mark 15:32 "see and believe" are used without objects (*hina idōmen kai pisteusōmen*).

- With a prepositional phrase, one believes "in him" (*eis auton*, in the accusative case, 2:11; 3:16; *en autō*, with the dative case, 3:15).[57]
- "That" (*hoti*) specifies the content of what is believed (8:24; 11:27, 42; 13:19; 14:10; 16:30; 17:21; 20:31).

Those who believe are by definition Jesus' disciples (see 6:64–66). Not only are disciples invited to initial belief; they are also exhorted to continue in faith as well (14:1). Believing (*pisteuein* without an object) essentially means commitment or trust.

There is also a strong confessional aspect to such commitment in John. Trusting Jesus, or believing in him or in his name, includes coming to own the confessions articulated by various figures in the Gospel, from the Baptist's initial witness (1:29, 30, 34, 36) to Thomas's climactic confession (20:28). One both believes in Jesus and believes certain things to be true about him. Often such statements are framed with the verb "believe" followed by "that" (*hoti*) and the content of belief or confession ("I believe that you are the Messiah," 11:27; "Do you not believe that I am in the Father?" 14:10). Virtually all such statements focus on Jesus' relationship to God (8:24; 11:27, 42; 13:19; 14:10; 16:30; 17:21; 20:31). Disciples follow after Jesus, and in doing so they come to understand who he is.[58] In this sense *pisteuō* ("believe") is at times indistinguishable from *ginoskō* or *oida* ("know"; e.g., 6:69). These two words for "knowing" and "understanding" are often interchangeable (7:27; 8:55; 13:7). The world does not know—accept, recognize, respond to—Jesus (1:26, 31, 33, 48; 8:55; 10:14–15, 27), but the disciples "know that" (*ginōskein* + *hoti*) Jesus is the Holy One of God (6:69), among other confessions about him. By following Jesus they come to "know the truth" (*ginōskein tēn alētheian*). "Knowing" is not merely knowing things about Jesus; it is also understanding who he is (see esp. 10:38, where "know and understand" translates *gnōte kai ginōskēte*; cf. 12:16).

John's vocabulary of faith—following, believing, knowing, and seeing—is used to refer both to the initial response and to ongoing commitment to Jesus. John's characteristic word "abide" (*menein*) denotes the persistence or faithfulness that must characterize disciples (15:4–10). Those disciples who have believed in Jesus will know the truth if they *continue* or *abide* in him (8:30–31). Knowing and understanding Jesus cannot be separated from the actual practice of discipleship: from following him, seeing what he does, and in being with him, coming to understand who he is.

Those who follow Jesus are exhorted to keep his commandments (14:15, 21, 23), above all the command to love him (14:15, 21, 23, 24; 21:15, 16, 17) and each other (13:34–35). John's metaphors further underscore the corporate dimensions of discipleship: Jesus gathers his sheep (10:16), the scattered children of God (11:52). On the cross, Jesus designates his mother and the disciple whom he loved as mother and son to each other, thereby establishing the family of God's children (19:26–27). When the man born blind is virtually disowned by his parents (9:21–23) and ridiculed and repudiated by others, Jesus seeks him out (9:28–35). Throughout the Gospel Jesus has spoken of his

57. See Matt 18:6 (*eis eme*); 27:42 (*ep' auton*).

58. See Mark 8:27–31 par.; note the plethora of designations for Jesus in the Synoptics: son of Abraham, son of David, Son of God, Son of Man, Messiah, King of the Jews, King of Israel, prophet, Lord.

death as the act whereby "all people" are drawn to him (12:32); the new family gathered by him is the result of his death.

In the Synoptic Gospels, Jesus admonishes his disciples to love their enemies; in John, the primary command given to them is to love each other (13:34–35). Both the Synoptic and Johannine traditions base these commands on the model of divine love (Matt 5:43–45; John 3:16). Even as the Father demonstrates his love for the world through the giving of the Son, so Jesus' followers bear witness to God's love as they together embody the kind of self-giving love for each other that Jesus has for them.

Thus, following Jesus includes:

- initial and ongoing commitment, being in his presence, coming to a certain understanding about him (that he is the Messiah, comes from God, and is spoken of in Scripture)
- faithful, persistent following after him (abiding in him; following him)
- keeping his commandments
- loving Jesus and loving one another

For one to become a disciple of Jesus, God must be active, "giving" and "drawing" people to Jesus (6:37, 44–45, 65; 10:27–29); God's spirit "blows where it wants" to quicken life and faith (3:8; 6:63). God bears witness to Jesus (5:37; 8:18); God's Spirit descends upon Jesus, identifying him as the one who baptizes with the Spirit, the Son of God (1:31–34). Jesus chooses his disciples (6:70; 13:18; 15:16). John not only emphasizes but also accords primacy to the initiative and action of God in bringing people to faith and sustaining them in it: God loves the world (3:16), seeks true worshipers (4:23), holds his flock (10:28–29), and tends the vine (15:1–8). Without the love, initiative, and continued sustaining action of God, there would be no life.

John also reckons with the instrumentality or agency of others: people bring disciples, friends, or neighbors to Jesus (1:35–37, 41, 45; 4:29; 12:21–22); similarly, the mutual love of Jesus' disciples for one another bears witness to Jesus (13:35). The Scriptures point to Jesus (2:22; 5:39; 20:9), as do his signs (20:30–31), calling for the human response of faith. Although John frequently uses the word "believe," the Gospel explicitly denies that the disciples "choose" or "decide" (*eklegomai* or *haireomai*) to be Jesus' disciples or to believe (6:70; 13:18; 15:16). There is genuine human response, but not without the enlivening work of God's Spirit. As God draws people to Jesus, so God's Spirit continues to teach them, through the Scriptures and in the context of the community, how to understand the person and ministry of Jesus (2:22; 13:7; 14:26; 15:26).

14:1–11 Jesus' Imminent Departure to the Father

Jesus' departure is now imminent. He promises his disciples that, if he departs, he will "come again and take you to myself, so that where I am you may be also" (14:3). This is a reference to Jesus' future return in order to gather the faithful to be with him in his dwelling with God. Later Jesus will speak of other ways in which the disciples will know and experience his presence. Now he assures them that, because he is returning to the Father, he will subsequently take his disciples there as well. Since he has mediated the presence of the Father to them in his earthly life, they can be confident that he will take them to be in the presence of the Father.

> 14:1 "Let not your hearts[a] be troubled. Believe in God and believe in me.[b]
> 2 In my Father's house there are many rooms.[c] If it were not so, would
> I have told you that I am going to prepare a place for you? 3 And if I go
> and prepare a place for you, I will come again and take you to myself,
> so that where I am you may be also. 4 And you know the way to where
> I am going."
>
> 5 Thomas said to him, "Lord, we do not know where you are going; how can we know the way?"
>
> 6 Jesus said to him, "I am the way and the truth and the life. No one
> comes to the Father except through me. 7 If you had known me, you
> would know my Father as well. From now on you will know him and have seen him."[d]
>
> 8 Philip said to him, "Lord, show us the Father, and it will be enough for us."
>
> 9 Jesus said to him, "I have been with you such a long time, and still
> you do not know me, Philip? The one who has seen me has seen the
> Father. How can you say, 'Show us the Father'? 10 Do you not believe
> that I am in the Father and the Father is in me? The words that I speak
> to you, I do not speak on my own, but the Father who abides in me does
> his works. 11 Believe me that I am in the Father and the Father is in me.
> Otherwise, believe on account of the works themselves."

a. While "hearts" is singular in the Greek (*kardia*), with the plural pronoun (*hymōn*) it is best translated in the plural.

b. *Pisteuete* can be parsed as imperative or indicative. Since the commands to believe (1) follow the imperative "Let not your hearts be troubled" and (2) are joined by *kai*, the most likely translation takes both instances of *pisteuete* ("believe") as imperatives.

c. BDAG: "a place in which one stays, dwelling (-place), room, abode." At the time of the KJV (1611), "mansions" carried that connotation in English, though it no longer does so.

d. The tenses of the verbs pose a challenge to translation: "If you had known (RSV; ESV) me [*egnōkate*, perfect tense], you will know [*gnōsesthe*, future] my Father as well. From now on you do know him [*ginōskete*, present] and have seen him [*heōrakate*, perfect]." One would not expect a perfect ("had known me") in the protasis to be followed by a future ("you will know the Father") or a present ("do know him") in the apodosis. Hence, the tenses here are not translated woodenly. John means to say that knowing (recognizing, understanding) Jesus leads to knowing the Father.

[14:1] After telling the disciples that his departure from them is imminent (13:33), that one of his disciples will betray him (13:21) and another will deny him (13:38), Jesus admonishes them to lose neither courage nor faith even though circumstances that are about to unfold will threaten their trust in him.[59] To be sure, the prospect of death troubles (*tarassō*) even Jesus (11:33; 12:27; 13:21); little wonder that it would also trouble the disciples. The command "Let not your hearts be troubled" (cf. 14:27) anticipates the disorientation brought on by the grief and shock caused by Jesus' crucifixion (see 20:1, 9, 11–13, 19). Jesus encourages them, exhorting them to continue believing in God and in him. Faith or trust in God and in Jesus are paired; to believe in one is to believe in the other, because Jesus is the one who has been sent by the Father, to make the Father known, and to lead people to the Father (cf. 5:23–24; 12:45; 14:10). Jesus implicitly cautions the disciples neither to fall away, as other disciples did (6:60, 66; 8:30–31), nor to betray him, as Judas did.

[2–5] Jesus' next words are clearly intended to provide reassurance and hope to the disciples in the face of his death, even if it is not entirely clear what he is promising. Referring to the "many rooms" (*monai*) in "my Father's house" or "household" (*hē oikia tou patros*; cf. 4:53; 8:35), Jesus informs the disciples that he is going to "prepare a place" for them, and that he will "come again" and take them to himself, so that they may be where he is. Although the New Testament regularly speaks of Jesus' *parousia* ("presence" or "coming"),[60] this is the lone instance where Jesus explicitly speaks of coming *again*.[61] Jesus promises to return and to take his disciples to "my Father's house" (or "household"), likely an allusion to the heavenly dwellings prepared for the righteous, so that they may be with him.[62] In John, when Jesus comes "again," he will complete his work as the good shepherd, gathering all his own together. In the Father's household there is room for all those whom Jesus will bring to be with him (10:16; 12:32).[63]

Because the Farewell Discourse persistently stresses that Jesus will "come" and be with the disciples (14:18, 23; 17:23, 26), some interpreters understand

59. See Parsenios (2005) for the consolatory elements of this discourse as reflecting Greco-Roman consolation literature (esp. 22–31, 90–109).

60. The word is not used in John; cf. 1 Cor 15:23; 1 Thess 2:19; 4:15; 5:23; 2 Thess 2:1, 8; Jas 5:7–8; 2 Pet 1:16; 3:4; 1 John 2:28; using *erchomai* in 1 Cor 11:26; 2 Thess 1:10, as in John 14:3.

61. The NT does not refer to Jesus' coming or "coming again" as the "second coming."

62. Jesus comes "from heaven" (3:13, 31; 6:41–42, 50–51, 58), but neither he nor believers are said to go there; Jesus returns to his Father; believers hope to be with Jesus in the presence of his Father. For heavenly dwellings, see *1 En.* 39.4–8; *2 En.* 61.2–3; *4 Ezra* 7.80, 85, 101; cf. Luke 16:9. Steven Bryan offers the intriguing suggestion that "my Father's house" refers to a heavenly temple that Jesus prepares to serve as the eternal dwelling place of the righteous with God. Philo (*Somn.* 1.256) speaks of the soul's return to "the paternal house" (*eis ton patrōion oikon epanelthein*; see also 1.135); Heraclitus, *Ep.* 5, to Amphidamas (in *Cynic Epistles* 194–95), refers to the immortal soul's dwelling in "ethereal dwellings" (*aitherioi domoi*).

63. Among the scholars who interpret Jesus' words as a reference to his (eschatological) coming are Barrett 457; Beasley-Murray 249–50; Frey 2000, 143–50; Lincoln 2005, 389–90; Schnelle 1998, 227–28; Talbert 204.

Jesus' promise to "come again" somewhat differently: for example, as the coming of Jesus to believers upon their death[64] or as Jesus' ongoing presence made possible by the impartation of the Spirit.[65] To be sure, Jesus' parting words are shot through with the promise of his presence; but here he explicitly promises that his future return will complete his work of gathering "the scattered children of God" (cf. 11:52) to their dwelling place with him and with the Father (14:3). In light of the fact that he later promises his disciples that he and his Father will "make our home" (*monēn par autō poiēsometha*, 14:23) with those who keep Jesus' commands, it may well be that even the promise here—that Jesus will take them to be with him—already entails his joining them to himself as the risen Lord.[66] While Jesus promises he will come again, in the meantime he will also be present with the disciples in other ways: they are never without his presence.

If Jesus has explained any of this to his disciples, if he has shared with them his knowledge that "his hour has come" to go to the Father (13:1), they seem not to have understood it; although Jesus asserts that they know *the way* to the place where he is going (14:4), Thomas responds with bewilderment that they do not even know *where* Jesus is going. How then can they know the way to it (v. 5)? Jesus' reply (v. 6) seems to answer a different question than the one Thomas implicitly asks.[67] The answer to Thomas's immediate question is that Jesus is going to the Father; he goes by means of his own death and resurrection. Jesus answers the question how *others* come to the Father: they come to the Father through him. Implicitly, then, Jesus interprets his death and resurrection, the means by which he returns to the Father, as the path by which others come to the Father.

[6–11] In one of the Gospel's distinctive "I am" statements, Jesus identifies himself as "the way and the truth and the life." The three predicative nominatives (way, truth, life), linked by the simple conjunction "and" (*kai*), could be understood to indicate three distinct but related predications regarding Jesus. But the following explanatory comment ("No one comes to the Father but by

64. Bultmann 1971, 602.

65. R. Brown 1970, 624–27. Keener (2:938–39) contends that the only possible way to read the text is as an example of present rather than future eschatology (14:23). O'Day (741) argues that the "heavenly dwellings" (as virtually all instances of "place" in John) symbolically depict relationship, here referring to the full communion with God made possible by Jesus' death and resurrection. In light of the equation of Jesus' body with the temple in 2:19–21, Kerr (298) argues that "my Father's house" (14:2) refers to Jesus' body and, by extension, to the community of believers; see also Coloe 2007, 108–12, 145–48; Grayston 115; McCaffrey 138–40.

66. Some interpreters believe that Jesus' promise to "come again" refers to all forms of the coming of Christ (Hoskyns 454; Barrett 457; Ridderbos 489–92).

67. A textual variant (see NRSV 14:4 mg.) arose to smooth the transition to Thomas's dual query about where Jesus is going and how he will go: "You know where I am going, and you know the way" (*hopou egō hypagō oidate kai tēn hodon oidate*; Metzger 207).

me") suggests that the three predicates could better be understood to indicate that Jesus is the way that leads to the Father, precisely because he himself embodies the truth and life that come from the Father (cf. 1:4–5, 17; 5:33; 11:25; 17:3). Thus we might translate, "I am the way that leads to truth and life." In the Psalms the "way" of God is spoken of frequently (see Pss 1:6; 5:8; 18:30; 25:8–12; 27:11), where the word in the LXX is *hodos* ("way," "path"), as here. The psalmist professes to "hate every false way" because God's word (*ho logos*) is "a lamp to my feet and a light to my path" (119:104–5 [118:104–5 LXX]). In John, Jesus is the Word, the light that illumines the true way to God and so gives life.

The assertion that Jesus is "the way to the Father" (14:6) is the result of, and gives expression to, Johannine Christology.[68] Because Jesus is the Word, and because he embodies truth, light, and life from the Father, he is also the way to the Father. Jesus is not extrinsic to the identity of God; he is not one of many prophets or agents who speak what is true. He is God's own Word, embodied. Because Jesus' identity is *intrinsic* to the identity of God, because God has made Jesus equal to him and one with him, because God has chosen to be made one with Jesus, Jesus is the way to the Father. To know Jesus is to know the Father who sent him; to know the only Son is to know the only God. Jesus' identity as the unique Son of the Father grounds the sweeping declaration that "no one comes to the Father except through me."

Jesus' remark that "from now on" (*ap' arti*, v. 7) the disciples will know and see the Father implies that something will soon change, or has changed, so that "from now on" something is possible that has not been possible before. But the statement is puzzling, because when Philip entreats Jesus, "Show us the Father" (v. 8), Jesus replies that if they have seen him, they have seen the Father. In other words, the disciples should already have "known" and "seen" the Father in Jesus. What, then, will change "from now on"? It may be that the temporal indicator "from now on" signals the imminent actualization of the conditions necessary for understanding Jesus more fully, conditions that include the resurrection of Jesus and the giving of the Spirit. These new realities alter the epistemological stance of the disciples, so that "from now on" they will see the Father because they will recognize Jesus more fully as both the *representative* and the *representation* of the Father (see comments on 2:17–22; 12:16, 44–50).

Jesus' statement "The one who has seen me has seen the Father" (v. 9) does not simply conflate the identities of the Father and the Son. Throughout the Gospel, Jesus has identified himself as the Son, the representative of God who speaks the words and does the life-giving works of the Father. To see the works of Jesus is to see the works of God because "the one who is sent is like

68. Rightly, Moberly 2008.

the one who sent him" (*m. Ber.* 5.5; see comments on 5:28–29; 13:16–20). But that is not all. Because the Father dwells in him, Jesus is also the representation of the Father. Thus, to see him is to see the Father. Indeed, no one sees God directly—that is, no one but the Son (1:18; 5:37; 6:46). Yet there remains a true, if mediated, vision of the Father through the Son, because the Son does the Father's work, and because Father and Son mutually dwell in one another (14:11). To see the works of Jesus is to see the work of God; to see the Son is to see the one in whom the Father dwells and who dwells in the Father. Because of their unity in work and their mutual indwelling, because they are one (10:30), to see the Son is to see the Father.

14:12–31 Jesus' Promises to His Disciples

Jesus continues his Farewell Discourse with a series of promises to his disciples:

- Those who believe in me will do greater works than I have done.
- I will do whatever you ask in my name.
- I will petition the Father, and he will give you another Paraclete, who will be with you and will teach you.
- I will not leave you orphans, but I will come to you.
- Because I live, you also will live.
- I will love you and reveal myself to you.
- I leave you my peace.

Taken together, Jesus' words promise his continued presence and peace with the disciples and his responsiveness to their needs and requests. Even though he is indeed going away and will not be among the disciples as he was before, they may nevertheless continue to know him, to see him, to be assured that they will live with him, and to expect him to act on their behalf. While after his death and resurrection the mode of Jesus' presence with the disciples will change, the fundamental reality that he is with them, making himself known to them, will not change. The disciples must learn what it means to "follow" the crucified and risen Lord, but it is the same Lord that they follow. As Hoskyns memorably put it, "What Jesus *is* to the faith of the true Christian believer, He *was* in the flesh."[69] All subsequent generations of disciples are also included in Jesus' promise of his presence, life, and peace.

> 14:12 "Amen, amen, I tell you; whoever believes in me will do the works that I do, and will do even greater works, because I am going to the Father.
> 13 Indeed, whatever you ask in my name, this I will do, so that the Father

69. Hoskyns 35.

might be glorified in the Son. 14 If you ask anything in my name, I will
do it.

15 "If you love me, keep my commandments. 16 And I will ask the
Father, and he will give you another Paraclete, to be with you forever, 17
the Spirit of truth, which the world is not able to receive, because it does
not see him or know him. You know him, because he remains with you
and will be in you.

18 "I will not leave you orphans: I will come to you. 19 Yet a little while
and the world will no longer see me, but you will see me. Because I live,
you also will live. 20 On that day, you will know that I am in the Father
and you are in me and I am in you.

21 "Whoever has my commands and keeps them is the one who loves
me. Whoever loves me will be loved by my Father, and I will love them
and reveal myself to them."

22 Judas, not Iscariot, said to him, "Lord, what shall happen that you
will soon reveal yourself to us but not the world?"

23 Jesus answered, "Whoever loves me will keep my word; and my
Father will love them, and we will come to them and make our home with
them. 24 Whoever does not love me will not keep my words. And the word
that you hear is not mine but belongs to the Father who sent me."

25 "I have said these things to you while I was with you. 26 And the
Paraclete, the Holy Spirit, whom the Father will send in my name, will
teach you all things and call to mind everything that I have said to you."

27 "Peace I leave you; my peace I give to you. I do not give to you as
the world gives. Do not let your hearts be troubled or afraid.

28 "You have heard that I said to you, 'I am going away, and I am
coming to you.' If you loved me, you would rejoice, because I am going
to the Father, for the Father is greater than I. 29 And I have spoken these
things to you before they happen, so that when they do happen, you will
believe.

30 "I will not speak with you much longer, for the ruler of this world is
coming. And he has no part in me, 31 but that the world may know that I
love the Father, and that I do what the Father has commanded me, I do this.

"Rise; let us go from here."

[14:12–14] Here Jesus makes two astonishing promises. First, he promises that those who believe in him will not only "do the works that I do," but that they will do "even greater works." Jesus' "work" or "works" includes all that he does or says. Elsewhere Jesus has already included others in his work (e.g., 9:4), so it is not surprising that he envisions the disciples as carrying on and furthering his "works," which are the works of the Father who abides in him (14:10). By analogy, the disciples will do Jesus' life-giving works only because he who is life dwells in and with them (see 14:20; 15:4–5). Their works are greater,[70] either because the many followers of Jesus will effectively multiply the number of his works or will extend the range of his work. Jesus' resurrection means that he now carries out his work as the risen one; therefore, his own ministry is not confined to first-century Judea, Samaria, and Galilee, any more than worship of the one true God is confined to worship in a temple or on one mountain (cf. 2:19–21; 4:21).

Second, Jesus promises to do whatever his disciples ask "in my name" (14:14).[71] Elsewhere in the Gospels, Jesus promises his disciples that, with certain qualifications, they will receive what they ask for (Matt 7:7–8; 21:22; Mark 11:22–24; Luke 11:9–10). In John, all such instructions on prayer are placed in the Farewell Discourse and anticipate Jesus' death and glorification, making it clear that it is the risen Lord, ever at the Father's side (1:18), who acts on behalf of his disciples in granting their requests.

Moreover, the disciples are instructed to pray in the name of Jesus. In Scripture one can do many things "in the name of the LORD": serve as a priest (Deut 18:5, 7); prophesy (Deut 18:20–22; 2 Chr 33:18; Ezra 5:1; Jer 11:21; 26:9); pronounce a blessing (Deut 21:5; 2 Sam 6:18; Ps 129:8) or a curse (2 Kgs 2:24); fight in battle (1 Sam 17:45; Ps 118:10–12); swear an oath (1 Sam 20:42; 1 Kgs 22:16; Neh 13:25); in New Testament accounts, baptize (Acts 2:38; 10:48; 1 Cor 1:13–15), heal and exorcize (Mark 9:39; Acts 3:6; 16:18), and proclaim the word of God (Acts 4:18; 5:40; 9:27; 10:28). What is done "in the name of" the Lord is done by the Lord's authorization. Even as Jesus does his Father's work because his Father has sent him and is with and in him (14:10), so the disciples will continue to do the works that bring light and life to the world and glory to the Father and the Son (9:4; 11:40). As they carry out that mission, authorized by Jesus as his representatives, their prayers will be granted because of his love for them and his position with the Father.[72]

[15–17] Jesus' next promise is that if the disciples love him and keep his commands, he will ask the Father to send "another Paraclete" to them.[73] This is the first reference in the Gospel to "the Paraclete," a distinctively Johannine term for the Spirit. Earlier the Spirit's coming had been relegated to the future, after Jesus' glorification (7:39). Since Jesus' glorification is imminent, he now promises that the Father will indeed send the Spirit, even though that sending still lies ahead.

Jesus' promise that the Father will send "another" Paraclete assumes the presence of a previous "Paraclete." Although Jesus is never called "Paraclete"

70. *Meizona*, 14:12; see BDAG under *megas* (1a), "of any extension in space in all directions."

71. See also the comments on 15:7; 16:24.

72. See also Lincoln 2005, 392–93.

73. For the meaning and background of *Paraclete*, as well as summary comments on the role of the Spirit in John, see also Excursus 9: "The Holy Spirit in John."

in this Gospel (cf. 1 John 2:1), he has served in this capacity. Jesus and the Spirit serve as advocates for the disciples, bearing witness to the truth, in the face of the world's opposition (cf. 16:7–11).[74] "Spirit of truth," unique to the New Testament's Johannine literature (John 14:17; 15:26; 16:13; 1 John 4:6; cf. 1 John 5:6), is found also in certain Jewish sources; it indicates that the Spirit empowers truthful speaking in bearing witness, prophecy, or judgment.[75] The prepositional description "of truth" emphasizes the origin, character, and function of the Spirit: the Spirit comes from God, who is truth; this Spirit can be distinguished from the spirit of error or deceit; it serves to bear witness to and instruct the disciples in the truth. Thus "Spirit of truth" virtually defines "Paraclete" in the Gospel. The Paraclete, the Spirit of truth, will abide "with you" (alternatively, "beside" or "near you," *par' hymin*) and be "in you" (*en hymin*) forever (14:17): that is, the Spirit will never leave or depart from them. The Spirit both accompanies them and dwells within them.[76]

The world does not receive, know, or see the Spirit. These statements are parallel to what has been said about the world's failure to receive or know either Jesus or the Father (1:10; 7:28; 8:55), or to have seen the Father (6:46). The world has of course "seen" Jesus, although it has not recognized or understood who he is. It is in this sense that one should take the statement that the world has not seen the Spirit: the world has not understood who or what the Spirit is. Even as the Spirit remained on Jesus at his baptism (*menon ep' auton*, 1:33), so now the Spirit remains with (*meth' hymōn*, 14:16; *par' hymin*, v. 17) and in (*en hymin*, v. 17) the disciples. The Spirit is God's ongoing presence and power with the disciples; yet the world acknowledges neither the revelation of God in Jesus nor the presence of God with the disciples through the Spirit.

There are three striking features of the usage of the characteristic Johannine word *kosmos* ("world") in the Farewell Discourse: (1) "World" appears frequently, although not exclusively, in conjunction with the work of the Paraclete (14:17–19, 26–27; 16:7–11). (2) "The world" designates those who do not believe in Jesus and who are the source of opposition and hostility to his disciples after his departure (14:17–19, 31; 15:18–19; 16:20, 33). In the Farewell Discourse, opposition comes not from "the Jews" (the term *hoi Ioudaioi* does not appear in chs. 14–17), as elsewhere in John, but from "the world." (3) The world is the arena of both the disciples' and Jesus' witness (14:22, 31; 16:8; ch. 17). As both the source of opposition to the disciples and the arena of their witness,

74. For this definition of *paraklētos*, see BDAG, with numerous examples and discussion.

75. *Jub.* 25.14; 1QS IV, 21–23; *Jos. Asen.* 19.11; *T. Jud.* 20.5 (perhaps a Christian interpolation).

76. For the fluid characterization of the Spirit in first-century Jewish texts, see Levison 1997, 238–48.

the recurrence of "the world" (*ho kosmos*) indicates the broader audience of the mission and work of the disciples following the death and resurrection of Jesus (cf. 3:16; 4:42).[77]

[18–20] Having warned his disciples that he is going away, leaving them behind in a perpetually challenging situation, Jesus makes his disciples yet another series of promises: he will not abandon them; he will come to them; they will see him; they will live. They will not be bereft of his life-giving presence. Specifically, Jesus promises his disciples several things:

1. Although he is going away, they will see him again, a promise that refers initially to the resurrection appearances: tellingly, the disciples confess Jesus' resurrection with the announcement "We have seen the Lord!" (20:18, 25; see comments there).[78] His death is the end neither of his life nor of his presence with them. As Jesus' words shift from the promise of seeing him (14:19) to the reality of indwelling (14:20) and to keeping his commandments and living in love (14:21), these promises encompass future generations of believers. The resurrection appearances will cease, but the disciples will continue to perceive Jesus' presence with them.

2. Jesus will not leave the disciples alone, as orphans, without any help or protection, but will "come to them" (v. 18). To be sure, Jesus promises them the Spirit, who will teach, guide, and be with them, but he also promises them his own presence. As Augustine rightly observes, "After his promise of the Holy Spirit, in order that no one might think that the Lord was going to give him as a substitute for himself in such a way that he would not also be with them, he added and said, 'I shall not leave you orphans; I shall come to you.'"[79] In other words, the risen Jesus should not be identified *as* the Spirit; the promise of the Spirit's coming does not fully exhaust the promise that Jesus will come to them.[80] Jesus does not here explain *how* he will be with them: later imagery and language will explicate his presence in terms of the disciples' dependence on and receptivity to Jesus (15:1–7), the reciprocity of friendship (15:14–15), and mutual indwelling (14:20; 15:5; 17:23, 26).

3. Finally, although Jesus will die, he will live again; he is life and resurrection, for the present and the future. Jesus' statement "Because I live" refers to

77. As Schnelle (1998, 166 n. 77) observes, "the Jews" do not appear in the portion of text that treats the situation of Jesus' followers after his departure most intensively; the fact that the role of "the Jews" in Jesus' ministry is taken over by "the world" (*ho kosmos*) in the situation of the church suggests that the conflict with Judaism and/or the synagogue lies in the past. See his discussions in "Exkurs 6: Die Ἰουδαίοι im Johannesevangelium" and in "Die Juden im Johannesevangelium," summarized by Kierspel 57–59; see also comments on 16:2 above.

78. For further discussion, see M. M. Thompson 2007; Zumstein 2008.

79. Augustine, *Tract. Ev. Jo.* 75.1.1.

80. See here also Frey 2000, 175–76.

his own resurrection;[81] the promise "You will live" grounds the disciples' hope of life and resurrection in Jesus himself.

"On that day" (14:20; 16:23, 26)[82] they will know that he is "in the Father and the Father is in me," because his resurrection will signal his union with God, "the living Father," and his participation in the life of God. As they remain in Jesus and he remains in them, the disciples will live. Hence, Jesus' resurrection, his return to life with the Father, assures them that his life will be in them.

[21–24] Jesus explains what it means to love him: it is to keep his commands (14:15; 15:10), even as God's people are called to love God (Deut 6:4) and keep his commandments (e.g., Deut 11:27–28; 12:28; 15:5). He further declares that those who love him will be loved by God, thus rounding out the Gospel's assertions that God loves the world (3:16), that the Father loves the Son (3:35; 5:20; 10:17; 15:9), and that Jesus has loved his own (13:1, 34; 15:12). Furthermore, Jesus will "reveal himself" to those who love him and keep his commands. The question of Judas ("not Iscariot," 14:22), how Jesus can reveal himself to them and not to the world, indicates that the disciples do not yet understand that they will "see" him because he has risen, but that his resurrection will not imply a return to life as before. Here is a contrast with Lazarus, who resumes his life as before, eating and drinking in public, and becoming an object of public curiosity (12:2, 9). As in the other Gospels, Jesus appears only to his disciples; at least they alone recognize who he is (21:7). The resurrection appearances are not manifestations of Jesus for all to see, any more than all see the glory of Jesus in the flesh. "Seeing" or recognizing Jesus depends upon his revelation or manifestation of himself to them.[83]

As we shall see, John interprets the resurrection appearances of Jesus to testify to his living presence, here pictured in terms of Jesus and his Father "making our home" with the disciples. If Jesus has "revealed" himself to the disciples, he can do so because he is living and will continue to live among and with the disciples. The promise to the disciples that Jesus will come again to take them to dwell with the Father (*monai*, 14:2–3) is now supplemented, but not replaced, by the promise of the divine presence dwelling (*monē*) on earth

81. The present tense ("because I live," 14:19) may, in the NT, be used as a future ("Because I will live"). Here, however, the present tense may also underscore that it is Jesus' ongoing life, present and future, that assures the resurrection of those who are in him.

82. While elsewhere in the NT "that day" typically refers to Christ's return (Matt 7:22; 24:36; Mark 13:32; Luke 10:12; 2 Tim 1:12, 18), here it refers to the eschatological hour inaugurated by Jesus' resurrection (cf. Isa 2:11, 17; 24:21; 25:9; Zech 2:11; 3:10; 9:16; 12:3); Jesus' appearances are one of the ways in which he comes to his disciples after his death. See comments on 14:20.

83. The word translated "reveal" (*emphanizein*, "to lay open to view, make visible" [BDAG]) is used only here in John (14:21–22). For the verb's use in relationship to resurrection, see Matt 27:53; Heb 9:24. On the theme of recognition generally, see Larsen.

(14:23; cf. Rev 21:3, 9, 22–23; 22:3). The dwelling or continued presence of Father and Son with the disciples will come to its fruition in the future when Jesus takes them to be with him where he is, in his Father's house (John 14:2–3).

[25–26] In addition to the promise of his own presence, Jesus reminds the disciples of additional tasks that the Paraclete will accomplish: to "teach you all things" and "call to mind everything that I have said to you." The Spirit's twofold work looks backward, calling to mind what Jesus said to the disciples while he was with them, and forward to things yet to be disclosed (see 16:13: the Spirit "will guide you into all the truth"). Presumably "all things" include the meaning of Jesus' words and work, done or spoken in the past, but understood only after his death and resurrection and the coming of the Spirit (2:22; 7:37–39; 12:16; 13:7; cf. 1 John 2.27; 4:1–2). The understanding that the disciples are said to acquire "later" may be attributed to the work of the Paraclete, the Spirit of truth, even when the Spirit is not explicitly named as the source of such insight (John 2:22; 12:16; 13:7; see 1 John 2:27; 4:1–2). But in order to grasp the teaching of the Spirit granted after Jesus' departure to the Father, one must turn back to the reality of the Word made flesh, his life, words, death, and resurrection. The Gospel itself is undoubtedly the product of the Spirit's guidance to understand the significance of Jesus' person, life, death, and teaching.

[27–29] Jesus now repeats his earlier exhortation (14:1) to the disciples not to let their hearts be troubled, adding a promise: he will give them his peace and they will rejoice. John's language calls to mind both Synoptic and Pauline descriptions of the blessings of the kingdom of God, especially Paul's description of it as "righteousness and peace and joy in the Holy Spirit" (Rom 14:17; cf. John 16:5–33, where righteousness, peace, and joy all occur).[84] In the present context peace is clearly the opposite of being "troubled" or "afraid." Hence, peace is a disposition, a state of well-being. In biblical sources peace is often found in words of greeting (Ezra 5:7; 7:12; Luke 10:5; 24:36; John 20:19, 21, 26) and farewell (Judg 18:6; 2 Sam 3:21; Jdt 8:35; Mark 5:34; Acts 16:36; 1 Cor 16:11; Jas 2:16), as well as in more general formulas of benediction or greeting (e.g., 1 Chr 12:18; Esth 9:30; Rom 1:17; 1 Cor 1:3; 2 Cor 1:2; Gal 1:3; Eph 1:2; Phil 1:2; Col 1:2).

Equally important, peace was believed to be a feature of righteous royal rule and of the messianic age.[85] God is the one who effects or gives peace (1 Chr 22:8–9, 18; 2 Chr 14:7; Pss 4:8; 29:11; 85:8, 10). As Messiah, the Holy One of God, the King of Israel, Jesus' promise to give his disciples peace is coupled with the promise of his ongoing presence. Jesus may appear to be absent from the disciples, but he will be there with them: they can be

84. For further discussion, see Beutler 2001, 169–73.

85. See BDAG, *eirēnē*; see esp. Ps 85:8, 10; Isa 9:6–7; 26:2; 32:17; 52:7; 54:10; 55:12; 57:19; Zech 8:12, 16, 19; 9:10.

assured of his presence and in that presence have the peace that characterizes the messianic age.

Jesus also urges his disciples to participate in the joy of the coming messianic age by rejoicing that he is "going to the Father, because the Father is greater than I" (14:28; for Jesus' return to the Father, see 13:1; 16:10; 17:5, 11, 13; 20:17). But the reason given for the disciples' rejoicing is scarcely transparent. Does Jesus give them the ground for rejoicing ("the Father is greater than I; hence, you should rejoice that I am going to him") or does he explain why is he going to the Father ("I am going to the Father because the Father is greater than I")? The answer depends to a large extent on what is meant by Jesus' characterization of the Father as *greater* than Jesus is. Jesus comes from the Father (6:46) and returns to the Father (13:1; 16:10, 28; 17:11); he is sent by the Father (5:37; 6:44, 57; 8:18; 12:49; 20:21), does the work of the Father (5:19–20, 36; 10:32, 37), speaks the words of Father (7:16; 8:28; 12:49–50), receives his commission to give life and to judge from the Father (5:21–22), and has "life in himself" as the Father has it (5:26) because the Father has given it as well as "all things" (3:35; 5:20, 22; 6:39; 13:3; 16:15) to him. These statements cannot be turned around: the Father is not sent by the Son, the Father does not receive a commission from the Son, and so on.[86] Hence, the Father is "greater" than the Son.[87] In returning to the Father, Jesus returns to the one who sent him after accomplishing the work that the Father has given him. Therefore the disciples should rejoice with Jesus.

[29–31] One section of Jesus' discourse now draws to its close: Jesus alerts his disciples that his time with them is short. He has sought to prepare them for his imminent departure, so that when the events that lead to his death unfold, the disciples will not cease to believe in him; and when they see him and experience his presence and the work of the Holy Spirit among them, the truth of his word will be confirmed, and they will have their faith deepened.

Now "the ruler of this world,"[88] the devil, is coming (v. 30). In his death on the cross, Jesus will encounter and triumph over the power of darkness, embodied in the "ruler of this world," which seeks to extinguish the light and to deceive and mislead people from coming to the light. Jesus assures his disciples that the ruler of this world "has no part in me" (lit., "has nothing in me," *en emoi ouk echei ouden*), where the sense may well be "has no claim on me" or "has no power over me." Nothing that the ruler of this world may do ultimately

86. Thus Barrett 468: "The Father is *fons divinitatis* [the 'fount of divinity'] in which the being of the Son has its source; the Father is God sending and commanding, the Son is sent and obedient."

87. John Chrysostom represents interpreters who argue that the statement "the Father is greater than I" contrasts the *Un*begotten Father with the *only-begotten* Son (*Hom. Jo.* 85); Augustine, citing Phil 2:6, represents those who take the statement to refer to the Son's humility in his humanity (*Tract. Ev. Jo.* 78).

88. On "ruler of this world," see the earlier comments on 12:31.

challenges Jesus' own claim on the world or the efficacy of his death for the life of the world. As Augustine declares, "The whole world from the heights of the sky even to the depths of the earth is subject to the Creator, not to the deserter, to the Savior, not to the slayer, to the Deliverer, not to the subjugator, to the Teacher, not to the deceiver."[89] For the world was made through the Word (1:10), who became flesh (1:14) in order to save the world (3:16). He now gives that flesh for the life of the world (6:51–58). To perceive Jesus' death on the cross not as his defeat and death, but as his victory that brings life, is to judge with right judgment (7:24). But that judgment can hardly be deduced from the spectacle of the crucified Jesus: it is the judgment granted by seeing from the perspective advocated by the Gospel itself.

Jesus seems to close his remarks as he invites his disciples, "Rise; let us go from here."[90] But Jesus keeps talking, and at some length, about his departure and the difficulties the disciples will encounter; his actual departure with his disciples from their supper is not narrated until later (18:1, "After Jesus had spoken these words, he went out with his disciples").[91] Jesus' departure to his arrest, trial, and crucifixion is anticipated but delayed.[92] In the interval between the expected and actual departure, Jesus addresses his disciples at length with a series of promises and exhortations regarding his continued presence despite his (imminent) absence. Jesus' delayed exit to his death, which has been anticipated throughout the Gospel, underscores the weightiness of the words that he now speaks to his disciples. Jesus' end is drawing ever nearer. One is reminded again of Echecrates's question to Phaedo, "I wish you would tell me about [Socrates's] death. What did he say in his last hours?"

Excursus 9: The Holy Spirit in John

In John, the Holy Spirit[93] bears a distinctive designation, "Paraclete" (*paraklētos*). In pre-Christian and extra-Christian literature *paraklētos* means "mediator, intercessor,

89. Augustine, *Tract. Ev. Jo.* 79.3.2. For the devil as deceiver, see the comments on 8:44–50.

90. Some interpreters speculate that the Farewell Discourse originally ended here (R. Brown 1970, 656). If so, John 14:1–31 is the first version of Jesus' parting words; 15:1–16:33 comprises added material or a deliberate rereading of the first version, inserted between 14:31 and 18:1.

91. The note that Jesus then departed (in 18:1) makes it difficult to adopt the suggestion that 14:31 signals that Jesus and his disciples are walking toward the garden as Jesus speaks (e.g., Carson 1991, 479).

92. Parsenios (2005, 55–70) argues that John here depicts a "delayed dramatic exit" roughly parallel to that found in ancient Greek and Roman tragedies; cf. Brant 216. On the effect created by Jesus' words, see also Moloney 1998a, 53; Lincoln 2005, 399; Schnelle 1998, 238. Lincoln and Schnelle are among those who note that John is basically following Mark's outline (in 14:42, Jesus says, "Rise, let us go"; but in 14:43 he is said to be "still speaking"); so also Barrett 469.

93. For recent studies, see Bennema 2002b; T. Brown; Levison 2009; M. M. Thompson 2001, 145–88.

helper."[94] The word is not found in the LXX.[95] Philo uses the word to mean both "intercessor, mediator" (*Ios.* 23; *Mos.* 2.134)[96] and "adviser, helper," or "advocate" (*Opif.* 23, 165), without locating such help or advocacy in a lawcourt. Grayston contends that the sense is closer to "patron" or "sponsor" (hence the Latin translation is typically *advocatus*), someone whose presence and person count in favor of another.[97] In rabbinic literature the word is transliterated as *pĕraklîṭ*, as in *m. ʾAbot* 4:11, where the context shows it is roughly the opposite of "accuser": "Whoever performs one precept gets for himself one advocate [*pĕraklîṭ*], but whoever commits one transgression gets for himself one accuser." Because it is difficult to find an adequate English translation, the term is often simply transliterated as "Paraclete" (as in this commentary),[98] though "helper" or "advocate" could serve well.[99]

John's distinctive designation of the Spirit as "the Paraclete" occurs only in the Gospel's Farewell Discourse, where the Spirit is also designated "the Spirit of truth" and "the Holy Spirit" (chs. 14–16). But in the narratives framing the Farewell Discourse (chs. 1–13; 18–20), the Spirit is called either simply "the Spirit" (1:32–33; 3:5–6, 34; 4:23–24; 6:63; 7:39) or the "Holy Spirit" (1:33; 20:22). Most intriguing is the way in which the designations "Paraclete" and "Spirit" tend to correspond, not only to different portions of the Gospel, but also to two distinct ways of describing the Spirit's role and work. On the one hand, primarily in those descriptions in the narratives, the Spirit has been understood, alongside "wisdom" and "word," as a way of speaking of God's activity or as the manifestation of a particular divine activity or power.[100] Hence, the Spirit is the means by which God effects new birth or brings life to the children of God (3:3–8; 6:63; 7:37–39). Jesus will baptize "with" or "by" the Holy Spirit, described by analogy with "water" (1:33; 3:5–6; 7:37–39); Jesus "breathes" the Spirit into his disciples (20:22).

On the other hand, the Spirit has also been conceived as "a divine being distinct from and in some degree independent of God."[101] Such a characterization of the Spirit takes its cue from the Farewell Discourse (14:16–17, 26; 15:26; 16:7, 13), where the Spirit is called the "Paraclete," as well as the Holy Spirit and Spirit of truth,[102] but never simply "the Spirit" (contrast 1:32–33; 3:5–6, 34; 4:23–24; 6:63; 7:39). The Spirit-Paraclete is a teacher (14:26), who reminds the disciples of Jesus' words (14:26), testifies on Jesus' behalf (15:26), glorifies Jesus (16:14), and accuses or convicts the world of sin (16:7–8).

94. So BDAG s.v., citing Demosthenes, Dionysius of Halicarnassus, Heraclitus, Dio Cassius.

95. In the LXX, Job's "comforters" are called *paraklētores* (Job 16:2 LXX); the cognate adj. *paraklētikos* is found in Zech 1:13 LXX.

96. In John, the Spirit does not explicitly intercede for disciples; contrast Rom 8:26–27, 34.

97. Grayston 122.

98. Latin authors such as Tertullian, Cyprian, and Augustine rendered the term *Advocatus*; the Vulgate transliterated the term as *Paraclitus* (14:16, 26; 15:26; 16:7).

99. The familiar translation "Comforter" (KJV), derived from the cognate verb *parakalein*, "to comfort, exhort, encourage," does not aptly characterize the Paraclete's functions in John.

100. E.g., Johnston 31–32.

101. Smalley 293.

102. "Spirit of truth" can be found in *Jub.* 25.14; 1QS IV, 21–23; *Jos. Asen.* 19.11; *T. Jud.* 20.5 (perhaps a Christian interpolation); the DSS and *Testaments of the Twelve Patriarchs* often refer to "the spirit of deceit" or "spirit of error." The similarity in terminology does not necessarily indicate John's dependence or borrowing; see Bauckham 1997.

The Paraclete "comes from" (15:26; 16:7, 13) and is "sent" by God (14:26; 15:26; 16:7);[103] in turn, the Spirit can be "received" or "welcomed"; and believers are said to "know" and, most peculiarly, to "see" or "perceive" (*theōrei*) the Spirit (14:16–17). Here, the Spirit is described, not by analogy with water and breath, but rather as a prophet or emissary—much as Jesus himself is depicted in John.

Clearly, the functions of the Spirit change upon Jesus' death and departure. In Jesus' absence the Paraclete continues to teach the disciples, as Jesus did; but the Spirit particularly causes the disciples to recollect and understand all the truth of Jesus' words and deeds. Because the Paraclete comes as a successor to Jesus, it is not uncommon to describe the Paraclete as a "replacement" for Jesus.[104] The correspondences between Jesus and the Spirit have been taken to suggest that Jesus' activities are carried on by the Spirit, or perhaps even "as the Spirit."[105] One might call this a "christological interpretation" of the Spirit, since it alleges that the portrait of the Spirit and the Spirit's work are painted from the model of Jesus himself. The overlapping functions of Jesus and the Spirit are primarily those of teaching and disclosing God's word.[106]

1. Jesus teaches (7:14–15; 8:20; 18:19), as does the Spirit (14:26).
2. Jesus gives testimony (5:31–32; 8:13–14; 7:7), as does the Spirit (15:26).
3. Both Jesus (7:17; 8:26; 14:10) and the Spirit (14:26; 16:13–14) speak of what they have heard.
4. Both Jesus (1:18; 4:25) and the Spirit (16:13) disclose and reveal.

However, many of the functions attributed to the Spirit are elsewhere predicated, not of Jesus or of Jesus only, but also of the *Father*.

1. The Father testifies to Jesus (5:37; 8:18; 1 John 5:9), as does the Spirit (15:26–27).
2. The Father glorifies Jesus (5:44; 8:54; 12:23, 28; 13:31–32; 17:1, 5), as does the Spirit (16:14).
3. The Father will be with the disciples (14:23; 17:11, 15, 26), and the Spirit will be with them as well (14:17).
4. The Father has the authority and right to judge, but has handed judgment over to the Son (5:22, 27, 30; 8:16); so, too, the Paraclete convicts the world of judgment (16:8–11).
5. The Paraclete teaches (14:26; 16:13), as does God (5:45; 1 John 2:26–27; Jesus teaches what God tells him to teach (7:16–17).

In other words, the Spirit carries on the work of both the Son and of the Father. In John, not only is it true that "what the Father does, the Son does"; it is also true that "what the Father does, the Spirit does."[107]

103. For discussion of the "procession" of the Spirit, see the comments on 15:26–27 below.

104. R. Brown 1970, 1143. For a different understanding, see Beasley-Murray 257–58; M. M. Thompson 2001, 179–85.

105. See Burge 141.

106. For further discussion, see R. Brown 1970, 1140–41.

107. Cf. Irenaeus's apt characterization of the Son and Spirit as the "two hands of the Father" (*Haer.* 3.11.1; 4.7.4; 4.20.1; 5.1.3; 5.6.1; 5.28.4).

If, after Jesus' departure, the Spirit will exercise new and specific functions among the disciples, we might ask how the Spirit's role was identified and experienced then. At this point some interpreters have pointed out that the description of the Paraclete's functions correspond to those of the ideal Christian prophets or teachers in the church.[108] In other words, the Spirit's roles of teaching, revealing, speaking, and bearing witness are exercised in the company of disciples, most probably by those who were designated or looked to as leaders and teachers.[109] One might term this the *ecclesiastical* understanding of the Spirit. The Spirit's work is exercised through those who teach, bear witness, seek the truth, or among the disciples in studying Scripture, or through those who bear witness to the world (16:7–8).[110] Such an understanding of the Paraclete gains credibility in light of the situation alluded to in 1 John. The epistle urges its readers to "test the spirits," appeals to the anointing of the holy one that teaches "about all things," and reminds believers that the "Spirit of God" leads to truthful confession that "Jesus Christ has come in the flesh" (2:20–27; 4:1–3), all for the sake of combatting "many false prophets." Apparently, a rift in the community was accompanied by rival claims to have the Spirit, to know the truth, and to speak as "prophets," those inspired by the Spirit.[111] In John, if Jesus is the Word embodied as a human being, then the Paraclete is the Spirit "embodied" in, among, and through the community of disciples (14:16).

In summary, we note the following aspects of the Spirit's work in John:

1. The Spirit points resolutely to Jesus, bearing witness to him, and glorifying or honoring him (1:32–34; 15:26; 16:14). Since the disciples come particularly to understand the events of Jesus' death and resurrection only "later" (e.g., 2:22; 12:16; 13:7), "all the truth" surely includes deeper insight into Jesus' identity and work, elucidating what was latent in his life. It is altogether likely that the author of the Gospel understood the truth granted by the Spirit as including the robust presentation of Jesus' divine identity, characteristic of and recorded in the Gospel itself.

2. Since the Spirit does not come until Jesus departs to be with the Father, Jesus' descriptions of the Spirit's work in chapters 14–16 (cf. 7:37–39) anticipate that which is coming; outside the narrative frame of the Gospel, however, the Spirit is present: Jesus has departed and "breathed" the Spirit on his disciples (20:22). Thus readers of the Gospel experience the presence of the Spirit. The Spirit continues Jesus' work, purifying those who believe (1:33; 3:25–26), enacting Jesus' promises of new life (3:3–8; 4:14–15; 6:63; 20:22), quenching thirst for wisdom (4:15; 7:37–39), and empowering true worship (4:24). What Jesus in the Gospel promises, the readers of the Gospel know to be fulfilled.

3. The Spirit, whom Jesus breathes into the disciples as he sends them into the world (20:20–23), empowers a mission that reaches beyond the geographical and ethnic boundaries of his own work. The work of Jesus' disciples will extend and expand what he himself did. The Gospel promises that, as the disciples enter uncharted territory, they

108. For the Paraclete as teacher and examination of key terminology, see Bennema 2002b, 228–34.

109. The "gifts of the Spirit" in 1 Cor 12:4–10 include speaking wisdom, knowledge, prophecy, discernment; Eph 4:11 includes apostles, prophets, evangelists, pastors, and teachers.

110. See Boring 113–14; Johnston.

111. For discussion of prophetic inspiration and ecstatic experience in early Judaism and the Gospel of John, see esp. Levison 1997; 2009, 390–98.

can and must trust the Spirit to guide and instruct them, so that what they say and what they do always bears witness to the truth that is embodied in and through Jesus.

15:1–17 Jesus, the True Vine

The previous portion of Jesus' last words to his disciples ends with an invitation, "Rise; let us go from here" (14:31). Jesus anticipates his departure from the supper with his disciples to face his arrest, trial, and death, yet his departure is delayed: no one leaves as Jesus keeps talking at some length. In the portion of the discourse now under consideration (15:1–17), Jesus illustrates his promise to be with his disciples (14:18, 23) and the mutual indwelling of Father and Son, Son and disciple (14:20), with the picture of a vine that unerringly gives life to the branches. Drawing their life from Jesus and clinging closely to him, the disciples "abide" in him (15:7), keep his commandments (15:10, 12–17; cf. 14:15, 21, 23–24), imitate his example (15:13–16; cf. 14:12), know him as a friend (15:13–15), have joy (15:11; cf. 14:28), and live in his love (15:9–10, 12–13).

The image of the vine recalls the Old Testament's description of Israel as a vine (see below). The "true vine" represents faithful, fruit-bearing Israel (Isa 27:2). Even as Isaiah foresaw the glory of Jesus (John 12:41), so, too, Isaiah foresaw Israel's restoration to be a fruitful vine. As a vine whose branches bear much fruit, Jesus and his people fulfill the prophetic vision of God's people as thriving in faithfulness, love, and friendship with God.

> **15:1** "I am the true vine, and my Father is the vinedresser. **2** He takes away
> every branch in me that does not bear fruit, and he cleanses[a] every branch
> bearing fruit so that it may bear more fruit.[b] **3** You are already cleansed[a]
> because of the word that I have spoken to you.
>
> **4** "Abide in me, and I will abide in you. Even as the branch is not able to bear fruit on its own unless it abides in the vine, so neither are you able [to bear fruit] unless you abide in me.
>
> **5** "I am the vine, you are the branches. Those who abide in me, and I in them, these will bear much fruit, for apart from me you can do nothing.
>
> **6** "If anyone does not abide in me, that one is cast out even as a branch
> [is cast out]; it withers, and they gather them and throw them into the
> fire and burn them.[c] **7** If you abide in me and my words abide in you, ask
> whatever you wish, and it will be done for you. **8** This is how my Father
> is glorified, that you bear much fruit and become my disciples.
>
> **9** "Even as the Father loves me, so I have loved you. Abide in my love.
> **10** If you keep my commandments, you abide in my love, even as I have
> kept my Father's commandments and abide in his love. **11** These words I
> have spoken to you so that my joy may be in you, and that your joy may
> be complete.

12 "This is my commandment: Love one another, even as I have loved
you. 13 No one has greater love than this—laying down one's life for
one's friends. 14 You are my friends if you do what I command you.
15 "No longer do I call you servants, for the servant does not know
what his master does. I have called you friends, because everything that
I have heard from my Father I have made known to you. 16 You did not
choose me, rather I chose you and have appointed you that you should go
and bear fruit and that your fruit should remain. Then whatever you ask
in the name of my Father he will give to you.
17 "These things I have commanded you: love one another."

a. The Greek *kathairein* means "to cleanse" but in this context means "to prune, trim" (see below).

b. Lit. "every branch in me not bearing fruit, he takes it away, and every [branch] bearing fruit, he cleanses it so that it may bear more fruit."

c. Lit., "and it is burned."

[15:1–3] At this point in the discourse to his disciples, Jesus uses a new image to describe the way in which they will experience his presence and their mutual indwelling (14:18, 20, 23): he is the "true vine," his Father is the vinedresser (*geōrgos*), and "those who bear fruit" are the branches. John's description of the vine draws on depictions of Israel as a vine, or as a vineyard, in various passages in the Old Testament.[112] Those biblical descriptions often recount God's care for the vine in the past while lamenting its desolation in the present. God "brought a vine out of Egypt," cleared the soil, and then planted and cared for the vine, but now it has been cut down and burned with fire (Ps 80:8–16).[113] Isaiah laments that while God cared for his vineyard, it failed to produce appropriate fruit, leading to its apparent abandonment by God (Isa 5:1–10). Yet Isaiah foresees a day when the vine is once again cared for and protected by God, and so becomes abundantly fruitful (27:2–6; 60:21). Jeremiah speaks of a vine that had borne fruit "in all truthfulness" (*karpophoron pasan alēthinēn*) but had subsequently become degenerate and was in need of washing (*apoplynō*, 2:21–22 LXX; cf. Jer 5:10; 6:9; 8:13; 12:10–11; Hos 10:1; 14:6–7). Yet, like Isaiah, Jeremiah foresees a day when the Lord will again have compassion on that which he had plucked up (12:14–15). These various depictions of Israel as a vine highlight both the tenderness of God's care for the vine and the dire consequences that result if God ceases to care for and protect it.

112. Ps 80:8–16; Jer 2:21; 8:13; 12:10–11; Ezek 15:2–6; 17:5–10; 19:10–14; Hos 10:1; 14:6–8; Joel 1:5–7; 2:22; see also Sir 24:17; *Lev. Rab.* 36 (133a); 1QH XIV (formerly VI), 15–16; *2 Bar.* 39.7; *1 En.* 10.16–21; *4 Ezra* 5.23; *L.A.B.* 12.8–9.

113. Commentators on the Psalms debate which historical catastrophe is in view here: the demise of the northern kingdom (723/722 B.C.E.) or the fall of Jerusalem (587/586 B.C.E.).

Most typically, God allows the vine to be destroyed because it has not produced fruit. But that is not the whole story: the Scriptures also speak of the prophetic yearning for God's restoration of his vineyard so that it might be the fruitful vine it was intended to be. In John, this vision comes to fruition in Jesus, who is the true vine; his disciples yield the fruit that comes from his life in them.

There are striking correspondences in diction and theme with Ezekiel's description of the vine (15:2; 17:6–9; 19:10–14).[114] In Ezek 15:4 LXX, branches are cut off and thrown into the fire at the yearly pruning, where the word for "pruning" is *katharsis* (*tēn kat' eniauton katharsin*, "the yearly cleansing" or "pruning"). John uses the word *kathairein* ("to cleanse") to describe the "pruning" of the branches so that they are "clean" (*katharoi*, 15:2–3). In a play on words, John states that the branches remaining on the vine and bearing fruit are "cleansed" (*kathairei*), while those that do not bear fruit are "taken away" (*airei*). Pruning thus does not portend destruction, as it does in Ezekiel, or even punishment or discipline, but instead ensures that the vine is abundantly fruitful. The branches bear much fruit because they are attached to the life-giving vine and tended, or cleansed, by the vinedresser.

It comes as a bit of a surprise, however, to read Jesus' words, "You are *already* cleansed [*katharoi*] because of the word that I have spoken to you" (15:3).[115] What, then, does the vinedresser, the Father, do? Through Jesus' word, the disciples have come out of the realms of unbelief, mortality, and death into the realm of faith, Spirit, and life (5:24; 6:63): they have been "cleansed" by the Holy One of God (6:69). And having been cleansed initially by Jesus' word, they will be pruned or cleansed by the Father's loving care so that they may remain as fruitful branches on the vine.[116] Now that they have "passed from death to life" (5:24), they must "abide," remain faithful, lest they become like those disciples who once believed but fell away from following Jesus (6:66) or who had once believed but did not abide in him (8:30–31) and were cut off from the life-giving vine. The Father tends the branches so that they remain attached to the vine, vigorous, healthy, drawing life, and producing fruit (cf. 10:28–30).

[4–6] While continuing to appeal to the metaphor of the vine, branches, and fruit, Jesus now exhorts his disciples to remain faithful, to persevere in discipleship, as he says, "Abide in me" (8:31; see also 1:32, 33; 5:38; 6:27, 56). Such

114. John 15 is the only passage in the NT to use the word *klēma*; it is used six times for "branch" in Ezekiel (15:2; 17:6, 7, 23; 19:11), about as many instances as in the rest of the LXX (Num 13:23; Ps 79:12 [80:11 ET]; Joel 1:7; Nah 2:3 [2:2]; Mal 3:19 [4:1]; Jer 31:32 [48:32]). Forms of *klados* are about 5 times as common, including 6× in Ezek 31; *klados* is used 11× in the NT (Matthew, Mark, Luke, Romans). See further Manning.

115. In *1 En.* 10.16–21 the cleansing of the earth from its pollution allows the vine to flourish; in John the vine is cleansed and bears fruit even though it still dwells "in the world," the realm typically portrayed in John as hostile to God.

116. Hoskyns (475) also notices the "double element in the purification of the disciples."

faithfulness requires that Jesus abide in his disciples ("and I in you"). Even as the branches cannot bear fruit unless they are attached to the life-giving vine, so without Jesus' continued presence, the disciples will be unable to remain in him. In other words, the relationship of mutual abiding that Jesus calls for is not a relationship of equals, or of equal contributions: Jesus' indwelling makes abiding and obedience possible because he is the life of the Father given to the branches.

Strikingly, Jesus does not exhort his disciples to bear fruit; rather, he exhorts his disciples to remain attached to him, the source of life. Elsewhere in the New Testament, the fruit that is borne indicates what is within a person (see Matt 3:8–10; 7:16–20; 12:33–35; 13:23; cf. Heb 12:11);[117] here fruit is produced as a result of the life of the vine. As Lesslie Newbigin aptly puts it, "The fruit is not an artifact of the *disciples*; it is the fruit of the *vine*. It is the life of Jesus himself reproduced in the lives of the disciples in the midst of the life of the world. The presence of fruit is the visible evidence of the fact that the branch is part of the vine."[118] Hence, Jesus' exhortation "Abide in me."

John's distinctive use of "abide" (*menein*) to describe the relationship of Jesus to the disciples and the disciples to Jesus has two dimensions: (1) It implies receptivity; it is neither passive nor static, but entails an openness and responsiveness to Jesus' life-giving presence.[119] (2) As part of John's rich vocabulary for the varied aspects of discipleship—believing, following, and knowing—"abiding" implies perseverance, steadfastness, or faithfulness.[120] In John, the life of discipleship does not merely begin with receptivity to Jesus; such receptivity characterizes the entire life of the disciple from beginning to end. "Abiding" issues in bearing fruit, keeping Jesus' commands, and loving one another. As is typical of John, such language describes both what it meant to be a disciple of the earthly Jesus—that is, to be faithful and steadfast in following after him (in contrast to the disciples of 6:66)—and what it now means to be a disciple of the living Lord. While "abiding" involves faithful following or discipleship (see comments on 8:12), it also envisions a union of disciples with the risen and living Lord that can no longer be described in the physical act of following. It undoubtedly reflects early Christian experience.[121]

117. So Paul speaks of "fruit" as the result of belonging to Christ (Rom 7:4–5), the Spirit (Gal 5:22), and the gospel (Col 1:6–10); James speaks of fruit that comes from heavenly wisdom (3:17).

118. Newbigin 197, emphasis added; similarly Barrett 474; Bultmann 1971, 532–33; Schnelle 1998, 240; i.e., fruit does not refer to converts (contra, e.g., Hoskyns 476; followed by Beasley-Murray 273).

119. So Barrett 474 ("not a static condition"); Ridderbos 517: "Remaining in him" is not a state of rest . . . but an adherence to *him* as the vital source of help and strength, in order to bear much fruit."

120. See also Excursus 8: "The Johannine Vocabulary of Faith and Discipleship."

121. John presents conceptual and linguistic parallels to the Pauline characterization of the life of faith as being "*in* Christ Jesus" or "*in* Christ" (e.g., Rom 3:24; 6:11; 8:1; 12:5; passim) and Christ's dwelling *in* the believer (Gal 2:20; cf. 2 Cor 11:10; 12:9; 13:3).

Jesus warns his disciples that those who do not abide in him are "taken away." Here the picture of the vine and branches becomes somewhat more difficult to understand. The branches do not cease to bear fruit *after* they are removed; they are removed because they do not bear fruit. But how did a branch attached to the life-giving vine cease to show forth the life and fruit of the vine? How did it die? Can a branch "detach" itself from the vine? As elsewhere in John (cf. 3:13–14; 10:11), the image used is left behind in order to make a point not easily drawn from that figure itself. Here the point is that the life and fruitfulness of the branches depend upon the life-giving power of the vine; branches not firmly attached to the vine, or that have ceased to be receptive to the life that flows from the vine, will also cease to bear fruit. There is no failure on the vine's part to give life, but there is failure on the branches' part to receive it. The Gospel does not give a fuller account of how or why the branches died, anymore than it explains what caused Judas to turn away. While the phenomenon of apostasy, turning from following Jesus in faith or merely ceasing to be receptive to Jesus, can be observed and perhaps even explained circumstantially, its ultimate causes remain unaccounted for. The burning up of the withered branches (15:6)[122] belongs to normal viticultural practice (Ezek 15:4) but is without parallel in the rest of the Gospel as a description of the fate or destiny of those who turn away from Jesus.

[7–11] The withered branches stand in marked contrast to those that bear abundant fruit so that "my Father is glorified" or "honored" (*edoxasthē*, v. 8; see comments on 13:31). Disciples are known by the lives they live, particularly as they reflect the character and will of the one whom they follow (13:34–35). Abundant fruit is the product of the life that flows through the branch, enabled by the care that the vinedresser, the Father, has given the branches. Thus the flourishing of this vine honors or glorifies the one who tends it, since the branch cannot bear fruit on its own: it depends on both the vine and on the one who tends the vine.[123]

A series of conditional statements pair implicit exhortations with generous promises: if the disciples abide "in [Jesus]" (15:4, 5, 7, 9), "in [his] love" (vv. 9–10), and in the Father's love (v. 10); if they keep his commandments (v. 10); and if his words abide in them (v. 7)—then they will bear fruit, receive what they ask for, be assured of Jesus' love, and have joy. Although couched in conditional form, these statements are intended to produce assurance in the disciples, not anxiety. The disciples "abide" in Jesus because his life (15:4) and words (v. 7) abide in them; they abide in his love, because the Father has loved

122. The text moves between sg. passive ("is cast out" and "is burned") and active pl. ("they gather them and throw them into the fire"), describing what workers do with withered branches.

123. In *L.A.B.* 12.8–9, Moses pleads with God not to destroy his "vine," which has lost its fruit in the sin of idolatry with the golden calf; in 23.12–14, Israel is described as a faithful people, a desirable vine, a faithful flock, not chosen in vain, whose "lot" is "life eternal."

Jesus, who has, in turn, loved them (v. 9); they abide in the Father because they keep the commandments of Jesus, given to him by the Father (v. 10). Because Jesus' words are in them, they are encouraged to voice their requests, confident that Jesus will respond to them (cf. 14:13–14). This admonition is sandwiched between Jesus' assurances that those who abide in him bear much fruit (15:5) and that the Father is glorified when they do bear such fruit (v. 8). Perhaps, then, the promise that whatever the disciples ask will be done for them has to do particularly with petitions about remaining in the vine and bearing fruit to the glory of God. The model here is Jesus himself, who has assurance that the Father always hears him and so calls Lazarus out of the tomb to life so that God is glorified (11:22, 42; 12:30; 17:9–10, 20–21).

The result of remaining in Jesus, keeping his words, and knowing his love is the fullness of joy, such as was promised by the prophets to God's people in the time of their restoration. When God breaks the yoke of the oppressor, the people rejoice (Isa 9:3). Acknowledging God's salvation, God's just judgment upon the earth, and the presence of the Holy One of Israel among them, the people sing for joy (Isa 12:3, 6; cf. 24:14; 26:19; 29:19). When the wilderness blossoms abundantly and streams flow in the desert, when God's people are redeemed, there will be great joy as they see the glory of the Lord (Isa 35:1–2, 6, 10; 48:11, 20; 49:13; 51:11; 52:8; 61:3, 7). And in Isaiah's visions of the future, because God restores his people, the people in turn rejoice with great joy (*charēte chara*, 66:10 LXX). Hence, as in Isaiah, in John joy is full or completed because it accompanies that time when God fulfills his purposes for his people, when the vine again bears abundant fruit. The joy given to the disciples is the joy of the abundance of the messianic era (*hē chara hē emē*, "my joy," John 15:11; 1:16; 17:13).

[12–17] Jesus now summarizes his words to his disciples by repeating the earlier commandment that they are to love one another (13:34), again commending his self-giving love for his disciples as the prime model of their love for each other, as the hallmark of the conduct of the people whom he has chosen. Not only has he chosen this people to belong to him; he also has given his utmost for them, laying down his life as a shepherd does for his sheep. This is the greatest manifestation of love: to give one's life for another. Those who follow Jesus' example, keeping his command to love each other, are to be counted not as his servants but as his friends, his "loved ones."[124]

Jesus' designation of his disciples as "friends" can be understood by any who have experience with friendship, and by any who understand the difference between the status of "friend" and "servant" or "slave" (the Greek word *doulos*, as in 15:15, can be translated as "servant" or "slave"). Jesus regards

124. "Friend" translates the Greek word *philos*. John interchangeably uses two verbs, *phileō* and *agapaō*, both of which mean "love."

the disciples as companions who share his ideals and commitments, those who have seen and heard all that God has made known to Jesus. These friends are unlike the would-be disciples to whom Jesus did not entrust himself (2:23–25), as Jesus has entrusted himself to his disciples. As the good shepherd, Jesus is willing to lay down his life for his sheep (10:11, 18; 15:13), to risk his life for the sake of one of his friends (11:8, 11).

Jesus' words may also be understood against the backdrop of the Scriptures and of later Jewish literature. The biblical material explicitly dealing with friendship is surprisingly meager. There are accounts of friendship (David and Jonathan [1 Sam 18–20]); references to friends (the three friends of Job [2:11; 32:3; 42:10]); and proverbial utterances about friendship (Prov 14:20; 18:24; 19:4). Abraham was called a friend of God (Isa 41:8; 2 Chr 20:7); God spoke to Moses as to a friend (Exod 33:11).[125] Those who trust or believe in God are numbered as the friends of God; similarly, in John, those who trust in Jesus and have committed themselves to him are his friends. While they heed his words, they do so not as his slaves, but precisely as his friends: those who are as close to and dependent upon him as a branch is on a vine.

Friendship was a topic widely discussed by ancient Greek and Roman philosophers, rhetoricians, and moralists.[126] For them, as in Scripture, one could be a "friend of God." Thus the Greek philosopher Epictetus linked true freedom with being "a friend of God" (*Diatr.* 2.17.29; 3.24.60; 4.3.9): that is, conducting oneself in ways that would be approved by the deity. Greek and Roman writers also had much to say about the ideals and values of friendship on a purely human level. Aristotle approves the proverb "Friends' goods are common property," adding, "Community is the essence of friendship."[127] A friend is "one who exerts himself to do for the sake of another what he thinks is advantageous to him."[128] Reflecting such ideas, common ideals for ancient friendship included agreement, harmony, trust, openness (*parrēsia*) or honesty, good will

125. In *Jub.* 19.9, Abraham is "recorded as a friend of the LORD in the heavenly tablets." Philo uses various designations for "friend of God," including *philos tou theou* and *theophilos*, for Abraham and Moses (*Abr.* 89; cf. 273; *Cher.* 49; *Sacr.* 77, 130; *Mos.* 1.156). In Wis 7:14, 27 one attains friendship with God through means of wisdom. In the NT, Jas 2:23 quotes Gen 15:6, "Abraham believed [*episteusen*] God, and it was reckoned to him as righteousness," adding, "and he was called the friend of God [*philos theou*]."

126. Among the many who wrote at length on friendship are Plato (various dialogues, including the *Symposium* and the *Republic*); Aristotle (*Eth. Nic.* 8–9); Cicero (*Amicitia*); Seneca (*Ep.* 3, "True and False Friendship"; *Ep.* 9, "Philosophy and Friendship"; *Ep.* 24, "Despising Death"; *Ep.* 35, "Friendship of Kindred Minds"; *Ep.* 63, "Grief for Lost Friends"); and Plutarch (*Mor.* 93A–97B, "Having Many Friends"). For further study, see the essays in Fitzgerald.

127. Aristotle, *Eth. Nic.* 8.9.1. Seneca commented that friends "have all things in common, especially their troubles" (*Ep.* 6).

128. Aristotle, *Rhet.* 1.5.16.

and affection.[129] Virtue or goodness, it was thought, made friendship possible.[130] The Roman author Seneca insists that one makes friends of those whose character is known and whom one trusts; certain matters are to be revealed only to one's friends (*Ep.* 3). Some ventured that one might, in friendship, give up one's life for another.[131]

Jesus' calling his disciples his "friends" rather than his "servants" or "slaves" indicates the harmony and trust that exists between them. Interestingly, Jesus counts among his friends those who obey his commands. Generally obedience seems to characterize the relationship of a slave or servant to a master, not the relationship of two friends. Yet those who do Jesus' commands are his friends because they manifest an understanding of his will and his words, and so ultimately of Jesus himself: such understanding goes beyond that which a servant has of his master.[132] The disciples are Jesus' friends, not his slaves, if they do what he commands, because friends demonstrate a shared or common mind: an understanding of God's will. Jesus remains, as he said earlier, their Teacher and Lord, but as Teacher and Lord he willingly serves them, washing their feet, relinquishing his rightful status, and even laying down his life for them (13:13–14). Jesus' words to his disciples reflect the highest ideals of love in human friendship. In turn, these ideals reflect God's own love for the world.

From all that Jesus has said, one might conclude that it is by keeping Jesus' commands and doing as he does that one stands among his circle of friends or becomes a part of the flock for which he has given his life. Yet Jesus makes it clear that the disciples belong to him, not by virtue of what they have done, but

129. See Cicero, *Amic.* 1.5; 2.8. Reflecting the ideals of Greco-Roman friendship, Josephus (*Ag. Ap.* 2.207) writes, "There is no friendship without absolute confidence."

130. Aristotle begins his discussion of friendship in the *Nicomachean Ethics* (book 8) with a discussion of the relationship of friendship and virtue. Cicero ends his discussion in *Friendship* with this exhortation: "Be certain of this: Virtue (without which friendship is impossible) is first; but next to it, and to it alone, the greatest of all things is friendship."

131. Aristotle, *Eth. Nic.* 9.9: "To a noble man there applies the true saying that he does all things for the sake of his friends, . . . and if need be, he gives his life for them"; Plato, *Symp.* 179b: "Only those who love will consent to die for others." Seneca speaks of "the friendship in which and for the sake of which men meet death" (*Ep.* 6); "For what purpose, then, do I make a man my friend? In order to have someone for whom I may die, whom I may follow into exile, against whose death I may stake my own life" (*Ep.* 9). Cicero refers to a play in which one of the main characters "wished to be put to death instead of his friend" (*Amic.* 24). Diodorus Siculus comments on the "wonder of such a friendship" as that of Damon, who allowed himself to be given as surety for the condemned Phintias (*Hist.* 10.4.3–6).

132. Among many Greco-Roman writers, Seneca stresses the importance of learning from and imitating the character of the "sages." "Plato, Aristotle, and the whole throng of sages who were destined to go each his different way, derived more benefit from the character than from the words of Socrates. It was not the classroom of Epicurus, but living together under the same roof, that made great men of Metrodorus, Hermarchus, and Polyaenus" (*Ep.* 6). "Choose as a guide one whom you will admire more when you see him act than when you hear him speak" (*Ep.* 52).

by virtue of his love for them and the fact that he chose them (see comments on 6:70). Jesus' assertion that he has chosen his disciples recalls the biblical notion that God has chosen certain persons, including Abraham and David, and has chosen the people of Israel to be his holy people because he has loved them.[133] In this sense "chosen" refers to a call to service, a vocation. Jesus' command to his disciples that they are to love one another indicates that he has chosen them all and that they belong, not only to him, but also to each other. Jesus' words here are the Johannine development of the Old Testament picture of Israel as a people bound in covenant to God and to each other, now applied to Jesus' disciples as those who love God and their neighbors as themselves.

15:18–16:15 The Disciples, the World, and the Paraclete

Now Jesus anticipates the bleak situation in which the disciples will find themselves after his departure. Jesus speaks of the world's hatred and persecution of the disciples, and of the world's ignorance of Jesus and of the Father. As those whom Jesus has chosen, and who belong to him, the disciples find themselves charged to bear witness to him (15:27) in the face of opposition and ignorance. While Jesus promises that the Paraclete will come and bear witness to Jesus (15:26–27; 16:7–11), there is no promise that the Paraclete makes the task easier or assures an immediately satisfying outcome. Rather, the disciples should expect nothing different from "the world" than the rejection Jesus has experienced from his own contemporaries, as foreseen in Scripture (Ps 69:4, cited in John 15:25). But the disciples are to imitate Jesus in being faithful and persistent in bearing witness in and to the world that God loves.

> **15:18** "If the world hates you, know[a] that it hated me first. **19** If you were of
> the world, the world would love its own, but because you are not of the
> world—rather, I have chosen you out of the world—therefore, the world
> hates you. **20** Remember the word that I spoke to you: 'Servants are not
> greater than their master.' If they persecuted me, they will persecute you.
> If they keep my word, they will keep your word.
>
> **21** "They will do all these things to you on account of my name,
> because they have not known the one who sent me. **22** If I had not come
> and spoken to them, they would have no sin. But now they have no
> excuse for their sin.
>
> **23** "Whoever hates me also hates my Father. **24** If I had not done the
> works among them, works which no one else has done, they would have
> no sin. But now they have both seen and hated both me and my Father.
> **25** These things happened so that the word that is written in their law might
> be fulfilled: 'They hated me without cause.'

133. Among many passages: Abraham: Gen 18:19; Neh 9:7. David: 2 Sam 6:21; 1 Chr 28:4. Israel: Deut 4:37; 7:7; 10:15; 14:2; Pss 33:12; 135:4; Isa 49:7; Ezek 20:5; 1 Macc 7:37; 2 Macc 1:25.

26 "When the Paraclete comes, whom I will send to you from the
Father, the Spirit of truth who comes from the Father, that one will bear
witness to me. 27 And you also will bear witness, because you have been
with me from the beginning.

16:1 "I have said these things to you in order that you will not fall
away. 2 They will put you out of the synagogue. The hour is coming
when anyone who kills you will think they are offering worship to God.
3 They will do these things because they know neither the Father nor me.
4 I have said these things to you so that when their hour comes, you will
remember that I told you about them. I did not tell you these things from
the beginning, because I was with you.

5 "Now I am going to the one who sent me, and none of you asks me,
'Where are you going?' 6 But because grief has filled your hearts, I have
said these things to you. 7 I have told you the truth: it is good for you that
I go. For if I do not go, the Paraclete will not come to you. But if go, I
will send him to you.

8 "And when that one comes, he will expose the world concerning sin
and concerning righteousness and concerning judgment: 9 concerning
sin, because they did not believe in me; 10 and concerning righteousness,
because I am going to the Father and you will no longer see me; and 11
concerning judgment, because the ruler of this world has been judged.

12 "I still have many things to tell you, but you are not able to bear
them now. 13 When that one comes, the Spirit of truth, he will guide you
in all the truth. For he will not speak of himself, but whatever he hears,
he will speak; and he will announce to you the things that are to come. 14
For that one will glorify me, for he will take what is mine[b] and announce
it to you. 15 All things that my Father has are mine. Therefore, I told you
that he will take what is mine and announce it to you."

a. The Greek *ginōskete* can be understood as either indicative ("you know") or, as translated here, an imperative.

b. Lit., "from" or "of what is mine" (*ek tou emou*).

[15:18–21] Jesus' Farewell Discourse to his disciples aims to provide comfort and assurance for the period after his departure from them, but his next words are hardly likely to console them in his absence. Instead, he warns the disciples that they will experience the world's hatred, even as he himself has experienced it (cf. 7:7). Typical of John's oppositional or dualistic terminology, *hatred* is the opposite of *love*.[134] On the one hand, love can almost be identified with commitment to Jesus or belief in Jesus (8:42–45; 14:15–24); on the other hand, it refers to the conduct that is to characterize the disciples in imitation of

134. The prediction that the world will "hate" the disciples is not limited to John; cf. Mark 13:12–13; Luke 6:22.

their Lord, who gives himself for them. The community of the disciples is to be marked by love for the other, and the world hates precisely this community, even as it hates—rejects, spurns, turns away from—Jesus and seeks his destruction. While *misein* and its cognates may not carry the affective connotations that the English terms *hate* and *hatred* do,[135] such lexical qualification would prove little comfort to Jesus' disciples, in light of the fact that they can expect to be treated—mocked, persecuted, rejected—as the world has treated Jesus.[136] Especially because "hate" betokens the refusal of the world to join with Jesus and his disciples, that "hatred" is particularly painful when it entails being cut off from family, friends, or community.

We may briefly examine three reasons for the world's hatred of the disciples: (1) The disciples do not belong to the world; Jesus has chosen them out of it (15:19). (2) The disciples are Jesus' servants and so are aligned with him (15:20). (3) The world does not recognize Jesus as the one sent by God; because they do not know God, they do not know the one whom he has sent (15:21).

First, the disciples are "not of the world" (*ek tou kosmou*). Being "of" something (e.g., *of the world*) has to do with identity and allegiance.[137] Having been chosen out of the world by Jesus himself, they belong to him and not to the world: they are "not of this world" (cf. 15:16; 17:6, 14–15). Jesus himself is "not of this world" because he is from above, from God: because he comes from God, his identity is determined by God, not by the world (*ek tou anō*, 8:23; 13:1; 17:14, 16). In turn, those who wish to participate in the life of God or enter into the kingdom of God must be begotten "from above" (3:3, *anōthen*; cf. *ek tōn anō*, 8:23), "of water and Spirit" (3:5, *ex hydatos kai pneumatos*). In other words, one belongs either to the world above and thus to God, or to the world or realm that is below. The disciples cannot participate in the character and allegiances of "the world" inasmuch as it rejects the one who has chosen them so that they might belong to him and not to the world (1:10; cf. 9:5; 13:1; 16:33; 17:11, 13). John could have written what James did: "Friendship with the world is enmity with God" (Jas 4:4).

Second, servants cannot be expected to be treated differently from or better than their masters. Even as Jesus calls his disciples to imitate him (13:34–35), so the disciples can expect that they will be treated as Jesus was treated. Although the use of "servants" here is somewhat unexpected in light of the previous disclaimer that Jesus now regards his disciples as friends, not

135. See the comments on 3:20 and 7:7 above; and BDAG, s.v. *miseō*.

136. On translating *diōkō* as "persecute," see comments at 5:16 above. Though "persecution" in John is not a systematic attack on "Christians" for their beliefs, it does connote hostility or opposition.

137. Referring to the various constructions with *ek tou* in John, Keck (1996, 274) writes, "'Of-ness' implies that what is decisive about a person is neither self-generated nor self-defined."

servants, he also remains their master (or *kyrios*, "Lord," 13:13). As they follow him, they can expect to experience what he experienced, because they are committed to him and his ways. Yet there is a note of hope: those who have kept Jesus' words will also keep his disciples' words as they remain faithful to him; as they keep Jesus' words, they draw life from the vine. The promise does not aim to exalt the disciples but to ensure the faithful transmission of their witness to Jesus.

Third, those who persecute the disciples will do so "on account of my name" and because "they do not know him who sent me" (15:21). The disciples will be hated not because of what or who they are on their own, but because of Jesus ("on account of my name"). Those who persecute the disciples do so because they do not know "the one who sent me." They do not follow the ways of God; if they had, they would understand and accept rather than reject Jesus. Rejection of the disciples is rejection of the one who sent them, Jesus himself, even as rejection of Jesus is rejection of the one who sent him.

[22–25] There is therefore a chasm between the disciples and the world, which has paradoxically been created by the revelation of God through Jesus. Because God loves the world, God has acted through his Son to bring the world out of darkness, sin, death, and hostility into light, life, obedience, and love. To accomplish that, sin must be exposed, but people will shrink from such exposure, hiding in the darkness, because "the world loves darkness rather than light" (3:19) and is therefore indifferent or even hostile toward God's initiatives to rescue it from its predicament. God reveals the way of life, shining a light in the darkness, but there is no natural instinct to turn toward the light; instead, those whose home is in darkness, turned away from God's light, want to remain there.

According to John, rejection of God's revelation through the words (15:22) and works (vv. 24) of Jesus constitutes sin. If Jesus had not spoken to them, revealing God's truth and his own identity, the world could not have rejected him and his words, and hence would not be guilty of sin (v. 22). This is the crisis that God's Word creates. Now, because Jesus has spoken to them and they have rejected him and his words, those who are of the world have also rejected the one who sent him and are guilty of the sin of unbelief. Similarly, if Jesus had not done the works that reveal him to be the life-giving agent of the Father, those who saw them would not have had to form a judgment, to "judge rightly" about them and the one who did them (15:24; 7:24). They would not "have sin." But because Jesus has done these works, and people have not believed in him through their witness, they are guilty of the sin of unbelief. They have seen Jesus, and rejected him, and because they have done so, they have also rejected the Father (v. 23).

This rejection has been foretold in the Scriptures. In two psalms, which John here refers to as "their law" (v. 25), the psalmist speaks of those who "hated him without cause" (Pss 35:19 [34:19 LXX]; 69:4 [68:5 LXX]).[138] Psalm 35 speaks of those who seek the psalmist's life "without cause" (vv. 4, 7), "malicious witnesses" (v. 11) who mock him (v. 16) and speak deceitfully (v. 20). Psalm 69 refers to the psalmist's enemies who seek to destroy him (v. 4), who insult and dishonor him (vv. 19–20). They "judge me unjustly" and "hate me without cause."[139] Jesus' charge that "they hate me without cause" means that the world does not evince a pursuit of Jesus based on truth and righteousness. Instead, its hostility arises from a failure to perceive the truth and righteousness in Jesus, a failure that leads to unjust persecution of Jesus.

[26–27] In this situation, the disciples are called to bear witness to Jesus because they have been with him "from the beginning" of his ministry (15:27). They have heard what he has said and have seen what he has done; therefore they bear witness to him and against the world that does not see, know, or receive the Spirit of truth (14:17). The mission of the disciples reflects that of Jesus himself: to bear witness to God's life manifested and available through him. Even as the disciples bear witness congruent with that of Jesus himself, they will experience similar hostility. Though they will not be summarily rescued from persecution, neither will they be abandoned without any help. Jesus will send them the Paraclete (15:26), who will bear witness to him.[140]

Two characteristics of the Paraclete are particularly important for the disciples as they undertake their witness. First, the Paraclete comes "from the Father." The Paraclete is God's Spirit; thus, in the conflict between the world and God, the disciples can be assured that God will aid them. Earlier Jesus spoke of God's bearing witness to him (5:37; 8:18; cf. 1 John 5:9) and of God's glorifying him (5:44; 8:54; 12:23, 28; 13:31–32; 17:1, 5). Now God will send the Paraclete to bear witness to Jesus. Second, the Spirit is the Spirit of truth. Throughout the Gospel Jesus has been characterized as the one who is full of truth (1:14, 17), who speaks the truth (8:32, 40, 45–46; 17:8, 17), and who himself is the truth (14:6). The Spirit of truth bears witness to the one who is, speaks, and reveals the truth.

While this passage does not elucidate a doctrine of the Trinity, along with others in John it prompted theological reflection on the relationship of the Father, Son, and Spirit due in part to its use of particular verbs and prepositional phrases. The Father has sent Jesus (*ho pempsas me*, 15:21); the Spirit

138. John cites Ps 69 two other times in connection with Jesus' death (69:9 in 2:17; 69:21 in 19:28–29).

139. The LXX reads *hoi ekdiōkontes me adikōs*, "those who pursue [or 'persecute'] me unjustly." For just judgment in John, see 5:30; 7:24, 51; 8:15–16, 26.

140. For the meaning and background of Paraclete, as well as summary comments on the role of the Spirit in John, see also Excursus 9: "The Holy Spirit in John."

comes from the Father (*ekporeuetai para tou patros*, 15:26),[141] but will be sent by Jesus (*egō pempsō hymin*) from the Father (*para tou patros*, 15:26). While Jesus will send (*pempsō*) the Spirit from God, the text does not say that the Spirit "comes forth" (*ekporeuetai*) from Jesus. Throughout the Gospel, Jesus is said to be sent (from *pempō* or *apostellō*) by God and to have come from God (*ēlthon*, *elēlytha*, or *exēlthon*: 8:14, 42; 12:27; 13:3; 16:28) or come down from heaven (*katabebēka*, 6:38). The Spirit is also said to be "sent" (*pempō*, 14:26; 15:26; 16:7) and to "come" (*elthē*, 16:13). But the verb *ekporeuomai* ("come out of, proceed from") describes the Spirit's "coming out from God" and not "from the Son": in John, the Spirit does not "proceed from" the Son.[142] Rather, the Spirit is the life-giving power that comes forth or "proceeds" from God.[143]

[16:1–4] If the disciples bear witness (*martyreite*, 15:26) to Jesus, they will also encounter opposition and hostility, presumably for that witness (cf. Luke 21:12–18).[144] Jesus wishes to prevent them from falling away when that happens. "Fall away" translates the Greek word *skandalisthēte* (John 16:1), used earlier to characterize the response of some of Jesus' disciples who ceased to follow him (6:60–61, 66). Jesus is the good shepherd who does not want any of his sheep to be lost (16:4; 6:12; 10:28; 17:12).

Jesus warns that they "will put you out of the synagogue"; more starkly, he warns that "they" will seek to "kill you," thinking that by doing so they are "offering worship to God" (16:2). John does not specify to whom "they" refers. Throughout the Farewell Discourse, Jesus speaks of the animosity that the disciples can expect from "the world," not "the Jews"; here, however, "they" who would put others "out of the synagogue" are clearly Jews (16:2; cf. 7:13; 9:22; 12:42). Still, those who think that they are offering worship (*latreian*

141. The verb *ekporeuomai* is used in Ezekiel (LXX) to describe the streams flowing out from the throne of God (47:1, 8, 12) and in the NT to speak of the words that "proceed" or "come out from" one's mouth (Matt 4:4; 15:11; Luke 4:22; Eph 4:29; so also Ezek 33:30: the prophet's message that "comes forth" from the Lord), as well as those thoughts and actions "that come out " from one's inward being" (Mark 7:15).

142. But Jesus "breathes" the Holy Spirit on the disciples (20:22).

143. Early Christian writers distinguished the *procession* of the Spirit and the *generation* [*begottenness*] of the Son from the Father. Thus the so-called Niceno-Constantinopolitan Creed confesses "one Lord Jesus Christ, the only-begotten Son of God, begotten of the Father before all worlds, Light of Light, very God of very God, begotten, not made," and "the Holy Spirit, the Lord and giver of life, who proceeds from the Father" (*ek tou patros ekporeuomenon*). The Western Church's later addition of the so-called *filioque* clause, "who proceeds from the Father *and the Son*," accelerated the schism between the Eastern and Western branches of Christianity in 1054, since the Eastern Orthodox Church insisted that the Spirit comes *from* the Father, *through* the Son. For discussion of the "double procession" of the Spirit from the Father and the Son, consult Kelly (1972, 358–67) and relevant articles (Double Procession; *filioque*; Nicene Creed) in *ODCC*.

144. In Acts 22:20 Stephen, who had been stoned to death, is called a witness (*martys*); in Rev 2:13 the slain Antipas is called "my faithful witness" (*ho martys mou ho pistos mou*).

prospherein)[145] to God by pursuing Jesus' followers to death need not be limited to Jews.

From Jesus' vantage point, expulsion from the synagogue lies in the future.[146] Other New Testament books narrate incidents of mistreatment and opposition to Jewish Christians from other Jews, including Paul's persecution (*ediōkon*) of them (Acts 8:1–3; 9:1–2; 26:10; Gal 1:13; 1 Thess 2:14–16) and his references to synagogue discipline (2 Cor 11:25). The New Testament also records the stoning of Stephen (Acts 7:56–8:1) and Herod's execution of James the son of Zebedee around the year 44 (Acts 12:2; cf. Mark 10:35–45). Josephus recounts the stoning of James the brother of Jesus and a number of others as "breakers of the law" under Ananus the high priest in the year 62 (*Ant.* 20.200).[147] The implicit scriptural precedent for such action was Phinehas, who was "zealous for his God" and killed those Israelites who had "yoked themselves to Baal" (Num 25:1–13; *m. Sanh.* 9.6; *Num. Rab.* 21.4). It will be no surprise if those who follow Jesus, a man deemed guilty of blasphemy and hence worthy of death, are deemed guilty of the same charges.

Far more believers in Jesus were put to death by the Romans. Roman historians and early Christian authors recount the torture and killing of "an immense multitude" of Christians in the mid 60s under the emperor Nero and possibly later, under Domitian.[148] In the early second century, Pliny, governor of Bithynia, asked the emperor Trajan how to treat those who had been denounced to him as Christians. Trajan counseled Pliny that while Christians were not to be sought out, if they were denounced to him and did not recant their Christian faith and return to proper worship of the Roman deities, then they were to be punished, even executed.[149] Somewhat later, Justin Martyr also speaks of the torture and killing of the "worshipers of God through the

145. *Latreia* appears four other times in the NT (Rom 9:4; 12:1; Heb 9:1, 6); when coupled with "offer" (*prospherein*), it connotes offering a sacrifice.

146. Cf. Matt 5:10; 10:21–23, 28; 24:9; Mark 13:9–12; Luke 6:22; 12:4; 21:12; see comments on 9:22.

147. Justin (*Dial.* 95.4; 133:6) claims that the Jews curse Christians in their synagogue prayers and put them to death; cf. *Mart. Pol.* 13.1.

148. Tacitus (*Ann.* 15.44) writes that when Nero blamed Christians for the fire that destroyed Rome in 64 C.E., "an immense multitude was convicted," tortured, and killed. Suetonius (*Nero* 16.2) reports that Nero inflicted punishment on Christians (but does not link that to the fire); *1 Clement*, written from Rome in the late first century, recounts the martyrdom of Peter, Paul, and "a great multitude of the elect" (5.1–6.2). Both Suetonius (*Dom.* 12.2) and Dio Cassius (*Hist.* 67.14) speak of the persecutions of Domitian (emperor in 81–96 C.E.); Dio reports that a number of persons who "drifted in Jewish ways" were charged with "atheism." Writing in the early fourth century, Eusebius, bishop of Caesarea, says that the emperor Domitian persecuted and killed a large number of Christians (*Hist. eccl.* 3.17–18; 4.26.9, citing Melito, bishop of Sardis [d. ca. 190 C.E.], *Oration to Antoninus Caesar*).

149. For the exchange of letters between Pliny, governor of Bithynia in 111–113 C.E., and the emperor Trajan, see Pliny, *Ep.* 10.96–97.

name of Jesus" who were crucified, beheaded, and thrown to wild beasts (*Dial.* 110.5), and he defends Christians against the charges of "atheism" (*1 Apol.*). At least in some of these cases, the explicit justification for putting Christians to death was their failure to worship as Rome required. If the Christians would not sacrifice to the Roman deities, then their lives would be forfeit: offered as sacrifice, as it were.

If those who had Jesus' followers put to death, whether Jews or Gentiles, thought they were "offering worship" to God by sacrificing these believers in Jesus, then Jesus counters that they "know neither the Father nor me" (John 16:3). If they had known the Father, they would not have pursued Jesus even to death; if they had known Jesus, they would not hate and harass his followers. Hostility toward the followers of Jesus arises not from knowledge but from ignorance of God. The world's "hatred" (15:18) may manifest as dismissal of or indifference toward the disciples; yet it may entail suffering and even death for them, even as it will do for Jesus.[150] If Jesus' primary opposition comes from "the Jews," his disciples can expect to experience the same from both the Jews and "the world" into which their mission now expands.[151]

[5–7] Once again Jesus speaks of his departure to "the one who sent me," adding a puzzling comment, "None of you asks me, 'Where are you going?'" Peter had asked this very question earlier (13:36). In fact, this is precisely the question that originally triggered Jesus' discourse. But the disciples have not asked Jesus anything since Peter, Thomas, Philip, and Judas (not Iscariot) made their initial inquiries about Jesus' departure to the Father (13:36; 14:5, 8, 22). They do not ask because they are filled with grief (16:6), anticipating Jesus' departure. Now, at the end of the discourse, they should once again ask, "Where are you going?" They would be reminded that (1) Jesus is going to the Father and that (2) he will send the Spirit to aid them in their witness in and to the world (16:8–12). The disciples need to be reminded not so much about Jesus' destination as about the consequences of his return to the Father for them; they need to think not so much about his absence as about how he will continue to be present with them.

[8–11] Earlier Jesus had spoken of the Spirit's role in helping the disciples to understand his teaching for the present and the future (14:26; 15:26; cf. 16:13); now he speaks of the Spirit's forensic (legal) function to "expose the world concerning sin and concerning righteousness and concerning judgment." The word translated "expose" comes from the Greek *elenchō*, which can mean "reprove, rebuke, expose, convict."[152] As used earlier in John (3:20; 8:46), the

150. On "hate" (*misein*), see the earlier comments on 3:18–20; 7:7; 15:18.

151. For discussion of "the world," and the parallels between "the Jews" and "the world," see the comments on 14:17 and 15:18.

152. Matt 18:15; Luke 3:19; 1 Cor 14:24; Eph 5:11, 13; 1 Tim 5:20; 2 Tim 4:2; Titus 1:9, 13; 2:15; Heb 12:5; Jas 2:9; Jude 15; Rev 3:19.

sense here is to "expose" sin or "bring it to light." The Spirit vindicates Jesus' righteousness and exposes the world's sin by exposing the world's unbelief, its error in condemning Jesus, and its false judgments about Jesus' relationship to God. The Spirit thus bears witness to Jesus while reproving the world, and the Spirit reproves the world by bearing witness to Jesus. Hence the three phrases explaining the Spirit's work can be understood as follows:

1. "Concerning sin, because they did not believe in me" (16:9): Inasmuch as "sin" in John refers almost exclusively to the rejection of the one whom God has sent (8:21, 34; 9:41; 15:22–24), the Spirit exposes the world as sinful because the Spirit exposes the world's unbelief (8:24). Through the witness of Jesus' disciples (20:20–23), the Spirit furthers Jesus' work of speaking the truth (8:46), so that those who hear are without excuse for their unbelief (15:22–24).

2. "Concerning righteousness, because I am going to the Father and you will no longer see me" (16:10): The world condemns Jesus to death because it judges him guilty of various charges leveled against him (5:18; 10:33; 18:30; 19:7). Ultimately it does not believe that he has come from the Father. Jesus' return to the Father bears witness to his righteousness: if he were not righteous, he would not now be going to the righteous Father (*dikaios*, 17:25); if he were not holy (6:69), he would not be returning to the Holy Father (*hagios*, 17:11).

3. "Concerning judgment, because the ruler of this world has been judged" (16:11): The Spirit testifies that the world has passed false judgment in its condemnation of Jesus. It is not Jesus but rather the ruler of the world, and the world along with him, who has been exposed as sinful, unrighteous, and hence meriting judgment (12:31). "The ruler of this world," the devil, tries to deceive people, leading them away from the truth and from following Jesus (see comments on 8:44; 12:31; 13:2; 14:30).

Although John speaks of the Spirit's work of exposing and reproving the world, that work must be perceived through the right judgment of faith (7:24). The world cannot see the Spirit of truth; those in whom the Spirit dwells may know and perceive the work of the Spirit (14:17). Given Jesus' impartation of the Spirit to his disciples (20:20–23), the Spirit's presence and work continue through the prophetic witness of the church: the Spirit creates a new family (3:3, 5), empowers true worship (4:24), enlivens its practices (of purification and proclamation) so that they are fruitful (6:63), and bears witness to Jesus as the Word made flesh.[153] Inevitably the argument is circular: to perceive the work of the Spirit, one must have the Spirit. As the branches abide in the vine, as Jesus' disciples faithfully cling to and follow him, their corporate practices and proclamation testify to the Spirit's presence in and among them.

153. In 1 John, false prophets deny that "Jesus Christ has come in the flesh" (2:18–23; 4:1–3; 5:6–12); but the Spirit bears witness to the Son, calling to mind the truth known "from the beginning" (2:24).

[12–15] In spite of all that Jesus has already told his disciples, he now adds the cryptic note that, while he has "many things" left to tell them, they cannot "bear them now." In their current situation the disciples are unable to grasp all that Jesus has yet to say, not only because of their grief (v. 6), although that is not to be downplayed, but also because understanding Jesus and the significance of his life, death, and resurrection will occur (1) after his death (2:22; 13:7), and (2) by means of the Holy Spirit's instruction (7:39; 16:7). The disciples must wait for the coming of the Spirit, whose task is to "guide you in all the truth" (16:13).

Presumably "all the truth" includes both the "many things" not yet fully understood and "things that are to come" or to be revealed (v. 13). Together, these things are described as "what is mine" and "all things that my Father has." In other words, the Father makes known or gives "all things" to Jesus (3:35; 13:3); the Spirit in turn takes what belongs to Jesus and makes these things known to the disciples (16:15). The Spirit guides into "all the truth" because the Spirit does not speak "on his own," any more than Jesus has acted or spoken "on his own" (5:30; 7:17, 28; 8:28, 42; 12:49; 14:10). Instead, the Spirit takes all the truth that belongs to Jesus and makes it known to the disciples.

Unfortunately, John does not specify what constitutes "all the truth." Since the Paraclete testifies to Jesus and brings his words to mind, "all the truth" must encompass the truth about Jesus and his significance. Such understanding comes "later," after his death, resurrection, and return to the Father, when he sends the Spirit to be with and teach the disciples (2:22; 7:37–39; 12:16; 13:7; 14:16–17, 26; 15:26; 16:7–13). Because Jesus will send the disciples into the world as the Father has sent him (17:18; 20:21), they will need the Spirit to point them continually to Jesus, that they might bear faithful witness to the one who is life for the world. With Jesus' departure, the disciples find themselves in uncharted territory, beset by unknown challenges and obstacles to witness and faith. The Gospel promises that the disciples can and must trust the Spirit to guide and instruct them so that what they say and what they do always bears witness to the truth that is embodied in and through Jesus.

16:16–33 Jesus' Departure

Jesus now repeats much of what he has already said: he is going away; the disciples will not see him for a brief period; when they see him again, they will experience great joy (vv. 16–22). The resurrection appearances will resolve the initial problem of the pain experienced at Jesus' death. But with the resurrection, Jesus has not returned to life as before: he is leaving the world and returning to the Father (16:28): he will no longer be present with the disciples as he has been. And while the disciples finally claim to understand what Jesus is saying (vv. 29–31), Jesus warns them again that the coming days will bring challenges to faith: the disciples will be scattered, experience hostility, and need peace and courage (vv. 32–33). In speaking directly to his disciples, Jesus also addresses all future disciples, all those reading the Gospel, who struggle in Jesus' absence to persevere in following him. What Jesus promised to those sharing that last meal with him, he promises to all who continue to draw their life from him.

16:16 "Yet a little while and you will no longer see me, and again a little
while and you will see me."
17 Then some of his disciples said to each other, "What is he saying
to us? 'Yet a little while and you will no longer see me, and again a little
while and you will see me?' and 'Because I am going to the Father?'" **18**
So they said, "What is this 'a little while'? We do not know what he is
saying."
19 Jesus, knowing that they wanted to question[a] him, also said to them,
"Are you trying to find out from each other what I meant when I said this:
'Yet a little while and you will no longer see me, and again a little while
and you will see me'? **20** Amen, amen, I say to you, you will weep and
mourn, and the world will rejoice. You will have pain, but your pain will
turn to joy. **21** Whenever a woman gives birth, she has pain, for her hour
has come. But when the child is born, she no longer remembers her dis-
tress because of her joy that a human being has been born into the world.
22 "And so you have pain now. I will see you again, and your hearts
will rejoice, and no one will take your joy from you. **23** And on that day
you will not question me. Amen, amen, I tell you, whatever you ask the
Father in my name, he will give to you. **24** Until now, you have asked[a]
nothing in my name. Ask and you will receive, so that your joy may be
complete.
25 "I have said these things to you in figures. The hour is coming when
I will no longer speak to you in figures, but I will tell you plainly of the
Father. **26** On that day, you will ask in my name. I am not saying that I
will ask the Father on your behalf. **27** For the Father himself loves you,
because you have loved me and have believed that I have come from the
Father. **28** I have come from the Father and have come into the world.
Again, I am leaving the world and going to the Father."
29 His disciples said to him, "Look, now you are speaking plainly and
not in figures. **30** Now we know that you know all things and that you have
no need that anyone should question you. This is how we know that you
have come from God."
31 Jesus answered them, "Do you now believe? **32** Look, the hour is
coming, and has now come, when you will be scattered, each of you to
your own home, and you will leave me alone. But I am not alone, because

the Father is with me. 33 I have said these things to you that you may have peace in me. You will have distress in the world. But take heart, for I have conquered the world."

a. Throughout this passage, *erōtaō* is translated as "question" (as in vv. 23 and 30), referring to the disciples' many queries to Jesus; it is distinguished from *aiteō* ("ask"), used of petition or prayer in vv. 23–24, 26.

[16:16–19] It is time for Jesus' departure to the Father (16:4–5). Jesus warns the disciples that "in a little while" they will not see him; yet after another little while, they will see him again (v. 16). Their expressions of bewilderment and Jesus' reiteration of their questions emphasize their incomprehension: they simply cannot understand what Jesus means: "We do not know what he is saying" (v. 18). For anyone who knows the story, things are clear enough: Jesus' death is imminent, and when he is taken away, crucified, and buried, the disciples will not see him. What the disciples do not know is that "in a little while" they will see him again as the risen Lord.[154] But how could they know? Curiously, Jesus has not told them explicitly that he will be killed and raised to life:[155] he tells them that they will "see" him. In keeping with that promise, in John the disciples report their encounters with the risen Lord by announcing that they "have seen the Lord" (20:18, 25). Jesus' resurrection makes it possible for the disciples to see him and to rejoice.

Soon Jesus will tell them that he is "leaving the world and going to the Father" (16:28). The "little while" of Jesus' absence that his disciples endure before his resurrection will then give way to a prolonged period of absence. Jesus' death creates a crisis resolved by Easter; but Jesus' subsequent departure creates a fresh crisis. In the Farewell Discourse the promises made both to those who look forward to Easter and to those now looking back to Easter are couched in the same terms: "You will see me."[156] In the indefinite period of Jesus' absence, Jesus' disciples will "see" him as they perceive him, living and present (14:19–23), and will acknowledge the ministry of the Paraclete among them (14:16, 26; 15:26; 16:7), while still expecting Jesus' return to gather them into the household of his Father (14:3).

154. For the argument that the resurrection appearances are in view in 16:16–21, see, among others, Zumstein 2008; Keener 2:1043; Lincoln 2005, 423–24; O'Day 778; Ridderbos 538; Schnackenburg 3:156; D. Moody Smith 1999, 300.

155. Cf. John 14:19. In the Synoptic Gospels, where Jesus foretells his crucifixion and resurrection, the disciples are no more comprehending than here (Mark 8:31; 9:31; 10:33–34).

156. Barrett (491) notices the "studied ambiguity" of the language: Jesus' words about "going away" and "coming again" can be as easily interpreted of the parousia as of the resurrection; Schnelle (1998, 250) contends that at the level of the text, "seeing Jesus again" refers to Easter; but for those who read or hear the Gospel, "seeing Jesus again" refers to the parousia.

[20–22] In the meantime, however, Jesus' death will lead to mourning, even as Lazarus's death did (v. 20). "The world" that opposed Jesus will not mourn; rather, it will rejoice, thinking that it has vanquished Jesus who exposed its sin and unbelief (3:20–21). The situation of the disciples will be reversed, however, upon the occasion of Jesus' resurrection: now the disciples' very real pain arising from Jesus' death will turn to joy, even as Mary's weeping dissolves into joy when she encounters the risen Jesus at the empty tomb (20:11–18). The disciples will see Jesus not crucified and dead, but living and by implication victorious. Jesus compares the disciples' pain with that of a woman in labor, who perseveres through it in order to bring a child into the world (16:20–21). Labor in childbirth is a biblical image for anguish and struggle, as well as for the sense of being overwhelmed and fearful (Ps 48:6; Isa 13:8; 21:3; 26:17; 42:14; Jer 4:31; 6:24; 13:21; 22:23; 30:6; 48:41; 49:22, 24; 50:43; Hos 13:13). The comparison may simply serve to evoke the pain that precedes birth as an image of the anguish associated with Jesus' death preceding the joy of encountering him alive.

In the prophetic tradition, a woman's labor also serves as an image of the travail and pain that precedes the deliverance of God's people. For example, the prophet Isaiah compares the distress of God's people in waiting for God's salvation to a "woman with child, who writhes and cries out in her pains when she is near her time" (Isa 26:17). Isaiah refers also to Zion's birth pains and labor (66:7–9), which finally lead to rejoicing when God's presence allows his glory to be seen (66:10–19; Jer 30:5–9; Mic 5:2–4; cf. 4:9–10; in the NT see Matt 24:8; Mark 13:8; Rom 8:22–23; 1 Thess 5:3).[157]

With the note that the "hour has come" (John 16:21), the image of birth pangs that give way to joy depicts the arrival of God's salvation as the life assured by the resurrection of Jesus from the dead. Hence the joy that the disciples now have is not merely the joy that follows relief from great pain; it is also the joy that belongs to the era of salvation, pictured now as the rebirth of God's people (see comments on 14:27–29; 15:11). Even after Jesus has returned to the Father, the disciples will continue to have joy because Jesus lives and is with them. Although elsewhere Jesus regularly promises the disciples that they will see him again, now he assures them, "*I* will see you again" (16:22). They will not see apparitions or visions of Jesus: they will see him, and he will see them. Their encounters will be the genuine encounter

157. Both Jeremiah and Micah link the birth pangs to the end of exile and return of God's people to their land; in later Jewish literature, the labor pains of a woman precede the birth of a "wonderful counselor" (1QH XI [formerly III], 7–10) or "that Son of Man" sitting on his throne of glory (*1 En.* 62.4–6); see Pitre 2005, 223–53. R. Brown represents commentators who think that John's imagery may allude specifically to the birth of the Messiah (1970, 731–32), but that interpretation is rightly rejected by others as lacking exegetical support (O'Day 780; Ridderbos 539; Schnackenburg 3:158).

of friends with each other (15:15). "It is really Jesus who comes back and sees them."[158]

Jesus' promise to the disciples that they will have joy that cannot be taken away (16:22, 24) reiterates the earlier promise that his love and presence will give them fullness of joy (15:11). These promises call to mind the prophetic vision of the great joy experienced in God's redemption of his people (Isa 35:1–2, 6, 10; 48:11, 20; 49:13; 51:11; 52:8; 61:3, 7; 62:5). As Isaiah writes, "You will see, and your heart shall rejoice" (66:14). "On that day" in which God restores "the remnant of Israel, . . . the LORD" himself "will rejoice over you with gladness" and "exult over you with loud singing" (Zeph 3:11–17). Now God grants the fullness of joy and peace that has been promised to his people, even while they live in this world. This is the distinctive announcement, indeed the "obscurity and scandal" of Christian faith: that the world's redemption has been accomplished in the midst of an unredeemed world, accomplished by the death and resurrection of the Lord Jesus.[159] Jesus' Farewell Discourse provides hope and encouragement to those living in such a situation.

[23–33] If the disciples are full of questions now, the day is coming when they will have no more questions for Jesus; he will speak plainly, and they will understand (John 16:23, 30).[160] Jesus also repeats the mind-boggling promise that whatever the disciples ask the Father "in my name" will be given to them (v. 23). Earlier Jesus had told them that he will do whatever they ask him in his name, to the glory of the Father (14:13–14); here he instructs them to ask the Father "in my name" (16:23). Jesus distinguishes between asking something of himself and asking something of the Father; however, given the mutual indwelling that characterizes Father and Son, the harmony of their will and purposes, and the admonition to pray to the Father in Jesus' name, it is impossible to imagine that Father and Son would give different answers to the disciples' prayers. Characteristically, John grounds the Father's responsiveness to his children's requests in his love for them: the Father from whom Jesus comes and to whom he returns will grant the disciples' requests because he loves them (cf. 14:21, 23), even as Jesus has loved them.[161] Jesus' assurance of God's love directs the disciples' attention not to the plethora of things for which they might ask, but to the relationship that they will have with the Father. The gifts received point to the Giver who bestows them (cf. 6:34–35).

Jesus alludes to "the hour" when he will no longer speak to them "in figures" but "plainly" (16:25; cf. comments on 7:13–26). To speak or work "plainly"

158. D. Moody Smith 1999, 300.

159. Hoskyns 487.

160. "You will not question me" (*eme ouk erōtēsete*), but they will pray ("ask," from *aiteō*) to the Father in Jesus' name. For "in that day," see the comments on 14:20.

161. In Matt 7:7–11 and Luke 11:9–13 the heavenly Father's willingness to grant petitions surpasses that of earthly fathers.

or "openly" stands in contrast with doing so (1) in secret (cf. 7:4, 26; 11:54; 18:20) or (2) in imagery or figures (10:24; cf. 11:14). It is the second meaning that is in view here, as is clear from the contrast with speaking *en paroimiais*, in figures or parables (16:25; reinforced in 16:29; cf. 10:6). When Jesus speaks figuratively, he is often misunderstood and asked to speak plainly (10:24), even as the signs are misunderstood by those who fail to grasp their witness to Jesus (6:26–35; 9:16; 12:37). But "the hour is coming" when Jesus will speak of the Father without using figures or images, so that the disciples will comprehend clearly what he is saying; no one will need to "question him" (16:23, 30). When coupled with the promises that the Spirit will teach them all things (14:26; 16:13), Jesus' pledge to speak plainly indicates that the Spirit will enable the disciples more fully to comprehend the Father, whom Jesus has made known (1:18). Their capacity to understand will be due as much to the Spirit's work within and among them as to the changed character of Jesus' speech (see comments on 2:22; 12:16).[162]

When Jesus promises that (1) the disciples may petition the Father in Jesus' name, (2) the Father loves them, and (3) he has come from the Father and is leaving the world to go to the Father, the disciples exclaim that he is indeed "speaking plainly" and acknowledge Jesus' divine origins and omniscience (16:30; cf. 17:7). Their confession (for that is what it is) that Jesus knows "all things" and "has come from God" is certainly correct, even if the immediate impetus for it is hard to detect.[163] But those who voice such enthusiastic acknowledgments elsewhere in the Gospel (1:49; 3:2) often show that their faith needs to be tested and deepened by the events of Easter and the tutelage of the Spirit. Jesus' question, "Do you now believe?" (16:31), alerts the disciples of the threats to their steadfastness in faith (see 13:38; 14:1). Their confidence that they now understand Jesus will not keep them from abandoning him in the coming hour: having abandoned him, they will be scattered (cf. Zech 13:7, cited in Matt 26:31 and Mark 14:27; and comments on John 10:11–16). Since Jesus' death and mission serve to gather the sheep, this "scattering" that severs relationship with Jesus and with each other will be only temporary, yet nonetheless real and a harbinger of what they must avoid.

Even if the disciples abandon Jesus, the Father has not abandoned him (16:32). Just as the risen Lord will not abandon his disciples (14:18) but will always be with them (14:23), so also God does not abandon the Son whom he loves. In Mark and Matthew the dying Jesus cries out from the cross with the words of the psalmist, "My God, my God, why have you forsaken me?" (Ps

162. Barrett 495; Hoskyns 490; Ridderbos 540–42; Schnackenburg 3:162; D. Moody Smith 1999, 303, 306.

163. Michaels (863) deems Jesus' prayer "itself an operation of divine grace, transforming the shaky faith of the disciples into something firm and lasting."

22:1 in Matt 27:46; Mark 15:34). While John gives hints of Jesus' distress in the face of his upcoming death (11:33; 12:27; 13:21), this Gospel does not present Jesus as experiencing the anguish of God's absence on the cross; rather, Jesus is presented as boldly testifying to God's constant presence with him (cf. Luke 23:46). When read in light of the resurrection and confession of Jesus' unity with the Father, the cross shows that Jesus has been glorified by God, not abandoned or discredited. Once again, the Gospel is written "from back to front," narrating events from the perspective of the end and, here, the resurrection.

Now at the end of his words to his disciples, Jesus comes full circle, exhorting them to "take heart" or, perhaps more loosely, "have confidence" (14:1, 27; 16:33). Earlier Jesus has encouraged his disciples not to be troubled (14:1, 27) and has promised them his peace toward that end (14:27). They may have peace because, in spite of the world's persecution or hostility, the world does not control their destinies any more than it has controlled Jesus' life. The world has not overcome Jesus: Jesus has overcome or "conquered" the world (16:33),[164] a counterintuitive interpretation of Jesus' death possible only from the vantage point of his resurrection and the pedagogical role of the Spirit (16:7–11). To perceive only a crucified man, persecuted by the world, is to interpret Jesus' story neither from its end nor from God's perspective, but from the world's viewpoint. Faith, directed by the Spirit, perceives Jesus' death as his victory over the cosmic powers of death and darkness (12:31; 14:30; 16:11). As an instrument of execution and Roman subjugation of conquered peoples, the cross symbolizes defeat and shame. Through it, however, Jesus attains his victory over evil and receives glory or honor from God because through that cross God, out of his love for the world, brings life to the world.

Jesus' last words before going to his death invite his disciples to understand the significance of the events that will unfold from the vantage point of the victory of God's life over death that is won through and on the cross. Both Jewish and early Christian eschatology expected a period of trials and testing before God's ultimate salvation. Such a schema of suffering preceding judgment and redemption can be found in Jesus' discourses in the Synoptic Gospels (Matt 24–25; Mark 13; Luke 21:5–36). These so-called apocalyptic discourses expect a period of turmoil, followed by judgment and an era of blessedness for the faithful. To be sure, the Synoptic accounts do not deem the disciples bereft of such blessing in the present, as Jesus' various beatitudes make plain: "Blessed are the eyes that see what you see!" (Luke 10:23; cf. 11:28; Matt 5:1–11; 13:16). But John boldly and explicitly presents the cross and resurrection of Jesus as that which overcomes the powers of the world: the disciples who remain *in* the

164. "Conquered" (*nenikēka*) comes from *nikaō*, which in 1 John describes the "victory" of faith over the evil one, the antichrist, or the world (2:13–14; 4:4; 5:4–5). In Revelation the believer who remains steadfast is described as one who "conquers" (2:7, 11, 17, 26; 3:5, 12, 21; 21:7).

world are thus able to interpret their own real sufferings and struggles from that vantage point. That hope instills peace, confidence, and courage.

17:1–26 Jesus' Final Prayer for His Disciples

Jesus turns to address the Father in prayer, making a number of requests pertaining to his death and to his disciples' continuing life in this world.[165] Above all Jesus prays that God may "glorify" or bring honor to him in and through his death (17:1, 5) so that, in turn, he may glorify God (17:2). Jesus then prays for his disciples, asking that God will (1) protect them after his departure, leaving them in a hostile world (17:9–14, 25); (2) sanctify or consecrate them so that they may be sent for the mission he is entrusting to them (17:17–19, 26); and (3) unite all his disciples with one another and with him (17:20–26). In praying for the work and mission of his disciples in the world, Jesus reveals the striking parallels between his status, mission, and purpose and theirs: sanctified by the Father, they are sent into an indifferent or hostile world; they will bear witness to the life that the Father gives to the Son, in order that together the Father and the Son may be glorified and others may be brought to faith and life.

Elsewhere in the Gospels, Jesus prays to God regarding his mission and for his disciples, entrusting himself and his mission to the Father's will, while acknowledging its mysterious yet gracious character (Matt 11:25–26; Luke 10:21). The Synoptics also recount prayers uttered in Jesus' final hours. According to Luke, Jesus prays for Simon's strength, knowing that he will be tempted by Satan to fall away (22:31–32). Just before his arrest, Jesus petitions God to "remove this cup" from him, yet he leaves the final disposition of his life in the hands of God, with the heartwrenching prayer "Your will be done" (Matt 26:36–45, esp. v. 42; Mark 14:32–42; Luke 22:40–46). Jesus also instructs his disciples to pray that they will not succumb to temptation (Matt 26:41; Mark 14:38; Luke 22:40, 46).[166] These prayers present Jesus as (1) committed to doing the work and will of his Father and (2) praying for his disciples in the face of temptations that will come.

Jesus' long prayer in John 17 addresses those two concerns. In other words, Jesus prays here much as he does in the Synoptics. But this prayer is as much declaration as petition, uttered under the conviction that Jesus did the will and work of his Father and thus brought glory to the Father. As is typical of John as a whole, this prayer elaborates traditional material and motifs while looking back on past events from the perspective of faith granted by the resurrection, and

165. See Hera for a recent study of this prayer, including its various titles. The most common name, the "High-Priestly Prayer," is typically attributed to David Chytraeus (1531–1600), but adumbrated by patristic references to Christ's intercession as high priest in John.

166. So also the petitions in the Lord's Prayer (Matt 6:10, 13; Luke 11:4).

it is cast in the distinctively Johannine idiom (cf. comments on 12:27–28).[167] Jesus speaks of what he *will* do as that which he *has already done* or *is in the process of doing*: there is no disjuncture between his petition and his faithful embodiment of God's will and work to bring life to the world.

17:1 When Jesus had said these things, he lifted up his eyes[a] to heaven and
said, "Father, the hour has come. Glorify your Son, so that the Son might
glorify you, 2 even as you have given him authority over all flesh, so that
[to] all that you have given to him, he might give eternal life. 3 And this
is eternal life:[b] that they know you, the only true God, and him whom
you have sent, Jesus Christ.
4 "I glorified you on earth, having completed the work that you have
given me to do. 5 And now glorify me, Father, in your own presence with
the glory that I had with you before the world came to be. 6 I have made[c]
your name known to those whom you gave me from the world. They were
yours, and you gave them to me, and they have kept your word. 7 Now
they know that all things that you have given me are from you. 8 For I have
given them the words that you have given to me, and they have received
[them] and truly understood that I have come from you, and they have
believed that you have sent me.
9 "I am asking on their behalf; I am not asking for the world, but rather
for those whom you have given to me, because they are yours, 10 and all
that are mine are yours and yours are mine, and I am glorified in them.
11 "And I am no longer in the world, but they are in the world, and I am
coming to you. Holy Father, keep them in your name that you have given
to me, so that they may be one even as we are. 12 When I was with them,
I kept them in your name that you have given to me, and I have guarded
[them], and none of them has perished, except the son of perdition,[d] so
that the Scripture might be fulfilled.
13 "Now I am coming to you. I have said these things in the world so
that they may have my joy fulfilled in them. 14 I have given them your
word, and the world hated them, because they are not of the world, even
as I am not of the world. 15 I do not ask that you should take them out
of the world, but rather that you should keep them from the evil one.[e] 16
They are not of the world, even as I am not of the world.
17 "Sanctify them in your truth; your word is truth. 18 Even as you sent
me into the world, so I have sent them into the world. 19 I sanctify myself
for their sake, so that they themselves may also be sanctified in the truth.

167. Characteristically Johannine vocabulary includes "give" (*didōmi*), "send" (*apostellō*), "glory" and "glorify" (*doxa, doxazō*), "world" (*kosmos*), "Father" (*patēr*) and "Son" (*huios*), as well as expressions of the mutual indwelling and unity of Father and Son.

20 "I do not ask for these only, but also[f] for those who will believe in
me through their word, **21** so that they may all be one, even as you, Father,
are in me and I also am in you, that they also may be in us, so that the
world may believe that you have sent me. **22** And the glory that you have
given to me I have given to them, so that they may be one even as we are
one. **23** I in them and you in me, so that they may be perfectly one, so that
the world will know that you have sent me and that you have loved them
even as you loved me.

24 "Father, I desire that they also, whom[g] you have given to me, may
be with me where I am, so that they may see my glory that you have
given me because you have loved me before the foundation of the world.
25 Righteous Father, the world does not know you, but I know you, and
these know that you have sent me. **26** And I have made your name known
to them, and I will make it known, so that the love with which you have
loved me may be in me as I also am in them."

a. Lit., "Jesus said [*elalēsen*] these things and, having lifted up his eyes to heaven, he said." The translation here renders the aorist indicative (*elalēsen*) as an aorist participle (as is *eparas*, "having lifted up his eyes").

b. "Eternal life" in 17:2 translates *zōēn aiōnion*, with this sequence of Greek words ("life eternal") as elsewhere in John; in 17:3 *hē aiōnios zōē* occurs, the only instance of this word order in the Gospel, suggesting to some a redactional gloss.

c. The aorist *ephanerōsa* ("I have made known") views Jesus' ministry as a whole; cf. Wallace 1996, 557.

d. There is a play on words in the Greek: none has "perished" (*apōleto*, from *apollymi*) except the son of "perdition" (*apōleias*).

e. As is the case with one of the Matthean petitions of the Lord's Prayer (Matt 6:13 and mg.), *ponēros* can be translated as "the evil one" (as here, understood to refer to the devil) or more generally as "evil."

f. The adversative *alla* ("on the contrary, but, rather") with *kai* is rendered here as "but also, moreover."

g. A number of MSS (including $\mathfrak{P}^{60}$ ℵ B D W) read *ho dedōkas moi* ("what you have given me") instead of the easier *hous* ("whom"), which is the sense here in spite of this reading's weaker attestation.

[17:1–3] Having finished his instructions and admonitions to his disciples, Jesus turns to address his Father, looking up to heaven in the formal posture of prayer (cf. 11:41–42; Ps 123:1; Mark 6:41; Luke 18:13) and declaring that "the hour has come."[168] The hour that has been anticipated, forestalled, and imminent is finally present. Its arrival scarcely catches Jesus unawares (John 12:23; 17:1; cf. 13:1; Mark 14:41). He purposely and knowingly faces the

168. Moses' farewell address to Israel in Deut 27–32 ends with a "song" of praise (32:1–44).

hour of his death and, in keeping with the will of his Father, sets the things in motion that lead to his crucifixion. His prayer, "Father, glorify your Son," echoes, with slight but important modification, the earlier petition, "Father, glorify your name!" (John 12:28). Jesus now prays for God to glorify him, but the result ("so that the Son may glorify *you*") shows that the glorification of one entails the glorification of the other: if the Father is honored, then so is the Son, and vice versa. To honor God is to honor Jesus; to honor Jesus is to honor God (5:23; 8:49, 54; 12:26; 13:32). Although the obviously declaratory aspect of Jesus' prayer seems to render it as much discourse as prayer, it shows that Jesus knows and accomplishes the will of the Father so fully that petition and declaration are virtually identical: to ask that something be done is equivalent to declaring that it will be done (cf. 11:41–43).

Specifically, the work that will bring glory to God is the giving of eternal life to all those whom God has given to Jesus (vv. 2–3). In this pithy formulation, several factors are noteworthy:

1. God is glorified by Jesus' work in giving eternal life. Throughout John the living and life-giving God, who created the world and gave it life through the Word, is glorified by the life-giving signs and words of the Son. God does not will death for the world, but life (3:16–17; 9:3; 11:4, 40).

2. Eternal life is knowing "the only true God" and the one sent by him, Jesus Christ. John does not write that knowing God leads to eternal life, as if it were the reward for faith, but that knowing God, to be in communion with God, *is* life, because God is the source of all life (cf. Col 3:4). Such a formulation lends itself to a view of salvation as participation in the divine life typical especially of the Eastern Church. Thus Clement of Alexandria expounds, "To know [the Father] is eternal life, through participation in the power of the incorrupt One. And to be incorruptible is to participate in divinity."[169]

3. As from the very beginning of the Gospel, John emphasizes the all-encompassing work and authority given to the Son by the Father: "All things came into being through him" (1:3). As the light "of all people" (1:4), the Son has authority over "all flesh" (17:2) because the Father has put "all things" into his hands (3:35), has shown him "all things" (5:20), and entrusted "all judgment" to him (5:22). As Hilary of Poitiers wrote, "The Father gave all; the Son

169. Clement, *Strom.* 5.10 (*ANF* 2:49). The Lord "has given a share of his own divinity" (Origen, *Comm. Jo.* 19.25) to believers, who through faith are "partakers of the divine nature" (Cyril of Alexandria 1874, 106). The first-century Alexandrian Jewish exegete Philo, who certainly influenced the entire Alexandrian school of interpretation, asserted that "eternal life [*zōē aiōnios*] is to find refuge with the one who is [*to on*]" (*Fug.* 78). But Dodd (1953, 163) also points out the genuine parallel to John 17:3 in the Septuagint—which Philo used extensively—of Hos 6:2–3: "We shall rise from the dead [*anastēsometha*] and shall live [*zēsometha*] before him [*enōpion autou*], and we shall have knowledge [*gnōsometha*]. We shall press on to know the Lord [*diōxomen tou gnōnai ton kyrion*]."

received all."[170] The destiny of every human person lies in the hands of Jesus, because God has entrusted every person ("all flesh," 17:2) into his hands.

4. Even as the Father wills to give life, so Jesus gives life to those whom the Father has given to him. They are variously referred to as those born of God (1:13; 3:3, 5), the children of God (1:12; 11:52), the sheep of God's flock (10:26–29), and the branches on the vine tended by God (15:1–11). The world was created by God through the Word; life is given by the Father through the Son.

5. Father and Son are here referred to, respectively, as "the only true God" and "Jesus Christ" ("Jesus the Messiah," 17:3). These terms, "only true God" and "Messiah," give voice both to scriptural affirmations of the uniqueness of Israel's God (cf. 5:44) and to the contemporary hope for the coming of God's anointed agent of deliverance, the Messiah, whose mission in John is construed as granting life to those threatened by death (11:25–27). By linking the acknowledgment of Jesus as Messiah to knowing the one true God, and by joining both to having eternal life, John reshapes the messianic role to emphasize the Messiah's deliverance as the work of giving life, to gather in and protect all the children of God.

A definition of eternal life is given in what appears to be a parenthetical explanation.[171] To be sure, the designation of God as "the only true God" reflects the Gospel's insistence that there is one God (5:44; 8:41, 54), who alone is true (3:33). But while Jesus is regularly referred to, if sometimes only tentatively or questioningly, as the Messiah (1:41; 4:25, 29; 7:26–27, 31, 41–42; 11:27), the conjoined name "Jesus Christ" occurs elsewhere only one other time in John (1:17), voiced by the narrator. The fuller designation, "Jesus Christ" (i.e., "Jesus the Messiah") or "Christ Jesus," occurs rarely in the Gospels (Mark 1:1) but regularly in Acts, the Epistles, and Revelation, suggesting that this designation was common in early Christian parlance, as a formal declaration of Jesus' identity. Its occurrence shows that this prayer reflects the confessional language of those who openly acclaim Jesus as the Messiah after his resurrection.

[4–8] In the next portion of his prayer, Jesus affirms once more that he has brought glory to God by completing the life-giving work that God has given him. In an emphatically phrased petition, Jesus asks that God will glorify him "with the glory that I had with you before the world came to be." Jesus has always shared in God's glory, a continuous participation in the divine identity of God: he had such glory prior to creation (1:1–4), he revealed it as the one made flesh (1:14; 2:11), he will receive such glory as he gives his life on the cross (12:23, 28), and he will return to the Father's presence in glory (1:18; 17:24). Jesus does not surrender his glory at any time.[172] Even though that

170. Hilary of Poitiers, *On the Trinity* 9.31.

171. See also Excursus 4: "Life and Eternal Life in John."

172. Schnelle 1998, 256.

glory cannot always be seen or discerned by human eyes, especially when it appears in unexpected ways—including in the death of this man on a Roman cross—there is never a time when Jesus does not manifest the glory of God, because it is intrinsic to his identity. Yet there is a peculiar hiddenness to the manifestation of his glory: the light shining in the darkness is visible only to faith.

Jesus has all that he has and does all that he does because God has given it to him (v. 7). Jesus has been given God's work (v. 4), certain persons "from the world" (v. 6), and words from God (v. 8); he has been given "all things" from the Father (v. 7; cf. 16:30). While this relationship cannot be reversed—the Son does not give life or "all things" to the Father—the extent to which the Father gives the Son his authority, entrusting to him his creative and sovereign work, nevertheless makes the Son "equal" and "one" with the Father.

Jesus expands the assertion that he has completed God's work: he has done so by (1) making God's name known (v. 6) and (2) giving his disciples God's words (v. 8). Therefore they believe he has come from God (v. 8; cf. 16:30). "Making God's name known" may simply mean making God known; according to John, the only Son has made the Father known (1:18) because Jesus has acted and spoken in the Father's name (5:43; 10:25) or by the Father's authority (see also 17:12).[173] To say that Jesus makes God known does not mean that God has never been known, but that the revelation of God through Jesus is *now* a revelation of God as the Father of the Son.[174] Everything in the formulation of Jesus' identity here links him with God and points ultimately to God.

[9–16] Because he is going away, Jesus prays for his disciples' protection. In his prayer Jesus reiterates the point that he is going to the Father; he is not departing to his "fathers" or ancestors (a euphemism for death), as Josephus has Moses say.[175] Jesus grounds his petition to God, the "Holy Father" (17:11), in the fact that ultimately the disciples belong to God, who has given them to Jesus (vv. 9–10), so that God and Jesus share "possession" or "ownership" of these disciples. We find here a pattern typical of John: what Jesus has, be it the authority to judge or to have and give eternal life,

173. Among those who agree that "name" stands for the person as a whole are Barrett 505; Beasley-Murray 298; Carson 1991, 558; and Schnackenburg 3:175. Hera (137) follows R. Brown (1970, 754–56) in proposing that the name is the divine "I AM [*egō eimi*]," yet this manner of divine speech is not precisely a name for God (see Excursus 5: "The 'I Am' Sayings of John"). Somewhat differently, Jesus will shortly speak of "your name that you have given to me" (v. 11), which cannot be the name "Father"; it must almost certainly be YHWH, or "LORD" (*kyrios*).

174. For this reason patristic authors tended to think of "Father" as God's name revealed in the advent of the Son (Tertullian, *Or.* 3; Cyril of Alexandria 1885, 11.7).

175. Josephus, *Ant.* 4.315 (*apeimi progonous*). Biblical texts speak of "lying down" or "sleeping with" one's fathers or ancestors (*paterōn*, LXX: Gen 47:30; 49:29). For the contrast between "fathers" (*pateres*) and "the Father" (*ho patēr*), see John 4:20–23; 6:31; 8:38–56.

he has by virtue of the Father's gift to him (3:27, 35; 5:22, 27; 6:39; 10:29; 12:49; 13:3; 17:2, 7–8). Those for whom Jesus prays are here designated as "those whom you have given to me" (v. 9). Because these disciples have been "given" to Jesus by the Father; they belong to Jesus. But precisely because the Father has "given all things" to the Son, there exists a mutuality between them, summarized as reciprocity: "All that are mine are yours and yours are mine" (v. 10). Those given to Jesus by the Father continue to belong to the Father even as Jesus holds them. As Father, God is the source of all that is; as Son, Jesus is the recipient of what the Father gives; as one, they share with each other all that the other has (cf. 14:28).[176]

Jesus prays for the disciples because, in his absence, they will need protection in a world that hates them, that rejects the message with which they are entrusted, and that sets itself against their witness (17:14–15). But why does Jesus add the note that he is praying only for his disciples and not for the world (v. 9)? Even if the disciples need God's protection, does not the world have equally urgent needs for God's care? Jesus prays for the disciples (1) because as their shepherd he is committed to their well-being and protection, a commitment that does not cease with his death; (2) because he desires to entrust them to the Father, who holds the sheep in his hand (10:26–30) so that they cannot be snatched from it (10:28–29; 17:11–12); and (3) because the disciples will carry on his mission in the world and need God's protection as they do so. Because Jesus prays for them in their witness in the world, his prayer for them will affect the world as well. If Jesus' own mission is the model for the disciples' mission, then that mission will lead them into deep engagement with, not withdrawal from, the world.

Addressing God as "Holy Father," Jesus petitions the Father to keep the disciples "in your name that you have given me" (17:11). To be kept "in your name" means to be protected or guarded as those who belong to the Father and so are identified, or marked, by the Father's name (see comments on 14:12–14; 17:6). The Father's name is "your name that you have given to me" (17:11–12). The Father who has given "all things" to the Son (3:35; 5:20, 22; 6:39; 13:3; 16:15; see on 14:28), who has made Jesus one with himself (5:18; 10:25–30), now gives his own name to Jesus. According to certain passages in the Old Testament, God's name is YHWH; this was read in Hebrew as *Adonai* (*ʾădônāy*, Lord), and often translated into the Greek as *kyrios* (Lord).[177] Thus, for example, in Exod 6:3 LXX, God refers to "my name Lord" (*to onoma mou kyrios*; cf.

176. Sheppard (113–14) intriguingly suggests that the passage could be read in light of Roman law, in which the father, as paterfamilias with *patria potestas*, retains legal control of *all* property of even adult children until his own death. But an adult son might receive jurisdiction over a fair amount of that father's estate by means of *peculium*, a kind of substantial allowance. Thus, though "owned" by the father, the property is also rightfully the son's.

177. For recent study of issues regarding the divine name, see Rösel.

MT, *šĕmî* YHWH). Since, in John, "Lord" nearly always designates Jesus,[178] it is highly likely that this should be understood as the name given to Jesus by God. Jesus is now known by God's own appellation, a telling indicator of the unity of Father and Son.[179]

The request that God may keep them so that "they may be one" (John 17:11) anticipates the possibility that people may leave the fold or be cut off from the vine, thus disrupting the unity of Jesus' community and working against God's purposes "to gather into one the children of God" (11:52; cf. 1 John 2:19). Unless God "keeps" the disciples (John 17:11) and guards them as Jesus has done (v. 12), the disciples are in danger of falling away, of being scattered and devoured by wolves, of withering on the vine like the branches that failed to bear fruit—indeed, of perishing (see 3:16; 6:12, 27, 39; 10:10, 28; 11:50; 12:25; 17:12; 18:9).

As if to quell the fear raised by the defection of Judas, Jesus emphasizes that "*none of them has perished*": there is only one exception (cf. 18:9), the "son of perdition" (17:12). "Son of perdition" (RSV) or "son of destruction" (ESV, NRSV mg.) means "one who is bound for perdition" or "doomed to destruction" (NIV).[180] In Sirach, Sodom is "a people of destruction" (*ethnos apōleias*, 16:9): a people doomed to destruction because of their wickedness. *Jubilees* refers to the wicked who perished in the flood as "children of perdition" (10.3), contrasting the "sons of the covenant" made with Abraham with the (uncircumcised) "children of destruction" (15.26). In 2 Thess 2:3, the "man of lawlessness" (NRSV mg.), the one who sets himself against God and God's law, is called "the son of perdition" (RSV; *huios tēs apōleias*), exactly as Judas is identified in John. In every case the idiom "children" or "people of destruction" refers to the wicked or disobedient, those outside the covenant. Judas has been "lost" to destruction because he has turned from following Jesus, like a branch that fails to bear fruit and so is "taken away" from the vine (15:2). Jesus petitions his Father to protect his disciples, to keep them within the flock or on the vine, and so guard them all as one.

178. There are exceptions in the OT quotations at 12:13 and 12:38; see the comments there and at 1:23; 6:23. In Phil 2:9, Jesus is given "the name that is above every name," which is YHWH, as Paul's statement suggests: "every tongue will confess that Jesus Christ is *Lord*" (*kyrios*, Phil 2:11; cf. Rom 14:11; Isa 45:23–25).

179. Compare the strikingly similar train of thought in 10:28–30: No one can snatch Jesus' sheep from his hand, because they are given to him by the Father; no one can snatch anything from the Father's hand; Jesus and the Father are one.

180. The idea of predestination to destruction is not here in view; Keck (1996) shows that in John predications of derivation reveal one's ultimate destiny; hence, those born "of God" (*ek theou*) are the "children of God" and destined to be with God. Judas is the "son of perdition," whose destiny is not life, but "perishing" or "death" (3:16–17) because he has turned from following Jesus (6:66–71).

Still, Judas's "loss" must have raised a question: Had Judas been lost to the evil one (13:2, 27; 17:15) because God had not "protected" him? Had Jesus prayed for Judas but had not been heard? Or had Jesus never prayed for Judas? John accounts for Judas's betrayal by affirming that it did not catch Jesus by surprise or thwart God's purposes, as the reference to the fulfillment of Scripture shows (17:12). This is likely an oblique reference to the same Scripture invoked earlier regarding the one who "lifted his heel against me" (Ps 41:9 = 40:10 LXX, cited in 13:18). One is lost, but the others are kept and guarded in the Father's name; no one can snatch from the Father's hand those who belong to him (10:26–29).

Jesus' prayer identifies the chief threat to the disciples as their continued existence in the hostile "world." On the one hand, they do not belong to the world: they have been "given" to Jesus (vv. 6, 7, 8, 9) "from" or "out of" the world (*ek tou kosmou*, vv. 6, 14, 16); thus, they are rejected or hated by the world (v. 14), epitomized in the "evil one" (v. 15). On the other hand, they remain *in* the world (*en tō kosmō*, vv. 11, 13). That world causes distress (16:33), not only through its treatment of both Jesus and his disciples, but also in the pressures, both subtle and obvious, that might divert the disciples from the path of Jesus.

This passage (esp. 17:14–16) contributes to the characterization of Christians as being "in the world but not of it."[181] Being "in the world" simply describes the disciples' circumstances: they are not yet with the Father or with Jesus after he leaves (14:2–3) but remain "in the world," even as Jesus was in the world for a period of time. However, like Jesus, the disciples are not "of the world" because the world, virtually by definition in John, stands opposed to Jesus and his followers. Jesus' disciples are oriented in their commitments and conduct to God's way, truth, and life, and not to the world's ways. Being "*in* the world" and being "*of* God" are not opposed to each other; but being "*of* the world" and "*of* God" are in opposition. In John, to be "of the world" is to stand against God.

[17–19] In order that the disciples remain faithful in the world, Jesus prays that God may *sanctify* (*hagiason*) them (17:17) even as he will sanctify himself for their sake (*hyper autōn*, v. 19; cf. 6:51). "Consecrate" or "sanctify" translates *hagiazō*,[182] a verb used sparingly in John, twice for Jesus being sanctified

181. For discussion of "the world" and being "of the world," see comments at 14:15–17, 15:18–21.

182. In the LXX *hagiazein* typically translates the Hebrew *qādaš*, to dedicate as a sacrifice or priest, to set apart for the service of God; as various lexicons indicate, the word is extremely rare in nonbiblical Greek, which more typically uses *hagizein* (for further lexical issues, see comments on 11:55). The LXX uses *hagiazein* of Jeremiah (Jer 1:5); God's servant, Israel (Isa 49:7); Moses (Sir 45:4); the "fathers" (ancestors, 2 Macc 1:25); yet also of the firstborn, Aaron and his sons as priests, the priestly garments, altar, furnishings in the tabernacles, and sacrifice (Exod 13:2; 28:41; 29:1, 21, 27, 37; Deut 15:19). While Hoskyns (503–4) and Thyen (697) insist that consecration for both service and sacrifice are clearly in view, in this context the emphasis falls on consecration or dedication for mission.

(10:36; 17:19a) and twice for the disciples (17:17, 19b). Its adjectival equivalent, "holy," refers only to the Spirit (1:33; 14:26; 20:22), the Son (6:69), and the Father (17:11). To be consecrated is to be dedicated for service to God. Jesus thus asks that God will do for the disciples what God has done for him, that God will sanctify or consecrate them in anticipation of their being sent into the world as Jesus was consecrated and sent into the world (cf. 10:36). The disciples are to be sanctified in or by truth, which is God's word (17:17, 19; Ps 119:142, 160). In other words, they are dedicated for their task by means of God's word, which they have received and believed; they have become part of God's purposes and mission through hearing and responding to God's words, given to Jesus, and subsequently to them (v. 8). Jesus' prayer recalls his earlier statement that the disciples have already been made clean through the word he has spoken to them (15:3). Having been cleansed by Jesus' word, now they are to be "sanctified" or dedicated to and by God (17:17, 19b), preparing them for the Son to send them into the world (v. 18). For the sake of their mission, Jesus consecrates himself: he sets himself apart for service to God (v. 19a). Because the disciples represent Jesus, who in turn represents God, their own consecration for mission depends on and results from Jesus' own self-giving to God (vv. 17–19).

In spite of the congruence, there is a great dissimilarity between Jesus' consecration and that of the disciples, since Jesus' consecration both precedes and effects theirs (Hoskyns 504). But there is also a point of comparison: *even as* (*kathōs*) the Father sent the Son "into the world" (17:18a; 10:36; 11:27; 12:46; 16:28; 18:37), so now Jesus sends the disciples "into the world" (*eis ton kosmon*, 17:18b; cf. 20:21). This is the world that was given life through God's Word but did not recognize him (1:5, 10; 17:25). Although God loves the world and gave his Son to bring it life (3:16; 12:47), this is the very world that rejects both the one through whom it was made and the disciples who follow that one (15:18–19). In other words, the mission of the disciples, like that of Jesus, springs from and expresses God's persistent will to bring life to the world, but their mission also anticipates an indifferent or hostile response. Nevertheless, they are sent and will be equipped by the Holy Spirit, the Spirit of truth, to persevere in their mission of speaking the truth in the world (16:8–13; 20:21–23).

[20–23] Having prayed for his disciples, Jesus then turns to pray for those who are not yet his disciples, but who will "believe in me through their word" (v. 20; cf. 10:16; 11:52). Throughout John, people are brought to Jesus by the witness of others (1:40, 44; 4:29–30); the Gospel itself serves as a witness to Jesus (20:31). Even as Jesus prayed earlier for his disciples to be one and to be protected from disintegration, so now Jesus prays in the same way for those who do not yet believe to become one with his disciples, part of "the communion of saints." Those "who will believe in me through their word" include any and all "disciples at second hand," those who did not see or hear Jesus themselves, whether separated by time or space. Through the testimony of the disciples, the written Gospel (20:30–31), and the Spirit, they may know and experience the risen Jesus, who is in fact present with and in them. Jesus' work as shepherd is to keep his flock together as one flock, protected from all forces that seek to destroy its unity (10:12, 16). To that end, Jesus prays "that they may all be one."

Their unity is organic: it exists, not because of human effort, but because of God's life-giving love for the world that is expressed through and in the mission of Jesus. Since the unity of Father and Son comes to expression in their saving work (10:26–30), Jesus may be understood to be praying that the disciples will be united in the mission entrusted to them, even as the common mission of the Father and Son in the world demonstrates their unity. But the mission of the disciples only expresses their unity: it does not create that unity.

The unity of Father and Son is described, not only as a mutual indwelling ("you in me and I in you," 17:21), but also in terms of love for each other; in turn, the unity of the disciples demonstrates that the Father has loved them as he has loved Jesus (v. 23). The love of the Father in the Son binds the disciples together because it is self-giving, not self-seeking; it is cohesive.[183] Furthermore, the disciples' unity with one another and with Jesus and the Father testifies to the world that Jesus has been sent by God. But these assessments are all the "right judgment" (7:24) of faith. The world, in fact, does not believe that the Father sent the Son; they do not believe that Jesus' teaching has been given to him by the Father (7:16; 8:47–48); they do not believe his works, even though he has "done so many signs in their presence" (12:37)—and yet he did them. The disciples' unity with one another and with the Father and the Son is intended to bring the world to know that the Father sent Jesus: that is its purpose, though not always its result. When faith is born, it will be faith that the Father sent the Son, and that the Son's mission exemplifies the unity of the Father and Son and their love for the world. The disciples participate in Jesus' mission, embodying God's love in order to bring life to the world, regardless of the response.

Jesus has also given to the disciples "the glory that you have given me" (v. 22). Jesus had this glory "before the world came to be" (17:5), and it was revealed abundantly through Jesus' signs of giving light and life to the world (1:14, 16; 2:11; 11:4, 40; 9:3). Although in Scripture "glory" typically connotes the visible manifestation of the divine presence, it may also mean honor and reputation.[184] Since Jesus is sending the disciples into the world so that he might be made known, his honor is intertwined with theirs. And because Jesus' disciples are one with him and in him, and because Jesus is one with the Father and in the Father (17:21, 23), the disciples have a share in all that belongs to

183. So Black (429–30) rightly describes God's love.
184. See Lincoln 2005, 438.

God and in all that God has given to Jesus. Not only is his reputation at stake in their mission; they also do share and will share in his own glory, life, and union with God.[185] These are truly staggering claims, similar to Paul's claim "All things are yours, . . . and you are Christ's; and Christ is God's" (1 Cor 3:21–23 RSV; for the hope of sharing God's glory, see Rom 5:2; 8:21; 9:4; Col 1:27; 3:4; 2 Thess 2:14; 2 Tim 2:10; Heb 2:10).

[24–26] Jesus now prays that the disciples "may be with me where I am" and that "they may see my glory" (v. 24), asking that the Father will fulfill the promise he has made to take the disciples to be with him "in my Father's house" (14:2–3). Jesus ends his prayer by underscoring the point that God has sent the Son into the world out of love. The Father has loved the Son "before the world came to be" (17:5), before the "foundation of the world" (v. 24). Love has always characterized the relationship of Father and Son; that very love now resides in the disciples, directing them toward the world to bring light into darkness. Jesus' mission to make God known is to make God's love known.

One of the dominant characteristics of Jesus' prayer is its striking theocentricity. Not only does Jesus address his prayer to the Father; from beginning to end, the substance of the prayer has to do with Jesus' relationship to the Father, the relationship of the Father to Jesus' disciples in their ongoing life in the world, and Jesus' mission to make the Father known (v. 25). To summarize: Jesus has all authority from God (vv. 1–2), gives life from God (vv. 2–3), accomplishes God's work on earth in order to bring glory to God (vv. 4–5), makes God known (v. 6, 26), receives everything he has from God (v. 7–10), is returning to God (v. 11), petitions God to protect the disciples he leaves behind (vv. 11–18) and to unite them to each other and to Jesus and the Father (vv. 19–26). As much as the Gospel focuses on the identity of Jesus, it also articulates his identity by relating him to God.

A second characteristic of Jesus' prayer in John 17 is its orientation of the mission of God to the world. The term "world" (*kosmos*) occurs 79 times in John, with almost half of those occurrences (38) found in chapters 14–17. Of those 38 uses, almost half (18) are found in this prayer. It is striking that as Jesus utters his final words to his disciples and prays for them, the world comes into such sharp focus. This is the world that God made, that God loves, and into which God sent the Son. Into this same world, Jesus now sends his disciples. To be sure, they are already "in the world," but they are commissioned by Jesus to bear witness in and to the world of God's love, made evident in the mission of the Son. If the world does not know God, receive the one whom he has sent, or give his disciples a hearing, nevertheless God has not turned his back on the world. The Father seeks true worshipers (4:23).

185. Barrett 513.

Jesus' prayer comes to its end, as do his words to his disciples about what they can expect from the world and from him in the coming days. Throughout the Farewell Discourse, Jesus speaks of the parallels of his own situation to his disciples' circumstances: sanctified and sent by God, Jesus embodies God's life and love so that what he says and does brings glory to God. Now, sanctified and sent by Jesus, his disciples are to embody God's love for the world as they bear witness to Jesus as the one who is the way, the truth, and the life (14:6), and thus bring glory to God. As they carry out their mission, the disciples can be assured of Jesus' constant and abiding presence. He does not abandon them (14:18).

Indeed, Jesus' work continues: even as he has made God known during his earthly ministry, so he will continue to mediate access to and knowledge of God, until he comes again in order to take his disciples to be with him where he is (14:2–3). For the present, he abides with them, giving life to them as a vine nourishes the branches (15:1–11). As he does so, the disciples can be assured of God's continued presence with them: the Father loves them, cares for them, and is with them. The disciples are also promised the Paraclete, the Spirit of truth, or Holy Spirit, to teach them, defend them, and lead them into all truth (14:16–17, 26; 15:26; 16:7–14).

In short, Jesus' last words and prayer reassure the disciples of his presence in spite of his absence. His absence is occasioned, first, by his death; second, by his departure to the Father. Yet he will be with the disciples, even if not as he was before. They will "see" him, but even seeing the risen one shows that everything is changing for the disciples, for he has not returned to live with them as before. Jesus is going to the Father. The experience of Jesus' first disciples becomes the experience of subsequent generations of disciples: all experience Jesus' absence; all have known and will know Jesus' presence; all are one with the Father and Son, and with one another; all will be taught by the Spirit; all hope for Jesus' return. The ongoing struggles of discipleship—to be steadfast, to bear witness, to love one another—are the same for all those who are "in" the world but not "of" that world.

John 18:1–19:42
The Arrest, Trial, and Crucifixion of Jesus

With the arrival of Jesus' "hour," the Gospel moves into the arrest, trial, and crucifixion of Jesus. It is clear from the New Testament and other early Christian literature that the death of Jesus was not only central to Christian proclamation, but also presented a formidable obstacle to faith (1 Cor 1:17–23; 15:3; Gal 3:13–14). To address that obstacle, the Gospel of John, like other early Christian literature, interprets Jesus' death not as the tragic end to his life, but as the result of faithfulness to his God-given vocation and the means through which God's salvation of the world was secured (Mark 10:45; Phil 2:8–11; 1 Tim 6:13; Heb 2:9–10; 4:14–16; 5:8–9; 1 Pet 2:4–8; 3:18; Rev 1:5; 5:12–13). It is on the cross that Jesus announced that God's work is finished (19:30); on the cross, therefore, Jesus is both glorified (12:23, 28; 13:31–32; 17:1, 4–5) and exalted (or "lifted up," 3:14; 8:28; 12:32, 34). John does not emphasize Jesus' suffering or mistreatment, yet neither does this Gospel deny Jesus' real death: blood flowed from his side (19:33–34). The Word who became flesh now gives his flesh: he dies, and he dies for the life of the world (6:51) in obedience to the Father's command (10:18). Looking backward from the resurrection, Jesus' death may be included in his victory, the means by which he overcomes the world and the power of darkness and death. It all constitutes his paradoxical triumph. From the perspective of that victory, John recounts the arrest, trial, and crucifixion of Jesus.

John's narrative begins with Judas's identification of Jesus in an unnamed garden (18:1), leading to Jesus' arrest, and ends with Joseph of Arimathea and Nicodemus placing Jesus in a tomb in another garden (19:41). Bookended by these two events, the narrative contains a number of elements common to all the canonical Gospels, such as Judas's betrayal, Peter's denial, and Pilate's scourging and sentencing of Jesus, as well as a number of distinctively Johannine features, including the presence of the beloved disciple at the foot of the cross and the spear thrust into Jesus' side to ascertain that he has died. In its present form, the narrative portrays Jesus as one who goes to his death willingly, in order to carry out God's purposes.[1]

1. On the questions of the sources and historical basis for John's Passion Narrative, see the discussions in R. Brown 1994, 75–93; Keener 2:1067–76; Lincoln 2005, 448–51.

Toward that end John's account underscores, first, Jesus' command of the entire situation. Although Jesus dies at the hands of Roman power, he is not its victim but superintends the unfolding of the events that lead to his crucifixion. He virtually orchestrates his own arrest (18:1–8),[2] entrusts the care of his mother to the disciple whom he loved while he is dying on the cross (19:26–27), and even seems to determine the moment of his own death (19:30). John thus narrates what it looks like for a good shepherd to willingly lay down his life for the sheep, keeping the command from the Father to "lay down his life."

Second, this Gospel emphasizes that Jesus' death accomplishes God's purposes. Jesus refuses to wield arms against those who want to arrest him, because he must "drink the cup that the Father has given" him (18:11). Unique to John, Jesus' last words from the cross ("It is finished!") demonstrate that Jesus has brought his work—God's work—to completion. Various passages are cited to show ways in which Jesus' death fulfills Scripture (19:24, 28, 36, 37). Jesus' death is no accident of history, as if he were simply in the wrong place at the wrong time. However much the cross attests to the powers of darkness in the world, it also embodies God's life-giving purpose for the world.

Finally, John's account presents Jesus as a king who gives his life for others. In John's Passion Narrative, Jesus' kingly identity is revealed on the cross. Pilate asks Jesus whether he is a king (18:33, 37); Jesus and Pilate converse about the source of their respective powers (18:36–37; 19:10–11). Jesus is mocked as king (18:37, 39; 19:3); Pilate repeatedly presents Jesus to the Jews and all onlookers as "King of the Jews" (18:39; 19:3, 14, 15, 19, 21). While kings have often died in the course of battles in which they seek to defend the lives of their people and to preserve their kingdoms, Jesus exercises his kingly office by preserving the lives of his people through giving his own life, rather than by taking the lives of others. Even in his death, he does not cease to be life for the world (1:4–5; 6:51–55).

18:1–14 Jesus Arrested in the Garden

In the narrative of Jesus' arrest in the garden, there are four main actors: Jesus, Judas, those who come to arrest Jesus, and Peter. Judas ostensibly serves to hand Jesus over to the authorities: the soldiers seize him, but Jesus dictates the action that leads to his arrest. Passively, the soldiers fall to the ground when Jesus identifies himself (18:5–6). Even Judas fades into the background, standing alongside the soldiers, but doing and saying nothing. Except for Jesus, only Peter, Jesus' own disciple, acts—and he acts against

2. Because John's account so emphasizes Jesus' initiative, Moloney (1998a, 129) deems the term "arrest" a misnomer; yet it is clear that Jesus is apprehended by the authorities, or allows himself to be apprehended by them.

the intentions of Jesus and of the Father by striking the high priest's servant with his sword in an effort to prevent Jesus' arrest. But Peter cannot halt the events that Jesus moves forward.

The conflict between Jesus and Peter reveals the difficulty of coming to grips with Jesus' death as the way that God's anointed king brings life to his people (cf. 6:51–60). Even at this point, Peter still fails to grasp the nature of Jesus' kingship. Earlier he had protested against Jesus assuming the role of a servant to wash his feet (13:6–8); now he protests against Jesus giving himself up to the Romans and certain death. Jesus washing his disciples' feet had graphically demonstrated the life of love and service to which Jesus calls his followers; it had also anticipated Jesus' self-giving on the cross: to protest the one is to protest the other. John now depicts Jesus as living out what he had said earlier, "No one takes [my life] from me, but I lay it down on my own" (10:18) and "No one has greater love than this—laying down one's life for one's friends" (15:13). Jesus gives himself over to earthly authorities in order to carry out the will of a higher authority.

[18:1] After Jesus had said these things, he went out with his disciples, across the Kidron Valley, where there was a garden. He and his disciples went into it. 2 Judas, who handed him over,[a] knew the place, because Jesus often gathered there with his disciples. 3 So Judas took a band of soldiers and servants of the chief priests and the Pharisees and went there with lanterns and torches and weapons.

4 Since Jesus knew all that was to come, he went out to him and said to them, "Whom are you looking for?"

5 They answered, "Jesus of Nazareth."[b]

He said to them, "I am he."

Judas, who handed him over, was standing with them. 6 And when he said to them, "I am he," they all drew back and fell to the ground.

7 So he asked them again, "Whom are you looking for?"

And they said, "Jesus of Nazareth."

8 Jesus answered, "I told you that I am he. If, then, you are looking for me, let these people go." 9 This was to fulfill the word that he had said, "Out of those whom you gave to me, I have lost none."

10 Then Simon Peter, who had a sword, drew it and struck the servant of the high priest and cut off his right ear. The servant's name was Malchus.

11 So Jesus said to Peter, "Put your sword into its sheath. Shall I not drink the cup that the Father has given me?"

12 Then the band of soldiers and their captain and the servants of the Jews took Jesus and bound him, 13 and they led him first to Annas, who was the father-in-law of Caiaphas, who was high priest that year.[c] 14 It

was Caiaphas who had advised the Jews that it was better that one person should die on behalf of the people.

a. "Handed over" translates the Greek *paradidous*, from *paradidōmi*; most often this is translated "betrayed." See textual notes at 6:64; 13:2; 18:30; 19:11.

b. While *Iēsous ho Nazōraios* is John's preferred form (18:5, 7; 19:19; cf. Luke 18:37), other NT references to Jesus as coming from or associated with Nazareth include *Iēsōus* [*Christos*] *toū Nazōraiou* (Matt 26:71; Acts 3:6; 4:10; 26:9); *Iēsous ho Nazarēnos* (Mark 10:47; 16:6; Luke 24:19); *Iēsous ho apo Nazareth* (Acts 10:38).

c. See the textual note at 7:32 on the translation of "high priest" and "chief priests."

[18:1–3] After finishing his last meal with his disciples and speaking his last words to them, Jesus sets out with them for a garden across the Kidron Valley. The valley is mentioned only here in the New Testament but appears several times in the Old Testament and twice in Josephus (*cheimarros tou Kedrōn*, LXX: 2 Sam 15:23; 1 Kgs 2:37; 15:13; 2 Kgs 23:6, 12; *Ant.* 8.17; 9.151). Although the word translated "valley" (*cheimarros*) designates a stream that flows during the winter season of rain (i.e., a wadi), the reference here may be to the ravine itself. The Kidron Valley runs along the east side of Jerusalem, separating it from the Mount of Olives.[3] Only John calls Jesus' destination a garden (18:1, 26); he does not name it "Gethsemane" (Matt 26:36 and Mark 14:32 call it a *chōrion*, "field"), nor does he explicitly locate it on the Mount of Olives (Luke 22:39–40).

According to John, Jesus frequently gathered there with his disciples, which explains how Judas knew the place and was able to lead "a band of soldiers" (*speira*, Matt 27:27; Mark 15:16) and the servants of the Jewish authorities there. The Greek word *speira* typically renders the Latin *cohors*, a tenth of a legion, or about six hundred Roman soldiers (but see Josephus, *J.W.* 3.67).[4] Some commentators have doubted that Pilate would allow Jewish authorities to commandeer his troops for such a venture or, if he had allowed it, that he would have sent such an enormous number and then permitted the troops to take Jesus to the high priest.[5] But Josephus refers to a *tagma* (brigade, detachment) of soldiers permanently located in the tower fortress known as the Antonia that overlooked the temple grounds, who were especially vigilant during festivals about potential uprisings of the people (*J.W.* 5.242–46). Given Jesus' popularity (11:48–50; 12:19), and since it was Passover, both Roman and Jewish authorities would be on high alert, eager to nip potential trouble in the bud. Even if the numbers of troops sent to confront Jesus are exaggerated, it is not unlikely

3. See BDAG; "Kidron, Brook of," *ABD* 4:37–38.

4. BDAG notes that *speira* may also translate *manipulus* (200 troops). In Jewish sources, *speira* also refers to the troops of a local military leader (such as Eleazar [2 Macc 8:23] or Judas [2 Macc 12:22]; cf. Jdt 14:11; 2 Macc 12:20). See comments and footnotes on 18:28.

5. Barrett 518; Keener 2:1080; Lincoln 2005, 443; Moloney 1998a, 130; Schnackenburg 3:222.

that Gentile and Jewish authorities together sought and secured Jesus' arrest and death.[6] Still, John's account dramatically heightens the contrast between the large armed band of servants and soldiers carrying torches, lanterns, and weapons on the one hand, and Jesus and his misguided defenders on the other hand. Peter has a sword and manages to wield it in an effort to protect Jesus until he is stopped, not by Roman or Jewish force, but by Jesus himself. Whatever happens, happens only because Jesus permits or wills it.

Judas does not need to identify Jesus to the authorities—there is no kiss (as in Matt 26:48–59; Mark 14:44–45; Luke 22:47–48)—since Jesus will identify himself to them. The Gospels never explicitly say what Judas does that constitutes "betraying" or "handing over" Jesus (see comments on 12:6). While Judas may have betrayed Jesus' whereabouts to the authorities, there have been plenty of previous opportunities to arrest Jesus in public places (18:20); these failed because Jesus' hour had not yet come (7:30; 8:20, 59; 10:39). The Gospel does make it clear that Judas's defection from the ranks of Jesus' disciples and his handing over of Jesus are two sides of one coin: what Judas does, he does not as a disciple, but as one who has ceased to follow Jesus and has been lured away from faithful discipleship (6:66–71; 8:44–50).

[4–9] Aware of what is to come, Jesus charts his own destiny in keeping with God's commands (13:1–4). Earlier, knowing that the Father had given all things into his hands, Jesus stooped to wash the feet of his disciples, thus foreshadowing his upcoming death as an act of self-giving love and of purification. Here, with the knowledge of what is to come, Jesus prods the band of soldiers: "Whom are you looking for?" (18:4). Jesus does not shrink from what is coming: he steps forward to meet his captors, who will hand him over to death. As he had said earlier, "No one takes [my life] from me, but I lay it down on my own" (10:18). Even if in the end the Romans do put Jesus on a cross, they do so only because Jesus allows and even wills it. The one who has and is life gives himself over to death.

Jesus identifies himself to those who have come to seek him. Twice he asks them, "Whom are you looking for?" (vv. 4, 7); twice they say, "Jesus of Nazareth"[7] (vv. 5, 7); twice Jesus identifies himself to them (vv. 6, 8). The first time he responds simply, "I am he" (*egō eimi*); the second time he states, "I told you that I am he" (*eipon hymin hoti egō eimi*). While *egō eimi* is simply an ordinary means of self-identification,[8] it is also the mode of God's

6. See Acts 4:27: "Both Herod and Pontius Pilate, with the Gentiles and the peoples of Israel, gathered together against your holy servant Jesus"; cf. Josephus, *Ant.* 18.64.

7. Or "Jesus the Nazarene."

8. "It is I" or "I am he"; cf. 4:26; 6:20. Some translators and commentators translate simply, "I am," perhaps intending a reference to Exod 3:14, where God identifies himself to Moses with the words "I AM WHO I AM." But *egō eimi* in John more likely represents the LXX's translation of the Hebrew *ʾănî hûʾ*, "I am he." See Excursus 5: "The 'I Am' Sayings of John."

self-identification in the LXX, especially in those parts of Isaiah where God asserts his uniqueness (Isa 43:10, 13, 25; 44:6, 24; 45:5, 18). With these words resonant of divine self-revelation, Jesus acknowledges himself to the troops who have come for him, and when he does, they fall to the ground. "Fell to the ground" does not necessarily indicate bowing in worship or subservience; for such acts the typical biblical expression is "fell on their faces."[9] Needless to say, it is unlikely that a contingent of Roman soldiers understood the significance of Jesus' self-identification as echoing the Septuagint translation of Isaiah. But the narrative does present these Romans unwittingly in the proper posture of honor and as powerless in the presence of Jesus.[10]

John depicts Jesus as confronting the formidable powers of Rome and of Israel: with neither lanterns, torches, nor weapons but only a word, he shows himself to be more powerful than all of them arrayed together against him. If Jesus is greater than Jacob (4:12) and Abraham (8:53), he is also greater than Caesar.[11] His word knocks a Roman cohort, along with the accompanying servants of the Jewish authorities, off their feet. Rome is confronting not merely a potential Jewish troublemaker, but the embodied Word of God: the one who speaks as God speaks, who has the unique powers to give life and to rule. In resisting Jesus, those who seize him are ultimately resisting God (cf. Acts 5:39). But Jesus does not destroy his captors; instead, he gives himself to them.

In order to set the course of events in motion, Jesus orders the soldiers to let his disciples go, demonstrating that he carries out the Father's will that he should lose none of those whom the Father has given to him (6:39; 10:28). Jesus' action of keeping and guarding those given to him by the Father—so that "none of them has perished, except the son of perdition" (17:12)—refers both to their physical lives in the present and the assurance of eternal life.[12] Like Scripture itself, Jesus' word "cannot be broken" and will be fulfilled (2:22; 10:35; 18:32). He did not "lose" any of them to death.

[10–14] While Jesus may have set events in motion, leading to his arrest and death, Simon Peter has other plans. Drawing a sword, he attacks the high priest's servant or slave (*doulos*), cutting off his right ear (cf. Matt 26:51; Mark 14:47; Luke 22:50). John's account names the man as Malchus. Malchus does not reappear in the Gospel, but named characters—except for well-known Jewish and Roman authorities, such as Caiaphas and Pilate—typically are or

9. Cf. Lev 9:24; Num 16:22; 20:6; Judg 13:20; 1 Kgs 18:39; Ezek 1:28; Dan 10:9; Matt 17:6; Rev 7:11; 11:16; 1 Macc 4:55.

10. Cf. the Roman centurion's acclamation of Jesus as "God's Son" (Matt 27:54; Mark 15:39) or as "righteous" or "just" (Luke 23:47).

11. To borrow the title from Thatcher's book, Jesus is *Greater than Caesar: Christology and Empire in the Fourth Gospel.*

12. Moloney (1998a, 130) argues that Jesus' claim not to have lost one of them includes Judas, and that Satan, not Judas, is the "son of perdition" of 17:12. But by this point in the narrative, Judas no longer belongs among Jesus' own (13:30).

become disciples of Jesus.[13] The implication within the narrative may be that, although originally part of the entourage that arrested Jesus and wounded by one of Jesus' own disciples, Malchus is one of the sheep that the shepherd calls "by name" and leads out of the fold (10:3).[14]

Commanding Peter to put his sword away, Jesus contrasts his disciple's sword with his Father's cup (*to potērion*) that Jesus must drink. Both sword and cup represent death, but the sword brings about death to others; the cup entails Jesus' death, which brings life to others. According to Mark, Jesus first prayed that "the hour might pass from him" (14:35), then that the Father would "remove this cup" from him; yet he also prayed that God's will would be done (Matt 26:39, 42; Mark 15:36; Luke 22:42). In John Jesus refuses to pray, "Save me from this hour" (12:27), the hour that marks the climax of his mission, and instead asserts that he will "drink the cup that the Father has given" to him (17:11). As is typical of the Gospel, John tells the story from back to front, rolling the results of what happened into the purposes or causes of those events. Under the conviction that Jesus' death has accomplished God's purposes for the world's salvation, John makes it clear that what God wills—that Jesus drink this cup—Jesus also wills and does, thereby demonstrating the Son's unity with the Father (10:30). Throughout this scene Jesus speaks as one who not only intends to do the will of God but also as one who has done it. Jesus does not, therefore, pray that the cup will pass; instead, he asserts his intention to drink the cup the Father has given him.

Once Jesus' intention has been made clear, the armed men and "their captain" (*chiliarchos*)[15] bind him and take him first (*prōton*) to Annas, the father-in-law of Caiaphas, "who was high priest that year." The office of high priest traditionally was hereditary, passed on at death; yet in the period of Seleucid and subsequent Roman rule, the high priest was subject to political appointment by the governing authorities. Deposing and replacing the high priest may have been a tool used to demonstrate Caesar's continued subjugation of the Jewish people; clearly it was also a way of exerting control over the Jewish authorities themselves.[16] While the tenures of some high priests were short and tenuous at best, there was no annual replacement of the high priest, as some have alleged that John thought, given his reference to Caiaphas's being "high priest that year." Rather, Caiaphas is high priest in "that year," that is, in the year that Jesus died (11:49, 51). Assuming that Annas is conducting this preliminary

13. In Josephus, Malchus is the name of an Arabic ruler (*Ant.* 13.131; 14.370–75; 15.167), and Malichus is the name of a Jew (14.84, 273).

14. According to John, one of Jesus' disciples was known to the high priest (18:15–16), which could also explain knowledge of this name. Schnelle (1998, 264) speculates that the name belonged to someone in the Johannine circle who had previously been its opponent.

15. Lit., "leader of a thousand soldiers" (Josephus, *Ant.* 17.215); BDAG, a Roman tribune, the commander of a cohort or 600 men; so also LSJM, "tribune" or "commander."

16. VanderKam 2004, 423.

investigation (vv. 13, 16, 19, 22, and esp. v. 24),[17] John actually refers to both Annas and his son-in-law, Caiaphas, as "high priest." Luke also links the two, speaking of the "high priesthood of Annas and Caiaphas" (3:2), suggesting that a former high priest could continue to be called "high priest" even if he was no longer in office.[18] John may also have in view a broader circle of "chief priests" (*archiereis*) to which he refers elsewhere, and in which he included both the former and present "high priest" along with other important priests (7:32, 45; 11:47, 57; 12:10; 18:3, 35; 19:6, 15, 21).

Even so, if Caiaphas is the acting high priest, then why is Jesus sent first to Annas? According to Josephus, a high priest named Ananus (known by the abbreviated name, Annas; see also Luke 3:2) was appointed by Quirinius and removed from office by the Roman prefect Gratus; the years of his tenure would have been 6–15 C.E. (*Ant.* 18.26, 34–35; 20.198).[19] Not only did Annas have a son-in-law, Joseph Caiaphas, who held the office of high priest from 18 to 36/37 C.E.; he also had five sons who held the office (*J.W.* 2.243). Even if not regarded by the Romans or the Jews as the high priest at the time of Jesus' death, Annas's influence clearly continued even after his deposition.[20] John's account of having Jesus questioned first by Annas may well reflect, as the Gospel does elsewhere, the political situation of Jesus' day (cf. 11:49–52).

Thus Jesus is taken to be interrogated by the chief religious and political authorities of the Jewish people. The "chief priests" first appear in the Gospel when they and Pharisees send servants (*hypēretas*) to arrest Jesus (7:32), but those servants had come back empty-handed (7:44–45). Now the chief priests, together with the Pharisees, have again sent servants (18:3) to apprehend Jesus; this time they do not come back empty-handed. While this may be attributed to the sheer numbers of armed troops sent to the garden with Judas, in John's account it is clear that Jesus has permitted his own arrest, as his hour in "that year" has finally come.

18:15–27 Peter's Denial and Jesus' Interrogation before Annas

One of the most poignant scenes in any of the Gospels is the account of Peter's denial of Jesus. In spite of Peter's earlier, fervent protests that he will lay down his life for Jesus (13:37), Peter now evades the opportunity to identify himself as

17. So most commentators. Michaels (896–97, 906–9), thinking that the initial interrogator is Caiaphas, reads v. 24 retrospectively: "Now Annas *had* sent him bound."

18. R. Brown 1970, 820; VanderKam 2004, 420. Josephus speaks of "Jonathan and Ananias, the high priests" (*J.W.* 2.243).

19. See VanderKam 2004, 420.

20. Bultmann considered Annas's prestige and influence to be sufficient to ascribe to him a pivotal role in Jesus' condemnation (1971, 643 n. 3); Hengel (1995c, 53) labels Annas the "éminence grise," the power behind the scene.

Jesus' disciple precisely in order to avoid sharing his master's destiny. Peter's threefold denial of Jesus, which spares his own life, stands in sharp counterpoint to Jesus' forthright public witness, which leads to his death. Throughout the Gospel, Jesus has spoken boldly and openly (7:26), while many of those who have come to believe in him remain timid and fearful of the consequences of open confession (7:13; 9:22; 12:42). Like them, Simon Peter fails to rise to the challenge of bearing witness to Jesus. Jesus may journey toward the cross without wavering in John, but few of his disciples display the same courage and faithfulness. Certainly Peter does not.

> **18:15** Simon Peter and another disciple followed Jesus. That disciple was
> known to the high priest, and he entered with Jesus into the courtyard
> of the high priest. **16** Peter was standing outside at the door. So the other
> disciple, the one known to the high priest, went and spoke to the maid
> who kept the door, and she brought Peter in. **17** The servant girl who kept
> the door said to Peter, "Are you not also one of this man's disciples?"
> He said, "I am not."
> **18** The servants and the assistants were standing by the charcoal fire
> that they had made, because it was cold, and they were warming them-
> selves. And Peter was also standing with them and warming himself.
> **19** Then the high priest asked Jesus about his disciples and about
> his teaching. **20** And Jesus answered him, "I have spoken openly to the
> world; I have always taught in the synagogue and in the temple, where
> all the Jews gather. I have said nothing in secret. **21** Why do you ask me?
> Ask those who heard me what I said to them. Look, they know what I
> said to them!"
> **22** When he had said these things, one of the assistants struck Jesus,
> saying, "Is that how you answer the high priest?"
> **23** Jesus answered him, "If I have spoken wrongly, bear witness con-
> cerning the wrong. But if I have spoken rightly, why do you strike me?"
> **24** Then Annas sent him, bound, to Caiaphas the high priest. **25** And
> Simon Peter was standing and warming himself. They said to him, "Are
> you not also one of his disciples?"
> But he denied it and said, "I am not."
> **26** One of the servants of the high priest, who was a relative of the man
> whose ear Peter had cut off, said, "Didn't I see you in the garden with him?"
> **27** Again Peter denied it, and immediately the rooster crowed.

[18:15–18] "Simon Peter and another disciple followed Jesus" (cf. 21:20). Because he is known to the high priest, the (unnamed) other disciple enters into the courtyard of the high priest; Peter is left standing outside (v. 16). This "other disciple" obtains Peter's entry into the courtyard. Who is this "other disciple"? Later, when Simon Peter runs to see the tomb on Easter morning, he is accompanied by "the other disciple" (*ho allos mathētēs*, 20:3, 4, 8), who is further identified as "the disciple whom Jesus loved" (20:2). That identification of "the other disciple" as "the beloved disciple" strengthens the case for seeing the figure who secures Peter's entrance into the high priest's court as "the disciple whom Jesus loved." This disciple bears witness to Jesus (21:24) and serves particularly as the guarantor of the traditions regarding the significance of Jesus' death (19:35; see further comments at 11:1–6; 13:23).

Once inside the high priest's courtyard, Simon Peter has the opportunity to bear witness to Jesus when the woman who let him in asks, "Are you not also one of this man's disciples?"[21] Earlier Jesus had boldly identified himself in the garden with the simple, "I am he" or "I am" (*ēgō eimi*, 18:5, 6, 8); now Peter denies knowing Jesus, using a similar phrase, "I am not" (*ouk eimi*; cf. vv. 17, 25, 27).[22] Peter has taken an initial step away from Jesus, and the narrative's wording indicates as much: Peter is "standing with" the servants and assistants of the high priest, warming themselves together around a charcoal fire, even as Judas had earlier been described as "standing with" the same officers in the garden (18:5, 18; cf. 19:25–26). Later in the Gospel, Peter will find Jesus cooking fish on a charcoal fire, there finding himself the uncomfortable target of Jesus' probing questions about Peter's love for him. Peter will be called to renew his earlier commitment to follow Jesus (13:37; 21:19, 22), as well as to keep Jesus' commandments to tend his flock.

[19–24] While Peter warms himself by the fire and denies being one of Jesus' disciples, the high priest asks Jesus about his disciples and his teaching (v. 19). Jesus responds that, having spoken openly and in public,[23] anybody who heard him speak, perhaps especially his disciples, should be able to report what Jesus had said (vv. 20–21). The narrative irony is palpable: Jesus refers the high priest to those who heard him, but one of those who has heard him has just denied being one of Jesus' disciples. Once, in response to Jesus' teaching, Peter had confessed him to be the Holy One of God, who has the words of eternal life (6:68–69). Now Peter acts exactly like those who, out of fear, say nothing at all. Again, whereas Jesus has spoken boldly and openly (7:26), many who have come to believe in him are fearful of the consequences of open confession (7:13; 9:22; 12:42).[24]

21. The question whether Peter is "also" one of Jesus' disciples (18:25) may indicate that "the other disciple" has already been recognized as such (cf. 18:16).

22. John (the Baptist) denies his identity as Messiah, Elijah, or the prophet with similar words (*egō ouk eimi ho christos* and *ouk eimi*), but his "confessions" (1:20) are positive statements of his relationship to Jesus rather than denials of it.

23. For "open" or "frank" speech (*en parrēsia*), see comments on 7:4, 26; 10:24; 16:25.

24. In Mark, Peter's interrogation (14:66–72) begins only after Jesus' has ended (14:55–65); but in John, Jesus' interrogation (18:19–23) is framed by the questions directed to Peter (18:17, 25–27); John thus contrasts Jesus' boldness in identifying himself with Peter's refusal to do so.

Clearly, Jesus' claim to have spoken openly, in the synagogue and temple, and to have said nothing "in secret" does not include his lengthy final discourse to his disciples. But his claims about his own mission from God and his call to believe have been laid out repeatedly in public discourse; these are indeed the substance of the written Gospel. What, then, could the high priest hope to learn about Jesus' teaching? Jesus does not answer Annas's question directly, but refers the high priest to his public teaching. Those who do not believe in him or accept his words will be able to recount his claims and teachings, even if they have found them "hard" or unacceptable. Jesus' words and signs are matters of public record.

Unlike other Gospel accounts, Jesus is not asked whether he is the Messiah, does not speak of the coming of the Son of Man, and is not charged with blasphemy (Matt 26:63–65; Mark 14:61–64; cf. Luke 22:67–71; 23:2). Nor is he charged with threatening to destroy the temple (Matt 26:61; Mark 14:58), perverting the nation, forbidding the payment of taxes to Caesar, or stirring up the people (Luke 23:5). In fact, at first glance Annas's questions seem ill designed to ferret out any reasons why the Jews might have pursued Jesus' arrest, let alone his death. Jesus' following dialogue with Pilate focuses on Jesus' kingship and kingdom, suggesting that, since the Jews handed Jesus over to Pilate (18:35), their concerns might have had to do with Jesus' intentions vis-à-vis Roman authority, especially with any claims to kingship that might attract unwanted Roman attention or forceful intervention. Earlier in the Gospel, Caiaphas worried about Roman interference and action if the Jews failed to curb Jesus' popularity; here, by advancing the process that will lead to Jesus' crucifixion, the chief priests ironically act in accord with Caiaphas's counsel that "one man should die for the people" (11:47–50). When Annas asks Jesus about his disciples, the implication may be that he is wondering whether they are inclined to mob action or armed conflict and thus pose a threat to the survival of the Jewish people. But when he inquires about Jesus' teaching, he may also be inquiring about his disciples' faithfulness to Moses, the law, and other characteristic practices and beliefs of Jewish faith, and asking what, exactly, being a disciple of Jesus entails—a concern expressed elsewhere in this Gospel (9:27–28). The question about Jesus' teaching aims to uncover what he has said and on what authority he has said it, and thus whether his words come from God or not. In short, the question is whether Jesus has deceived his disciples by his teaching and so merits punishment (7:12, 47).[25]

25. Cf. Justin, *Dial.* 69: "They dared to call him a magician and a deceiver of the people"; *b. Sanh.* 43a: "He beguiled and led Israel astray." According to the Mishnah, those guilty of capital offenses include "the one who beguiles," "the one who leads astray," and "the sorcerer [i.e., the one who does magic] and a stubborn and rebellious son" (*m. Sanh.* 7:4, 10–11; 8:1–7). Martyn (80) argues that the legal charge against Jesus was that he was a deceiver. Michaels (904) thinks the upshot of the question is to determine whether Jesus' disciples are a unified group who will keep his teaching alive after his death.

The terse interrogation ends with the assistant of the high priest striking Jesus for insolence. Exodus 22:28 (27 LXX) forbids blasphemy (*ou kakologēseis*) or speaking badly or evil (*ou kakōs ereis*) of the leaders of the people; Jesus demands to know whether he has "spoken wrongly" or "badly" (*kakōs elalēsa*), the opposite of speaking well (*kalōs*) or telling the truth (4:17; 8:48; 13:13). As he has elsewhere, Jesus appeals for a right or just judgment of his words and deeds (7:24; 8:46; cf. Acts 23:2–5). Annas says nothing: he does not pass any judgment; but he sends Jesus, bound, to Caiaphas. While the other Gospels report a hearing before Caiaphas (Mark 14:60–64 par.), John does not: the scene is set, but for Peter's denials and not for Caiaphas's interrogations.[26] Caiaphas serves only to send Jesus on to Pilate, the Roman governor and hence the final earthly authority in Judea.

[25–27] As Jesus' interrogation comes to an end, Simon Peter remains standing by the fire, again denying that he is also one of Jesus' disciples. Peter denies Jesus three times, thus fulfilling Jesus' prophetic word (13:38). John does not recount Peter's memory of Jesus' prediction (Luke 22:61) or his remorse (Matt 26:75; Mark 14:72; Luke 22:62); the emphasis falls on two sharp contrasts: the first between Peter's taking up the sword at Jesus' arrest and his subsequent failure to confess his allegiance to Jesus; the second, between Peter's cowardice and Jesus' boldness. On his way to giving himself to death, Jesus models the courage and frankness that his disciple cannot.

In his correspondence with the emperor Trajan, Pliny, governor of Bithynia, reports that he gives Christians three chances to deny that they are Christians:

> I have asked them in person if they are Christians; and if they admit it, I repeat the question a second and third time, with a warning of the punishment awaiting them. If they persist, I order them to be led away for execution. (Pliny the Younger, *Ep.* 10.96.3)

Some early Christians staunchly maintained their confession of allegiance to Jesus; others, succumbing to understandable fear or weakness, denied their allegiance to Christ, even cursing him at the governor's behest. While this correspondence belongs in the early second century (ca. 112 C.E.), the Gospel's portrayal of Peter's denial of Jesus would surely have struck a chord with those who were faced with the threat of death for their confession of Jesus. The Roman governor sought to persuade obstinate Christians to invoke the (Roman) gods, offer prayer with incense and wine to the image of the emperor and to statues of the gods, and to curse Christ (Pliny, *Ep.* 10.96). It was as Jesus had warned: the hour is coming "when those who kill you will think that they are offering worship to God" (John 16:2; cf. 4 Macc 12:14).

26. See the footnote at 2:12 regarding similar "vestigial scenes."

But in spite of Peter's denials, he never comes to be identified by a moniker such as that carried by Judas, who is always "the one who handed over" Jesus. Peter never becomes "the one who denied" Jesus. To be sure, the story of his denial lives on in this and other Gospels, but his denial is not the last or definitive word written over him. Peter will meet Jesus again and will be commissioned to service and called to follow Jesus on the way of costly discipleship (John 21). The subsequent story of Peter is the story of his faithful discipleship.[27]

18:28–19:16 Jesus and Pilate

In the long narrative of Jesus' encounter with Pilate, there are three main characters: Pilate, Jesus, and the Jewish authorities, who speak with a single voice. The scene is set at the praetorium, Pilate's headquarters in Jerusalem. The action moves from the outside to the inside, as Pilate moves between the Jews, who remain outside the praetorium, and Jesus, who has been taken into the praetorium to be examined, as the following overview demonstrates:

- Outside: The Jews bring their accusation against Jesus.
- Inside: Pilate enters the praetorium to ask Jesus whether he is the King of the Jews.
- Outside: Pilate declares Jesus' innocence and offers to release him.

[*Pilate has Jesus flogged.*]

- Outside: Pilate again declares Jesus' innocence and presents him, dressed in a purple robe and with a crown of thorns, with the words, "See the man!"
- Inside: Pilate enters the praetorium to ask Jesus about his origins.
- Outside: Pilate again brings Jesus out to the Jews, this time presenting him with the acclamation, "See your king!"

[*Pilate hands Jesus over to be crucified.*]

Pilate is the dominant figure in this dramatic narrative, going in and out of the praetorium to talk alternately with the Jews and with Jesus. Pilate asks questions, passes judgment, and orders Jesus to be first flogged and then crucified. In the political situation of Jesus' day, the Roman governor held ultimate authority in the administration of provincial affairs that were otherwise left to

27. See Bockmuehl 2010.

the jurisdiction of local authorities. In this case the Jews cannot act apart from Pilate's approval; as they themselves acknowledge, they cannot put Jesus to death. But if from one vantage point Pilate is the one in charge, from another vantage point he is virtually a puppet, being pulled in and out of his own headquarters by the puzzling statements of Jesus on the one hand and the pointed demands of the Jews on the other.

"The Jews" remain outside the praetorium, ostensibly in order to preserve their ritual purity. But the fact that they remain on the outside also scores the point that they do not have final authority in this matter. Subject to Rome, they remain outside the halls of power. Nevertheless, even though they are subject to Rome's authority, ultimately Pilate acts in accordance with their wishes and petitions. Although crucifixion was a way for the imperial government to terrorize and subjugate its provincial subjects, here those subjects participate in the Roman government's destruction of one of their own.

Jesus has been arrested by Roman and Jewish authorities; therefore, he is at the mercy of both. Pilate examines, flogs, and condemns Jesus to death; the Jewish authorities demand and obtain the death sentence for him. Hardly a commanding figure of power and authority, Jesus is instead subject to the authorities, both Roman and Jewish, ultimately succumbing to their judgment to execute him. But things are not what they seem. Pilate is not calling the shots in this drama: Jesus is. Rome does not have the ultimate authority and power it claims for itself: only God does. There is nothing that the Jews or the Romans can do to Jesus that will demonstrate their superior power or authority. In fact, the drama they are playing out is a scenario that Jesus has foreseen and even chosen before it ever begins to unfold.

Thus neither the Romans nor the Jews hold the power here: Jesus does. Jesus never protests the legitimacy of either Roman or Jewish power, nor is he shown contesting the validity of the charges against him or of his trial. Rather, he declares that his kingdom has a different manifestation in this world than does the kingdom that seeks his death: Jesus' kingdom is characterized not by taking life, but by giving life; not by fighting to avoid death at the hands of others, but by dying for others; not by dominating power, but by bearing witness to the truth. What comes to light in the trial narrative in John is not merely the question whether Jesus is the king of the Jews, but rather the entire character of his kingship and his kingdom.

18:28 Then they led Jesus from Caiaphas to the praetorium. It was early in
the morning. And they did not go into the praetorium, lest they be defiled
so that they could not eat the Passover. **29** Pilate went out to them and said,
"What accusation do you make against this man?"

30 They answered, "If he had not done evil, we would not have handed
him over[a] to you."

31 Then Pilate said to them, "You take him and judge him according
to your law."

The Jews said to him, "We are not permitted to put anyone to death."
32 This was to fulfill the word of Jesus that he had spoken, showing by
what sort of death he would die.

33 Again Pilate went into the praetorium and summoned Jesus and said
to him, "Are you the King of the Jews?"

34 Jesus answered, "Are you asking this on your own, or did others say
it about me?"

35 Pilate answered, "I'm not a Jew, am I? Your own people and the
chief priests handed you over to me. What have you done?"

36 Jesus answered, "My kingdom is not from this world. If my king-
dom were from this world, my servants would have fought so that I might
not be handed over to the Jews. But my kingdom is not from here."

37 Pilate said to him, "So then you are a king?"

Jesus answered, "You say that I am a king. I have come into this world,
so that I might bear witness to the truth. Whoever belongs to the truth
hears my voice."

38 Pilate said to him, "What is truth?"

And when he had said this, he went out again to the Jews and said to
them, "I do not find any ground for a charge against him. 39 But it is a
custom that I should release for you one [prisoner] at Passover. Do you
want me to release the King of the Jews to you?"

40 They cried out again, saying, "Not this one, but rather Barabbas!"
Now Barabbas was an outlaw.

19:1 Then Pilate took Jesus and scourged him.[b] 2 And the soldiers
plaited a crown of thorns and put it on his head, and put purple garments
on him. 3 And they came to him and said, "Hail, King of the Jews!" And
they struck him.

4 And Pilate went outside again and said to them, "Look, I am bringing
him out to you, so that you will know that I find no ground for a charge
against him."

5 Then Jesus came out, wearing a crown of thorns and a purple gar-
ment. And Pilate said to them, "See the man!"[c]

6 When the chief priests and the servants saw him, they cried out, say-
ing, "Crucify! Crucify!"

Pilate said to them, "Take him yourselves and crucify him. For I have
found no ground for a charge against him.

7 The Jews said to him, "We have a law, and according to the law he
ought to die, for he made himself the Son of God."

8 When Pilate heard this, he was even more afraid, 9 and he went into
the praetorium again and said to Jesus, "Where are you from?" And Jesus

did not answer. 10 Then Pilate said to him, "You won't speak to me?
Don't you know that I have the authority to release you and the authority
to crucify you?"

11 Jesus said to him, "You do not have any authority over me except
what has been given[d] you from above. But the one who handed me over[a]
to you has the greater sin."

12 From that point on, Pilate sought to release him. But the Jews cried
out, saying, "If you release this man, you are not a friend of Caesar!
Everyone who makes himself a king opposes Caesar." 13 When Pilate
heard these words, he led Jesus outside and sat down on the judgment
seat, in the place called the Stone Pavement,[e] and in Hebrew,[f] Gabbatha.[g]

14 Now it was the day of preparation for the Passover, and it was noon.
And he said to the Jews, "See your king!"

15 So they cried out, "Away! Away! Crucify! Crucify!"

Pilate said to them, "Shall I crucify your king?"

The chief priests answered, "We have no king but Caesar." 16 Then he
handed him over[a] to them to be crucified, and they received Jesus.

a. For the translation of *paradidōmi* as "hand over," see textual notes at 6:64; 13:2; 18:2.

b. Grammatically, "Pilate" is the subject of the verb "he scourged"; the sense is surely "he had him scourged."

c. "Man" here translates the Greek *anthrōpos*, "human being"; one could also translate "Look at this person!" or simply "Look at him!"

d. "Authority" (*exousia*) is feminine; "what has been given" is neuter (*ēn dedomenon*); but it is difficult in the context of the sentence to construe the neuter phrase as referring to anything other than "authority." Carson (1991, 601) takes it to refer to the entirety of the events surrounding Jesus' betrayal.

e. The Greek *lithostrōton* means "stone pavement" or "mosaic"; cf. 2 Chr 7:3; Esth 1:6; Song 3:10; Josephus, *J.W.* 6.85, 189.

f. *Gabbatha* is Aramaic in its form.

g. The meaning of this word is uncertain; John does not say that *lithostrōton* translates *Gabbatha* (cf. "translated" in 1:41). Josephus mentions that *Gabbath Saoul* (i.e., the Gibeah of Saul; cf. 1 Sam 11:4) is to be translated in Greek as *lophos Saoulou* ("hill of Saoul," *J.W.* 5.51). Gibeah is a place name; the Hebrew noun *gibĕʿâ* means "hill."

[18:28] The scene now shifts to Pilate's "praetorium." In the Gospels, the "praetorium" refers to the official residence of the governor (Matt 27:27; Mark 15:16; John 18:28, 33; 19:9).[28] Although the Roman governor of Judea was

28. Some have identified the praetorium with the fortress Antonia, which stood on the northwest corner of the Temple Mount; others, with the ancient royal Hasmonean palace, used by Herod the Great until 23 B.C.E. and taken over by Roman prefects in 6 C.E. after Archaelaus, the son of Herod, was banished; still others, and most commonly today, with Herod's "Upper Palace" in the area today called the Citadel (near the Jaffa Gate).

typically quartered in Caesarea Maritima,[29] a Roman cohort was stationed in Jerusalem; during festivals the governor would make his way there in case of civil unrest[30] and to hear judicial cases. Pontius Pilate served as the Roman governor of Judea for eleven years, from 26 or 27 until 37 C.E.[31] Not only does he figure prominently in the Gospel narratives of Jesus' trial, but he also is mentioned by the Jewish authors Josephus and Philo, as well as the Roman historian Tacitus.[32] An inscription bearing his name and giving his title as "prefect," indicating his military functions and role in maintaining order, was discovered at Caesarea Maritima in 1961.[33] In the New Testament, Pilate is remembered as the one before whom Jesus "made the good confession" (1 Tim 6:13) and in the Apostles' Creed as the one under whom Jesus suffered.

Pilate was governor of Judea, which was neither very large nor prosperous. Because its population was viewed as difficult to control, it was classified as an imperial province (i.e., belonging to Caesar rather than the Senate).[34] On the one hand, Judea was beholden to its larger and more powerful neighbor, the province of Syria and its legate[35] (cf. Luke 2:2), who would have had higher rank and greater military power at his disposal.[36] The legate's troops were not stationed in Jerusalem but could be moved there if the Judean governor or the people appealed to him for help. On the other hand, the high priests were granted authority to administer local affairs. But the Roman governors could—and did—depose and appoint the high priests as they wished, underscoring the ultimate power of Rome in the province. In the Johannine account, we see Pilate concerned for maintaining the peace of the province and quelling any sources

29. See Josephus, *J.W.* 2.169–74; 2.332; *Ant.* 18.55–59; Acts 23:23–24; 25:1–13.

30. Cf. Josephus, *J.W.* 2.224; *Ant.* 20.106. Josephus notes that Pilate "moved the army from Caesarea to Jerusalem to take up their winter residence" (*Ant.* 18.55).

31. His 11 years was a relatively long tenure; most of the 14 governors served for 2 years or so. For further details and discussion, see D. Schwartz; and Bond.

32. See Philo, *Legat.* 299–305; Josephus, *J.W.* 2.169–75; *Ant.* 18.35, 55–54, 87–89, 177; Tacitus, *Ann.* 15.44.

33. The governor of a minor imperial province was called a "prefect." Under Claudius (41–54 C.E.), the governors of these provinces received the civilian title of "procurator." The change explains the confusion about this official's appropriate title in various literary sources (see Bond 12 n. 64; see *OCD* s.v. *praefectus*; procurator).

34. See Strabo, *Geogr.* 17.3.25.

35. A *legatus* was a senator, with the rank of consul, appointed by the emperor to govern one of the provinces, and particularly those with permanently stationed legions; hence, the commander of a legion (see *OCD* s.v. *legati*; procurator).

36. According to Tacitus (*Ann.* 4.5), Syria had four legions (of about 5,000 men each). The province of Judea had 5 infantry cohorts and 1 cavalry regiment, or about 3,000 men; one of those cohorts was permanently located in the Antonia fortress in Jerusalem (*J.W.* 5.244–45; cf. Acts 21:31; 23:23). Other troops were scattered throughout the province at various fortresses; see Josephus, *Ant.* 18.55 (Caesarea); *J.W.* 2.408 (Masada); 2.484–85 (Cypros, near Jericho); *Ant.* 18.111, 119 (Macherus, the fortress where John the Baptist was put to death).

of potential unrest. In overseeing the trial of Jesus and ultimately condemning him to death by crucifixion, Pilate is portrayed as acceding to the wishes of the priests, while also wishing himself to remain in good graces with the emperor (cf. *Ant.* 18.64).

The Jews who brought Jesus to Pilate are unwilling to enter his residence because they are soon to eat the Passover meal, which requires a state of ritual purity (see comments at 11:55).[37] Since the praetorium is the residence of the Gentile governor, the priests would be defiled if they enter it.[38] The comment regarding the need to maintain purity makes it clear that, in John's chronology, Jesus' last meal was not a Passover meal (see also 13:1), and that Jesus was crucified before Passover. Because the chief priests will not enter the praetorium, Pilate, aware of Jewish scruples, comes out to meet them. Although Josephus and Philo present Pilate as at times inflaming Jewish sensitivities, especially with respect to the sanctity of Jerusalem, they also show that, when pressured, Pilate would change course so as not to provoke further incidents (Philo, *Legat.* 299–304; Josephus, *Ant.* 18.55–59). Throughout Jesus' trial, Pilate appears as one who seems incredulous at the claims of both Jesus and the Jews regarding his identity as the King of the Jews and the existence of his kingdom. At the end of it all, he bows to the Jewish threat that, were he to release Jesus, he would be no friend of Caesar. But if Pilate fears the Jews, he fears Jesus more.

[29–32] Pilate initially asks the Jewish authorities what they are accusing Jesus of having done. They offer no specific charges, merely claiming that he has "done evil." Elsewhere Jesus' opponents charge that he is

- a violator of the Sabbath and of the law, a "sinner" (5:1–18; 9:14–16, 24)
- a blasphemer (5:17–18; 8:58; 10:24–38; 19:7)
- a false teacher, who leads the people astray (7:12, 45–49; 18:19–24) and
- a threat to the survival of the Jewish people and their temple (11:47–53).

Because these charges reflect particular Jewish concerns regarding their Scripture and laws, Pilate instructs the Jews to judge Jesus accordingly (cf. Acts 18:12–16, where Gallio passes the same judgment in the matter of the Jewish charges against Paul). The unwillingness of the Roman prefect to become involved in the case of a provincial Jewish teacher fits with the Roman willingness to leave the administration of local affairs to local authorities, as

37. Hence, "they" (v. 28) likely refers to the Jews alone, rather than to the soldiers who were part of the contingent who seized Jesus in the garden.

38. The Mishnah states, "The dwelling-places of Gentiles are unclean" (*m. ʾOhal.* 18:7); cf. Acts 10:28, "It is unlawful for a Jew . . . to visit a Gentile."

long as these do not impinge on Roman sovereignty or the maintenance of law and order.

But the Jews now offer Pilate a reason why he must be involved: they are seeking a death sentence, and they lack the authority to carry it out.[39] They acknowledge Rome's greater authority when they admit that they are "not permitted" (i.e., by Rome) to put anyone to death.[40] They also acknowledge Rome's ultimate authority over Jesus: whether he lives or dies will be decided by the Romans, not by the Jews. As we shall see in the course of Jesus' dialogue with Pilate, however, not even Pilate has such authority over Jesus. To be sure, Jesus will be put to death by crucifixion, which is a Roman rather than a Jewish form of execution. The Jewish authorities acknowledge that they need the Romans in order to put Jesus to death, and eventually the Romans comply.[41] In doing so, the Romans inadvertently fulfill Jesus' own words regarding the "sort of death" that he would die: he would suffer the Roman penalty of crucifixion, being "lifted up from the earth" (3:13; 8:28; 12:32–34). Once again the way the narrative unfolds underscores the point that Jesus does not die as a victim. He is aware and even in control of his own destiny.

The claim of the Jews that they "are not permitted to put anyone to death" has occasioned considerable discussion. Smallwood argues that the Jews did have the right to carry out a sentence in capital cases, but that this right was limited to cases involving breaches of Jewish law (as here). So, while the Romans granted the Jews freedom to act in matters of religion, they retained for themselves the right of the death penalty in political matters.[42] There have already been two attempts on Jesus' life in John; twice the Jews sought to stone Jesus for blasphemy, a matter both Jewish and religious (8:59; 10:31). In Acts, the Jews stone Stephen to death (7:58–8:1); and seek to kill Paul for desecrating the temple (21:31).[43] Herod has James the brother of John "killed with the sword" (Acts 12:1–2). And Josephus describes the execution of James the brother of Jesus under Ananus ben Ananus on the charge of breaking the law (*Ant.* 20.197–203).

39. Somewhat differently, Hoskyns (518–19) argues that they are seeking to have Jesus crucified, as per Roman practice, rather than stoned to death in accord with Jewish law—thus unknowingly they verify the declarations that Jesus must be "lifted up."

40. Augustus granted Coponius, the first governor of Judea, the power of capital punishment (Josephus, *J.W.* 2.117).

41. Josephus writes, "Upon indictment brought by the leading men among us, Pilate sentenced him to the cross" (*Ant.* 18:64).

42. So Smallwood 149–50; see further discussion in Keener 2:1107–9.

43. See Josephus, *J.W.* 6.124–8: Titus reminds the Jews that at the temple they have the power to kill Gentiles who pass the boundary that prohibit Gentiles from entering the Court of the Israelites, even if the offender is a Roman. In other words, Josephus thinks that, at the time of the first revolt (66–73 C.E.), the Jews still have the right of capital punishment for desecration of the temple, but the fact that he portrays a Roman emperor as singling this case out suggests that it is an exception to the otherwise prevailing norm.

Such cases seem to support Smallwood's point, since these matters fall under local Jewish jurisdiction. The implication, then, is that the Jews could have had Jesus put to death, at least on such charges as the blasphemy to which John refers, although not on the charges brought at his trial.

Others have argued that John is correct and that the Jews did not have the right of capital punishment at the time of Jesus' death.[44] John's description of Jewish attempts to stone Jesus, as well as the stoning of Stephen, can be described as mob action. The attempt to kill Paul (Acts 21:31) would comport with the allowed exceptions, since the charge is that Paul has brought a Gentile into the temple. And while Josephus describes the execution of James under Ananus ben Ananus, he also reports that the populace protested Ananus's action because it occurred in the interim after the death of the Roman governor Porcius Festus, but before Albinus arrived on the scene. According to Josephus, Albinus was furious because it was clear that Ananus had taken advantage of the situation and flouted Roman authority (*Ant.* 20.197–203).

If the Jews actually had the right of capital punishment, then John's note that they did not is in error, unless it implicitly includes the kinds of exceptions that Smallwood suggests: Jewish jurisdiction in religious but not political cases. While Christopher Bryan rightly protests the anachronistic and neat distinction between "religious" and "political," it is also worth noting that, even in those Gospels where the Jewish authorities deem Jesus to have committed blasphemy, they do not put him to death.[45] Other persons were put to death by the Jews in this period, but Jesus was not. Moreover, Jesus was crucified, and he was crucified by the Romans. None of the other persons who are executed by Jewish authorities in the New Testament is crucified; none was handed over to Rome. Jesus was almost certainly crucified as "King of the Jews,"[46] a charge that reflects Roman concern for maintaining their political sovereignty, even if in the Gospel accounts they are routinely shown as mocking Jesus and the claims that he is a king. These facts—that Jesus was crucified, by the Romans, as King of the Jews—require some sort of causal explanation. Either the Jews did not have the right of capital punishment at all; or they did not think Jesus' crimes merited death at the hands of a Jewish court; or they had

44. See the discussion in C. Bryan 71–75.

45. In Matthew and Mark, the Jewish authorities pronounce Jesus worthy of death (Matt 26:65–66; Mark 14:64–65). In Luke, Jesus' identification of himself as Son of Man, and perhaps as the Son of God (22:69–70), seems sufficient for his condemnation (22:71). In John, no Jewish court condemns Jesus as worthy of death. In other words, no matter how the Gospels portray the Jewish interrogation of Jesus, and even when he is condemned on apparently "religious" charges, the Jewish authorities do not actually execute him. For further discussion and references, see Keener 2:1107–9.

46. In all four Gospels the charge brought to Pilate is that Jesus is called "King of the Jews"; this is also what the placard on the cross, announcing his crime, states (Mark 15:2; Matt 27:11; Luke 23:2–3; John 18:33; 19:3, 14, 15, 19).

the right but preferred to shift the responsibility for Jesus' death to Rome. If Pilate had simply rubber-stamped a Jewish religious condemnation of Jesus as a deceiver or blasphemer, it is not clear that he would have agreed to Jesus' death, let alone his crucifixion: a form of execution intended by the Romans as a dramatic deterrent to would-be lawbreakers for crimes against the state. But the understanding that the Jews did not have the right of capital punishment at the time of Jesus' death explains the various accounts in all the Gospels, including the Gospel of John.

[33–38a] Pilate now turns to Jesus with the question: "Are you the King of the Jews"? Prior to this point, the only charge brought against Jesus by "the Jews" is that he has "done evil" (18:30). Hence, while Pilate's query "Are you the King of the Jews?" seems to come out of nowhere, it aptly summarizes a charge that could lead to Jesus being branded as "evil" or "criminal" (18:30 NRSV) by the Romans. Although the Roman senate had allowed Herod to be called "king of the Jews,"[47] since the deposition of his son Archelaus (6 C.E.) and the appointment of a Roman prefect in the province of Judea, there was no "king of the Jews." Anyone who claimed to be such a king, or for whom that claim was made, would find himself at odds with Roman authority.

Pilate's question contains the first occurrence of the title "King of the Jews" that begins to loom large in the narrative (18:33, 39; 19:3, 19, 21). To be sure, the designation of Jesus as "king" has appeared earlier in John (1:49; 6:15; 12:13, 15), although never on the lips of Jesus himself. Others claim that Jesus is a king; Scripture corroborates that claim (12:15). Typically Jesus does not directly answer Pilate's question whether he is the King of the Jews: instead, he asks what has prompted it, since Jesus himself has not actually made such a claim. The implied and most likely explanation is that "the Jews" who brought Jesus to Pilate also brought this indictment against him. Yet they are unwilling to claim Jesus as their king (19:15, 21). Pilate's disclaimer—"I'm not a Jew, am I?" (18:35)—distances him from the Jews who have brought Jesus to him.[48] Pilate is not one of "them"; "the Jews" have handed Jesus over to him. Hence, like it or not, he has been drawn into their affairs. But Pilate's words make it clear that he passes judgment, not as a Jew, but in another capacity: that of Roman prefect. From Pilate's point of view, Jesus is one of "the Jews"; they are his "own people" (1:11). And yet soon Jesus will speak of being "handed over to the Jews" (v. 36), as if he were not one of them. Neither Pilate nor the Jews grant Jesus the status "King of the Jews."

47. Josephus uses the designation "king of the Jews" for David (*J.W.* 6.439; *Ant.* 7.72), Jeconiah (*J.W.* 6.103), Alexander (Janneus) (*J.W.* 7.171; *Ant.* 14.36), Antigonus (*Ant.* 17.92), and Herod (*J.W.* 1.282, 388; *Ant.* 14.9; 15.373, 409; 16.291, 311). See the comments on 6:14–15.

48. The Greek (*Mēti egō Ioudaios eimi?*) expects a negative answer: "Of course not!"

The questioning has not ended, and the dialogue continues with Jesus' description of the character of his kingdom and kingship. For Jesus even to claim to have a kingdom (*basileia*) sets him potentially at odds with Rome and its sovereignty. Jesus describes his kingdom as "not from this world" (*ouk estin ek tou kosmou toutou*) and "not from here" (*ouk estin enteuthen*, 18:36).[49] Jesus' assertion that his kingdom is "not from this world" means that it cannot be identified with any earthly kingdom: Jewish, Davidic, or otherwise. Nor does Jesus' kingdom derive its authority from earthly powers, kingdoms, or authorities; it certainly does not derive its legitimacy from Rome. Other client kings of the Mediterranean world, including Herod, depended on Rome's good graces for their continued existence. But Jesus' kingdom does not, since it is a kingdom that is neither established nor lost through political machinations or military victory.

Instead, Jesus' kingdom will be brought about through the death and resurrection of its king. In that sense, also, this kingdom is "not of this world": kingdoms "of this world" do not follow that path of surrender rather than domination, of giving up life rather than taking the life of others. Neither the Caesars of Rome nor the kings of Israel had done so. Jesus' kingdom is unlike any the world recognizes or admires. Although Jesus' kingdom is "not from this world," it does manifest itself in this world, even as he (18:37) and his disciples (17:11) are "in this world." In this world, Jesus' kingdom manifests itself as self-giving and life-giving love.

Seizing on Jesus' description of his kingdom, Pilate presses his question: "So you are a king?" (18:37). But instead of responding "yes" or "no," Jesus offers an enigmatic reply: "You say that I am a king." That can either mean (1) "It is as you say: I am indeed a king"; or (2) "These are your words, not mine." It may be that Jesus' declaration, "I have come into the world, so that I might bear witness to the truth," demonstrates that Jesus prefers to identify himself as a "witness to the truth" rather than as a king. But in light of the pattern found elsewhere in John—others bear witness to Jesus as a king, but he himself does not claim the title—Jesus should be understood to acknowledge that he *is* a king but does not attain his kingship by seizing the throne or allowing others to do it for him. In fact, his kingly vocation is carried out in bearing witness to truth. Earlier the crowds tried to make Jesus king (6:14–15), but he withdrew and hid himself. Upon his entry into Jerusalem, the crowds hailed him as King of Israel, but Jesus himself did not make the claim (12:15). The way to his royal acclamation, to his exaltation, lies through his death on the cross. He will be crucified, not because he has done evil (18:30, 38; 19:4, 6), but because he has borne witness to the truth, publicly and openly (18:20). Those who hear

49. On the latter, Augustine writes, "He does not say, 'Now, my kingdom is not here, but 'not from here.' In fact, it is here unto the end of the world. . . . But despite this it is not from here, because it is a stranger in the world" (*Tract. Ev. Jo.* 115.2).

him and follow him acknowledge him as king; those who do not listen to his voice, do not.

With his next question, "What is truth?" (18:38),[50] Pilate cements his position as one who does not hear or understand Jesus at all, let alone acknowledge him as king. Is the question meant to mock Jesus, or ridicule Jesus' claim to know the truth? Is it asked sincerely, with a genuine desire to know? The best cue for interpreting Pilate's question here is the context of John, for Jesus has identified himself not only as the one who speaks the truth and who testifies to it (18:37) but also as truth itself (14:6). Pilate's question demonstrates that he does not begin to understand who Jesus is: he does not recognize the Truth standing in front of him. If Pilate belonged to the truth (v. 37), he would listen to Jesus.

[38b–40] If Jesus will not explicitly claim to be a king, or to demonstrate his intention of challenging Caesar by using instruments of power and weapons of death, then Pilate cannot find Jesus guilty of any crime, certainly not one punishable by death. Jesus has done nothing to demonstrate any interest in usurping Roman power, which, presumably, Pilate can only conceive as mounting armed revolution of one sort or another. But it is not clear why, if Jesus cannot be charged with a crime, Pilate does not simply release him without virtually asking the Jews' permission to do so. Lincoln's comment is worth repeating, "Pilate's declaration of Jesus' innocence . . . means that from this point the trial is being carried out with the judge explicitly aware that the accused is innocent and so constitutes a travesty of justice."[51]

According to "custom," Pilate offers to release Jesus; but the crowd prefers Barabbas. In John, this "custom" is presented as belonging to the Jews ("You have a custom"), whereas the Synoptic Gospels seem to suggest this custom was the Roman governor's (Mark 15:6, 8; Matt 27:15; cf. Luke 23:17 mg., 18, 25). There is no other attestation of such a practice, but that need not mean that it was not a custom practiced by Pilate.[52] In any case, the Jews are not interested in having Jesus released. They want Barabbas, who, John explains, "was a *lēstēs* [outlaw]."[53] In the LXX, *lēstēs* refers to a lawless or violent person,

50. Pilate speaks in accord with the philosophical school known as skepticism. In Cicero (*Nat. d.* 1.67), Cotta, speaking for skepticism, asks, "Where is truth to be found?" (*Sed ubi est veritas?*), and declares it much easier to prove something false than true (1.57, 60). Pyrrhon (Diogenes Laertius, *Lives* 9.83) contends that the skeptic's stance should be "suspension of judgment about truth" (cf. 9.10.58; 9.107). Sextus Empiricus (*Pyr.* 1.232) proffers the maxim that to every argument an equal argument should be offered.

51. Lincoln 2005, 464.

52. Keener (2:1116–17) discusses the power of prefects to issue amnesties and other relevant historical precedents.

53. Matthew (27:38) and Mark (15:27) report that Jesus was crucified between two *lēstai*; Luke (23:33) calls them *kakourgoi* (evildoers, criminals). John calls Barabbas a *lēstēs* (18:40); Mark (15:7) and Luke (23:19) describe Barabbas as taking part in a revolt and as a murderer, but they do not call him a *lēstēs*.

including those who had polluted the temple (Jer 7:11); in Josephus the term has a somewhat wider range of meaning (see comments on 10:1). At his arrest in the garden, Jesus eschews the path of violence and murder committed by various others whom Josephus labels *lēstai*.[54] The charge against Barabbas is not levied against Jesus. But in spite of Barabbas's reputation, the crowd calls for his release. In choosing Barabbas, the crowd chooses a man whose path may well have been characterized by overt resistance to Rome, possibly even violent resistance. Ironically, Pilate—the delegated defender of order, stability, and Roman government—colludes with them in this decision. Pilate and Rome understand would-be kings who speak the language of power demonstrated in weapons and military might better than those who use the language of surrender and self-giving.

[19:1] In reaction or response, Pilate has Jesus flogged. According to all the Gospels, Jesus is whipped or scourged (*mastigoō*) before his crucifixion. Ancient sources note that crucifixion was often preceded by such torture.[55] John places the scourging in the middle of Pilate's investigation of Jesus rather than at its end, perhaps because the scourging is also offered as an alternative to crucifixion.[56] The Romans were not adverse to the use of torture in the course of judicial procedures[57] and interrogation, especially for slaves or others not protected by citizenship, such as Jewish subjects in the provinces.[58] Torture of various sorts was not intended to lead to the victim's death but to coerce a confession, thus eliciting the "truth" about a suspected or known wrongdoing. Pilate's scourging of Jesus, following the line of questioning regarding Jesus' kingdom and claims related to it, could be read as his last attempt to ferret out the truth regarding the discrepancy between the Jews' charges against Jesus and his own claims. It could also be seen simply as the use of gratuitous torture, a way for Rome to humiliate and flex

54. Josephus also relates the crucifixion of many *lēstai* by Felix (*J.W.* 2.253). On the perception that Jesus was crucified as a brigand, see Chapman 225–28.

55. Plato, e.g., wrote, "The just man will have to be scourged, racked, fettered, blinded, and finally, after the most extreme suffering, he will be crucified" (*anaskolopizō*, "fix on a pole or a stake, impale"; *Resp.* 2.361e–362a). Cicero described the treatment of a Roman citizen prior to his crucifixion: violent scourging "on all sides," in a public arena (*Verr.* 2.5.162). Josephus reports that Florus, the Roman governor, had several thousand citizens of Jerusalem whipped and then crucified (*J.W.* 2.306).

56. See also Luke 23:16, 22, where Pilate proposes to punish, and then release, Jesus.

57. Elsewhere Jesus warns his followers that they will be flogged "in the synagogues" (Matt 10:17; 23:34). In the Gospels, Jesus is struck or beaten by Jewish guards (Matt 26:67; Mark 14:65; Luke 22:63–65; John 18:22), but scourged by the "Gentiles" or Romans (Matt 20:19, 26:26; Mark 10:34; 15:15; Luke 18:33; 23:22; John 19:1).

58. Josephus narrates the flogging of Jesus ben Ananus, who for seven years appeared at various festivals, proclaiming an unending litany of woes against Jerusalem, the temple, and the holy people. When this flogging apparently accomplished nothing, the Jewish authorities took him to the procurator Albinus, who had him brutally flogged but then released (*J.W.* 6.300–304).

its muscles over its provincial subjects, especially since Pilate has already declared that he cannot find any "ground for a charge" against Jesus (18:38) and will soon do so twice more (19:4, 6).[59] Crucifixion has itself been labeled "state-sponsored terrorism,"[60] the state-authorized infliction of fear and pain to deter and control its subjects.

[2–5] After Jesus is scourged, the Roman soldiers dress him in the purple robe of royalty, crown him with a wreath of thorns, and pay him mock homage as "King of the Jews." By positioning Jesus' flogging and mocking in the middle of Pilate's investigation, John can then have Pilate present Jesus, beaten and dressed in royal robes, to the Jews as their king—thus mocking both Jesus and the Jews at the same time. Such a king—beaten, humiliated, mocked—is neither much of a threat to the Romans nor much of a credit to the Jews. The other Gospels portray a more thorough dishonoring of Jesus: he is spit upon (Mark 14:65; Matt 26:67), struck on his face and head (Mark 14:65; Matt 26:67; John 19:3), ridiculed and mocked (Mark 15:20, 31; Matt 27:29, 31, 41), insulted (Mark 15:32; Matt 27:44), and despised ("treated with contempt," Luke 23:11). John's account, however, focuses the mocking of Jesus specifically on the claim to be a king and depicts the soldiers as paying mock homage to him. For John, this ignorant mocking of Jesus ironically acknowledges who Jesus is: King of the Jews. And it is precisely in his death that he is glorified, or honored, rather than dishonored. Since it is God who honors or glorifies Jesus, nothing that any human being, including the representatives of the most powerful empire of that time, can do will discredit or dishonor him.

Once Jesus has been flogged and dressed in the robes of royalty, Pilate presents him to the Jews in order to show them that he can find no grounds for condemnation, that he has done nothing wrong. Pilate's words, "See the man!" (*idou ho anthrōpos*, 18:5), echo 1 Sam 9:17 LXX, when the Lord identifies Saul as king, pointing him out to Samuel with the assertion, "Behold the man [*idou ho anthrōpos*] whom I have told you shall govern my people."[61] While Pilate will soon identify Jesus explicitly as king (19:14), he now presents Jesus simply as "the man." The Gospel is replete with references to Jesus as "this man," a term used sometimes disparagingly, sometimes innocently, but usually ironically (cf. 4:29, "a man"; 5:12, "the man"; 10:33, "you, being a man"; 11:47, "this man"). In the healing of the man born blind in John 9, Jesus is repeatedly referred to as "the man" or "this man" (vv. 11, 16, 24). Peter is asked whether he is one of "this man's disciples" (18:17); Pilate asks what charge the Jews

59. See Harries 33.

60. E.g., Horsley and Silberman 86.

61. Pilate's statement has also been understood as intended to arouse pity and compassion for Jesus, a harmless caricature of a king (Bultmann 1971, 659; Haenchen 2:181). Others have taken "the Man" as a throne name, a title of honor and dignity, perhaps equivalent to "Son of Man" (cf. Meeks 1967, 70; cf. Dodd 1953, 473; and Moloney 1978, 205–7).

bring against "this man" (18:29). Pilate's mocking presentation of Jesus, with the invitation to "see the man," brings this theme to a climax. Pilate has no idea with whom he is actually dealing: Jesus is indeed a king whose kingdom is not "from this world"; indeed, he is the Son of God (19:7). The Jews will soon inform Pilate that Jesus has made this claim as well. Pilate sees only another Jew, powerless, beaten, and humiliated before the Romans. In goading the Jews by presenting Jesus to them with the declaration "See the man," Pilate means just this beaten and humiliated man, and surely he is not worthy of condemnation. Pilate, in fact, declares that he has found no grounds on which to condemn Jesus, since he claims only a "kingdom" that is "not from here," which offers no visible threat to Rome. Ironically, in his attempts to exonerate Jesus, Pilate's actions and words are self-incriminating: he has had an innocent man beaten; he will soon have an innocent man crucified.

[6–9] The chief priests and their servants renew their efforts to secure Jesus' crucifixion; meanwhile Pilate renews his protestation of Jesus' innocence: they have charged Jesus with doing evil, but he can find no evidence of such evil. Therefore he tells the Jews that they should take Jesus themselves and crucify him. Having already been reminded that the Jews do not have the authority to put anyone to death, Pilate mocks them with their impotence to carry out the sentence that they seek. In response, the Jews offer another charge against Jesus that merits death: he has made himself the Son of God. The charge is that Jesus has usurped for himself a prerogative not rightfully his, or exalted himself into such a position.

Earlier in the Gospel, the Jews have charged Jesus with "calling God his own Father," thus "making himself equal to God" (*ton theon ison heauton poiōn tō theō*, 5:18) and with "making himself God" (*poieis seauton theon*, 10:33). On the second occasion, Jesus counters their charge with the assertion "I am the Son of God" (10:36). That claim is reflected here, as is Jesus' frequent use of the absolute "Son" throughout the Gospel. In John, as in the other Gospels, "Messiah" and "Son of God' are linked because the king of Israel, David's son, was regarded as a son to God (John 11:27; 20:31; 2 Sam 7:12–14; Ps 2:7; see Matt 16:16; Mark 1:1). Here, however, Jesus' identity as Son of God is distinguished from his identity as king (so also Luke 22:67–71). Pilate mocks the acclamation of Jesus as "King of the Jews" (19:14–15, 19), but he quakes before Jesus at the possibility that he is the Son of God (v. 8). And rightly so: for while Jesus is the Messiah, the King of Israel, John highlights his identity as Son of God, not as a son of David.

Pilate's increased fear might initially seem to be clarified with reference to the first-century Roman context. "Son of God" (Latin, *divi filius*, translated in Greek as *theou huios*) was used of those Roman emperors in the first century—Augustus, Nero, Titus, Domitian, and Trajan—who were the appointed heirs or sons of a divinized emperor.[62] A Roman governor might then legitimately worry that someone calling himself a "son of God" deemed himself to be a king, a potential rival to Caesar. But Pilate's question to Jesus, "Where are you from?" suggests that the identification of Jesus as "Son of God" triggers the suspicion that Jesus' power has the potential to surpass and even supplant Caesar's. Earlier, without fully understanding Jesus' claims or identity, the soldiers sent to arrest Jesus fell to the ground when he declared, "I am" (*egō eimi*); now Pilate unknowingly quails before the one who is Son of God.

[10–12] In spite of Pilate's needling, Jesus refuses to answer him (cf. Mark 15:5; Isa 53:7). Speaking as the Roman governor of a relatively small province, Pilate reminds Jesus that he holds the power of life and death: he has the authority to release or to crucify Jesus. Presumably Pilate expects Jesus to answer him by denying the charges against him, since his very life lies in Pilate's hands—or so says Pilate. And in one sense, Pilate's statement is true. Pilate has the power to crucify or release Jesus—but only because that power has been given to him "from above," that is, by God. But Pilate does not get the acquiescence he is expecting: Jesus' assertion that Pilate does not have "any authority over me except what has been given . . . from above" (19:11)[63] echoes a common theme that runs throughout the Bible and Jewish literature: all the governments of the earth, and this includes the kings and kingdom of Israel, exist only by God's permission and authority. Because they do, they are answerable to God for their conduct and actions and can and will be judged or replaced as they fail to honor the God who gives them authority and to practice justice in their dealings with all people (cf. Dan 2:20–23; Rom 13:1–7).

Those kings who set themselves against God's people, Israel, or their king cannot expect their dominion to endure (Ps 2:8–9; Dan 7:11–12, 26). But interestingly, these kings are not advised to surrender their power but to "serve the LORD with fear," lest he be angry and destroy their kingdom (Ps 2:10–11). God grants authority to rulers or nations so that they will serve his purposes, not their own. By the same token, the Bible warns the Israelites that if they forsake the law of God, they will be punished (Ps 89:31–33). Josephus explains the destruction of Jerusalem and the ascendancy of the Roman Empire in terms of both Jewish intransigence and God's providence (*hēgemonia*, *J.W.* 2.390;

62. The Latin, *divi filius*, means "son of the divinized one." While Greeks could speak of the living emperor as both *theou huios* ("son of God") and *theos* ("god"), in Latin *divus* applied only to dead emperors (or their families), who had been acknowledged as divine by determination of the Roman Senate, based on testimony that the deceased emperor's soul had been seen departing to heaven (Price 1994a, 83–84). Price also discusses the differences between the Greek *theos* and Latin terms *deus* and *divus*; Peppard (esp. 31–49) challenges the distinction.

63. Cf. Jesus' statement at 14:30: "The ruler of this world has no part in me" (*en emoi ouk echei ouden* [lit., "has nothing in me"; ESV, "has no claim on me"; TNIV, "has no hold over me"]).

4.622; 6.310–11; *Ant.* 1.14). Apocalypses such as *2 Baruch* and *4 Ezra* lament God's permitting or decreeing the destruction of Jerusalem and its temple by Rome, but they also expect Rome's final overthrow by God. Unjust powers will be judged and their authority taken away.

Jesus derives his authority from God, as do the governments of the world. Jesus has demonstrated that he does the will of God in all things; unwittingly, Pilate is about to demonstrate that, while he thinks himself to be exercising his authority or Rome's authority in condemning Jesus, he is doing no such thing because (1) Jesus lays down his life of his own volition (2) in response to his Father's command (10:18). In John's view that Jesus' death was the result of God's purposes and Jesus' own volition, as well as the act of those hostile to Jesus and to God, this Gospel reflects the New Testament's understanding of the mysterious confluence of divine purpose and human agency that brought about Jesus' death.[64] Even if Pilate's actions serve the purposes of God, he is not thereby exonerated nor is "the one who handed me over to you." This one has "the greater sin," implying that Pilate's own action in "handing Jesus over" is likewise culpable.

Who "handed Jesus over" to Pilate? Judas is said to "hand over" (from *paradidōmi*) or betray Jesus (6:64, 71; 12:4; 13:2, 11, 21; 18:2, 5; 19:11; 21:20). But the chief priests (18:30, 35–36; 19:11) and Pilate (19:16) also "deliver" or "hand over" Jesus to be crucified. If all instances of the verb *paradidōmi* are translated with "hand over," then Judas "hands over" Jesus to the Jewish authorities along with the Roman soldiers; they in turn "hand over" Jesus to Pilate; and Pilate "hands over" Jesus to be crucified.[65] Pilate is therefore the last in the line of those human agents who bring about Jesus' death. In that light, the one who has handed Jesus over to the Romans could be the chief priest, either Annas or Caiaphas, or perhaps the Judean elite viewed as a whole.[66] Since the Romans have reserved the right to pass a capital sentence, the actions of the priest in delivering Jesus to Pilate are intended to seal Jesus' death sentence. But since Judas set the whole chain of events in motion, and since elsewhere in John he is identified simply as "the one who handed Jesus over" (*ho paradidous*, as in 18:2, 5), he is more likely the one in view here (19:11). He has "the greater sin" because his action initiated the events that led to Jesus' arrest and eventual appearance before Pilate. Pilate stood at the end of this series of actions, but Judas stood at its beginning. In either case, no single individual shoulders all the responsibility or blame for Jesus' crucifixion.

64. Thus Matt 26:24 and Luke 22:22: "For the Son of Man goes as it has been written of him [Luke: "determined"], but woe to the person by whom he is betrayed!" (or, "handed over," *paradidotai*); cf. Acts 2:23; 4:27–28.

65. See also the comments on 6:64 and 13:11; R. Brown 1994, 1:211; Keener 2:1127.

66. Keener 2:1127.

Pilate wants nothing to do with this numinous figure before him, who claims to have a kingdom "not from this world" and seems impervious to Pilate's threats against his life. But even as Pilate redoubles his efforts to free Jesus, the Jewish authorities insist that releasing Jesus constitutes enmity against Caesar, on the grounds that anyone who "makes himself a king opposes Caesar" (v. 12). If Jesus has made himself a king, then he has set himself up as a rival to Caesar. Such opposition would not be a matter of indifference to Caesar or his provincial governor, who is specifically charged with maintaining peace, order, and stability, and with quelling exactly the sort of riots or insurrections for which would-be kings are responsible. If Pilate is willing to overlook the aspirations of even such a pitiful king, then he is no "friend of Caesar."[67]

"Friend of Caesar" (Latin, *amicus Caesaris*) is a semitechnical term and is here illumined by its contrast with "[the one who] opposes Caesar." One is either for or against Caesar, and being against Caesar would certainly end one's career, and perhaps more. Epictetus, a first-century Stoic philosopher, reports that, although people are anxious to be Caesar's friend, their anxiety does not disappear once they are. Caesar requires the time, attention, and ministrations that a patron expects of a client. Something can provoke Caesar to become one's enemy; when Caesar dies, the security thought to be offered by his friendship will cease (*Diatr.* 3.4.2; esp. 4.1.45–49, 95–97). If, in theory, being Caesar's friend ensures some measure of protection, in practice one needs to be ever vigilant not to lose Caesar's patronage and friendship.[68] The Roman historian Tacitus demonstrates the value of being Caesar's friend when he recounts how Piso appealed to the emperor Tiberius "as one who is your friend" to spare the life of his son; Tiberius obliged by absolving him from the charge of civil war (*Ann.* 3.17.1). Tacitus also demonstrates that the perks of being Caesar's friend could disappear: Decimus Silanus experienced "exclusion from the emperor's friendship" (*amicitia Caesaris*, 3.24.2–4); and in old age, Caius Sallustius, a Roman historian, and Maecenas, a senator, retained only "the shadow rather than the substance of the emperor's friendship." Tacitus sums up the matter: "Rarely is it the destiny of power to be lasting." John presents Pilate as anxious about preserving his power. A false move or a wrong step in managing provincial affairs could destroy Pilate's standing as Caesar's friend and bring his power—and perhaps his life—to an end.

[13–14] The appeal to Pilate to preserve his political capital with Caesar quashes the attempt to free a man he deems innocent. The hour has come to render an official verdict, and so John explains: "When Pilate heard these

67. In *J.W.* 2.34, Josephus states that to become an enemy of Archelaus or his kingdom is to become an enemy also of Caesar.

68. Rome euphemistically designated subservient states as "friends," not "clients." The phrase "friend of the king" is used frequently in 1 Maccabees, where the Hasmoneans are "friends and allies" of the Romans (cf. 8:20, 31; 10:16, 20; 13:36; 14:40; 15:17, 32).

words, he led Jesus outside and sat down on the judgment seat, in the place called the Stone Pavement, and in Hebrew, Gabbatha." John writes as though the place of Jesus' judgment is well known, identifiable from either its Greek or Aramaic ("Hebrew") name. But the Greek *lithostrōton* need not be a place name, and Gabbatha is otherwise unattested: the point seems to be that Pilate now brings Jesus outside, to that public space in which he would pass judgment on Jesus. Some translate the Greek word *ekathisen*, "sat down," as "seated," effectively rendering the phrase "Pilate seated Jesus on the judgment seat" [*bēma*; Matt 27:19; Acts 12:21; 18:12, 16, 17; Rom 14:10; 2 Cor 5:10]. Then the sense is that Jesus, rather than Pilate, is acting as judge.[69] While such a reading is attractive if Jesus is thought to be passing judgment on the Jews for rejecting him as their king, on balance it is more likely that Pilate is depicted here as finally taking his place as judge in order to pass judgment on Jesus.

This is a Roman tribunal, and Pilate must determine Jesus' fate. He does not cede this right, nor Rome's power, to Jesus. But by now it is clear that Pilate can scarcely claim to be speaking on his own authority. Even if Pilate occupies the judgment seat, he is hardly exercising his powers autonomously. On the one hand, Pilate is answerable to Caesar, and he not only knows this but also knows that his position is therefore always precarious. But on the other hand, Pilate is answerable to God: this is what he does *not* know, and precisely this ignorance renders his position far more precarious. How he deals with Jesus shows how he positions himself with respect to the God who gives all power to human beings and expects them to use that power with justice. If Pilate treads on precarious ground with Rome, he is unwittingly treading on far more precarious ground with God.

John's next note, "It was the day of Preparation for the Passover, and it was the sixth hour," presents the timing of Jesus' trial, crucifixion, and death differently from the Synoptic accounts. According to Mark, Jesus is crucified at nine o'clock in the morning (15:25), on the morning after eating the Passover meal with his disciples (cf. 14:12, 14, 16), and dies about three o'clock in the afternoon. Thus in Mark, Jesus' arrest, trial, and crucifixion happen after this meal is eaten. According to John, Jesus' last meal with his disciples takes place "before Passover" (13:1; 18:28). Thus Pilate passes sentence on Jesus at about noon "on the day of preparation for Passover" (19:14).[70] Jesus is crucified; he dies and is buried before sundown and the Passover meal.

69. However, see *J.W.* 2.302, 308, in which Josephus describes the Roman procurator Gessius Florus as setting up a *bēma* ("tribunal-platform") before the Jewish people and seating himself (*kathezetai*). Afterward the chief priests, powerful men, and notables of the city gathered around as he prepared to decide the fate of certain Jews. See also the comments on 11:50 above.

70. The Passover lambs are slaughtered on Nisan 14, then eaten at sunset at the end of that day and the beginning of Nisan 15.

There are various explanations of these chronological differences. One of the most common takes John's chronology to reflect his determination to present Jesus as sentenced to death at noon ("the sixth hour") in order to align the timing of his death with the slaughter of the Passover lambs, understood to have begun at noon.[71] In other words, Jesus dies during the exact hour when the Passover lambs are slaughtered. But this interpretation requires the coherence of three questionable points: (1) the lambs for Passover actually begin to be slaughtered at noon; (2) this fact is widely known to or appreciated by John's readers; (3) John's Gospel actually intends the comparison. While the issues are complicated, the evidence counts against this interpretation of John's reference to the sixth hour, and John does not sufficiently explain his cryptic reference to "the sixth hour" so as to render that interpretation plausible.

1. No ancient Palestinian source actually states that the lambs for Passover began to be slaughtered at noon. In *Jubilees* (2d c. B.C.E.), the Israelites are instructed to "sacrifice [the Passover] before it becomes evening" (49.1, 12); and "at evening when the sun is setting on the third part of the day" (49:19; cf. 11Q19 XVII, 7). Josephus, a priest, places the sacrifice "from the ninth hour until the eleventh" or what we might call mid to late afternoon.[72] According to the Mishnah, the Passover lambs were sacrificed after the daily burnt offering. The earliest permissible time for such offerings occurs when the eve of Passover coincides with the eve of Sabbath; then the daily burnt offering is slaughtered at "half after the sixth hour" and offered at "half after the seventh hour" (1:30). The Passover offering was slaughtered after that: sometime after 1:30 in the afternoon (see *m. Pesaḥ.* 1:4; 4:1, 5).[73] Philo does speak of the offering of myriads of lambs from noon (*mesēmbria*) till eventide (*hespera*, in *Spec.* 2.145), but the comment notes the duration, rather than the beginning, of the appropriate time for sacrifice.[74] In other words, no ancient source unequivocally locates this sacrifice of Passover lambs at noon.

2. The exact hour of this sacrifice was unlikely to have been known (or have mattered) to the readers of John's Gospel. Of course, that depends to some extent on how we envision the audience of John's Gospel. If Christians from the Roman Empire surrounding the Mediterranean were in view, it can be doubted whether the vast majority of them knew or cared about details such as the exact hour at which the Passover lambs were sacrificed. For that matter, it is doubtful

71. So R. Brown 1970, 556, 895; cf. Moloney 1998a, 141; Stibbe 1994, 38; Talbert 241.

72. Josephus, *J.W.* 6.423. Sanders (1992, 135) takes Josephus's reference to reflect first-century practice; so also Safrai 892.

73. The Mishnah specifies that "sixth hour" marks the cessation of work and the burning of leavened things (*m. Pesaḥ.* 1:4).

74. Ezekiel the Tragedian (2d c. B.C.E., Alexandria) notes that animals selected on the tenth day of the month are kept until "the fourteenth day has dawned," then sacrificed at evening (175–92).

that even pilgrims who went up to Jerusalem for the feast knew the details of fixing the precise hour of this sacrifice. For what readers would John's allusion have been instructive?

3. One could argue that while John's readers would not have made the connection, John nevertheless intends to indicate the solemnity of the hour and the significance of Jesus' death as the Passover lamb by noting that it was the hour when the slaughter began that Jesus was sent to his death. But John does not signal to his reader that "the sixth hour" is either unusually significant, or if it is, what its significance might be. John includes three other references to precise hours (1:39; 4:6, 52; see comments on 4:52–53). Jesus' "hour" has been anticipated throughout the Gospel; with the unfolding events of Jesus' passion, that hour clearly has come (12:23, 27; 13:1; 17:1). Pilate's sentencing of Jesus at "the sixth hour" adds to the momentous movement toward his death.[75]

There is no mistaking the importance of the moment. Pilate has not yet sentenced Jesus to death. He offers the Jews one more opportunity to acknowledge their King. Presenting Jesus, flogged and dressed in purple robes and a crown of thorns, Pilate acclaims, "See your King!" This statement joins with Pilate's earlier pronouncement, "See the man!" The two announcements go together: this man is their King.

[15–16] But they will not have their King. They persist in their demand to have Jesus crucified, so that Pilate inquires, once more, whether they really mean to give up their king to the Romans to be put to death. While Pilate may wonder about their resolve, this course has already been charted by the council, when Caiaphas counseled that it would be better for Jesus to die than for the whole nation to be destroyed (11:47–52). The irony of the situation is that Pilate does not seem to have agreed with the earlier judgment that Jesus' continued activity is a threat to the survival of the people or their holy place. Instead, Pilate wishes to release Jesus on the grounds that he can find no charge to levy against him, while the Jews insist that Jesus has made himself a king and has set himself up against Caesar. Rejecting Jesus as their king, the Jews make the fateful declaration, "We have no king but Caesar!" If they are willing to live by Caesar's rule, they will find that they also suffer under Caesar's rule. The one they now claim as king, the Roman Caesar, will demonstrate his power over his subjects when, several decades later, he and his troops besiege and destroy

75. Note Josephus's tendency to record the precise dating of certain solemn events: "At the time when the people were assembling for the Feast of Unleavened Bread, on the eighth day of the month of Xanthicus, at the ninth hour of the night, so brilliant a light shone round the altar and the sanctuary that it seemed to be broad daylight" (*J.W.* 6.290). Later he comments on the spontaneous opening of the bronze gate: "It could scarcely be moved by twenty men; fastened with iron-bound bars, it had bolts which were sunk to a great depth into a threshold consisting of a solid block of stone—this gate was observed at the sixth hour of the night to have opened of its own accord" (*J.W.* 6.294).

Jerusalem and its temple, killing scores of Jews and selling the survivors into slavery. Caiaphas's worst fears about the possible destruction of "the people" or "the nation" (*ethnos*) will tragically be realized. The efforts of the Jews, a small and subject people, to appease the Romans, a powerful empire, will in the long run come to nothing.

In claiming the emperor as their only king, are the Jews knowingly and deliberately turning their backs on God? Throughout the Old Testament, God is proclaimed as a great king over all the earth, king over the nations (Ps 47:2, 7–8). A frequent refrain in the Psalms is, "The LORD is king!" (Pss 10:16; 93:1; 96:10; 97:1; 99:1; cf. 1 Chr 16:31; Isa 33:22; Zech 14:9; Tob 10:13; Add Esth 13:9). It is therefore possible to read the statement of the Jews in John, "We have no king but Caesar," as rejecting God's rule altogether, even as the prophet Samuel interpreted the Israelites' request for a king "to govern us" as rejecting God "from being king over them" (1 Sam 8:6–7, 10). Much later, Judas the Galilean led a revolt against direct Roman rule and the payment of taxes to them, berating his countrymen "because they were subjecting themselves to the Romans after God," since God was to be "their only ruler [*hēgemōn*] and master [*despotēs*]."[76] When the Jews declare, "We have no king but Caesar," they could be viewed as opting to give their loyalty to a human king—here, the Roman emperor—rather than to God.

But, of course, the Old Testament is also replete with narratives about the kings of Israel and their anointing by God to rule over his people. Even while God is acknowledged as king, various individuals served as "king over Israel," and they had been placed in or removed from these positions by God (1 Kgs 4:1; 12:20; 1 Chr 12:38; 14:8; 28:4; Neh 13:26). Indeed, the coming Messiah was to be a king like David, under the authority of God, who was and is King over all. Thus, for example, Psalm 17 of the *Psalms of Solomon* opens and closes with the declarations, "Lord, you are our king forevermore" (17.1, 46), but those two affirmation enclose (1) the assertion that this same Lord "chose David to be king over Israel" (17.4) and (2) the prayer for God to "raise up" a "king, the son of David, to rule over your servant Israel" (17.21). One could simultaneously acknowledge both God and God's anointed one as king, as long as one understood that God is king over all the earth, while the anointed king of Israel rules on earth as God's delegate.

John's point is that, in rejecting Jesus as their king and turning to Caesar, the Jews reject the God who is the King over all the earth. To honor the Son is to honor the Father (5:23); to reject the Son as King is to reject the one who sent him. As Jesus said to Pilate, whatever authority to which Pilate may lay

76. For Judas's revolt (6 C.E.), see *J.W.* 2.118, 433; *Ant.* 18.23; 20.102. Josephus views Judas's stance as something of an anomaly, since it foreshadowed the disaster of the Jewish revolt. Judas was protesting the subjugation of the Jews to Roman, or foreign, rule.

claim has been given to him "from above," that is, from God; the same would hold true for Pilate's superiors and for Caesar himself. Nowhere in John does Jesus deny that Pilate or Caesar has authority, but they have it "from above" and therefore only as subordinates to God—and ultimately to Jesus, the Son of God, to whom God has given *all* judgment (5:22). Caesar and Jesus have both been appointed to positions of authority, but Jesus exercises the full authority of God; Caesar's authority, superficially superior and more far-reaching, can neither challenge nor compete with that of Jesus. But the Jews prefer both Barabbas and Caesar to Jesus: they prefer to deal with the kingdom of Rome. Even at Passover, in effect, they embrace Pharaoh rather than the king whose truth can make them free.

And so, pressured by the Jews but subject ultimately to a higher authority, Pilate plays his part in the drama as a Roman appointee and hands Jesus over to be crucified, presumably to the soldiers and not to the Jewish authorities.[77] John writes, "They received [or, 'took'] Jesus." The chain of agency that begins with Judas, who betrayed (or "handed over") Jesus,[78] now comes to its climax with Pilate's handing Jesus over to those who will carry out the sentence of death by crucifixion.

Crucifixion is a predominantly Roman form of execution, and John, like all the other Gospels, acknowledges that the Romans carried it out. It is worth pausing on this point a bit, for much ink has recently been spilled over the role of the Jews and the question of "anti-Judaism" in the Gospels, particularly in the Passion Narratives and especially in John. But the Roman authorities figure prominently as adversaries in the Johannine Passion Narrative. A detachment of Roman soldiers come with "lanterns and torches and weapons" to arrest Jesus; Pilate judges Jesus to be innocent but orders him beaten anyway; in spite of his determination that the charges against Jesus are baseless, Pilate orders his crucifixion. The Jewish authorities warn Pilate about losing his privileged status as a friend of the powerful Caesar. It will be Rome that crucifies Jesus; Roman soldiers gamble for his garments as he hangs on the cross, are willing to break his legs to hasten his death, and thrust a spear into his side to determine that he is indeed dead. Rome both orders and oversees Jesus' death. The Fourth Gospel anticipates the death of Peter, apparently also by crucifixion (21:18–19). Jesus does speak of an hour that is coming when "they will put you out of the synagogues" and when "those who kill you will think that by doing so they are offering worship to God" (16:2); yet the two deaths John narrates or alludes to, those of Jesus and Peter, occur at the hands of Roman rather than Jewish authorities.

77. In context, "to them" (*autois*, 19:16) could mean that Jesus is being handed over to the chief priests. But as the narrative shows, the Romans, not the Jews, carry out the crucifixion.

78. As noted elsewhere, "hand over" and "betray" come from the same root (*paradidōmi*); see the comments at 6:64; 13:11; 18:2; 19:11.

19:17–42 The Crucifixion and Burial of Jesus

The Romans take Jesus to be crucified, a form of execution reserved mostly for slaves, dangerous criminals, mutinous or cowardly troops, and traitors or rebels. Ancient sources testify to the public character of crucifixion, as well as to the shame and humiliation that attended it. Although other early Christian authors call attention to these aspects of crucifixion,[79] they feature rather differently in John's Passion Narrative. In John, the crucifixion of Jesus is not a cause for shame (or dishonor); instead, Jesus is glorified (or honored)[80] as the King of the Jews as he dies on a cross. Only from the vantage point of Jesus' resurrection can the cross be interpreted as the climax of God's mission to bring life to the world through the Son. It is the life-giving work of the Father through the Son that glorifies both.

Like other early Christian authors, John reads the Old Testament as foreshadowing or foretelling Jesus' rejection and death, especially as the Messiah of God. With few exceptions,[81] the passages that John cites in connection with Jesus' crucifixion come from the book of Psalms, particularly Pss 22, 34, 41, and 69.[82] While these psalms provide the texture of the Passion Narrative in the Synoptic Gospels, John explicitly quotes various passages from them (John 13:18; 15:25; 19:24, 28, 36; less directly, 2:17). John never states that these quotations come from the Psalms (cf. Luke 20:42; 24:44; Acts 1:20), nor does he make reference to David, their alleged author (contrast Matt 22:43; Mark 12:36; Luke 20:42; Acts 2:25; 4:25; Rom 4:6; 11:9).[83] For John, these passages are important because they are *Scripture.* Moreover, they describe the checkered pathway of Israel's king and in so doing prefigure Jesus' destiny as the one who "came to his own home" but was not acclaimed by his own people (1:11).[84] Although the true King of Israel (1:49), Jesus was betrayed by a disciple (13:18), "handed over" to the Jewish authorities, who handed him over to

79. Paul speaks of the cross as foolish, a sign of God's curse, an offense (1 Cor 1:23; Gal 3:13; 5:11); Heb 12:2 mentions the "shame" of the cross. Justin Martyr (ca. 100–165; in *1 Apol.* 13.4) defends Christians against the charge that they are mad for honoring a crucified man; Melito, bishop of Sardis (died ca. 190), observes that the body of the Lord had been treated "in unseemly fashion" (*Peri pascha* 96–97). In *Contra Celsum* (6.10), Origen says that Jesus was "bound in the most ignominious fashion" and "executed in a shameful way." See further Chapman.

80. *Doxa* can be translated as either "glory" or "honor"; cf. 5:41; 8:49–50, 54–55; 12:23, 43; and comments ad loc.

81. John 12:38–40 quotes Isa 6:9–10 and 53:1; John 19:37 quotes Zech 12:10.

82. For a list of other possible allusions to the Psalms in the Gospel Passion Narrative, see the discussion in R. Brown 1994, 1451–65.

83. But see the demurral of Daly-Denton 318: "Davidic 'authorship' of the Psalms was a 'given' so obvious that it did not require reiteration every time a psalm was cited."

84. On the point that the Psalms in the Passion Narratives are invoked not to present the "paradigmatic righteous sufferer" but rather the suffering and death of the king (or messiah), see Hengel 1981, 40–41; Juel 102–3; Daly-Denton 238–39; Lincoln 2000, 54.

Pilate (18:30, 35, 36; 19:11, 16), and finally was put to death by the Romans. John finds Jesus' path to the cross laid out in the Psalms.

> **19:17** Carrying the cross himself, he went out to the place called "of the
> skull," which in Hebrew is called Golgotha,[a] **18** where they crucified him.
> And with him were two others, one on either side, with Jesus in the
> middle.
>
> **19** And Pilate wrote an inscription and put it on the cross. It was written,
> "Jesus the Nazarene,[b] the King of the Jews." **20** Many of the Jews read
> this inscription, for the place where Jesus was crucified was near the city;
> and the inscription was written in Hebrew, Latin, and Greek.
>
> **21** Then the chief priests of the Jews said to Pilate, "Do not write,
> 'The King of the Jews,' but rather, 'This man said, "I am the king of
> the Jews."'"
>
> **22** Pilate answered, "What I have written, I have written."
>
> **23** When the soldiers had crucified Jesus, they took his clothes and
> divided them into four parts, a part for each soldier, and the tunic. The
> tunic was seamless, woven from top to bottom in one piece. **24** And they
> said to each other, "Let us not tear it, but rather let us cast lots for whose
> it shall be." This was to fulfill the Scripture, "They divide my clothes
> among them, and for my clothing they cast lots." So then the soldiers did
> these things.
>
> **25** And Jesus' mother was standing by the cross, and his mother's
> sister, Mary the wife of Clopas, and Mary Magdalene. **26** So when Jesus
> saw his mother, and the disciple whom he loved, standing there, he said
> to his mother, "Woman, see your son!" **27** Then he said to the disciple,
> "See your mother!" And from that hour, the disciple took her into his
> own home.
>
> **28** After this, Jesus, knowing that all things had been accomplished,
> in order to fulfill[c] the Scripture, said, "I am thirsty." **29** A vessel full of
> sour wine[d] was there. So they[e] offered him a sponge full of it, lifting it on
> hyssop, to his mouth. **30** When he had received the sour wine, Jesus said,
> "It is finished."[c]
>
> And he bowed his head, and he died.[f]
>
> **31** Since it was the day of Preparation, in order that the bodies would
> not remain on the cross on the Sabbath (for that Sabbath was a high day),
> the Jews asked Pilate that their legs might be broken so that they could
> be taken down. **32** So the soldiers went and broke the legs of the first
> one and of the other one who was crucified with him. **33** But when they
> came to Jesus, they saw that he had already died, so they did not break
> his legs. **34** Rather, one of the soldiers pierced his side with his spear, and
> immediately blood and water came out.

35 The one who has seen this has testified, and his testimony is true,
and he knows that he speaks the truth, so that you might believe.
36 These things happened so that the Scripture might be fulfilled, "Not
one of his bones shall be broken." 37 And yet another Scripture says,
"They shall see the one whom they have pierced."
38 After these things, Joseph from Arimathea, who was a disciple of
Jesus, but secretly for fear of the Jews, asked Pilate that he might take
the body of Jesus. And Pilate gave him permission. So he came and took
his body. 39 And Nicodemus, the one who had come to him by night the
first time, came bearing a mixture of about a hundred pounds of myrrh
and aloes. 40 Then they took the body of Jesus and bound it in linen cloths
with the spices, according to the burial custom of the Jews. 41 And in
the place where he was crucified, there was a garden, and in the garden
there was a new tomb in which no one had ever been placed. 42 So since
it was the Jewish day of Preparation, and the tomb was nearby, they laid
Jesus there.

a. "Of the skull" translates *kraniou*, Greek for skull (Matt 27:33; Mark 15:22; Luke 23:33; the Latin is *calvaria*, hence, "Calvary"). The Hebrew for skull is *gulgōlet* (Judg 9:53; 2 Kgs 9:35); the Aramaic *gulgultā* appears in the Targums.

b. See the textual note on *Iēsous ho Nazōraios* at 18:5.

c. The words here translated "accomplished" and "finished" (from *teleō*) and "fulfill" (from *teleioō*) are cognates in the Greek. John uses *teleō* twice (19:28; 19:30; cf. *telos* in 13:1 and comments there). While *teleō* can mean simply "bring to an end, complete, finish," Jesus' last word from the cross, *tetelestai*, "It is finished!" (19:30) surely means "it has been accomplished" or "it has been completed" with reference to completing God's mission and work. Elsewhere John uses *teleioō* (4:34; 5:36; 17:4, 23; 19:28), to mean "fulfill," "complete," or "bring to its goal." The use of *teleioō* in 19:28 is the only time it is used with reference to the fulfillment of Scripture; elsewhere the verb used is *plēroō*.

d. BDAG, "Sour wine" or "wine vinegar"; LSJM, "poor wine" or vinegar made from it.

e. "They" probably refers to the soldiers (v. 23), and not Jesus' mother and the disciple whom he loved (v. 27).

f. "Gave up his life" (CEB); lit., "handed over [*paredōken*] his spirit" (KJV, "gave up the ghost").

[19:17–18] Pilate has pronounced his sentence on Jesus, and Jesus is now taken to be crucified.[85] Evidence from the ancient world indicates that crucifixion, a way of executing criminals that emphasized subjugation of conquered

85. The NT almost always uses the verb *stauroō*; in Heb 6:6, the verb is *anastauroō*. Josephus uses both; Philo uses only *anaskolopizein* (a *skolops* is a stake; the NT uses only the word *stauros* for the cross on which Jesus was crucified).

peoples and instilled fear in them, was practiced before the Roman period. Alexander the Great, for example, was said to have crucified two thousand survivors of the long-drawn-out siege of Tyre.[86] Antiochus Epiphanes, the man blamed for the edicts that launched the Maccabean revolt, crucified some Jews who kept the forbidden ancestral customs.[87] Subsequently, Alexander Jannaeus, one of the Hasmonean kings, the descendants of the Maccabees, ordered the crucifixion of some eight hundred Jews who had resisted him.[88]

In the Roman world, crucifixion was reserved especially for dangerous criminals (such as murderers) or robbers; slaves, no matter whether their offenses were serious crimes or minor infractions; troops who threatened mutiny or did not fight with appropriate vigor and valor; and persons guilty of rebellion or treason. For example, six thousand followers of Spartacus, the leader of an army of runaway slaves, were crucified along the Appian Way "from Rome to Capua" after several years of fighting (73–71 B.C.E.) and the death of Spartacus himself.[89] The Roman legate of Syria, Varus, executed two thousand Jews who revolted after the death of Herod the Great.[90] Roman soldiers caught, tortured, and crucified Jews trying to escape from the siege of Jerusalem in their first war against Rome (66–70 C.E.).[91]

Crucifixion carried out en masse contributed to its alleged deterrent effect. According to John and the other Gospels, Jesus is crucified between two others, making his execution somewhat unusual and possibly less dramatic in its effect.[92] Still, since Jesus has a certain notoriety, his public crucifixion is evidence of Rome's swift reprisals against any whose activities garner significant support, stimulate opposition, or even raise questions regarding their intentions vis-à-vis Rome. Caiaphas's shrewd calculation that sacrificing one man would appease the Romans (John 11:47–53) rings true to the situation of the Jewish people under Roman rule in the first century.

Plutarch, the first-century Greek essayist, writes that every condemned criminal bears his cross,[93] apparently alluding to the practice of a condemned criminal carrying the horizontal beam (*patibulum*), which was then affixed to a vertical pole or stake (*stipes*) at the site of the crucifixion. John states emphatically that Jesus carries his own cross; in the Synoptic Gospels, Simon of Cyrene is pressed

86. Curtius Rufus, *Hist. Alex.* 4.4.17.

87. Josephus, *Ant.* 12.256.

88. Josephus (*J.W.* 1.97; *Ant.* 13.379–80) describes Alexander Jannaeus's action as "one of the most savage of all acts." On whether crucifixion was legal in ancient Jewish law, see Chapman 5–7, supplementing Hengel 1977, 84–85.

89. Appian, *Bell. civ.* 1.116–120.

90. Josephus, *J.W.* 2.75; *Ant.* 17.295.

91. Josephus, *J.W.* 5.449.

92. But see Josephus, *J.W.* 5.289, where Titus orders a single Jew crucified in front of the walls of Jerusalem to see whether the Jews under siege would surrender.

93. Plutarch, *Sera* 9 (*Mor.* 554B).

into service to do so (Matt 27:32; Mark 15:21; Luke 23:26). Although John's account fits with his portrayal of Jesus as initiating and superintending the events that lead to his arrest and condemnation (and is therefore often viewed as historically dubious), its details nevertheless cohere with ancient practice. Still, it is striking that John writes, "*He* went out . . ." (John 19:17). Even though Pilate has handed Jesus over to "them" (*autois*, 19:16), the verb "went out" (*exēlthen*) is singular, and Jesus is the subject of the action. Here John depicts in narrative form what is asserted elsewhere: Jesus lays down his life on his own (10:18).[94]

Jesus goes to the place called Golgotha, the place of "the skull." The place name is not attested outside the New Testament, and the precise reason for this name, as well as its location, remains unknown.[95] The traditional site of the crucifixion (and nearby burial) of Jesus is now marked by the Church of the Holy Sepulchre in Jerusalem. Now inside the walls of Jerusalem, this area was outside its walls in Jesus' day. Helena, mother of the emperor Constantine, was present when the church was built (325/6 C.E.) and claimed to have found the True Cross and a tomb there. Eusebius reports the discovery of this tomb (or cave), but also alleges that the site had earlier been venerated by Christians until a temple to Venus had been built on it, thus effectively ensuring that Christians had not forgotten where Jesus had been crucified and buried.[96] However, both the New Testament and earliest Christianity lack evidence of tomb veneration, or of marking the site where these momentous events had transpired. Given the fact that Jesus was not thought to be in the tomb, the lack of such commemoration is hardly surprising. At this place called Golgotha, Roman soldiers crucified Jesus of Nazareth between two others, whose names remain lost to history.

[19–22] The charge against Jesus, however, is written on a placard of some sort (*titlos*) and placed on the cross: "Jesus the Nazarene, the King of the Jews."[97] John alone mentions the fact that the charge is written in three

94. In the account of Abraham's intended sacrifice of Isaac, Isaac carries the wood to the place of sacrifice (Gen 22:6). A number of ancient Jewish sources stress Isaac's own role in this event, with some claiming that he went knowingly and willingly toward his death; Philo, *Abr.* 172; Jdt 8:26–27; *L.A.B.* 32.2–3; 4 Macc 7:12–14; 13:12; 16:20; *Ant.* 1.225–32; *Tg. Neof.* 22.8–10; *Tg. Ps.-J.* 22.1, 10; cf. *1 Clem.* 31.2–4.

95. The place may be named for its shape (Barrett 548) or its locale as a place of execution (Keener 2:1135).

96. Eusebius, *Vit. Const.* 25–28.

97. Cf. Suetonius, *Cal.* 32: Caligula ordered the hands of a slave—convicted of theft—cut off, and the slave displayed "with a placard [Lat. *titulus*] giving the reason for his punishment." In *Dom.* 10, Suetonius reports that a gladiator was consigned to the arena with a placard charging that he spoke impiously. Eusebius describes the martyrdom of Attalus as follows: "He was led around the amphitheater, a tablet being carried before him on which was written in the Roman language, 'This is Attalus the Christian'" (*Hist. eccl.* 5.1.44). In Matt 27:37 one finds the "accusation" or "charge" (*aitia*) against Jesus; Mark 15:26 gives the "inscription of the charge" (*hē epigraphē tēs aitias*); Luke 23:38 reports the "inscription" (*epigraphē*). In John, Pilate can find no grounds for a charge (*aitia*) against Jesus (cf. 18:38; 19:4, 6).

languages: Hebrew, Latin, and Greek. On the one hand, these three languages attest the exchange of Jewish, Hellenistic, and Roman language, culture, and architecture in the eastern end of the Mediterranean, including first-century Jerusalem. On the other hand, the three languages on the placard show that the death of Jesus is intended for all the world, and that when Jesus is "lifted up," he will draw "all people" to himself (12:32). In any case all literate passersby could read the charges against Jesus. Even if they could not read, the point remains: the one crucified as King of the Jews is king not just of the Jews.

The chief priests, however, apparently complain that what Pilate has written—or ordered to be written[98]—will appear to be a formal declaration of Jesus' identity rather than a charge against him. Since they do not believe Jesus to be the King of the Jews, neither do they wish the placard under which he is crucified to present him as such. Instead, the charge they have brought against him is that he made himself king, thus usurping a position not rightfully his and positioning himself as a rival to Caesar (19:12, 15). Indeed, throughout the Gospel, Jewish charges against Jesus come in just that form: Jesus *made* himself equal to God; he *made* himself God, or the Son of God, or King.[99] From the Jewish vantage point, these statements summarize Jesus' false claims and illicit actions, not true statements of his identity. But Pilate calls the shots, and he refuses to change what is written. In any case, like others in the narrative who do not understand what they are saying (cf. 11:51–52), Pilate has unknowingly written the truth about Jesus' identity.

Handed over by Judas (*Ioudas*), Jesus dies as king of the Jews (*tōn Ioudaiōn*). The play on Greek words (*Iouda, Iouaios/oi*) should not be missed: it shows that Jesus dies precisely for "his own" (1:11; 4:9, 22), those who betray, reject, and crucify him. This is the ultimate way, then, in which salvation is "from the Jews" (4:22). In spite of the unequivocally negative portrayal of the Jews in chapters 18–19—or better, precisely in light of that portrayal—Jesus dies to reveal and manifest the saving love of God, who "gave his only Son." If the saving love of God the Father is revealed in the death of the Son as the king of those who have most deeply betrayed him, ultimately in John's view also misrepresenting the witnesses they have claimed to represent (e.g., the law, Moses, Sabbath, the festivals), then nothing can stop this love from reaching the entire world. In fact, the cross becomes the means of "drawing all people" to Jesus (12:32).

[23–25a] The terse account of Jesus' crucifixion reflects various practices commonly associated with it: probably crucified naked,[100] victims were nailed

98. *Ho gegrapha gegrapha*, "What I have written, I have written" (18:22). The verb is first-person sg., but it is unlikely that Pilate himself physically wrote the charge.

99. John 5:18; 10:33; 19:7, 12. In every case the verb is *poiēin*, "to make."

100. John 19:23. Martial, *Epigr.* 7; Artemidorus, *Oneir*. 2.53.7 (2.61).

to the cross.[101] After the grim deed is done, the Roman soldiers divide Jesus' clothing into four parts and cast lots for his seamlessly woven tunic, in keeping with the two actions described in Ps 22: "They divide my clothes among themselves, and for my clothing they cast lots" (22:18).[102] This actual quotation is distinctive of John, who further notes that this event happened "to fulfill the Scripture."[103] The verb "fulfilled" translates *plēroō*, characteristic of the quotations of Scripture in the second half of the Gospel that are especially connected with Jesus' death (12:38–19:42). What the Scripture wrote about or foresaw came to fruition here: Scripture has been fulfilled. The tunic (*chitōn*) is an inner garment; it is described here as woven "from top to bottom" (*ek tōn anōthen*) without a seam (*araphos*).[104] While the "seamless garment" has often been interpreted symbolically (e.g., as symbolizing the unity of the church), in the context of the Gospel the description simply explains why the soldiers gambled for it, but the irony is inescapable: while willing to nail a man to a cross, they are unwilling to tear his robe.

[25b–27] Standing near the cross are several women and the disciple whom Jesus loved.[105] Among the women are Jesus' mother and Mary Magdalene, mentioned for the first time, who will also be the first to see the risen Lord on Easter morning. Additionally the Gospel names "his mother's sister, Mary the wife of Clopas," but it is not possible to tell whether these are two persons ("his mother's sister; and Mary the wife of Clopas") or the same person ("his mother's sister, that is, Mary the wife of Clopas"). The Gospel never refers to the mother of Jesus as Mary and hence could conceivably think of Jesus' mother's sister as named Mary. Although Jesus is (mistakenly) referred to as the "son of Joseph," neither Jesus' mother nor brothers are named in the Gospel (2:1, 3, 5, 12; 6:42; 7:3, 5, 10; 19:25–27); it is possible that John here leaves the sister of Jesus' mother unnamed as well.

While all the Gospels refer to women near the cross as Jesus died, John also mentions the presence of the disciple whom Jesus loved. From the cross, Jesus sees his mother and this disciple, and he presents them to each other now

101. John 20:25. On the practice of nailing victims to the cross, see Josephus, *J.W.* 2.308; 5.451; Philo, *Post.* 61; *Somn.* 2.213.

102. John's citation matches that of the LXX exactly. In the Synoptic accounts, the soldiers divide all Jesus' clothing by casting lots (Matt 27:35; Mark 15:24; Luke 23:34).

103. "Scripture" is used 12 times in John, 4× in Matthew, 3× in Mark, 4× in Luke. Except for 5:39, John always uses the sg. (*graphē*) rather than the pl., likely because "Scripture" denotes for him a particular verse. On the contrary, Beutler (1996, 148, citing others) contends that John is more interested in the fulfillment of Scripture as such than in fulfillment of individual passages.

104. Josephus (*Ant.* 3.161) notes that the high priest's *chitōn* was "one long garment," and not *raptos* (hence, *araphos*).

105. Elsewhere in John, the description of someone "standing" with or by another often indicates allegiance to that person (e.g., 1:35; 3:29; 18:5, 16).

as mother and son, thus establishing a new relationship between them.[106] The statements reflect traditional material known from the Synoptic Gospels, where Jesus' mother and brothers are defined as those who do the will of God, and the bonds of the family extend beyond the lines of consanguinity (Matt 12:46–50; Mark 3:31–35; Luke 8:19–21).[107] In the ancient Mediterranean world, the sense of family or kin extended beyond the limits of father, mother, and their naturally born children.[108] Jesus here defines the family, or household, that is created by means of his death; the point is reiterated when the risen Jesus commands Mary Magdalene to report to his "brothers" (that is, his disciples) that he has risen (20:17). Through his death and resurrection, Jesus gathers together the children of God who are brothers and sisters to each other and to him, and the claims of this family outweigh biological claims (1:12–13; 3:3, 5; 9:22–23, 35; 11:52).

[28–30] For the second time in the Gospel, Jesus is thirsty (4:7). Some have thought it ironic that Jesus, who can supply living water to those who thirst (4:13–15), experiences thirst himself. But it is precisely the Word *made flesh*, capable of thirst, that offers thirst-quenching living water. Knowing that his mission and life are drawing to their end (cf. 13:1; 18:4), Jesus now utters the words "I thirst" in accord with the description of the rejected king of the Psalms cited elsewhere in John's Passion Narrative (see n. 6 above). But Jesus' words "I thirst" do not match any single passage in the Psalms, generating considerable discussion about the text in view.[109] Perhaps most frequently, since John cites Ps 69 three times in connection with Jesus' death,[110] Jesus' declaration of thirst has been taken as implied by the words of Ps 69:21 (68:22 LXX): "For my thirst they gave me vinegar to drink" (cf. John 19:29).

The clause "in order to fulfill the Scripture" could be taken with what precedes ("knowing that all things had been completed in order to fulfill the Scripture") or with what follows ("in order to fulfill the Scripture, he said"). The fact that Jesus does not directly quote the psalm indicates that John does not mean that Jesus woodenly spoke these words, "I thirst," simply in order to

106. Jesus' statements ("See your son!" and "See your mother!") are parallel to each other, as well as to the statements of Pilate ("See the man!" and "See your king!") in 19:5, 14.

107. In Matt 12:49 and Mark 3:34 the wording is "See my mother and my brothers!" (*ide hē mētēr mou kai hoi adelphoi mou*).

108. See the discussions, with many texts, in deSilva 157–240; Barton; comments on 9:18–23 above. Note also the emphasis on common (religious) commitments and conduct that strengthen and even outstrip the bonds of family, in 4 Macc 13:24–27; Philo, *Virt.* 195: "Kinship is not measured by blood alone."

109. Those who think John's citation comes from Ps 69:21 include Barrett 553; Carson 1991, 619; Lincoln 2005, 477; Lindars 581; O'Day 832; Ridderbos 617; Schnelle 1998, 290; Talbert 244. Some see a double allusion to Pss 22:15 and 69:21; among them are Beasley-Murray 351–52; Blomberg 253; Brant 253; D. Moody Smith 1999, 361. L. Jones (203) points to Ps 42:2 or 63:1, where "thirst" is the thirst for God.

110. John 15:25 cites Ps 69:4; John 2:17 cites Ps 69:9; John 19:28 cites Ps 69:21.

quote Scripture as he died. Rather, the psalm's description of the one who is dishonored and rejected is being "fulfilled" in Jesus as he dies, thirsty, on the cross. According to John, Jesus speaks in full awareness of the unfolding of his mission, knowing that it is now coming to its end. The one who knows he will raise Lazarus still weeps at the tomb; the one who knows "all things had been completed" still thirsts as he accomplishes God's purpose.

Those standing nearby—most likely the soldiers—offered Jesus a sponge full of sour wine on a branch of hyssop. This vinegary or sour wine diluted with water, probably the drink known in Latin as *posca*, was a common drink of the Roman army.[111] It served to slake thirst, not exacerbate it. Thus Plutarch describes Cato the Elder as drinking water on his campaigns, except for occasions while, "in a raging thirst, he would call for vinegar [*oxos*]."[112] Again, the action of offering Jesus a drink of wine correlates to the words of the psalm, although there the offer of vinegar to drink provides a parallel to the offer of poison for food. But John does not envision a malicious act,[113] and Jesus takes the sponge of wine that is offered to him.

The sponge is lifted up to Jesus on "hyssop." Hyssop was the plant used to smear the blood of the Passover lamb on the doorposts of the Israelites (Exod 12:22). It is doubtful that the simple reference to hyssop, without any other verbal links to its use in smearing blood on the doorposts, would have been understood in this way. More frequently in the Bible, hyssop is associated with purification both from the impurity contracted from leprosy and from a corpse (Lev 14:4, 6, 49, 51–52; Num 19:6, 18; Heb 9:19), and from moral defilement caused by sin; thus the psalmist prays, "Purge me with hyssop, and I shall be clean" (Ps 51:7). Perhaps hyssop here connects Jesus' death to purification from sin, but the Gospel provides no clue that the hyssop should be understood symbolically.

After receiving the wine, Jesus said, "It is finished" (*tetelestai*; see textual note), bowed his head, and "gave up his spirit" (*paredōken to pneuma*). In Matthew and Mark, the dying Jesus quotes the opening line of Ps 22, "My God, my God, why have you forsaken me?" Neither in John (nor in Luke) does Jesus voice this lament. Instead, Jesus' final utterance from the cross declares the mission that the Father has given him has been completed or finished: he has drunk the cup that the Father has given him (John 12:27; 13:1; 18:11; cf. Matt 20:22–23; 26:39; Mark 10:38–39; 14:36). And while Jesus has been abandoned

111. Here and Mark 15:36 par., *oxos*; cf. Ruth 2:14 LXX. In Matt 27:34 Jesus is given wine (*oinos*) mixed with gall, which he refuses; later he is given "sour wine" (*oxos*, 27:48).

112. Plutarch, *Cat. Maj.* 1.10; cf. Suetonius, *Vit.* 12.1 (*posca*); *Historia Augusta: Life of Hadrian* (10.2) describes camp fare as "bacon, cheese, and vinegar" (*posca*).

113. Michaels therefore argues that Ps 69:21 cannot be in view, noting that the persistent assumption of its importance is allowed to "override" what the Gospel actually says, that the action was not hostile (against Keener 2:1146).

by his disciples, the Father has not abandoned him (16:32).[114] Jesus' unity with the Father is such that it cannot be severed. True, Jesus' resurrection and return to the Father are yet to come, but they are virtually implicit and contained in Jesus' "laying down his life," since he lays it down *only* to take it up again, as the Father has charged him (10:18). The pronouncement that his work has been completed appropriately summarizes both Jesus' purposeful, willing engagement of his destiny and his inseparable unity with God.

The phrase "gave up his spirit" is similar to the idiom "to give up one's life" (*paradidonai tēn psychēn*)[115] and probably means simply, "He died." Because the Gospel has stated earlier that the Holy Spirit will be given upon Jesus' glorification, some have seen "the spirit" as a reference to the Holy Spirit: as Jesus dies, the Spirit is given.[116] But that seems to stretch the idiom "gave up his spirit" too far[117] and leaves little room for the later account in John, where Jesus "breathes" the Spirit on the disciples with the explicit charge "receive the Holy Spirit" (*labete pneuma hagion*, 20:22). Taken together, Jesus' pronouncement "It is finished," his bowing of his head, and giving up his spirit picture him as willingly giving his life: "No one takes it from me" (10:18).[118]

[31–35] And so Jesus dies. It is Friday afternoon, and the Sabbath is imminent. According to Deut 21:22–23, no corpse that is hung on a tree may remain there all night, or else the land will be defiled. In Deuteronomy it is apparently the corpse of a person already executed that is hung on a tree, for purposes of further exposing and shaming the wrongdoer; the Mishnah follows this interpretation (*m. Sanh.* 6:4). But in the *Temple Scroll*, the passage from Deuteronomy is interpreted with reference to crucifixion, or hanging a living person (11Q19 LXIV, 6–12; cf. 4Q169 frgs. 3–4). Although the Romans often left victims of crucifixion unburied, Jewish practice, in keeping with the dictates of

114. It is arguable whether either Matthew or Mark intends to say that God abandoned or forsook Jesus as he died. Jesus' prayer of lament expresses genuine anguish, an appeal to God for help and deliverance; but it is not an assertion of God's abandonment of the suffering righteous one; and the Synoptics, too, understand the cross as completing Jesus' mission.

115. Isa 53:12 LXX, *paredothē eis thanaton hē psychē autou*, "his life was handed over to death"; cf. Acts 15:26.

116. E.g., R. Brown 1994, 2:1082.

117. Note the parallel expressions in Matt 27:50, Jesus "released his spirit" (*aphēken to pneuma*), and Luke 23:46, "I commit my spirit" (*paratithemai to pneuma mou*).

118. The last verb in John 19:30, *paradidōmi*, is used of Jesus' being "handed over" to death: Judas "hands over" Jesus to the authorities (6:64, 71; 12:4; 13:2, 11, 21; 18:2, 5), who "hand over" Jesus to Pilate (18:30, 35–36), who in turn "hands over" Jesus to be crucified (19:16). Jesus' "handing over" of his spirit could then be taken as the last act of "handing over": although others have handed him over, Jesus now hands his own spirit over (to the Father) and "lays down his life on his own" (10:18). This interpretation is largely correct, even if it reads too much out of the verb taken apart from its object. Indeed, Jesus has been handing himself over all along the way toward his death.

Deut 21, required burial before sundown.[119] Not only was Sabbath approaching; this Sabbath was also a high day: it was time to keep the Passover.

Apparently in order to hasten death, the Jews ask that Pilate allow the soldiers to break the legs of those being crucified. Breaking the legs (*crurifragium*) was a brutal act that accompanied other forms of torture, mutilation, and execution.[120] The Roman statesmen Seneca advised his readers not to condemn their slaves or to break their legs;[121] this is exactly what Augustus ordered done to his secretary, Thallus, for taking a bribe.[122] Even if designed to hasten death, *crurifragium* was scarcely an act of mercy (the coup de grâce), but one more mark of the brutality of crucifixion. Given the fact that Pilate has acquiesced to all that "the Jews" have asked him to do, it is not surprising that he apparently grants their petition here as well. The soldiers comply, breaking the legs of those crucified with Jesus. But they find Jesus already dead.

The Jews have requested that the legs of all the victims, not just those of Jesus, be broken; John notes that the soldiers break the legs of the other two men before turning to Jesus. In other words, all the parties (the Jewish authorities, Pilate, the soldiers) assume that the three men are still living. The reader of the Gospel, of course, knows that Jesus is already dead. Having expected to find Jesus alive, one of the soldier's thrusts his spear into Jesus' side either to establish or ensure Jesus' death, or perhaps both.[123] The two additional notes that "blood and water" come out of Jesus' pierced side, and that there is a witness to it, serve to verify Jesus' death. But how?

The answer depends partially on how one construes the significance of the flow of blood and water: is it a token of any normal death, or does it portend a miraculous event? Since, in the narrative, the soldiers expect to hasten Jesus' death, instead find him already dead, and seek to verify his death, the "water and blood" should be construed as corroboration that Jesus has indeed died.[124] But Jesus' death completes his mission: it gives life to the world (6:52–59); it

119. Josephus (*J.W.* 4.317) contrasts Roman impiety, discarding dead bodies without burial, with Jewish care in burying the condemned and crucified before sundown. See also Philo, *Flacc.* 83; and comments at 19:38 below.

120. Polybius, *Hist.* 1.80.13.

121. Seneca, *Ira* 3.32.1.

122. Suetonius, *Aug.* 67.2; cf. Polybius, *Hist.* 1.80.13.

123. R. Brown (1994, 2:1177) suggests that the soldier "stabbed" (*enyxen*) at the body to see if there would be any reaction (contrast *exekentēsan*, "pierced," 19:37); he cites Quintilian (*Decl.* 6.9), who refers to crucified victims who had been "pierced" [*percussos*].

124. Talbert stresses that *ichōr* ("serum") not *haima* ("blood") was thought to flow in the veins of gods and thus argues that the attestation of water and blood flowing from Jesus' side establishes his humanity; Plutarch, *Alex.* 28.2 (when wounded, Alexander tells onlookers, "This is blood, not *ichōr*"; quoting Homer, *Il.* 5.340; the story is repeated in Plutarch, *Mor.* 180E, 341B); but Koester (2003, 201) suggests that ancient physiology held that *ichōr* or *hydōr* (water) flowed in the veins of human beings along with blood. In either case, the point remains the same.

completes the cleansing of his own (13:1–11). Hence the flow of "water and blood" from Jesus' side signals the purificatory and life-giving power of Jesus' death.[125] To say, then, that the one who saw these things has testified to them is to say that he bears witness, not merely to the fact of Jesus' death, but also to the life-giving work of Jesus effected through his death.

Throughout the Gospel, "seeing" refers both to physical sight and to deeper insight or understanding (e.g., 9:39–41), and likely both such "sight" and "insight" are in view here as well. The one who *has seen* has *testified*.[126] He reports what he saw, but as a witness he does more: he provides testimony that serves as an appeal to faith. Both the reality of what was seen and its proper understanding are emphasized: but it is less clear why this is needed. Had someone denied that Jesus was a human being of flesh and blood, had actually died on the cross, or that his death on the cross had brought his purifying work to its climax? Such views are known in early Christianity; and 1 John may be written to combat some of them (see 1 John 1:8–10; 2:1–2; 3:3; 4:2; 5:7–8). The witness whose testimony is reported is surely "the disciple whom Jesus loved," the only male disciple said to be at the cross.[127] The editorial observation, "He knows that he speaks the truth," may be the beloved disciple's oblique way of asserting his own truthfulness; or it may be the comment of others about him (cf. 21:24 and comments there). This disciple figures particularly in John's Passion Narrative: he appears at the Last Supper, the cross, and the empty tomb, and he is present when Jesus appears to the disciples at the Sea of Galilee. Not surprisingly, his testimony focuses particularly on the significance of Jesus' death.

[36–37] The events that transpire after Jesus' death fulfill two scriptural passages. The first explains why Jesus' legs were not broken; the second concerns the soldier's spear thrust into Jesus' side. The first citation, "Not one of his bones shall be broken," alludes either to the Lord's instructions to Moses and Aaron regarding the Passover lamb: "You shall not break any of its bones" (Exod 12:46) or to the promise of God's protection of the righteous in the Psalms: "[The LORD] keeps all their bones; not one of them will be broken" (Ps 34:20 [33:21 LXX]). While John's citation may echo both Old Testament passages, the Greek wording of John points first of all to the promise in the

125. In keeping with 7:37–39, the water that flows from Jesus' side may symbolize the Spirit, given after Jesus is glorified (20:22), the means of cleansing (13:1–11), new birth (3:3, 5), instruction of the disciples (14:26; 15:26; 16:13), and conviction of the world's unbelief (16:8–10). See further Koester 2003, 200–203.

126. In 3:31–32, the one who is "of/from the earth" (John the Baptist) "testifies to what he has seen and heard"; for the linkage of "seeing" and "testifying," see also 1:32, 34; 3:11; on the eyewitness as interpreter, see comments on 12:37–43 above.

127. The nouns and pronouns identify the disciple whom Jesus loved and the one who testified as male.

psalm.[128] The quotation from the psalm serves the purpose of demonstrating God's protection of the righteous, in spite of appearances to the contrary.

Among those contrary appearances are the crucifixion itself and the Roman soldier's piercing of Jesus' side, which is interpreted by a quote from Zech 12:10, "They shall see the one whom they have pierced." Although Scripture has foreseen the soldier's action, it is taken not so much as foreshadowing the spear thrust itself as its result: they "shall see [*opsontai*] him whom they have pierced."[129] This quotation from Zech 12:10 may refer to the piercing of one from the house of Judah by the nations (12:9). But in John's context, the prophecy—or promise—that they will "see him whom they have pierced" also anticipates Jesus' appearance to Thomas, who is invited to see the wounds left by nails and spear, and believe that this crucified victim is now living, in keeping with the testimony of his fellow disciples: "We have seen the Lord!" (20:25; cf. "pierced" in Rev 1:7).

Taken together, these two quotations from Scripture demonstrate that, while the Romans take action to ensure that Jesus has died, to the bitter end no one has taken Jesus' life from him; he and no other has given it up. They do not need to break Jesus' legs; the piercing of Jesus' side does not cause his death. Yet he indeed does die, and they may see him as the one whom they have pierced. But if they truly see the crucified one, they may live, even as those who looked upon the brass serpent in the wilderness would live (3:14–15; 8:28; 12:32, 34). The one they will see is the righteous King, unjustly crucified, but guarded by God and raised again to life.

[38–42] Following Jesus' death, Joseph of Arimathea, a "secret" or "hidden" disciple (12:42) takes the initiative to ask Pilate whether he might remove Jesus' body for burial; Joseph's status as "one of the authorities" might explain why Pilate grants his request. The Jews considered it impious to abandon the corpses of the dead; to be left unburied was a humiliation, often evidence of divine judgment.[130] Roman law allowed the bodies of those executed to be

128. The passive form of the verb "shall be broken" (*syntribēsetai*) in 19:36 is identical to the verb in Ps 33:21 LXX (34:20 ET), whereas in Exod 12:46 the verb *syntripsete* is in the imperative mood. Elsewhere in John where Jesus is portrayed as "the Lamb" (1:29, 36), Passover is not mentioned; where Passover is in view (chs. 2, 6, and the Passion Narrative), there is no explicit reference to a lamb. In connection with Passover in John 6, Jesus is likened to the manna that provided sustenance for the wilderness pilgrimage; 6:51–58 may allude to the Passover lamb whose blood secured Israel's release from Egypt.

129. The quotation reflects the Hebrew; the LXX reads quite differently: John 19:37, *opsontai eis hon exekentēsan*; Zech 12:10 LXX, *epiblepsontai pros me anth' hōn katōrchēsanto*. For thorough discussion of this quotation and text types, see Bynum.

130. Even those condemned and executed were to be buried; Deut 21:22–23. See further Deut 28:25–26; 1 Kgs 14:11; 21:23–24; 2 Kgs 9:33–37; Jer 7:33; 8:2; 14:16; 16:4; 22:19; 25:33; Ezek 29:5; Josephus, *J.W.* 1.594; 4.317, 360; *Ag. Ap.* 2.205, 211. Philo (*Ios.* 22–23) has Jacob lamenting that he would have buried Joseph sumptuously. Tobit's special virtue was burying the dead (1:18–20; 2:3–8; 4:3–4; 6:15; 14:10–13).

given to their relatives for burial.[131] Philo reports that the bodies of the condemned and crucified were taken down and given to their relatives so that they might receive a proper burial (*Flacc.* 83). Joseph's request underscores the point that neither Pilate nor the soldiers would have taken any pains to see to the disposition of the body. Joseph's action is therefore an act of honoring Jesus.[132]

In John's account, Nicodemus—the Pharisee who had earlier come to Jesus by night (3:1) and later pleaded that Jesus be given a just hearing, as the law requires (7:50–51)—joins Joseph, bringing an exorbitant quantity of perfumes and spices, to be placed within the linen cloths wrapped around Jesus' body. Burial with spices and ointments was customary.[133] In describing Herod's burial, Josephus refers to the "sweet spices" carried by five hundred servants and freedman.[134] This is not the practice of embalming, but of masking the odors of decay. Nicodemus's generous provision of myrrh and aloes corresponds to Mary's extravagant use of costly perfume to wash and anoint Jesus' feet (12:1–8). Both Mary and Nicodemus expend enormous sums of money to see that Jesus is properly and honorifically buried as king. There is a tinge of irony even in the actions of Jesus' well-meaning friends: while they ensure that Jesus is buried with all dignity and honor, they will soon find that the tomb in which he was laid after their careful preparation of his body is empty. Still, his death is no mere illusion: his body is prepared to be entombed and then laid in a nearby tomb, a "new tomb" in which no one had ever been laid.[135]

The description here and later of Mary and the disciples going "into" the tomb, suggests one of the many "rock-cut tombs [that] are artificially hewn, underground caves cut into the bedrock slopes around Jerusalem,"[136] with niches (*loculi*) intended for a single body. Because of the expense involved in the preparation of such tombs, they belonged to and were used by families over the generations with the means to pay for them.[137] This tomb may have been the family tomb of Joseph, perhaps an indirect mirroring of Jesus' reconfiguring of his family when, as he dies, he entrusts his mother and the disciple whom he loved to each other. This tomb is located in an unnamed garden, even

131. *Dig.* 48.24.1; 48.24.3. The *Digest* (of Roman laws) was compiled by command of Justinian (527–65) and gathered up earlier laws; what happens in John fits with laws recorded there.

132. Contrast Josephus's description of the execution and burial of Achan: *en nykti taphēs atimou*, "he was buried at night in disgrace" (*Ant.* 5.44; see Josh 7:25).

133. In the other Gospels, Joseph buries Jesus after wrapping the body in linen cloths. It is the women who come early on Sunday morning, intending to treat the body with spices and ointments (Matt 27:57–61; 28:1; Mark 15:43–16:2; Luke 23:50–24:1).

134. See Josephus (*J.W.* 1.671–73) for the elaborate ornamentation of Herod's bier and body in kingly regalia.

135. The so-called Garden Tomb, just outside the Damascus Gate, cannot mark the site of Jesus' entombment: that tomb, from the period of the First Temple (ca. 830 B.C.E.), is hardly a "new" tomb.

136. See Magness 145–80.

137. Note that Matt 27:57 describes Joseph as "rich."

as Jesus was accosted by the Romans in a garden across the Kidron Valley (18:1). John does not identify these two gardens with each other, and neither is named Gethsemane. Because of the imminent approach of the Sabbath and the proximity of the tomb to the cross, Jesus is buried there. Joseph's request to Pilate to bury Jesus and Nicodemus's contribution of myrrh and aloes have ensured a proper burial for the one who has been crucified as "King of the Jews."

While John does not narrate the placement of the stone over Jesus' tomb, once they had prepared Jesus' body and placed it in the tomb, Joseph and Nicodemus would have sealed it with a stone (cf. 20:1; 11:38–39, 41). Neither those who crucified Jesus nor those who buried him have any reason to believe that this is anything other than the end of Jesus' life. If they had heard Jesus' final words, "It is finished," they surely would understand them to indicate just that: "It is finished."

John 20:1–21:25
The Resurrection of Jesus

"Suffered under Pontius Pilate, was crucified, died, and was buried": neither the Apostles' Creed nor the Gospel ends there. Indeed, the Gospel of John has anticipated an afterlife to the story of Jesus in the life of Jesus' disciples. They will need comfort (14:1, 27), instruction (14:26; 16:13), prayer (14:13–14; 16:23–24), faith (14:1, 11), love (15:12–17), perseverance (16:1), courage (16:33), protection (17:9–12, 15), and unity (17:20–23) for their ongoing life together and in the face of various challenges to faith (15:18–25; 16:2). With Jesus' death, the story of Jesus' followers has just begun.

But Jesus has not abandoned the disciples (14:18). The accounts of the discovery of the empty tomb and Jesus' appearances testify that he lives (6:57; 14:19). His disciples bear witness to his resurrection in the form of the confession "We have seen the Lord!"[1] Jesus' tomb has been found to be opened and empty, and the disciples have *seen* the risen Lord (cf. Acts 26:16; 1 Cor 9:1), even as they *saw* his glory throughout the course of his ministry (John 2:11; 11:40; 14:9). So while Jesus will be with and among the disciples (14:23), he will be with them as the one who has been raised to life with the Father (1:18; 7:33; 8:21; 13:33–36; 14:4, 12, 28; 16:5, 10, 17; 17:11, 13; 20:17). The mode of Jesus' presence with his disciples differs after his death and resurrection.

John's account of Jesus' resurrection appearances links seeing and believing, and it calls for faith in the risen Lord. The disciple whom Jesus loves believes when he sees the empty tomb (20:8). Mary responds to Jesus when he calls her by name (20:16, 18). Those to whom Jesus appears in the upper room rejoice when they see the Lord (20:20). Upon seeing Jesus, Thomas confesses him as "My Lord and my God" (20:28). Even as the signs point beyond themselves, bearing witness to Jesus as the life-giving Son of the Father and thereby inviting faith, the resurrection appearances attest that the Son now lives and similarly call for faith.[2] But recognition of the risen Jesus requires his self-disclosure.

1. Compare "The Lord has risen indeed!" (Luke 24:34); "He has been raised" (Matt 28:6–7; Mark 16:6).

2. On the resurrection appearances in John, see esp. Lincoln 1998; Attridge 2008; Painter 2008; Koester 2008a; Wright 662–82.

Jesus must address his own by name, speak to them, show them his hands and side, or invite them to eat with him. Without Jesus' self-manifestation, the disciples do not recognize him. Now, as before, Jesus takes the initiative and reveals himself, seeking the response of faith.

John's accounts of Jesus' resurrection appearances also emphasize the restoration of personal relationship with Jesus that have appeared to be broken by the events of Good Friday. In John, unlike the other Gospels, individual disciples are singled out in Jesus' appearances: the risen Jesus calls Mary by name (20:16), directly addresses Thomas and invites him to believe (20:27–29), and commissions Peter to take care of his flock (21:15–18). But Jesus' appearances and invitations do not signal a return to the past. The disciples now enter into a relationship with the one whom death cannot destroy, who has and gives eternal life: they can now receive the promise of having "life in his name" (20:31).

Without the resurrection, the whole of the Gospel's witness collapses: if the one who has revealed himself repeatedly as life now lies dead in a tomb, then the promises that he will be with the disciples, confer the Spirit, and give and sustain them in life—indeed, that he himself *is* the resurrection and the life—will come to nothing (11:25). The resurrection testifies that Jesus is living, that he has "life in himself" and can confer this life on others. He has not returned to life as it was, but both enters into and inaugurates the life of the resurrection. Trusting in God and the one whom he has sent, infused with the Spirit and sent in his name, the disciples are to continue to follow Jesus and to bear witness to him, participating in the Father's life-giving work through the Son by offering the forgiveness of sins and by tending Jesus' flock.

With the resurrection of Jesus, everything has changed: Jesus will not be with the disciples as he was before, because he has not returned to life as before. And yet nothing has changed: Jesus' call to the disciples is still "Follow me!" (1:43; 21:19, 22). The circumstances differ, and the mode of Jesus' presence with the disciples in those circumstances differs radically. But even after Jesus' resurrection some things remain unchanged for all disciples: they are called to believe, to respond to the voice of the master, to confess him as Lord, and to follow him faithfully.

20:1–10 The Discovery of the Empty Tomb

Only John contains the account of Simon Peter and the beloved disciple's hurrying together to the tomb in response to Mary Magdalene's report that the tomb has been opened and the body of Jesus removed (20:1–2).[3] Here, as elsewhere, when the beloved disciple features in the narrative, he appears to surpass Peter

3. Luke reports that upon hearing the reports of the women that they had found the tomb empty, Peter runs to the tomb and finds only the linen cloths (Luke 24:12).

in some way: he lies closer to Jesus at the Last Supper, remains at the foot of the cross when the other (male) disciples have abandoned or denied Jesus, bests Peter in a footrace to the tomb, and "believes" when they find it empty; when fishing together on the Sea of Galilee, he is the first to recognize the risen Jesus. All that constitutes the beloved disciple's alleged superiority—his proximity and faithfulness to Jesus, his presence at the empty tomb and early belief in Jesus—show him to be the ideal witness to testify to the crucified and risen Lord. That is how he functions throughout the Gospel and with respect to Simon Peter (19:35; 21:24). Like the Gospel itself, the beloved disciple serves as a witness to lead others to faith (20:30–31).

20:1 On the first day of the week, when it was still dark, Mary Magdalene
went to the tomb and saw that the stone had been removed from the tomb.
2 So she ran and went to Simon Peter and the other disciple, whom Jesus
loved, and said to them, "They have taken the Lord from the tomb, and
we do not know where they have laid him."

3 Then Peter and the other disciple set out toward the tomb. **4** The two
ran together. And the other disciple ran more quickly than Peter and came
to the tomb first. **5** And stooping down, he saw the linen cloths lying there,
but he did not go in.

6 Then Simon Peter came, following him, and he went into the tomb.
And he saw the linen cloths lying there, **7** and the facecloth, which had
been on his head, not lying with the linen cloths, but folded up by itself,
in another place.

8 Then the other disciple, who had come first to the tomb, also went
in, and he saw and believed. **9** For as yet they did not know the Scripture
that it was necessary for him to rise from the dead. **10** Then the disciples
returned[a] to where they were staying.[b]

a. "Returned" translates "went away again" (*apēlthon . . . palin*).

b. Lit., "to them" or "to themselves" (*pros autous*); sometimes translated "home," the sense is that they returned to their quarters, to the places that they had been staying. "To them" could conceivably mean "to the others" (i.e., the other disciples), but it is not clear that they had all been staying or gathered together when Mary first made her report (cf. 20:1–2).

[20:1–2] The week begins: it is early in the morning, and the darkness has not yet lifted when Mary Magdalene[4] goes to Jesus' tomb. She was among those who kept vigil as Jesus died (19:25); it is not clear whether the Gospel

4. In Luke (8:2), Mary Magdalene, "from whom seven demons had gone out," is one of the women accompanying Jesus. Neither in Luke nor in John is she called a sinner or prostitute; cf. Haskins for a survey of the development of patristic and medieval traditions about her.

implies that she was present as Jesus' body was wrapped in linen and laid in Joseph's tomb. Nor does the Gospel say why she went to the tomb early in the morning on the first day of the week: she is not carrying spices or ointments. She may have gone to the tomb to mourn, as Lazarus's sisters and the Jews from Jerusalem had done at Lazarus's tomb (11:31). Whatever the motivation for her early morning visit, Mary surely expects to find a sealed tomb. She discovers that the stone has been taken away from the tomb and that the body she has expected to find in it is no longer there.

Assuming that someone has removed the body of Jesus from the tomb, she hurries to report the news to Simon Peter and to "the other disciple, whom Jesus loved." Simon Peter was last seen in the courtyard of the high priest (18:15); the disciple whom Jesus loved was one of those at the cross along with the women (19:26, 35). It is appropriate, therefore, that they be the first to learn that the tomb in which Jesus had been buried has been opened. Mary reports her finding dramatically: "They have taken the Lord out of the tomb and we do not know where they have laid him" (20:2; cf. Matt 27:63–66; 28:11–14). The plural "we" may suggest that (unnamed) others accompanied Mary Magdalene that morning, or it may simply be an assertion of a fact that would have puzzled any and all of Jesus' followers that morning. Just who Mary imagines "they" might be who took Jesus' body remains unspecified.[5] But someone must be responsible, since a dead body cannot move on its own (cf. 11:34).

[3–10] Mary's report galvanizes Peter and "the other disciple" to hurry to the tomb together. In John's account, "the other disciple" runs more quickly than Peter, arriving at the tomb first. He then peers into the tomb without entering it and sees the linen cloths in which Jesus' body had been wrapped. There is an implicit contrast with the description of the newly raised Lazarus, who emerges from the tomb still wrapped in the trappings of burial (11:44). What happened to Jesus is not identical with what happened to Lazarus: Lazarus was raised to life again; Jesus was raised to life anew. But this will become clear as the narrative progresses.

Up to this point no one has apparently entered the tomb.[6] When Simon Peter does, not only does he see the same cloths that the other disciple had seen; he also sees the cloth that had covered Jesus' head (*soudarion*, 20:7) lying folded up by itself. Again the contrast with Lazarus, whose face is "wrapped in a cloth" (*soudarion*, 11:44), comes to the fore. At this point the "other disciple" also goes into the tomb, and "he saw and believed." Naturally this raises the question, believed what?

5. Maccini (125) notes Mary's accurate visual perception (the tomb is empty) but her limited comprehension of the events.

6. On the kind of tomb implied by such statements, see comments on 19:38–42 above.

Perhaps the beloved disciple simply believes Mary's report that Jesus' body had been removed from the tomb. Even as the disciple had seen and could bear witness to Jesus' death and to the blood and water that flowed from Jesus' side (19:34–35), so now he (unknowingly) provides preliminary testimony to Jesus' resurrection: the very body that had been crucified, wrapped, and buried cannot be found in the tomb. Though he also sees the empty tomb and the gravecloths, Peter is not said to "believe" at this point. But if the beloved disciple only believes Mary Magdalene's report, then he believes what is not true: namely, that they "have taken the Lord from the tomb." Nobody has taken the body of Jesus: that is a misunderstanding that the resurrection appearances will soon correct. Such a description of the beloved disciple would be out of character with the Gospel's consistently positive depiction of his understanding and recognition of Jesus.[7]

If, unlike both Mary and Peter, the beloved disciple draws the appropriate conclusion that Jesus has risen, then he understands what they do not.[8] He understands that the opened tomb and the abandoned burial cloths bear witness that Jesus lives, as he had said he would (14:19), and that he will return to his Father (13:1, 33, 36–38; 14:3; 16:28; 17:11, 13; 20:17). Even as Jesus' signs bear witness to the life-giving Lord, so the stone now removed from the tomb, the empty tomb itself, and the burial cloths testify that the Lord is living.[9] They testify, not that Jesus' body is *missing*, but that he *has risen*, in keeping with the expectation of a bodily resurrection such as Jesus spoke of elsewhere (5:29), and as the raising of Lazarus has foreshadowed (11:24–25).

The beloved disciple believes in the resurrection before and apart from seeing the risen Lord, thus providing the initial witness to the resurrection.[10] Later Jesus reminds Thomas that some will believe—that is, believe in him—having never seen him (20:29). Here, then, the beloved disciple serves as a model for

7. The beloved disciple has continued to believe, as Jesus exhorted his disciples to do (14:1); there is no evidence that "even the Beloved Disciple . . . had to struggle toward belief" (Moloney 1998b, 543).

8. For the view that the beloved disciple believed in the resurrection, see Barrett 561, 563–64; Carson 1991, 638; Keener 2:1184; Lincoln 2005, 490–91; Lindars 602. Michaels (992) suggests that this disciple has the preliminary belief that Jesus has gone to the Father (14:28–29), but not yet a full-fledged belief in the resurrection, which includes Jesus' return to his disciples (14:18; 16:16, 22); according to Schneiders (2008, 164–65), the beloved disciple believes that on the cross Jesus was truly glorified; O'Day (841) claims he believes that "Jesus has conquered death and judged the ruler of this world," but not yet in the resurrection. The Gospel contains numerous instances of "believe" without an object: 1:7, 50; 3:12; 4:42, 53; 5:44; 6:36, 64; 9:38; 10:25–26; 11:15; 12:39; 16:31; 19:35; such usage denotes "believing" or "trusting" in Jesus and his identity as the one sent from God to bring life to the world.

9. See Koester 2008a, 47–74.

10. So also Lindars 602.

later generations, believing that Jesus has risen without seeing him. He is, in fact, the only disciple in John, or in any of the Gospels, who does so. In the episodes that follow, both Mary Magdalene and Simon Peter will see the risen Jesus and respond to him in faith: they see and believe. In fact, everyone who sees the risen Jesus in John comes to faith. But initially, and without seeing Jesus, neither Mary nor Peter believes.

After declaring that the beloved disciple believes, the Gospel explains, "For as yet they did not know the Scripture" that Jesus "must rise from the dead" (20:9; cf. 2:22), signaling that Scripture will provide further testimony to the resurrection of Jesus. John does not indicate which Scriptures are in view, but it is likely that earlier citations from the Psalms and Zechariah exemplify the point that the Scriptures at least anticipated the resurrection of Jesus (see comments on 19:36–37).[11] The beloved disciple believes without seeing Jesus or receiving the testimony of others that they have seen him, and perhaps without the witness of Scripture.[12] But he has grasped the promises spoken by Jesus to his disciples in his last words to them (14:19).[13] Later generations of disciples come to faith without seeing the empty tomb or the risen Lord, but on the basis of the joint testimony of the disciples, now recorded in the Gospel itself, and of Scripture, which confirm Jesus' own promises that he will live. Together the Scriptures (5:39), the disciples and especially the beloved disciple (19:35), and the Gospel that inscribes his witness (20:30–31; 21:23–24) point to Jesus, confirming his words and bearing witness so that others might believe. Following their discovery of the empty tomb, Simon Peter and the beloved disciple return to the other disciples. Mary remains at the tomb.

20:11–18 Jesus Appears to Mary: The Good Shepherd Calls His Own

Jesus appears first to Mary Magdalene as she is weeping at the tomb in the garden. When she does not recognize him, he simply speaks her name, "Mary!" Then she recognizes and responds to him: the good shepherd who calls his own by name, has laid down his life, but has taken it up again (10:3, 18). The encounter between Jesus and Mary attests the new situation that obtains after the resurrection. Jesus is alive, but he is departing, ascending to his Father,

11. Cf. Luke 24:25–27; Acts 2:27, 31, citing Ps 16:10; and 1 Cor 15:4.

12. It is not clear whether the statement "for as yet they did not know the Scripture" (20:9) refers to the other disciples only or includes the beloved disciple as well; if the former, it may be implied that the beloved disciple did indeed know or believe the witness of the Scriptures.

13. The beloved disciple implicitly understands what Jesus meant in such statements as "I lay down my life, in order that I may take it up again. . . . I have this authority to lay it down, and I have authority to take it up again" (10:17–18).

returning to the glory that he had before the world was made (17:24). Mary is to announce that she has seen the Lord, clarifying that the tomb was empty, not because the body had been stolen, but because Jesus had risen from the dead: he is alive. But he is not returning to his life with them as in the past: he is returning to his Father. She is to interpret the meaning of the empty tomb and of Jesus' appearance to her to his disciples.

20:11 Mary was standing outside the tomb, weeping. As she wept, she
stooped and looked into the tomb. 12 And she saw two angels in white,
sitting, one at the head and one at the feet, where the body of Jesus had
lain. 13 And they said to her. "Woman, why are you weeping?"

14 She said to them, "They have taken my Lord, and I do not know
where they have put him." After she said these things, she turned around
and saw Jesus standing there, but she did not know that it was Jesus.

15 Jesus said to her, "Woman, why are you weeping? Whom are you
looking for?" Thinking he was the gardener, she said to him, "Sir, if
you have taken him away, tell me where you have put him, and I will
take him."

16 Jesus said to her, "Mary." Turning, she said to him, in Hebrew,[a]
"Rabbouni!" (which means "Teacher").

17 Jesus said to her, "Do not touch me, for I have not yet ascended to
the Father. But go to my brothers and say to them, 'I am ascending to my
Father and to your Father, and to my God and to your God.'"

18 And Mary Magdalene went, announcing to the disciples, "I have
seen the Lord!" and that he had said these things to her.

a. The Greek has *Hebraisti*, but the form of the word is Aramaic.

[20:11–14a] Apparently Mary has remained alone at the tomb, weeping; only John refers to Mary (or any of the women) weeping at the tomb (20:11, 13, 15; cf. 11:31; 16:20). When Mary stoops to look into the tomb, she sees two angels, dressed in white, marking the place where the body of Jesus had lain (20:12). Their presence signals that God has been at work, not grave robbers, thus providing an initial impetus toward understanding that the empty tomb bears witness that Jesus is alive. The Gospel does not say that the angels have opened the tomb. Neither do the angels announce that Jesus has risen nor offer any word of comfort or exhortation (cf. Matt 28:5–7; Mark 16:6–7; Luke 24:5–7). The first words of comfort and commission will come from Jesus himself (20:16–17). In any case, Mary does not think the angels have taken Jesus' body, but that someone else has. Thus in answer to their question, "Woman, why are you weeping?" (v. 13), she repeats to them what she has first told Jesus' disciples, "They have taken away my Lord, and I do not know where they have laid him" (v. 14).

Mary's weeping verifies what Jesus had foretold: the disciples will weep and mourn (16:20). Even as Jesus loved Lazarus and wept at his tomb, so Mary Magdalene weeps at Jesus' tomb (11:31, 33–36). Thus her lament: "They have taken away *my* Lord" (20:14). But grief will turn to joy when she sees Jesus again—and that will happen soon. Thus the angels' question may gently nudge Mary toward understanding that it is not appropriate to weep, but for sorrow to turn to joy (16:20). Jesus' earlier promise, like so many others in the Farewell Discourse, anticipates the resurrection both as his triumph over death and as betokening his ongoing presence with the disciples. Mary need not lament Jesus' absence; she may rejoice that he lives.

[14b–16] Mary turns and sees but does not recognize Jesus. Failure to recognize the risen Lord is a motif familiar from other resurrection appearances (21:7; Luke 24:16, 31). Jesus repeats the angels' question ("Woman, why are you weeping?") while adding, "Whom are you looking for?" This question recalls the same question asked earlier in the Gospel (1:38; 18:4, 7) and ironically points out that the one she is looking for is standing right before her, albeit not in the form she expects. She is still seeking the body of Jesus, presumably so that she might bury it once more, thus preventing the shame of Jesus' not having a proper burial. But to paraphrase Luke, Mary is looking for the dead among the living (Luke 24:5). There has been much speculation about why Mary does not recognize Jesus: perhaps her tears blur her vision or her grief blinds her to the impossible reality of his presence; perhaps he has been so changed through the process of death and transfigured by his resurrection so as to render him unrecognizable. Whatever the explanation, as elsewhere in John, Jesus must make himself known so that he will be recognized; he must correct Mary's misunderstanding that he is dead, as he has corrected prior misunderstandings in the Gospel through revealing himself (e.g., 4:13–14, 25–26; 6:34–35).

Jesus makes himself known simply by speaking the weeping woman's name: "Mary." At this, Mary turns to Jesus: she recognizes him when he calls her by name. The good shepherd "calls his own sheep by name"; the sheep follow him "because they know his voice" and listen to it (10:3–5, 8, 16, 27). Mary responds to Jesus as *Rabbouni* (Aramaic for "my Teacher"), a form of address not found elsewhere in John. Some of the first disciples who follow Jesus address him as "Rabbi," which John translates as "Teacher" (*Didaskale*, 1:38); Martha tells her sister, Mary, that "the teacher" (*ho didaskalos*) is calling for her (11:28); after Jesus washes the disciples' feet, he speaks of himself as their teacher (*didaskalos*, 13:13–14). There Jesus also refers to himself as Lord (*ho kyrios*), a designation one might have expected Mary Magdalene to use in addressing the risen Jesus, especially since "Lord" is a common term for addressing Jesus in this Gospel (6:68; 9:38; 11:3, 12, 21, 27, 32, 34, 39; 13:6, 25, 36, 37; 14:5, 8, 22). Mary has lamented, "They have taken away my Lord" (20:2, 13; cf. v. 15); she will subsequently announce that she has seen the Lord (20:18). Now, however, she simply addresses Jesus with the designation that she has probably used most frequently: "Teacher." Even as the disciples have learned the meaning of Jesus' death from their Teacher and Lord, so they will learn the meaning of his resurrection from their Teacher as well.

[17] Jesus' response, in a nutshell, informs Mary that his appearance to her does not constitute a return to things as they were before his death and resurrection. While that overall point seems clear enough, prickly problems remain in understanding Jesus' words "Do not touch me" (*mē mou haptou*):[14] what, exactly, does Jesus forbid Mary to do, and why?[15] In the light of Jesus' later invitation to Thomas to put his finger into the wounds of the risen Jesus, Jesus' subsequent words to Mary, "For I have not yet ascended to my Father," are sometimes taken as explanatory: once Jesus has ascended, Mary will be able or invited to touch him. But that explanation causes more problems than it solves: it assumes that Jesus' return to the Father has taken place between his appearances to Mary and Thomas, and that it is somehow possible to touch the ascended Jesus, who is with the Father, but not the risen Jesus, who stands in front of her. The text seems to assume, rather, that both Mary and Thomas *can* touch Jesus: if not, why the prohibition to Mary?[16]

The thrust of Jesus' command not to touch him may be illumined by juxtaposing it with Jesus' command to "go to my brothers" in order to tell them that he is about to ascend[17] "to my God and your God, to my Father and your Father." For the risen Lord whom Mary now sees, and who can indeed be touched, has not returned to be with her or the disciples but is ascending to his Father. This is what Mary must go and tell Jesus' "brothers." She has not found Jesus' corpse; she has encountered the risen Lord. But there is more: Jesus is now returning to the Father. Although often spoken of together, Jesus' resur-

14. For a survey and analysis of various interpretations of John 20:17, see Bieringer 2008.

15. *Haptomai* means "touch" (see BDAG; LSJM). Other translations suggest "Do not hold me" (RSV; "Do not hold on to me," NRSV, NIV; cf. CEB) or "Stop clinging to me" (NASB), perhaps with an eye toward the account in Matthew, where Mary Magdalene and "the other Mary" have taken hold of (*ekratēsan*) Jesus' feet (Matt 28:1, 9). Bieringer (2008, 231) shows that in the LXX *haptomai* ("I touch") sometimes translates the Hebrew *qārab* ("to come near, approach").

16. Notice the striking contrast to Homer's descriptions of the dead as phantoms: Achilles could not embrace (*amphibalounte*) the deceased Patroclus, for the spirit vanished like a "wisp of smoke"; Patroclus was only a "spirit [*psychē*] and semblance of a man [*eidōlon*]" (*Il.* 23.94–104). When Odysseus met his deceased mother, Anticleia, and three times tried to "clasp" (*heleein*, from *haireō*, "take with the hand, grasp, seize") her, "three times she flitted from my arms like a shadow [*skiē*] or a dream [*oneiros*]" (*Od.* 11.206–8). Cf. Isa 14:9.

17. The present tense "I am ascending" may be so read, or even as "I will ascend."

rection and ascension are not a single event in John; Mary sees the living Lord, and he must now return to his Father.[18]

The form of the announcement she is to relate to Jesus' disciples is peculiar to John in two ways. First, Jesus himself, and not a heavenly messenger, reveals that he is alive (cf. Matt 28:6; Mark 16:6; Luke 24:5). Second, Jesus does not say, "I have been raised" (perhaps because that is revealed by his appearance to Mary), but "I am ascending to my Father." In Jesus' farewell to his disciples, he spoke of going away (14:2, 4, 28; 16:7) and of going to the Father (14:12, 28; 16:5, 10, 17, 28; 17:11, 13). When he spoke of his own resurrection, he did so not by saying he would "rise from the dead" but that he would live (6:57; 14:19). Jesus' appearances mean that he is living, but he has not returned to his previous existence on earth: he will return to the Father, who sent him.

As much as Mary wants to stay with Jesus, to have him restored to her, she cannot hold on to him or cling to the relationship that existed prior to his death and resurrection, because he has not returned to the same mode of existence as he had before. Jesus is, instead, ascending to the Father; now glorified, participating in the new life of the resurrection, he returns to the glory he had with the Father (17:5, 24). If "touching" or "holding" Jesus signals Mary's expectation of a return to the state of affairs before Jesus' crucifixion, then his charge to "go and say to my brothers, 'I am ascending to the Father'" interprets the new situation in which she now finds herself.[19] In effect, Mary is to tell the other disciples that she has seen the Lord *and* that this does not mean that he has returned to live with them as before: rather, he is returning to his Father, even as he said he would. To bear witness to the risen Lord is to testify that his mission has been completed, and that he has returned, as promised, to the Father who sent him (14:28; 17:13).

In a striking formulation, Jesus refers to God as "my God and your God, my Father and your Father," thus simultaneously joining himself with, and distinguishing himself from, the disciples. This is the Gospel's first use of "brothers" (*adelphous*)[20] to refer to Jesus' disciples, and in speaking to the disciples, the

18. So also Barrett 566; Moloney 1998a, 167; Ridderbos 638; D. Moody Smith 1999, 378; somewhat differently, R. Brown 1970, 1014–15. Since John does not narrate the ascension as an observable incident (cf. Acts 1:9–11), it is difficult to discern when John thinks that Jesus has indeed returned to the Father.

19. See especially Lindars 607: "The Resurrection appearances attest the new situation, but they are not a substitute for it. The desire to hold Jesus must be restrained, because it is an attempt to recapture the conditions of the incarnate life in place of the universal and abiding relationship which is the object of his mission."

20. If the Twelve (or the Eleven, without Judas) are in view, then "brothers" would be an accurate translation. However, *adelphous* can include men and women, thus identifying all disciples of Jesus as members of his family, with God as their common Father. The same term in 21:23 includes the entire fellowship (hence, "the community" [NRSV] or "the believers" [NIV]).

first and only reference to God as "your Father" (contrast 8:41, 42, 44). There is no reference in John to God as "our father," by which Jesus includes the disciples with himself in such address. The differences between the relationship of Jesus and of the disciples to the Father remain, but through the life-giving work of the Son, the disciples—and others—may enter into the relationship of kinship granted to them by the Son.[21] They are children of God (*tekna tou theou*), begotten of God (1:12–13; 3:3, 5) through the life and work of the Son of God (*huios tou theou*), who is from God—a terminological distinction that John consistently maintains. After Jesus' resurrection, anticipating the giving of the Spirit, Jesus' disciples are referred to as *adelphoi* ("brothers and sisters"), a term that plays an important role in 1 John as the basis for the call to unity and love among believers (3:13, 14, 16). God's purpose to call together a family, a people who will honor the Son as they honor the Father, begun in Jesus' mission (3:3, 5) and anticipated in his crucifixion (19:26–27), has been realized through Jesus' resurrection.

[18] Curiously, in spite of Jesus' instruction that Mary is to tell the disciples that he is returning to the Father, Mary's report neither repeats nor alludes to Jesus' words to her. Instead, she declares, "I have seen the Lord!" (20:18; cf. v. 25). John frames encounters with the risen Lord in terms of having "seen" Jesus, because seeing, or being with Jesus and in his presence, grounds his disciples' testimony to him.[22] Even as Jesus' disciples saw his glory in his earthly life (1:14; 20:30), so now they see the risen Lord and will bear witness to him, interpreting to others what they have seen.

20:19–23 Jesus Appears to His Disciples: The Giving of the Holy Spirit

At this point in the Gospel, only Mary Magdalene has seen the risen Lord. But on the evening of the same day, Jesus appears to "the disciples." The appearance to these disciples is similar to that recorded in Luke 24:36–43, but it has several distinctive features: (1) Jesus sends the disciples as he was sent by the Father; (2) he "breathes" the Holy Spirit on them; and (3) he tells them that they are to forgive sins. With the giving of the Spirit, Jesus thus fulfills the promise made earlier to his disciples in the Gospel, that upon his return to the Father, he would send the Holy Spirit (14:26). Having received the Spirit, Jesus' disciples act on Jesus' behalf, extending his ministry to take away sin (1:29, 36; 8:31–36) by offering forgiveness to others. The disciples are said to be glad

21. The same can be said of the other Gospels as well; the distinction may go back to the peculiar identity of Israel's king as a son of God (2 Sam 7:12–14; Ps 2:7), distinguished from the Israelites as God's children; see M. M. Thompson 2000.

22. Cf. 1 Cor 9:1: "Am I not an apostle? Have I not seen Jesus our Lord?"

(cf. 16:16–22) and to have peace (cf. 14:1). What Jesus had promised before his death comes to fruition through his presence with the disciples and giving of the Holy Spirit after his resurrection.

> **20:19** When it was evening on that day, the first day of the week, and the
> doors were shut where the disciples were for fear of the Jews, Jesus came
> and stood in their midst and said to them, "Peace be with you." **20** When
> he had said this, he showed them his hands and his side. And the disciples
> were glad when they saw the Lord.
> **21** Then he said to them again, "Peace be with you. Even as the Father
> sent me, so also I send you." **22** And when he had said this, he breathed
> and said to them, "Receive the Holy Spirit. **23** If you forgive the sins of
> any, they are forgiven; and if you keep the sins of any, they are kept."

[20:19–20] Mary's encounter with the risen Jesus occurs on the morning of the first day of the week; Jesus' first encounter with the rest of his disciples occurs in the evening of that same day. Thomas, "one of the Twelve," is not with them (20:24). The Gospel does not specify who "the disciples" are; elsewhere they comprise a larger group than the Twelve (6:66–67; 20:24). Whoever "the disciples" may be, and however many of them are in view, they are gathered together, behind locked doors, "for fear of the Jews." Elsewhere in the Gospel, certain persons do not speak openly or publicly acknowledge Jesus out of "fear of the Jews" (7:13; 9:22; 12:42) or "of the Pharisees" (19:38). Here the disciples share that fear and, as a result, hide themselves. In the aftermath of Jesus' execution, the disciples fear for their own lives (cf. 16:2). Apparently they do not accept Mary's testimony that she has seen the Lord; at least her report has made no difference to their conduct or faith.

Jesus simply "came and stood among them." John does not say that Jesus walked through the door; he is neither a phantom nor a ghost. Yet clearly John portrays Jesus' presence with his disciples as occasional: they can neither predict nor control his appearances. In spite of closed doors and the seclusion of the frightened disciples, Jesus finds them, even as he found the man who had been driven out by the Pharisees, and appears among them. Nothing keeps Jesus, the good shepherd, from finding his own (see 9:22, 34–38; 10:4, 15–16, 27–28).[23]

Calming the disciples' fear with the traditional greeting of peace (Greek, *eirēnē*; Hebrew, *šālôm*),[24] Jesus identifies himself by showing them the wounds

23. Hoskyns 544.

24. Cf. Luke 10:5; 24:36; salutations in NT Letters (Rom 1:7; 1 Cor 1:3; 2 Cor 1:2; Gal 1:3; Eph 1:2; Phil 1:2; 1 Tim 1:2; 2 Tim 1:2; Titus 1:4; Phlm 1:3; 1 Pet 1:2; 2 Pet 1:2; 2 John 1:3; Rev 1:4).

in his hands and side, confirming that the one standing in front of them is the one who was crucified on the cross, whose death was corroborated by the thrust of the Roman spear into his side. Since only the beloved disciple and the women at the cross had witnessed these events, it is curious that Jesus would show the gathered disciples the tokens of his crucified body. But the disciples knew Jesus had been taken away, so the wounds left by the nails, and other signs of abuse or torture, would remind them of what happened to him after he had ordered their release (18:8). In any case, the point is clear, especially for the reader: the crucified Jesus is now the risen one, whose presence with the disciples is not restricted by the conditions of fleshly existence or earthly mortality. And the disciples rejoice because they "saw the Lord," fulfilling the promise of Jesus that although they would grieve, their grief would turn to joy (16:20–22). In Jesus' presence, there is joy (3:29) and there will be joy (15:11; 16:20–24; 17:13).

[21–23] Repeating his greeting, Jesus emphasizes that he brings peace, as he has promised (14:27; 16:33). But he has also come to send the disciples on a mission that has parallels to his own: now Jesus sends them *even as* the Father has sent him (v. 21); the disciples are given the Holy Spirit, even as the Spirit had descended and remained on Jesus (v. 22; 1:32–33); their mission has to do with forgiving sins, even as Jesus' had to do with taking away sin (v. 23; 1:29).

Echoing words from his prayer to the Father,[25] Jesus directly commissions the disciples, sending them as the Father sent him. The conjunction *kathōs* ("even as") indicates a parallelism between the way in which the Father sent Jesus and the way in which Jesus sends the disciples.[26] There is, first, the simple parallelism of being sent: Jesus is sent by the Father; the disciples are now sent by Jesus. Even as the Father sent Jesus into the world to bring life to the world (3:16; 5:26) and gave him the Spirit (1:33; 3:34), so now the glorified (i.e., crucified and risen) Jesus (7:37–39) breathes out the life-giving Holy Spirit and commissions the disciples to extend his life-giving work in the world through the forgiveness of sins (cf. 8:21; 16:8–11; 14:12). Prior to his arrest, Jesus had prayed that the disciples be "consecrated," set apart for the work and purposes of God, even as he had been consecrated (or sanctified) by the Father (10:36) and had consecrated himself (the Greek word throughout is *hagiazein*; 17:17,

25. John 17:18, "Even as you sent me into the world, so I have sent them into the world."

26. "Even as the Father sent [*apestalken*, from *apostellō*] me, so also I send [*pempō*] you." Both *apostellein* (e.g., 5:36, 38; 6:29, 57; 7:29; 8:42; 11:42) and *pempein* (e.g., 4:34; 5:24, 30, 37; 6:38, 39, 44) are used in John of Jesus' being sent by the Father, apparently without distinction. In the participial phrase "the one who sent me," the verb is always from *pempō*; hence, *ho pempsas*, whether for Jesus or John the Baptist (1:33). Cf. Barrett 569.

19). As the one who baptizes,[27] or purifies, with the Spirit, and as the Lamb of God who takes away the sin of the world (cf. 1:24–34), Jesus breathes out the purifying Spirit. As recipients of the life that Jesus bestows, the disciples now participate in conferring that life on others (cf. 2 Cor 5:20). "The sending of the Son *into* the world both establishes and demands the sending of the disciples *within* the world."[28]

The description of Jesus' breathing the Spirit uses the Greek word *enephysēsen* ("he breathed," from *emphysaō*), the word that describes God's "breathing" into Adam the "breath of life" (*pnoēn zōēs*) so that Adam becomes "a living being" (*psychēn zōsan*, Gen 2:7 LXX). The account of the creation of humankind in Genesis becomes, in turn, the template for the description of God's breathing life into the desiccated bones of the people of Israel (Ezek 37:9; cf. 1 Kgs 17:21; Wis 15:11). Since in both Hebrew and Greek, the same words can mean "spirit" and "breath" (*rûaḥ*, *pneuma*), when God "breathes" into someone, God infuses "spirit."[29] God's breath, God's spirit, brings about the life and renewal of God's holy people.[30]

Those who understand the present passage to be about Jesus' equipping of the disciples for mission generally dismiss the view that Jesus' "breathing the Spirit" into the disciples signifies their "new creation."[31] But mission and identity are inseparable. In John, not only is there a parallel between the mission of Jesus and his disciples, but there also are parallels between who and what Jesus is and who and what the disciples are: both the disciples' mission and their identity are derivative of and dependent on Jesus' mission and identity. As the Son sent by the Father, Jesus sends those who are his brothers and sisters, the children of God; as the one who has the Spirit, he confers the Spirit on others; as the Holy One of God, who is consecrated by his Holy Father, he consecrates his disciples. The following table illustrates these parallels and demonstrates the inseparability of the identity and mission of Jesus on the one hand and of his disciples on the other:

27. Cf. Matt 3:11; Mark 1:8; Luke 3:16; Acts 1:5; 11:16.

28. Schnelle 1998, 304, AT.

29. Carson (1991, 652–55) argues that in the LXX the word *enephysēsen* ("he breathed") always requires a prepositional phrase or dative object in order to indicate that God breathed *into* or *upon* someone. Thus in Carson's view, Jesus' breathing or exhalation (of *pneuma*: "breath" or "Spirit") symbolizes the coming full gift of the Spirit (at Pentecost, as portrayed in Acts 2). For different constructions with *emphysaō* outside the LXX, see Philo, *Opif.* 135; and entries cited in BDAG.

30. In Isaiah the outpouring of the Spirit effects eschatological re-creation and renewal (32:15–17; 44:3–6). The restoration and renewal of God's people through the Spirit is promised in *Jub.* 1.23–25; 1QS IV, 20–22; cf. *Jos. Asen.* 8:11; 12.2; 15:6.

31. So, e.g., Ridderbos 643. For a different view, see Dunn 1970, 180; Painter 2008, 45; M. M. Thompson 2004.

Table 3 As the Father Sent Me, So Also I Send You

"As the Father sent me, so also I send you" (20:21)	
God sends Jesus to bring life to the world (3:16–17; 5:23–24, 37; 6:39).	Jesus sends the disciples (13:20; 17:18; 20:21).
The Father has granted the Son to have life in himself (1:4; 5:26).	Jesus gives life to those who are dependent on him and abide in him (3:16; 6:57; 10:10; 14:19).
The Spirit remains on Jesus (1:32), the Son (1:34; *huios*) who comes from above, from God (3:2; 8:23).	Children (*tekna*) of God are "born from above" through the Spirit (1:12–13; 3:3–7; cf. 10:16; 11:52).
Jesus will baptize with or give the life-giving Spirit (1:32–33; 3:3–5; 7:37–39).	Jesus breathes out the Spirit (20:23).
Consecrated by God (10:36), the "Holy Father" (17:11), Jesus is the "Holy One of God" (6:69), who further consecrates himself for the sake of his disciples (17:19).	Jesus asks the Father to consecrate the disciples in word and truth (17:17); he consecrates himself so that they may be consecrated (17:19).
Jesus is the Lamb of God who takes away the sin of the world, so that the world may live (1:29; 3:16; 8:21).	The disciples receive the Spirit and Jesus' commission: through them sins will be forgiven and retained (20:23).
Jesus' words are spirit and life; they are the words of eternal life (6:63, 68).	Through the work of the Paraclete, who convicts the world about sin, the disciples bear witness to Jesus, who is and gives life (16:7–8; 20:23).

The disciples' mission reflects and extends Jesus' own mission by participating in God's mission to bring life to the world, here expressed in terms of the forgiveness of sins. This is the only reference in John to the forgiveness of sins. Jesus himself does not tell anyone that their sins are forgiven (cf. Mark 2:10; Luke 7:48), nor does he instruct his disciples in the course of his ministry that they are to forgive others (cf. Matt 6:12–15; 18:21–22). Jesus' mission does deal with sin: as the Lamb of God, Jesus "takes away the sin of the world." In that formulation John expresses the totality of Jesus' work with respect to sin: "take away" designates the removal of sin; the singular "sin" brings into view the whole of sin and its power; "of the world" designates the universal scope of Jesus' work. Since, in John, sin is understood primarily as unbelief that leads to death (8:21, 34; 9:41; 15:22, 24; 16:9), Jesus takes away sin by revealing, in word and deed, that he is the agent of God's life, and Jesus calls for faith in himself. It is the work of God in Jesus, through the Spirit, to bring people to faith, and so to take away sin and to confer life.

Having been cleansed by Jesus' word (15:3) and having been given the life-giving Spirit, the disciples extend the blessings of Jesus' salvific work into the world: "If you forgive [*aphēte*] the sins of any, they are forgiven [*apheōntai*]; and if you keep [*kratēte*] the sins of any, they are kept [*kekratēntai*]." They do not "take away" sin; but in light of Jesus' all-encompassing work, they forgive sins. If the passive verbs ("they are forgiven," "they are retained") are divine passives, then it becomes apparent that God stands behind the disciples' mission as he did behind Jesus' mission. As Jesus' own deeds and words were to lead people from unbelief to belief, from death to life, so his disciples present him—with his promises of life and hope, and his acts of healing and restoration—to those who cannot see him so that they may believe (20:30–31).[32]

20:24–31 Jesus Appears to Thomas: The Call to Faith

The Gospel records an appearance to Jesus' disciples a week after his first appearance to them, this time with Thomas present. Jesus speaks pointedly to Thomas, showing him his hands and his side, and inviting him to believe; that is, to believe that Jesus is indeed risen and living and so to believe in him. To that invitation, Thomas responds with the climactic confession of the Gospel, "My Lord and my God!" Although elsewhere people have spoken of Jesus or addressed Jesus as Lord, and even "my Lord," here is the first instance where someone explicitly acknowledges him as "my God." Thomas is called to "believe," to join with the beloved disciple, with Mary, and with the other disciples in acknowledging that he has indeed seen the Lord because the Lord is risen. Although Thomas does see the Lord and come to believe, Jesus reminds him—as the Gospel reminds all its readers—that there are many who will not see and will yet believe. They depend upon the apostolic testimony, enshrined in the pages of the Gospel, and the life-giving work of the Spirit in order to present Jesus so that they, too, may make the confession that Thomas here offers.

32. According to Calvin (2:204), "The only subject handled here is the preaching of the Gospel." Calvin's foil was the Roman Catholic use of John 20:22–23, which was cited in the canons and decrees of the Council of Trent (1545–63) as warrant for the sacrament of penance; for ET, see Schroeder 39, 89.

20:24 But Thomas, one of the Twelve called the Twin,[33] was not with them
when Jesus came. **25** So the other disciples said to him, "We have seen the
Lord!" But he said to them, "If I do not see in his hands the mark of the
nails, and put my finger into his side, I will never believe!"

26 And after eight days his disciples were again inside, and Thomas
was with them. And though the doors were shut, Jesus came and stood in
their midst and said, "Peace to you." **27** Then he said to Thomas, "Reach
your finger here, and see my hands, and reach your hand, and put it into
my side. Do not be unbelieving but believing."

28 Thomas responded, "My Lord and my God!"

29 And he said to him, "Because you have seen me, you have believed.
Blessed are those who believe although they do not see."

30 Jesus did many other signs in the presence of his disciples, which are
not written in this book. **31** But these things are written so that you may
believe[a] that Jesus is the Messiah, the Son of God, and that by believing
you may have life in his name.

a. There is early textual evidence for both the present subjunctive *pisteuēte* (adopted here; $\mathfrak{P}^{66}$ ℵ B) and aorist subjunctive *pisteusēte* (a corrector of ℵ, A, C, D, and the majority of MSS); if the aorist is adopted, one could translate "come to believe."

[20:24–25] Thomas was not among the disciples who encountered the risen Lord on Easter evening (20:19). The disciples report their encounter with Jesus to Thomas, with the typical Johannine confession of the resurrection, "We have seen the Lord!" Although "seeing" can be used in John to designate both sight and insight, in postresurrection confessions it refers to seeing the Lord in his risen state. John stresses the continuity between the Jesus into whose hands nails were driven and into whose side a spear was thrust, and the Jesus who now stands before the disciples.

When the disciples tell Thomas what they have seen, he refuses to believe their testimony, declaring emphatically, "If I do not see in his hands the mark of the nails, and put my finger into his side, I will never believe!" (*ou mē pisteusō* is an emphatic construction). Thomas's adamant refusal ought not to be very surprising. Up to this point, only the beloved disciple has believed without seeing the risen Lord (20:8). Mary and the other disciples have seen the risen Lord. Thomas simply wants what the others have been granted: an encounter with the risen Jesus. No doubt he gives voice to the desires, the longings, of many believers since his day, who simply want to see Jesus (cf. 12:21; Heb 2:9).

[26–29] A week later, Jesus again appears to the disciples in similar circumstances: the doors are shut, and Jesus comes and stands in their midst. He

33. See comments on 11:16 for discussion of Thomas's designation as "Twin."

speaks the same, traditional greeting, "Peace to you." Then he turns directly to Thomas, inviting him to verify for himself that the one he sees is the same one who died on the cross. He is indeed living. Thomas can see for himself.

In his Farewell Discourse, Jesus had warned the disciples that upcoming events would trouble their faith and had exhorted them to hold fast to their belief in God and in him (14:1). Now he exhorts Thomas to be "believing" (*pistos*) rather than "unbelieving" (*apistos*, 20:27).[34] Although frequently referred to as "doubting," Thomas's problem is not doubt in the sense of struggling with perennial obstacles or challenges to faith. Rather, Thomas faces the alternative posed to all figures in the Gospel and to its readers as well: belief *or* unbelief. Jesus' death threatens to end Thomas's faith because Thomas cannot accept the reports that Jesus has risen; he cannot believe on the basis of the testimony of others; and faith cannot be directed toward a dead man. If he persists in unbelief, Thomas will find himself in the perilous situation of those before whom Jesus has done so many signs, yet who have not believed (12:37).

It was Thomas who earlier lamented to Jesus, "We do not know where you are going" (14:5); now Thomas is implicitly invited to verify Jesus' own promise that he will both live and return to the Father (14:19; 20:17). Interestingly, the Gospel does not tell us whether Thomas complies with Jesus' invitation to reach his hand into Jesus' wounds. Instead, it simply reports that Thomas responds to Jesus' exhortation with the confession "My Lord and my God!" Although Jesus is frequently designated as "Lord," or "the Lord,"[35] in John, "my Lord" occurs only in postresurrection contexts (20:13). Similarly, the address to Jesus as "my God" is distinctive to the postresurrection setting. Although "the Jews" have challenged Jesus because he made himself equal to God, or made himself God, no one—not even Jesus' disciples—has addressed Jesus as "my God" until now.

Thomas's confession cannot mean that the risen Jesus alone is God, since earlier Jesus had distinguished himself from "the only true God" and from "my God and your God" (cf. 17:3; 20:17). The Father and Son are not simply "collapsed" into one; nor has the one whom Jesus himself so recently identified as "my God" (20:17) become the crucified and risen Lord himself. But the acclamation of the risen one as "my Lord and my God!" acknowledges the inclusion of Jesus, the Word made flesh, in the identity of that one called "the only true God" (1:1, 14), thus marking the other end of the confessional arc begun in the Gospel's opening verses (1:1, 14). The narrative of the Gospel has demonstrated how the Father has entrusted to the Son all authority to give

34. John never uses the noun *pistis* ("faith, belief"); there are 98 occurrences of the verb *pisteuein* in the Gospel; the adjectival forms *pistos* and *apistos* occur only here.

35. John uses "Lord" for God only when quoting the OT (see 12:13 and comments on 1:23; 6:23; 12:38).

life and to judge: the Father has, therefore, made the Son "equal to God" (cf. comments on 5:18; 10:33). Thomas now articulates the Gospel's Christology as personal confession.

As is typical of John, Thomas's confession can be read in various contexts, including scriptural, Jewish, and Roman settings. First, and most important, Thomas's words echo the psalmist's address to God as "my God and my Lord" (*ho theos mou kai ho kyrios mou*, 34:23 LXX [35:23 ET]). One of the most common descriptors attached to "God" in the Old Testament and Jewish sources is either the singular or plural personal possessive pronoun: hence, "my God" or "our God." "Our God" frequently identifies YHWH, the LORD: a notable example is the Shema, where "the LORD" (YHWH) is identified not simply as "God" but as "our God" (Deut 6:4). "My God," both with and without LORD, is especially prominent in the Psalms, in petition, lament, and praise. Additionally, there are numerous examples in the Old Testament of the phrase "the LORD our God" (passim); "the God of Abraham, Isaac, and Jacob" or variations thereof; "the God of Israel" (passim); or "God of my/our ancestors." The "god" in question is thus identified with a specific person or people who honor and worship that particular deity as God.[36] In John, then, those who honor the Son as they do the Father (5:23) acknowledge God as "our Father" and "our God" (20:17) and Jesus as "my Lord and my God."

Thomas's confession may also echo Jewish speculation on the names of God, especially as that speculation is connected with the "two powers" or "two measures" of God.[37] In rabbinic literature, these two powers are judgment and mercy: Elohim (God) denoted God's judgment, and YHWH (LORD) pointed to God's mercy. Philo, on the other hand, took *theos* (God; Hebrew, *ʾĕlōhîm*) to signify the creative power of God, and *kyrios* (LORD; Hebrew, YHWH) to refer to the royal or sovereign power of God. Philo further asserted that these two powers emanated from the Logos, the visible manifestation of God.[38] The Gospel of John envisions the powers to give life and to judge as the distinctive

36. In Jewish sources one may add other designations: "the Lord, the God of Joseph" (*Jos. Asen.* 3.4; 6.7; 21.4); "Lord God of my father Israel" (*Jos. Asen.* 8.9); "O Lord God and King, God of Abraham" (Add Esth 13:15; 14:18); "The Lord Almighty, God of Israel" (Bar 3:1, 4); "Lord God of my ancestor Simeon" (Jdt 9:2); "God of my ancestor, God of Israel's heritage" (9:12 AT); "Lord, the God of Daniel" (Bel 41); "Lord God of Shem" (*Jub.* 8.18). Ignatius often refers to Christ as *theos*, with which he frequently uses a possessive pronoun, such as "our God" (Ign., *Eph.* proem; 15.3; 18.2; Ign., *Rom.* proem [2×]; 3.3; Ign., *Pol.* 8.3) or "my God" (Ign., *Rom.* 6.3).

37. On the "two powers" of God, see Marmorstein; Dodd 1953, 320–23; Dahl and Segal; Segal 1977; Urbach 448–61.

38. In *QG* 1.57, Philo speaks of "the two original virtues which belong to the Deity, namely, his creative and his royal virtues. The one of which has the title of God, the other, or the royal virtue, that of Lord. Now the form of the creative power is a peaceable, and gentle, and beneficent virtue; but the royal power is a legislative, and chastising, and correcting virtue." In *QE* 2.68, Philo comments that the Logos has two powers, designated as "Lord" and "God"; see also *Fug.* 103–6.

powers of God active in and given to Jesus, the Word (*Logos*) made flesh (cf. John 5:25–27). Thus, when the Gospel of John asserts that Jesus brings both life and judgment, it evokes the biblical portrait, emphasized in Jewish interpretation, of God as creator and ruler.

The resurrection confirms Jesus' identity as the living and life-giving one, the incarnation of the Word of God that was in the beginning (1:1), the one who has the Father's life in himself (5:26), to whom God has given all judgment (5:27), and who now lives with the living Father (1:18; 6:57). The resurrection confirms Jesus' identity as the one who has the divine prerogatives to give life and exercise God's rule: because he lives, he indeed has "life in himself" and so can truly confer it on others (5:26; 10:18). Unless he had been raised to life, he could not continue to exercise these prerogatives; hence, without the resurrection, Jesus' work would have been ended, brought to a full stop, rather than finished or brought to its goal (19:30).[39]

Finally, Thomas's confession may direct the reader's attention to imperial Rome and especially claims made by or for emperors.[40] According to the Roman historian Suetonius, the emperor Domitian (81–96 C.E.) was styled by himself and others as "our lord and god" (*dominus et deus noster*).[41] Whether that particular claim can be verified historically or not, "lord" and "god" were used of various emperors; and Suetonius thinks the claim possible, even if outrageous.[42] Read against similar designations for the emperor, Thomas's acclamation of Jesus as "my Lord and my God!" asserts that such honors rightfully belong to Jesus, not to Caesar (cf. 19:12, 15). While Thomas's confession quite naturally articulates Jesus' identity as it has been developed in John from its scriptural contexts, it indirectly refutes the attribution of similar designations to Caesar.[43]

[29] In response to Thomas's acclamation, Jesus remarks that Thomas's "seeing" has led to his "believing."[44] This is no criticism of Thomas. After all,

39. Cf. the comments on *teleō* and *teleioō* at 19:30.

40. See esp. Cassidy; Salier; for the imperial cult in Ephesus, see Friesen; for imperial cult more generally, see Price 1984b.

41. Suetonius, *Dom.* 13. The Greek writers Dio Chrysostom (*Def.* [*Or.* 45] 1) and Dio Cassius (*Hist.* 7.13.4) speak of Domitian as *despotēs kai theos* ("master and god"), but not as *kyrios mou kai theos mou* ("my Lord and my God"). Pliny the Younger (*Pan.* 49.1) notes that even Domitian's divinity (*divinitas*) could not save him from assassination and condemnation by the senate; see also Tacitus, *Agr.* 45. A number of scholars (e.g., B. Jones 118–19) argue that such claims were part of an agenda to vilify Domitian.

42. See Price (1994a) for seminal discussion of the terms *deus*, *divus*, and *theos*; Friesen 29–49; Carter (2008, 202 nn. 86 and 88) provides information on Ephesian inscriptions that name an emperor as either god (more common) or lord (less common).

43. As Moloney (1998a, 177) states, "At best, the rejection of emperor worship serves as the background."

44. The sentence could be a question: "Have you believed because you have seen me?" (NRSV).

he follows the pattern of his fellow disciples: when they saw the risen Lord, they rejoiced and believed. At Jesus' exhortation, Thomas now joins their company. Jesus then pronounces a benediction on those "who believe although they do not see." Jesus does not say that those who believe, although they do not see, are *more* blessed. Such faith simply arises in different circumstances or is catalyzed by different experiences.

The period in which Jesus' disciples saw him and his signs is drawing to an end; the period when they will not see him now approaches. This is true for Mary Magdalene, for Thomas, for the other disciples, and for any and all who will come to believe in Jesus through their word (17:20; cf. 4:40–42). The disciples to whom Mary Magdalene announced that she had seen the Lord do not believe without seeing the risen Jesus—but they do have Mary's testimony. Thomas does not believe without seeing the risen Jesus—but he does have the testimony of his fellow disciples. The Gospel shows that such testimony can be trusted, a particularly important point since, from now on, that is precisely how people will come to believe: without seeing the risen Jesus except as he is presented by the testimony of others, and in and through the Gospel narrative itself (20:30). Since the witness of the beloved disciple, the first to believe in the risen Lord and to believe without seeing, is also the witness behind the Gospel, to believe the witness of the Gospel is to believe the witness of this one who saw Jesus (21:24).

[30–31] There now follows a statement, directly addressing the Gospel's readers, that appears to summarize the Gospel, here referred to as a "book" (*biblion*)—and yet another chapter follows. Some interpreters have therefore understood the statement in 20:30–31 as the original ending to an earlier edition of the Gospel, with chapter 21 added later.[45] While the summary does cast an eye back over the entire Gospel, it also echoes the earlier summary that marked the end of Jesus' public ministry of signs (12:37). Both statements speak of Jesus' many signs; both assume that the desired response is belief, even if that response is not always forthcoming:

> Even though Jesus had done so *many signs* before them, yet *they did not believe.* (12:37)
>
> Jesus did *many other signs* in the presence of his disciples, which are not written in this book. But these things are written *so that you may believe. . . .* (20:30–31)

While in the first statement *sēmeia* ("signs") denotes Jesus' various deeds of provision and healing in the Gospel that point to his life-giving power from the

45. E.g., Barrett 575; R. Brown 1970, 1057; Lincoln 2005, 507; Schnelle 1998, 310; D. Moody Smith 1999, 385, 389; Bultmann 1971, 452, 698, 700, argues that it is the ending of the signs source used by the evangelist. See the discussion below.

Father, in the second statement the *sēmeia* include Jesus' resurrection appearances, which point to the reality that Jesus lives.[46] Every manifestation of Jesus' identity as the one who has and gives life calls for faith.

The Gospel's selectivity is acknowledged: "Jesus did many other signs not written in this Gospel."[47] The statement may simply indicate that these are among the many signs that Jesus did. Perhaps the statement also recognizes the other kinds of signs, such as demon exorcisms and cleansing of lepers, that are well known from the other Gospels but missing from John. Since *sēmeia* ("signs") in 20:30 also include Jesus' resurrection appearances, the statement may signal that Jesus was known to appear to others at other places and times. These, however, are some of the signs that Jesus did "in the presence of his disciples." These signs were seen by his disciples, and such "seeing" has led them to continue to believe in him.

But the Gospel has been written for those who did not see Jesus' signs, who were not privy to his resurrection appearances. The written Gospel serves to re-present Jesus' signs, his ministry, and his person to its readers. The Gospel narratives serve to foster an encounter not just with the Jesus of the past, by recounting stories of the Jesus who once lived, spoke, and acted, but to foster an encounter with the Jesus who lives and who is present to his disciples even after his death. The Gospel offers testimony so that all may believe, bearing witness to Jesus, as do John the Baptist (1:7, 15, 19; 5:33–36), the Samaritan woman (4:39), the Scriptures (5:39), Moses (5:46–47), the crowds (12:17), the Spirit (15:26), Jesus' disciples (15:27), the beloved disciple (19:35; 21:24), Jesus' works (5:36; 10:25)—and the Father (5:37; 8:18), who testifies to Jesus as the Messiah, the Son of God. Not only does the Gospel tell its readers about Jesus; it also presents Jesus so that its readers may see Jesus' deeds, hear his words, encounter the risen Lord, trust in him, and so receive the life that he offers.

That the likely readers of the Gospel are already believers is suggested by Jesus' extensive Farewell Discourse to his followers regarding their life in him and with each other (chs. 14–17). Throughout the Gospel there has been a

46. A minority of scholars argue that "signs" in 20:30 refers exclusively to the resurrection appearances of ch. 20 (Bauckham 2007c, 78; Hoskyns 549–50; O'Day 850–51, 854; Michaels 1020–23). Others propose that the term here encompasses both the signs of Jesus' public ministry (12:37) and his resurrection appearances (Beasley-Murray 387; R. Brown 1970, 1058; Lindars 617; Lincoln 2005, 507–8; Schnelle 1998, 311). Ridderbos (651) argues that *sēmeia*, "signs," refers to "any event in which Jesus' divine glory is manifest." Still others view Jesus' resurrection (Wright 669), or his death and resurrection, as signs; Carson (1991, 661), Thyen (774), and Bruner (1198) suggest that the passion-resurrection complex together constitutes Jesus' seventh or eighth sign. Finally, some take "signs" as summarizing the entirety of Jesus' words and deeds (Schnackenburg 3:337; Moloney 1998a, 181 n. 86; D. Moody Smith 1999, 386). The diversity of views points up the ambiguity in the Johannine use of "signs."

47. Cf. 1 Macc 9:22: "Now the rest of the acts of Judas, and his wars and the brave deeds that he did, and his greatness, have not been recorded, but they were very many."

persistent emphasis on the need to continue to believe, to hold fast, to abide in Jesus and a concomitant, if often implicit, warning against falling away from Jesus (e.g., 8:30–31). Discussions of the purpose of the Gospel have focused in part on the evaluation of a textual variant in 20:31: the verb translated "believe" may render either the present or aorist subjunctive (*pisteuēte*[48] or *pisteusēte*[49]). Those who opt for the former reading, and who understand the Greek present to indicate ongoing action, tend to suggest that the Gospel was written primarily to encourage its readers to continue to believe in the face of all the challenges to faith. Those who argue for the originality of the aorist read it as pointing to the initial act of coming to faith and thus construe the Gospel primarily as an evangelistic document. Although this commentary assumes the originality of the present subjunctive, it is doubtful that one can draw rigid lines between the two interpretive options based on the tense of the verbs alone. Jesus' signs call for faith in him—as do his deeds, his resurrection appearances, and the Gospel's subsequent accounts of them—whether initial or continuing faith.

Coming as it does after Thomas's confession of Jesus as "my Lord and my God," the designation of Jesus as Messiah and Son of God seems to retreat from Thomas's climactic formulation. But it does not: the confession to which the Gospel calls people is identical to Martha's affirmation of Jesus as "the Messiah, the Son of God," an affirmation she makes in response to Jesus' query whether she believes that he is "the resurrection and the life" (11:25–26). Both Martha's response and the summary statement here show that John defines "Messiah, Son of God" to characterize Jesus as the one who delivers people from death to life—as indeed early Christian tradition has done (cf. Gal 2:20)—and that one receives life through faith.[50]

Moreover, the confessions of Jesus as Messiah and Son of God (20:31) and as Lord and God (20:28) mutually interpret each other. As Messiah, the King of Israel (1:49), Jesus is ruler not only of Israel but is also "Lord" and "my Lord": these biblical designations for God are now appropriated for Jesus. As Son, Jesus shares fully in the divine activity of giving life and judging (5:25–26), the two characteristic activities of God in Scripture that are now exercised through, and entrusted to, the Son. Through his Word, God brings life to the world; through the Word made flesh, crucified, risen, and glorified, God brings new life to all his world. The Son's identity is conferred by and derived from the Father: he is wholly and fully what God is. He who is Messiah and Son of God

48. E.g., Barrett 575; Lindars 617; Moloney 1998a, 179 n. 84; Michaels 1022; Ridderbos 652; D. Moody Smith 1999, 386–87.

49. Esp. Carson 1991, 661–63.

50. On the messianism of John, see Bauckham 2007c, 207–38.

is Lord and God. That is the mystery of the person of Jesus and of the identity of God in the Gospel of John.

21:1–25 Jesus Appears to His Disciples in Galilee: The Call to Follow

Although Jesus' appearance to his disciples at the Sea of Galilee is numbered as his third (21:14), it is somewhat unexpected since the Gospel has already been brought to satisfying closure: Jesus has appeared to his disciples, fulfilling the promise that he would live and they would see him and rejoice (14:19; 16:20–24; 20:18, 20, 25); again, as he promised, he has given them the Spirit (14:26; 15:26; 20:20–23); Thomas has confessed the risen Jesus as "Lord and God," forming an inclusio with the opening sentences of the Gospel (1:1; 20:28); and a summary statement, addressing the Gospel's readers, has invited them to share the faith of the disciples that Jesus is indeed Messiah and Son of God (1:41, 49; 4:25–26; 11:27; 20:30–31). With that invitation, the Gospel comes to a fitting conclusion: it does not seem unfinished; the reader does not anticipate more.

And yet there is a third appearance, loosely connected to the preceding accounts by the vague chronological marker "after these things," and set not in Jerusalem but in Galilee, a move anticipated in Mark and Matthew (Mark 14:28; 16:7; Matt 28:10, 16–20) but not in John. The disciples decide to go fishing. But Jesus' disciples have not been portrayed as fishermen in John, nor has their future mission been described in those terms (cf. Mark 1:16–20; Luke 5:1–11). Some care is taken to validate Peter's good standing with Jesus, which in some ways seems oddly out of place, since Peter (along with the other diciples) has already been given the Spirit and sent into the world with the mission of forgiving and retaining sin (20:21–23). Almost as an afterthought, the beloved disciple is identified as the author of the Gospel—a note that could have been expected to accompany the earlier statement of purpose (20:31). Moreover, while Simon Peter and the beloved disciple have been paired in various scenes, this final chapter focuses sharply on their relationship to each other and to Jesus, on their distinct roles, and on the ultimate fate of each.[51]

Taken together, these features—the plausible ending of the Gospel at 20:30–31; the unanticipated narrative elements introduced in chapter 21; the focused articulation of the distinctive roles of Simon Peter and the beloved disciple, and the anticipation of their deaths—have led some interpreters to

51. Additionally, there are stylistic variations between chs. 1–20 and 21; see Barrett (576) for a list of Greek terms found in ch. 21 but missing from the rest of the Gospel; further discussion in R. Brown 1970, 1077–80.

regard John 21 as an extended epilogue to the Gospel, added after it was essentially finished, either by the author of the earlier chapters or by someone else.[52] Most though not all interpreters who take chapter 21 as part of the Gospel's original design concede that either vv. 24–25, or 23–25, are a postscript identifying the author of the Gospel as the beloved disciple.[53] If chapter 21 was a later addition, it was added before the Gospel circulated widely; there are no extant manuscripts that simply end after chapter 20.[54] For that reason, more recently interpreters have been inclined to read the Gospel as a unity. Such an interpretive stance does not settle the source-critical question, but it does focus on the Gospel as presented to most, if not all, of its readers. It is therefore worth probing how chapter 21 continues the narrative—if not by the design of the (original) author, then in the experience of reading it—that has already appeared to come to a fitting conclusion.

The following chart presents the parallels and differences between the accounts of Jesus' appearances in chapters 20 and 21:

Table 4 Jesus Appears in Jerusalem and Galilee

John 20: Jesus appears in Jerusalem	John 21: Jesus appears in Galilee
The beloved disciple is the first (implicit) witness to the resurrection when he "believes" (20:8).	The beloved disciple now explicitly bears witness to the risen Jesus (21:7).
Jesus' appearances at the tomb and behind closed doors lead his disciples to recognize that he is living (20:16), to believe in him (20:8), and to confess him as the risen Lord and God (20:18, 25, 28).	Jesus' appearance in the ordinary course of life leads the beloved disciple to recognize the risen Lord when he provides abundantly for his disciples (21:7).

52. Among those who consider ch. 21 as part of the Gospel's original design are Carson 1991; Hoskyns; O'Day; Whitacre. Others claim it was added as an appendix to the original Gospel by the author himself: Westcott; Ridderbos (656) calls it "a striking . . . addition to a provisionally concluded whole"; or by an editor: Barrett; Beasley-Murray; R. Brown 1970; Bultmann 1971; Grayston; Lincoln 2005; Lindars; Schnackenburg; and D. Moody Smith 1999.

53. Bauckham (2006, 369–83) argues that the beloved disciple wrote all of ch. 21, including vv. 24–25; O'Day (863) states that ch. 21 is part of the original plan of the Gospel but was not written by the beloved disciple.

54. Among those who deem the source-critical problem inconclusive or irrelevant for reading the Gospel are Brant; Keener; Michaels; Moloney (1998a; 1998b), who nevertheless thinks that the chapter is an obvious addendum; and Talbert.

As Jesus promised his disciples, they would see him and have peace and joy (20:18, 19–21, 25–26, 29; see 14:19, 27; 15:11; 16:10, 16, 20–24, 33; 17:13).	As Jesus promised his disciples, they would see him and he would be with them (21:1–22; see 14:19, 23, 28; 16:10, 16).
Jesus sends the disciples as he was sent (20:21).	Jesus commissions Peter to take care of his sheep (21:15–18).
The Gospel, containing only some of the many signs that Jesus did (*polla . . . alla sēmeia epoiēsen*), bears witness to him (20:30–31), so that people may believe.	The Gospel, containing only some of the many things that Jesus did (*alla polla ha epoiēsen*), is ascribed to the beloved disciple (21:24–25).

Three aspects of the resurrection appearances in John 21 stand out:

1. There is a particular concern to validate the role of the beloved disciple as a witness to the risen Jesus, and to do so with respect to Peter's pastoral charge to tend Jesus' flock. For the first time the beloved disciple is explicitly portrayed as both seeing and identifying the risen Lord. He thus carries out the role for which he has been uniquely equipped, by means of his proximity to Jesus: having believed in Jesus (20:8), he now also sees and identifies him as the risen Lord to others. He thus acts as the ideal witness to Jesus, and his testimony will be inscribed in the Gospel itself.[55] The beloved disciple exercises his primary function after the resurrection.

2. The appearances in Jerusalem (ch. 20) demonstrate that Jesus is alive: the disciples express their faith with the confession, "We have seen the Lord!" and "My Lord and my God!" Jesus is the living Lord, and the disciples are called to believe in him. The summary statement (20:30–31) makes clear that Jesus' signs (those done throughout his ministry, as well as his resurrection appearances) are written to evoke faith. But the appearance at the Sea of Galilee underscores Jesus' ongoing presence and provision for his own. He is the life-sustaining Lord, who feeds his disciples.[56] They already know that he is alive, and they rejoice; the ongoing challenge is to recognize, trust, and follow him

55. For the beloved disciple as "ideal witness," see Hengel 1989, 78, 125; Lincoln 2005, 522. Bauckham (2007c, 73–91) labels him the "ideal author"; Resseguie (2013, 537) suggests that he represents "the ideal point of view."

56. Brodie (582) and Moloney (1998a, 190–91) rightly read John 21 to be depicting Jesus as present but (in my view) wrongly assume that this presentation undermines or contradicts the implication of Jesus' earlier appearances that (with the end of the original Gospel at 20:30–31) Jesus is now absent.

in the ordinary routines of life.[57] Jesus thus calls Peter: "Follow me!" (21:19, 22; cf. 1:43, addressed to Philip).

3. After his resurrection Jesus sends his disciples as he was sent; now he specifically sends Peter to tend his flock. The commission to Peter has to do not with the forgiveness and retention of sin—that is, not with the mission of bearing witness so that others may believe and find life (20:23, 31)—but with Peter's ongoing care for Jesus' flock (21:15–18). Jesus' Farewell Discourse anticipates his death, resurrection, and departure, thus providing directives to the disciples for their life together and their witness in the world; so also the resurrection appearances of chapter 20 confirm that Jesus is alive and that he sends the disciples into the world to bear witness to the life he has and gives. Subsequently, chapter 21 envisions the long haul of discipleship and witness, while demonstrating that Jesus makes provision for both: Peter tends the flock; the beloved disciple writes the Gospel.

Thus, whereas the accounts in John 20 bear witness that Jesus is alive, the accounts in John 21 show that Jesus' life-giving and life-sustaining work continues. From Jerusalem to Galilee—and perhaps implicitly beyond their boundaries—Jesus will be present with his disciples, providing for them. As the disciples engage in the mission that Jesus has given to them, Peter will serve as a shepherd in tending the flock, and the beloved disciple will offer his distinctive witness, a testimony that underwrites the Gospel itself.

21:1–14 Jesus' Provision for His Disciples

Jesus' third appearance again underscores the continuity between his provision for his disciples before and after his death and resurrection. Earlier Jesus provided more than enough bread and fish for five thousand, with twelve baskets left over; now he fills the nets of his disciples with a prodigious catch of large fish and prepares breakfast for them. If the narratives of the Johannine resurrection appearances establish the new relationship that now obtains between the risen Jesus and his disciples, they also demonstrate Jesus' continual provision for his disciples as well as their continued need for and dependence upon the one who is and gives life. Indeed, apart from him, they can do nothing (15:5).

> **21:1** After these things, Jesus showed himself again to the disciples by
> the Sea of Tiberias. He showed himself in this way. **2** Simon Peter and
> Thomas, called the Twin, and Nathanael from Cana of Galilee, and the

57. The verb *pisteuein* ("to believe, to have faith"), used 98 times in the Gospel, is not found in ch. 21 (nor in ch. 15 nor 18), further illustrating that, while the resurrection appearances of ch. 20 are aimed at confirming and calling forth faith, the appearance narrated in ch. 21 serves a different function.

sons of Zebedee, and two others of his disciples were together. 3 And
Simon Peter said to them, "I am going fishing." They said to him, "We
also will come with you." And they went and got into the boat, but that
night they caught nothing.

4 And when it was morning, Jesus stood on the shore; yet the disciples
did not know that it was Jesus. 5 Jesus said to them, "Children, you have
not caught anything, have you?"

They answered him, "No."

6 He said to them, "Throw the net on the right side of the boat, and you
will find some." Then they threw [their net], and they were no longer able
to draw it in, because of the many fish.

7 Then that disciple whom Jesus loved said to Peter, "It is the Lord!"
So when Simon Peter heard that it was the Lord, he girded himself, for
he was stripped for work,[a] and he jumped into the sea. 8 And the other
disciples came in the boat, dragging the net of fish, for they were not far
from the shore, about a hundred yards[b] off.

9 When they came up on shore, they saw a charcoal fire there, with
fish lying on it, and bread. 10 Jesus said to them, "Bring some of the fish
that you have just caught." 11 So Simon Peter went and drew the net, full
of 153 large fish, to shore. And even though there were so many, the net
was not torn. 12 Jesus said to them, "Come and have breakfast." None
of his disciples dared to inquire,[c] "Who are you?" For they knew it was
the Lord.

13 And Jesus came and took the bread and gave it to them, and the fish
also.

14 And this was the third time that Jesus appeared to his disciples after
he had been raised from the dead.

a. "Stripped for work" translates *gymnos*, "naked."

b. "Two hundred cubits": a cubit is the length from the point of the elbow to the tip of the middle finger.

c. Found elsewhere in the NT only in Matt 2:8; 10:11; BDAG, "scrutinize, examine, inquire."

[21:1–7] Jesus' third (v. 14) resurrection appearance to "his disciples" occurs not in Jerusalem, but on the shores of the Sea of Tiberias,[58] more commonly known in the Gospels as the Sea of Galilee (John 6:1; cf. Mark 14:28; 16:7). The appearance occurs "after these things" (*meta tauta*), a phrase that often indicates temporal passage in the Gospel's narrative without specifying how much time has elapsed (3:22; 5:1, 14; 6:1; 7:1; 19:38). In some instances,

58. On "Sea of Tiberias," see comments on 6:1.

however, considerable time elapses between the events so connected (cf. 7:1: from spring to autumn). Jesus encounters the disciples, not behind locked doors in Jerusalem, but at the shore of the lake in Galilee (cf. Mark 14:28; 16:7; Matt 28:7, 16).

The Gospel names some of the seven disciples present, including Simon Peter, Thomas, and Nathanael, all of whom have figured earlier in the Gospel.[59] For the first time in John "the sons of Zebedee" are mentioned; the list also includes "two others" of Jesus' disciples. Later in the narrative, it becomes apparent that the "disciple whom Jesus loved" (v. 7) is among this group of seven. Since he cannot be Simon Peter, and presumably is neither Thomas[60] nor Nathanael, who are both named, the beloved disciple could be one of the sons of Zebedee, or one of the two "other disciples." Given the possibility that elsewhere the beloved disciple is also called "another disciple" or "the other disciple,"[61] the likelihood is great that he is one of these two unidentified "other disciples." This is the first time that he has figured in a scene set in Galilee.

Simon Peter decides to go fishing, and the others join him. While it is often assumed that the disciples have returned to their previous occupations, John has not introduced any of the disciples as fishermen (Mark 1:16–17; Luke 5:1–11).[62] It may be that this tradition was widespread, known at least to the Gospel's readers. The disciples are fishing at night, which allows them to sell their fresh catch in the morning. But their foray yields nothing. When morning dawns, Jesus addresses them from the shore, although the disciples do not yet know who he is.

Jesus' resurrection appearances to Mary Magdalene at the tomb and now to the seven at the lake in both cases call for recognition of the risen Jesus. Mary recognizes Jesus when he speaks her name; the beloved disciple recognizes Jesus especially by what his word effects. Jesus' word has accomplished healing (4:50, 53; 5:8), called Lazarus forth from the tomb (11:43), purified the disciples (15:3), and now calls forth the abundance that has characterized the "fullness" given by Jesus throughout the Gospel (1:14, 16; 2:7; 6:13). Jesus addresses the disciples as "children" (*paidia*; cf. the synonym *teknia* in

59. Although John does not call attention to the number seven, many commentators do; thus Beasley-Murray (399): "Doubtless a symbolical number, representing the whole disciple group, and indeed the whole Body of disciples, the Church"; Schnackenburg 3:352; Grayston (173) deems it more important than twelve (= Israel).

60. But Charlesworth (1995) argues that the beloved disciple is Thomas.

61. John 18:15–16; 20:2–4, 8; 13:23, "one of his disciples"; discussion and bibliography in Resseguie 541.

62. The Gospel does not say why the disciples go fishing; commentators have imaginatively filled in the gaps: R. Brown (1970, 1096) speaks of "aimless activity undertaken in desperation"; Hoskyns (552) labels the incident "a scene of complete apostasy" (fulfilling Jesus' earlier prediction in 16:32); Whitacre (490) suggests they are doing "what is right in their own eyes"; Beasley-Murray (399) thinks they are hungry.

13:33).[63] Although Jesus has called them "friends," he is still their Teacher and Lord, as his address to them as *children*, emphasizing their continued dependence, now recalls (15:15).

The beloved disciple, the first to understand the significance of what they all have seen, testifies to Peter: "It is the Lord!" The beloved disciple regularly "sees what others do not see."[64] In keeping with a recurring pattern in the Gospel, it is the witness of others that enables people to recognize Jesus and to believe and follow him (1:41, 45; 4:39; 20:30–31). Peter responds to the beloved disciple's testimony and "girds himself" (*diezōsato*), or fastens his garment securely around him, so that he may swim or wade ashore without difficulty. Although the word *gymnos*, here translated "stripped for work," can mean naked, it seems unlikely that Peter would have put on his clothing before jumping into the water; moreover, Palestinian Judaism resisted public nudity.[65] The Gospel does not hint that Peter was embarrassed and tried to hide his nakedness, whether that be construed physically or metaphorically (i.e., as Peter's "shame" before Jesus). Peter's leap into the sea demonstrates the simple desire to be with Jesus. Jesus has been absent from them: now he is present, and Peter yearns to be in his presence.

[8–11] While Peter swims ashore to meet Jesus, the other disciples struggle to haul in the catch of fish. Arriving on shore, they see a charcoal fire (*anthrakia*), with fish cooking on it, and bread. The description recalls two previous scenes in the Gospel: first, the feeding of the five thousand with bread and fish (6:1–14); second, Jesus' interrogation in the courtyard of the high priest, where Peter, gathered with others around a charcoal fire (18:18), three times denied that he was a disciple of Jesus (18:17, 25, 26–27). When Jesus asks for some of the fish from the catch, presumably to cook them along with those already on the fire, Peter himself hauls the net ashore.[66] The narrator supplies the enigmatic note that the net contained 153 large fish and that, although it contained so many, the net was not torn.[67] Suspecting that the number functions

63. *Paidia*, "children" (21:5), which can also be used of infants, occurs twice in 1 John (2:14, 18; cf. 3:7, MSS); *teknia* ("little children"), the diminutive of *tekna* ("children"), occurs regularly in 1 John; *tekna* occurs in all three Johannine Epistles. The terms are probably used synonymously.

64. Resseguie 546.

65. Michaels (1034) argues that *gymnos* ("naked") means "stripped for work"; similarly, Keener 2:1229–30.

66. On "Fishing, Nets," see Rousseau and Arav 93–97; cf. Mark 1:16 (nets thrown from shore) and 1:19–20 (nets cast from boats, as here).

67. Some interpreters have proposed that the account of the abundant catch of fish symbolizes the disciples' mission work—and possibly its failure (Brown 1970, 1097; Lincoln 2005, 511, 515; Michaels 1027–28; Moloney 1998a, 183; Talbert 260; Thyen 778). The unbroken net means that none must be lost (cf. 6:12, where none of the fragments of bread are lost; 17:12, "none of them has perished"). Since elsewhere John does not describe the disciples' mission in terms of fishing (contrast Mark 1:16–17; Luke 5:1–11), this interpretation seems strained. But notice Bruner's comment: "Jesus comes, precisely, to disciples disappointed in their work" (1208).

symbolically, commentators have offered a wide range of suggestions for understanding the significance of the number 153, none of which has commanded universal assent. In virtually every proposal, however, the number is understood to indicate fullness or abundance.

1. Jerome thought that Greek sources of his day indicated that there were 153 kinds of fish;[68] the catch was thought, then, to symbolize the universal scope of Jesus' mission.

2. Many have followed Augustine, who pointed out that 153 is the sum of the successive numbers from one to seventeen. But there is less agreement why the number seventeen might be important. Augustine posited that seventeen itself was the sum of ten, the number of the commandments of the law, and seven, the day of creation first associated with sanctification and hence symbolic of the Holy Spirit. Thus ten and seven represent, respectively, the old and new covenants, law and grace, letter and spirit; or the full number of the saints who will enjoy eternal life.[69]

3. Others have suggested that John was employing the technique of gematria, where each letter of the alphabet has a numerical value (cf. Rev 13:17–18). For example, the numerical value of the Hebrew phrase *bĕnê ha-ʾĕlōhîm* ("sons" or "children of God") is 153; here they (like the fish) are gathered in (see 11:52).[70] One of the more intriguing suggestions was made by J. A. Emerton,[71] who also exploited Augustine's observation that 153 is the sum of the numbers from one to seventeen. Emerton argues that the sum of the numerical value of the Hebrew letters in the name En-gedi comes to 17, and in En-eglaim, 153, and that these names evoke Ezekiel's description of a great river flowing from the temple: "People will stand fishing beside the sea from En-gedi to En-eglaim; it will be a place for the spreading of nets; its fish will be of a great many kinds, like the fish of the Great Sea" (Ezek 47:9–10). Ezekiel does not mention the number 153, and John never cites or names Ezekiel (here or elsewhere in the book), or either of these places named in Ezekiel.[72] But the great catch of fish in John 21 at least shares Ezekiel's vision of the abundant provision of fish.[73]

4. Finally, some commentators dismiss all symbolic interpretations.[74] Elsewhere, in narrating miracles of "supply" or "provision," the Gospel calls atten-

68. Attributed to Oppianus Cilix, in Jerome's commentary on Ezek 47:6–12 (in PL 25:474C); cf. Grant, who says Jerome may have derived the number from the Gospel of John itself.

69. Augustine, *Tract. Ev. Jo.* 122. Augustine offers additional suggestions how the number symbolizes the Trinity, Pentecost, and the Spirit.

70. Bauckham 2007c, 278.

71. Emerton 1958.

72. For allusions to Ezekiel in the Gospel, see the comments at 3:5; 6:41–44; 10:11–18; 15:1–7. For further discussion, see Manning 189–94.

73. So also Lincoln 2005, 511.

74. Grayston 173 n. 5; Ridderbos 663; Lindars (631) thinks it is symbolic but inexplicable.

tion to the size and volume of the water jars (2:6) and the number of baskets of bread gathered after the feeding of the five thousand (6:13). Here the reference to both the size and number of the fish caught demonstrates that there is nothing meager about Jesus' provision. Even as the fragments were gathered up in baskets after the feeding in the wilderness, so here the fish are caught without tearing the nets: nothing is lost, evocative of both Jesus' abundant provision and sovereign care.

[12–14] Jesus invites his disciples to breakfast. Although they apparently had not recognized him at first, now they "knew it was the Lord." Yet the comment "none of them dared to ask him," coupled with their initial failure to recognize him, suggests that Jesus' appearance was unexpected or perhaps unrecognizable. As Jesus fed the multitudes with bread and fish so that they ate "as much as they wanted" (6:11), Jesus now serves a small group of his disciples bread and fish (v. 13; cf. 6:11). Notice the parallel:

> Jesus took the bread and, having given thanks, distributed it to those sitting down; likewise also the fish, as much as they wanted. (6:11)

> And Jesus came and took the bread and gave it to them, and the fish also. (21:13)

In keeping with his promise that the disciples would see him, he now stands among them and feeds them, continuing to provide for them after his resurrection that which he had provided them before his death.[75]

This was "the third time" that Jesus appears, or shows himself (*ephanerōthē*) to the disciples. *Phaneroō* ("show, reveal") can aptly be translated "made known" here and elsewhere in John, but only in this chapter is it used to characterize one of Jesus' resurrection appearances.[76] While this may simply reflect stylistic variation, some have thought that it betrays the fact that John 21 comes from a different hand than the rest of the Gospel. Even so, it demonstrates that Jesus takes the initiative to make himself known so that he may be recognized.

But if this is the third appearance, what are the other two? If we count the appearance to Mary in the garden (20:11–18), the appearances to Jesus' disciples on Sunday evening (20:19–25), and then again a week later (20:26–29), this appearance by the lake (21:1) would be the fourth. Probably

75. There are similarities to Jesus' appearance on the Emmaus road (Luke 24), where Jesus is recognized as he breaks bread. Among those detecting eucharistic allusions in John 21:9–13 are Bruner 1211; Bultmann 1971, 710; Michaels 1027–28; O'Day 858–59; D. Moody Smith 1999, 394.

76. John baptizes so that Jesus might be "revealed" (*phanerōthē*) to Israel (1:31); Jesus "manifested [*ephanerōsen*] his glory" at Cana (2:11); Jesus' brothers exhort him to "show" (*phanerōson*) himself publicly (7:4); Jesus has "made known" (*ephanerōsa*) God's name (17:6).

Jesus' appearance to Mary, the only appearance to a single witness and not to a gathering of disciples, has not been counted.[77] In John, there will be no more resurrection appearances: they are effectively ended. Yet this particular appearance underscores that, as he had promised he would do, Jesus remains with his disciples, wherever they are and whatever they are doing: he has not left them alone; he continues to provide for them (14:18; 15:1–11). The Johannine resurrection appearances establish the continuity between Jesus' relationship to his own both before and after his death and resurrection.

21:15–22 Three More Questions for Simon Peter

Jesus then turns to Peter with three questions and three commands. While the number three is a familiar narrative device—stories, parables, and jokes often have three main characters—here it recalls the three questions that Peter was asked during Jesus' interrogation by the high priest (John 18:15–18, 25–27). Peter did not acquit himself well on that occasion, denying three times that he was a disciple of Jesus. Jesus now gives him the opportunity to answer a different set of questions, a set equally aimed at testing his faithfulness to Jesus. This faithfulness will be demonstrated first in his love for Jesus and then in his willingness to follow Jesus' commands to care for Jesus' flock. Jesus alone is the good shepherd; Peter will not usurp Jesus' place, but he must exercise a comparable function as shepherd on Jesus' behalf, which will include laying down his life, even as the good shepherd did. In multiple senses Peter must follow Jesus (21:19). While Peter will not die a natural death in old age, that is apparently the destiny marked out for the beloved disciple (vv. 21–22). But his fate does not concern Peter: his only concern is obedience to Jesus' call: "Follow me!"

> 21:15 Then when they had eaten breakfast, Jesus said to Simon Peter,
> "Simon, son of John, do you love me more than these?" And he said to
> him, "Yes, Lord, you know that I love you." He said to him, "Feed my
> lambs."
> 16 He said to him a second time, "Simon, son of John, do you love
> me?" He said to him, "Yes, Lord, you know that I love you." He said to
> him, "Tend my sheep."
> 17 He said to him a third time, "Simon, son of John, do you love me?"
> Peter was grieved that he said to him the third time, "Do you love me?"

77. Paul does not mention separate resurrection appearances to women in his catalog in 1 Cor 15:3–7, but women are surely included in the 500 *adelphoi* ("brothers and sisters").

and he said to him, "Lord, you know all things. You know that I love
you." Jesus said to him, "Feed my sheep."

18 "Amen, amen, I say to you, when you were younger, you girded
yourself and walked wherever you wanted. But when you have grown
old, you will stretch out your hands, and another will gird you and take
you where you do not want to go." 19 He said this to show by what sort of
death he would glorify God. And when he had said this to him, he said,
"Follow me."

20 Peter turned and saw, following [them],[a] the disciple whom Jesus
loved, who had reclined at his side at dinner and said, "Lord, who is the
one will betray you?" 21 And when Peter saw him, he said to Jesus, "Lord,
what about him?"

22 And Jesus said to him, "If I will that he remain until I come, what
is that to you? *You* follow me."

a. "Following" lacks an object in the Greek; most English translations supply "them."

[21:15–17] Jesus now addresses Simon Peter as "Simon, son of John" (21:15, 16, 17; cf. 1:42).[78] Three times Jesus asks Peter, "Do you love me?" Three times Peter responds affirmatively, and three times Jesus gives him a charge or command. In the first question, "Do you love me more than these?" Jesus asks Peter whether he loves Jesus more than the other disciples do.[79] Earlier Peter insisted he would lay down his life for Jesus (13:37–38), and in response Jesus predicted Peter's threefold denial (13:38). Now Peter is given the chance to acknowledge his love for Jesus, which will lead to Jesus' commission to tend his sheep, tied together with a prediction that Peter will indeed make good on his earlier vow by laying down his life for Jesus. That will take great love—both for Jesus, and for the flock entrusted to Peter's care.

What has attracted the most attention, however, is the fact that the Greek word for "love" varies; in Jesus' first two questions, a form of the verb *agapaō* is used, whereas in the third question, the verb is *phileō*:

78. Matt 16:17 has *Simōn Bariōna,* "Simon, son of Jonah." Bockmuehl (2012b, 22) argues that John takes *Yonah* as short for the more common *Yohanan*; cf. idem 2010, 141–48.

79. In Jesus' question *Agapas me pleon toutōn?* "Do you love me more than these?" the demonstrative *toutōn* ("these") can be the subject of an implied clause, "Do you love me more than these [other disciples love me]?" or the object of a second, implied verb "love," "Do you love me more than [you love] these?" referring either to (1) Peter's fishing paraphernalia or (2) the other disciples.

Table 5 Love: *Agapaō* and *Phileō*

Jesus' question	Peter's response	Jesus' charge
"Do you love [*agapas*] me?"	"Yes, Lord, you know that I love [*philō*] you."	"Feed my lambs [*boske ta arnia mou*]."
"Do you love [*agapas*] me?"	"Yes, Lord, you know that I love [*philō*] you."	"Tend my sheep [*poimaine ta probata mou*]."
"Do you love [*phileis*] me?"	"Lord, you know all things. You know that I love [*philō*] you."	"Feed my sheep [*boske ta probata*]."

Building on the view that *agapē* and its cognates refer to a kind of divine, self-offering love, while *philia* and cognates designate friendship or fraternal love, interpreters have sometimes rendered the dialogue between Jesus and Peter as follows: Jesus asks Peter whether he loves him (*agapas*): that is, whether Peter truly loves Jesus with the kind of self-sacrificing love that Jesus has shown for him. While Peter answers affirmatively ("Yes, Lord"), he uses the verb *phileō*, showing that he is not capable of or cannot commit to the level of love that Jesus himself has manifested. Jesus repeats the (theologically charged) question; Peter gives the identical (more tepid) response. The third time, however, Jesus changes the question, now using the verb that Peter himself has used: *phileō*. In other words, because Peter cannot rise to Jesus' level, Jesus condescends to Peter's level. Peter grieves that, in this third query, Jesus has lowered his expectations to account for Peter's failure to render what Jesus asks; nevertheless, Peter emphatically affirms his love for Jesus.

This subtle interpretation founders on the evidence in the Gospel itself. (1) Throughout John the verbs *agapan* and *philein* are used interchangeably. Both are used of God's love for human beings (3:16; 16:27), the Father's love for the Son (3:35; 5:20), Jesus' love for human beings (11:5, 36), the love of human beings for each other (13:34; 15:19), and the love of human beings for Jesus (8:42; 16:27). (2) In his threefold charge to Peter, Jesus uses two verbs for "feed" and "tend" (*boske, poimaine*) and two nouns for "sheep" or "lambs" (*arnia, probata*). No clear pattern distinguishes these charges, even as no clear pattern differentiates the words for love in this passage. (3) Jesus takes each of Peter's responses at face value, without varying his charge to Peter. Because Peter loves Jesus, he is entrusted with the care of Jesus' flock;[80] Jesus does not vary or lower his expectations in keeping with Peter's replies. (4) Finally,

80. In 1 Pet 2:25 Jesus is the "shepherd and guardian" (*poimēn kai episkopos*); in 5:4 he is the "chief shepherd" (*archipoimenos*).

Peter's grief that Jesus asks "a third time" probably recalls an earlier set of three questions and answers, around another charcoal fire, in which Peter denied his discipleship (18:15–18, 25–27).

In short, Jesus interrogates Peter, not about the quality of his love, but about his willingness to demonstrate that love by keeping Jesus' command to take care of his flock. Jesus called all his disciples to manifest their love by keeping his commandments (14:15). But if Peter loves Jesus and still wants to follow him to death (13:37), then he may demonstrate it by carrying out the particular command to care for Jesus' flock, even to the point of giving his life for the sheep (10:11). Jesus' command to Peter has been generalized to encompass the pastoral office of the church;[81] yet in the context of this chapter, Peter and the beloved disciple are set in sharp and clear contrast: the beloved disciple does not exercise Peter's role, but exercises his own role of witness in service to Peter and the other disciples. Peter and the beloved disciple do not compete for the same roles.

[18–22] The task of shepherding the flock entrusted to Peter draws on Jesus' role as the good shepherd, who guides the sheep to pasture and protects them from predators (10:1–18). Jesus subsequently foretells Peter's destiny: by his death, Peter will "glorify God," even as Jesus' death on the cross "glorified" God (12:16, 23, 28; 13:31–32; 17:1, 4). The description of Peter "stretching out his hands" and being led by another where he does not wish to go probably alludes to the practice of tying a condemned person's arms to the crossbeam, which he then carried to the place of crucifixion.[82] According to tradition, Peter died by crucifixion during the Neronic persecutions of Christians in 64–65 C.E.[83] By the time John was composed, Peter had kept his vow to follow Jesus, wherever that path might lead.

Jesus repeats the summons given to disciples at the outset of his ministry: "Follow me!" (1:43). Now, however, it is the risen Jesus who summons Peter to follow him. If Peter's footsteps lead him on the path of following Jesus, the good shepherd, that path leads through death to life: "Because I live, you also will live" (14:19). With the call to "follow me" (*akolouthei moi*) ringing in

81. Ridderbos (666) sees "nothing unique" in the designation of Peter as shepherd; yet Schnackenburg (3:365) speaks of Peter's "prominent position" and "office" of "earthly representation." On Peter's distinctive office, see esp. Bockmuehl 2012b, 58–67; also Labahn 2013.

82. That Peter's "stretching out his hands" hints at death by crucifixion is doubted by R. Brown 1970, 1107–8; Michaels 1048. In *Barn.* 12.1–5 and in Justin (*1 Apol.* 35; *Dial.* 90–91), several OT passages about "stretching out" hands or arms are read as figures of the cross; Epictetus (*Diatr.* 3.26.22) describes a crucified man as "stretched out."

83. For Peter's martyrdom, see *1 Clem.* 5.4 and Tertullian, *Scorp.* 15.3; for the tradition that Peter was crucified upside down, see *Acts of Peter* 9.35.6–9.38.9; Eusebius, *Hist. eccl.* 2.25.8; 3.1.2 (citing Origen, *Comm. Gen.* 3). Seneca (*Marc.* 20.3) speaks of seeing crucified victims suspended heads downward and in other grotesque ways; cf. Josephus, *J.W.* 5.450–451; Bockmuehl 2012b, 66; 2010, 114–32, 200–202.

his ears, Peter turns to see "the disciple whom Jesus loved following [*akolouthounta*]." This may be a play on the word "following": the beloved disciple is shown actually doing what Peter has just been called to do in a figurative sense. Having learned of his own destiny, Peter is understandably curious about that of the beloved disciple: "What about him?" (v. 21). Jesus leaves that question unanswered and the future of the beloved disciple open: he may "remain" (*menein*, "abide") until Jesus comes—one of the few explicit references to Jesus' return in the Gospel[84]—but that will be determined by Jesus. Jesus emphatically repeats his command to Peter: "*You* follow me!"[85]

"Follow me!" was one of the first commands Jesus gave to a would-be disciple (1:43); now it is the last command given to any of the disciples (21:19, 22). The Gospel thereby reiterates the point that, even in spite of the obvious differences in the relationship of Jesus to his own after Easter, the character of discipleship has not fundamentally changed. Being a disciple of Jesus still, and always, means following after him (12:26). Following Jesus began in response to the invitation "Come and see!" (1:39). In the course of the narrative, the disciples have seen, as the Gospel states, the many signs that Jesus did in their presence, and they have struggled to discern what they mean and who he is. Now the Gospel itself calls its readers to "come and see!" through the signs that are "written in this book" (20:30). Those readers are also addressed in Jesus' call: "Follow me!" The call that came to Jesus' first disciples in John now comes to all those who know him through the testimony of the Gospel.

21:23–25 Yet Once More: The Disciple Whom Jesus Loved

The Gospel could have ended with Jesus' call "Follow me!" But there is a brief epilogue. Apparently a misunderstanding about the death of the beloved disciple has arisen and must be addressed. Correcting that misunderstanding provides the occasion to identify the "beloved disciple" as the one who has written the Gospel. Additionally, there is a brief note that, although this Gospel has now come to an end, there are yet a multitude of traditions about Jesus that could have been told.

> **21:23** The rumor[a] spread among the brothers and sisters[b] that this disciple
> would not die. But Jesus did not say to him that he would not die, but
> rather, "If I will that he remain until I come, [what is that to you?]"[c]
> **24** This is the disciple who is bearing witness concerning these things
> and who has written them, and we know that his testimony is true. **25** But

84. See comments on 14:2–3.

85. The command in 21:19, *Akolouthei moi*, becomes in 21:22 <u>*Sy*</u> *moi akolouthei*. The use of the personal pronoun (*sy*) and its position in the sentence communicate emphasis: "*You* follow me!"

there are many other things that Jesus did. If each were written, then all the books in the world could not hold the things that would be written.[d]

a. "Rumor" translates *logos*, "word."

b. *Adelphous*, "brothers and sisters" (cf. 20:17). See textual note on 2:12 and comments on 20:17.

c. The bracketed words translate the Greek *ti pros se?* ("What is that to you?"). They are missing in א* C[2] and other MSS and versions. Although textually better supported, the question makes the reading easier and may be an addition.

d. Some MSS and versions locate John 7:53–8:11, the account of the woman taken in adultery, after the end of verse 25.

[21:23–25] Jesus' words to Peter about the beloved disciple, "If I will that he remain until I come, what is that to you?" (v. 21), had apparently been misunderstood by the time this Gospel is being written. Some had thought that Jesus meant, "This disciple will not die." Whatever the misunderstanding, it must be corrected. It is unlikely that they believed Jesus had meant that the disciple would never die: the Gospel promises eternal life after resurrection, not unending life without death (e.g., 11:25–26). And Jesus' qualification "until I come" shows that "would not die" has a temporal limit (vv. 22–23). A likely explanation for the confusion reported among the disciples is that some thought the beloved disciple would live to see the return of Jesus, but the disciple had died before Jesus returned.[86] Perhaps, then—some may have reasoned—Jesus would not come back, as he had promised. The death of Christians prior to Jesus' return caused problems in other early Christian communities. Paul had to promise the Thessalonians that the resurrection of Jesus ensured the resurrection of those who had "fallen asleep" or died before Jesus' coming (1 Thess 4:13–15). Second Peter reminds its readers that the delay of Jesus' return can be attributed to God's distinctive way of reckoning time (2 Pet 3:4).

[24] Whoever identifies the beloved disciple as the one "bearing witness concerning these things" deliberately echoes an earlier description (19:35):

> The one who has seen this has testified, and his testimony is true, and he knows that he speaks the truth, so that you might believe. (19:35)
>
> This is the disciple who is bearing witness concerning these things and who has written them, and we know that his testimony is true. (21:24)

Throughout the Gospel, the beloved disciple has both proximity to Jesus and often deeper or immediate understanding of events or of Jesus himself: reclining

86. Those who question the assumption that the beloved disciple has died include Carson 1991, 682; Hoskyns 559; and Keener 2:1241. The present tense ("the one who bears witness," *ho martyrōn*) need not imply that the beloved disciple is still living (cf. 1:15); he "bears witness" even through that which has been written.

next to Jesus at the Last Supper, he learns the identity of Jesus' betrayer (13:23); standing at the foot of the cross, he witnesses the death of Jesus (19:26–27); discovering the tomb empty, he believes in the resurrection of Jesus (20:8); recognizing the effectiveness of Jesus' word, he identifies the risen Lord to Peter and the others (21:7). The beloved disciple's proximity to Jesus qualifies him as the ideal witness: his witness is true; it can be trusted.

The claim made for this disciple is not merely that he is the witness to "these things" but also that he "has written them" (*ho grapsas tauta*).[87] On the surface, that claim seems simple enough: the beloved disciple is the author of the Gospel. And yet someone other than the beloved disciple must have written the words "We know that his testimony is true" (v. 24), even if he has not died (v. 23). The late intrusion of this voice into the narrative raises the question of just who is heard speaking elsewhere. Does this editorial addition include only vv. 24–25 or 23–25?[88] Or does it include all of chapter 21? Should other passages in the first-person plural (cf. 1:14, 16) be attributed to the beloved disciple, or to the "we" who here testify to his trustworthiness?[89]

Because of such vexing questions, some have appealed to the earlier statement that Pilate had denied the Jews' request to change the wording of the charge against Jesus with the assertion, "What I have written, I have written" (*ho gegrapha, gegrapha*, 19:22). Doubtless the words mean, "What I have ordered" or "what I have caused to be written, I have written." If such an interpretation of "who has written them" (*ho grapsas tauta*) were to be adopted, then the beloved disciple "ordered" or "caused" the writing of the Gospel that inscribes his witness, while someone else wrote it.[90]

And yet this late postscript (vv. 23–25) claims more: the Gospel bears the stamp of the beloved disciple, not only as the witness whose authority underwrites the Gospel, but also as its author. One other authorial or editorial voice—perhaps a student of the beloved disciple or someone within his ecclesial circle—can be heard as well ("we know," v. 24; "I suppose," v. 25).[91] He

87. In Rom 16:22, Tertius calls himself *ho grapsas tēn epistolēn*, "the one who has written this letter" (AT); he is the scribe or amanuensis. But more is claimed for the beloved disciple.

88. For a cogent argument that whoever added vv. 24–25 must also have added v. 23, see Bauckham 2007c, 81–82; Barrett (583) notes the intrinsic connection between vv. 23 and 24.

89. Resseguie (2013, 548) helpfully distinguishes between the beloved disciple as character in and writer of the narrative.

90. Commentators who think the beloved disciple is here presented as the author of the Gospel include Barrett 587; Carson 1991, 685; Lindars 641; Michaels 1054–56; Ridderbos 671. Among those reckoning him as the authority somehow responsible for the Gospel are Beasley-Murray 415; Lincoln, 2005, 523; O'Day 863; Schnackenburg 3:373; Talbert 263. See also "Authorship" in the introduction to this commentary.

91. In agreement with Bauckham (2007c, 79): "A single editor speaks for himself in the first-person singular of verse 25 and on behalf of the Johannine school in the first-person plural of verse 24." Bauckham (2006, 369–83) argues that the beloved disciple wrote all of ch. 21, including vv. 24–25.

verifies the Gospel as the written testimony of the one who appears in its pages as the disciple beloved by Jesus.

[25] The closing words of the Gospel are somewhat anticlimactic, especially when compared to the earlier statement summarizing the Gospel's purpose to evoke faith in Jesus as the Messiah, the Son of God (20:30–31) or the majestic opening to the Gospel that sets the entire narrative on a cosmic canvas. Someone—now speaking in the first-person singular—simply asserts that there are many more things that could have been recounted about Jesus.

> Jesus did many other signs [*polla . . . alla sēmeia epoiēsen*] in the presence of his disciples, which are not written in this book. (20:30)

> But there are many other things which Jesus did [*alla polla ha epoiēsen*]. If each were written, then all the books in the world could not hold the things that would be written. (21:25)

Both statements are instructive for understanding the character of the Gospel of John. Admittedly selective, the Gospel has focused on a few themes to the virtual neglect of many others and has underscored certain aspects of Jesus' identity in order to foster and encourage faith in him. At the same time, the Gospel's acknowledged selectivity demonstrates that there is more to say about Jesus. The Gospel offers a reliable witness to Jesus, but it cannot contain all that could be said about him. The closing remarks here allow for other traditions, perhaps even other ways to tell the story of Jesus, so long as they are consonant with the truthful witness borne to him here: in the Word who was with God, who became flesh, and is now ever at the Father's side, there is life.

INDEX OF SCRIPTURE AND OTHER ANCIENT SOURCES

In this index, Scripture follows the book order and verse numbers of the NRSV.

NEW TESTAMENT

PATRISTIC WORKS

GRECO-ROMAN LITERATURE

INDEX OF SUBJECTS AND AUTHORS